Robert John (Bob) Hunter was born in rural Meath in 1938 and was educated at Wesley College and Trinity College, Dublin. After graduation in 1960, he began research on the Ulster Plantation in the counties of Armagh and Cavan, 1608–41. This interest in the Plantation, and early modern Irish history generally, was to dominate his life.

In 1963 he was appointed Assistant Lecturer in History at Magee College, thus beginning an association with the city of Derry/Londonderry that was to continue for the rest of his life. The creation of what was to become the University of Ulster also saw him teaching regularly in Coleraine.

Through his meticulous research, he developed an encyclopaedic knowledge of his subject, traversing such themes as the development of towns, the role of the English planters, the history of trade and migration and the intellectual and cultural life of Ulster more generally.

Though his untimely death in 2007 was to cut short his ambitions for further writing, he was nevertheless to leave behind more than thirty articles, essays, reviews, etc., which were the result of painstaking study conducted with a careful eye for detail and relevance.

David Edwards is Senior Lecturer in History at University College Cork, and a Director of the Irish Manuscripts Commission. His previous publications include: *Age of Atrocity: Violence and Political Conflict in Early Modern Ireland*, named among *The Irish Times'* Books of the Year in 2007, and *The Ormond Lordship in County Kilkenny, 1515–1642: The Rise and Fall of Butler feudal power*, a Book of the Year in 2003. He is currently Principal Investigator of the Irish Research Council collaborative project 'The Colonial Landscapes of Richard Boyle, 1st Earl of Cork'.

The Ulster Plantation

in the Counties of Armagh and Cavan, 1608–41

R.J. Hunter

Foreword by

David Edwards

ULSTER HISTORICAL FOUNDATION

Published in association with the R.J. Hunter Committee.
The Committee works to acknowledge the contribution R.J. Hunter made to the study of our past by making more widely known the results of his research, as well as giving limited support to others engaged in associated endeavours.

The Committee is grateful for the assistance of Dr. David Edwards and Dr. Margaret Curtis Clayton in producing this volume.

First published 2012. Reprinted in paperback 2016
by Ulster Historical Foundation,
First Floor, Corn Exchange,
31 Gordon Street, Belfast, BT1 2LG
www.ancestryireland.com
www.booksireland.org.uk

ISBN: 978-1-903688-96-0

COVER IMAGES

Front: Tombstone of Bishop William Bedell (d. 1642),
Kilmore, County Cavan (courtesy of William J. Roulston)

Back: 'The Barony of Ardmagh', 1609
(The National Archives, ref. MPF1/63)

Printed by SPRINT-print Ltd.
Design by Cheah Design

CONTENTS

TABLES AND MAPS

Tables:

Maps in plate section:

ABBREVIATIONS

AFM	*Annala rioghachta Eireann; Annals of the kingdom of Ireland by the Four Masters*
Anal. Hib.	*Analecta Hibernica*
App.	Appendix
Arch. Hib.	*Archivium Hibernicum*
bars	baronies
BIHR	*Bulletin of the Institute of Historical Research*
BL	British Library
Bod. Lib.	Bodleian Library, Oxford University
Cal. Carew MSS	*Calendar of Carew MSS preserved in the archiepiscopal library at Lambeth, 1515–1624*, ed. J.S. Brewer & W. Bullen 6 vols, (London 1867–73)
Cal. fiants Ir.	'Calendar to fiants of the reigns of Henry VIII–Elizabeth'
Chas	Charles
cos.	counties
Cott.	Cottonian
CPRI, Chas I	*Calendar of patent and close rolls of chancery in Ireland, Charles I, years 1 to 8, ed. James Morrin* (Dublin, 1864).
CPRI, Eliz.	*Calendar of the Patent & Close Rolls of Chancery in Ireland from the 18th to the 45th of Queen Elizabeth*, ed. James Morrin (Dublin 1861)
CPRI, Jas I	*Calendar of Irish patent rolls, James I* (Dublin 1830)
CSP Dom	*Calendar of State Papers, Domestic*
CSPI	*Calendar of state papers, Ireland, 1509–1670*, ed. H.C. Hamilton et al. (24 vols., London 1860–1912)
DKRI	*Report of the Deputy Keeper of the Records, Ireland*
d.s.p.	died without issue
edn.	edition
EHR	*English Historical Review*
fol./ff	folio/folios
fn.	footnote
IER	*Irish Ecclesiastical Record*
IHS	*Irish Historical Studies*
Inq. cancel. Hib. repert.	*Inquisitionum in officio rotulorum cancellariae Hiberniae asservatarum reportorium*, ii, (Ultonia), (Dublin 1829).
Ir.	Irish
Jas	James
JCHAS	*Journal of the Cork Historical and Archaeological Society*
jnl.	*journal*
JRSAI	*Journal of the Royal Society of Antiquaries of Ireland*
JRHAAI	*Journal of the Royal Historical & Archaeological*

	Association of Ireland
Lam. Pal. Lib.	Lambeth Palace Library, London
MS/MSS	Manuscript/Manuscripts
NAI	National Archives of Ireland
n.d.	no date
NLI	National Library of Ireland
OED	*Oxford English Dictionary*
PKIAS	*Proceedings and papers of the Kilkenny and south-east of Ireland Archaeological Society*
PRIA	*Proceedings of the Royal Irish Academy*
PRONI	Public Record Office of Northern Ireland
RCB Lib.	Representative Church Body Library, Dublin
RIA	Royal Irish Academy
SHR	*Scottish Historical Review*
ster/stg	sterling
Stud. Hib.	*Studia Hibernica*
TCD	Trinity College, Dublin
TNA	The National Archives, London
UJA	*Ulster Journal of Archaeology*

FOREWORD

Once upon a time in Ireland, in the days before desktop publishing, it was relatively unusual for a dissertation – even a history dissertation – to be published in full book form. Thumbing through the back issues of the periodical *Irish Historical Studies*, which each year supplies a hand-list of 'Theses on Irish history completed in Irish universities', it is striking how few of the dissertations completed during the 1950s, '60s and '70s achieved much notice after their completion. Only a minority would later reappear as monographs, published by some university press or other (usually English), or a commercial publishing house (very often English). The great majority of dissertations had to settle for more limited public exposure, in the form of articles derived from the main body of the dissertation text which might be accepted for publication by a variety of national and international peer-reviewed periodicals and specialist journals. Yet even those dissertations that produced an article or two can hardly be said to have achieved their full potential. Indeed, more often than not, once published, the extracted articles were viewed by many who read them as a convenient substitute for having to consult the dissertations from which they derived. As a result, for several decades, a very large proportion of the very best scholarship on Irish history went mostly unread.

For the early modern period the non-publication of one dissertation in particular has seemed especially regrettable, R.J. Hunter's 'The Ulster plantation in the counties of Armagh and Cavan, 1608–1641', completed in Trinity College, Dublin in 1969. As anyone who has attempted to teach it at third level can attest, the plantation in Ulster has long continued to be one of the most contested episodes of Ireland's past. Early in my career, as a tutor in Modern History at Trinity in 1988–9, I found the task of teaching the plantation to be poorly served by most of the available secondary literature. Simply put, much of what had been published was unequal to the questions raised in class by bright freshman students curious about the actual mechanics of seventeenth-century colonisation and its political justification and who were mindful of the plantation's lingering presence behind much more recent events. Most popular histories of the plantation era were unreflectively partisan, either pro- or anti-colonist in approach, while supposedly more balanced academic writings tended to avoid the very questions that students most often asked about the plantation scheme in order to make sense of it: Why was it done? Did it make Ireland easier to govern from Whitehall, or more difficult? How was it done? To what extent did the transfer of millions of acres that it entailed rely on the use of coercion? What sort of opposition did it face, and how easily was this overcome? Frustrated at being unable to answer the students' questions satisfactorily, I raised the matter with Aidan Clarke and Ciaran Brady: it was through them that I discovered R.J. Hunter's dissertation, hidden away in the stores of Trinity's library.

I was aware of his name. A few years earlier I had been introduced to Bob at a college prize-giving and had briefly chatted with him and his friend Kenneth Nicholls over dinner, since which I had read three or four of his articles as background to my research. His dissertation, however, proved a revelation. It was not just that it provided answers to many of the questions I had been confronted with as a tutor. Looking over the notes that I took from it, I see that I filled nearly forty pages of foolscap with Hunter's insights into a range of issues that went beyond my immediate teaching needs – I was struck by his detailed knowledge of the background of his English, Scottish and Irish protagonists; his careful scrutiny of the series of surveys commissioned by the government immediately before the plantation began, and throughout its subsequent development; his grasp of the various legal (and extra-legal) mechanisms that underpinned the plantation and how they affected peoples' lives, from the greatest of the planters to the humblest of tenants and those that were made landless; and I was clearly impressed by his observations on the disparity between the government's assumptions about the positive impact of the plantation and the reality of its introduction on the ground in Cavan and Armagh.

Hunter's command of his subject – in places magisterial – was grounded on a strong chronological foundation, in which each development was located in its proper time and place, a meticulous process which allowed even minor details to gain added meaning as, expertly, they were fitted in to a larger sequence. By the 1980s some studies of colonisation in early seventeenth-century Ulster had moved away from chronological or 'narrative' history, adopting instead a thematic approach to the subject. While this approach did yield some important new insights, it was largely dependant on there being a fully rounded chronology of often very complex occurrences. Reading Hunter, it was clear that the accepted chronology on which such studies rested was deficient – what scholars had identified as key trends were sometimes interpreted out of sequence or, more often, without proper awareness of other relevant developments.

His chapters on the period 1619–1637 (Chapters 4–5, and much of Chapter 6) are a case in point. Too often the historiography had concentrated on the early years of the plantation, from its inception in 1608–09 to Pynnar's Survey of 1618–19, before cutting hastily to the late 1630s, to Wentworth's campaign against the Scottish settlers and the run-up to the plantation's overthrow by the Irish in 1641. By ignoring the crucial 'middle period' after 1619, a succession of scholars had helped to create a mostly false impression that little of moment had occurred in Ulster before the Scottish crisis erupted – that is to say, that the plantation had settled down, and that the Irish rebellion, when it came, was unexpected, a terrible shock, 'a bolt from the blue'. Hunter knew otherwise. By giving equal coverage to the middle years he was able to observe a very different scenario, in which the plantation underwent a series of emergencies due to fear of invasion or local rebellion (or a combination of both), and which continued until shortly before the Scottish crisis. Characteristically, he did not place a heavy emphasis on this point, preferring instead to let the facts, arranged in sequence, do the work.

But it is not just his treatment of the background to 1641 that stands out. His careful tracing of events provides important elucidation of much else besides. For instance, discussing the evolution of the plantation project before 1610, he anticipated the work of later scholars (notably John McCavitt) in revealing the distaste of the lord deputy, Sir Arthur Chichester, for the scale and form of the plantation scheme that was eventually approved in Whitehall, and after 1610, the deputy's constant support of the army interest in Ulster over that of the planters. Early in Chapter 3 Hunter shows that the 1615 conspiracy was far more serious than is sometimes thought, and probably shocked James I into renewing the plantation, whereas just a little earlier royal enthusiasm for the colony had been visibly flagging. A few pages later, Hunter throws an especially penetrating light on the post-1615 situation in Ulster in his treatment of George Allen's hopelessly unrealistic militia project, and the abject failure of the planters and the crown to agree on an agent or official to mediate between them. Historians have long noted the mutual incomprehension and suspicion that gradually emerged between the planters and the state during the 1610s and 1620s, particularly over the retention of Irish tenants, yet few have described this as well as Hunter. He shows how government plans to keep the Irish segregated from the 'British' heartland were confounded by the economic realities that pressed on many planter families unable to attract enough English or Scottish tenants, and in Armagh and Cavan the proliferation of Irish of all sorts appears to have reached peak levels by *c.* 1630, to the alarm of Dublin and London. Yet even here Hunter brings fresh light and deeper understanding, able through careful sifting of the evidence to suggest that on some estates planters had endeavoured to co-operate with the requirement to limit the number of natives to a quarter of the available land. Plainly, inter-ethnic relations varied widely from estate to estate, accommodating and business-like on one, cold and guarded on another; the tension and volatility that this engendered lurks between the sentences.

At the end of his chronological narrative Hunter's treatment of Wentworth is no less striking. According to many discussions of the subject, Wentworth was harsh towards the planters, oppressing most of the Scots but antagonising the English too, so much so that English Ulster planters were prominent among his adversaries and played a significant part in his downfall. In Hunter's hands this familiar tale is significantly altered. The governor is shown to have initially intended to bring the colonists to book; however, as his proposed plantation of Connacht ran into difficulties and came more and more to consume him, Wentworth is depicted as modifying his position over Ulster, and in Armagh and Cavan – though not in Londonderry – his administration adopted a more conciliatory attitude than is generally realised.

The second section of the dissertation is just as accomplished, attempting nothing less than a comprehensive social and economic history of the two counties in order to measure the full impact of the plantation on everyday life in Ulster before 1641. Re-reading it recently as it was being prepared for publication, I was just as impressed as when I first read it twenty years ago. While some fine studies of aspects of the plantation's economy have been published since the 1970s, few are better than Hunter is here. Beginning with an overview of the native Irish experience that ranges from the main Irish grantees included within the plantation to the thousands of Irish that it left landless (Chapter 7), he explores in detail the main ways in which the English and Scottish newcomers set about the task of transforming the region and eking out livelihoods for their families and followers – their trades and occupations, their uneven record of building activity, their disputes over terms and conditions of occupancy, their frequent recourse to litigation and the courts. The chapter on towns (Chapter 8) will be partly familiar to students of the period, some of its contents having appeared in Hunter's well-known essay 'Towns in the Ulster Plantation', published in *Studia Hibernica* in 1971, but even so the chapter contains much added information on Armagh, Charlemont, Mountnorris, Tandragee, Cavan, Belturbet and Virginia, which was otherwise omitted from the article.

The depth of understanding that Hunter brings to these and other aspects of plantation society is matched by the depth of the archival research that underpins it. Not content to confine his inquiry to standard primary sources such as the State Papers or the Carew Manuscripts, he ranged far and wide in search of new material. Just look at the bibliography at the end: it provides one of the most extensive listings of manuscript materials in the National Archives of Ireland, the National Library of Ireland, Trinity College Library, and Armagh Archiepiscopal Library ever produced by an Irish early modern historian. To this day few scholars have discovered as much material in these repositories as Hunter did. This is not to say that he managed to find everything. At the time of his research little was known of the survival of Irish historical papers in the United Kingdom, outside the British Library, TNA, or the Oxford and Cambridge libraries, as the system of county and local record offices was still in its infancy. Accordingly, he was unaware of the Valentia papers, now at Oxfordshire County Record Office, which contains important estate documents from Cos Armagh, Cavan and Down that would have added significantly to his analysis; likewise the Culme papers in Dorset County Record Office have valuable private papers concerning planter families in Co. Cavan.[1] Yet even these sources will probably only augment what Hunter found elsewhere. The enduring quality of his dissertation is a testament to his huge appetite for what Kenneth Nicholls calls digging, and what I prefer to call sleuthing – constantly sniffing about, asking more questions, looking for new evidence in places that no-one else has looked.

It is deeply regrettable that the exceptional calibre of Hunter's work was not better recognised when it was submitted as a thesis in 1968. Shockingly it was only awarded the degree of M. Litt and not the PhD it so richly deserved, due, it is believed, to the harsh assessment of its external examiner, but also possibly to a difference of opinion in relation to the interpretation it deployed between Hunter and his supervisor, the late T.W. Moody. Hunter never really recovered from this setback. He would not attempt to publish the thesis, even in modified form, because his confidence was weakened. It gives me great pleasure to see the thesis in book form at last. Its appearance helps to right an injustice; better still, it makes for an excellent book. In the current slew of publications marking the quadricentennial of the plantation it will take a very special work to top it. I think you will agree, once you have read it.

Finally, for their assistance with this project I would like to thank Dr. Margaret Curtis-Clayton, Aine Sheehan and David Heffernan at University College Cork (UCC).

David Edwards

[1] For a listing see Brian Donovan and David Edwards, *British Sources for Irish History 1485–1641: A Guide to Manuscripts in Local, Regional and Specialised Repositories in England, Scotland and Wales* (IMC Dublin 1997), 44–5, 209–13.

PREFACE

Since Professor Moody's comprehensive study of the Londonderry plantation was published, almost thirty years ago, there has been no attempt to examine the plantation in any of the other escheated counties of Ulster. This thesis, undertaken at his suggestion, seeks to extend the treatment to two counties, each with distinctive features, where individual settlers rather than corporate bodies were the predominating agents of colonisation.

Apart from my own limitations in evaluating the surviving materials, I have been hampered throughout by the very limited amount of surviving estate materials and sources of local and legal administration from which systematic data could be drawn. As a result the treatment of many social and economic aspects has been necessarily incomplete and inconclusive. However, much that is suggestive has been included in the hope that studies of other counties will reveal complementary information from which a general picture of the plantation can eventually be built up.

The development of settlement in both counties has been examined against a background of the history of the plantation as a whole. The separation of particular and general aspects has presented difficulties, but in so far as possible both have been considered in different sections of each chapter. Considerations of space, in an already lengthy thesis, precluded detailed treatment of the British background of the settlers.

Two maps of each county are presented to indicate ownership at the outset of the plantation and also to show the effect by 1641 of intervening changes. Similarly, to give the thesis a statistical basis the areas of land held by the different types of owners at the beginning and in 1641 have been calculated. Reproductions of contemporary plans and maps have not been included, with the exception of Netherclift's map of Cavan town, *c.* 1593. A reconstruction of the town of Armagh in 1618 from a rental of that year, made by Mr. H.D.McC. Reid, MA, vice-principal of Armagh Royal School, which forms part of his unpublished MA thesis 'The historical geography of Armagh' (QUB, 1954) is presented here by his kind permission. I am specifically indebted to Mr. C.J.W. Edwards, MA, lecturer in Geography at Magee University College, whose draftsmanship has given my maps their highly professional appearance.

I am indebted to many people for advice on source material and for numerous helpful suggestions. In particular I would like to thank Dr. John Andrews, Dr. L.J. Arnold, Professor J.C. Beckett, Mr. John Brown, Dr. Aidan Clarke, Dr. William Crawford, Dr. M. Perceval Maxwell, Professor

J.L. McCracken, Mr. K. W. Nicholls, Dr. J.G. Simms, and Mr. Joseph Starr. To the staffs and curators of all the libraries and manuscript repositories in which I worked, I wish to express my thanks. I owe special thanks to the staff of the library of Magee University College, Londonderry. My primary debt, for both advice and kindness, to my supervisor Professor T.W. Moody, I gratefully acknowledge.

R.J. Hunter, 1968

CHAPTER 1

Introduction

1. The plantation scheme

The background in Ulster to the Flight of the Earls, which precipitated the adoption of the policy of plantation there, is well known.[1] Already since the battle of Kinsale British institutions and laws were being introduced and the very progress of these played some part in the earls' decision to embark for the continent.

The Flight of the Earls on 3 September 1607 suggested an all-out confiscation of their territories. Immediate steps also had to be taken to fill the power vacuum created by their departure. Thus on September 7 a proclamation was issued assuring the inhabitants of Tyrone and Tyrconnell that they would not be disturbed in the possession of their lands so long as they behaved as dutiful subjects,[2] and also a commission was issued to the archbishop of Armagh and sixteen others, bishops, local commanders, and Gaelic Irish, for the government of Tyrone, Tyrconnell, and Armagh.[3] Suggestions for re-settlement took various forms, a division of the land between natives and servitors being commonly suggested, with forts and towns to guarantee security, though it was also felt that British colonists should be imported.[4] With the drift of these early plans the London government concurred, requesting further information.[5] The precedent of the Munster plantation was also examined.[6] In December the territory of the fugitives, indicted of treason, was found, by local juries, to be forfeit to the king.[7] In April 1608 the rebellion of Sir Cahir O'Doherty, lord of Innishowen,[8] and the sympathetic outburst at the end of May of Oghy Oge O'Hanlon in Armagh[9] both soon suppressed, gave incentive to the scheme

1 T.W. Moody, *The Londonderry Plantation, 1609–41* (Belfast, 1939), provides a general introduction which is re-worked here to bring out certain issued not relevant to the Londonderry situation, 23–40.

2 *CSPI, 1606–8*, 263.

3 Ibid., 263–4; *CPRI, Jas I*, 118.

4 *CSPI, 1606–8*, 266, 268, 276, 281, 304, 339–43.

5 Ibid., 286, 290, 331.

6 Ibid., 325–6.

7 Ibid., 343–4, 335, 361, 389–93, 406, 434, 555–6.

8 Moody, *Londonderry*, 29–39.

9 See below, 21–2.

for plantation.[10] By March 10 Chichester had drafted his 'notes of remembrance' for the guidance of the privy council in London.[11] These recommendations were essentially moderate both in the amount of the escheated territory with which they dealt and as to the proportion of each county covered which was recommended for plantation. At this time the province was governed in ten units by local commanders[12] and the establishment of a presidency was being suggested, to be located at either Dungannon or Armagh.[13] Sir Josias Bodley, the overseer of fortifications, was sent to examine and report on the serviceability of the Ulster forts.[14]

O'Doherty's rebellion underlined the need for a new settlement and caused a hardening in attitudes towards the Ulster Irish.[15] On July 20 the privy council ordered Chichester to abstain from making promises of any of the escheated lands.[16] On the same day in a letter to Sir Geoffrey Fenton Salisbury, recognising that the logic of conquest was plantation, that 'a free passage [was] prepared to the ... settlinge' of Ulster, expressed the hope that the lord deputy would not be 'over facile' in granting pardons to those who would afterwards 'crosse the courses of plantacon his majesty intendeth.'[17] On August 5 Sir John Davies informed Salisbury that the king had six entire counties in Ulster at his command 'which is a greater extent of land than any prince in Europe has to dispose of'.[18] The next two years saw the working out of the plantation scheme, the choice of settlers, and the allocation of land.

Between July and September 1608 in an official tour through the six counties of Armagh, Tyrone, Coleraine, Donegal, Fermanagh, and Cavan[19] surveys of the state of landownership were taken in each county.[20] These surveys differentiated lay from clerical land, and investigated the amount of land within each barony and within each Gaelic territory of which the baronies were composed. They listed monastic property in each county, examined the parochial organisation, inquired into the amount of land over which the bishops had control, and stated on what grounds the temporal land was available for plantation. On October 14 Chichester dispatched

10 *CSPI, 1606–8*, 480–4, 485–7, 499–514, 516–20, 524–27, 541–5, 563.
11 'Ulster Plantation Papers' no. 73, *Anal. Hib.* viii.
12 *CSPI, 1606–8*, 401–3.
13 Ibid., 397–8, 405, 487.
14 Ibid., 502, 514, 526.
15 *CSPI, 1608–10*, 81.
16 *CSPI, 1606–8*, 617. Chichester assented in September (*CSPI, 1608–10*, 34).
17 A.B. Grosart (ed.), *The Lismore Papers*, 2nd ser., 1, 127–8.
18 *CSPI, 1608–10*, 17.
19 Ibid., 14–17, 25–29.
20 A contemporary abstract of these is published in *Anal. Hib.* iii. The survey in detail for Armagh is in TCD, MS 582, ff 177–96.

Sir James Ley, the chief justice, and Sir John Davies, the attorney general, to London armed with his revised 'notes of remembrances' on the state of each of the six escheated counties, as well as with general recommendations, to confer with the privy council in drawing up the scheme for colonisation.[21] The claims of landholders within each county were discussed, and places deserving of special care mentioned. It was an essay in political geography. Chichester recommended that the principal natives in each county be taken into consideration, noting that although their claims to freehold status could not be justified in law, it would be almost impossible to displant them. The rest of the land should be granted to well-chosen undertakers from England and Scotland as well as servitors from Ireland, on fixed conditions and with annual rents to the crown which should be remitted for the first years. All grantees should take the oath of supremacy, except, perhaps, some of the natives. Estates should not be very large or of especially unequal size. The servitors should be located in places of most danger, those of inadequate means to be given temporary military appointments in their localities. When these servitors had been placed, and such natives as should receive land chosen, the remainder of the land should be allocated to undertakers in equal proportions, their location to be determined by lot. The English and Scottish undertakers should be required to build castles and strong houses, erect towns and villages, and enclose and manure the land in a civil fashion and should accordingly be required to pay less rent than the Irish from which it would be optimistic to expect such improvements. The Irish, however, should be obliged to refrain from their 'creatinge' a transhumance practice, settle in towns and villages and build houses like those of the Pale. Special care should be taken of the church, both in the re-building of places of worship and the allocation of adequate endowments to parochial clergy and bishops. In the granting of land to the bishops, whose temporalities were not obscured and 'out of order' it would be best to begin afresh 'as if his Majesty were to begin a new plantation in America from which it does not greatly differ'. On October 18 Chichester suggested that Scottish grantees should not be allowed to bring over islanders as their tenants.[22]

A committee was now formed in London to prepare the details of the plan, which was completed by January 1609 when two fundamental documents were produced, one of which was printed. These were 'A Collection of such Orders and Conditions as are to be observed by the undertakers upon the distribution and Plantation of the Escheated lands in

[21] 'Ulster Plantation Papers' no. 75, *Anal. Hib.*, viii; *CSPI, 1608–10*, 54–65, 68.

[22] *CSPI, 1608–10*, 85.

Ulster',[23] and 'A Project for the Division and Plantation of the Escheated lands in … Ulster',[24] the latter an extension to the six counties of the specimen project drawn up by 20 December 1608 for County Tyrone.[25]

The 'Orders and Conditions' laid down that the estates, or proportions, should be of three sizes: great, middle, and small, containing 2,000, 1,500 and 1,000 English acres respectively, quantities of bog and wood to be granted in addition rent free depending on local availability. Beneficiaries under the scheme were to be of three types: English and Scottish who were to settle their proportions with English and inland (or lowland) Scottish tenants, servitors of Ireland who might take Irish or British tenants, and natives of Ireland. The king should decide in what county each undertaker should have his grant, but indicated that within each county the allocation should be by lot.

The English and Scottish undertakers were to have their estates in fee farm paying an annual quit-rent to the crown at the rate of £5. 6. 8. per thousand acres, with exemption from payment for the first two years. Great and middle proportions were to be held by knight's service in capite though to be exempt from wardship for the first two descents, small proportions in common soccage. Every undertaker of a great proportion was, within two years of his letters patent, to build a castle enclosed with a strong court or bawn; of a middle proportion a stone or brick house and bawn; of a small proportion a bawn at least. They were to plant within the same two-year period 'a competent number' of British tenants, who should be obliged to build their houses near the undertakers' strongholds. All were to be allowed timber from the king's woods in the province for their buildings. Each undertaker should have in his house 'a convenient store of arms' for the defence of his colony, which should be mustered half-yearly. The undertakers should take the oath of supremacy and conform to the official religion. Each undertaker or an accredited agent must reside on his lands for five years after his grant. They should have power to erect manors, and hold courts baron twice in the year and create tenures. One-third of their estates should be held in demesne, one-third alienated in fee-farm and the remainder for forty years or under. They should not grant any land to the mere Irish. No part of their estate should be demised at will, and they should not reserve uncertain rents or Irish exactions. For seven years they

[23] TNA, SP 63 226, ff 30–39v; it is printed, with notes, in G. Hill, *Plantation papers* (Belfast, 1889), 78–89.

[24] 'Ulster Plantation Papers' no. 74, *Anal. Hib.* viii; *Cal. Carew MSS, 1603–24*, 13–22; Hill, *Plantation*, 90–116.

[25] *CSPI, 1608–10*, 117, 129.

should have power to export all produce without payment of custom and similarly to import food, utensils, materials, and stock.

The servitors should have their estates at a rent of £8 per thousand acres and rateably, but if they planted with British tenants they should pay at the same rent as the undertakers. Apart from the freedom to plant with Irish tenants, their conditions were not different from those of the undertakers. Irish grantees should pay at the rate of £10. 13. 4. per thousand acres, with exemption for one year only. They should build on and inhabit their lands as the undertakers were required to, and practice the agricultural methods of the Pale.

Commissioners were to be appointed to put the plantation into effect, all undertakers to appear before them at or before the coming midsummer. Every undertaker before receiving his patent should enter into a bond or recognizance to perform the conditions of his grant. In each county 'a convenient number' of market towns and corporations should be established, and there should be at least one free school in each county. There should likewise be a 'convenient' number of parishes and parish churches, all tithes to be paid to the incumbents.

The 'Project' began with five basic points. In each county half of the escheated land should be divided into small proportions, the remaining half to be divided equally into middle and great proportions. Each proportion was to be constituted a parish, a parish church erected on it, and glebe land assigned to each incumbent at the rate of sixty acres in every thousand. The 'Project' then examined each of the six counties. For each the acreage and number of local land units derived from the survey of the previous year was stated; the amount to be reserved for the church both episcopally and parochially, the area of monastic lands, the amount undertakeable divided into proportions, and the number of these to be given to each type of grantee, being also set down. The number of towns in each to be incorporated was defined, and land reserved to be granted to them. These should receive rights to hold markets and fairs, and 'other reasonable liberties' including the power to return burgesses to parliament, and to establish them there should be a 'levie or prest' of tradesmen and artificers out of England. Land was also to be reserved for one free school per county and Trinity College, Dublin, was to be endowed. The native population in each county was to be settled on the lands of the servitors, the native grantees either under or prior to the plantation, or on the bishops' lands and the glebes. 'Swordsmen', however, were to be transplanted to Connacht or Munster or impressed as soldiers.

Difficulties were encountered at this point. In March Chichester submitted his observations on the scheme as formulated. While approving in general of the sizes of proportions, he was not entirely in favour of a rigid 'popular equality' in division. Provision should be made for powerful undertakers to receive larger scopes. He brought forward objections to the method of assigning land by lot: groups of planters united by ties of friendship or blood might wish to live together; it was important that grantees be satisfied with the location of their lands; the servitors, previously anxious for land, were now unwilling to apply unless they could choose where to live, those in command of forts particularly desiring land nearby. The amount of time for building was too short. In particular the tenure by knight's service in capite, which had not been imposed on the Munster settlers, was objected to. Grants of land to the church would need further consideration. Also he felt that inadequate provision had been made for the native Irish, who were consequently very restive. Many more of them, especially in Cavan, Fermanagh, and Donegal, were claiming and expecting freeholds than appears to have been taken account of. In the solving of many of these problems much should be left to the discretion of the commissioners who would put the plantation into effect.[26] At the same time a rumour of the return of Tyrone provided added explanation for the lack of enthusiasm for the plantation.[27] Consequently, in May, the government decided to soften some of the conditions.[28]

Fresh difficulties now came into prominence. It became apparent that the 1608 survey had not been an accurate one. Further it had been merely a survey of the counties, it remained for the land to be divided into proportions, an essential preliminary to plantation. Also, a paralyzing problem had arisen through the claims of the Ulster bishops who brought forward a fundamental criticism of the findings of the surveyors. In 1608 the termon and erenagh lands had been uniformly pronounced crown property.[29] From these quasi-ecclesiastical lands, a peculiarity of Irish Christianity,[30] the bishops had received traditional rents but it was found that they were see property and so that they had escheated and were open to confiscation.[31] By a calculation made in March 1609 it was found that there were 7,986 acres of demesne and mensal lands in the escheated area, and 60,946 acres of termon and erenagh land.[32] This land, too, lay

26 *CSPI, 1608–10*, 149, 155–61, 176–9.

27 Ibid., 193.

28 Moody, *Londonderry*, 35; *CSPI, 1608–10*, 212.

29 *CSPI, 1608–10*, 16, 17.

30 For the medieval background of these lands and the institutions related to them see a series of articles by J. Barry in *IER*, series 5, lxxviii, 17–25 (1957); lxxix, 24–35, 424–32 (1958); xci, 27–39 (1959); xciii, 361–5 (1960); xciv, 12–16, 90–5, 147–53, 211–18 (1960).

31 Henry Morley, (ed.), *Ireland under Elizabeth and James I* (London, 1890), 364–7; *CSPI, 1608–10*, 280–1.

32 *CSPI, 1608–10*, 180. 293; *Cal. Carew MSS, 1603–24*, 40.

interspersed throughout the escheated area, and so presented added administrative difficulties.[33] The bishop of Derry, George Montgomery, one of those who drew up the 'Project' claimed these as outright demesne property. With such problems outstanding, it was decided to defer the granting out of the land until spring 1610.[34] By then it was felt a resurvey would have been conducted, the problems of church lands solved, the capacities of claimants for land investigated, the natives 'drawn into' reserved areas and a more peaceful environment assured, and new conditions of plantation, more attractive to servitors whose value to support the undertakers was recognised, promulgated.[35] At this point, the London government entered into negotiations with the city of London which resulted in its undertaking the entire county of Londonderry.

In June 1609 instructions were issued to the deputy, followed by a commission of July 21, to complete preparations in Ireland.[36] They were now to hold fresh inquisitions to remedy omissions and defects in the 1608 survey. Temporal land was to be divided into proportions according to the 'Project', each to be delineated by known mears and bounds, and the name of every ballyboe and other land measure in it recorded. Names should be chosen for the proportions, and in estates lying near highways, fit places on which undertakers should build selected. Because the principle of selection by lot discouraged potential undertakers wishing to live together, every county was to be divided into precincts, containing several proportions, to which consorts of undertakers might be appointed, lots to be drawn by precinct rather than proportion. Bog and wood over and above the acreage of proportions was to be allotted to each, though great woods were to be preserved for the king. The commissioners were to establish the boundaries of parishes and allocate glebe land at the rate of sixty acres in every thousand. They were to allot the lands to be granted to towns, schools, and the college at Dublin, and to reserve 12,000 acres as endowment of a hospital for maimed and diseased soldiers. They were to make maps of every county, indicating the boundaries of precincts and proportions by name. The commissioners should adjudicate disputes and controversies. They were to investigate complaints that clerical land had been granted out as monastic and where this had happened take steps for its restitution. Furthermore, they were particularly instructed to regard all lands from which the bishops 'have had heretofore rent, certentie of refecc'ons or penc'ons' as ecclesiastical

33 *CSPI, 1608–10*, 211.

34 Ibid., 211–12.

35 Ibid.

36 *Cal. Carew MSS, 1603–24*, 42–3; *CSPI, 1608–10*, 181–4, 213; *Inquisitionum in officio rotulorum cancellariae Hiberniae asservatarum reportorium*, ii, (Ultonia), (Dublin, 1829), App.; Moody, *Londonderry*, 36, n. 2.

property to be annexed to the appropriate sees. Royal title to all the areas of escheated land was to be drawn up by the lawyers. They were to report on what pensions or otherwise should be granted to the widows of special individuals. They were to arrange for the allocation of fishing rights. Their business should be concluded by 'hallowmass' and two copies of their findings made, one to be transmitted to London, the other to remain in Dublin.[37] At the same time the deputy was to send to England a list of such servitors as were willing to undertake for lands.[38] He was also to procure the removal of Ulster swordsmen to other parts of Ireland, or have them enlisted to serve abroad. Those authorised to levy soldiers for foreign service should particularly draw them from Armagh, Tyrone and Coleraine. Swordsmen who could not be transplanted should be confined to special places within the escheated counties at the discretion of the lord deputy.[39]

The commissioners devoted the period from July 31 to September 30 to their task, taking inquisitions in each county.[40] The jurors found universally, as before, that the bishops had no just claim to the erenagh lands in demesne despite pressure from the bishop of Derry,[41] Chichester reporting that 'some of them sought that of right which they must have of grace if they possess at all'.[42] In Fermanagh a dispute arose on this between the elderly Miler McGrath, archbishop of Cashel, who claimed Termon Magrath as erenagh, and Montgomery, who then held the bishopric of Clogher, claiming it as demesne.[43] In each barony they selected men who assisted the surveyor-general, Sir William Parsons, and Sir Josias Bodley and his cartographic associates in the construction of maps.[44]

Finally, in February 1610 Davies and Sir Thomas Ridgeway, the vice-treasurer, were sent to London with the commissioners' findings and with

37 *Inq. cancel. Hib. repert.*, ii, App.; *CSPI, 1608–10*, 236–7, 245–7, 253–4, 255–6; *Cal. Carew MSS, 1603–24*, 43.

38 *Cal. Carew MSS, 1603–24*, 43–3; *CSPI, 1608–10*, 213.

39 *Cal. Carew MSS, 1603–24*, 48–9.

40 *CSPI, 1608–10*, 293–5; *Inq. cancel. Hib. repert.*, ii, App.; TCD, MS 595.

41 *CSPI, 1608–10*, 280–1.

42 Ibid., 285. He stated that he wished they could have this land at the king's pleasure, but he could not 'digress from the duty and service he owed to his sovereign as to feed the insatiable humours of craving men, when they tend to his majesty's loss or dishonour, in order thereby to preserve himself from their envy and complaints' (ibid.). Whatever the justice of the bishops' claims it should be noted that the termon and erenach lands in the diocese of Dromore, outside the plantation are of Ulster, were not granted outright to the bishops (W. Reeves, *Ecclesiastical Antiquities of Down, Connor and Dromore* (Dublin, 1847), 310–11).

43 *CSPI, 1608–10*, 288, 292. In the 1590s and in the early years of the seventeenth century some of the Ulster termon and erenach lands, especially in Cavan and Fermanagh, had been granted out as monastic property. In 1596 the McGraths had surrendered and received a regrant of Termon Magrath (*DKRI*, 7–22 (Dublin, 1875–90)), nos 5993, 5997; *Calendar of patent and close rolls of chancery in Ireland, Elizabeth, 19 year to end of reign*, ed. James Morrin (Dublin, 1861), 361–2.

44 *CSPI, 1608–10*, 280–1, 293.

recommendations from Chichester on a wide range of details of the scheme.[45] The delay resulted from the fact that Chichester had been engaged after the commissioners' return to Dublin in rounding up swordsmen, one thousand of whom were dispatched to Sweden.[46] The two most important items returned by the commissioners were a set of barony maps of the six counties, made under Bodley's supervision,[47] and a detailed declaration of the king's title to the forfeited land in each county, the work of Davies,[48] as well as the inquisitions for each county.

The maps were described at the time in glowing terms, Davies stating that 'the most obscure part of the king's dominions is now as well known and more particularly described than any other part of England.'[49] Bodley, however, in a letter to Salisbury, indicated awareness of some defects of the work which later became apparent. He stated that while they had found 'many thousand more acres' for the king than in any previous survey their acreage estimates had been based on local computation as well as on Irish rather than statute measure. He accordingly advised that a clause be inserted in undertakers' patents reserving the right to take a more exact survey later, whereby he felt the king's revenue could be augmented by one-third.[50] It is sufficient to state here that the total acreage of the escheated counties found in 1609 was 424,643, which exceeded that of 1608 by 38,345 acres.[51] However, the maps had the immediate value that the temporal land had been divided into proportions, and ecclesiastical land, and land for other uses was demarked. The lawyers, in brief, found that the king's title to the lands in Armagh, Tyrone, and Coleraine, stemmed from the attainder of Shane O'Neill, to Donegal and Fermanagh from the flight of the chieftains, and to Cavan from the death of Philip O'Reilly in rebellion in 1596.[52]

At the end of January Chichester sent over a list of servitors, divided into eight categories, who were willing to undertake Ulster lands. These people, of varying positions and competencies, were 171 in number. In some cases he recommended where they should be located.[53] He attempted to restrain suitors for lands, British and Irish, from going to London by

45 Ibid., 389–91.

46 Ibid., 251, 263, 264–5, 281, 286–7, 296–7, 300, 303–6, 334 (some of them escaped).

47 TNA, MPF, 35–64; *Maps of the Escheated Counties in Ireland [Ulster], 1609* (Ordnance Survey Office, Southampton, 1861). The coverage for Donegal and Londonderry did not come to light. Two maps of Donegal have since been located amongst the muniments of Trinity College, Dublin (F.H.A. Aalen and R.J. Hunter, 'Two Early Seventeenth Century Maps of Donegal', *JRSAI*, xciv, 2, 199–202).

48 *CSPI, 1608–10*, 389, 552–77.

49 Ibid., 409.

50 Ibid., 392–3.

51 Ibid., 404.

52 Ibid., 552–77.

53 Ibid., 365–8.

undertaking to present their cases himself.[54] He also, in common with other members of the Irish administration, sent a wide range of general and specific recommendations. Soccage tenure should be adopted rather than grants in capite. Powerful men should be induced to supervise a barony (or precinct), each to select suitable undertakers, who should not make leases for less than twenty-one years or three lives. Previously he had stressed that the success of the plantation scheme would depend on subsidisation from England.[55] Tenants should not be allowed to 'struggle or disperse' into unsafe places as they had done in Munster, but should dwell together beside the principal undertaker, thereby deriving a strength out of unity against 'the common enemy'.[56] He felt the time for building should be extended to four years, during which time also measures of land enclosure should be effected. The period of exemption from rent should also be extended. The Irish, since they would be difficult to transplant to other parts of Ireland, should be removed to segregated areas within the six counties and reformed from their social customs. They should not be settled amongst the British population, which Munster experience had shown to be unsuccessful. To preserve the cultural identity of the settlers, they must be kept separate from the Irish, forbidden to intermarry with them, 'and if possible … exceed them in multitude'. His attitude to the Irish was, however, within the limits of his commitment to the plantation policy, more liberal than their subsequent treatment would suggest, pointing out that it was a matter of 'great consequence and necessity' to make 'meet provision' for them.[57] However, precautions must be taken for the defence of the colony and he recommended that if an Ulster presidency were to be established, it should be located at Dungannon.[58] He urged that the division of land should be made by baronies, rather than by individual proportions, which would cause paralyzing administrative difficulty. Sir Edward Brabazon, writing to Salisbury in March, pointed to the dangers of tension stemming from the conflicting purposes of undertakers and servitors: '… the captains wishing for war to supply them and the undertakers for peace are two contrarities which can hardly be brought into fashion unless the martial men may be placed by themselves.'[59]

Dealing with the church Chichester emphasised again that the bishops' claims to the erenagh lands were unfounded though he pointed out that the erenaghs were not worthy to be grantees. If the bishops were to receive these

54 Ibid., 390–1.
55 Ibid., 269–70.
56 Ibid., 355–9.
57 Ibid.
58 Ibid., 368–72.
59 Ibid., 407–8.

lands the parish clergy should have allocations of glebe from them. The bishops should be enjoined to build a substantial house for their own use in each diocese and plant British on their lands and compel their Irish tenants to live a settled life. The bishops should have the donation of benefices except for a small number to be granted to the college and the lord deputy.[60]

Fortified with such wide-ranging recommendations the commissioners in London worked out the final arrangements in the spring of 1610. It was decided that the termon and erenagh lands should be granted to the bishops 'as of his Majesty's free donation' and on a negotiated basis. The outcome was that the bishops consented to plant one-third at least of these lands with British under the plantation conditions, being free to demise the remainder to Irish. In the first instance they might make leases for sixty-year periods but succeeding leasings should not exceed twenty-one years or three lives.[61]

The temporal lands in the five counties were divided into twenty-eight precincts, sixteen to be allocated to British undertakers, in equal proportions to English and Scots, and twelve to servitors and native grantees. Each of the precincts allotted to undertakers was to be supervised by a substantial figure – members of the English or Scottish privy councils – who should select a group of undertakers, a consort, and allocate to each his proportion. The servitors and native grantees were to be planted together. Three reasons were given for this: that the servitors, being familiar with the Irish, could 'carry a better hand and eye' over them than the undertakers; that it would be advisable to separate the servitors from the undertakers to avoid dissentions; that since the servitors might receive Irish tenants they should not be intermingled with the undertakers who should only plant with British.[62]

In April a revised set of conditions was produced, under which the grantees accepted their lands later in the year. These revised conditions for undertakers were printed in London,[63] the corresponding regulations for servitors and Irish natives exist only in manuscript. The form of the previous set was followed but certain changes were made. Each precinct for undertakers was to be assigned to a principal undertaker and his consort, the chief undertaker being allowed two middle proportions if he desired. Lands should be held in free and common soccage as of Dublin castle. The time limit for building castles and planting tenants was extended to three years, rent payment to begin at Michaelmas 1614. Each undertaker of one-

[60] Ibid., 355–9, 362–5, 368–72, 389–90, 390–1.

[61] Ibid., 409–11; *Cal. Carew MSS, 1603–24*, 38–40 (incorrectly ascribed to March 1609).

[62] *CSPI, 1608–10*, 404–6, 409–11.

[63] BL, Lansdowne MS 159, ff 217–23; T.W. Moody, 'The revised articles of the Ulster plantation, 1610', *BIHR*, xii, 178–83.

thousand acres was by the time limit to have twenty-four male British tenants aged eighteen and over and forming at least ten families upon his proportion, with corresponding increases for larger estates. These ten families should be divided as follows: two fee-farmers with one hundred and twenty acres each; three lease-holders, for twenty-one years or three lives, of one hundred acres each; and four families of husbandmen, artificers, or cottagers whose land was to be assigned at the discretion of the undertaker, who should himself have a demesne of three hundred acres. Undertakers and tenants should take the oath of supremacy. The undertakers or their agents should present themselves before the lord deputy and plantation commissioners before the ensuing midsummer day, and occupy their proportions before Michaelmas. The revised conditions for servitors and natives embodied corresponding modifications.[64]

In the months of April and May the baronies assigned for undertakers were allotted to consort groups by superintending members of the English and Scottish privy councils.[65] The selecting of servitors and native freeholders took longer, posed specific difficulties, and involved both the Dublin and London governments. From the list of servitors sent over by Chichester a short list of suitable candidates, with accompanying instructions, was returned to Dublin in April 1610. It was laid down that no servitor with a current martial position in Ulster, unless a privy councillor, should be a grantee. The deputy was given discretion to omit from the list returned unsuitable candidates.[66] In general, however, the placing of the servitors was to fall within the competence of the Dublin government, the consort principle was not applied. Recommendations of individuals from London, not all of which were accepted and some of which were received after the land had been allotted, were common,[67] but within the framework of the list of servitors and the accompanying instructions, the deputy and plantation commissioners had considerable initiative in the selection and placing of servitor grantees.

The selection of native freeholders and the treatment of the Ulster Irish generally had, as we have seen, occupied attention for a considerable time before 1610. Chichester regarded the settlement of the natives as a political problem of the utmost importance. In a letter to the privy council in February he urged that careful consideration be given to their location in each county 'and how the dependence of a multitude may … be so taken

64 'Ulster Plantation Papers' no. 18, *Anal. Hib.* viii; *Cal. Carew MSS, 1603–24*, 50–2.
65 'Ulster Plantation Papers' no. 21, *Anal. Hib.* viii.
66 *CSPI, 1608–10*, 428–9.
67 See for example, 'Ulster Plantation Papers' no. 23, *Anal. Hib.* viii; *CSPI, 1608–10*, 450, 455.

away from all the great ones, as they may chiefly depend upon the king and his laws'. This could be done, in his opinion,

> by creating many petty freeholders among them, with parity of estates, by making few or none of them equal with the rest of the undertakers, therein, by overtopping them in multitudes if it be possible.[68]

As a guide to 'your lordships and us' in the selection he forwarded a list of names of freeholders which had been drawn up for him previously by the earl of Tyrone and other northern chiefs.[69] In March it was felt that the choice of native grantees should be referred to the deputy and plantation commissioners.[70] While, as in the case of other grantee categories, the number of baronies to be assigned was decided in England, the selection of suitable natives clearly demanded a degree of local knowledge which could not be shared by the English government. However, in a number of important instances the lord deputy requested that government decide on the amount and location of land to be granted,[71] and was advised accordingly.[72] Also certain of the substantial native gentry appear to have gone to London to plead their cases and come back with recommendations to the deputy.[73] However, apart from such important instances and within the limits of available land, the choosing and siting of native grantees was left to the deputy and the commissioners for implementing the plantation.

Certain further problems were considered in the spring before responsibility for the inauguration was transferred to Dublin. Particular points concerning the granting of land to the church were cleared up, and it was ordered that the bishoprics and other spiritual livings in Ulster should be rated for first fruits. It was decided that although tradesmen were not apparently to be transplanted from England to live in them, the proposed Ulster towns should be incorporated as planned, their importance in returning members to parliament being recognised. Steps should also be taken for the transplantation of Ulster natives to other parts of Ireland, or indeed to Sweden or Virginia.[74] It was decided that the deputy should nominate the commissioners to put the plantation into effect.[75] Its

68 *Calendar of patent and close rolls of Chancery in Ireland, Charles I, years 1 to 8*, ed. James Morrin (Dublin, 1864), 636–9.

69 Ibid. The list has not been found.

70 *CSPI, 1608–10*, 411.

71 Ibid., 362–5.

72 Ibid., 429; *Cal. Carew MSS, 1603–24*, 52–3.

73 *CSPI, 1608–10*, 431–2, 438–9, 440–1, 443.

74 Ibid., 415–16, 425.

75 Ibid., 424.

implementation now had a special urgency because there were fears that the Irish regiment in Flanders would be disbanded and that its members might return to Ireland and raise a new war.[76] Finally in June Davies and Ridgeway were returned to Ireland and a commission was issued for the transference of the land to grantees. In July Chichester and his fellow commissioners set out for Ulster to inaugurate the new dispensation now so lengthily planned.[77]

It may be noted that Ulster had not been entirely unprofitable to the crown in the interval since the Flight of the Earls. Sir Toby Caulfeild was appointed to collect the rents due to the earl of Tyrone from the counties of Armagh, Tyrone and Coleraine from the flight until 1 November 1610. These ranged from £2,100 Ir. to nearly £2,900 Ir. per annum,[78] though much of this was disbursed in maintaining order in this interim period.[79]

2. Historical background

A. Armagh, 1543–1610

It is well known that Henry VIII's surrender and regrant policy created untold dynastic problems and had little permanent effect. The creation of Conn O'Neill earl of Tyrone in 1543[80] may have seemed likely to introduce momentous changes in central Ulster. However, the succession arrangement – to his illegitimate son Matthew – which his patent incorporated, did not commend itself to his other son Shane, who in 1559 had himself styled O'Neill, symbolic of his wide popular support. The Dublin administration found itself with little power against him, the garrisoning of Armagh in 1551 and again 1561, when the cathedral was fortified and 200 men placed there by Sussex, had little effect. In 1556 an expedition led by Sussex into Ulster proved unsuccessful; the deputy in fact decided that Ulster could only be subordinated by a chain of forts along the coast from Dundalk to Lough Foyle. A further journey in 1557 proved equally inconclusive. While Armagh was burned twice by Sussex, Shane O'Neill ravaged the Pale. As Shane's power developed he achieved recognition from the queen in 1562 of this title as O'Neill and only the most nominal measures were taken to

76 B. Jennings (ed.), *Wild Geese in Spanish Flanders, 1582–1700* (IMC, Dublin, 1964), 48–50, 542, 548, 549, 550.

77 *CSPI, 1608–10*, 433, 460–1, 497–80; *Cal. Carew MSS, 1603–24*, 54–5.

78 *CSPI, 1608–10*, 532–46.

79 Ibid. It is clear that the plantation, whatever its other advantages, was not markedly more profitable to the crown than such an arrangement might have become with usage and in a more settled environment. For the income under the plantation, see below 144–45. In 1625 the English privy council requested information on what the pre-1610 rents had been *CSPI, 1625–32*, 62–3).

80 T. Rymer, *Foedera*, xv (1728), 7–8. The patent does not define the territorial limits of his earldom.

restrain his claims over the territories of the O'Reillys and the Maguires. In 1566 lord deputy Sydney made a further descent on Ulster from which Armagh suffered a further burning, this time at the hands of Shane. The downfall and death of Shane in the following year was due, perhaps, more to the structure of power in Ulster than to any capacity of the Dublin administration to achieve his destruction.

However, in the parliament of 1569 an act of attainder was passed against Shane, the title of O'Neill declared extinguished, and an elaborate case rehearsed to establish a royal claim to the O'Neill territories including all of the present county of Armagh. The act left no doubt that not only were Shane's lands forfeited, but also those of his adherents, the territories of the O'Hanlons, the O'Neills of the Fews, and the McCanns, amongst others, being specifically mentioned.[81] This act had a special value in 1609 when the case for confiscation of O'Neill territory was being worked out.

In December 1567 Cecil made proposals for the conserving of peace in Ulster involving the settling there of well-disposed persons of Irish or English birth, the erection of a residence for the deputy at Armagh, to be occupied in his absence by a soldier of rank governing with the aid of a permanent council, and the establishment of forts at strategic points both inland and on the coast.[82] Sydney concurred with much of this thinking, particularly for the erection of forts and bridges.[83] However, Shane's cousin and tanist Turlogh Luineach succeeded him with government recognition, and the eruption of James Fitzmaurice Fitzgerald in Munster, which had led by 1585 to the downfall of the Desmonds and the Munster plantation, distracted government attention from any elaborate plans for colonisation in Ulster, following on the Leix and Offaly precedent.

There were, however, some schemes for colonisation on a local scale[84] one of which concerned part of Armagh. In October 1571 a certain Capt. Thomas Chatterton, a Wiltshireman who had probably seen service in Ulster, made an agreement with the queen, confirmed by patent of 10 June 1573, whereby he received a grant of O'Hanlon's country of Orior, the Fews or Hugh McNeill Mór O'Neill's country, as well as the gallowglass country, an area within the present Fews barony. Chatterton covenanted to conquer and colonise this territory before 28 March 1579, undertaking to distribute the land at the rate of two ploughlands to every horseman and one to every footman, and to have there before 28 March 1579 horsemen

81 W.F. Cullinan (ed.), *The Irish Statutes Revised, 1310–1800*, (London, 1884), 761–74.

82 R. Bagwell, *Ireland under the Tudors* (3 vols, London, 1885–90), ii, 126–7.

83 Ibid., 149.

84 R. Dunlop, 'Sixteenth century schemes for the plantation of Ulster', *SHR*, xxii (1925), 50–60, 115–26, 197–212.

and footmen in appropriate numbers suitably armed. Any ploughlands not so divided should revert to the crown. He should not grant leases to any mere Irish or Scots for a longer term than five years.[85]

The scheme foundered on inadequate resources and lack of government backing. Its intention was essentially military, designed against both Gaelic Irish and mercenary Scots. By 1575 Sydney felt that Chatterton's ineffective efforts were merely an irritant to the O'Hanlons, who might otherwise be induced to make peace with the government and pay an annual rent.[86] Agreement with O'Hanlon 'a dutiful subject since the overthrow of Shane O'Neill',[87] with whom negotiations were then in progress, would have political advantage in the circumscription of the power of Turlogh Luineach. In July 1576 the grant to Chatterton, who continued 'to wrestle and work and go to the worse', was revoked.[88] Chatterton appears to have continued in Ulster, however, being killed by a Scottish Islesman in 1585.[89] Such small scale private schemes were no adequate answer to the Ulster problem, having no place amongst the details of either of two possible policies, conquest or conciliation. The former was clearly a necessary precursor to colonisation, the latter logically excluded it.

The value of negotiating with the O'Hanlons, and other Ulster families including the O'Neills of the Fews, as a counterbalance to Turlogh Luineach, was grasped by Pelham in 1579,[90] and pursued further by Perrot in the next decade. The outcome was a surrender by Oghy O'Hanlon, now knighted, of all his lands in Orior, which led to a regrant from the crown in December 1587 at an annual rent of £60 stg and with obligations of military service, the titles of O'Hanlon and tanist to be abolished.[91]

Such a policy of planned attrition of the area of O'Neill's suzerainty was all the more important as Turlogh Luineach aged and Hugh O'Neill, an English protegé and the son of Matthew the baron, developed his power. In April 1587 Sir Francis Walsingham boldly visualised the restriction of Turlogh Luineach to an area west of mid-Tyrone allowing Hugh's influence to run from there to the Blackwater and with superiority over Fermanagh. The area 'from the Blackwater to the Pale' manifestly crucial for the extension of crown power, and particularly the lands of the O'Hanlons, McCanns, O'Neills of the Fews, Magennises and MacMahons, in effect the

85 Ibid.; Cal. fiants Ir., Eliz., no. 2354; *CSPI, 1608–10*, 553.

86 Dunlop, 'Sixteenth century schemes', 118; *Cal. Carew MSS, 1575–88*, 36, 180; see Cal. fiants Ir., Eliz., nos. 967, 1108, 2485.

87 Sydney to privy council, [27] February 1576 (*Cal. Carew MSS, 1575–88*, 43).

88 *CSPI, 1574–85*, 97; *Cal. Carew MSS, 1575–88*, 53, 129.

89 *Cal. Carew MSS, 1575–88*, 403; Dunlop, 'Sixteenth century schemes', 118.

90 *Cal. Carew MSS, 1575–88*, 190.

91 Cal. fiants Ir., Eliz., nos. 5041 (surrender), 5090 (regrant); see also 2485, 3270; *Cal. Carew MSS, 1575–88*, 473; *CSPI, 1586–88*, 548.

counties of Armagh, Monaghan, and part of Down, should be brought under direct crown dependence. This, in his opinion, would not only limit the overlordship of the O'Neill but secure the Pale from invasion.[92] Such a plan was, however, beyond the bounds of political practicability, and Hugh's grant of the earldom of Tyrone in May contained no territorial restriction from Armagh, though the fort recently built on the Blackwater was reserved from his patent and his political rights over the smaller chiefs were to be exercised subject to the consent of the lord deputy.[93]

In 1593 Hugh persuaded Turlogh Luineach, who died two years later, to resign the title of O'Neill in his favour, and, in alliance with Red Hugh O'Donnell, emerged rapidly as a powerful threat to the queen's influence in Ulster. The war when it came was one of unprecedented Tudor proportion. Most expeditions rarely proceeded far west of the Blackwater and the importance of the garrison at Armagh is continually stressed. In 1596 in negotiations with Hugh O'Neill the government offered to concede, as he had persistently required,[94] that Armagh and Tyrone should be made one county rather than divided as two following on Perrot's previous arrangement, but O'Neill was unwilling to countenance the continuous presence of a garrison at Armagh[95] which had been regarrisoned in the previous year.[96] With the renewal of hostilities the town remained an objective of importance to both parties, and suffered accordingly. After the battle of the Yellow Ford in 1598 Armagh was abandoned and although proposals were made to garrison it in 1599, it was not retaken until 1601 under Mountjoy.[97] At this time also three forts were erected and garrisoned in the county, at Charlemont, Mountnorris and Moyry. After the war had ended in 1603 these military installations remained, with caretaker garrisons, as reminders of changed times.

At the restoration of Hugh O'Neill following on the treaty of Mellifont there were exempted from his patent two small areas assigned to the forts of Charlemont and Mountjoy (in Tyrone), and the lands of Henry Oge O'Neill in Armagh and Tyrone as well as those of Sir Turlogh McHenry O'Neill of the Fews. These had been previously promised to them at the time when they submitted, to hold directly from the crown.[98] Sir Turlogh McHenry had campaigned with the lord deputy in 1597,[99] held a captaincy

92 *CSPI, 1586–88*, 336–7.
93 *CPRI, Eliz.*, 123, 130; Bagwell, *Tudors*, iii, 170–1.
94 *CSPI, 1592–96*, 172.
95 *Cal. Carew MSS, 1575–88*, 172–3; Bagwell, *Tudors*, iii, 260–3.
96 *CSPI, 1592–96*, 343.
97 *CSPI, 1600–01*, 404.
98 *CSPI, 1603–6*, 12–14.
99 *AFM*, 2023.

in 1601,[100] and received a pardon in 1602,[101] and Sir Henry Oge who submitted in July 1602,[102] was later to die in the campaign against O'Doherty. Their patents were issued in 1603 and 1605 respectively.[103] Both patents implied restrictions of Tyrone's overlordship, and while his relations with Sir Turlogh and Sir Henry Oge did not deteriorate as radically as with O'Cahan[104] there is evidence that he resented their direct dependence on the crown.

In April 1604 Sir John Davies asserted that Tyrone was behaving provocatively towards Sir Turlogh McHenry[105] though in December of the same year he noted a quietness in Tyrone's country which was in marked contrast to the situation in Donegal.[106] Nevertheless in January 1605 Hugh O'Neill was in Dublin seeking redress in grievances against Sir Henry Oge.[107] Part of the purpose of the journey into Ulster of the deputy and members of the administration accompanying the justices of assize in 1605 was to 'settle' disputes in which O'Neill was involved.[108]

This important expedition embraced counties Armagh, Tyrone, Londonderry, and Donegal.[109] Not only were assizes held, but various efforts were made to 'beget in the people a disposition to live in obedience and civility'.[110] In Armagh they found the cathedral decayed, the clergy practicing under papal authority, and tithes misappropriated. The archbishop was instructed to install a minister there forthwith, and to reside and preach there himself every 'summer season'.[111] In consultation with the earl and others, they divided the county into five baronies, annexing Clanbrassil, an area previously of doubtful ascription to either Armagh or Down. The order for this purpose was made on August 3.[112] Three coroners for the county were appointed, John Fleming, Daniel McCasy of Tynan and Patrick oge Macgillran of the Fews. As constables for each barony substantial members of local families were chosen. Thus Rory O'Hanlon was constable of Orior, Neil McCoddan for Armagh, Patrick McCuls

100 *CSPI, 1601–3*, 201.
101 Cal. fiants Ir., Eliz., no. 6662.
102 *CSPI, 1601–3*, 459.
103 *CPRI, Jas I*, 67, 75; *CSPI, 1603–6*, 296.
104 Moody, *Londonderry*, 56–7.
105 *CSPI, 1603–6*, 160.
106 Ibid., 215.
107 Ibid, 245.
108 Ibid., 300–1.
109 *CSPI, 1603–6*, 317–23.
110 Ibid., 317.
111 In a later dispatch of October 4 it was noted that the primate was building in Armagh and intended to live there as required (ibid., 328–30).
112 Armagh Archiepiscopal Registry, a.2a.28 no. 7 (very damaged); a transcription by W. Reeves is in Armagh Public Library, Armagh Papers, 427–9.

Carrach McArdill for the Fews, Donell O'Hugh for Tiranny, and Neill O'Quin for the barony of Oneilland. The amalgamation of the Irish territories into baronies and the appointment of officers were 'published in open assizes'.

The lord deputy and council also adjudicated the dispute between Hugh O'Neill and Sir Henry Oge, establishing the latter in all the lands he held at his submission. No dispute, however, came to light between the earl and Sir Turlogh McHenry. Finally they allocated lands to Charlemont and Mountnorris forts,[113] in the latter case with the consent of Patrick O'Hanlon, whose father had been killed on the queen's side in the previous war and who held a pension from the crown,[114] on promise of a grant of the lands he held nearby. These forts and lands were subsequently leased to the commanders there for twenty-one years with covenants to maintain the buildings in repair. Capt. Henry Adderton, 'a gentleman that hath carried himself well and very honestly …, and is now a good help unto them both for execution and administration of justice in those parts'[115] received such a lease of Mountnorris in February 1606,[116] similarly Capt. Anthony Smith received the fort and lands of Moyry in June,[117] and Sir Toby Caulfeild the fort and lands of Charlemont in June 1607,[118] some months before the Flight of the Earls.

These were the ways in which the impact of external authority was being felt in Armagh. Back in Dublin in October Chichester felt prompted to write in general terms to Salisbury about the need to extend the planted area in Ireland. Only thus could justices of the peace and other dependable agents of anglicisation in state and church be provided in the localities. The king should 'more confirm and strengthen his estate, and leave a more honourable memory behind him by reforming and civilising of Ireland than in regaining France'. It was either 'absurd folly' or 'wilful ignorance' to plant Virginia or Guiana 'and leave this of our own waste and desolate.'[119] Clearly he saw social and political change as dependent ultimately on change in landownership. Two years, however, were to pass before this tentative suggestion could be pressed with conviction as having a realistic relevance to the Ulster situation.

However, small areas of Armagh were coming under British control in various ways in the years before the plantation. It has been seen that land was

[113] Marsh's Library, Dublin, Z 4.2.6, 4, 15–16.
[114] *CSPI, 1603–6*, 129; *CPRI, Jas I*, 5, 30.
[115] *CSPI, 1603–6*, 318.
[116] *CPRI, Jas I*, 78.
[117] Ibid., 96.
[118] Ibid., 102.
[119] *CSPI, 1603–6*, 325–6.

reserved for the three forts in the country. The most significant area was, however, monastic property, and it must be remembered that the effective dissolution of Armagh monasteries had awaited the reign of James I. The abbey of St. Peter and St. Paul located in Armagh, with its extensive lands in Armagh, Tyrone and Londonderry, was leased for twenty-one years to Sir Toby Caulfeild, commander of Charlemont, in June 1607.[120] In July 1606 the monastery of Kilsleve was leased for the same period to Marmaduke Whitechurch, a servitor with local connections.[121] In February 1610 he received an outright grant of this property.[122] In May 1612 Caulfeild also received an outright grant of his abbey lands,[123] but was obliged in December to surrender that part which lay within the territory granted to the city of London despite energetic protest and the intervention of the lord deputy.[124] There were also lands in Armagh which had belonged to the monastery of the Blessed Virgin and St. Patrick at Newry which had been granted to Sir Nicholas Bagnal, the marshal of the army, in 1553.[125] Bagnal's successor, Arthur, received a regrant in February 1612.[126] Another piece of monastic apparent property, Kilmore, was granted to Edward Trevor of Narrow-Water, County Down, in February 1611.[127] The complicated history of the property of the Culdees or vicar choral in Armagh at this time is discussed elsewhere.[128] The granting out of the termon and erenach lands was not taken in hand for this county as in Cavan.[129] Otherwise only the archbishop's land was in Protestant ownership. There were not grants of attainted land in this county, unlike Cavan.

Two members of the O'Hanlon family who had served the crown during the war received grants of land in Orior in 1609. One of these, Patrick O'Hanlon who had been captain of a king's ship,[130] had a pension from 1603.[131] In September 1603 a letter from the English privy council directed that he should be granted a patent of his lands with other land in compensation for the amount he had surrendered for the erection of

120 *CPRI, Jas I*, 102; see *Inq. cancel. Hib. repert.*, ii, Armagh (4) Jas. I.
121 *CPRI, Jas I*, 97.
122 Ibid., 159.
123 Ibid., 229.
124 See below, 295.
125 *CPRI, Eliz.*, 154–5. Bagnal seems also to have purchased some land from the O'Hanlons (*Inq. cancel. Hib. repert.*, ii, Armagh (2) Jas. I).
126 *CPRI, Jas I*, 246–7. Bagnal received a licence of alienation in March 1606 for the property (*CPRI, Jas I*, 86), and in March 1609 a small part of it was granted to Sir Oliver Lambert (*CPRI, Jas I*, 133). However, Bagnal appears to have recovered it all by February 1612.
127 Ibid., 190.
128 See below, 306–08.
129 See below, 9.
130 *CSPI, 1608–10*, 338.
131 *CPRI, Jas I*, 30.

Mountnorris fort.[132] His grant dated from 26 October 1609.[133] The other grantee, Redmond O'Hanlon, received his patent on December 15 'in consideration of his faithful services'.[134] These patents were belatedly taken out; it is unlikely that grants would have been made otherwise to native Irish so close to the time of plantation.

Little can be said about the financial relationships of the Irish in this area with people from outside in the decades before 1610. In 1609 Sir John Davies states that the earl of Tyrconnell had mortgaged 'great scopes of land for small sums of money' to merchants of the Pale.[135] No such statement was made about O'Neill, though his post-war poverty was pointed to by the same prolific commentator.[136] It was noted, however, in 1608 that three townlands in the Fews had been leased by him to Capt. Henry Adderton.[137] Archbishop James Ussher working over the 'diminicle' of the 'great office',[138] provides some further information. Thus we find that about 1604 Sir Oghy O'Hanlon had mortgaged five townlands in Orior to an Old English Newry merchant called Fleming and a smaller area to Marmaduke Whitechurch who lived at Carlingford.

The conclusion of war saw the granting of pardons on a very considerable scale.[139] No disturbances were reported from the county in the ensuing years, and in December 1604 Sir John Davies reported that the earl of Tyrone's country was more quiet and 'void of thieves' than any other part of the province.[140] With the Flight of the Earls the control of Armagh and parts of Tyrone was entrusted to Sir Toby Caulfeild and Sir Francis Roe.[141]

However, the revolt of Sir Cahir O'Doherty in April 1608 had significant reverberations in Armagh. Both Sir Henry Oge, who was killed in June,[142] and Sir Turlogh McHenry O'Neill, were sent in arms against him, and at the end of May, Oghy Oge O'Hanlon, son of Sir Oghy and husband of O'Doherty's sister, with about one hundred supporters went

[132] Ibid., 5.

[133] Ibid., 156.

[134] Ibid., 156.

[135] *CSPI, 1608–10*, 282–3.

[136] *CSPI, 1603–6*, 160.

[137] TCD, MS 582, fol. 184.

[138] A background document now lost. Ussher's amended copy, profusely annotated but much dilapidated is in Armagh Archiepiscopal Registry, A.2a.28.

[139] Cal. fiants Ir., Eliz., nos 6489, 6662, 6734; *CPRI, Jas I*, 1–153 *passim*.

[140] *CSPI, 1603–6*, 215. The sheriffs of Armagh at this time were local servitors, Marmaduke Whitechurch (1606), Anthony Smith (1607 and 1609), Henry Adderton (1608) and Robert Cowell (1610), PRONI, T808/14926.

[141] *CSPI, 1606–8*, 402.

[142] Ibid., 559, 567, 605.

into rebellion in Orior, being active from Newry to Armagh. Chichester dispatched soldiers but found them difficult to suppress because of their extreme mobility.[143] By June O'Hanlon's supporters had increased to 200, and had moved into Tyrone,[144] where Sir Henry Oge's town of Kinard (Caledon) was burned.[145] Although O'Doherty was killed early in July,[146] O'Hanlon and his followers in eastern and central Ulster continued in arms. In July Chichester himself was in the field against them,[147] forcing O'Hanlon to retreat beyond the Blackwater.[148] O'Hanlon's wife, recently pregnant, was captured 'by an Irish soldier who knew her not'. Stripped of her clothing she died of exposure.[149] O'Hanlon continued to elude capture, but in February 1609 Chichester reported to London that the county of Armagh had petitioned him to pardon their woodkerne or else allow them to leave the country. He stated that he had informed them that the ringleaders, particularly Oghy Oge, would be neither pardoned nor suffered to depart, but that the others could secure pardon by effecting the end of hostilities.[150] Later in the month he reported that Sir James Perrot had been employed against O'Hanlon,[151] and in March Brian oge McMahon was slain in south-east Armagh.[152]

Indeed by the end of March 1609 the rebellion had been to all intents and purposes suppressed, though Oghy Oge remained at large.[153] In April Sir Robert Jacob, the solicitor general, reported that O'Hanlon was still active in Armagh though he had but four or five supporters. He felt that Sir Turlogh McHenry could easily capture him, but was deterred by ties of kinship and by the calculation that should he wish to stand for the title of O'Neill, O'Hanlon would be a strong supporter. O'Hanlon, he felt, was continuing his rebellion in order to procure a pardon.[154] Finally, in September, Chichester accepted his submission, as that of a person 'of a malicious, stubborn, mutinous disposition, and without doubt a traitor in his heart',[155] and he was one of the contingent of swordsmen which was dispatched to Sweden at this time.[156]

143 Ibid., 545.
144 Ibid., 563.
145 Ibid., 567–70.
146 Ibid., 606–8.
147 Ibid., 612–13.
148 *CSPI, 1608–10*, 5–10.
149 *CSPI, 1606–8*, 613; *CSPI, 1608–10*, 15.
150 *CSPI, 1608–10*, 143.
151 Ibid., 150.
152 *CPRI, Jas I*, 198; *Inq. cancel. Hib. repert.*, ii, Armagh (1) Jas I.
153 *CSPI, 1608–10*, 177–8.
154 Ibid., 195–6.
155 Ibid., 305.
156 *CSPI, 1608–10*, 287.

If O'Hanlon, then, extricated himself alive from a situation foredoomed to failure, his rising did, of course, destroy his prospects as a native grantee under the plantation. Furthermore it ensured that his father, Sir Oghy, could also be dealt with severely. Chichester, in fact, in October 1608 negotiated his surrender of the O'Hanlon territory in return for an annuity of £80 for life with a promise to pay his debts to the extent of £300. In this he felt he had made a 'good bargain for the king and a fair way for the plantation.'[157]

While Chichester was in Armagh in July 1608 he revived a device for maintaining order which had been adopted there two years previously. By an order of July 18 the chiefs of 'every name and sept' were required to present the names of all their tenants and followers twice yearly to the sheriff of the county and undertake to be responsible for their good behaviour. The sheriff should retain one copy of this list for himself and present another to the lord deputy. This was to be done twice yearly to record all changes, the chiefs and landlords having refused to be accountable for those people who had been previously listed as their dependents.[158]

Another order made on the same day was directed against the practice of transhumance in Ulster generally. It was an order

> for the inhabitants of Ulster livinge dispersedly and removinge w'th theyr creates and cattell from place to place to cohabite and continew theyr dwellinge in certayntie.

The disadvantages of the practice of transhumance and dispersed settlement were rehearsed: rebels were 'receaved and releeved' in these 'creaghts' and were not easily arrested; constables of baronies were hindered in their duties in a way they would not be if all inhabitants lived in towns and villages; people living dispersedly were not able to defend themselves against 'rebells, woodkerne, or outlawes'; this 'loose and unsettled manner of living' accounted for the absence of trades and handicrafts which were essential to a civil life and which would flourish in villages and towns.[159] Again, this order can hardly have taken much effect.

O'Hanlon's rising, at any rate, had allowed of a more extensive plantation of the county than might otherwise, perhaps, have been effected. In his 'notes of remembrances' of October 1608, Chichester, dealing with County Armagh, hoped that with the death of Sir Oghy there should be no more O'Hanlon chiefs, but rather that the territory should be disposed

157 Ibid., 67.
158 Bod. Lib., Oxford, Rawlinson MS A237, fol. 115; PRONI, T545/9, 9–10.
159 Bod. Lib., Oxford, Rawlinson MS A237, fol. 116; PRONI, T545/9, 11–13.

directly to some of the best affected of the family and to planters. He went on to state that much of the rest of the county, controlled by Art McBaron O'Neill, Hugh's brother, was available for plantation because of the forfeiture of the earl, the lands of the primate, Sir Henry Oge, and Sir Turlogh McHenry only excepted. The sons of these O'Neill leaders, as well as those of Sir Cormac McBaron, some of whom were in foreign service, should be provided for to prevent subsequent disaffection. The principal residents of Clancan and Clanbrassil (in Oneilland barony) claimed to be freeholders and he felt would willingly accept tenancies from the crown and pay a good rent. He advised that Sir Turlogh McHenry's territory should be augmented by a grant of part of Toaghy (in Armagh barony) adjoining the Fews. He felt that care should be taken in the settlement of Sir Henry Oge's territory. However, for the other inhabitants of the escheated lands, the O'Hagans, O'Quins, and Clandonnells no recommendation were made. Armagh should be given corporate status and the forts in the county preserved.[160]

The years 1608 to 1610, between the planning and the implementation of the plantation were ones of impending revolution when the claims of Armagh Irish landholders, and servitors in Ireland were being considered by Chichester and his government and in some cases by the London administration. Order in the meantime was maintained by the local commanders and the sheriffs in the county. It was in these years, too, that the two inquiries, in 1608 and 1609, into the amount of land available in each county for confiscation were carried out. It has been seen above that the inquiry in 1608 had major defects, but it did amass an amount of topographical detail which in the case of Armagh has been preserved.[161]

The 'Project' of plantation stated that the county contained 77,800 acres which would make 61 proportions as follows: 10 great, 13 middle, and 38 small. Church lands were to be deducted as follows: archbishopric, 2,400 acres (i.e. excluding the termon lands), glebe, 4,650 acres, and monastic lands, 430 acres. Further deductions were Sir Turlogh McHenry O'Neill, 9,900 acres, and Sir Henry oge, 4,900 acres. Thus there remained, it was considered, 55,620 acres to be divided to grantee groups as follows: to English and Scottish undertakers 28 proportions or 35,000 acres, to servitors 6 proportions or 7,500 acres, and to natives 8 proportions or 10,000 acres. The remaining 3,120 acres were to be divided amongst 4 corporate towns, 1,200 acres, Trinity College, Dublin, 1,200 acres, and a 'free school at Armagh, 720 acres.'[162] The mathematics were by no means

[160] *CSPI, 1608–10*, 62–3.
[161] TCD, MS 582, ff 177–96.
[162] Hill, *Plantation*, 114–6.

entirely accurate, but it can be seen that the share of the native Irish in the county was conceived as to be about 32 per cent.

From 1609 the consideration of native claimants for land in the county and the selection of servitor and undertaker grantees was taken in hand, dovetailing with the general planning of the plantation. At the end of March 1609 Chichester, writing to Davies who was then in London, recommended him to ensure that the planners there should decide on the treatment of the sons of Sir Art O'Neill, to ensure that the grant to Sir Turlogh McHenry should be expanded, and that the sons of Sir Henry oge O'Neill, whose heir Phelim, his grandchild, was an infant, should receive lands, for otherwise they would be 'thorns in their feet and pricks in their sides.'[163]

By January 1610 Chichester's suggestions for some of the leading O'Neills in Armagh were perhaps more crystallised and less generous.[164] He wished that Sir Turlogh McHenry (who was seeking more land) could be removed from the Fews to the 'plains' or otherwise be 'hemmed up' in his present position.[165] In August the idea of moving him to Cavan was mooted.[166] Art McBaron O'Neill, Turlogh McArt O'Neill, Henry and Conn McShane O'Neill, and Brian Crossagh O'Neill expected more than was fitting to be given them. Turlogh and Henry, he felt, should be treated more liberally, but neither should have more than two or three townlands. Art McBaron must be satisfied by reason that he had sons in military service on the continent. Chichester requested that decisions on these people be taken in London, and their demands satisfied so as the Dublin government would be freed from blame should 'they play the knaves upon discontent hereafter.'[167]

In the spring of 1610 some of the O'Neills, either by petition or personal visit, tried to influence the London administration in their favour. Thus in March Henry McShane O'Neill one of the sons of Shane, applied to Salisbury to be his tenant should Salisbury receive land in Ulster.[168] Sir Turlogh McHenry and others returned from England in June[169] and the information divulged by them about the imminent plantation was a cause of unrest in Armagh at this time.[170]

From April instructions were being received from England defining the amounts and locations of lands to be granted to 'principal natives' whose

[163] *CSPI, 1608–10*, 177–8.
[164] Ibid., 362–5.
[165] Ibid.
[166] Ibid., 489.
[167] Ibid., 362–5.
[168] Ibid., 408.
[169] Ibid., 474–5.
[170] Ibid.

fates had, by Chichester's request, been decided there. Hence Art McBaron was to have one great proportion in Orior for his life only. Henry McShane O'Neill was to have one great proportion in Orior and his brother Conn one small proportion in Fermanagh.[171] The choice of the native grantees otherwise fell to the deputy and plantation commissioners.

Armagh was particularly popular amongst applicants for land as undertakers or servitors, doubtless on account of its geographical location. In a list of undertaker candidates a high proportion requested land in Oneilland.[172] In April 1610 Lord Saye and Seale, stating that he had been requested by many undertakers to procure land for them there diplomatically put it to Salisbury that the latter should take charge of the barony, take a title from it, and 'let them live under his protection'. The undertakers, he stated, were resolved to build a town or city called Sarum or Cranborne, and a fort called Cecil's Fort.[173] One applicant for land as an undertaker who was not selected, Marcell Rivers,[174] is of interest in that he was married to the heir of Capt. Thomas Chatterton, the Elizabethan adventurer. He subsequently received belated backing from the English privy council for land as a servitor in Orior or elsewhere.[175]

From January 1610 Chichester was making proposals for those whom he felt should be servitors in the county. In Orior he recommended Sir Oliver St. John master of the ordnance and subsequently lord deputy; Sir James Perrot (possibly an illegitimate son of Sir John), author of the *Chronicle of Ireland, 1584–1608*, captain of a company at Newry, who conducted Delvin to England in 1608, and was engaged against Oghy Oge O'Hanlon;[176] Sir Thomas Williams, who as a captain had campaigned in south Armagh in 1600[177] and was in command of the Blackwater fort from 1601;[178] and Sir Garret Moore, who had many Cavan connections, a background of military service, and whose lands in Louth were not far distant from Armagh. Chichester was anxious to have Sir Toby Caulfeild settled in Clancan.[179] The deputy's list of possible servitors sent to England at this time included these and others as candidates for land in Armagh.[180] The finally chosen grantees will be discussed in the following chapter.

171 Ibid., 429, 431–2; 'Ulster plantation papers', no. 23, *Anal. Hib.*, viii.
172 *CSPI, 1608–10*, 548–51; Hill, *Plantation*, 146–49; see also *CSPI, 1608–10*, 180–81.
173 Ibid., 425.
174 Ibid., 550.
175 Ibid., 455.
176 H. Wood (ed.), *The chronicle of Ireland, 1584–1608*, (IMC, Dublin, 1933), vi; *CSPI, 1608–10*, 150.
177 *CSPI, 1600*, 191, 527–30.
178 *CSPI, 1601–3*, 55, 117, 201, 487, 523.
179 *CSPI, 1608–10*, 362–5.
180 Ibid., 365–8.

B. Cavan, c. *1550–1610*

The present county of Cavan formed in Irish political geography the eastern part of the large area called Breifne, or the Brenny in anglicisation, and had for ruling chieftains the family of O'Reilly. It is the most south-westerly of the Ulster counties bordering on the Pale with which it had many contacts, and on Connacht, and until the seventeenth century was regarded as part of the province of Connacht. During the reign of Elizabeth the attitudes of the O'Reillys were formed in large party by their reactions to the Dublin government on the south and the power of the O'Neills, who claimed rights over their territory, to the north. By the end of the century, however, they had committed themselves sufficiently to the O'Neills for the county to be included in the plantation scheme.

The relations of the O'Reillys to the Dublin government from the reign of Henry VIII had not been markedly different from that of other chieftains. It is perhaps strange that they did not participate in the surrender and regrant scheme, though proposals for a viscountcy of Cavan were discussed at that time.[181] However, it was with the rise of Shane O'Neill that the O'Reillys began to turn for support to Dublin. Instructions from the queen to Sussex in 1560 and 1561 commanded him to take steps against Shane O'Neill and to 'restore our faithful subject O'Reilly to such losses and damages as he had sustained by means of the said Shane.'[182] An encounter between Shane and 'Cale' O'Reilly took place early in 1561 as a result of which O'Reilly received a 'letter of thanks' from Dublin.[183] In September 1560 amongst 'opinions for the reformation of Ireland' Sussex had recommended that the queen should impose levies on such Irish chieftains as O'Reilly, O'Ruairc, and Maguire, with the eventual intention of 'reducing the government as to come from the Prince.'[184] The view was common that O'Reilly and others might sympathise with the government owing to the activities of O'Neill.[185]

With the submission of Shane in 1562 it was agreed that his dispute with the O'Reillys and also the Maguires should be submitted to commissioners.[186] The queen was anxious that no deterioration should result in relations with the O'Reillys and urged Sussex to arrange with O'Reilly, Maguire, and O'Donnell to 'repair hither and to receive their lands from us as of our gift, in such sort as the earls of Clanrickard and

[181] P. Wilson, *The beginnings of modern Ireland* (Dublin & London, 1912), 263.
[182] *Cal. Carew MSS, 1515–74*, 297, 309–11.
[183] *CSPI, 1509–73*, 166–7.
[184] *Cal. Carew MSS, 1515–74*, 300–4.
[185] Bagwell, *Tudors*, ii, 11.
[186] Ibid., 63.

Thomond did in our father's time.'[187] In November 1562 Maelmora O'Reilly and his son Hugh Connelagh along with Maguire, protested to the queen against the renewed pressures of Shane, asserting that they would 'maintain their faith to her majesty to the last.'[188] However, Maelmora O'Reilly died – in 1565 – before any scheme of surrender and regrant had been concluded. But Sussex ended his deputyship convinced that the O'Reillys had been pacified and English power significantly pressed forward on the Ulster borders.[189]

Yet although important steps had been taken by Sussex towards the reconciliation of the O'Reillys, complications following on the renewal of hostilities with Shane O'Neill, followed immediately by war in Munster, delayed the finalisation of Sussex's policy. In 1565 three sons of Maelmora, Cahir, Owen, and John, went into rebellion and despoiled the Pale.[190] Shane O'Neill undertook to compel restitution of the spoils[191] but Sir William Fitzwilliams reported to Cecil that Cahir O'Reilly, the most active of the insurgents, was supported by Shane.[192] Severe pressure, argued in some quarters as excessive,[193] was brought to bear of Maelmora by lord justice Arnold,[194] but after his death and with the appointment of Sir Henry Sydney as deputy, an agreement was reached in November 1566 between Sydney and Maelmora's son and successor Hugh Connelagh and Hugh's brother and tanist Edmund,[195] commissioners having been appointed in 1565 to conduct negotiations.[196]

This agreement not only dealt with the military problem, but also involved the Dublin administration in settling a range of local disputes in which the O'Reillys were engaged. Hugh Connelagh and his brother undertook to prosecute the three rebels and promised to be bound by the adjudication of commissioners appointed by Sydney in disputes with the inhabitants of Monaghan and with the baron of Delvin. Hugh undertook that the castle of Tullevin, recently taken by the lord deputy from Owen O'Reilly, and committed by him to Edmund the tanist, should be maintained for the queen's use. Hugh undertook to live in that part of Cavan which bordered on the Pale for the length of the rebellion of his

187 *Cal. Carew MSS, 1515–74*, 327–30.
188 *CSPI, 1509–73*, 209–10; see also 236.
189 *Cal. Carew MSS, 1515–74*, 330–44, 344–9.
190 *CSPI, 1509–73*, 251, 253.
191 Ibid., 265.
192 Ibid., 266.
193 Ibid., 270, 280.
194 Ibid., 267.
195 *Cal. Carew MSS, 1515–74*, 373–7.
196 Cal. fiants Ir., Eliz., no. 732.

brothers and Shane O'Neill 'in order that the English parts may be secured by his protection against the said rebels.'[197]

In December Sydney, writing to the privy council with propositions for planting settlers on the Ulster coast, reported the goodwill of Hugh Connelagh O'Reilly whose son John (later Sir John) had been given as a hostage, stating that he had made an inroad on the three O'Reilly rebels.[198] In January 1567 Cahir O'Reilly received a pardon and a grant of English liberty to him and his heirs.[199] However, no further steps were taken to implement the surrender and regrant policy and the Irish method of government through chieftain and tanist continued in operation. One step taken, however, was to confer official recognition on Edmund's position as tanist. In May 1567 and again in January 1568 Edmund was appointed 'secundarious or tanist of the country of the Brenny, to hold during good behaviour.'[200]

Turlogh Luineach O'Neill, who succeeded Shane, reasserted his claims over Cavan, claims which the Dublin government was unwilling to see validated. Thus in an agreement made with him in 1571 he undertook not to invade O'Reilly, O'Hanlon (in Armagh), O'Donnell and others, who should 'remain upon the peace of the lord deputy.'[201] It is not possible to provide a full account of the events of these years in a brief introduction, but Sydney had a high appreciation of Hugh Connelagh O'Reilly whom he saw in 1575 as 'the justest Irishman and his country the best ruled.'[202]

In 1579, at the time of the Fitzmaurice rising, O'Neill, who was in touch with Fitzmaurice, threatened to invade Cavan. One of his followers did so in May,[203] and in the autumn plans were made to meet an attack on the Pale and Cavan.[204] In the same year the shiring of the county, 'where never writ was current and almost sacrilege for any Governor to look in' took place.[205] In June Hugh Connelagh presented himself to lord justice Drury and was knighted, and it was agreed that justices should hold session in the county.[206] However, by the end of the year O'Reilly was complaining about depredations in Cavan of a certain Capt. Hollingworth, and doubts were expressed about his reliability – though he submitted in December,[207]

[197] *Cal. Carew MSS, 1515–74*, 376–7.
[198] *CSPI, 1509–73*, 321.
[199] Cal. fiants Ir., Eliz., no. 982.
[200] Ibid., nos. 1047, 1206.
[201] *Cal. Carew MSS, 1515–74*, 404–6.
[202] *CSPI, 1574–85*, 85; see also Bagwell, *Tudors*, ii, 310.
[203] *CSPI, 1574–85*, 169.
[204] Ibid., 184, 186, 193.
[205] Ibid., 169.
[206] Ibid., 171.
[207] Ibid., 199, 202.

– as well as that of his brother Phillip.[208] At this time Pelham was trying to forge an Ulster alliance of O'Reilly, O'Hanlon, Magennis, as well as members of the O'Neill family, to resist Turlogh Luineach.[209] In September 1580 O'Neill required O'Reilly to come to his support, which he refused, turning to Dublin to lord deputy Grey for assistance.[210] In the following September Shane oge O'Neill, a supporter of Turlogh Luineach, was slain in Cavan, and Sir Nicholas Malbie, reporting the incident to Burghley described Hugh Connelagh as 'the best Irish subject in the land.'[211]

It was in such unresolved conditions of tension that Hugh Connelagh died in 1583. As early as 1576 Sydney had foreseen that 'at his death there will be much trouble.'[212] Maelmora had been a prolific father and a contest for the succession was not unlikely. At the same time Edmund (or Eamon), Hugh's brother, who was still alive, had been recognised as tanist in both 1567 and 1568. However, in 1583 John or Shane O'Reilly, the son of Hugh Connelagh, was fully supported in Dublin. In June Sir Henry Wallopp dismissed Edmund's claims and commended Shane, who was then going to England to sue for backing, as a man who 'lives by industry after the English manner, speaketh the English tongue, [and] maintaineth no thieves.'[213] John returned, knighted by the queen,[214] and by September he had been established as his father's successor and Edmund was continued as tanist.[215] At this time also steps were taken to introduce the English legal system. In July 1583 Richard Bellew of Bellewstown received a fiant for a grant of the office of clerk of the crown and peace in County Cavan, the office being created by his patent.[216] However, Bellew does not appear to have exercised the office and in November Patrick Moore of Dowanstown, County Meath, was appointed.[217] On the arrival of Perrot as lord deputy in June 1584 Sir John O'Reilly was one of a group of Irish chieftains who came to present their services to him.[218]

Such a solution, however, did not commend itself to Edmund whose position as tanist had been already recognised by the Dublin government. In 1582 he had sued and received a pardon,[219] presumably to establish

208 Ibid., 195, 197.
209 Ibid., 204.
210 Ibid., 248, 250.
211 Ibid., 230.
212 Ibid., 92.
213 Ibid., 450.
214 Ibid., 454.
215 Ibid., 455, 468; Cal. fiants Ir., Eliz., no. 4197.
216 Ibid., no. 4185.
217 Ibid., no. 4259. He received a similar appointment for Down at the same time.
218 *CSPI, 1574–85*, 517.
219 Cal. fiants Ir., Eliz., no. 3914.

his case for the succession. In the autumn of 1583 an eruption took place between him and his nephew, and by November Capt. Anthony Deering[220] with 150 soldiers had been sent to Cavan to impose order, as a result of which Edmund came to Dublin and agreed to accept the *fait accompli*.[221]

It was left to Perrot, however, to devise a new policy towards Cavan. The obvious logic from the government viewpoint of a situation where one member of the family was being maintained as chieftain effectively with military support from Dublin, was that the territory should be divided amongst the rival contestants each to hold from the crown. The opportunity for such immediate re-thinking present itself to Perrot when in August Sir John, Edmund, and Phillip, Edmund's brother, appeared before him in Dublin and 'submitted their controversies to his order.'[222]

Perrot's scheme had been worked out by November 28, when a series of agreements were reached. By one of these Sir John O'Reilly undertook to surrender 'O'Reilly's country', and to receive a grant from the crown of the towghe (tuath, in effect the barony) of Loughtee, and of the towghe of Tullygarvey. He was also to hold the 'seignories and rents' of the baronies of Tullyhunco and Tullyhaw.[223] Hugh Reoghe O'Reilly, Cahir Gare O'Reilly and Mulmora O'Reilly, sons of 'the Prior' were to surrender the towghe of Clanmahon, and have it granted to them.[224] The barony of Clankee was arranged to be granted to Phillip O'Reilly[225] who received a pardon on November 24.[226] All should allow any persons who had grants of land in the county to occupy such lands. Obligations of military service were imposed. As a result of the settlement 220 beeves were payable to the crown annually as rent, which according to Sir John Davies in 1607, had ever since been received.[227] Davies regarded the settlement as it affected Tullyhunco and Tullyhaw, the territories of the McKiernans and the McGaurans, as of nominal import: 'being remote and bordering upon O'Rorke's country they were neglected and left subject still to the Irish exactions of the chief lord'.[228]

Certain limitations on the powers of the O'Reillys under this rearrangement were implied by appointments made at this time. In December 1584 Walter Brady, subsequently sovereign of Cavan, was

[220] In 1582 he was in charge of the ward of Ballinasloe (*CSPI, 1574–85*, 344).
[221] *CSPI, 1574–85*, 477.
[222] Ibid., 522.
[223] *Cal. Carew MSS, 1575–88*, 391–2; *CSPI, 1574–85*, 539, 543.
[224] Cal. fiants Ir., Eliz., no. 4541.
[225] Morley, *Ireland*, 349. Davies's account is not entirely accurate.
[226] Cal. fiants Ir., Eliz., no. 4534.
[227] Morley, *Ireland*, 349.
[228] Ibid.

appointed constable and jailer of the jail at Cavan.[229] The Bradys, a merchant as well as landholding and clerical family, had many contacts with the government and were subsequently grantees under the plantation.[230] On December 18 Henry Duke (of Castlejordan, County Meath[231]) as sheriff of Cavan was appointed to execute martial law in the county.[232]

The new arrangement did not apparently commend itself to either Sir John or Phillip O'Reilly. In November 1585 Phillip was incarcerated in Dublin Castle,[233] where he remained until the end of 1592. Also Sir John complained about the restriction of his rights and on 1 April 1585 commissioners met him at Cavan to inquire into the duties and customs he had previously received.[234] The outcome was that out of the three baronies – Clanmahon, Castlerahan, and Clankee – which he no longer held, it was decided he should receive a chief rent of 10/- per poll or townland.[235] The scheme, however, never took official effect; none of the grantees taking out patents.

In March 1588 the appointment of John Kearnan, a leading member of the McKiernan family, to the office of seneschal of the territory of Upper Tullyhunco or McKiernan's country, was a tentative step in the extension of English influence to the northwest of the country.[236] Kearnan was a lawyer who had been associated with the Dublin administration and had lived in the Pale for some years. He stated in a petition to Burghley that he had, on the entreaty of his kinsmen, left the Pale to live among them

> hoping ... to bring them through dutiful exhortation and examples of husbandry and other civil trades, from their disorders and disobedience to the due regard of loyalty and obedience.[237]

Contacts with the McGaurans of Tullyhah were made by 1586 when pardons were issued to members of the family.[238]

Little or no further steps were taken towards the reorganisation of the county before the outbreak of the O'Neill war transformed a partly political

229 Cal. fiants Ir., Eliz., no. 4547.

230 In 1586 Patrick McDonagh Brady, for example, was appointed to receive a fine on behalf of the crown from Cowchonaght Maguire (ibid., no. 4810).

231 Cal. fiants Ir., Eliz., no. 5157.

232 Ibid., no. 4556.

233 *CSPI, 1574–85*, 585; *1586–88*, 110.

234 *Cal. Carew MSS, 1575–88*, 402; *AFM*, 1804–6, note b; J. O'Donovan (ed.), *Leabhar na g-ceart or the book of rights* (Dublin 1847), xx–xxii.

235 Morley, *Ireland*, 349.

236 Cal. fiants Ir., Eliz., no. 5156; *CPRI, Eliz.*, 143–4.

237 *CSPI, 1586–88*, 430–1.

238 Cal. fiants Ir., Eliz., no. 4813. Pardons to O'Gowans, O'Lynchs, McCabes (defined as galloglasses) and others from Cavan were also issued in these years (ibid., nos. 4812, 4891, 4892, 4934).

situation to an essentially military one. Some indication of growing tension in Cavan towards the end of the 1580s can be got from the reports of Henry Duke, the sheriff. In January 1588 Duke, Sir John and Edmund O'Reilly, and Thomas Betagh, were commissioned to take the muster and array of the inhabitants to Cavan[239] following on a threat of invasion of Cavan by Cormac McBaron, the brother of Hugh, earl of Tyrone, Turlogh McHenry and others.[240] In February 1587 Duke had written to Burghley informing him of his services in Cavan. Before his coming there 'the Brenny' had been 'a nursery of all Rome runners, and all others, robbers, spoilers, and burners of his Majesty's good subjects of the Pale', but now all were reformed and 'every man brought to be answerable to assize and sessions'.[241] Such tactics of English influence, however, were not palatable to the O'Reillys and even Sir John was reported by Duke in December 1589 and by Sir Lucan Dillon in January following as being 'discontent against the officers of Cavan.'[242] The heads of Brian McFerrall oge O'Reilly, son-in-law to Sir John, and 'a man among the lewd sort both of the Pale and the Irish greatly lamented' and three others were sent to Dublin Castle by Edward Herbert, Duke's successor as sheriff, in October 1589.[243]

Meanwhile Phillip O'Reilly, who had been placed in Dublin castle in 1585, was petitioning the queen to be released.[244] Duke, from local knowledge, assured the lord deputy in 1588 that if he were released 'her Majesty should command no more in the Brenny ... than she did in Shane O'Neill's time.'[245] In September 1590 the lord deputy firmly opposed his release, pointing out that he was

> a dangerous neighbour to the Pale and most to be doubted of all the Irish borderers as well for his malice against the state and specially religion wherein he is most perverse, as for his great wit, stirring spirit, and courage to execute, besides great ability if he enter into any bad action.[246]

However, he was released at the end of 1592.[247] In January 1594 he evinced a desire, not pursued further, to take out a patent, and commissioners were

[239] Cal. fiants Ir., Eliz., no. 5130.

[240] *CSPI, 1586–88*, 466–7. Duke's attitude was clearly uncompromising: 'Whosoever will believe that the Irishry will be dutiful and obedient, although they swear it never so much, except there be a present force of men to command them, will be greatly deceived.' (ibid.)

[241] Ibid., 264–5.

[242] *CSPI, 1588–92*, 283, 302.

[243] Ibid., 253, 261–2.

[244] Ibid., 11, 45, 48, 108, 360, 362, 446, 462.

[245] *CSPI, 1586–88*, 467.

[246] *CSPI, 1588–92*, 362.

[247] *CSPI, 1592–96*, 14.

appointed to investigate the extent of his property.[248] In 1591 Sir John O'Reilly had petitioned, also inconclusively, for a patent of the baronies allotted to him under Perrot.[249]

With the outbreak of the O'Neill war a major recession in English influence in Cavan took place. On the death of Sir John in 1596 Phillip assumed the title of O'Reilly and proved intractable to government direction.[250] Official opinion was that Maelmora, Sir John's son, should be supported against his uncle.[251] However, Phillip was killed in October,[252] and Edmund, who captured Cavan castle, the seat of chieftainship, from his kinsmen, was created O'Reilly by Hugh O'Neill immediately afterwards, Maelmora being likewise appointed as tanist.[253] The possibility that Maelmora, on dynastic grounds, might solicit royal support to displace Edmund, was keenly felt,[254] but Maelmora himself was slain at the battle of the Yellow Ford in 1598, leaving a young son, Maelmora oge, as the claimant in English eyes. It was on the basis of the death of Phillip in rebellion in 1596 that crown title to the county, prior to its confiscation for plantation, was subsequently found.

In 1600, when Edmund was very old, further contention arose over the succession, in which O'Neill again intervened appointing Owen, a son of Hugh Connelagh, to be tanist.[255] Owen, accordingly, succeeded Edmund in 1601, was pardoned in 1602,[256] and died without issue in 1603.[257] His brother Maelmora McHugh Connelagh, attainted[258] and later a grantee under the plantation, succeeded as chieftain and died in 1635.

It is not the purpose of this introduction to do more than show how the complex dynastic problems of the O'Reillys were affected by the O'Neill war. Two members of the family Capt. John and Capt. Hugh held positions in the English army, though both defected, Capt. John early in 1600[259] and Capt. Hugh in 1601.[260] Continuous stress was laid on the strategic importance of the area, facilitating the passage of northern armies into the

248 Cal. fiants Ir., Eliz., no. 5843.
249 *CSPI, 1588–92*, 450.
250 *CSPI, 1592–96*, 523, 529–30, 535. In June 1596 the bishop of Meath reported to Dublin that Phillip had 'more mind to settle himself in O'Reilly's seat and renew his old Irish orders than to perform any covenants with the state' (ibid., 530).
251 Ibid., 537.
252 *CSPI, 1596–97*, 140, 143, 146.
253 Ibid., 143, 145, 156, 164–6.
254 Ibid., 164–6.
255 *CSPI, 1600*, 365.
256 Cal. fiants Ir., Eliz., no. 6657.
257 RIA, MS E.iv.i.
258 *Inq. cancel. Hib. repert.*, ii, Cavan (1) Jas I.
259 *CSPI, 1599–1600* 439.
260 *CSPI, 1601–3*, 13, 18, 133, 350.

south and allowing of the devastation of the Pale. Sir Francis Shane in February 1601 emphasised the importance of placing a strong garrison at Cavan.[261] O'Neill himself, returning through Cavan after Kinsale, complained of the failure of the O'Reillys 'and the other borderers' to invade the Pale during his absence.[262] In a list of places requiring garrisons drawn up in 1599 Cavan featured prominently as requiring 1,000 foot and 100 horse. A small detachment should be placed at Belturbet, who, with the help of two 'good boats', could control the river-basin area between there and Enniskillen.[263]

By May 1601 Mountjoy had reported to the privy council that a garrison had been placed in Cavan and that some of the O'Reillys had been already reduced.[264] In the following April Capt. Lawrence Esmond, later knighted and constable of Duncannon fort,[265] stated that the O'Reillys were anxious to be received to mercy. In June 1603 Sir Garret Moore, who had seen service in Cavan during the war, was appointed seneschal of 'the Brenny' and of the town of Kells.[266] In October 1603, John Bingley, of the Donegal servitor family, received a grant of a Tuesday market at Cavan town.[267]

In all, some forty-nine O'Reillys were attainted during the Nine Years' War period, and their lands recorded in many cases by inquisition in January 1604.[268] In addition, fourteen other landowners were attainted, including McCabes, O'Lynches, O'Sheridans, and Bradys.[269] However, large numbers of pardons were also secured.[270] Unlike the restoration of Hugh O'Neill (as earl), no appointment or recognition as chieftain was made, nor was the division of 1584 revived. Thus, although plans were made for the settlement of the county in 1606, the years between the end of the war and the decision to confiscate left Cavan in an unsettled state from the government viewpoint.

The earliest land to be held by crown grant in Cavan, prior to 1610 was monastic. In February 1571 Hugh Connelagh O'Reilly, then chieftain, received a twenty-one year lease of the monastery of the Holy Trinity in Loughowter with four appertaining townlands and their tithes, and also of

261 *CSPI, 1600–1*, 197.
262 *CSPI, 1601–3*, 283.
263 *CSPI, 1599–1600*, 328.
264 *CSPI, 1600–1*, 303.
265 J.L.J. Hughes (ed.), *Patentee officers in Ireland, 1173–1826* (IMC, Dublin, 1960), 47.
266 *CPRI, Jas I*, 30.
267 Ibid., 12.
268 *Inq. cancel. Hib. repert.*, ii, Cavan (1) Jas I.
269 Ibid. The property of people attainted between 1590 and 1593 is recorded in exchequer inquisitions (NAI, Calendar to exchequer inquisitions of the counties of Ulster, Cavan (3–6), Eliz., 6–16).
270 Cal. fiants Ir., Eliz., nos. 6458 (*CPRI, Eliz.*, 597), 6525 (ibid., 576), 6554 (ibid., 592), 6559 (ibid., 591), 6573 (ibid., 597), 6657, 6661; *CPRI, Jas I, passim.*

the monastery of Drumlahen with eight townlands, their tithes, and two rectories.[271] In 1582 O'Reilly forfeited his lease, rent having being unpaid for seven years, and in August both monasteries were leased, again for twenty-one years[272] to Hugh Strowbridge, who in 1597 was appointed clerk of first fruits and searcher of the towns of Youghal and Dungannon.[273] The monastery of Cavan, with half a townland adjacent, was granted in perpetuity to Edward Barrett in *c.* 1592.[274] Barrett may well have been the sheriff of Cavan, he is referred to in 1592[275] and in 1596 he wrote to Dublin about conditions there.[276]

The effectiveness of the lease of Loughowter and Drumlahen is conjectural. In September 1586, both were leased for sixty years to Sir Luke Dillon, to take effect at the termination of the lease to Strowbridge.[277] A grant of the ownership of both places was made in January 1604 to William Taaffe, who like Dillon was Old English and who was subsequently a plantation grantee in Castlerahan, who had acquired Dillon's interest in these and other properties. In March 1605, Theobald Bourke received a grant in soccage of the monastery of Cavan.[278] Shortly after the plantation the two former monasteries were owned by James Dillon, earl of Roscommon, and the Cavan monastery by Sir Thomas Ashe.[279]

Impropriate rectories in Cavan had also been granted before the end of the sixteenth century. The abbey of Kells, County Meath, had been granted to Sir Gerald Fleming in 1541,[280] but five rectories in Cavan impropriate to this abbey do not appear to have accompanied the grant so that in 1587 a twenty-one year lease of these, being 'waste and not leased to any since the suppression', was granted to Gerald Fleming.[281] In 1603 Fleming received a regrant of them for a further twenty-one year period 'in consideration of his services to Queen Elizabeth.'[282] He received an outright grant and a patent of other lands in Cavan in December 1608.[283] The abbey of Fore in Westmeath to which eleven rectories in Cavan were impropriate was held

271 Cal. fiants Ir., Eliz., no. 1681. In 1569 a grant of the custody of the Holy Trinity monastery had been made to Turlogh McCable of Flinstown, County Meath (*CSPI, 1509–73*, 399–400).

272 Possibly from the date of O'Reilly's original lease (see *CPRI, Jas I*, 2–3).

273 *CPRI, Eliz.*, 456.

274 Ibid., 219.

275 *CSPI, 1588–92*, 462.

276 *CSPI, 1592–96*, 529–30.

277 *CPRI, Jas I*, 2–3. It is clear from a fragment of a chancery bill that Strowbridge had not been able to collect at least some of the profits of these monasteries (NAI, Chancery salvage, D.54).

278 Ibid., 53–5. See Hill, *Plantation*, 113 (inaccurate?).

279 TCD, MS 570, fol. 312; *CPRI, Jas I*, 199.

280 Cal. fiants Ir., Henry VIII, no. 223.

281 Cal. fiants Ir., Eliz., no. 4956.

282 *CPRI, Jas I*, 10.

283 Ibid., 134.

by the Nugent family, barons of Delvin, by lease or otherwise, (with possible intermissions) from 1567.[284]

Through grants of attainted land patentee ownership or leasehold of lay property was also appearing in the county from *c.* 1592. Following an inquisition held at Cavan in September 1590 which found that the lands, two townlands in Castlerahan, of one Brian McPhelim O'Reilly who had been attainted, had come to the crown,[285] these lands were granted to Edward Barrett in *c.* 1592.[286]

Further inquisitions were held in 1592 and 1593, finding that the lands, and in some cases chief rents, of ten of the O'Reillys, and three others (one of whom held termon land) had come to the crown by attainder, or in a few cases by death without issue.[287] In March 1594 a sixty-year lease of the lands of nine of these proprietors with an additional area not found escheated by any surviving inquisition was granted to John Lee of Rathbride, County Kildare.[288] Lee was an anglicised Irishman who was 'interpreter of the Irish tongue' to the Dublin administration.[289] Lee's tenure of these lands may not have been very effective, at any rate in November 1603 a twenty-one year lease of two of the properties was made to Sir Thomas Ashe[290] a member of an English family whose father had acquired property in Meath by marriage under Elizabeth, and who in this way began a connection with Cavan landownership, subsequently considerably strengthened.

It was not however until after the war that land in any quantity became available through attainder and that conditions propitious for its occupation by grantees prevailed. These lands were granted in 1609 to two substantial Old English landowners, Gerald, earl of Kildare, 'in consideration of his services'[291] and Mary, Lady Delvin and her son Sir Richard Nugent, baron of Delvin and subsequently earl of Westmeath.[292] Delvin retained the land, with some adjustments, after the plantation. Kildare assigned most or all of his grant to Delvin.[293]

The grant to Delvin and his mother had a controversial background. In 1597 they had received royal authority for a grant of attainted lands in

[284] Cal. fiants Ir., Eliz., nos. 1089, 3478.

[285] NAI, Exchequer inquisitions, Ulster, Cavan, (3) Eliz., 6–9.

[286] *CPRI, Eliz.*, 219.

[287] NAI, Exchequer inquisitions, Ulster, Cavan, (4–6) Eliz., 9–16.

[288] Cal. fiants Ir., Eliz., no. 5849; *CPRI, Eliz.*, 274–5. Lee was a crown leaseholder of his Kildare lands (*CSPI, 1603–6*, 184).

[289] H.F. Hore, 'A chronographic account of … Wexford…', *PKIAS*, new series, ii (1858), 17–21. He died in 1612 (ibid.).

[290] *CPRI, Jas I*, 10.

[291] Ibid., 140–1.

[292] Ibid., 145.

[293] TCD, MS 570, fol. 311.

Cavan and Longford to the annual value of £100.[294] However, no grant could be made until after the peace in 1603 and the claims of the Delvins to lands in Longford, which engendered considerable ill-feeling, were ultimately not accepted, the O'Farrells of Longford being considered by Salisbury no less good subjects than the Nugents themselves.[295] In July 1607 the king ordered that the O'Farrells be repossessed and that Delvin and his mother should receive escheated lands in Cavan or elsewhere to the value of £108 per annum.[296]

In the autumn of 1607, however, Delvin, whose relations with authority were now embittered, was accused of inciting the earl of Tyrone to flee to the continent, and of plotting to seize Dublin castle. He was arrested in November, and it was planned to send him to England to stand trial, but he escaped and with a small following fled to Cloughowter in Cavan. Sir Garret Moore and the marshal of the army were dispatched against him. At the end of December Cloughowter and Delvin's young son were captured and the baron of 'enforced as a woodkerne in mantle and trouses to shift for himself.'[297] By February 1608 Salisbury conceded that he should be pardoned, and Chichester, finding him impossible to apprehend, feared that this 'young Robin Hood' could be a dangerous rallying point in the event of invasion or the return of the fugitive earls. Finally, on May 5, shortly after the outbreak of O'Doherty's rising, he submitted. A charge of complicity in O'Doherty's rising was not proved against him, and he was sent to England where on July 18 he was pardoned.[298]

This incident caused delay in the granting of the lands in Cavan to Delvin, and the patent, to Sir Richard and his mother, was dated 20 July 1609.[299] Smaller portions of attainted land were granted in 1606 to Sir John Kinge, the mustermaster general.[300] Kinge subsequently transferred his land to Roger Downeton,[301] a clerk of the pipe in the exchequer.[302] It can be seen then that although New English were acquiring land in Cavan prior to the plantation, the bulk of the land which had become available for distribution – attainted land – was granted to two Old English landowners, Kildare and Nugent.

[294] *CPRI, Eliz.*, 439–40.

[295] *CSPI, 1603–6*, 74, 312–14, 418–20, 529–30, 536; *1606–8*, 45, 111, 116, 134, 220, 522–3.

[296] *CSPI, 1608–8*, 220, 522–3; *1608–10*, 519, 581.

[297] *CSPI, 1608–8*, 362.

[298] Ibid., 45, 134, 157–60, 187–8, 256, 264, 320–1, 326, 327, 333, 334, 335, 337, 338, 348, 348–62, 398–9, 407, 415–16, 429–38, 459, 473, 482–3, 486, 502, 515, 529, 547–51, 583, 611–12, 614; R. Bagwell, *Ireland under the Stuarts* (3 vols, London, 1909–16), I, 40–6.

[299] *CPRI, Jas I*, 145.

[300] Ibid., 80–2.

[301] TCD, MS 570, fol. 311.

[302] Hughes, *Patentee Officers*, 43.

The termon and erenagh lands came in for official interest from 1590, when an inquisition was held at Cavan to investigate their extent.[303] These lands, some forty areas, were held to belong to the queen, as if they were monastic property. Some slight doubt about the validity of the categorisation must have existed, however, because an inquisition held in 1593 found one piece of termon land to have escheated to the crown through death without heir.[304] Seisin of these termons with their tithes was granted to Edward Barrett as part of an extensive grant throughout Ireland by two patents in June 1595 'in consideration of his wounds and for his services in the war manifoldly rendered.'[305] A twenty-one-year lease of one piece of termon land, Killdallon, was made to Sir Thomas Ashe in November 1603.[306] However, both Barrett and Ashe appear to have surrendered their leases and in March 1606 Sir Garret Moore, the seneschal of the county, received a twenty-one, year lease of all the termon land in Cavan at a rent of £17. 0. 0.[307] This lease appears to have passed to Sir Oliver Lambert, a prominent servitor figure and subsequent grantee in Clonmahon barony, because in November 1607 and again in March 1608 king's letters were written directing that he should have a regrant for forty-one years of termon lands in Cavan on the expiration of leases he then held.[308]

The granting out of confiscated land had thus introduced people of both Old English and New English grouping as owners or lessees in the county. Land had also been acquired by purchase, or was of longstanding ownership, by Old English from the area to the south of the county. The Plunketts, barons of Killeen, owned the territory of Munterconnaght, south of Lough Ramor.[309] Capt. Garret Fleming, who held the abbey of Kells, had purchased land in Clankee, and petitioned the lord deputy to be granted a patent. His suit was commended to London in January 1607 particularly because he had begun to build a castle on his new lands.[310] In the following year he went to London in person again recommended by Chichester, who referred to his 'maymes' received in the O'Neill war and his recent services against Delvin,[311] and in April a royal directive was issued in

303 NAI, Exchequer inquisitions, Ulster, Cavan (3) Eliz., 6–9.
304 Ibid., (6) Eliz., 12–16.
305 Cal. fiants Ir., Eliz., no. 5935; *CPRI, Eliz.*, 312–13, 313–14.
306 *CPRI, Jas I*, 10.
307 Ibid., 83. This crown lease was renewed in August 1607 (ibid., 107).
308 Ibid., 114, 133–4; *CSPI, 1606–8*, 330, 443.
309 NLI, J. Ainsworth, 'Reports on Private Collections, no. 6: Fingal papers'. The ownership of this land was in dispute with some of the O'Reillys at the time of plantation (NAI, Repertory to the decrees of chancery, i, 279; chancery salvage, R.159, U.103), and adjudged in favour of Christopher, Lord Killeen ('Ulster plantation papers', *Anal. Hib.*, viii).
310 *CSPI, 1606–8*, 79–80.
311 Ibid., 410.

his favour,[312] and his patent followed in December 1608.[313] Capt. Richard Tirrell, who had fought for O'Neill but surrendered in April 1603, was another of this type, being described as 'the most sufficient soldier and of the greatest reputation through all Ireland.'[314] He had acquired lands by purchase in Cavan and his position came into prominence in the spring and summer of 1610.[315] The New English Sir John Elliot, a baron of the exchequer, had also purchased some land in Cavan.[316]

Cavan, then, on the eve of plantation had a less homogeneous character than more northern counties. Thus, although there had been no scheme for colonisation in the county in the sixteenth century, as in Armagh, land ownership in Cavan had been more affected by a number of processes than in Armagh prior to the plantation. Not only were Old English and New English landholders established there, some perhaps tenuously, but there were also well-forged commercial contacts. The town of Cavan was an established market centre by the turn of the century and its logical contacts were with Dublin and sea-board Pale towns like Drogheda and Dundalk. One of its leading merchants, Walter Brady, was appointed constable and jailer of Cavan in 1584.[317] He appears to have lived at Dundalk during the war period and when in 1600 he sought a pension doubts were cast on his loyalty by the bishop of Meath, who stated that although he had built a castle at Cavan he had also aided the rebels.[318] His loyalty, however, was sufficiently established for him to receive a pension after the war, and when the town received its charter in November 1610, Walter Brady became its first sovereign, presiding over a mixed corporation of Gaelic Irish, old English and servitor elements. An interesting letter in the TCD archives serves to illustrate Brady's contacts with Dublin institutions. In June 1605 Walter Brady and Barnaby Brady, 'merchants', bound themselves unto 'Mr. Doctor Challoner, Chiffe of the Trinity Colledge' to be responsible for the good behaviour of two students from the county then in the college.[319] One of the witnesses was John Brady, vicar of Kilmore. Members of the Brady family thus not only had political and commercial links with Dublin, but also some had accepted the official religious position.[320] Such facts are understandable from the geographical position of the county and the

[312] Ibid., 480.
[313] *CPRI, Jas I*, 134.
[314] *CSPI, 1603–6*, 25.
[315] Below, 46.
[316] 'Ulster plantation papers', *Anal. Hib.*, viii.
[317] Cal. fiants Ir., Eliz., no.4547.
[318] *CSPI, 1600*, 418–20.
[319] TCD Muniment Room, Mahaffy Collection, c.12a. The students were John Jordan and Phillip McConin.
[320] *CPRI, Eliz.*, 277.

responses of its ruling family to English influences from the reign of Elizabeth. Sheriffs were appointed probably from the shiring of the county in 1579 and sessions were held there intermittently also from that time. These facts, cumulatively, indicate the peculiar position of Cavan on the eve of plantation and give the subsequent application of the plantation policy to this area a special significance.

We have seen that with the peace in 1603 no restoration of an O'Reilly chieftain or division of the county took place. In October 1605 Chichester, writing to Salisbury on the state of Wicklow, held it to be of 'especial consequence' to settle that county, as well as Cavan, Monaghan, Fermanagh, and Antrim.[321] Thus for two counties, Cavan and Fermanagh, subsequently planted, schemes were being devised following on the 1591 precedent of Monaghan (now in need of revision) whereby the land would be divided into small units amongst the native landholders, each to hold directly from the crown and the political powers of the chieftains to disappear. The plan, in short, was to establish a direct freehold relationship between all individual landholders and the crown. In July 1606 the deputy, Chichester, assisted by Davies, the attorney-general, and others, set out on a tour of Cavan, Monaghan, and Fermanagh, with this end in mind.[322] The implications of this policy were to be of profound importance after the plantation scheme had been adopted.

In August at Cavan a jury was assembled which included a large servitor element which found that the whole county had escheated to the crown through the successive deaths in rebellion of Sir John, Phillip, and Edmund O'Reilly.[323] In the autumn the deputy and council and Davies personally communicated their findings and plans for the three counties to Salisbury and the privy council.[324]

As to Cavan they felt that the division by baronies amongst the O'Reillys in 1584 had been inequitable and bred contention. An opportunity was now available, following on the findings of the jury, to make a more thorough and radical settlement. This was based upon a fundamental re-interpretation of the rights of the chieftains, not only in these three counties, but in Ulster in general. The journey in 1606, then, had general implications for Ulster as a whole. As Davies put it to Salisbury in November:

> we made so exact an inquiry of the estates and possessions of the Irishry that it appeared unto us plainly that the chief lords of every

[321] *CSPI, 1603–6*, 342.
[322] Ibid., 528.
[323] Ibid., 537, 538–39; *CPRI, Jas I*, 118.
[324] *CSPI, 1603–6*, 558–66; *1606–8*, 19–21; Morley, *Ireland*, 343–80.

> country had only a seigniory consisting of certain rents and duties, and had withal some special demesnes, and that the tenants or inferior inhabitants were not tenants at will, as the lords pretended, but freeholders, and had as good and large an estate in their tenancies as the lords had in their seignories and that the uncertain cuttings and exactions were a mere usurpation and a wrong and were taken *de facto* and not *de jure*, when the lords made war one upon another or joined together in rebellion against the crown.[325]

There was thus, it was argued, ample justification from within the Irish system itself for the restriction of the ruling families to particular defined areas of land paying quit rent for these to the crown, and for the circumvention of their political claims by the division of the remainder, with the same direct rent-paying relationship to the crown, amongst the subordinate occupiers. This analysis was applied equally to the O'Neill territories and had a particular relevance at that time in view of the impending crisis between O'Neill and O'Cahan.[326]

In Cavan, as in the other two counties, the deputy and his train set themselves, on the above assumption, to establish and record the amount of land possessed by each occupier or 'freeholder', to be used as the basis for a subsequent division of the county under patent.[327] They also planned that a part of the county – as of the other two – should be granted to servitors on condition of building castles. These servitors should either be dispersed in each barony, or in the barony of Loughtee, 'the best in the county', in which Cavan town was located.[328] Such a reorganisation of landholding and the presence of servitors would, it was felt, in short time transform a county,

> hitherto … little better than a den of thieves infesting the two counties of East and West Meath with continual spoils and robberies … to the condition of an English County, obedient to law.[329]

They furthermore decided to respect the expectations of the baron of Delvin to forfeited lands in Clanmahon, and suggested that captains Fleming and Tirrell who had bought land be granted patents and indeed receive 'somewhat more, for they have done more good by building and civil settlement than all the rest of the county.'[330] On their journey they

325 *CSPI, 1606–8*, 19–20.
326 Ibid., 20–21; Moody, *Londonderry*, 48–50, 56–7.
327 Morley, *Ireland*, 377.
328 *CSPI, 1603–6*, 558–66.
329 Ibid., 562.
330 Ibid., 565.

investigated also the state of the church, the termon lands, and monastic property.[331]

The programme for these three counties, as Davies envisaged it, was in effect that they should become extensions of the Pale, though including also a New English servitor element. The chieftainship of the O'Reillys, McMahons, and Maguires, 'three heads of that hydra of the north', should be abolished, and the customs of tanistry and gavelkind forbidden. Instead all land should be owned under the common law. Every man was to have a 'certain' home and know the extent of his estate. This would cause them to build better houses, improve their lands, and 'love neighbourhood'. In such an orderly environment villages and towns would prosper. These counties, he hoped, would in a short time 'not only be quiet neighbours to the Pale, but be made as rich and as civil as the Pale itself.'[332]

In November the privy council acknowledged receipt of the Dublin programme, approved the recommendations for Monaghan, and urged that the land in Cavan (as well as Fermanagh) should be distributed much more broadly than the division of 1584 had effected. They also approved of grants to servitors. However, the land was to be granted predominantly to the native inhabitants, and if any English were planted they should be placed on the church lands, which would cause less contention,

> lest if any strangers be brought in among them it should be imagined as an invention to displant the natives, which would breed a general distaste in all the Irish.[333]

The division, or settlement, should be carried out by 'commissioners of indifferency' so that the scheme should 'wear the appearance of agreement rather than enforcement.[334] The adoption of the plantation policy later involved a change in attitude, in the rejection of the view that the Irish landholders were freeholders.

The implementation of this scheme for Cavan (and Fermanagh) never took place. In January 1607 the lord deputy and council stated that the project would take time to implement.[335] By June the division of Monaghan had been completed and a record of the landholding pattern thus established was submitted to London,[336] but the scheme for Cavan and

[331] Morley, *Ireland*, 377.
[332] Ibid., 379.
[333] *CSPI, 1606–8*, 23–4.
[334] Ibid.
[335] Ibid., 87.
[336] Ibid., 161–87.

Fermanagh remained still at the preparatory stage.[337] In December the drafting of the division scheme for Fermanagh and Cavan, the latter disordered by Delvin's escapade, was postponed until the following summer or spring.[338] By then the Flight of the Earls had allowed proposals for a much more radical policy of plantation in which Cavan was included.

The plan to settle Cavan amongst the native Irish thus proved abortive, but it has a certain interest in relation to the plantation which followed. The plantation involved the clear reversal of the policy, and also the theory – that the subordinate Irish landholders in Ulster were of freehold status – on which it was based. Sir John Davies in Cavan in 1610 found himself obliged to argue from an opposite viewpoint to that which he had held in 1606.

The years from 1608 to 1610 were ones of active planning of the plantation for the county. After the Flight of the Earls Sir Garret Moore retained his position as seneschal of the county.[339] Moore was for a while accused of complicity in the flight. Tirrell made complaints against him,[340] and Sir Edward Herbert, who had been sheriff of the county in 1591, applied for his position,[341] but Moore was not removed. O'Doherty's rising barely affected Cavan, though Delvin was accused of having contacts with him, and the need for precautions was expressed.[342] In the summer of 1608 small numbers refused to account to the sheriff or governor[343] but there was no serious disruption. In July 1608, however, it was noted that the death of O'Doherty had opened the way for a 'universal settlement' of Ulster.[344]

In his 'notes of remembrances' of September 1608 Chichester indicated that he still visualised a settlement of much of Cavan amongst the native inhabitants, as well as the introduction of settlers. In the original version of these 'notes', drawn up in March, he had recommended that the division of Cavan – and Fermanagh – should follow as much as possible the form adopted for Monaghan.[345] Of the O'Reillys he said there were many septs, most of them 'cross and opposite one unto another'. This dynastic unrest would facilitate a careful division of the land amongst freeholders, who, unless a few were made too powerful, would come to depend directly and individually on the crown. The natives of the county were not adequate to

337 Ibid., 164.
338 Ibid., 361–3.
339 Ibid., 401–3.
340 *CSPI, 1608–10*, 115.
341 *CSPI, 1606–8*, 461, 585.
342 Ibid., 486.
343 Ibid., 568–70.
344 Ibid., 609; *1608–10*, 46–7.
345 'Ulster plantation papers', *Anal. Hib.*, viii.

utilise the half of it, hence areas in each barony, or one entire barony, could be planted, with 'civil and well-chosen' men whose way of living would be exemplary to their Irish neighbours. Particular care should be taken of the town of Cavan, then anxious for incorporation, and a ballibetagh of land should be granted to it, as well as to the castle there, which should be granted to a settler. Belturbet, strategically placed on Lough Erne, should be similarly treated, and Cloughowter also reserved and 'regarded for'. He proposed that the rest of the barony of Cavan [Loughtee] should be granted to Maelmora O'Reilly, the grandson of Sir John and the chief in English eyes. However, there were many residents there who claimed freeholds, the Bradys and McCabes and others, and they should also receive land grants. Hence if Maelmora, whose father, it was pointed out, had died on the English side at the Blackwater and whose mother was a member of the Ormond family, were not to be reduced to very minor status, he should also receive grants in other baronies or some chief rents from the inferior freeholders. Ballinecargie, at which a small garrison was located, should be treated as Belturbet or Cloughowter, though the ward retained until the county became settled. The purchases of Capt. Fleming, Capt. Tirrell, Walter Talbot, and others unnamed should be respected, though it was noted that some doubt existed as to the validity of the baron of Delvin's claim to lands. If it was felt wise to reserve any other places for the king's service it should be done at the time of division and settlement.[346]

The 'Project' of plantation stated that the county contained 40,500 acres, which would make 32 portions – 25 great, 7 middle, and 20 small. Of this 40,500 acres, 3,500 were termon land, 2,500 should be granted as glebe, and 500 acres were monastic. There was thus 34,000 acres to be allocated to grantees under the plantation. Of this English and Scots should receive 6 proportions or 8,000 acres, servitors similarly 6 proportions or 8,000 acres and native Irish 14 proportions or 16,500 acres. Of the remaining 1,500 acres, 250 each should be allotted to three corporate towns, 250 acres to the castle at Cavan, 150 acres to the castle at Cloughowter, and 350 acres for a free school at Cavan. By this calculation the native Irish were to be granted some 40 per cent of the county.[347] While these acreage figures bear little relationship to reality, they were those with which the planners operated, and proportionate allocations based on them indicate the kind of mixed society which was visualised for the county.

From 1609 claims for land in Cavan from native and servitor elements as well as old English were pressed on both the Dublin and London

[346] *CSPI, 1608–10*, 54–6.
[347] Hill, *Plantation*, 112–14.

administrations. In April 1609 Sir Robert Jacob informed Salisbury that the Irish generally claimed to be freeholders,[348] an argument which would have found favour in 1606. The most radical claim rested in a petition presented to the deputy in June 1609 by Richard Plunkett of Rathmore.[349] Plunkett indicated his descent from Sir Theobold de Verdon, who he asserted had been lord of Cavan. Plunkett required that the county should be granted to him in regard of his inherited title. Chichester, in an endorsement, instructed Davies to investigate the claim. This fantastic demand does not appear to have been pressed further, and Plunkett did not become a grantee under the plantation scheme.

Early in April 1610 Capt. Tirrell who had acquired land in Cavan and who was a kind of 'petty chieftain' over some of the O'Reilly's, went to England without the deputy's permission to secure his title and also, it was suspected in Dublin, to petition for lands for the O'Reillys as well.[350] The Irish chancellor warned Salisbury against him stating that 'it is certain that if the fugitive arch-rebel have confidence with any man in this kingdom he has it in Captain Tirrell', and urging that he should not be permitted to live in Cavan any longer.[351] However, at the end of June he returned to Dublin with an official letter accepting his personal suit.[352]

In March 1609 Chichester had pointed out that the chief members of the O'Reilly family would not be content without substantial grants.[353] It was felt that portion should be allotted to Catherine Butler, widow of Maelmora O'Reilly, and to the widow of Sir John O'Reilly.[354] In the spring of 1610 an O'Reilly pedigree was prepared and sent to England.[355] At this time also John O'Reilly and Connor McCahir O'Reilly returned from England, where they had sued for land, bearing a letter from the privy council.[356] This recited that they had owned twenty townlands and were chiefs of one-third of Clanmahon, and recommended the deputy and his advisers to grant them such quantity of land as they thought expedient since both were to be removed elsewhere for the convenience of the plantation.[357] A recommendation of one Lysaghe O'Connor, who had petitioned for land

348 *CSPI, 1608–10*, 193–7.
349 Ibid., 221.
350 Ibid., 426–7.
351 Ibid.
352 Ibid., 468–9. His patent dated 25 May 1612 is abstracted in Hill, *Plantation*, 347.
353 *CSPI, 1608–10*, 178.
354 Ibid., 183, 237–8.
355 Ibid., 419.
356 Ibid., 440; 'Ulster plantation papers', *Anal. Hib.*, viii.
357 Another recommendation from London was on behalf of a certain Owen Carnan, possibly the Wony McThomas McKiernan who received land in Tullyhaw (*CSPI, 1608–10*, 441).

in Cavan, but can hardly have had land there, was dated July 25 and must have arrived when the land had already been allotted.[358] Otherwise the choosing of native grantees for the county is relatively undocumented and was left to the deputy and plantation commissioners.

The final plan for the allocation of land in Cavan differed from that embodied in the 'project'. One barony, Loughtee, was allocated to English undertakers, and was divided into 11 proportions, 8 small and 3 middle making 12,500 acres as then calculated. Two baronies, Tullyhunco, 6 small proportions: 6,000 acres, and Clankee, 2 great and 2 small proportions: 6,000 acres, were allotted to Scots. The remaining four, Tullyhaw, Castlerahan, Clanmahon, and Tullygarvey, comprising in all 4 great, 7 middle, and 16 small proportions: 32,500 acres, were for servitors and natives.[359]

In the earlier stages of planning the colony, most energy seems to have been devoted to more northern counties. Hence, in 1609, a list of possible undertakers and lands they might receive passed over Cavan with the statement that by reason of its contiguity to the Pale it would be 'easily' undertaken.[360] Only one consort group, however, applied for land there, and of these only one, John Taylor from Cambridgeshire, subsequently received an estate in Cavan.[361] In his list of candidates suitable for grants as servitors drawn up early in 1610, Chichester made only two recommendations for this county: that Sir Francis Ruish should get land near Belturbet, with which he had connections, and that Capt. Culme should also receive the rewards of his profession in Cavan.[362] However, no delay in implementing the scheme ensued, and when in July 1610 the plantation commissioners began their task of allocating the escheated lands, the first county they dealt with was Cavan.

358 Ibid., 483.
359 Ibid., 404–6.
360 Ibid., 180–1.
361 Ibid., 550.
362 Ibid., 366–7.

CHAPTER 2

The Beginnings of Plantation, 1610–13

1. Allocation of land and grantees

The spring and summer of 1610 saw the climax of preparations for the plantation. In April and May the choice of consorts was made and the names of those English and Scottish undertakers with the baronies to which they were assigned forwarded to Dublin.[1] The undertakers, or accredited agents, were required to present themselves to the lord deputy and plantation commissioners before 24 June 1610.[2] In May and June instructions were received from the privy council authorising Chichester to issue a commission and make the necessary arrangements for the allocation of land to the grantees. He was to assemble forces to attend the commissioners on their journey and leave companies in Ulster for the planters' security.[3] He was also to impress and despatch further swordsmen to Sweden.[4]

The task of the commissioners, to be accomplished with minimum delay and involving incidental and complex problems, was not an easy one. They were to settle estate, barony and county boundaries where doubt or dispute existed, to define for settlers in strategic areas the locations of their strongholds, and to arbitrate in all suits concerning the escheated lands. They might re-organise parochial boundaries to coincide with the new structure of planters' estates. They were, *inter alia*, to allocate suitable glebe to each parish to allot the land granted for towns, and to restore church land alienated as monastic property.[5]

Chichester was aware of the difficulties involved. In letters to Salisbury in June and July he stated his fears. The undertakers were slow in arriving,[6] and the natives could not be removed from undertakers' land without difficulty and disturbance – 'the word of removing and transplanting being to the natives as welcome as the sentence of death.'[7] His fears for the native

1 'Ulster plantation papers', no. 21, *Anal. Hib.*, viii.
2 BL, Lansdowne MS 159, ff 217–23, T.W. Moody (ed.), 'The revised articles of the Ulster plantation, 1610', *BIHR*, xii.
3 *CSPI, 1608–10*, 452; *Cal. Carew MSS, 1603–24*, 54–5.
4 *CSPI, 1608–10*, 458–60, 460–61.
5 'Ulster plantation papers', no. 26, *Anal. Hib.*, viii; *CPRI, Jas I*, 195.
6 *CSPI, 1608–10*, 470–73.
7 Ibid., 479–80.

Irish reaction were not without substance. In June Sir Toby Caulfeild, fitly placed to assess the local reaction, reported to Dublin the effect of the news of the impending plantation on the people of central Ulster.[8] Not only was he having difficulty in controlling the 'woodkerne', but since the news of the plantation had been divulged by Sir Turlogh McHenry O'Neill there was not 'a more discontented people in Christendom.' They foresaw that it would shortly be their predicament 'to be woodkerne out of necessity, no other means being left to them ... than to live as long as they can by scrambling.' They hoped to maintain their position until the spring of 1611 when aspirations centred on the return of O'Neill and the reversal of the entire situation by military force.

In such circumstances the implementing of the plantation was an immediate necessity. Towards the end of July Chichester and his associates set out for Ulster to allot the lands, deciding to begin with Cavan where there was more land to be allotted to the natives than elsewhere in Chichester's opinion, and where he felt the people were 'more understanding and pliable to reason than in the remoter parts.'[9]

The commissioners' reception in Cavan on August 4 proved of significance because here an attempt was made to defeat the plantation scheme by legal means. The success or failure of the natives of Cavan would be a precedent of general importance. Davies discussed this affair in a series of lengthy letters, September–November 1610.[10] The Cavanmen through proximity to the Pale had acquired a knowledge of English law not known in more distant parts of Ulster. Thus when the commissioners, meeting in Cavan, announced that the natives would be removed from the undertakers' lands to facilitate the plantation a Pale lawyer, employed by them, argued that they had estates of inheritance in their land which could not have been forfeited by the O'Reilly attainders. He therefore demanded for his clients the benefits of freeholders in England law, and pleaded also the proclamation of pardon and oblivion made in 1605. Such a claim if allowed would have overthrown, in large measure, the whole legal pretext for the plantation.

Davies impressed by this very case in 1603,[11] now entirely opposed it. The king, he argued was lord paramount of all the land in the kingdom, and where a tenant's estate 'doth fail and determine' he may dispose of the land at pleasure. As to Cavan, because two of the O'Reilly's had been

8 Ibid., 474–5.

9 Ibid., 480.

10 Ibid., 497–501; BL, Cotton MSS, Titus B X, ff 202–5v; Morley, *Ireland*, 383–90. See also G.A. Hayes-McCoy, 'Sir John Davies in Cavan in 1606 and 1610 ', *Breifne*, vol. 1 no. 3 (1960), 177–91.

11 Above, 41–3.

recently killed in rebellion, all these lands had reverted to the crown. The plaintiffs, Davies contended, had no estates of inheritance 'because neither their chiefries nor their tenancies did ever descend to a certain heir.' Their custom of gavelkind had already been declared illegal and they had 'only a scrambling and transitory possession at the pleasure of the chief of every sept.' The claimants could, he insisted, substantiate no title by common law to their estates, and if they had no legal rights in their lands, the proclamation which received these lands into the king's protection did not give them any better estate than they had had previously. Even by brehon law their claim was untenable.

Furthermore the king was bound in conscience to implement a project which would convert his people from barbarism to civility. The land, half of which was now waste, would with the coming of the planters, be fully stocked and infinitely more productive. Also the plantation would mean a financial loss to the state: the rents recently collected from the earl of Tyrone's lands were higher than the settlers' quit rents would be.

Davies's altered attitude was a clear indication of the change in government policy since 1606. With the defence

> the natives seemed not unsatisfied in reason, though in passion they remained ill-contented, being grieved to leave their possessions to strangers which their septs had so long, after the Irish manner enjoyed.[12]

However, the deputy 'so mixed threate with intreaty' that they promised to give way to the undertakers if the sheriff, by warrant of the commissioners, put them in possession. This crisis in Cavan represents an important stage in the development of the native reaction to the plantation. 'The eyes of all the natives in Ulster were turned upon this county.'[13]

The undertakers were required to be in Ireland by June 24, and although all may not have been punctual, most came over the presented themselves to the commissioners on their journey of assignment.[14] From the schedules of the grants of the commissioners[15] we can establish the number of undertakers who received possession in 1610, which can be presented in tabular form.[16] It is likely that most of the servitors received possession at the same time.

12 Morley, *Ireland*, 389.
13 Ibid., 499.
14 *CSPI, 1608–10*, 497–501.
15 'Ulster plantation papers', no. 11, *Anal. Hib.*, viii.
16 The certificates are in some cases undated or ambiguous. The last column (b) gives numbers for which the evidence is clear though the larger figures in (a) are more likely to be correct.

County	Barony	Nationality	No. of grantees	No. present (a)	No. present (b)
Armagh	Fewes	Scots	5	2	1
Armagh	Oneilland	English	10	7	6
Cavan	Loughtee	English	7		7
Cavan	Clankee	Scots	4		0
Cavan	Tullyhunco	Scots	5		2

These certificates of 1610 are dated variously from the camps of the commissioners as they moved about Ulster. They range from August 4 to September 24. John Taylor of Loughtee was the first undertaker to be assigned his lands. The majority of undertakers of both counties did not arrive in Ulster until September. Most striking is the low initial attendance of Scots. Clankee barony remained unclaimed until after Carew arrived back in Dublin, after surveying the plantation, in September 1611.

The impetus towards plantation of those who acquired land is not part of this study, but a brief introduction of the grantees with reference to the sizes of their estates and the overall proportions of the land of each county held by the different proprietor types is essential.[17] The incomes some of the grantees claimed to have are stated below. It would seem that, not unexpectedly, they were not people of special substance. It is not easy to find comparative figures for England or Scotland at this time, but in a recent study of the Kent gentry between 1640 and 1660 it has been shown that the average income of 135 families with well-documented fortunes was £656 per annum, though the author states that hundreds had an income of under £250 a year.[18]

In Armagh, where the confiscated land in two baronies, Oneilland and the Fews, was allotted to English and Scottish consorts respectively, in all fifteen undertakers, ten English and five Scots, received estates. There were also eight servitor grantees in Orior.

In Oneilland two grantees, John and William Brownlow, were father and son. John, who came from Nottingham, put in for 2,000 acres and claimed to have a income of £150 per annum.[19] Three, John Dillon, Richard Rolleston, and William Powell whose estate Rolleston subsequently acquired, came from Staffordshire. Rolleston, a clergyman, claimed an income of £100 per annum and property to the value of £500. Powell was a royal servant, one of the equerries of the king's stable.[20] He was, in a sense,

17 For a list of all proprietors see Appendix 1.

18 A. Everitt, *The community of Kent and the great rebellion, 1640–60* (Leicester, 1966), 41, 329.

19 *CSPI, 1608–10*, 548–51 (Hill, *Plantation*, 146–9).

20 Hill, *Plantation*, 145. In 1604 he received a reversionary grant 'of the keeping of the race at Malmesbury' (*CSP Dom., 1603–10*, 114; Hill, *Plantation*, 26).

a servitor in England and it is not surprising that he quickly disposed of his Armagh lands. Two, James Matchett, the second clerical grantee, and William Stanhowe, came from Norfolk. Matchett, whose income was £84 a year,[21] clearly received no great preferment, and Stanhowe (with his son Henry) in applying for land represented himself as having £150 per annum and £500 in goods.[22] Francis Sacheverall, from Leicester, had, of those who declared it, the highest income with £300 per annum.[23] Joseph Warde, also from Norfolk, with £2,000 in goods, was selected as a grantee,[24] but exchanged his lands with John Heron who does not feature on the lists of applicants for lands and whose origin and fortunes are unknown. The remaining person allotted land in this barony, Sir Richard Fines, Lord Saye and Seale, had earlier proposed himself as a consort leader,[25] but now simply became an undertaker and in fact quickly disposed of his lands. He was later to be involved in colonising schemes in North America.[26]

Two of the five Scottish grantees in the Fews, Sir James Douglas and Sir James Craig, accompanied King James to England and had established themselves in good positions for further advancement. Douglas, from Haddingtonshire, became a gentleman of the bedchamber. In 1608 he received a grant of the recusancy fines of certain individuals and also license to prospect for gold and silver in Hampshire and the Isle of Wight. He received other emoluments of royal service in 1609 and in the following year land in Ulster.[27] Craig had the advantage of similar royal proximity and held positions in the wardrobe from 1603.[28] He not only became an Ulster undertaker, but also subsequently received many grants of land throughout Ireland.[29] The other grantees, William Lawder, Claud Hamilton, and Henry Acheson were Scots residents who were not royal servants, though Henry Acheson's brother, Sir Archibald, who was to acquire Douglas's estate, was a leading Scottish public official.[30]

Of the eight servitor grantees in Orior, two, perhaps three, were men of considerable distinction. Sir Oliver St. John had been a soldier in Flanders, was sent to Ireland in 1601, was now master of the ordnance, and was subsequently lord deputy.[31] The career of Sir Garret Moore has already been

21 *CSPI, 1608–10*, 550; Hill, *Plantation*, 261 is incorrect.
22 *CSPI, 1608–10*, 550.
23 Ibid., 549.
24 'Ulster plantation papers', no. 21, *Anal. Hib.*, viii.
25 *CSPI, 1608–10*, 425, 500.
26 C.P. Nettels, *The roots of American civilization* (2nd edn., London, 1963), 121–2, 174.
27 Hill, *Plantation*, 283; *CSP Dom., 1603–10*, 379, 415, 437, 462, 524, 527.
28 *CSP Dom., 1603–10*, 55, 127, 170; Hill, *Plantation*, 284.
29 *CPRI, Jas I*, 460, 529, 531–2, 558, 561, 563, 569, 574.
30 John Lodge, *The peerage of Ireland*, ed. Mervyn Archdall (1789), vi, 81.
31 Hill, *Plantation*, 310; Hughes, *Patentee Officers*, 115.

noted. Lord Audley, Sir George Touchet, the 18th baron, was of a Staffordshire family, had acquired land in Munster, and was the father-in-law of Sir John Davies.[32] He made an extravagant application for 100,000 acres in Tyrone in July 1609 which was at first welcomed by the English privy council.[33] However, Chichester was sceptical stating that his limited achievements in Munster did not 'promise the building of substantial castles nor a convenient plantation in Ulster.'[34] By June 1610 he had declared himself willing to receive a grant as any other servitor,[35] and he received 500 acres as then computed in Orior, with the reversion of the land granted to Art McBaron O'Neill.[36]

Of the remaining five, Sir Thomas Williams has been already mentioned. Marmaduke Whitechurch who had fought at the Blackwater,[37] had already acquired monastic property in Armagh. John Bourchier was the second son of Sir George Bourchier, the Irish master of the ordnance who had died (as also had his eldest son) 'a very poor gentleman' in 1605.[38] Charles Poyntz was a lieutenant who proved an extremely active landowner and Francis Cooke was a captain who developed close connections with the Londonderry plantation, and married the widow of Sir Edward Dodington.[39]

In Cavan the forfeited land in one barony Loughtee (apart from small areas) was granted to seven English undertakers and that in two baronies Clankee and Tullyhunco (again with excepted areas) was assigned to nine Scottish undertakers. The forfeited land in the remaining four baronies, Tullygarvey, Clonmahon, Tullyhaw, and Castlerahan were granted to servitors and natives, of whom there were eighteen British servitors.

Three of the seven Loughtee undertakers, Sir John Davies, the attorney-general, Reynold Horne, and William Snow almost immediately disposed of their lands. Davies received land as a servitor in Fermanagh[40] – the distinction between servitor and undertaker was not always a hard and fast one – and transferred his interest in Loughtee to a fellow undertaker, Richard Waldron who in turn disposed of his own allotment to Reynold Horne.[41] Horne received a grant of possession on 4 September 1610, but

32 Hill, *Plantation*, 135.
33 *CSPI, 1608–10*, 258–9.
34 Ibid., 297–8, 319.
35 Ibid., 467.
36 Ibid., 494. He was also consort leader and a grantee as an English undertaker in the barony of Omagh, County Tyrone ('Ulster plantation papers', no. 21, *Anal. Hib.*, viii.).
37 *CSPI, 1598–9*, 241, 244, 491.
38 *CSPI, 1603–6*, 343, 346: Sir George committed his son's care to Chichester.
39 Moody, *Londonderry*, 110, 140, 162, 174, 178, 280, 313, 314–15, 317, 349, 447.
40 Hill, *Plantation*, 330.
41 'Ulster plantation papers', no. 21, *Anal. Hib.*, viii.

by September 24 had passed his lands to Sir Nicholas Lusher.[42] Snow did not come to Ulster but disposed of his lands to Lusher's son, William.[43]

Of the seven grantees to receive land in Loughtee after these initial re-arrangements two, the Lushers, came from Surrey.[44] Sir Nicholas had probably had a previous association with another grantee Sir Hugh Wirrall from Enfield in Middlesex – income £200 a year – because they, and others, received an office in the customs administration of England in 1611.[45] Richard Waldron was the son of an Elizabethan adventurer in Ireland, John Waldron, who received an extensive grant of lands throughout the country in 1607.[46] Of the remaining three, two, John Fishe and Stephen Butler, came from Bedfordshire. Fishe, claiming an income of £300, applied originally for land in Oneilland.[47] Butler similarly applied for Armagh land but represented himself as having an estate of £1,500.[48] The remaining grantee, John Taylor, came from Cambridgeshire, submitted his income as being 200 marks per annum, and was one of a group who actually applied for land in Cavan.[49]

Of the four Scots grantees in Clankee, one, Esme Stuart, Lord Aubigny, was the second son of the first duke of Lennox, a member of the Scottish privy council.[50] The others, William Bailie, William Dunbarr, and John Ralston, were of less clear origin, though the latter was the son of the lord (or laird) of Ralston.[51] In Tullyhunco Sir Alexander Hamilton and Sir Claud, father and son, were undertakers. There were also two brothers Alexander and John Auchmooty, the latter a groom of the bedchamber from 1603.[52] The fifth, John Browne, a man without title or royal connection, quickly disposed of his estate.

The British servitors in Cavan numbered eighteen. Two were men of considerable standing in public service. Sir John Elliot, who received land in Castlerahan having purchased land in the county before the plantation,[53] was a baron of the exchequer and had been involved in drawing up the indictment against the fugitive earls.[54] Sir Oliver Lambert was a man of outstanding energy and a privy councillor. A nephew of Sir Henry Wallopp,

42 Ibid., no. 11.
43 Ibid.
44 Hill, *Plantation*, 282.
45 *CSP Dom., 1611–18*, 67; *CSPI, 1608–10*, 551.
46 Hill, *Plantation*, 280.
47 *CSPI, 1608–10*, 549.
48 Ibid.
49 Ibid., 550.
50 'Ulster plantation papers', no. 21, *Anal. Hib.*, viii; Hill, *Plantation*, 308.
51 'Ulster plantation papers', no. 21, *Anal. Hib.*, viii
52 Hill, *Plantation*, 307.
53 Above, 42.
54 Hughes, *Patentee Officers*, 46; Hill, *Plantation*, 343.

he first appeared in Ireland in 1581, later serving against Spain and in the Netherlands. He assisted Essex in Ireland in 1599, was made governor of Connacht in 1601, and fought in the Ulster wars. He received a number of grants of land throughout the country before and after the plantation, already had Cavan connections, and had his home at Kilbeggan in Westmeath on monastic property.[55] In 1610 Davies described him as 'a worthy servitor … like to prove a good planter in … Cavan.'[56]

Some of the other servitors, like Lambert, had had previous connections with the county. Capt. Hugh Culme was constable of Cloughowter castle,[57] of which with its lands he received a twenty-one-year lease in November 1610.[58] In the same year he was provost-marshal of County Cavan 'and parts adjoining'.[59] Sir Thomas Ashe of Trim, who with his brother John of Kilmessan received land in Tullygarvey, had acquired crown leases of Cavan land before the plantation.[60] Archibald and Brent Moore, the former constable of Ballynecargy in Cavan,[61] were relatives of Sir Garret Moore,[62] who had been seneschal of the county.

Of the other grantees, Nicholas Pynnar, a captain who had been at Lifford and Omagh forts in 1602,[63] was subsequently appointed an overseer of fortifications and plantations,[64] and was made responsible for the survey of the Ulster colony conducted in 1618–19. John Ridgeway, a grantee in Castlerahan, was a brother of Sir Thomas Ridgeway, the vice-treasurer[65] who with Davies had acted as liaison officer between Dublin and London in planning the plantation in the spring of 1610. Sir Edmund Fettiplace as a captain had fought at the Blackwater;[66] by 1605 he was a pensioner and knighted.[67] Sir Richard and Sir George Graham belonged to the famous Scots border and Cumberland clan that had been transplanted to Roscommon 1606.[68] However, they had both had a military career in Ireland in Elizabeth's reign,[69] Sir George (or possibly his father Sir George)

55 Lodge, *Peerage*, i, 348–53; *CPRI, Jas I*, 89.
56 Morley, *Ireland*, 390.
57 *CSPI, 1608–10*, 80.
58 *CPRI, Jas I*, 182, see also 92.
59 *CSPI, 1608–10*, 512; see also *CSPI, 1601–3*, 535.
60 Above, 37, 39.
61 'Ulster plantation papers', no. 11, *Anal. Hib.*, viii; *CPRI, Jas I*, 327.
62 Hill, *Plantation*, 346
63 *CSPI, 1601–3*, 525.
64 BL, Add. MS 4794, ff 390–91.
65 Hughes, *Patentee Officers*, 111.
66 *CSPI, 1598–9*, 253–4.
67 *CSPI, 1603–6*, 256.
68 *CSPI, 1608–10*, xcv–ciii; P. William, 'The northern borderland under the early Stuarts' in H.E. Bell & R.L. Ollard (eds.), *Historical essays, 1600–1750 presented to David Ogg* (London 1963), 1–17.
69 *CSPI, 1601–3*, 347–8, 487.

had got land at Naas in Kildare[70] and in 1617 Sir Richard received a controversial grant of O'Byrne land in Wicklow.[71]

The remaining grantees had had minor military careers. Four, Anthony Atkinson, Edward Rutledge, John Russon (or Russell), and Roger Garth were lieutenants.[72] Thomas Jones, a serjeant, received lands as in Tullyhaw which are in modern Tullyhunco, and Joseph Jones was a grantee in Clanmahon.[73] They were now reaping the rewards of previous service.

There were also ten Old English proprietors in Cavan, some of whom, as has been seen, had acquired land previously to the plantation. The positions of Richard Nugent, baron of Delvin, Christopher Plunkett, baron of Killeen, Capt. Garret Fleming, Capt. Richard Tirrell, Walter Talbot[74] and Luke Dillon have already been discussed. Christopher and Edward Nugent as grantees were presumably also retaining earlier acquisitions. Richard Fitzsimonds was a Drogheda merchant who acquired the fishings of the Bann and Foyle in the Londonderry plantation in 1613 and was also a tenant to the archbishopric of Armagh.[75] His grant in Cavan was probably also a confirmation of a previous acquisition.

There was no systematic buying out of private interests as in Londonderry,[76] though it will be seen below that in 1638 one person, also Old English, claimed that his father had surrendered land in Cavan to facilitate the plantation on alleged promise from Chichester of compensation in a later plantation.[77] The remaining Old English grantee, Sir William Taaffe, who received land in Castlerahan as a servitor, had had little previous contact with the county.[78] He owned property in Louth and Connacht (the latter by grant of 1592) and also between 1603 and 1620 received grants in a number of Irish counties.[79] He distinguished himself as a captain during the O'Neill war and in 1606 was constable of Ardee castle.[80]

The fact that the Old English retained or received so much land in Cavan would indicate something of the government's attitude towards them at this

70 Hill, *Plantation*, 327; also in Galway (*CPRI, Jas I*, 90).

71 H.F. Kearney, *Strafford in Ireland, 1633–41* (Manchester 1959), 175–6.

72 *CSPI, 1611–14*, 212–13.

73 A certain Capt. Lyons as associated with him for a time (ibid.).

74 Talbot held his lands for some time in partnership with Hugh Culme. The original patent was in fact issued to Culme alone (*CPRI, Jas I*, 193–4). By 1630, the year in which Culme died, it was owned entirely by Talbot's son, James (*Inq. cancel. Hib. repert.*, ii, Cavan (29) Chas I), and he received a patent for it in 1638 (NAI, John Lodge, Records of the rolls, vi, 123). Hill, *Plantation*, 338 is confusing.

75 Moody, *Londonderry*, 151, 173; below 355.

76 Moody, *Londonderry*, 114–18.

77 Below, 191–2.

78 Above, 36.

79 NAI, Lodge, Records of the rolls, iv, 290–91; Hill, *Plantation*, 343.

80 *CSPI, 1603–6*, 432.

time, though two years later, in 1612, the baron of Delvin was described by Barnaby Rich as one of the six 'pryncypall pyllers that doth enterteyne prystes and gyveth support and countenance to popery in Ireland.'[81]

The subsequent role of the consort leaders in the cases of baronies granted to groups of English undertakers and of the Scottish privy council with regard to groups of Scots grantees after the initial stage of assembling those who would receive land, seems to have been very slight. There is no evidence that the earl of Worcester as supervisor of Oneilland took any active interest in the colony there, though Chichester in writing, in October 1610, to the earl of Northampton, who had selected the grantees in Loughtee, referred to his good choice of those sent 'to undertake his precynct';[82] and as late as February 1614 Sir Robert Jacob informed him that the undertakers he had recommended for that barony had 'built and planted very well.'[83] The Scots privy council appointed a 'chief undertaker' in each barony allotted to their countrymen.[84]

In order to give a statistical basis to this thesis an attempt has been made to establish the acreage of each estate in statute measure. The methods employed and problems encountered are described below,[85] where lists of proprietors are given. Proprietors have been classified, and the percentages of the total acreage of each county held by each category at the beginning and end of our period calculated. A tabular abstract of the state of landownership in Armagh and Cavan following on the plantation is presented here. The figures are necessarily presented with an appearance of accuracy which must, however, be qualified. The evidence on which identifications of seventeenth-century place names with the modern Ordnance Survey equivalents has been made has varied in quantity and quality. These figures are furthermore presented in terms of real acreages; owing to defects in the seventeenth-century statistical material, the amount of land in profitable occupation in the early seventeenth century is difficult to establish. However these statistics and the maps which accompany them are the outcome of careful investigation and are presented as a fundamental part of this study.

The figures below are given the date period *c.* 1610–*c.* 1620 to take account of various adjustments, grants of small areas overlooked in 1610, and the like which are discussed in the early chapters. The categories are

[81] C.L. Falkiner (ed.), 'Barnaby Rich's "Remembrances of the state of Ireland, 1612"', *PRIA*, xxvi, C, no. 8 (1906), 140–41.
[82] *CSPI, 1608–10*, 521.
[83] HMC, *Hastings MSS*, vol. iv (1947), 14.
[84] 'Ulster plantation papers', no. 21, *Anal. Hib.*, viii.
[85] Below, 407–10.

generally self-explanatory, though a few points must be made. Under the heading British servitors have been grouped not only those British granted land as servitors,[86] but also all those British who in 1610 or subsequently held lay land without obligation to plant British tenants, i.e. those British proprietors of small areas who were not tied to the conditions of undertakers. These include the holders of fort lands, a small number of pre-plantation British proprietors of non-ecclesiastical land, and grantees after the plantation of small areas, one of whom in Cavan was, in fact a Scot. Although mountain land was granted to a person of ordinary servitor type,[87] it is here placed in a particular category in order not to weight the proportion held by servitors unrealistically since its value to its grantee is known to have been very slight. Although grantees of monastic land could be fitted into other categories, ex-monastic land is here particularised to show the extent of monastic property prior to the plantation.[88]

Armagh, *c.* 1610 – *c.* 1620

Proprietor groups	**% of total acreage**
English undertakers	21.33
Scottish undertakers	5.05
British servitors	8.97
Native Irish	25.21
Archbishopric	15.44
Trinity College, Dublin	7.36
Ex-monastic	9.57
Glebe	2.11
Other ecclesiastic proprietors	2.77
School	0.50
Mountain	0.32
Unidentified ownership	1.37

Cavan, *c.* 1610 – *c.* 1620

Proprietor groups	**% of total acreage**
English undertakers	11.95
Scottish undertakers	16.12
British servitors	20.59
Native Irish	22.49
Old English	13.73
Bishopric	6.86

86 Above 52–3, 54–7.

87 Below, 99.

88 It may be slightly exaggerated in Armagh at the expense of servitors.

Ex-monastic	0.90
Glebe	2.95
School	0.20
Town of Cavan	0.15
Mountain	3.63
Unidentified ownership	0.40

It can be seen that in both counties undertakers were granted somewhat more than one-quarter of the total acreage. In Londonderry, their equivalents, the Irish Society and individual companies received 63.2 per cent of the land.[89] Native Irish in both counties received somewhat less than the share of undertakers, but more than twice the 10.2 per cent granted them in Londonderry.[90] In Armagh two-thirds of the land Irish-owned (some 50,000 acres) was granted before the plantation, all but 6,000 of this being held by Sir Turlogh McHenry and Sir Henry oge O'Neill, hence the amount distributed to Irish under the plantation in this county was smaller than the table suggests.[91] In Cavan British servitors, who received one-fifth of the land, were a very substantial group, with proportionately twice the share of their Armagh counterparts. However, monastic land in Armagh, which accounted for about 10 per cent of the area, was, unlike Cavan, granted to people exclusively of servitor type. In Cavan the Old English occupied a special position. They had received almost all the monastic land, which with their share of lay land, gave them an almost 15 per cent stake in the proprietorship of the county. Thus native Irish and Old English catholics owned some 37 per cent of the county – the Catholic (and native Irish) share of Armagh was 25 per cent. In Armagh, Trinity College, a unique though Protestant proprietor received 7 per cent of the land. In Armagh the share of the church, some 20.32 per cent, was considerably higher than in Cavan, where it was almost 10 per cent, but was similar to the 22.8 per cent of Londonderry.[92] In all three counties incumbents' glebes occupied a similar proportion of the land. The approximate area of ecclesiastical land before the plantation can also be stated. This is the total of episcopal (including termon and erenagh land), monastic, and of other ecclesiastical proprietors. Glebe, being largely non-existent before the plantation, should be excluded. The figures are, thus, 24.78 per cent of Armagh, and 7.76 percent of Cavan.

[89] Moody, *Londonderry*, 455.

[90] Ibid.

[91] This throws light on Chichester's opinion (below, 61–2), that only in Cavan had the Irish received an adequate share of the land.

[92] Ibid.

The acreages of individual estates are provided in Appendix 1. It can thus be seen how much larger than the amounts they were granted the real acreages of estates turned out to be.[93] In Oneilland estates were generally about three times, though occasionally very much more, the size of the acreage they were granted as. In the Fews estates, apart from Douglas's, ranged from being almost twice to somewhat more than twice the figures they were granted as. Scots' undertakers estates in Armagh were thus smaller than those of their English equivalents. The TCD lands in County Armagh were five times the size of their calculated acreage. Servitor grants in Orior were generally about three times their granted size.

In Cavan estates proved to be even larger. In Loughtee the estates of English undertakers were from over three to over four (in one case more) times the sizes recorded in the patents. Scots' estates in Tullyhunco were, with one exception, four to six times their official acreage, and in Clankee they ranged from five to ten times the 1610 acreage. Servitors' estates in Cavan were similarly large. Estates in Cavan would have been even larger but for a change made in the official estimate of the acreage of the poll between 1609 and 1610. The 'Project' for the plantation of January 1609 assumed that each poll contained twenty-four acres.[94] However, the patents in 1610 granted polls as having an acreage of about double this assumption.[95]

The fact that estates proved so much larger than the planners designed had a number of consequences. Firstly, from the standpoint of public finance, it meant that the government got a smaller return from quit rent than need have been necessary. It also meant that the density of settlement to which the undertakers were bound – twenty-four men per small proportion – was in effect greatly reduced. More specifically, as in Londonderry,[96] estates of this size did not lend themselves to settlement in villages as the plantation conditions required.

Government officers were not long in detecting these defects in the Ulster plantation. Sir Oliver St. John, lord deputy when the Longford plantation was being planned in 1618, and himself a grantee in Armagh, proposed that estates to be granted in Longford should be very much smaller than they had been in Ulster, where

93 This also applied in Londonderry (Moody, *Londonderry*, 451–6).

94 'Ulster plantation papers', no. 74, *Anal. Hib.*, viii.

95 *CPRI, Jas I*, 163–7. An inquisition in 1601 relating to Mulmory oge O'Reilly's land, had stated that each poll contained sixty acres (NAI, Exchequer inquisitions, Ulster, Cavan (7), Eliz., 17–24).

96 Moody, *Londonderry*, 310.

> experience hath taught us that ... the undertakers' buildings have not been so readily performed as was expected, nor the British brought over in sufficient numbers to inhabit those great scopes ...[97]

The plantation in Ulster, it was seen, had begun with an in-built disadvantage.

2. The First Year

The prospects of the colony received mixed assessment. Davies on September 24, with moderate optimism, hoped for a peaceful resettlement of the native population stating

> that if they were once settled under the servitors, the bishops, and others who may receive Irish tenants, they would ... rest as well contented under their wings, as young pheasants do under the wings of a house-hen, though she be not their natural mother.[98]

As for the native freeholders he hoped also for transformed attitudes after they had moved to their new lands so that as transplanted trees they would 'like the ground better and yield pleasanter and sweeter fruit than they did before.'[99] The majority of the undertakers had come over and were preparing to begin their buildings in the spring. Servitor grantees had been chosen from many competitors and were men 'of merit and ability and for the most part such as have set up their rests in Ulster.'[100]

Chichester's appraisal was perhaps more accurate. The plantation, involving an extensive displanting of the natives, imposed in his opinion an undue strain on private initiative and especially that of the present grantees. He felt it demanded much more state sponsorship. 'To remove and displant the natives ... is not a work for private men, who expect a present profit, or to be performed without blows or opposition.'[101] Only in Cavan, he felt, had the natives, and also the servitors, received fitting proportion of the land:

> in the distribution of the precincts made ther [i.e. in England] I can not but thinke that the servitors and natives were greatly neglected in all counties but the Cavan, for wee conceived here that the one

[97] *Cal. Carew MSS, 1603–24*, 368.

[98] *CSPI, 1608–10*, 497–501.

[99] Ibid.

[100] Ibid.

[101] Ibid., 519–21. For the ideas of an undertaker thinking along similar lines see T. Blenerhasset, 'A Direction for the plantation in Ulster, 1610' in J.T. Gilbert, *A Contemporary History of Affairs in Ireland* (1879), I, i, App. x, 317–26. It is noteworthy that a scheme for the removal of the natives from undertakers' lands by state initiative was put forward in 1628.

> half at least of each countie woulde have been left and assigned for them but nowe they have but one baronie in a county … which hath grieved the servitor and so discontented the natives that they, the natives I meane, wyll do what spite and malice can invent to hinder the proceeding and good successe in a work so commendable in itselfe and profeatable to all posterities …

The contrast of Cavan with Armagh in this respect was not, as we have seen,[102] as sharp as Chichester suggested.

Chichester was thus dissatisfied both with the plantation scheme and its beneficiaries. Northampton's consort in Loughtee appeared an able one, but in another barony, presumably Oneilland, two of the planters were churchmen and one a youth in his late teens.[103] In general he felt that the English undertakers were plain country gentlemen with little promise of ability to perform the conditions. Some had already exchanged or sold their proportions. His first impressions of the Scots were in part more favourable. They came in a more business-like manner and with larger followings. However, they may have had less money to expend than the English and many had begun to bargain with the natives promising, in return for supplies, to obtain permission for them to remain on their lands as tenants.[104]

Under the plantation scheme the native inhabitants were to remove from the undertakers' lands in 1610. This they did not do. At the same time their military position had been revolutionised, and the failure of the Cavan men to arrest the plantation by judicial means was noted throughout Ulster. To the planters, however, the situation was perilous and Thomas Blenerhasset, a Fermanagh grantee, wrote in the autumn of 1610:

> … although there be no apparent enemy, nor any visible main force, yet the wood-kerne and many other (who have not put on the smiling countenance of contentment) doe threaten every house, if opportunitie of time and place doth serve … and besides them there be two, the chief supporters of all their insolencie, the inaccessible woods and the not passible bogs: which to subject to our desires is not easie …[105]

The native freeholders, particularly in Armagh, Tyrone, and Londonderry were dissatisfied with the sizes of their grants and Chichester sympathised with their complaints.[106] Natives' hopes and planters' fears that the

[102] Above, 59.
[103] Ibid.
[104] *CSPI, 1608–10*, 525–7.
[105] Blenerhasset, 'Direction', 319.
[106] Below, 203.

plantation would be swept away, that it had been a self-destructive policy, were great in the autumn of 1610. Foreign intervention was expected, and attempts were being made to amass arms.[107]

Barnaby Rich, who had local knowledge of Ulster, was the only person to make a reassuring comparison of the power of the Irish at this juncture: with their strength under Elizabeth Ireland was as quiet as Cheapside and where 'a thousand menne in times past would have been intercepted, I dare now undertake to passe myselfe and my boy.' The Irish were cruel and 'bloudie minded', they were trained in treason and superstition 'and nuzeled from their cradles in the very puddle of Popery', their wood-kerne were 'the very Hags of Hell fit for nothing but the gallows,' but their capacity to maintain a full-scale war was negligible. They were without military supplies and the money to buy them 'their greatest wealth, wherewith to maintaine a warre, consisteth in otmeale and butter.' However, he opposed the granting of pardons and saw that in the event of insurrection quick and consistent action would be essential.[108]

If the lack of foreign aid prevented general revolt the hope of it combined with the natives' grievances encouraged local resistance. The attempt to control Ulster by a non-military and so inexpensive tactic would, initially at any rate, need military backing. Before the commissioners left Ulster they doubled the garrisons at Charlemont (in Armagh), Mountjoy, and Coleraine.[109] In Armagh there were 100 foot at Charlemont, a constable and ten warders at Mountnorris, and at the Moyry fort a constable, a porter, and twelve warders.[110] Cavan was considered less in need of garrisons.[111] The number of foot in all Ulster, 1,100, was at this stage over half of the total for the whole country.[112]

To the incoming settler the triple scourge of 'the cruel wood-kerne, the devouring woolfe, and other suspitious Irish'[113] appeared as terrifying dangers. Even lands in the immediate vicinity of Charlemont were subject to spoliation. Blenerhasset described the situation as it affected Caulfeild:

> Sir Tobye Caulfeild he dwelleth in Charlemount a forte of many other the best, and well furnished with men and munition; yet now (even in this faire clame of quiet) his people are driven every night

[107] *CSPI, 1608–10*, 501–4, 518–21, 525–27.
[108] Barnaby Rich, *A new description of Ireland* (London, 1610), 15, 37, 94–5.
[109] *CSPI, 1608–10*, 505.
[110] Ibid., *1611–14*, 7–9, 10.
[111] Ibid., 5–7.
[112] Ibid., 7–9. A second attempt was made in September 1610 to round up Ulster swordsmen when Capt. Richard Bingley impressed about 600 men. This press-ganging itself, of course, caused discontent (*CSPI, 1608–10*, 458–60, 496–97).
[113] Blenerhasset, 'Direction', 318.

> to lay up all his cattle as it were in warde, and doe hee and his what they can, the woolfe and the wood-kerne (within caliver shot of his forte) have oftentimes a share; yet I do verily believe no man keepeth better order, as well for the safeguard of himselfe and his neighbors as for the government of all those parts about him.[114]

Howeve, although there were depredations in the early years, the situation never became unmanageable. The local commanders appear to have used stern measures where necessary. Hence on 1 February 1611 Chichester gave instructions for the pardoning of Sir Toby Caulfeild and others who within their localities had commanded the execution of 'seu'll p'sons' by martial law, and now sued for pardon fearing the legality of their action might be questioned.[115]

Palliative measures were also resorted to to pacify unrest. In November 1611 Sir Oghy O'Hanlon received, on the authorisation of the king, a regrant of an annual pension of £8.[116] Pardons without fine were issued. Thus between 20 November 1610 and 25 May 1612 various members of the O'Hanlon family, some of them grantees, received pardons.[117] On 6 June 1611 the deputy issued a warrant for the pardon of forty-six Irish (including five from Armagh), being pardoned to ease their lot as Irishmen who were not grantees and who were to be removed from their traditional abodes as a result of the plantation.[118]

The natives' discontent with their share in the scheme was a principal cause of discontent;[119] however, their immediate removal from undertakers' lands would cause great inconvenience to settlers – through disruption of food supplies and loss of rents – who made virtually no colonising efforts in 1610. Accordingly the government extended the time in which natives might remain on undertakers' lands to May 1611.[120] This proclamation also took a more uncompromising account of the native freeholders' discontent with the sizes of their grants. Those who would rather leave than 'tye themselves to the plantac'on thereof' might hand in their tickets of assignment to the sheriffs and receive passports to their stated destinations. A major modification, the result of economic necessity rather than policy change, was thus introduced, albeit temporarily, in the plantation scheme.

114 Ibid., 319.

115 Bod. Lib., Carte MSS, vol. 61, fol. 523.

116 Bod. Lib., Carte MSS, vol. 62, fol. 10 (*CSPI, 1611–14*, 70); *CPRI, Jas I*, 212.

117 *CPRI, Jas I*, 183, 227–8.

118 Bod. Lib., Carte MSS, vol. 62, ff 124–25.

119 T.W. Moody, 'The treatment of the native population under the scheme for the plantation in Ulster', *IHS,* vol. 1 no. 1 (March 1938), 59–63.

120 'Ulster plantation papers', no. 5, *Anal. Hib.*, viii; *Cal. Carew MSS, 1603–24*, 63.

It may also have served to reduce tension. Also the Irish who had been allotted land were by about November beginning to reconcile themselves, for a number of reasons, to the *fait accompli* of the plantation and were considering the acceptance of their grants.

In such an uncertain environment little was achieved by the planters before spring 1611. In most cases possession was taken and then after preliminary reconnaissance the undertaker returned to Britain. Stephen Butler had a deputy and 'some twelve or sixteen men' resident on his proportion throughout the winter.[121] More typical, however, is the fact that almost all the undertakers in our counties who received possession in 1610 also received licences to appoint deputies.[122] One Cavan planter, Richard Waldron, applied for permission to be an absentee for five years.[123] Some estates changed hands rapidly. Hence while some British settlers arrived in 1610, on a large number of estates the land had been simply let to the Irish and little further done. A new landlord class had been introduced at any rate by the end of 1610.[124]

In the spring of 1611 there were hopes that this would quickly become an effective colonising influence. On January 21 Davies wrote that new colonists were arriving on every passage 'so that by the end of the summer the wilderness of Ulster will have a more civil form'.[125] Chichester was also hopeful for development, the country he felt was quieter, though he and others noted the activities of counter-reformation priests.[126]

Reports of work done in the spring and summer of 1611 are fragmentary and sometimes inconsistent. In April a proclamation was required ordering the undertakers to repair to Ireland before the beginning of May.[127] A temporary letting of some of their lands in Armagh had been made by Trinity College to Caulfeild in 1610.[128] At the end of May, on the account of Davies, the servitors and such undertakers as had arrived were diligently planting, but many were still absent and so likely to lose 'the fairest time and weather, and fittest for this work, that hath been seen these many years past in Ireland.'[129] Those who had come over, according to instructions on matters to be discussed in England given by Chichester to Sir John Bourchier at this time, had as yet achieved little except to provide

121 Lam. Pal. Lib., Carew MSS, vol. 630, fol. 61v.
122 'Ulster plantation papers', no. 11, *Anal. Hib.*, viii.
123 *CSPI, 1608–10*, 477; 'Ulster plantation papers', no. 37, *Anal. Hib.*, viii.
124 This was, of course, consistent with the modified regulations regarding the natives.
125 *CSPI, 1611–14*, 5.
126 Ibid., 5–7, 11–12, 80–2.
127 *CSPI, 1611–14*, 28; *CSP Dom, 1611–18*, 23.
128 Below, 329.
129 *CSPI, 1611–14*, 59–60.

building materials in some places.[130] However, land and boundary disputes, indicative of colonial beginnings, start about this time.[131] Also personal predicaments begin to impinge on the uniformity of the plantation. For example, one Cavan undertaker, Wirrall, detained in England by a lawsuit, was allowed to substitute another deputy for one who had died.[132]

There were also numerous problems concerned with details of the plantation which had to be dealt with at this time.[133] The most major one still arose from the provision of tenants. In May the moratorium on the removal of the natives was due to expire, and the undertakers, pleading ambiguity in the plantation conditions, sought to retain Irish tenants and servants in addition to the legal number of British colonists. This was forbidden. However, the natives were still indispensable to the undertakers and to Chichester's inquiry whether he should remove them by force the privy council replied ambiguously in May that he should proceed in the 'constant execution' of the articles of plantation, but might use his discretion in cases of 'sudden urgency'.[134] In July the council concurred with his suggestion and permitted the retention of the natives for another year.[135]

Thus if one problem was solved by procrastination, others, smaller, were settled immediately. The undertakers were demanding the rents due at Michaelmas 1610 as well as at Easter 1611. It was decided that they should not receive the former because they had not been in Ireland to receive them, and because they had already been collected for the crown.[136]

According to the plantation conditions, undertakers and tenants were to take the oath of supremacy. The schedules of grants in 1610 indicate that the undertakers when receiving their lands took the oath,[137] but no machinery was devised for proffering it to tenants as they arrived. In May 1611 Stephen Butler and James Craig petitioned the deputy to appoint commissioners in each county to take the oath of the tenants, lest their titles be endangered.[138] The deputy in his reply undertook to issue a commission for this purpose.[139] Two reports exist, one of Sir Hugh Wirrall and Stephen Butler, 30 March 1612, and the other of Stephen Butler and

130 Ibid., 63–67.
131 Below, 76–88.
132 *CSPI, 1611–14*, 34.
133 A list of these was submitted by Chichester through Sir Oliver Lambert, himself a Cavan servitor, to the English privy council for consideration in 1611 (*CSPI, 1611–14*, 35–44).
134 Ibid.
135 Ibid., 63–67; *Cal. Carew MSS, 1603–24*, 79–83, see also 87–88. Swordsmen and followers were to be removed and such native labourers as the undertakers were willing to see displaced for the settling of British families.
136 *Cal. Carew MSS, 1603–24*, 82; 'Ulster plantation papers', no. 36, *Anal. Hib.*, viii.
137 Ibid, no. 11.
138 Ibid., no. 36.
139 Ibid.

James Craig, 23 October 1612, as commissioners for Cavan.[140] They deal with only four estates. There is no evidence of this for Armagh or any other county. Thus, while the government appears to have been unable to have the oath administered widely to incoming tenants, at a later stage failure to take the oath was noted as a serious defect in the plantation.[141]

3. Carew's Survey

An investigation of Irish affairs including the plantation was made by Sir George Carew in 1611. He was sent over in June as the king's special commissioner with a seat on the Irish council and an allowance of £5 per day. He was especially to concentrate on the plantation in the prosecution of which the king had heard there was great slackness.[142] Carew's report is the first of a series of surveys conducted between 1611 and 1622. Although an estate by estate investigation, its value is vitiated by a failure to be consistent in the type of information provided for each proportion, and this, combined with inexactness in stating numbers, makes systematic analysis difficult. It was also conducted quickly. He passed through both counties between August 30, when he was at Dungannon, and September 3, when he was at Ardee.[143] For Armagh, at any rate, it was in part based on the certificates of the undertakers, attested by the sheriff and Sir Toby Caulfeild.[144]

The general picture of Ulster as it appeared to Carew and the deputy may be noted. To Carew, writing from Derry in August, the country seemed quiet, and 'theft, murder and rebellion were asleep.'[145] However, even a reduction of 100 foot and 29 horse in the army in Ulster quickly resulted in unrest and planter uneasiness.[146] In September and October Chichester heard of more instances of depredation, cattle driving and the like, than in almost the entire seven years of his government.[147] The planters petitioned Chichester not to reduce the army stating that they had been promised protection during the time given to build their castles and settle colonists.[148]

Timidity and slackness as well as absenteeism amongst the planters was noted. Chichester was persuaded that if

> three or four undertakers should be feloniously burned or spoiled by wood-kerne in any part of the province … it would so discourage

[140] Ibid., nos. 68, 69.
[141] Below, 135, 166–7.
[142] *Cal. Carew MSS, 1603–24*, 68–9, 70–3; *CSPI, 1611–14*, 73–4, 75.
[143] *Cal. Carew MSS, 1603–24*, 218–19.
[144] Lam. Pal. Lib., Carew MSS, vol. 630, ff 58v–59.
[145] *CSPI, 1611–14*, 94–5.
[146] Ibid., 151–52, 160.
[147] Ibid., 96–7, 148–51, 156–57; *Cal. Carew MSS, 1603–24*, 131–34.
[148] *CSPI, 1611–14*, 156–57.

> the rest, who are not yet come over, that this design would be interrupted for many years.[149]

The progress of the plantation offered him little satisfaction. Many undertakers were absentee, unwilling

> to adventure their persons or substance … and those that go about to plant themselves here and there do it with such weakness as if they were … either not able or not willing to go straight with what they ought and are bound to do.[150]

The weakness of the undertakers was most apparent in their tendency to appoint deputies, adopt native tenants, and even sell their lands to others.[151]

In May 1611 necessity had again demanded the procrastination of the native problem. On October 1 the commissioners instructed the sheriffs to remove the native freeholders only with their dependants, and two-thirds of the labourers or ploughmen on November 1. The others might continue on the undertakers' lands until 1 May 1612.[152]

The planters were also wracked by disputes over land. 'The multiplicity of differences between themselves and others for land' struck Carew forcibly.[153] Such litigiousness and contention must have had a deleterious influence on the plantation enterprise. Carew's report in the autumn of 1611 indicates the state of the plantation at the end of its first year. It (and succeeding surveys) have been examined by taking the barony as the most convenient unit.

In the English barony of **Oneilland** in Armagh Carew found fairly consistent evidence of visible achievement.[154] Although two of the ten proportions had changed hands since 1610, on only one of these had nothing been done and eight of the ten afforded clear if variable evidence of activity. By one change of ownership Richard Rolleston had acquired Powell's estate. The new proprietor Sir Anthony Cope, a member of a family from Northamptonshire and Oxfordshire,[155] had acquired Lord Saye and Seale's estate and took out a patent on 5 July 1611.[156] On five estates the owners

[149] *Cal. Carew MSS, 1603–24*, 131–34.
[150] Ibid.
[151] *CSPI, 1611–14*, 178.
[152] *Cal. Carew MSS, 1603–24*, 115–16 (directive to sheriff of Donegal).
[153] *CSPI, 1611–14*, 100–101.
[154] Lam. Pal. Lib., Carew MSS, vol. 630, ff 58–60. The calendared version is generally incomplete. Since the report is brief reference is given only to the section covering the barony under discussion; brief quotations are not given individual references.
[155] Burke, *Peerage* (103rd ed.), 579. He died in 1615. His brother, Sir Walter, master of the court of wards, had built Cope Castle (later Holland House) in London (ibid.).
[156] *CPRI, Jas I*, 167.

were resident. Three settlers, Stanhowe, Matchett, and Heron were represented by members of their families. Rolleston who had acquired Powell's estate was resident in person on his own and while active there were no settlers on his second acquisition. Though Cope was not resident he had a 'very sufficient overseer' and his estate afforded clear evidence of activity.

On five estates the building of bawns and houses was under way. Timber, bricks, stone, and lime were being prepared. Sacheverall had built three houses for tenants, and on Rolleston's estate a tenant had built his own house '40 foote longe and 12 foote broade of stone and clayemorter, the eaves of the house being 12 foote high.' On the Cope estate a 'fayre castle of freestone' had been begun.

The number of males involved in the plantation of this barony was 136 or 137.[157] These can be sub-divided as follows: 81 or 82 workmen and tradesmen, 44 tenants, and 11 either owners or their agents. The proportion of workmen to tenants indicates the priorities being pursued. The distinction is not a hard and fast one, but it indicates the intention of the undertakers to impress their position visibly upon the area. Thus if in their building operations their achievement was promising, in the bringing over and estating of tenants they had broken the plantation conditions. The number of Englishmen required by 1 November 1611 was 396. Carew's total (some of whom might have been Irish labourers), only just exceeded one-third of this stipulation. They were also unequally distributed, Heron, Matchett, and Stanhowe as well as the estate previously Powell's being noticeably defaulting. While some stock had been imported they were not numerous.[158] There were also some arms.

The situation in the colonised area of the **Fews** barony,[159] south of Oneilland presented one contrast to its neighbour. Here the main preoccupation of its Scottish owners was with farming. This is clear from the fact that there were about 50 tenants or occupiers, ten artificers and workmen, and six owners or agents. The total present, about 65,[160] was about half of the 144 required for the estimated 6,000 acres involved. Two owners, Craig and Henry Acheson, and almost certainly a third, Claud Hamilton

[157] There were also four (unmarried) women.

[158] Below, 261–2.

[159] Lam. Pal. Lib., Carew MSS, vol. 630, ff 103–3v, 105.

[160] The main problem in establishing this figure has been to decide on the number of adult males per family. In some cases Carew refers to families rather than individuals. It has been assumed that a family young enough to emigrate in 1610 probably contained only one adult male in 1611. It has recently been shown that seventeenth-century people married later and that the average family size was 4¼ – 4½ people (P. Laslett and J. Harrison, 'Clayworth and Cogenhoe' in Bell & Ollard (eds.), *Historical essays*, also P. Laslett, 'What is so special about us now' in *The Listener*, vol. LXIX, no. 1767, 7 February 1963, 235–37).

were resident. The other two estates were supervised by agents. On one of these, Douglas's, the largest proportion, no colonising effort was attempted until after Carew's return to Dublin. On the other four estates there was considerable uniformity of achievement, most markedly agricultural. On three of these there were 170 cows and 47 horses and mares. On the fourth, Craig's, grain crops, oaths and barley, had already been harvested. Buildings suitable for such pursuits were also in evidence on some estates. Craig was building a mill, and had provided accommodation for four tenants. Claud Hamilton was building a stone barn.

In this barony, though building was less under way, the planters were nearer to fulfilling the conditions. About half the required number of people were present higher than Oneilland, though not necessarily with leasehold tenures, whereas building operations would not be finalised until 1613. However, while their pursuits showed a concern for profitable activity, in failing to fortify their estates they were not taking sufficient account of the unsettled state of the country.

In Oneilland and the Fews can be seen the contrasting priorities of the two national groups in the county at this time. Amongst the servitors in **Orior**[161] there is little evidence of more than cautious efforts. Activity was still limited to elementary preliminaries, and no building appears to have been completed by autumn 1611. Audley had done no more than 'sett out' his land. St. John was actively preparing timber and stones for building, but on no estate had building operations proceeded at a faster rate. Williams had 'sett' most of his land to Capt. Anthony Smith of Moyry fort, and Bourchier had taken responsibility for Cooke's estate. It is unlikely that there was much personal residence, especially of people such as St. John and Moore. There were not British colonists, indeed the façade of landlordry appears only flimsily established. Evidence of the fortunes of native Irish grantees from this and subsequent surveys, will be examined in a separate chapter.[162]

Comparable achievements to those of the English undertakers in Armagh can be seen in **Loughtee** in Cavan,[163] although here there had been much initial interchange and re-organisation of grantees.[164] Carew found two proprietors, Butler and Fishe, resident. Another, Wirrall, whose family was on the estate, was temporarily absent. The Lushers made a belated arrival at the end of September when the survey had been completed. Two

[161] Lam. Pal. Lib., Carew MSS, vol. 630, ff 67v–68.
[162] Below, 203–17.
[163] Lam. Pal. Lib., Carew MSS, vol. 630, ff 61–3.
[164] Above, 53–4.

estates, Taylor's and Waldron's were in charge of agents. On both Lusher estates nothing had been done.

Activity similar to, though more diverse, than that in Oneilland prevailed in Loughtee. The main preoccupation was again constructional. About 130 adult males were present, some 40 per cent of the required 300. There were about 86 artificers and workers, 35 tenants, and 7 owners or managers. The preparing of bricks and stones and the processing of timber was in hand on the five occupied estates. Fishe had carpenters felling trees in Fermanagh and had made 140,000 bricks. Butler and Wirrall had each built houses at Belturbet. They had also jointly built five boats. In all 17 houses had been built, most for tenants, and preparations were being made for two manor houses. On Waldron's estate an Irish house had been restored and equipped. There were two mills and a forge. Carew found arms for about 80 men. On all five estates freeholders are referred to, some having returned to England for their families. The processing of timber, the providing of stones and burning of lime, all indicated a degree of dynamism in Loughtee not found, except in isolated instances, elsewhere in the entire county.

The state of the Scots-appointed **Tullyhunco**[165] was far from dynamic. Two estates, those of the brothers Auchmooty, had been sold in August 1610 to Sir James Craig[166] who was also a grantee and resident in Armagh. Sir Claud Hamilton, also a grantee in the Fews was managing his father's estate, and on October 30 sold his own proportion in this barony to John Hamilton brother of Sir James of Clandeboy.[167] Browne was an absentee.

The total male population did not reach 40 (about 20 of them artificers and workmen), about one-quarter of the required 144. Some building preparations – palely in accord with Scots practice in Armagh – are recorded for two estates, Sir Alexander Hamilton's and those of James Craig. Hamilton was building a mill and Craig preparing to do so. He had also built a 'watled' house and a blacksmith's forge. Of stock no more than four horses and mare, on Craig's estate, are recorded.

Claud Hamilton had brought over a minister 'not yet allowed by the bishop'. However, the plantation had involved little more than a change in ownership of the land. Some building efforts afforded scattered evidence of this change, but the local pattern of living had been otherwise, it would seem, little altered. Those who had been active had established their position on small areas, but the rest of the land was let to the Irish. Browne had sent over an agent who let the land to the Irish and returned to

[165] Lam. Pal. Lib., Carew MSS, vol. 639, ff 104–4v, 105.

[166] *Inq. cancel. Hib. repert.*, ii, Cavan (27) Chas I.

[167] Ibid., (24) Chas I. Carew stated that he met Hamilton in Dublin after the survey and that he had brought people with him to plant the land.

Scotland. On 1 May 1611 Craig appointed out his entire estate of thirty-five Irish tenants.[168] These included one native freeholder in Tullyhaw.[169]

The entire barony of Clankee was unclaimed and unoccupied at this time.[170] Not only had the grantees not attended the commissioners in 1610 but they appear to have taken no action in the intervening year. On 30 July 1611 Lord Aubigny granted his lands to Sir James Hamilton,[171] later Viscount Clandeboy, but he had done nothing on the estate. In Dublin Carew encountered an agent of the consort who stated that he had brought over inhabitants, cattle and provisions. At this time also Dunbarr, Bailie, and Ralston were rumoured to be in Ulster. Bodley's report, however, reveals that nothing had been done even by 1613.[172]

In Cavan the servitors as a group had done little more than take possession of their estates. Of the seventeen mentioned by Carew[173] only three had been in any way markedly active.

The achievement of Capt. Ridgeway was atypical as it was impressive. He had felled and 'squared' 120 oak trees in Fermanagh, and had drawn 280 'garran' loads, enough to make a mill and a house. He had made a watercourse for his mill costing £25. He had burned bricks and provided stones at the site for his house and bought 500 barrels of lime in Meath and had sand and clay ready. The construction of his castle necessitated the removal of five Irish houses, but he had built 2 others elsewhere. He had also brought over a group of English tradesmen, about six or seven with their families and tools, as the nucleus of his settlement – the origin of Virginia. He had contracted at Belturbet for the building of a boat of three tons for use on Lough Ramor.

The brothers Sir Thomas and John Ashe in Tullygarvey were building a bawn of sods and earth and intended to draw water from an adjoining lake as an added fortification. They had already constructed a watercourse two miles long to the site of a mill and were felling and preparing to build 'a good house' in the spring. In Tullyhaw the only activity of note was that of Capt. Hugh Culme and Walter Talbot who had built a strong timber house and two wattled houses. Apart from felling 40 trees this was the limit of their achievement. These servitors showed in varying degree an initial energy noticeably lacking in their fellows.

[168] *Inq. cancel. Hib. repert.*, ii, Cavan (27) Chas I.

[169] The man concerned, called here Eugen McThomas Reagh is doubtless the same as Owen McThomas Reaught, or Owny McThomas McKiernan.

[170] Lam. Pal. Lib., Carew MSS, vol. 639. fol. 104v.

[171] *Inq. cancel. Hib. repert.*, ii, Cavan (19) Chas I.

[172] Below, 92–3.

[173] Lam. Pal. Lib., Carew MSS, vol. 630, ff 68v–70.

Carew's inquiry in 1611 revealed in general that the plantation was only slowly becoming established. In Armagh the undertakers had on the whole been more active than in Cavan, and in Oneilland and the Fews Carew found some 200 men or 37 per cent of the required total of 540. In the three baronies allotted to undertakers in Cavan one was still derelict, and in only one, Loughtee, was there evidence of vigour. The achievement of the Scots in Tullyhunco and Clankee, except in two cases, was very dilatory, and gave little indication that the natives' occupation of the land was in jeopardy. On all three baronies there were some 165 men or 28 per cent of the required 588. The colony was still a tentative one and many owners were absentee; however, the tone of the report was not markedly censorious.

There are a number of cases of ownership change; however, greater variation is evident in the way in which the planters used their lands. Apart from the general variations already noticed, the Scots' pre-occupation with farming and the English with building, there was considerable variety in individual endeavour. While in some baronies a relatively uniform pattern can be seen, in others personal resourcefulness – or its absence – gave the plantation a character which inhibits generalization. It would seem clear that the capital and labour resources of the planters were inadequate to their task.

As yet little movement and resettlement had taken place among the native grantees. This in itself is some indication of the inadequacy of the undertakers. However, Carew's evidence forces the conclusion that the servitors were the most dilatory planter category. Apart from a few instances of rare enthusiasm, their impact, especially in Cavan, had been slight. They complained to Carew that they were suffering through the undertakers retaining the natives as tenants:

> The servitors being charged by us with backwardness and having done so little on their portions answered for the most p'rte that they had not taken out their patents until the end of Candelmas tearme last, and that by reason the British undertakers doe yet retaine the natives (who ought to be their tenants) they are disabled to put things forward as otherwise they would, but they will goe roundlie in hand with their workes this next springe as they have promised us ...[174]

This complaint was legally justified if in practice a flimsy one.

[174] Lam. Pal. Lib., Carew MSS, vol. 630, fol. 70v.

4. Friction in Armagh between servitors and undertakers

An uneasiness between the servitor and undertaker elements in the plantation was not, as we have seen,[175] an entirely unexpected problem, and it was decided to place the servitors in the same baronies as the native grantees and not interspersed with the undertakers, though the servitors' positioning vis-à-vis the natives was a logical one. However there were areas where there was some initial tension. The protracted ill-feeling between Sir Thomas Phillips, servitor, and the London companies is well known, and there was also tension between Sir Toby Caulfeild and the same undertaker authorities. The servitors, too, felt they had not received an adequate share in the plantation with which Chichester sympathised,[176] and the king later made provision for a few unrewarded in 1610.[177] It was in fact only in Cavan that Chichester felt that an equitable distribution had been reached.[178]

Defects in the plantation became quickly apparent, most notably the incapacity of the undertakers to do without native tenants. This gave the servitors ground for complaint.[179] The undertakers complained that concealed lands were being granted to servitors and natives.[180]

In the spring of 1612 tension came to a head in Armagh through the protest of the Scots undertakers in the Fews. Sir James Douglas on behalf of himself and his fellows complained to the king that they were being subjected to the depredations of the natives 'through the connivance or slackness of the English servitors who were willing enough to see them so discouraged and supplanted.'[181] The undertakers intimated that many of their tenants were in consequence preparing to leave the country.

The king was impressed by these grievances, and on June 4 Henry Acheson, a neighbour to Douglas, presented Chichester with a letter from James of March 11.[182] In it the king asserted that the servitors were abusing their right to have native tenants, by not protecting the undertakers from their depredations. Chichester was instructed to

[175] Above, 10.

[176] *CSPI, 1608–10*, 521–22.

[177] Below, 99. The problem would have been greater had not some servitors previously received grants of land in Down.

[178] Above, 61–2.

[179] Above, 73.

[180] *CSPI, 1611–14*, 157–58. The only person in our counties to be thus rewarded was Francis Annesley, subsequently chief secretary and Baron Mountnorris. In October 1611 he had acquired a lease of the fort of Mountnorris (*CPRI, Jas I*, 203), and in January 1612 he received a grant of two contiguous townlands (ibid., 207).

[181] R. Dudley Edwards (ed.), 'Chichester letter-book, 1612–14', no. 14, *Anal. Hib.*, viii, Chichester to Humphrey May, 8 July 1612.

[182] *CSPI, 1611–14*, 253–56.

> lay his [the king's] express command upon all the servitors there to aid the undertakers to the uttermost of their power in defence of their lands and goods.

He was to publish a proclamation to this effect.[183]

Chichester did not find the allegation as convincing. He felt that it was a 'confused complaint', that the king had been 'unworthily troubled', and that it should have been submitted to him.[184] He accepted that the natives were refractory, but felt that the difficulties of the undertakers stemmed in large measure from their own failure either to take precautions or to muster themselves and pursue their goods. Also Armagh presented peculiar difficulties in that it was much wooded and also still contained many followers of Oghy oge O'Hanlon whom Chichester hoped to pacify by granting pardons. But basically he claimed that the real fault lay with the undertakers themselves who neglected to build 'strong houses' and bawns on their estates. Indeed, he asserted, they took advantage of the situation

> ... if one of them lost a cow, garran, or other goods ... that could not justly be esteemed at forty shillings, they would not be contented under five or six pounds, and that not from the felons themselves (whom they would neither attack not justly accuse in any place) but from the natives of some of the next baronys ... indifferently whether freeholders or tenants to the servitors, exempting their own Irish tenants which may be culpable rather than any other, as their ill affections towards them is the same with those that dwell further off.[185]

The issue was tied up in his eyes with the undertakers' retention of Irish tenants. Nonetheless to gratify the king and the undertakers he had caused £200 to be levied upon the natives of Armagh and £200 also on the natives of Tyrone to replay 'those pretended losses'.[186] The natives had considered this unfair and entered complaints.

Chichester thus did not accept the undertakers' contention. He found none who would directly charge any of the servitors with neglect. The servitors as a group, he claimed, had no obligation specified in their conditions of plantation, to protect the undertakers and yet

[183] R. R. Steele (ed.), *Tudor and Stuart proclamations, 1485–1714* (2 vols, Oxford, 1910), ii, 20 (no. 205). Steele merely prints what is in effect the relevant extract from this letter as a proclamation, stating it to be 'not found'.

[184] 'Chichester Letter-Book', no. 14, *Anal. Hib.*, viii.

[185] Ibid.

[186] Ibid. Elsewhere he speaks of £140, possibly another sum? (*CSPI, 1611–14*, 294–96).

> many servitors without any other obligation than the publique regard [had] not fayled to lend them their money, their houses, their beds, with all their pains and good endeavours at their occasion.[187]

The undertakers' complaint therefore implied the negligence of Sir Toby Caulfeild and the 'servitors of command' in the county. Chichester would not entertain the notion of their guilt. He affirmed that they 'would esteem themselves unworthy to live any longer than they would give unto the undertakers all possible assistance in their plantation there.'[188] To the king's command that a proclamation be issued strictly obliging the servitors to protect the undertakers, Chichester replied ingeniously that he would couple with it a proclamation for the removal of the natives from the undertakers' lands.

The outcome is not known or indeed the rights and wrongs of the incident. Chichester would appear at any rate not to have been entirely impartial. There is no further evidence of servitor-undertaker uneasiness. The baronial segregation began to break down with time and distinctions must have become reduced, though in Wentworth's time a differentiation between English and Scots had significance. There are cases of people of servitor origin acquiring undertakers' land, and the undertaker group failed ever to be able to dispense with native tenants, and some servitors did have a number of British tenants. Further in 1641 it became clear that all groups had failed to take adequate precautions for defence.

5. Disputes and Concealments

Land disputes began to spring up immediately after the settlers occupied their estates. For two years or more these deflected much energy into highly unproductive channels. Disputes were of various types. First, altercation over titles, two settlers often laying claim to the same places. Secondly, there were difficulties over 'concealed' lands. It was often found that small areas had been unallotted, and the disposal and discovery of these raised difficulties. There were also occasional assertions by planters that they had received defective measure and there were also the claims of people asserting rights by patents dating from before the plantation. These latter, not unexpectedly, were more prevalent in Cavan than in any other county.[189] By 1612 disputes had reach such a spate that the government was obliged to take special measures to deal with them.

187 'Chichester Letter-Book', no. 14, *Anal. Hib.*, viii.

188 Ibid.

189 *CSPI, 1611–141, 63–7.*

Inaccurate and incomplete knowledge of the countryside at the time of plantation was the chief cause of these problems. Bodley's Ulster survey, though hailed at the time as a special achievement,[190] did not withstand trial when proved in detail. Since the maps were drawn more from verbal evidence than by the techniques of surveying the relative locations of places sometimes proved incorrect, and the maps sometimes gave the estates of planters a more compact appearance than was justified. Since the undertakers' patents appear to have been drawn up from lists of place names derived from the inquisitions of 1608 and 1609 as well as from the maps, estates did not always follow the proportion divisions there represented. Also it is evident that a complete coverage of places had not been achieved. The discovery of 'concealed' – or unplotted – lands was common. How these unallocated lands should be disposed of caused much inquiry.[191] The factor of geographical imprecision was then a fundamental one, and these problems all became pressing as the settlers began to investigate the extents of their estates. Numerous cases survive of appeals to high authority.

Previous experience had suggested that concealed lands could present difficulties. On 1 August 1610 the English privy council directed that concealed lands found within proportions should be granted to the appropriate proprietor. Concealments not within any proportion were to be placed with the 'reserved' land – presumably that for towns, glebe, and the like – of the precinct.[192] Just previously three of the plantation commissioners had made the same recommendation for lands within proportions. Lands outside of proportions, they advised, should be granted to adjoining proprietors with appropriate rent adjustments. Chichester in September urged that if any more land became available in Armagh, Tyrone or Londonderry it should be granted to the natives. A year later the undertakers complained that concealed lands were being granted to servitors and natives.[193]

As to disputes within the colony, the deputy and plantation commissioners were to adjudicate. Suits concerning church lands were to be decided with the consent of the deputy, the archbishops of Dublin and Armagh, and the bishop of Clogher then elect of Meath, or the deputy and any two of these.[194] However, disputes arose both in number and complexity to an extent which can hardly have been anticipated. Litigation, then, was

190 Ibid., *1608–10*, 419.

191 For a brief discussion of some of these problems see Aalen & Hunter, 'Two early seventeenth century maps of Donegal'.

192 *CSPI, 1608–10*, 488–89.

193 Ibid., *1611–14*, 158–58.

194 'Ulster plantation papers', no. 26, *Anal. Hib.*, viii.

not only to absorb much of the settlers' energy, but to tax the administrative machine as well.

In the spring of 1611 a number of cases came before the deputy and commissioners and appeals were also made to London for the adjudication of disputes. None arose in Armagh, but three Cavan suits have each an interest. Capt. Hugh Culme claimed a townland in Fishe's proportion as being included in his lease of the fort and lands of Cloughowter.[195] The matter came before the English privy council and Fishe arrived in Dublin in May bearing a letter instructing Chichester to guarantee possession to him, to grant it to the servitor Culme being considered 'expressly contrary to the articles of plantation'.[196] Fishe's patent was issued in July 1610,[197] Culme's lease dated from November,[198] the difficulty having arisen through a failure to correlate the two documents. A somewhat similar case was that between Sir Thomas Ashe and John Ridgeway where two townlands committed to Ridgeway for the town of Virginia were also in Ashe's patent. Here the deputy and commissioners adjudicated, deciding that Ridgeway should pay the rent of these place, £6 per annum, to Ashe until such time as Ashe could receive compensation either out of concealed land or to be purchased for him by the crown.[199]

The largest of these early problems was one which was to recur. The 1609 barony maps of Cavan did not record the recent grant[200] of areas of attainted property throughout the county made to Richard Nugent, Baron Delvin, and the plantation commissioners in allotting lands to the new grantees took inadequate care of his prior claim. Accordingly a number of disputes arose between him and some of these and also because some of his land was reserved as glebe. In May the deputy and commissioners made an order which only went some way towards solving the problem. Delvin was to have all the land contained in his patent except for seven and one-half townlands granted to Waldron, Sir Claud Hamilton and Snow (i.e. William Lusher). The ownership of these was to be sequestered pending further order. A similar order was made for three townlands projected for glebe.[201]

In lists of plantation problems sent to England in the care of Sir Oliver Lambert and Sir John Bourchier and returned in May and July (in the latter case in the care of Carew)[202] problems arising from the claims of pre-

[195] *CPRI, Jas I*, 182.
[196] *CSPI, 1611–14*, 33.
[197] *Inq. cancel. Hib. repert.*, ii, Cavan (26) Chas I.
[198] *CPRI, Jas I*, 182.
[199] 'Ulster plantation papers', no. 33, *Anal. Hib.*, viii.
[200] Above, 37.
[201] 'Ulster plantation papers', no. 35, *Anal. Hib.*, viii.
[202] *CSPI, 1611–14*, 35–44, 63–7.

plantation patentees, especially in Cavan, to lands allocated to planters were submitted for decision. The privy council advised that if a patentee's lands were situated in such a way within a proportion as to be prejudicial to the planter then an attempt should be made to procure for the patentee the equivalent amount, if available, on the fringes of the proportion. However, if the lands were not prejudicially situated and no exchangeable unallocated land could be found the patentee was to keep the land and the planter to receive an abatement of rent.[203]

At first, at any rate, suits had not been of unmanageable quantity, but as the grantees settled down to identifying their property disputes arose in far greater number. The perambulation of Ulster by Carew, accompanied by Chichester, brought a plethora of disputes into prominence. Carew commented specifically on 'the multiplicity of differences' for land which had come to his notice. These were still in 'rough papers'.[204] In Dublin in September Carew was a member, with the deputy, of a group of the plantation commissioners who attempted to reconcile these disputes. Apart from complaints about undermeasurement,[205] seven disputes or groups of disputes between owners in Armagh and eight between Cavan grantees were adjudged at this time.[206] These disputes had a variety of causes, most of them in the last resort indicating imprecise geographical knowledge, and reflecting on the inaccuracy in detail of the investigation, mapped and otherwise, of the escheated land prior to the plantation.

One case can be taken to reveal a particular type of failing. The ballyboe of Drumnaleg (or Downlege) which was not marked on the 1609 map of the barony of Orior was allotted in 1610 to Irish grantees, Ardell McFelim O'Hanlon who received two-thirds of it as the total extent of his grant, Cahir O'Mellan and others. It would seem that a concealment had been found on the journey of allocation and was being handed over to Irish proprietors. However, Drumnaleg was an alternative name for Magherycreevagh which had appeared on the map – where it was indicated as part of a proportion (this proportion was subsequently granted as two: to Bourchier and St. John) – but which had been chosen as glebe for Tawnaghtally parish. Bourchier claimed it under the name of Skeoghmurry Crivagh.[207] The commissioners in 1611 stated that O'Hanlon had received it in the previous year as a concealment. However, it was not found to be one and the same as

[203] Ibid., 63–7.
[204] Ibid., 100–101. 'Ulster plantation papers', no. 45, *Anal. Hib.*, viii, would appear to contain some or all of the material to which Carew referred.
[205] Below.
[206] *Cal. Carew MSS, 1603–24*, 244–51; 'Ulster plantation papers', nos. 50, 53, *Anal. Hib.*, viii.
[207] 'Ulster plantation papers', no. 45, *Anal. Hib.*, viii.

Magherycreevagh, already reserved as glebe, and so it was decided that it should not be confirmed to either contestant.[208] This decision necessitated that a person (O'Hanlon), considered a suitable beneficiary under the plantation in 1610 should be deprived of his grant in the following year.

The subsequent struggle for ownership was a prolonged one between the parish minister and other contestants, and may be outlined here. In 1616 it was described as 'supposed' glebe land.[209] In 1622, O'Hanlon having lost his claim completely, the parish minister stated, with disgruntlement, that by a recent order in council he was to occupy the land on condition of paying £20 compensation to three claimants, Sir Henry Bourchier, Lord Moore, and Cahir O'Mellan.[210] The matter was still unsettled by October 1623 when a local jury returned that the land had alternate names, had been intended for the church, and had been acquired by O'Hanlon 'by some sinister ill-dealing'.[211] 'Magherycreevagh' was later, in 1628, granted as glebe.[212] It is not clear how the dispute had been resolved by 1641. It is notable, however, that although the land as granted should have been held by either of claimants, Irish or ecclesiastical, subject to confiscation under the Commonwealth, it does not appear at all – a generally reliable indication of confiscability – on the map of the Down Survey. The case indicates the kind of difficulty that could arise from a failure to record sub-denominational and alternate names of places before the land was allocated. It was only with inquisitions at a local level preparatory to regrants throughout the plantation period that this deficiency was redressed.

Another Armagh case in 1611 arose directly from cartographic deficiency. The barony rather than the county had been taken as the unit for map-making purposes in 1609 and in Armagh at any rate no successful attempt was made to ensure that uniformity of barony boundaries was achieved. As a result a townland was indicated in both Oneilland and the Fews and was granted in two patents, those of Henry Acheson and Richard Rolleston. Carew's perambulation established that there was only one such townland, but there was no decision in 1611 other than that one of the claimants must lose it with appropriate abatement of rent.[213] A similar case arose in Cavan between a servitor in Castlerahan and an undertaker in Loughtee.[214]

208 *Cal. Carew MSS, 1603–24*, 246.
209 *Inq. cancel. Hib. repert.*, ii, Armagh (5) Jas I.
210 TNA, Manchester papers, 30/15/2/182.
211 *Inq. cancel. Hib. repert.*, ii, Armagh (8) Jas I.
212 *CPRI, Chas I*, 323.
213 *Cal. Carew MSS, 1603–24*, 247.
214 Ibid., 248.

Disputes about ownership between layman grantees and ecclesiastical owners were also common. The most substantial of these was a historic claim asserted by the dean of Armagh, Robert Maxwell, and accepted by the king in England to five and one half townlands in the Fews which had been granted to Claud Hamilton. Hamilton argued that to concur in the decision would be the 'overthrow of his plantation' because he had built a bawn and sixteen houses on the land to be surrendered. The plantation commissioners could not rescind the general effect of the order,[215] but they decided to appoint Sir Toby Caulfeild and the archbishop of Armagh as commissioners to procure a settlement whereby Hamilton would surrender another townland of equal value to that on which he had built his settlement.[216] The dean's patent was taken out in February 1613.[217]

There were also a number of disputes between settlers in both counties and the bishop.[218] Sir Toby Caulfeild, the grantee of the abbey of St. Peter and St. Paul asserted claims to small pieces of land in Armagh as monastic property. It would be harsh to see all these claims as arising from faulty geography. The disentanglement of the abbey lands presented many difficulties arising from the disorganisation of the late sixteenth century. The decision with regard to one of Caulfeild's claims, at any rate, upheld the decisions reached at the time of the survey.

> The general survey found many parcels for that abbey never before found and yet this could not then be found and therefore I think the tenant of the abbey must be concluded by the survey.[219]

Although Cavan was where the claims of pre-plantation patentees caused most difficulty,[220] two of these also came to light in Armagh at this stage. Capt. Edward Trevor and Sir Arthur Magennis both claimed lands in Brownlow's estate as being their property, and in County Down. Trevor had a patent dating from February 1611,[221] but Magennis had not received a patent. The lands granted to Trevor were at the time of survey found by the local juries to be part of Armagh and to have been O'Neill property and so were considered forfeited and 'accordingly cast into proportions' and granted to Brownlow in the summer of 1610. However, in February 1611 'being not thought to be the same' they were granted to Trevor. Subsequently it

[215] Ibid., 247.
[216] 'Ulster plantation papers', no. 50, *Anal. Hib.*, viii.
[217] *CPRI, Jas I*, 245–46.
[218] Ibid., 244–51; 'Ulster plantation papers', no. 53, *Anal. Hib.*, viii.
[219] *Cal. Carew MSS, 1603–24*, 249.
[220] *CSPI, 1611–14*, 63–7.
[221] Above, 20.

was decided that Brownlow should be maintained in possession and Trevor compensated in some other way.[222] Magennis's claim, it was decided, was less substantial, he having procured no patent of the lands in question.[223] Both disputes recurred later. Both arose from a failure to decide on prior claims and establish beyond question the amount of land available for plantation.

Claims that land had been over-measured were abruptly dealt with. A number of cases arose in Armagh in which it was argued that places granted had been rated as whole ballyboes for purposes of quit rent that were in fact smaller. The case of James Craig in the Fews was dismissed unceremoniously and with the threat of a re-measurement:

> This may be a sufficient tale to pass the time withal in the country but my answer must be that they are found by the country upon oath [to be whole ballyboes] and being passed to the undertaker, sine plus sine minus, he must be satisfied, otherwise at his charge I will undertake to find him so many acres by due measure, as are contained in his patent.[224]

Such claims had the effect of casting doubt in official quarters on the views held in 1608 and 1609 about the acreages of Ulster townlands on which the grants of proportions in 1610 purporting to represent measurements by acres, had been based.[225] When now reconsideration of the whole quantitative basis of the plantation scheme forced itself, it was too late to correct the error. That the land had been under-measured became apparent, but it was only during Wentworth's administration that serious consideration was given to the question of having the lands re-surveyed.[226] The social as well as the financial implications of this were recognised in 1618 when the Longford plantation was being planned,[227] but ten years later when it was agreed that undertakers might receive new patents it was conceded that no new measurement of their estates as a preliminary to a re-calculation of rents should take place.[228]

As to concealed lands, in proposals sent to England by Chichester and returned in May 1611,[229] there was the suggestion that these should be granted to servitors and natives. The reply indicated that concealed lands

222 *Cal. Carew MSS, 1603–24*, 251.
223 Ibid.
224 *Cal. Carew MSS, 1603–24,* 248. With regard to John Dillon's complaint on this score it was noted that the crown had no advantage if some townlands proved to be undermeasured, 'for they are apt to complain for a little but will be loth to suffer strict survey for the king' (ibid., 249).
225 Bodley himself had pointed this out in 1609.
226 Below, 180–85.
227 *Cal. Carew MSS, 1603–24*, 367–70.
228 Below, 157–66.
229 *CSPI, 1611–14*, 35–44.

within baronies allotted to undertakers should be granted to them and to servitors and natives if found within their baronies. The privy council recognised that the survey – the maps of 1609 – had been inaccurate but felt that to grant concealments in undertakers' precincts to servitors and natives would cause dispute between them and the undertakers. Also it would lead to a mingling of servitors and natives with undertakers which was contrary to the plan for the colony.[230]

However, concealed lands were only part of the general problem caused by disputes over ownership and by the summer of 1612 these had become so numerous as to tax the council or plantation commissioners in Dublin, and so complex that it was found necessary to appoint special commissioners to go to Ulster and carry out a local investigation of the problems. Recourse to the official records in Dublin was clearly considered to be inadequate, and already in March 1612 the king had instructed Chichester that the justices of assize when next on circuit in Armagh should adjudicate the dispute between Acheson and Rolleston.[231]

The outcome was that in June 1612 special commissioners were appointed to go to Ulster to resolve disputes and settle certain outstanding problems.[232] The three so appointed were Christopher Sibthorp, a justice of the king's bench, William Parsons, the surveyor-general, and William Roullfe.[233] They were to 'heere and determine all differences, suits, and demands' for land, seeing to it that the king's revenue should not if possible be diminished but increased and that the planters, through the settlement of their disputes, might be enabled to proceed with colonisation in accordance with their covenants. If any suit arose which could not be settled without prejudicing these conditions they should examine it, but forbear final decision until it had been considered by the deputy and plantation commissioners. They were to allocate land for glebe to the parish ministers and if the land so designated should prove remote from the parish churches they were to 'labour an exchange' by negotiation with other owners. As to concealments they were to announce the royal pleasure that when the proportions assigned to grantees were complete – i.e. when they had had full measure – they should also be given grants of the concealments within or near their estates. These should be certified to the surveyor-general by Easter 1613, so that their rents could be adjusted, otherwise the king would grant them to 'whomsoever can finde and first discover them'. Finally, they were to ascertain if the native inhabitants had removed from the undertakers'

230 Ibid.

231 Ibid., 256–58.

232 'Ulster plantation papers', no. 55, *Anal. Hib.*, viii.

233 Their report is in TCD, MS 806, ff 9–31.

baronies and order those remaining to remove by September 30 on pain of forfeiture of one-third of their goods.[234] At the same time a letter was written to the Ulster bishops explaining that they and other local figures had not been placed in the commission to avoid any possible taint of partiality.[235] In this letter the bishops were informed that the commissioners might settle disputes involving them if the bishops were satisfied with the decisions otherwise the commissioners had been instructed to refer it to the deputy (and commissioners) for decision. In a general letter to the grantees, British and Irish, Chichester requested them to provide for the board and lodgings of the commissioners when in Ulster.[236]

The commissioners' report indicates that in five counties (excluding Londonderry) they heard 180 'differences' of which 152 were 'fully determined'. For each county they listed those grantees whose numbers of townlands fell short of those required to complete their proportions, i.e. they accepted the conventions, varying with locality, about the acreages of townlands, and they also listed the concealments by name and barony discovered in each county. They also noted that all the glebes had been assigned.[237]

In Cavan they dealt with 77 cases and in Armagh 20. Thus more than one-third of the land disputes arose in the former county. Fermanagh with 41 was the next highest and Donegal and Tyrone presented approximately similar numbers to Armagh. Extensive concealments were found in Fermanagh and Tyrone. In Armagh, which had more concealments than Cavan, and in Cavan concealments were roughly similar to those found in Donegal.

Defects were found in roughly similar numbers throughout the five counties, though there were slightly more in Armagh than in Cavan. In Armagh 12 owners were found to have defective measure, amounting in all to 22 and one-third ballyboes. This included Trevor's claim to six ballyboes and the land taken from Claud Hamilton through the dean's claim. Four Irish grantees including Henry McShane O'Neill, three of whose townlands were 'detained' by Whitechurch and Bagnal, featured in the list as wanting six ballyboes. In all 19½ ballyboes of concealments – 'means to supply theis defects' – were found in the county most of which were in Oneilland. In Cavan defects amounting to 34 polls were found in 14 properties, three of which were native Irish, and 5½ polls of concealments were discovered.

234 'Ulster plantation papers', no. 55, *Anal. Hib.*, viii.
235 Ibid., no. 56.
236 Ibid., no. 57.
237 Below, 284–97.

The disputes are too numerous for individual treatment. Also, in some cases, the report records that decisions were taken but in whose favour it is not stated. In Armagh many of the cases not unexpectedly concerned lands in Orior where so many grants of small areas were made to native Irish. A number of cases arose between native grantees and Bagnal, who held monastic property, in south Orior. These were suspended because Bagnal was not represented, and their resolution referred to the plantation commissioners. It does not appear that any partiality was exercised in favour of servitor claimants. Thus, for example, a piece of land claimed as school land by Sir John Bourchier, its 'supposed lessee', was ordered as the property of Donell McCarbery McCann 'uppon due examination'. The dispute between Rolleston and Acheson was referred to be heard by the judges 'being a suite in law'.[238] A dispute between Acheson and the primate was 'examined and certified,' but because it concerned episcopal title it was not decided by the commissioners in accordance with their instructions. However, in another case between the archbishop and the agents of Trinity College, a decision was made in favour of the latter on the evidence of a jury. The same method was used to resolve a dispute between the primate and Sir Toby Caulfeild. The disputes between Brownlow, and Trevor and Maginnis which again came into prominence, were referred to the lord deputy.

In Cavan a very wide variety of cases involving all types of grantees, individual and institutional, were heard. Many of these concerned small parcels of land. The method, seen also in Armagh, of using local juries and thereby tapping local knowledge, features in the resolution of a number of cases. In one dispute, a difference between the corporation of Cavan and Sir Oliver Lambert, where defective measurement was in question, it is recorded that the land was measured and the dispute determined. A number of other cases arose between the townsmen of Cavan and other grantees. 'Divers differences' between the townsmen of Cavan 'amongst themselves' were 'decided and quietned', and a 'general order at large' was made in each case for the 'settlement' of the towns of Cavan and Belturbet. A case between the schoolmaster of Cavan and Stephen Butler was resolved. Disputes between parish clergy and Mulmony McHugh, Connelagh O'Reilly and Mulmony oge O'Reilly for glebe were, in two of three cases at any rate, ordered in favour of the clergy. Disputes between the parish clergy and British settlers also occurred, and there were a considerable number involving the bishop of Kilmore. Cases involving Irish grantees featured prominently as elsewhere. One was between two brothers, Phillip McPhillip and Shane McPhillip O'Reilly, concerning six polls of land

[238] 'Ulster plantation papers', no. 71, *Anal. Hib.*, viii.

'intended to be divided between them'. A complaint made by Donnogh Magauran (McGovern) that he had received defective measure was 'answered and determined'. A dispute between two servitors, Garth and Fettiplace, was in part determined and 'in parts respited till conference be had with the judges.' One of the largest sources of conflict continued to be claims of the baron of Delvin arising from his grant of attainted land. He was engaged in dispute with nine different grantees.

Many difficult cases were referred by the commissioners to the deputy and plantation commissioners in Dublin and these were tackled between October 1612, after the commissioners' return from Ulster, and February 1613.[239] On November 27 they made an order that the 'great office' – the inquisitions taken in 1608, with which those of 1609 may be included – should hold good and not be modified or 'impeached'.[240] Numbers of the cases examined above were settled at this time. Thus, for example, Trevor was obliged to surrender the lands he claimed on promise of receiving compensation out of the concealed lands found in Armagh.[241] Rolleston, rather than Acheson, was ordered the townland in dispute between them.[242]

Delvin solved his problems by recourse to the king. He returned bearing a king's letter of 11 July 1612 authorising Chichester to grant him so much of the lands of the dissolved abbey of Fore, which he held in lease, as should amount to the value of the 24 polls in Cavan which he had consented to surrender 'for the benefit of the plantation.'[243] He received a patent accordingly in January 1613.[244] Waldron, one of the planters benefiting most from Delvin's surrender, received a king's letter for the surrender and regrant of 'the lord of Delvin's and other lands' in August 1614.[245]

As to the concealments found by the special commissioners, the deputy and plantation commissioners ordered in November 1612 that no concealments found 'neere or adjoyninge' to any undertaker's proportion be granted to him before defects of quantity found in other proportions be first made up to their owners out of the concealments found, and that concealments found amongst undertakers should be granted to them, and those found amongst servitors and natives unto them.[246] In February 1613,

239 'Ulster plantation papers', nos. 59–67, 71–72, *Anal. Hib.*, viii.
240 Ibid., no. 64.
241 Ibid., no. 60.
242 Ibid., no. 72.
243 *CSPI, 1611–14*, 275; *CPRI, Jas I*, 249.
244 Ibid., 238. The acreage figures and maps presented to indicate ownership at the beginning of the plantation have been arrived at by taking as much account as possible of the legal decisions of these years.
245 Ibid., 300. He received a further king's letter for a regrant on 1 December 1616 (ibid., 326; BL, MS 4794, 359–60).
246 'Ulster plantation papers', no. 63, *Anal. Hib.*, viii.

in a letter to the privy council, Chichester reverted to the problems caused by concealments and defects.[247] He stated the problem that where there was most want of measure amongst the settlers[248] there were least concealments available to satisfy the deficiencies and the settlers were demanding abatements of rents. However there was enough concealed land in the plantation counties to satisfy all demands and Chichester put forward an administratively-difficult way in which this could be done:

> If any of them having a full proportion, shall have any concealment within the same, I mean to put that parcel or parcels into this account, and again to deduct as much more upon the outskirts or border of his lands as shall supply the defects of his next neighbours, if any be, and so to proceed in this manner of separation and addition untill every one be fully satisfied …

Remaining concealments were to be granted to those to whose lands they were closest. If Chichester expected authority to implement this scheme he was to be disappointed and it was some time before concealments were finally granted out.[249]

By 1613 the main burden of the problem concerning disputes, at any rate, had lifted. However, it may reflect on the efficiency with which the plantation was inaugurated, litigation over boundaries was obviously a problem to be associated with the early years of the plantation. The very universality of the problem, however, had necessitated special treatment. Disputes were to recur and we shall see that not all concealments had been found at this stage.[250] However, as the colony settled down recourse was had much more to the ordinary processes of law. Indeed by February 1614 Sir Robert Jacob, the solicitor general, writing from Cavan, could recommend that suits should be dealt with by the courts of law and not by the privy council.[251]

That the massive volume of disputes reflected badly on the implementation of the plantation and particularly on the surveyor-general was implicit in a letter of July 1613 written by Parsons to Sir Richard Boyle, then in England.

> If you hear anie things of the plantation of Ulster I pray you say it was dispatched with a great deale of paines and though [I] say yt, dexterity, consideringe the tyme allowed and vastness of the work.

[247] 'Chichester Letter-Book', no. 45, *Anal. Hib.*, viii.
[248] There has obviously been a change in official attitudes here since 1611.
[249] Below, 99–105.
[250] Below, 166, 172.
[251] *Hastings MSS*, iv, 14–16.

Errors which had 'escaped' had been 'but few and smale' and the disputes settled by himself and Sibthorp had been largely due to early-arriving settlers holding others' lands until compelled by these commissioners to relinquish them.[252] It was a letter which smacked of apologia.

6. Bodley's survey, 1613

From the petitions of individuals the king, in a letter of Chichester in December 1612,[253] stated that he was getting a series of impressions of the plantation, however garbled, but lacked a 'general' picture of how the scheme was developing. He had fears that the planters were making slow progress. He therefore commissioned Chichester to provide him with an 'exact survey of the whole state of the plantation' detailing the achievements and defects of each grantee so that 'being truly certified … where the obstructions lie, he [might] the better know how to remove them.' He had gathered that some of the undertakers had sold their proportions to 'men of meane ability and unfit for that service', and that others had acquired land from their fellows which they were not capable of undertaking. Chichester was to 'take particular cognition of the severall transactions in this kind.'

The person chosen by the deputy to carry out the investigation was Sir Josias Bodley. He had recently received a permanent grant of the office of director-general and overseer of fortifications previously held in a temporary capacity.[254] The survey was carried out between February 2 and 25 April 1613.[255] The report on Cavan is dated February 6. It was produced just at the time when the deadline for building and planting – Easter 1613[256] – was being reached. The report will be examined by barony as in the case of the Carew survey.

In **Oneilland**[257] Bodley found that since Carew's survey ownership had remained unchanged. However, as to tenants we are informed that on the Brownlow estate there were 'very few' and that 'those which John Brownlow brought over, which were 40 or 50, by reason of the hardness of the country [had] all forsaken him.' This may not be entirely accurate, Carew had found 19. On Sir Anthony Cope's estate no tenants had 'as yet come over', yet Carew recorded the presence of some 37 workmen who were to become tenants. While recognising that the reports are not very consistent, it does

[252] Grosart, *Lismore Papers*, 2nd ser., 1, 161–64.

[253] *CSPI, 1611–14*, 309–10; 'Ulster plantation papers', no. 70, *Anal. Hib.*, viii.

[254] Hughes, *Patentee Officers*, 13.

[255] *Hastings MSS*, iv, 159–82. The section for Londonderry is missing (see Moody, *Londonderry*, 159).

[256] Moody, *Londonderry*, 37.

[257] *Hastings MSS*, iv, 174–75. Barony references only are again given.

seem clear that set-backs had been encountered. However, on a number of estates he found the 'full number of tenants' or 'sufficient persons' present. John Dillon had planted 28 families 'who are for the most part of them enjoined to convenient building and arms. Heron, Stanhowe and Sacheverall who were absentee were expected to return from England with tenants.

By a conservative estimate there were 128 adult males present, excluding owner or agents. Five of the nine owners were present, three absentees were expected to return with tenants, and two, Cope and Stanhowe (one of the three), were represented by agents. There were thus some 135 present, a figure almost identical with that of 1611. They were not evenly distributed, Cope, Sacheverall, and Stanhowe, as well as the Brownlows having few or none. Cope had apparently made over part of his land to 'certain gentlemen in England' who were to bring over tenants. However, on Bodley's evidence many of the tenants had been 'estated', i.e. given documentary title to their holdings.

In the building recorded a marked development had taken place since 1611. On all estates except Stanhowe's building skills had been mobilised. Bawns (sometimes made of 'timber clefts') and manor houses were being erected, and also in some cases framed houses for tenants and windmills were being provided. Rolleston had erected a windmill and Brownlow was about to do so. Cope's house, made of 'hewn stone with clay', had fallen and was not yet being rebuilt 'with lime'. On Rolleston's acquired estate 200,000 bricks were being manufactured. In some cases the adaptation of previous sites, or the provision of improvised structures is referred to. In three cases, Dillon, Matchett, and Rolleston estate, there are references to there being stock and goods upon the lands.

That there was reasonable activity on all estates except Stanhowe's is apparent, but viewed in the light of the plantation conditions defects are evident. The natives had not been removed and only one-third of the stipulated population was present.

In the Fews[258] Henry Acheson had acquired Douglas's proportion, the latter preferring to remain in royal service in England.[259] Acheson, though energetic and resident on his own proportion, had as yet built nothing on Douglas's. Claud Hamilton, who had land in Cavan also, which was currently engaging his attention, also had larger responsibilities than he could handle. However, there were extenuating circumstances: building work had been suspended on account of his dispute with the dean.[260] Acheson was

[258] *Hastings MSS,* iv, 175–76.

[259] The date of sale is not clear. Bodley said Acheson 'answereth' for Douglas's lands. An inquisition of *c.* 1630 dates it as 3 May 1611 (*Inq. cancel. Hib. repert.*, ii, Armagh (42) Chas I), but Douglas appears to have been owner up to the spring of 1612.

[260] Above, 81.

resident, Hamilton was in Cavan, Lawder was represented by his son, and as for Craig Bodley 'found none that could inform [him] of his purposes'.

As to tenants there were about 73 present,[261] or some 10 more than in 1611. The increase was largely due to Acheson, who had 47 'British families' on his proportion. The returns for the other undertakers suggest that some of their tenants had either returned to Scotland, gone elsewhere, or moved to Acheson's estate. On Craig's lands there were 'a dozen Scottish men, then newly arrived', and not estated.

The report indicates that the Scots in the Fews had continued the disregard for building shown in 1611. This is of interest in the light of Chichester's comments in 1612.[262] As yet on no estate had a bawn been completed, two were in construction, and there was no 'strength' built on Lawder' estate. Apart from the fact that Craig had completed a mill, the report indicates little improvement on the 1611 situation.

By 1613 the building record of the servitors in **Orior**[263] no longer compared unfavourably with that of the Armagh undertakers. Six of the eight grants are mentioned, excluding those of Poyntz and Whitechurch. Ownership had remained stable since 1611.[264] Of the five owners dealt with, representing six estates, one, Audley, had still made no visible impact on his grant. The other four estates presented variable impressions. Williams (or Smith) had 'only' built a small unflanked bawn. Moore was assembling materials and had 'divers' masons and labourers at work. The efforts of St. John and Bourchier, both unlikely residents, considerably outstepped those of their neighbours. St. John had already completed a bawn, albeit of earth and sod, but 'substantially flanked and ditched' and had on the site stone and materials for building a 'pile or castle'. Bourchier's bawn, a considerably larger affair, 80' by 100', was at an advanced stage of construction. He had also drawn and quarried stones and prepared lime for building a stone house. Timber had been felled and drawn and arrangements made with carpenters 'for sawing and squaring and fitting the same'. A millwright had been commissioned to construct a watermill. While Bodley gives no evidence either way it is unlikely that more than three of the Orior servitors were resident at this time.

In the rich lakeland barony of **Loughtee**[265] in Cavan ownership had remained unchanged since 1611. Five of the seven undertakers were

[261] The assumption is still made that there was one adult male per family.

[262] Above, 75.

[263] *Hastings MSS,* iv, 176–77.

[264] Curiously Williams who, by Carew's evidence, had made over most of his lands to Capt. Anthony Smith now features as owner. Smith is recorded as owner in Pynnar's survey.

[265] *Hastings MSS,* iv, 161–63.

resident and active; the other two, the Lushers, though represented by a 'factor' had no tenants and only a minimal achievement in building. Bodley provides evidence for 99 tenants of various kinds, of whom about 90 were resident. There were some 83 servants of various types including Waldron's personal entourage of about 50, some of whom must have been women. There was thus present an adult male colony approaching 170, an increase of 40 since 1611, and some 57 per cent of the norm. The increase since Carew's day was in the tenant class, hence a comparatively solid basis was being laid in his barony. Bodley understood that Sir Stephen Butler had no Irish tenants. However imported tenants were generally supplemented by native Irish. With regard to Taylor's proportion he wrote that 'divers of the Irish are yet remaining both on this proportion and others, without whose assistance for a while they pretend impossibility of proceeding in their undertakings.'

All estates except the Lushers's provided evidence of diversified building. Thus five planters had manor houses either built or in course of construction. One of these, Waldron, was actively replacing a thatched house with a more permanent structure and another, Wirrall, was living in an 'English thatched house' in Belturbet 'to serve till the accomplishment of his greater work.' Taylor and Butler had erected substantial bawns, and on two estates improviseable natural features had been availed of. Waldron was, notably, causing his tenants to build together in two places 'for their better safety'. Taylor had built '3 or 4 houses of English frames which are set to tenants' – the origin of Ballyhaise. One windmill, one horsemill, and one watermill, this an elaborate defended structure on Butler's estate, had been constructed, and a further windmill was being erected. Five boats of four to ten tons, owned by Butler and Fishe, were a response to the potentialities of inland navigation. Butler, Waldron,[266] Fishe, and Wirrall were adequately supplied with arms.

Four planters are reported as well stocked with cattle and horses, it being stated of Waldron that he had 'stocked his ground with English and Irish cattle.' For five of seven estates in this barony Bodley's statement about Stephen Butler that he had 'laid the ground work of a good plantation' is perhaps the fairest generalisation. It still remained true that the plantation stipulations were only partly fulfilled.[267]

266 For a dispute involving Waldron at this time see *CSPI, 1611–14*, 370–72.

267 In February 1614 Sir Robert Jacob, the solicitor-general, wrote to [the earl of Northampton], consort leader of Loughtee, stating that the undertakers there had 'built and planted very well'. As to Waldron's efforts he stated: 'I lay last night at Mr. Waldron' house who has built a very fair house of stone for himself and 27 houses for English tenants and has made a very handsome village where there was not only stone laid within these twelve months, and intends to enlarge his own house a great deal more' (*Hastings MSS,* iv, 14–16).

The Scots in **Tullyhunco**[268] provided a disappointing contrast to the English in Loughtee. Only Sir Claud Hamilton, who was resident on his father's estate, had a substantial achievement and this at the neglect of his lands in Armagh. The estate of John Browne had been acquired by 'one Achenson' (Acheson of the Fews), but had been for the most part leased to 'one Taylor' (hardly the English undertaker in Loughtee?), who was non-resident, had done nothing, and of whose prospects Bodley was dubious. Craig retained his acquisitions and was reported as 'being now gone into England to bring over with him more inhabitants'. He had already 'about a dozen tenants'. John Hamilton had done nothing.

On the two large estates, those of Claud Hamilton and Craig, there was reasonable evidence of activity. Their building styles were stated to be identical and Craig's house and bawn admitted 'no exception for strength and conveniency'. Hamilton's stone house 'of exceeding good strength [and] on all parts well flanked' was already 'raised to the sole of the window of the third storey'. The site was a strategic one, and masons, carpenters, and labourers were actively at work. Both castles, it may be noted, played a very prominent role in the defence of the plantation in 1641.[269] Both proprietors were adequately supplied with arms. Both were engaged in cattle rearing, Craig having 'a good stock of cattle' and Hamilton 'above eighty head'.

Craig had 'had out a dozen' tenants and had gone to England to recruit others. Sir Claud Hamilton in addition to 36 artisans had 'divers other' both English and Scottish, not yet estated. The total can hardly have exceeded 55, or under 40 per cent, of the requirement. The foundations of a colony were thus only being laid, and it seems that planters were turning to England rather than Scotland as a source of man-power. Dependence on native tenantry was still widespread.[270] Only two owners had so far been adequate to their task, and had made building a primary objective. The link-up in ownership with the Fews was manifestly an unhappy one, Claud Hamilton and Craig tending to neglect their Fews properties.

The entire Scots planted area of the barony of **Clankee**[271] was still visibly unaffected by the plantation. Bodley found no inhabitants other than the 'mere Irish' and no preparations in hand although 'the settling of that place, and the strengthening thereof be of special consequence and import'. By letter from Lord Killeen, an Old English Catholic and Cavan proprietor, he was informed that he had undertaken the duties of Sir James Hamilton and

[268] Ibid., 164.
[269] E.W. Hamilton, *The Irish rebellion of 1641* (London, 1920), 153–60. Hamilton's castle was called Keilagh, Craig's Croughan.
[270] *Inq. cancel. Hib. repert.*, ii, Cavan (27) Chas I.
[271] *Hastings MSS*, iv, 159–60.

intended to build and plant in the coming summer. Otherwise Bodley found this Scots-allocated barony unregulated by its new owners.[272]

In Cavan Bodley reported on seventeen servitor (and old English) grantees.[273] In general progress had remained limited and individualistic. It is noteworthy that two estates in **Castlerahan**, those of Sir Edmund Fettiplace and the Old English Sir William Taaffe had both been acquired by Edward Dowdall an Old English and Catholic lawyer.[274] Taaffe had got into debt, the earl of Cork noting in his diary on 1 November 1612 that Taaffe had failed to replay £88. 13. 4. borrowed from him.[275] On neither estate had buildings been erected. Of two other Old English referred to, captains Tirrell and Fleming, Tirrell had done nothing, though Fleming had a 'strong pile' and other buildings in hand on the lands in Clankee which he had acquired before the plantation.

In **Tullyhaw** Sir Richard Graham's share of the joint Graham grant was reputed to have been made over to his son-in-law. Both were absent, a bawn 'of ill stone and worse lime', 5½ feet high, was incomplete and there was no agent present, though the surrounding countryside was 'exceeding fast'. Pynnar had done nothing, but was said to have had his plantation obligations respited in favour of public service. Culme was one of the few energetic grantees reported on. He and his partner Walter Talbot[276] in this barony had already built '3 or 4 handsome Irish houses' – possibly the origin of Ballyconnell – and were also making preparations for building a castle, expected to be complete by the summer, at a strategic position previously undefended and 'by which in times past that country was much infested.'

In **Tullygarvey** Culme had joined with Archibald Moore through purchasing Brent Moore's share of the estate, and had already made preparations at a strategic point, Tullyvin. A 'fair and large Irish house' had already been built. In 1620 Brent Moore received a grant of land in the Longford plantation.[277] The brothers Ashe were building a bawn of claywork, substantially proportioned, but threatened by overlooking hills.

In **Castlerahan**, where Dowdall had acquired so much land, only one settler, like Culme in Tullyhaw, had made any pronounced impact. Ridgeway was accumulating building materials for a bawn 'in a fit place' near Lough Ramor. He had about five English tenants and had built three thatched houses, one-storeyed, with walls of stone and clay. However, stone and clay were inadequate building materials and one of these houses had

[272] In June Ralston sold his estate to John Hamilton (*Inq. cancel. Hib. repert.*, ii, Cavan (18) Chas I).
[273] *Hastings MSS*, iv, 159–61, 163–64, 165.
[274] Below, 104.
[275] Grosart, *Lismore Papers*, 1st ser., i, 14.
[276] Above, 56.
[277] *CPRI, Jas I*, 468.

already fallen and the other was 'declining'. He had done no more than choose the name Virginia for his prospective town. The rest of the barony in which there were two servitor owners, Elliot and Garth, was yet 'in statu quo prius' except that Garth had begun a bawn which he seemed likely, in Bodley's view, to finish speedily.

In **Clanmahon** the four estates evidenced only the most ineffectual of efforts. The most active, Sir Oliver Lambert who did not live there, had started quarrying operations, manufactured lime and was preparing timber for an Irish house. Russell had built a bawn of earth and sod to six feet in height, and had timber and wattle ready to build an 'Irish house'. Atkinson, who did not take out his patent until February 1615,[278] and Jones were making tentative attempts by improvisation and otherwise to belatedly fulfil their building obligations. The general impression of servitor initiative in Cavan is unfavourable.

In conclusion it may be stated that the British male population in both counties was somewhat similar. In Armagh there were some 210, and in Cavan about 235.

7. Aspects of the native Irish reaction

However much some of the Irish might have been able to mitigate their position in local practice, it was clear by 1613 that the plantation, however defective, was a *fait accompli*. It is not surprising then that plans very tentative and localised, though associated with hopes for foreign intervention, for an appeal to arms can be seen in that year. The local reaction of the elections of 1613 must also be examined.

There is no evidence that any plans embracing the entire province had been formulated, but there are cases of limited and localised insurgency at this time. Counter-Reformation clergy urged adherence to Catholicism and promised continental support. It was widely known that a parliament was about to meet which would consolidate the titles of the Ulster planters and perhaps introduce penal religious legislation. The deputy was fully aware of the unpopularity of this policy.[279]

Sir John Wishart, an undertaker in a part of Fermanagh which bordered on Cavan, informed the king in February 1613 of 'secret resolutions' to 'disturb the peace'.[280] Arms, it was alleged, were being accumulated at Belturbet 'and in the woods and other secret places thereabouts'. The king instructed Chichester to give Wishart a 'secret warrant' to search suspicious

[278] Ibid., 272.
[279] 'Chichester Letter-Book', no. 41, *Anal. Hib.*, viii.
[280] *CSPI, 1611–14*, 324.

places.[281] In the summer and autumn a Franciscan friar, Turlogh McCroddin, carried out a preaching crusade in Ulster urging religious revival and promising foreign intervention, though the nature of his activities is only derived from depositions taken before Sir Toby Caulfeild in October.[282]

No rebellion materialised though some small groups did attempt local action. Surviving jail delivery returns[283] give some evidence of its nature. With regard to Cavan various people had judgment passed on them at Cavan on 30 March 1613.[284] Apart from cases of larceny and rape, a number of cases of people who had 'levied war' in the county between 20 August 1612 and 20 January 1613 were heard. Two Irish are mentioned as having 'levied war' 'with other traitors' and abetted by two others at Lough Ramor on 20 August 1612. One of the abettors was found guilty and sentenced to execution, the rebels having presumably been executed earlier probably by martial law. In two cases those presented for rebellion were acquitted. Seven incidents of this nature are recorded involving nineteen named people, with 'other traitors' unnamed. These names include O'Reilly, Bradys, and McMahons.

A delivery held in Armagh on 13 April 1614[285] reveals similar though less numerous incidents for County Armagh. Two McCanns and one descendant of Turlogh Brassilogh O'Neill who were assisted by Turlogh groom O'Hanlon, a grantee under the plantation, were all acquitted for incidents in Oneilland and Orior in December 1613. The existence of the depositions referred to above testifies to the energy of Sir Toby Caulfeild.

At the same time attempts were made to conciliate the current unrest by the granting of pardons. From the end of 1612 until about mid-1614 pardons were a widely used expedient. In December 1612 Sir Francis Ruish, who had Monaghan connections, submitted the names of three O'Reillys from Cavan stating that they had 'stood long upon protection and carried themselves well' and recommending their pardon 'in hope of their honest loyal behaviour hereafter'.[286] Chichester issued a warrant for their pardon.[287] Settler certification had also been given for a group for

[281] Ibid.

[282] TNA, SP 63/232, ff 137–38 (*CSPI, 1611–14*, 429–31); BL, Cotton MSS, Titus B, x, fol. 236; J. Lodge (ed.), *Desiderata curiosa Hibernica* (2 vols, Dublin, 1772), i, 394–96; C. Maxwell, *Irish history from contemporary sources, 1509–1610* (London 1923), 150–51.

[283] J.F. Ferguson (ed.), 'Ulster roll of gaol delivery, 1613–18', *UJA*, 1st series, i (1853); 260–70, ii (1854), 25–28.

[284] Ibid., i, 266–67. Ferguson misdates the Cavan roll of 30 March 11 James I as 1614. Other dating errors have also been corrected here.

[285] Ibid., i, 269–70.

[286] *Hastings MSS*, iv, 42.

[287] Ibid.

whose pardon a fiant was ordered by the deputy in July 1613.[288] Three O'Reillys from Cavan in this list had been certified by Sir Oliver Lambert and Ruish.[289] They received their pardon on July 23.[290] Within the period above mentioned in all 26 Irish from Cavan and some 61 from Armagh received pardons.[291] A number of grantees under the plantation feature in these lists including Mullmory oge O'Reilly from Cavan,[292] and Calvagh McDonnell,[293] Patrick modder O'Donnelly, Henry McTurlogh O'Neill, and Art McTurlogh O'Neill[294] from Armagh.

These pardons offer some indication of the scale of native opposition in Armagh and Cavan at this time. It lacked cohesion and was not markedly more serious than petty violence. Local commanders and settlers seem to have intervened where necessary, and there was no foreign assistance. Also, more generally, the native Irish could count on no support from the Old English who agitated for a political solution to their grievances about the parliament at this time. By 1614 conditions appear to have been more peaceful, and at the Armagh jail delivery of March 1615 no cases of 'open war' came up.[295]

The acute sense of crisis, however, of early 1613 provoked in Chichester profound misgivings about the security of the plantation. In January 1613 in a letter to the lord privy seal[296] he stated that:

> the undertakers ... goe slowly on with the works of the plantation, labouring rather for the most part to make profit of the lands then to erect strong buildings for their subjects or bawns and court lodges for their goods and cattle, so as they lye open to the will of their ill affected neighbours who undoubtedly would cut many of their throats and thrust the rest clean out of the country if they were assured of assistance from fforeign parts, or had arms and munition to make a war.

Some had begun houses of stone and lime, but in the meantime lived in 'weak' thatched houses. They did not live in townrids as required, but lived 'scattered up and downe ... where every man affects best his ease and profit, from which I cannot withdraw them, neither could he with his 'small

288 Bod. Lib., Carte MSS, vol. 61, fol. 43.
289 Most of those listed had been 'repreived by the judges'. One had 'byne in Sweden' (ibid.).
290 *CPRI, Jas I*, 258.
291 Ibid., 239–40, 258, 261, 267, 267–68; *Hastings MSS,* iv, 43, 43–4.
292 *CPRI, Jas I*, 239–40.
293 Ibid.
294 Ibid., 261.
295 Ferguson, 'Ulster roll', ii (1854), 27–8.
296 'Chichester Letter-Book', no. 41, *Anal. Hib.*, viii.

fforces' protect them in emergency. Many were absentee and must be required to return and finish their building by the summer, when commissioners should be appointed to examine the plantation – which would be 'comfort and incoragement' to those who had performed the conditions and allow the punishment or reproof of those who had not.

The 1613 parliament had already been the subject of a thorough study in which it is shown that the catholics took sharp objection to the conduct of the elections and made a number of charges of 'violence and unfairness'.[297] It emerges clearly that these elections caused tension between the native Irish electors (and also the Old English in the case of Cavan) and the New English elements in both of our counties. For both counties and their boroughs – Armagh and Charlemont, Cavan and Belturbet – English, either settlers or government nominees, were returned as members by the sheriffs.[298] With regard to both counties and also the town of Cavan charges of intimidation and other malpractices in the conduct of the elections were made.[299]

The king appointed a commission of inquiry on 27 August 1613 which conceded only that the burgesses returned for Cavan, Hugh Culme and George Sexton (the deputy's secretary), had been miselected and ordered that their opponents, Water and Thomas Brady, both landowners in the neighbourhood, should take their place. The king in August 1614 disfranchised Charlemont for the remainder of the parliament because it had not received its charter until after the issue of the election writ.

Such change was in the circumstances the most that could be secured. The charters of the new boroughs were such that they could not but be, in Davies's words 'perpectual seminaries of protestant burgesses',[300] and in the succeeding elections of 1634 and 1640 Armagh constituencies returned all new English members,[301] though Cavan county in 1634 returned the Old English Sir Lucas Dillon[302] who in 1640 was replaced by Phillip O'Reilly.[303] If the elective system could guarantee it the plantation was assured.

297 T.W. Moody, 'The Irish parliament under Elizabeth and James I', *PRIA*, vol. xlv, C, (1939–40), 41–81.

298 *Journals of the house of commons of the kingdom of Ireland, vol. 1, 1613–66* (Dublin 1796), 18 May 1613, 7.

299 For details see TNA, SP 63/232, ff 97–9 (*CSPI, 1611–14*, 357–64).

300 *CSPI, 1611–14*, 516.

301 Kearney, *Strafford*, 256, 262.

302 Ibid., 257.

303 Ibid., 262.

CHAPTER 3

Development of the Plantation, 1614–19

1. Introduction

Bodley's survey revealed defects in the plantation at the end of its initial phase. The settlers were doubtless conscious that their efforts were under scrutiny and from about 1614 a number were attempting to regularise their positions by the mechanism of surrender and regrant. Also there were a number of sales in these years.

The English government, too, was displaying further interest in the Ulster project. In June 1614 the deputy was instructed to have a further survey of the plantation taken by Bodley 'about Michaelmas next'.[1] At the same time Chichester was given detailed instructions concerning important aspects of the plantation. Cognizance was taken of the fact that the undertakers still retained Irish tenants and these were to be removed as expediently as possible. It had also come to notice in England that some of the undertakers, especially the Scots, were intermarrying with the Irish. This, an aspect of the native problem, could have serious repercussions. The deputy was to 'reprove' all offenders 'until order may be taken for their further punishment.' Chichester was also to tender the oath of supremacy to all undertakers and their tenants and also to servitors 'and if they refuse to take the oath or to go to church to give order that they may be returned from whence they came.' Two delinquents in particular, here, were singled out, neither in Armagh or Cavan.[2]

Bodley's report has only come to hand for Londonderry.[3] Only one case of the penalisation of intermarriage has been found for our area. On 29 January 1617 William Brownlow and Elinor O'Doherty his wife were given a pardon in return for a small fine.[4] As to the proffering of the oath of supremacy there is no evidence that any action was taken by the Dublin government.

1 TNA, SP 63/232, ff 157–61v, copy ff 163–66v (*CSPI, 1611–14*, 481–84); *CPRI, Jas I*, 277; BL, Add MS 4819, ff 285–89v. These instructions followed on a report by Chichester (BL, Add. MS 4819, ff 281–84v; 4673, ff 168–70v).

2 They were Sir George Hamilton, a Catholic and a brother of the earl of Abercorn who was an undertaker in Strabane barony (Hill, *Plantation*, 530) and one of two Robert Stewarts who also held land in Tyrone (ibid., 287–88).

3 Moody, *Londonderry*, 159–60.

4 *CPRI, Jas I*, 320.

2. Granting of concealments, surrenders and regrants

At the same time the problem of concealments was again taken in hand. In the instructions of June 1614 Chichester and the commissioners were empowered to dispose of concealed lands first to all whose proportions were defective and the remainder to the grantees within whose allocations they were found.[5] In December Sir Oliver St. John concurred with this policy. To grant concealed pieces of territory to others than contiguous planters – that is, in effect, to accept Chichester's proposal of 1611 that concealments should be granted to additional servitors and natives[6] – would cause 'much complainte ... besides much disagreement and expense of money in sutes of law' and would not encourage the settlers to performance of conditions.[7]

In Armagh and Cavan grants followed, in effect, both policies. In these counties the granting of concealments was in hand between 1615 and 1620. It is some commentary on government efficiency that though the concealed lands had been recorded in some systematic way in 1612[8] it was to be some two years before action began to be taken towards their conversion to crown profit. Even the king, too, was prepared to make some exceptions to the London policy. In March 1613, for example, he empowered Chichester to make a grant of un-allocated mountain, bog, or woods in Ulster to Capt. John Sandford who had been engaged in the transportation of swordsmen to Sweden at the time of the distribution of land and so had gone unrewarded.[9] Another exception was also made by the king in October 1614, that is some months after the June directive.[10]

5 *CSPI, 1611–14*, 482.

6 Above, 82–83.

7 TNA, SP 63/232, ff 268–68v. The calendared version omits this – St. John's handwriting is difficult (*CSPI, 1611–14*, 540). His appraisal of the Ulster venture as a whole was as follows: 'The plantation in Ulster goes slowly forward, the buildings not half performed, the natives lingered upon undertakers' lands ...'

8 Above, 84.

9 Bod. Lib., Carte MSS, vol. 62, ff 308–308v (*CSPI, 1611–14*, 329). Inquisitions were taken finding the extent of these mountains (*Inq. cancel. Hib. repert.*, ii, Appendix), and Sandford received a patent on July 7 (*CPRI, Jas I*, 257). The grant did not prove a lucrative one. In the exchequer court in November 1617 he claimed that 'divers persons interrupt his assigns being very many in number having no residence but only pasture upon the same with their creaghts ... so that they cannot be brought to answer in a legal manner.' An injunction forbidding them was ordered to be issued to the sheriffs (NAI, Ferguson MSS, xi, 246). He had received mountains in all the planted counties except Londonderry. Shortly afterwards Sandford assigned his grant to Sir Toby Caulfeild (TCD, MS 570, fol. 303).

10 This was in favour of Andrew Dikes, a Scottish merchant, who had petitioned the king for compensation for losses sustained in Derry at the time of O'Doherty's rising. The king ordered Chichester to grant him 'as much concealed or escheated lands in Ulster or elsewhere ... as shall amount to ... £35 by the year' (BL, Add. MS 4794, fol. 310v. However he did not receive such a grant in Ulster. He later renewed his petition and the king in 1618 (ibid., ff 411v–12v) ordered the granting to him of lands or chantries, or impropriations, or tithes anywhere in Ireland to the yearly value of £40.

In Armagh three English undertakers, Dillon, Cope, and Brownlow, received concealments grants in 1617.[11] John Hamilton, brother of Sir James, who had acquired the Lawder estate in the Fews in 1614,[12] got a grant of concealments there in 1616.[13] Other previous owners in the county to receive grants of concealments were Marmaduke Whitechurch,[14] and Francis Annesley who, in 1615, acquired concealed lands[15] close to other concealments which he had been granted in 1612.[16]

Of new owners who received concealments in the county, Trevor, who received the largest grant of all, in 1615,[17] had already been promised these in 1613,[18] as compensation for lands he had been obliged to surrender. Richard Atherton, brother of Henry Atherton late constable of Mountnorris, but who had had no previous connection with Armagh proprietorship, received two grants of concealments, one in 1617,[19] and the other in 1618.[20]

Similar numbers received concealments in Cavan, between May 1615 and June 1620. One established owner was John Hamilton, who had also purchased land in Cavan, and who was granted related concealments in 1615.[21] Three newcomers were Sir Robert Stewart who received concealments in Clankee in 1617,[22] and was possibly one of two Scottish undertakers of that name in Mountjoy, Tyrone,[23] William Binde,[24] and George St. George.[25] The latter two were servitor-type grantees. St. George came from Cambridgeshire, had property in Leitrim, and was vice-admiral of Connacht in 1634.[26]

The lands granted in these years in both counties bear a close relation to those found by the commissioners in 1612.[27] It may be noted that no Irish proprietor received a grant of concealments and that no new proprietor

11 *CPRI, Jas I*, 324, 339–40.
12 Below, 102.
13 *CPRI, Jas I*, 309.
14 Ibid., 299–300.
15 Ibid., 272.
16 Above, 74.
17 *CPRI, Jas I*, 299.
18 Above, 86.
19 *CPRI, Jas I*, 314.
20 Ibid., 359. This small area in Orior has not been identified.
21 Ibid., 300.
22 ibid., 317.
23 Hill, *Plantation*, 287–88.
24 His grant was in Loughtee (*CPRI, Jas I*, 317).
25 His grant was in Clankee, and he also received concealments in Tyrone and Fermanagh (ibid., 468–69).
26 Burke, *Peerage*, 2140; *CSPI, 1633–47*, 129, 434; Lodge, *Peerage* (ed. Archdall), i, 144, iii, 111, *CPRI, Jas I*, 434.
27 TCD, MS 806, ff 21–21v (Cavan), 23–23v (Armagh).

was Irish. In only one case, that of John Hamilton in Cavan, were concealed lands granted to previous proprietors without rent, that is to say, the notion that these could be granted to redress defects of measure was not accepted. It should also be noted that not all concealments had been discovered or declared and were granted in these years. In 1628 the government again attempted to inquire into concealed lands and areas held without quit rent payments were subsequently found, especially in Cavan.[28]

In these years also many planters surrendered their holdings to the crown and received greater security of tenure by regrant. The government was making itself aware of defaults by periodic survey and there was some reason for uneasiness. In the summer of 1614 instructions were given for them to have their patents enrolled in the Irish chancery,[29] and a copy of the conditions of plantation appear about this time among Carew's manuscripts.[30]

In the years between 1614 and the time of Pynnar's survey and after, a considerable number of settlers surrendered their estates and received regrants. This, in some cases at any rate, indicates that the government was unwilling to undertake the task of displacing defaulters and instating substitutes.

The procedure was straightforward. The landowner wishing to 'strengthen his estate' petitioned the king who, in return, by letter to the lord deputy and chancellor indicated that a surrender be accepted and regrant made. These king's letters show the conditions of the regrants. They were to be without fine, at the same rents, and rateably for concealments where involved.[31] There was to be no mention of the surrender in the new patents to avoid allegations of defective title.[32] Regrants were not to involve any action contrary to the conditions of plantation.[33] The proprietor might have a commission out of chancery to inquire into place names and land quantities, the findings of which might be incorporated in the patent.[34] The latter was a tacit admission – admittedly specifically in one instance[35] – that the surveys of 1608 and 1609 were inadequate or inaccurate. A side effect therefore was increased topographical knowledge.

28 Below, 166, 172.

29 *CSPI, 1611–14*, 491.

30 *Cal. Carew MSS, 1603–24*, 269–70.

31 BL, Add. MS 4794, ff 419v–20v (king's letter on behalf of William Bailie, 6 October 1618).

32 Ibid., ff 348–48v (king's letter on behalf of Charles Poyntz, 18 July 1616).

33 *CSPI, 1615–25*, 35 (king's letter on behalf of earl of Abercorn and the undertakers in Strabane barony, Tyrone, 18 July 1615).

34 BL, Add MS 4784, ff 419v–20v (Bailie).

35 In the case of Sir Toby Caulfeild, king's letter, 17 May 1619 (BL, Add MS 4794 ff 468–69; 36,775 ff 80v–81; *CPRI, Jas I*, 434).

Sometimes a surrender and regrant reflected a landowner's desire that his patent should contain the most definitive listing of his lands, and so ensure his advantage in local disputes. Thus by king's letter of 12 May 1619 Sir Toby Caulfeild, then engaged in dispute with the archbishop of Armagh, was to have a 'new and enlarged' grant, including all 'particular and knowen names', of his lands conferred.[36] Four original patentees or their descendants in Cavan and three in Armagh (excluding Caulfeild) on these grounds, and also to acquire grants of concealments, secured king's letters. In Cavan these were Sir Stephen Butler,[37] William Bailie,[38] Richard Waldron,[39] and the widow and heirs of Lord Lambert.[40] In Armagh they were Brownlow,[41] Audley,[42] Moore,[43] and Caulfeild. Sometimes they decided that a king's letter was ample insurance and did not actually take out new patents.

More importantly perhaps, the permitting of surrenders and regrants can be seen as a giving of official recognition to new owners who had acquired plantation land by commercial transactions. Surrenders and regrants also allow us to date such transfers.

One such new owner was John Hamilton, a brother of Sir James Hamilton of County Down, who acquired extensive lands in Armagh and Cavan. On 30 October 1611 he acquired Sir Claud Hamilton's proportion in Cavan.[44] This, however, he passed, on 4 December 1614,[45] to William Lawder, the Scottish undertaker in Armagh, acquiring in exchange the Lawder estate in Armagh.[46] On 11 June 1613[47] he had got Ralston's lands in Cavan and on 22 November 1615 he also acquired Craig's proportion in Armagh.[48] Before Pynnar's survey and probably after his regrant of 18 December 1617 which does not include it, he acquired Claud Hamilton's Armagh estate.[49] In 1615 and 1616 he received concealments grants.[50] He

36 Ibid.

37 BL, Add MS 4794, ff 358v–59; *CPRI, Jas I*, 326 (king's letter, 6 April 1617 – no patent was taken out).

38 BL, Add MS 4794, ff 419v–20v; *CPRI, Jas I*, 389 (king's letter, 6 October 1618 – no patent was taken out).

39 BL, Add MS 4794, ff 359v–60; *CPRI, Jas I*, 326 (king's letter, 1 December 1616 – no patent was taken out).

40 Ibid., 454 (king's letter, 17 July 1619), 473 (further king's letter, 22 May 1620). The patent was issued on 16 February 1622 (ibid., 516–17).

41 *CPRI, Jas I*, 339–40.

42 BL, Add MS 4794, ff 490–90v (king's letter, 17 July 1619).

43 Ibid., ff 498v–99v (king's letter, 28 June 1619).

44 *Inq. cancel. Hib. repert.*, ii, Cavan (24) Chas I.

45 Ibid.

46 Ibid., Armagh, (4) Chas I.

47 Ibid., Cavan, (18) Chas I.

48 Ibid., Armagh (4) Chas I.

49 This purchase is dated incorrectly as 3 May 1610 in ibid.

50 *CPRI, Jas I*, 300, 309.

had thus accumulated a considerable estate in two plantation counties. On 18 October 1616 a king's letter in his favour authorised a surrender and regrant.[51] His surrender took place on 10 December 1617,[52] and the regrant followed on December 18.[53] In the regrant he is styled of Ballirobert, County Down, though he later lived in Cavan.[54] A Scottish settler from Down had thus moved into a substantial area of plantation land.[55]

The process of surrender and regrant was also availed of at this time by people who had acquired lands granted to native freeholders. One example, also otherwise complicated, may be cited. At the time of plantation Francis Annesley, who had become a patentee officer in Ireland since 1606,[56] received a comparatively small grant as a servitor in Tyrone.[57] However, he quickly acquired a footing in Armagh which proved the basis for expansion. On 12 October 1611 on the death of Henry Atherton, constable of Mountnorris fort, he acquired the fort and lands by the same conditions as Atherton had held them, for twenty-one years.[58] On 31 January 1612 he received a grant to two contiguous concealed townlands.[59] On December 31 he was appointed governor of the fort, with a daily emolument of eight shillings and the command of ten soldiers at eight pence a day each.[60] On 24 February 1615 he was granted a small adjoining area of concealed land.[61] He had also acquired the lands granted in 1609 to Patrick O'Hanlon.[62] On 22 October 1616 a king's signet letter took cognizance of his position and ordered a surrender and regrant 'of all his lands which shall be found by office or inquisition'.[63] Nothing was done at this stage, and on 21 September 1618 – he was then Irish chief secretary and knighted – he got

51 Ibid., 326.
52 Ibid., 343.
53 Ibid., 340.
54 The 1622 government survey states that he was resident there at that time (BL, Add. MS. 4756, ff 100–100v).
55 Another newcomer of this period was Sir George Mainwaring from Shropshire who on 14 March 1616 purchased Sir Nicholas Lusher's proportion in Loughtee (*Inq. cancel. Hib. repert.*, ii, Cavan (23) Chas I). Hill (*Plantation*, 466) mistakenly dates this transaction as 14 March 1613. However, he was an absentee in 1622 and in 1627 he sold the estate to Thomas Moynes, bishop of Kilmore and Ardagh, without having taken out a patent in his own name (*Inq. cancel. Hib. repert.*, ii, Cavan (23) Chas I).
56 Hughes, *Patentee Officers*, 3.
57 Hill, *Plantation*, 551.
58 *CPRI, Jas I*, 203.
59 Ibid., 207.
60 BL, Add. MS 36,775, ff 87–8v; Hughes, *Patentee Officers*, 3.
61 *CPRI, Jas I*, 272.
62 O'Hanlon appears to have forfeited his lands for treason. They were granted in June 1615 to Sir John Kinge, the muster master general, and Sir Adam Loftus, later lord chancellor (*CPRI, Jas I*, 280–82), from whom Annesley presumably acquired them.
63 BL, Add. MS 4794, ff 348v–49; *CPRI, Jas I*, 314.

the benefit of a further king's letter.[64] The letter recited that he had previously had command of the fort for life:

> But being informed by some of our officers of trust that the said forte was not now, nor is ever like to be, of any such consequent use for our service we have thought fitt amongst other abatements of our army to discharge the said fort of Mountnorris,

and it was thus with its related territory to be granted to Annesley as private property. As compensation for the loss of employment as governor he was to receive a pension of five shillings a day for life. He was to have a regrant in his own name of O'Hanlon's lands and of all his other property in Ireland. This followed on 9 January 1619.[65] It included also a nunnery in the town of Armagh. He had also by this stage acquired property in Cavan. Charles Poyntz at this time also legalised purchases of native territory in Armagh.[66]

In Cavan a purchaser who was Old English secured his title in this way. The two estates in Castlerahan granted to Sir Edmund Fettiplace and Sir William Taaffe became objects of speculation before becoming the property of Edward Dowdall, a Catholic lawyer. In Bodley's report they are stated as being under Dowdall's control, Taaffe's estate having come to him, it was understood, by way of Sir John Kinge.[67] By an inquisition of May 1614 Dowdall was stated to be in possession of both.[68] By the following year the property had come into the hands of Francis Annesley,[69] who received a regrant on November 25.[70] At the time of Pynnar's survey, 1618–19, both proportions were held by Sir Thomas Ashe,[71] the servitor grantee, who had bought them from Annesley[72] and on 12 May 1620 we find a king's letter for a surrender by Ashe of one of the estates 'and other lands in County Cavan', as assignee of Sir Francis Annesley, and directing that a regrant be made to Edward Dowdall as assignee of Ashe.[73] In 1622 the plantation surveyors noted that Dowdall held both properties 'by late letters patent'.[74]

64 Ibid., ff 420v–22, 432v–34v (copy; 36,775, ff 87–8v; *CPRI, Jas I*, 410, also 389 (inaccurate).

65 *CPRI, Jas I*, 407. Sometime later he acquired the land of Donogh reogh O'Hagan.

66 BL, Add. MS 4794, ff 348–48v; *CPRI, Jas I*, 314 (king's letter, 18 July 1616, for surrender); ibid., 412 (surrender, and regrant, 14 December 1618). The undated inquisition (*Inq. cancel. Hib. repert.*, ii, Armagh (10) Jas I) was probably taken for the purpose of this regrant.

67 *Hastings MSS*, iv, 160.

68 *Inq. cancel. Hib. repert.*, ii, Cavan (4) Jas I.

69 *CPRI, Jas I*, 292 (king's letter, 7 May 1615).

70 Ibid., 294.

71 Hill, *Plantation*, 457.

72 BL, Add. MS 36,775, ff 110v–12.

73 Ibid. BL, Add, MS 4794, 44 600–601; *CPRI, Jas I*, 512.

74 BL, Add. MS 4756, ff 100–101. A fragment of Fettiplace's estate was apparently retained by Ashe and subsequently sold. It was held by George Garland in 1641 (NAI, Books of Survey and Distribution: this would appear to be inaccurate in calling him an 'Irish papist').

Such a transfer of plantation land into old English hands was hardly in accordance with the intention of the plantation.

Accumulation of land by settlers was also condoned. For example, Sir James Craig, who sold his lands in Armagh to John Hamilton in 1615,[75] had acquired in August 1610 the two proportions in Cavan granted to Alexander and John Auchmooty.[76] Later, in 1615, he acquired the lands of a neighbouring native freeholder.[77] On 18 July 1618 the king gave instructions, on his petition, for a regrant on these lands and their concealments.[78] Another case is perhaps more interesting. Sir Oliver St. John, now Viscount Grandison and later lord deputy, had received a grant as a servitor in Orior. Before Pynnar's survey he also acquired Matchett's undertaker's lands in Oneilland, and in February 1622[79] he received a regrant of all his lands following on a king's letter of the previous December 22.[80] Such an acquisition was in breach of the differentiation of servitors and undertakers into separate baronies.

By way of conclusion it may be noted that a condition under which the settlers received their lands was that for the first five years they should not be sold.[81] Procedure by king's letter arose from the apparently unregulated breach of this condition. The vast majority of surrenders and regrants were in the period covered by this section. So far as undertakers were concerned there was a plan, first mooted in 1619[82] and finalised in 1628 for systematic regrants to these under modified conditions of tenure and at double rents.

3. Irish unrest, 1615–16

One reason, it seems, why the government did not adopt a more forceful line with the settlers lay in the uncertain local background of their relations with the Gaelic population. The incapacity of the government to meet concerted opposition if backed by foreign support was a cause of concern in Dublin. In 1615 when optimistic plans for a rising had been formulated the lord deputy wrote:

75 *Inq. cancel. Hib. repert.*, ii, Armagh (4) Chas I.

76 Ibid., Cavan (27) Chas I.

77 Ibid.

78 *CPRI, Jas I*, 402; BL, Add. MS 4794, ff 428–29.

79 *CPRI, Jas I*, 515–16. He had also by this time acquired the lands originally granted to Lord Audley in Orior, and the concealed land granted to Richard Atherton, who was now Grandison's estate agent.

80 BL, Add. MS 36,775, ff 97–8; *CPRI, Jas I*, 518. The inquisition dated 22 January 1621 (*Inq. cancel. Hib. repert.*, ii, Armagh (7) Jas I) was obviously connected with this regrant, and so must have been pre-dated one year in transcription.

81 Moody, 'The revised articles', *BIHR*, xii, 178–83.

82 Marsh's Library, Dublin, MS Z4.2.6, 420–21; Moody, *Londonderry Plantation*, 192.

> we are a handful of men in intartaynement here so ill payde that everie one is discontented and out of hart ... and what service I can performe w'thout men and monie if occasion require it, is easily conceived.[83]

Outrages had proliferated and without reinforcements he would soon be 'wearied in a tempest when commands, law, and proclamations are of no use without the sword to make them obeyed.'[84] There were rumours that Tyrone was about to return with forces to regain lost lands.[85] Earlier, to relieve the Ulster undertakers, to appease the natives, and convinced that 'the church and clergy of Ulster is at this day far otherwise provided for than this kingdom has ever known before',[86] Chichester had absolved them from paying certain tithe exactions.[87]

When the suspected plot was uncovered it was found to have been unlikely of success and limited to Ulster. The outline of the conspiracy has already been reconstructed by Professor Moody[88] who stressed the ineffectiveness of the conspirators and also that County Londonderry was not only the chief centre of disaffection, but also the area which it was considered most essential to overcome initially. However, in aspirations it was conceived as involving all of Ulster, and presumably all of Ireland, and receiving backing from outside.

The preliminary tactics were to capture Derry and Coleraine, take certain hostages, 'and then to proceed to a rebellion'.[89] As far as Armagh was concerned a major objective was to release Hugh O'Neill's son, Conn, who was under the custody of Sir Toby Caulfeild in Charlemont fort, and send him to Spain.[90]

In its second phase it was hoped that the rebellion would spread generally in Ulster. Schemes were formulated for sacking Carrickfergus, Lifford, Massereene, Dungannon, and Mountjoy.[91] While many of the Maguires of Fermanagh seem to have been implicated, no evidence has survived to indicate that any agitation of note was carried out in Armagh or Cavan. However, there were doubtless small isolated incidents. At a jail delivery at Armagh in March 1615 judge Gerard Lowther found numerous cases of theft, but none of 'open rebellion'.[92] No jail delivery records have survived for Cavan at this time.

83 Chichester to Winwood, 18 March 1615 (TNA, SP 63/233, ff 29–30v; *CSPI, 1615–25*, 19–20).
84 Ibid.
85 *CSPI, 1615–25*, 22.
86 Ibid., 22–4.
87 Ibid.
88 Moody, *Londonderry Plantation*, 165–67.
89 *CSPI, 1615–25*, 51.
90 Ibid., 82.
91 Ibid., 42, 74.
92 Ferguson, 'Ulster roll', ii (1854), 27–8.

As far as the general conspiracy was concerned secrecy was not maintained and the rising – 'a dangerous practice tending to rebellion' in the phrase of the English privy council[93] – never came to fruition. Between February and June 1615 a series of arrests were made, and the disaffection was in fact suppressed without extraordinary difficulty. The garrisons in the Ulster forts were not increased[94] and the threat was met by the use of provost marshals with small numbers of soldiers who were sent into 'sundry counties, especially Ulster'.[95] The local military commanders also played an active part, particularly two of them, Sir Toby Caulfeild in central Ulster and Sir Thomas Phillips in Londonderry, the sheriffs of the counties and the assize judges assisting in the arrests and interrogations.[96] Sir Oliver Lambert, the Cavan proprietor, was sent on an expedition to the island of Islay to ensure the inactivity of the Scots.[97]

Executions followed and the optimistic plans were forestalled. It was clear, however, that the government had been profoundly disturbed by the conspiracy though by the end of April when it had been manacled it was being turned to political advantage in Dublin as a means of expediting the deliberations of parliament.[98] Royal instructions were given in May and June that Conn O'Neill should be sent immediately to England[99] and on July 7 the English privy council reported to Chichester that he had been placed in Eton.[100] On 21 April 1615 the king gave order for the payment of an annuity of £30 to the widow of Sir John O'Reilly, to be paid out of the Ulster rents, provided she relinquished her claim to lands in Loughtee.[101] On June 30 Dame Mary O'Reilly was granted a pension for life of £80 a year.[102] The conspiracy also convinced the king of the need to extend the royal influence in Ireland. The 'remedy for the barbarous manners of the mere Irish', he felt, was to press on with the policy of either plantation (with British) or settlement (among the native Irish with definite quit-rents) and extend it immediately to Leitrim and Longford, and 'other Irish counties'.[103]

In Ireland pardoning continued to be a valued expedient for dealing with unrest, and a spate of these followed, usually in return for small fines,

93 *CSPI, 1615–25*, 53–4.
94 TNA, SP 63/233, ff 7–14v (*CSPI, 1615–25*, 10–13).
95 Ibid., ff 40–1v (ibid., 38–9).
96 *CSPI, 1615–25*, 41, 62.
97 Ibid., 47.
98 TNA, SP 63/233, ff 46–6v, 48–51v, 54–5v (*CSPI, 1615–25*, 49–50, 50–51, 52).
99 *CSPI, 1615–25*, 53–4, 65–6.
100 Ibid., 84.
101 Ibid., 47. Chichester had suggested this in January 1614 ('Chichester Letter-Book', no. 95, *Anal. Hib.*, viii).
102 *CPRI, Jas I*, 286.
103 *CSPI, 1615–25*, 35–6.

over the next few years. For want of more specific evidence they offer some rough way of assessing the extent of unrest in our counties. Between 26 June 1615 and 28 July 1617, twenty-seven Irish from Armagh and five Irish from Cavan received pardons.[104] These included Patrick O'Hanlon, the Orior proprietor, who was pardoned in July 1617.[105] He had presumably forfeited his lands in 1615 because in June of that year they were granted to Sir John Kinge and Sir Adam Loftus.[106] They subsequently became the property of Sir Francis Annesley.[107]

A return of the fines collected as a result of the lent circuit of the judges in 1616 presents what may well have been higher than average figures.[108] Archibald Moore, collector for Cavan, returned £262. 6. 0. Irish, and Marmaduke Whitechurch £185. 10. 8. collected from Armagh.

By the summer of 1615 the immediate threat had been suppressed though unrest continued in 1616.[109] In August 1616 one of the O'Hanlons was considered a possible threat.[110] In December the king acknowledged the 'former good services' of Sir Moses Hill as provost marshal of Ulster and instructed that he should have a regrant of this office for life.[111] Thus some form of military superintendence of Ulster was considered essential on a long-term basis. That Hill had been thorough in his task and not over-sensitive to strict legal rectitude is also clear. In March 1617 a pardon for him was authorised

> because in strictness of law he may be questioned for the execution of offenders by martial law, notwithstanding His Highness's commission authorising him thereunto.'[112]

However, by the end of 1616 Ulster had been restored to some quiescence. In October St. John, who had succeeded Chichester as deputy, wrote to Winwood that 'within the land things stand well without appearance of trouble or danger'.[113] There were still a few outlaws in the north, but he hoped that they would be 'scattered without any great labour'.[114] Also the

[104] Bod. Lib., Carte MSS, vol. 62, ff 320–20v, 390, 412–12v, 430; *CPRI, Jas I*, 299, 320, 325.
[105] Ibid., 325.
[106] Ibid., 280–82.
[107] Above, 103.
[108] TNA, SP 63/234, ff 46–7 (*CSPI, 1615–25*, 127–28).
[109] Between August 1617 and February 1618, nine people from Armagh and two from Cavan were pardoned (*CPRI, Jas I*, 325, 330, 341). In December 1615 there had been royal criticism that 'the multiplicity of pardons had multiplied offenders' and pardons were only to be granted after due deliberation and with reasonable fines (*CSPI, 1615–25*, 101–105).
[110] TNA, SP 63/234, ff 63–3v (*CSPI, 1615–25*, 135–36).
[111] Bod. Lib., Carte MSS, vol. 62, fol. 398 (*CSPI, 1615–25*, 153).
[112] *Hastings MSS*, iv, 48.
[113] TNA, SP 63/234, fol. 72 (*CSPI, 1615–25*, 139–40).
[114] Ibid. See Moody, *Londonderry Plantation*, 178.

death of Hugh O'Neill in 1616 may be seen as marking the end of a phase of native resistance to the plantation.

4. Government policy, 1615–18

The unrest of 1615–16 underlined the need for renewed pressure on the settlers to fulfil their conditions. At the same time the government was unwilling or unable to exert stern pressure and with the need to conciliate the native Irish little direct action was taken against them at this time.

Bodley's report of 1614 had not impressed the king and he wrote in March 1615 to Chichester expressing his dissatisfaction with the 'slow progress' of the plantation:

> Some few only of the servitors and natives [had] as yet performed the conditions of the plantation; the rest (for the greater part) [had] either done nothing at all, or so little, or ... to so little purpose that the work [seemed] rather to be forgotten ... than to be advanced, some having begun to build and not planted, others begun to plant and not build, and all of them in general retaining the Irish style, the avoiding of which was ... the fundamental reason of the plantation.[115]

He had made a list of defaulters who would 'be sure to feel the effect of his displeasure as there shall be occasion'. He would consider it no injustice to resume the lands of defaulters and allot them to worthier individuals, but for the meantime he would make a further concession. Though the deadline for performing the plantation conditions had passed he would permit an extension, which would be 'final and peremptory', until the end of August 1616. Bodley was then to conduct a further inquiry, when Chichester should dispossess all defaulters 'without respect of persons'. To ensure that no grantee should plead ignorance of his defects, Bodley should immediately inform each of his particular shortcomings.[116]

The king's letter did cause some anxiety though no concerted government action followed either then or in 1616. John Rowley, the agent of the Drapers' company in Londonderry urged his employers to action in May 1615. The king's letter he stated had not only activated the agents of the other London companies 'but also all the servitors and undertakers'.[117]

[115] *Phillips MSS*, 47–9; *CSPI, 1615–25*, 25–6, 120.

[116] Ibid. The king's criticisms were not the only ones. Chief Justice Denham in 1615 criticised the planters' slowness to create freeholders (*CSPI, 1615–25*, 67). In 1617 on the inauguration of a new Irish chief justice Francis Bacon pointed out that the 'bane of a plantation is when the planters ... make such haste to a little mechanical present profit, and disturb the whole frame and nobleness of work for times to come'. They must be therefore kept to their conditions (ibid., 166–67).

[117] Moody, *Londonderry Plantation*, 164–65.

There is evidence too that Bodley carried out his 1616 survey in about November[118] (it has not come to light) though the immediate action which the king had ordered seems to have been overlooked. If in July 1617 the Londoners were accused of breach of conditions,[119] this was by the English privy council, the Dublin government was less vigorous.

However, in August and September 1617 an attempt was made to ensure compliance with the regulation governing natives on undertakers' lands which may have resulted from a further royal direction. The evidence has only survived for Londonderry but it seems apparent that the intention was a general one. Local commissioners were instructed to give 'public warning' that all the natives within that county residing on undertakers' lands should 'immediately without any further stay' remove themselves to the lands of the church, the servitors, or the native freeholders. If they should 'importune' for a delay they might be given until 1 May 1618. For failure to comply at that date they should suffer such 'fines ... penalty or ... punishment' as the deputy or council should see fit to impose.[120] However, no removal took place.

In 1618 an important modification of policy was implicit in a proclamation issued on October 1 by the Dublin government.[121] The proclamation commanded the removal of the Irish from undertakers' lands before 1 May 1619. However, if they had not removed by that date they should be fined at the rate of ten shillings sterling and afterwards at whatever rate the deputy and council should appoint. This was, in effect, a tacit recognition by the government that it could not, or would not, enforce the plantation regulations on this crucial issue. Instead they would convert the necessity to petty financial advantage. Economic and indeed political necessity – the needs of the undertakers for tenants and the desire of the government not to create further tension – combined to assure the retention of the natives.[122]

In 1618, also, it was decided that the militia or outrising of Ireland should be mustered and trained regularly. The reason, however, was not primarily due to the Irish situation. The outbreak of the Thirty Years' War had caused alarm in England and a mustering of the English forces was ordered in February of that year.[123] The same reasons obviously dictated

[118] Ibid., 177–78.

[119] Ibid., 178.

[120] *Phillips MSS*, 49–50.

[121] Steele, *Proclamations*, ii, 22, no. 224.

[122] Carew noted in 1618: 'The British plantation already effected, although in the managing thereof the natives have been justly dealt with has left discontented humours in them.' (*Cal. Carew MSS, 1603–24*, 386–87).

[123] *Acts of the privy council of England, 1613–31* (14 vols, London 1921–64), *1618–19*, 362–69.

the decision with regard to Ireland. The Ulster settlers had been required to have arms available 'to furnish a competent number of men for their defence' who should be mustered every half year 'according to the manner of England.'[124] On 8 May the king, on the advice of the deputy, decided to appoint two muster masters, one of whom, Capt. George Alleyne, became responsible for Ulster and Leinster.[125] Alleyne's inspection was the first to be carried out in plantation Ulster.[126]

St. John was to negotiate with the localities for the payment of the muster masters who were to receive remuneration after the manner of England.[127] On 10 July he wrote to the justices of the peace of the counties in Ulster and Leinster informing them of Alleyne's appointment and intention to begin his duties immediately, and requiring them to inform the landowners in their counties of this, and make arrangements both as to time and place, for the mustering and training of the militia.[128] On July 18 Alleyne was given corresponding instructions, and required to report what defects he might fine.[129] Alleyne reached agreement with the counties along the following lines: that he should muster and train three times yearly, once in person and twice by deputy; that he should be paid at the rate of 6d. per ballyboe on muster days; that he should bring with him one drum and two sergeants to assist in training. The training centres were agreed on and the contract was to be in force from year to year until dissolved by the majority of the justices of the peace for the county.[130]

Alleyne proceeded to his task and provided figures of those who attended for the nine counties of Ulster with a report on the difficulties he encountered.[131] Calculating on the basis that the six escheated counties contained 197,000 acres, and that 24 men were musterable per 1,000 acres, he computed that 4,728 men should appear, that is he took the numbers of tenants required by the articles of plantation as being the norm also for muster purposes. By these calculations he concluded that Armagh should muster 528 and Cavan 588. However he found that there appeared in all only 1,966 men, with 230 muskets, 408 calivers, 664 pikes, 90 halberts, and 1,141 swords[132] only 41.5 per cent of his required total. Such a response

[124] For a study of this see L. Boynton, *The Elizabethan Militia, 1558–1638*, (London, 1967).

[125] Bod. Lib., Carte MSS, vol. 62, fol. 481. The other was Nicholas Pynnar.

[126] His report, with transcripts of related documents is BL, Add MS 18,735 (*CSPI, 1615–25*, 220–30).

[127] *CSPI, 1615–25*, 227.

[128] Ibid.

[129] Ibid., 228.

[130] Ibid., 229–30.

[131] BL, Add. MS 18,735.

[132] Ibid., fol. 5. The calendared version has slight inaccuracies. Faulty additions by Alleyne in his return for Cavan have also been corrected and these figures correspondingly modified.

would not be unexpected if English attitudes at this time may be taken as a guide. Writing with particular reference to the reign of James I, Dr. Boynton states 'during the seventeenth century the theme becomes one of growing slackness in the militia.'[133]

In Armagh and Cavan he found 238 and 541 men respectively, this is 44 per cent and 92 per cent of the required number. In Armagh there were mustered 25 muskets, 48 calivers, 92 pikes, 2 halberts, and 124 swords. In Cavan there were 55 muskets, 109 calivers, 235 pikes, 36 halberts, and 389 swords. Four undertakers in Oneilland produced no men at all for musterage: Cope, Brownlow, Stanhowe, and Heron. Sacheverall, with 48 men, mustered about three times as many as his fellows. The Scots in the Fews, John Hamilton, and Archibald and Henry Acheson, mustered between them 128 men which was only 4 less than the requirement.[134] In Cavan, as we have seen, the attendance rate was very much higher and was also fairly consistently so. None of the servitor grantees had mustered men or arms. Apart from the small attendance of men in Armagh, most noteworthy of comment is the small number of muskets shown. Both counties produced only 80 between them. It may be pointed out that in England in 1618 calivers as musterable weapons were forbidden and the changeover to muskets was proceeding rapidly.[135]

It is clear from his observations that Alleyne had not found his task an easy one. He found that there were no fines exacted for non-appearance at muster. He wished in future to be aided by two justices of the peace of each county, particularly to provide against more than one landowner mustering the same men and arms

> for let me muster in one county … today, tomorrow the most of these men and their arms do meet me in the next county to muster again. Thus they defraud your majesty.

He wished also for clarification as to the number of type of arms that each undertaker should muster. He found in both provinces a general reluctance to pay him his dues. Leinster and counties Londonderry and Down refused outright, and the other Ulster counties as a result became recalcitrant. Under-sheriffs and bailiffs were availing of the opportunity for extortion so that 'in levying six pence for [Alleyne they] extort twelve pence for themselves'.[136] He asked for confirmation in the office and emoluments for

[133] Boynton, *Elizabethan Militia*, 11–12.
[134] This takes account of the land lost by Claud Hamilton to the dean of Armagh.
[135] Boynton, *Elizabethan Militia*, 238.
[136] *CSPI, 1615–25*, 229.

life and also a proportion of the fines to be imposed on defaulters. He requested that the clergy should find men and arms 'as customably in England'.[137] He further observed that he had found Antrim and Down 'better planted with English and Scottish than some of the escheated counties of Ulster'.[138]

Another, though abortive, decision of 1618 is of considerable interest. This was that the Ulster planters should choose an agent who would channel their petitions and grievances to the king and transmit decisions back to Ulster, thereby dealing with the problems of 'all such new beginnings' as the plantation then presented. The idea arose out of a suggestion of the 'British undertakers' which was accepted by the king, as also was the person chosen to represent them, on 1 August 1618.[139]

> He saw that not only would it lead to the avoydinge of great chardges w'ch a journey hither might drawe them unto [but also] they may the better attend at home for p'forming of those condic'ons whereunto by covenant they are bounde.

The person chosen was a Scot, Sir William Alexander, later to be earl of Stirling. Alexander had apparently little or no connection with plantation Ulster at this stage. However, he later had claims to land in Donegal and acquired property in Armagh,[140] and was to be responsible for a major if abortive colonial scheme for North America.[141]

The relationship between the Dublin government and the agent was broadly defined in the king's letter to the deputy:

> our pleasure is whensoever at any tyme wee shalbe pleased to declare our will unto you … either for all the said undertakers or for ony one of them by the said Sir William that the same be obeyed as delivered by an officer whome we specially trust and this much you shall signifie unto them.[142]

It was not, manifestly, to be a startling limitation of the power of the Dublin government, though given the subsequent history of the plantation such an agency might have acquired some permanence.[143]

[137] Ibid., 228; though, see Boynton, *Elizabethan Militia, passim*, on this.
[138] Ibid., 228.
[139] BL, Add. MS 4794, ff 435v–36.
[140] Hill, *Plantation*, 507–508, 562–63.
[141] *DNB*, i, 275–80.
[142] BL, Add. MS 4794, ff 435v–36.
[143] Its mooting reflected somewhat on the efficiency of the Dublin administration, though the relationship of the Irish government to the parent body was by no means clearly defined.

However, on October 12 the king countermanded his decision:

> forasmuchas wee have since considered there is noe business of that kingdome of greater consequence and that more required a great experience in him that should deale in it, as also that, God be thanked, wee have found by experience since [August 1] that we are not so much importuned with theire complaints as might require a p'ticular men to bee designed for that purpose,

he was therefore well pleased to cancel the arrangement.[144] Perhaps this was in response to protest from Dublin. Sir Francis Blundell, a member of the Dublin administration, would be retained as general intermediary on Irish affairs between Dublin and the king.[145]

5. Pynnar's survey

In March 1618 the English privy council informed the deputy that the king required a full investigation of the plantation to be carried out, and that thus informed he intended to 'take that advantage of those that had so grossly failed as eyther in lawe or policy of state he may justly doe'.[146] Nicholas Pynnar, who had been appointed one of two joint successors to Bodley as overseer and director general of fortifications and plantations in February,[147] was assigned the task. Pynnar had some previous knowledge of Ulster. He was a grantee in Cavan, and he had visited the Ulster forts in 1617.[148]

The survey was postponed for a number of reasons. As St. John wrote on June 29 the Longford plantation was then in hand and 'the overseers … must spend a good part of this summer in measuring the escheated lands' there.[149] St. John also pointed out that most of the bonds and patents of the undertakers had not been sent from England or Scotland and requested that transcripts of these be sent to Dublin.[150] On August 11 when the bonds of the English undertakers had arrived, he wrote requesting the patents and also the bonds taken in Scotland. Thereby he would be the 'better enabled to give … an account of the state of the plantation.'[151]

In September the possibility that some of the settlers would forfeit their estates was seriously held. Lord chief justice Jones wrote on the matter in

144 *CSPI, 1615–25*, 214; BL, Add MS 4794, fol. 444.
145 Ibid. Perhaps also the appointment of a Scot to such a position provoked strong reactions in Dublin. He was also probably a person of dubious standing.
146 *Acts privy council, 1617–19*, 97; Moody, *Londonderry Plantation*, 184.
147 BL, Add. MS 4794, ff 390v–91.
148 TNA, SP 63/234, ff 44 154–55 (*CSPI, 1615–25*, 187–88).
149 Ibid., ff 185–86v (ibid., 200–202.
150 Ibid.
151 TNA, SP 63/234, ff 209–10 (*CSPI, 1615–25*, 207–208).

cryptic terms to Sir Richard Boyle at Youghal.[152] Manifestly these were people anxious to benefit from any dispossessions that might occur.

The inquiry was eventually carried in the winter–spring of 1618–19. On November 27 the lord deputy gave instructions to Pynnar and others unnamed who were entrusted with the task which included the administration of the oath of supremacy to the undertakers and their tenants and dependants.[153] The report, which seems to have been principally Pynnar's personal achievement, states that the survey was carried out between 1 December 1618 and 28 March 1619.[154]

His general conclusions hardly require restatement.[155] In the six counties he found planted 1,974 families, a figure resulting from faulty arithmetic and which should read 1,980, making in all 6,215 'bodies of men', and so implying on average 3.1 men per family. These he subdivided both by county and by type of tenure. His total of families was composed of 334 freeholders, 99 lessees for lives, 1,013 lessees for years, 464 cottagers, and 70 'families with no estates', a category presented for Donegal only. His totals of adult males per county were as follows: Armagh 642, Cavan 711, Fermanagh 645, Donegal 1,106, Tyrone 2,469, and Londonderry 642. His finding for Armagh and Cavan were sub-divided as follows: Armagh – freeholders 39, lessees for lives 18, lessees for years 190, cottagers 43 totalling 290 families stated to make 642 men and so implying 2.2 men per family; Cavan – freeholders 68, lessees for lives 20, lessees for years 168, cottagers 130 totalling 386 families and containing 711 men and so implying 1.8 men per family. Professor Moody has shown that his figure of 642 for Londonderry was miscalculated and too small,[156] and it will be seen below that Pynnar's totals for Armagh and Cavan are also difficult to reconcile with his figures for individual estates within those counties. However, Pynnar was himself sceptical of these figures, positing 8,000 adult males as the likely plantation population. At the same time he concluded that 'the fourth part of the land was not fully inhabited'.[157] As to buildings, these were 107 castles with bawns, 19 castles without bawns, 42 bawns without castles or houses, and 1897 dwelling houses of stone and timber after the English manner, in villages, 'besides very many such houses in

[152] Grosart, *Lismore Papers*, (2nd series), ii, 132–33.

[153] Hill, *Plantation*, 449–51. Hill failed to see that the mandate he quotes was issued by, and not to, the lord deputy.

[154] Ibid., 451. There are two MS versions of the report: (a) Lam. Pal. Lib., Carew MSS, 613 (*Cal. Carew MSS, 1603–24*, 392–423), and (b) TCD, MS 864, printed in W. Harris, *Hibernica*, 2nd edn. (Dublin 1770), 139–241 and Hill, *Plantation*, 451–590. References below are to Hill's edition.

[155] Hill, *Plantation*, 588–90; see Moody, *Londonderry Plantation*, 185–86.

[156] Moody, *Londonderry Plantation*, 187–90.

[157] Hill, *Plantation*, 589.

several parts which I saw not'.[158] Yet there was a great lack of houses both in villages and dispersed.

He appended also various telling observations. The permanence of the colony was not yet guaranteed. Many of the English tenants did not yet till their lands, and lacked the confidence to provide themselves with cattle or labourers. Similarly the Irish (on undertakers' land) felt insecure and so grazed the land rather than tilling it. But for the Scots, who were cultivators, the colony would be liable to starvation. Landlords were too prone to let land at high rents to the Irish. The colony was indeed in a two-fold way dependent on the natives:

> If the Irish be put away with their cattle the British must either forsake their dwellings or endure great distress on the suddain. Yet the combination of the Irish is dangerous to them, by robbing them and otherwise.[159]

Economics and security were thus precariously balanced. The Irish were to be found most densely in County Londonderry. For Armagh and Cavan the following assessment of the survey had been attempted, proceeding, as before, with the barony as the most convenient unit.

In **Oneilland** two estates had changed hands since Bodley's 1613 survey. St. John had, as has been seen,[160] acquired the Rev. James Matchett's estate, Matchett having in 1613 decided on a clerical career in the Armagh archdiocese.[161] The other sale, by Rolleston of Powell's proportion, brought in a new English owner, Michael Obbyns, from Rutlandshire.[162] John Brownlow's estate, with his death, had become joined to his son's. Two of the nine owners were definitely absentee, St. John as deputy in Dublin, and Stanhowe, who had been in England 'these seven years'.[163] Rolleston and Sacheverall appear to have been temporarily absentee. On all estates except Stanhowe's there was positive evidence of endeavour, but individual practice continued to offer variation.

Buildings of varying type and permanency and at differing stages of completion were evident on all estates except Stanhowe's, who had 'nothing at all built'.[164] Cope and Sacheverall had large bawns of either lime and stone, or stone and clay, each 180 feet square. Each had four flankers. Cope's arrangement (his earlier house had fallen) being to design these for

158 Ibid.
159 Ibid., 589–90.
160 Above, 105.
161 *CPRI, Jas I*, 234; PRONI, T975/2, 4.
162 PRONI, Lodge, records of the rolls, v, 521.
163 Hill, *Plantation*, 561–62.
164 Ibid.

habitation rising to three storeys. Sacheverall, more typically, had constructed a 'good house' of lime and stone within, the bawn being defensive in conception.[165] However, elsewhere the bawns were either made of timber or timber and sods some having pallazados and moated. Brownlow was replacing one such with the stipulated bawn of lime and stone. There were also two houses, one being on Dillon's proportion and incomplete, unenclosed by bawns. There were in all nine bawns. The manor houses were built either of stone, stone and brick, or, in St. John's case, of 'cage work'.

Some had produced small settlements, the nucleus of later villages and towns. Brownlow's Lurgan was the most impressive, consisting of forty-two houses, paved streets, and two water-mills and a windmill. Obbyns' Portadown was at this stage, more typically, a grouping of four houses around his own house and bawn. All of the undertakers, save Stanhowe, had caused small clusters of houses to be built. Thus, for example, Sacheverall had twelve houses, Rolleston nine, and Cope fourteen. John Dillon had 'great store of tenants' who had made two villages and dwelt together. The settlement pattern revealed on St. John's proportion is well described.[166] He had two strong timber bawns in each of which there was an 'English house' of cage work, with two English families in them. Near to one of these there was a grouping of five houses 'inhabited with English families'. In the return for his tenants he is stated as having four cottagers each with a 'tenement', a 'garden plot', and commons for their cattle. The rest of the tenants lived 'dispersedly upon the land [though in this case] three or four families together'.

Since the numbers of houses in these villages correspond fairly closely to the numbers of cottagers recorded for estates it is safe to assume that the villages must have been for the most part occupied by people of this type. The pattern of settlement by tenants was apparently, for the most part, dispersed despite the requirements of the plantation conditions.

The number of tenants per landlord varied immensely. Brownlow had fifty-seven families who with their undertenants numbered 100 men; Stanhowe had 'not above three or four poor English men upon the land'. In Oneilland as a whole Pynnar found 30 freeholders, 155 lessees for years, 18 lessees for lives, and 11 cottagers whose families made up in all 390 adult men. This excludes the 'three or four' on Stanhowe's estate and the landlords. The required total was 396, and the required number of freeholders was 33. Apart from the fact that the settlement structure of each

[165] Hill omits part of the report on this estate. See, *Cal. Carew MSS, 1603–24*, 416.
[166] Hill, *Plantation*, 557–58.

estate did not always follow closely what was required, in numbers, the plantation in the barony had reached its norm, the lapses of individuals being counteracted by the modest excesses of their neighbours.

Pynnar's evidence in some points may be faulty both with regard to this barony and in general. His numbers of freeholders do not always withstand close scrutiny.[167] Beyond stating that Brownlow had 'good store of tillage' and three mills 'all for corn' – Cope also had three mills – he gives no indication of how the land was used. All the men he found in the barony were stated to have arms, and Brownlow had 'store of arms in his house'. It is unlikely, however, that such a uniform situation pertained.[168]

His statements, and omissions of them, about the numbers of Irish on the proportions also tend to undermine confidence in his thoroughness. Only in the cases of Brownlow and Stanhowe are the Irish referred to. With regard to the former that there was 'not one Irish family upon the land' is demonstrably false[169] though his statement for the absentee Stanhowe, that 'all the land is inhabited with Irish', was broadly inescapable. Further, he was instructed to administer the oath of supremacy yet only some of Cope's and St. John's and all of Brownlow's tenants are stated as having taken it. Thus he either neglected to proffer the oath widely, or encountered opposition to taking it. On the whole, however, the impression from his report of general energy and progress in this barony seems undoubtedly an accurate one.

The Scottish barony of the **Fews** where, as we have seen,[170] three estates had become the property of Sir James Hamilton's brother John, also provided evidence of general expansion. Only one original owner, Henry Acheson, who had by now disposed of his acquisition of Douglas's lands to his brother Sir Archibald,[171] retained possession of his 1610 grant. Hamilton, who lived either in Down or Cavan, was absentee, but the Achesons may both have been resident.[172]

[167] Below, 266–9.

[168] However, it would be dangerous to accept the evidence of musters as conclusive either.

[169] Below, 219.

[170] Above, 102–03.

[171] An inquisition of *c.* 1630 states that Douglas sold his estate to Henry Acheson in 1611 and that it was not until 28 August 1628 that Sir Archibald acquired it, acquiring his brother's at the same time (*Inq. cancel. Hib. repert.*, ii, Armagh (42) Chas I).

[172] Some scant notes on the Acheson family preserved in Belfast (PRONI, T906/2), and which make use of Hill's work, state that Henry's health did not allow him to live in Ireland. See also Hill, *Plantation*, 284 and Lodge, *Peerage* (ed. Archdall), vi, 81. He appears, at any rate, to have been temporarily present at this time. Sir Archibald was probably too much of a public figure in both Ireland and Scotland to be a permanent resident. In 1621 and again in 1625 he was appointed a master of the Irish chancery to facilitate the acclimatisation of his countrymen to legal procedure in Ireland (BL, Add, MS 4794, ff 584v–85; Hughes, *Patentee Officers*, 1). He was also for a time secretary of state for Scotland and had a house in Edinburgh. He died in Letterkenny in 1634.

Pynnar found some 285 men present, or more than double the required 132. This represented a fourfold increase on the 1613 figure, but 60 per cent of all resided on Archibald Acheson's estate. His 29 families of tenants with their undertenants made up 144 men and in addition he had built a 'town' called Clancarny – Markethill – where he had 29 tenants each with small parcels of land. However, Henry Acheson, while having a 'great number' of tenants had failed to grant leases 'but by promise and yet they have been many years upon the land'.[173] Two claiming freeholds and seventeen claiming leaseholds appeared before Pynnar, took the oath of supremacy, and petitioned to be granted their leases. This Acheson seemed willing to do 'presently'. Elsewhere in the barony leases seem to have been generally granted. In some instances on Archibald Acheson's estate there were joint tenancies. Pynnar found thirty-two cottagers in the barony (excluding the residents of Markethill), approximating closely to the number of houses found near the settlers' bawns. Each had a house and garden plot and commons for cattle. All the tenants except Archibald Acheson's are stated to have taken the oath of supremacy. All are reported as armed, Archibald Acheson being said to have 'great store' of arms in his bawn adequate for 129 men.

On each estate the building requirements with regard to bawns appear to have been adequately complied with, and substantial bawns had been erected in all cases but two with clusters of houses to the number of six or seven around them. The accumulation of five estates into the hands of three owners, however, seems to have affected the building of manor houses. These appear to have existed only the two Acheson estates. Archibald Acheson had a bawn with four flankers constructed for living in, and had begun a castle 80' x 22' which was then two storeys high. With regard to land use there is only the unqualified statement for Henry Acheson's estate that 'here is great store of tillage'.[174]

In **Orior** by this time Audley had transferred ownership to his son-in-law, Davies, and Capt. Smith is clearly accorded the ownership of Williams's proportion.[175] There had thus been no significant change of ownership.

Comparative equality in building was now being achieved through the belated, though it seemed pressing, action of Bourchier and Smith. Davies's property was unique in its conspicuous lack of development whereas Poyntz, who already had a house and bawn completed, but 'not liking of the seat', had begun a new bawn and brick house and had workmen 'labouring very

[173] Hill, *Plantation*, 565–66.
[174] Ibid.
[175] Above, 90.

hard' with the intention of completing it by August. St. John's stronghold, it was noted, had not progressed since Bodley's description, but the 'town' – Tandragee – had increased in buildings all filled with British tenants.

There were many absentees, Poyntz and Smith being present, but St. John, Davies, Moore, and Bourchier all had outside interests. An 'Irishman' was living in Moore's bawn. Nonetheless there are some indications, apart from building activities, that the plantation had not merely brought change of ownership. St. John's village had English inhabitants as well as nine Irish families 'who come to church' and had taken the oath of supremacy. However, Davies had 'not so much as an English tenant on the land.'[176] There should have been at least ten adult British males present.

In the English barony of **Loughtee** in Cavan three of the seven estates had changed hands since Bodley's inquiry. Sir Nicholas Lusher had sold his land in March 1616 to Sir George Mainwaring from Shropshire,[177] and his son William had disposed of his estate to Peter Ameas, a none-too-successful purchaser, by June 1618 when he appears as collector of the subsidy for the county.[178] Sir Hugh Wirrall's estate had been mortgaged or sold twice by this stage. It was held by Thomas Mountford, who had been an unsuccessful candidate for land at the time of allocation,[179] between December 1613 and November 1614[180] and was in the possession of a Mr. Adwick at this time. Otherwise the original owners remained actively in occupation, and the state of the barony gave evidence of their vigour. Only Mainwaring appears to have been absentee.

On all estates except two, Adwick's and Waldron's, bawns and 'castles' are described as 'long since finished' or of 'great strength'. Waldron's stone house was completed and occupied, but his bawn was of sods and 'much of it … fallen down'.[181] Adwick's house had remained unfinished for two years, and no bawn had been constructed.

The number of British males recorded by Pynnar was 439, which does not include the unspecified number of residents in Belturbet. It represents a substantial increase on the 1613 figure of about 170 and was about half as much again as the plantation requirements demanded. He breaks them down into the following sub-division: 41 families of freeholders (25 were required), 101 families of leaseholders (most were lessees for years, 15 held for three lives), and 63 cottagers. The latter would appear to have lived in

176 Hill, *Plantation*, 570.
177 *Inq. cancel. Hib. repert.*, ii, Cavan (23) Chas I.
178 NAI, Ferguson MSS, xi, 271.
179 Hill, *Plantation*, 149.
180 *Inq. cancel. Hib. repert.*, ii, Cavan (16) Chas I.
181 Hill, *Plantation*, 461–62.

the planters' villages. Waldron's town was composed of 31 houses inhabited with English, Fishe had two villages, one of them possibly Stradone, of 10 houses each. The existence of villages, in this barony did not then imply a strict compliance with the projected arrangement. However, Taylor had a group of 7 freeholders, 7 lessees for years, and 10 cottagers on his estate who lived 'most of them'[182] in a village of 14 houses, presumably Ballyhaise. In all there were 6 villages owned by 5 of the undertakers. They were essentially small dwelling settlements, but in two, which stood upon a 'road way' there was a 'good innholder' and in another a windmill was sited. The incorporated town of Belturbet which was not markedly different in character is examined in a separate section.[183]

There were five mills in the barony, two for corn and one, on Sir Stephen Butler's estate, which was a fulling mill. There are only two references to the rural economy, indicating that there was 'a little' or 'no great store' of tillage. The oath of supremacy is referred to only in the case of Taylor's tenants. Neither Mainwaring's, Ameas's, nor Adwick's tenants were armed. The others satisfied Pynnar in this respect, some being 'very well armed', and Sir Stephen Butler was 'able to arm 200 with very good arms which are within his castle, besides others which are dispersed to his tenants for their safeguard'.[184]

In **Tullyhunco** the impact of ownership change and death can be seen on two estates. Sir Claud Hamilton, who had taken over his father's, Sir Alexander's, estate had died *c.* 1616[185] leaving the land in the hands of his widow, who was resident, his son Francis being a minor. Sir Claud's own estate, Clonmeen, which had been sold in 1611 to John Hamilton who, in turn in 1614, had sold to William Lawder who moved there from the Fews and died in 1618, was at this point reacquired by Sir Alexander for the use of his grandson.[186] Craig and Acheson, who was absentee, retained their acquisitions in this barony the former having also purchased the lands of Brian McKiernan, some 2,225 acres, in 1615.[187]

Only on Hamilton's Clonmeen estate had no stronghold been erected. However, the other Hamilton structure and that of Sir James Craig, both commended in 1613, were now 'thoroughly finished'.[188] Craig had built a platform designed for two small pieces of cannon. Acheson had a bawn but no house. On Hamilton's Clonmeen estate there was a 'town' of twenty-

182 Ibid., 460–61.
183 Below, 252–4.
184 Hill, *Plantation*, 465.
185 *Inq. cancel. Hib. repert.*, ii, Cavan (37) Chas I.
186 Ibid., (24) Chas I.
187 *Inq. cancel. Hib. repert.*, ii, Cavan (27) Chas I.
188 Hill, *Plantation*, 469–70. Craig's castle was five storeys high.

two houses – Killashandra – and Craig appears also to have had a village of similar size.

The colony numbered about 200 adult males at this stage.[189] A large number were cottagers, but the minimum required, 144, had been well surpassed. It is clear, however, that there were serious defects in the organisation of estates in this Scottish barony. On the Clonmeen estate there were no estated tenants, Lady Jane Hamilton claiming that she could not grant valid leases and her son was underage. Acheson's tenants had not 'taken out' their leases (which Pynnar saw 'drawn and signed') and most of them refused the oath of supremacy until they received their leases. It is of interest, as a criticism of Pynnar, that although he makes this comment Pynnar nonetheless particularises Acheson's tenants as two freeholders and nineteen leaseholders. Pynnar reinforces Bodley's evidence about English tenantry being brought in as well as Scots[190] by stating that Acheson's following was English as well as Scottish in origin. Only some of the tenantry had taken the oath of supremacy. There is no reference to arms, or to the agricultural pursuits of the barony.

A very dynamic situation was revealed in the other Scottish barony of **Clankee**, presenting a marked contrast to the 1613 situation. Only one of the original four owners, William Bailie, remained and the other estates were in the hands of John and William Hamilton as well as their brother Sir James. This noteworthy incapacity of original Scottish grantees had been seen also in the Fews. John Hamilton acquired Ralston's lands in June 1613,[191] the precise date of William's purchase is not known. The Hamiltons had exploited the opportunities provided by their base in Down, and the size and energy of their family to expand into plantation Ulster and take over from their less able, substantial, or persevering countrymen.

The Hamiltons, a well-cooperating family, had now interests in three Ulster counties, Armagh, Cavan, and Down. John is described by the family historian as 'a prudent person and painful man',[192] and William as 'a prudent industrious and pious man, very useful in the country, and to my lord Clandeboy'.[193] Sir James, who clearly supervised the family enterprise, came in for praise for his methods of estate management. He was 'careful and wary' in granting leases for longer than three lives 'and went that length but with very few'.[194] He made 'great use' of his brothers and nephews as

189 In one case the number of men is not given, but only the number of families. In all there were 107 families, 85 of which produced 180 men.
190 Above, 92.
191 Above, 102.
192 T.K. Lowry (ed.), *The Hamilton manuscripts* (Belfast 1867), 44.
193 Ibid., 45.
194 Ibid., 36–7.

well as various business agents.[195] Both John and William were brought to Ireland by their brother. John was at first employed as Sir James's law agent and he seems to have continued in this capacity even after he acquired his own estates.[196] William was also employed in estate management[197] as well as acquiring land for himself in Down and Cavan.

On the estates vigorous, if belated, energy was being displayed. Each had its stone-built bawn, and all had houses or castles, some incorporating defensive arrangements, at various stages of building. Sir James Hamilton's Castle Aubigny, with the king's arms cut over the gateway and located 'upon a meeting of five beaten ways, which keeps all that part of the country',[198] was five storeys high, well defended with four round flanker towers, and was in use and completed save for slating. However, the other houses were at earlier stages of construction. On the estates of William and John Hamilton village building had begun. John had eight houses 'joining to the bawn' and also a water-mill and five house 'adjoining' it.[199] There were five houses near William Hamilton's bawn. Each had a roughly approximate number of cottagers.

Pynnar found in the barony 178 men. This exceeded the required minimum of 144 but a high proportion were cottagers. At the same time the required number of freeholders is recorded. Almost all are stated to have taken the oath of supremacy and to be armed. Bailie and Sir James Hamilton were stated to be in occupation. However, the latter's chief residence was at Killyleagh in County Down.[200] It is not known if John Hamilton was resident at this stage, though he was in 1621.[201] William lived chiefly in Down. With regard to three of the four estates – he makes no comment on Sir James Hamilton's – Pynnar found 'good tillage and husbandry after the manner of the English'.

The fortunes of the Cavan servitors continued to present mixed impressions. In **Castlerahan** two estates, those of Fettiplace and Taaffe, as has been seen,[202] were at the mercy of commercial transaction, being now held by Sir Thomas Ashe. Ashe had also acquired Garth's property, and Ridgeway's estate, and with it responsibility for the town of Virginia, had been purchased by Sir Hugh Culme. Only one original British servitor,

[195] Ibid., 31.
[196] Ibid., 12; John Hamilton to Lord Clandeboy, 10 May 1621 (PRONI, T808/2758).
[197] Lowry, *Hamilton Manuscripts*, 12.
[198] Hill, *Plantation*, 452.
[199] Ibid., 454.
[200] On 9 July 1619 in a letter written from Dublin he refers to having been in Clankee (Lowry, *Hamilton Manuscripts*, 12).
[201] PRONI, T808/2758.
[202] Above, 104.

Elliot, remained in possession, and the others' lands had, at least for the moment, been accumulated into the lands of Ashe and Culme.

Such discontinuity of ownership was not without effect. Not even Elliot could possibly have been resident. On all lands except Culme's the Irish were the exclusive tenantry. However, buildings of some kind were not in evidence on all estates. On Ashe's estates there were an old castle 'now monded',[203] a 'very good'[204] bawn of lime and stone, and a bawn of sods respectively. Elliot had a bawn of lime and stone and a 'small house'[205] within it. On Culme's purchase the foundations evinced in 1613 were now reaching completion. A bawn of lime and stone, flankered, and strategically placed had been erected and a house within of the same materials was being completed. On the estate there were four English families. The town of Virginia boasted eight timber houses built by Culme and inhabited by English. Reference is made to the minister who was a 'very good preacher' and kept a school.[206]

In **Tullygarvey** ownership had remained unchanged since 1613. On the Culme-Moore estate the bawn was 'thoroughly finished'[207] and the house almost so. Moore was resident but the brothers Ashe lived outside the plantation area and Culme elsewhere in the county. On the Ashe estate there were two bawns though not of masonry and no house. The Old English Capt. Richard Tirrell had built a 'strong'[208] bawn, but granted no leases. Apart from four English families on the Culme-Moore estate, the land in the barony was entirely in Irish hands.

In **Clanmahon** two of the smaller grantees, Atkinson and Jones, had disposed of their estates. The result was the accumulation of more land by Lord Lambert who acquired Jones's[209] and Archibald Moore who acquired Atkinson's.[210] Advances in building also altered the 1613 picture. Bawns and houses had been built on all estates except perhaps Russell's. On Lambert's original estate there was a stone house and bawn 'long since finished'.[211] Fleming, the Old English proprietor, had also built a bawn and house. None of the British servitors appears to have been resident. However,

[203] Hill, *Plantation*, 457.
[204] Ibid.
[205] Ibid., 458.
[206] This was most likely George Creighton who was admitted in 1619 and was there in 1641 (NLI, MS 2685, 283) rather than Benjamin Culme, Sir Hugh's brother, who became dean of St. Patrick's Dublin, in 1619, as Hill suggests (Hill, *Plantation*, 458).
[207] Hill, *Plantation*, 458.
[208] Ibid., 460.
[209] Lambert had died in June 1618 (*Inq. cancel. Hib. repert.*, ii, Cavan (6) Jas I).
[210] Pynnar appears to be incorrect in stating that Russell had also sold his land to Moore.
[211] Hill, *Plantation*, 468.

Lambert had 'and English gentleman' resident on each of his estates and on his recent acquisition there were three other families living 'about the bawn' each holding land for twenty-one years.[212]

In **Tullyhaw** it emerges that Pynnar had disposed of his own estate to the absentee surveyor-general William Parsons.[213] Otherwise the only development recorded since 1613 was on the Talbot-Culme estate where a castle and bawn had been completed.

The most general comment that can be made on the servitors in Cavan is that through the sales of the less substantial grantees, one of whom Pynnar, preferring to remain in public service, their land had, at this stage at any rate, with the exception of Pynnar's sale to Parsons, come into the hands of their more substantial fellow grantees in the county thereby decreasing the number of British proprietors. This was further an unhappy development because with the exception of Culme and Moore, these owners were not resident in the county. It is unlikely that there were more than thirty British males in all four servitor baronies.

By way of conclusion it may be stated that Pynnar's survey reveals that it was only at this stage that the plantation requirements in building and planting had been reached on most estates. There were also some conspicuous delinquents as well as hesitancies, and the ownership changes and land accumulations revealed were also discordant with the plantation scheme.

The numbers of British males present derived from an examination of Pynnar's report on each estate are not consistent with his own tabulated returns. Furthermore, Pynnar did not report on ecclesiastical, monastic, and college land and provides no figures for the towns of Armagh, Charlemont, Cavan and Belturbet. For Armagh Pynnar's evidence indicates the presence of 685 adult males in the baronies of Oneilland, Fews, and Orior, yet his own figure was 632. His returns for the planters' lands in Cavan suggest a population of some 847 British males which is considerably higher than his own figure of 711.

Densities of English in both counties, calculated on the basis of the real acreages of estates, were very similar. In Cavan the Scots had planted just somewhat more densely than their English counterparts. In Armagh, however, the Scots, with 5 per cent of the land, had planted 285 men, the English, with 21 per cent, having planted 390, i.e. the Scots had planted three times as densely as the English. The 'daily' departure of Scots to Ireland had been noted in 1615[214] yet at the same time it must be

212 Ibid. One tenant received a lease in April 1618 (*Inq. cancel. Hib. repert.*, ii, Cavan (6) Jas I).

213 Parsons took out a patent in October 1619 (*CPRI, Jas I*, 445–47).

214 *CSPI, 1615–25*, 85.

remembered that Scottish proprietors in Cavan had sought tenantry from England as well as Scotland.[215]

It is clear that at least a small number of estates in both counties had not measured up to the standards of the plantation conditions. Nevertheless there is little or no evidence that punitive measures were taken against offenders. Apart from government laxity or disinclination procedure by king's letter leading to regrants had presumably protected some delinquents. However, in January 1620 one Armagh undertaker, William Stanhowe, was summoned into the exchequer court for non-performance of his bond to build and plant, on his estate. He was given 'further time' until Michaelmas 1621 by the deputy and council.[216]

[215] Above, 92, 122.
[216] NAI, Ferguson MSS, xii, 27.

CHAPTER 4

Progress and Problems, 1619–25

1. Military Aspects

The progress of the colony must be viewed against a background in which the attitude of the native population is important. In 1618 a commentator, while admitting that 'all make a fair show of quiet', recognised that 'the hearts of the people are now (as ever heretofore) alienated from the crown of England' and that therefore 'treasons like snowballs crescent eundo'.[1] His immediate fear was for the reaction to the Longford and Leitrim plantation schemes, feeling that where colonies were already established there was least danger.

However, by the following year disaffection was rife in Ireland and in Ulster in particular. In February 1619 the government admitted that although the king had more power in Ireland than any of his predecessors, reports of 'stealths, robberies and outrageous acts' were coming in from all parts.[2] The 'poor army' was in arrears and the forts in disrepair, those in Ulster and Connacht being in 'so greate decay' that they were 'likely to become utterly unserviceable'.[3]

The outbreak of hostilities on the Continent – the Thirty Years' War – combined with events in Scotland presented some external stimulant to unrest in Ulster. In the spring of 1619 there was violence in the Scottish highlands and islands which was in part occasioned by the absence of Archibald Campbell, 7th earl of Argyll, who had left Scotland at the end of 1618. Argyll had previously been a powerful agent of royal expansion in Scotland but, seriously in debt and converted to Catholicism, he quitted Scotland and entered Spanish service.[4]

This went not unnoticed in Ulster. In March 1619 the Irish government reported to London that many people 'eager after alteration' had been 'easilie induced' by the priests to believe that Spanish plans included a descent on Ireland. The influence of Scottish disorder, and expectations from Argyll's defection were also pointed to:

1 *CSPI, 1615–25*, 233–34.
2 TNA, SP 63/235, ff 17–17v (*CSPI, 1615–25*, 240).
3 Ibid., ff 19–20v (ibid., 240–41).
4 R. Chambers, *Domestic annals of Scotland from the reformation to the rebellion*, vol. 1 (Edinburgh & London 1858), 499–500; *DNB*.

> the most suspected people of Ulster betake themselves to their swords ... and so much harken after the Erle of Argile, and ... the Redshanks of Scotland (by the ports under Sir Hugh Montgomery and Sir James Hamilton) more frequently convey themselves to-and-fro than they were wont.[5]

The areas in Ulster where disaffection spilled over into local insurgency were particularly the 'fastnesses' between Tyrone and Londonderry. By the autumn St. John was able to report some measure of success in dealing with the situation in the country at large. Order had been largely maintained, as it had been in 1615 and 1616, by the use of provost-marshals and the questioned expedient of pardons. In addition Irish spies had been employed and undesirables encouraged to enlist abroad.[6] No serious eruption took place and the situation in Ulster was characteristic of a supine social system under pressure. A considerable proportion of some £1,500 paid in concordatums in the year ending April 1619 was expended to provost-marshals for the maintenance of order in Ulster.[7] In June 1619 the government petitioned to be allowed spend £500 per annum in addition.[8] Beyond the evidence of pardons nothing specific can be said about unrest in Armagh and Cavan. Between July 1619 and February 1621 thirty-two people from Armagh, including O'Hanlons, O'Neills, O'Donnellys, and McCourts, and eight from Cavan, mainly O'Reillys and O'Gowans, received royal pardons on payment of fines.[9]

It was emerging, it would appear, at this time that unrest of the type affecting Ulster could best be dealt with by provost-marshals with ad hoc commissions. The Ulster forts, so important in the Elizabethan wartime strategy, were now in disrepair and whatever their value as a physical deterrent, the efficiency of their servitor-commanders had been previously, though it would seem unfairly, called into question.[10] It was at any rate unusual for a fort-commander to hold a commission as provost-marshal though Capt. Hugh Culme of Cloughowter was provost-marshal of Cavan and Monaghan in the years 1617–19.[11] Many of the commanders had acquired plantation land and developed lay interests. By 1619 the military

5 TNA, SP 63/235, 44 23–23v (*CSPI, 1615–25*, 242).

6 Ibid., 55–55v (ibid., 250); ibid., ff 86–8 (ibid., 262–63); ibid., ff 91–91v (ibid., 265); ibid., ff 98–98v (ibid. 265).

7 Ibid., ff 33–42v (ibid., 245–47).

8 Ibid., ff 53–53v.

9 *CPRI, Jas I*, 435, 460, 474, 497, 511.

10 Above, 74–6.

11 TNA, SP 63/234, ff 70–3v; /235, ff 35–42v (*CSPI, 1615–25*, 194–96, 245–47).

value of these forts was limited. In February and June St. John reported that the forts of Ulster and Connacht were likely to become 'utterly unserviceable' unless immediately repaired.[12] The problem was related to the provision of finance for the army.

Early in 1620 a proposal was made, or received, concerning the inland forts of Ulster and Connacht. This was by Sir Thomas Dutton, the Irish scout master general,[13] to the English privy council that he should be enabled to dispose of these to the commanders then in occupation who in return for payments to Dutton should become the owners and receive patents. The privy council informed Dublin of the proposal and asked for advice.[14] The Irish government replied ambiguously enough on May 20, but enclosed a statement on the current tenures of the forts.[15]

Three forts in Armagh and one in Cavan were reported on. As to Mountnorris it was stated that Annesley was now owner[16] and that the ward was discharged. Moyry castle and lands were held by Capt. Anthony Smith by twenty-one year lease from 1608. There was in the fort a constable, a porter, and eight warders, 'it being a fitt place to continue a ward'. Smith was bound to keep the castle in repair. Charlemont, held in lease by Caulfeild, and where his company lodged, was also considered a 'fitt place' to continue a garrison. In Cavan the island fortress of Cloughowter and its lands were held by Culme under a twenty-one year lease from February 1620.[17] He was required to keep the fort in repair, but the ward was discharged. It was stated that this fort had been chosen as a detention place for priests, that £200 had been consequently expended on it, and that it was now ready for use whenever 'it shalbe thought fitt'.

In July the privy council asked for a more exact account of each indicating which were necessary and which dispensable and also the amount of land allotted to each.[18] To grant them in perpetuity, they felt, could not save money:

> the saving must be either in repairs or in discontinuing the wards. For the first, those that have them in lease are always tied in covenants for reparation, and for the latter it is advised that the wards be continued.

[12] TNA, SP 63/235, ff 19–20v, 55–55v (*CSPI, 1615–25*, 241, 250).
[13] Hughes, *Patentee Officers*, 45.
[14] *Acts privy council, 1619–21*, 159.
[15] TNA, SP 63/235, ff 156–9 (*CSPI, 1615–25*, 283–6: inaccurate).
[16] Above, 104.
[17] *CPRI, Jas I*, 461.
[18] Marsh's Library, Dublin, MS Z4.2.6, 451–2; TNA, SP 63/235, ff 181–81v (*CSPI, 1615–25*, 293).

The Irish government had avoided any opinion on whether such action was militarily advisable.[19]

However, on October 29 the king informed St. John that he had approved Dutton's scheme.[20] He was therefore to make grants of the forts of Moyry and Charlemont in Armagh and Cloughowter in Cavan with others in Antrim, Fermanagh, Monaghan, and Leitrim, with their lands, to the present possessors. Since these grants were being made at the instance of Dutton any forts the occupants of which had not compounded with Dutton and taken out patents within one year should be granted to Dutton himself. By accompanying instructions[21] the grantees were to hold in free and common soccage, pay the present rents, and undertake to build castles and bawns, where absent, within three years. These were to be kept, under penalty, in continual good repair, the owners to maintain in them such number of men as should be necessary to defend them in time of peace. They should not alienate without license, or to people unconformable, or at all to the Irish and should not demise any part of the land to the Irish for longer than twenty-one years. In times of emergency the king should have power to put such garrisons into any of the forts as the deputy should think fit.

The working out of the arrangement took some time and came in for criticism before it was completed. Commissioners who conducted an inquiry into Irish affairs in 1622[22] were critical at least in some cases. Cloughowter – as well as Toome and Enniskillen – were considered 'very necessary' and the disposal of Mountnorris, earlier, and Moyry was also regretted.[23] In January 1623 a stay was put on the granting of all land in Ireland to prevent crown loss through dubious practices.[24] This was not specifically directed against the implementation of Dutton's scheme, but Falkland, the new lord deputy, commissioned Pynnar to examine the Irish forts generally and estimates for their reparation.[25] Falkland presented his report to London in September with the suggestion that if the forts were not

19 They further felt that 'they may not grant away that w'ch hath been won w'th much bloode … and that w'ch hath been excepted by name in all the king's grants especially his Ma'tie having so little crown land in that kingdom' (ibid.). On these see Marsh's Library, Dublin, MS Z4.2.6.

20 TNA, SP 63/235, ff 199–200 (*CSPI, 1615–25*, 292, 300). If the forts of Donegal and Lifford were found to be inland forts they were to be treated in like manner.

21 TNA, SP 63/235, ff 201–201v (*CSPI, 1615–25*, 300–301). *CPRI, Jas I*, 484–5.

22 Below, 135–56.

23 NLI, Rich Papers, MS 8014/5, Army: 24 July 1622 (see also TCD, MS 808, fol. 46 and Marsh's Library, Dublin, Z3.2.6, no. 43).

24 Below, 155.

25 TNA, SP 63/237, ff 113–13v (*CSPI, 1615–25*, 429). His estimates were lower than the earlier ones of Bodley, but totalled for all Ireland, £2,841. 13. 4. On Moyry, Mountnorris, and Cloughowter he recommended that £50, £40 and £150 respectively should be spent. The latter figure makes it seem unlikely that Cloughowter had been repaired as stated above.

repaired it were better that they should be razed.[26] In June Dutton petitioned the council in London about the 'stoppage' of the grants of the inland forts[27] and despite uneasiness in Dublin the arrangement was not contravened.

Sir Toby Caulfeild was the first in our area to compound with Dutton. In December 1622 he paid him £200,[28] and on 1 March 1623 took out a patent of the buildings and lands of Charlemont.[29] He was given rights to hold fairs and markets, an indication that the fort area was developing with a civilian centre. Smith also compounded for Moyry, though it is not formally recorded.[30] In December 1624 Culme received a grant of the fort and lands of Cloughowter, which referred to his agreement with Dutton of the previous year, under conditions which accorded with the general instructions.[31] The scheme thus took complete effect in our area, though not it seems so completely or smoothly elsewhere.[32]

The granting of the forts was not an act based on blind unawareness of danger. Scarcity of public money was a stark reality of the period. However, it was not as money-saving as expected. It seems that in many of the forts' garrisons were retained as accustomed at least for some years.[33] Expenditure on maintenance and repairs only was saved. The decision to dispose of the inland forts indicates presumably a confidence that there was less danger from insurrection than invasion.

There is no immediate subsequent evidence for the state of Cloughowter.[34] Charlemont appears to have been kept in good repair after it was granted to Caulfeild.[35] One irregularity was condoned in the case of Moyry. In 1623 Smith sought permission from the deputy to settle the lands on his son-in-law. The person concerned, a certain Charles Brennan, was a native Irishman and had paid £200 to the suppliant. Falkland and the council granted the request, Brennan being conformable in religion and known to be 'of very honest and civill carriage having been bred from his youth in and about the citty'.[36]

26 Ibid.

27 TNA, SP 63/237, fol. 54 (*CSPI, 1615–25*, 411).

28 *CPRI, Jas I*, 562–3.

29 Ibid.

30 Marsh's Library, Dublin, MS Z3.2.6, no. 60.

31 *CPRI, Jas I*, 586–7.

32 See ibid., 572; Marsh's Library, Dublin, MS Z4.2.6, 618–9; NAI, Lodge, Records of the rolls, v, 52–3.

33 NLI, Rich Papers, MS 8013/1 (establishment of 1622); TNA, SP 63/237, ff 34–5v (*CSPI, 1615–25*, 405–6) (establishment of 1623); *CSPI, 1625–32*, 195–9 (establishment of 1626).

34 Note in pencil reads 'on Cloughowter and Culme's patent in 1639 see NAI, Lodge, Records of the rolls, vi, 272–4.

35 BL, Add. MS 24,200, 37: 'The state of the forts in Ireland in 1624'. This report by Pynnar refers to 'the late Lord Caulfeild' and so was probably written after his death in 1627.

36 Marsh's Library, Dublin, MS Z3.2.6, no. 60.

In 1622 permission was given for enlisting Irish in foreign service. In May and June the king gave permission for recruiting in Ireland on behalf of the king of Spain for service in Flanders, by five captains of Irish or Old English descent.[37] The activities of one of these, John Maguire, in Ulster caused apprehension. Falkland reported on October 1 that he 'loitered' in Ulster and did not control his men 'whereby spoils and robberies were frequently committed, and the good subjects grieved and terrified.'[38] He was himself 'spying, prying, and riding' in Fermanagh, Monaghan, and Donegal 'and other countries', making contacts with 'all the principal and dangerous persons'.[39] The deputy placed restrictions on his actions and he left Ireland in the spring of 1623.[40] The affair had no serious consequences but it maintained contacts between the native Irish in Ulster and émigré Irish on the continent.

Apart from seasonal violence which in these years caused apprehensions for the security of the 'inhabitants of the plantations'.[41] Anglo-Spanish relations produced a heightening of tension which affected Ulster, though it is difficult to give it a locational reference. Anglo-Spanish marriage negotiations, commenced early in 1623, caused apprehension in England, but encouraged Catholic Ireland. Early in 1623 disaffection in Londonderry provoked government intervention.[42] It was not limited to Derry, however, and in July Falkland reported that in the planted areas of Ulster and Leinster the settlers were disheartened 'being continually terrified and oppressed with burglaries, robberies and outrages'.[43] The matter was the more serious, he felt, because of the general poverty and absenteeism amongst the planters.

In Armagh only one case of terrorism comes to light. Four O'Neills captured a certain Sir Benjamin Thorneborough near Armagh at Easter 1623 'and carried him away to the woods'. They offered to release him in return for a pardon. However, the government took energetic action, procured his release, and banished his captors 'to the service of foreign parts' for seven years.[44]

In Cavan and adjacent areas the implications of the proposed match were being drawn. In October Sir Hugh Culme reported that an assembly

37 *Acts privy council, 1621–23*, 233, 271; *CSPI 1615–25*, 363; Jennings, *Wild Geese*, 27–8. This was recommended by commissioners in 1621 (*CSPI 1615–25*, 328–30).

38 TNA, SP 63/236, ff 201–2v (*CSPI 1615–25*, 393–4).

39 Ibid.

40 TNA, SP 63/236, ff 215–16v; /237, ff 1–2 (*CSPI 1615–25*, 398).

41 Ibid., ff 201–2v (ibid., 393–4) deputy and council to privy council, 1 October 1622.

42 Moody, *Londonderry Plantation*, 212–15; *CSPI, 1615–25*, 428–9.

43 TNA, SP 63/237, ff 91–91v (*CSPI, 1615–25*, 423).

44 Ibid., ff 45–5v (ibid., 407–8).

of twelve friars in their robes had taken place in the town of Cavan attended by at least 2,000 people – doubtless an exaggerated figure – 'to the terror of the poor English that dwelt in those parts'.[45] The deputy, aware that such meetings were common 'out of confidence of the match', stated that he would make every effort, however difficult, to suppress them.[46]

The failure of the marriage negotiations in October 1623 heightened rather than alleviated apprehensions. There were now fears of invasion,[47] and 'the destruction of the plantations and the restitution of all men to their lands again'.[48] Fears that a Spanish invasion was imminent and would aim at Ulster were expressed in the following years:

> The north is the place most to be feared, where the counties of Tyrone and Tyrconnell bordering upon Londonderry is most affected by their chiefs, which places with the rest of the escheated counties and … Antrim should be well provided with armed and trained soldiers to resist them.[49]

Inland counties, such as Armagh and Cavan, did not pose the particular problems associated with invasion. However, there were some unsettling rumours current between the end of 1623 and 1625. In January 1624 a settler farmer in Cavan deposed before a justice of the peace that a friend 'one Humphrey Welch' who had moved to neighbouring Leitrim had, during a visit, affirmed that it was 'reported by the Irishe in that place … that the earl of Westmeath [previously baron of Delvin and a Cavan landowner] should be the king of Ireland'.[50] However, Westmeath protested his loyalty, and (despite Falkland's suspicions of him and the earl of Antrim with whom he had marriage ties)[51] Welch, 'one singular baggage fellow'[52] was taken prisoner and confessed that he had spoken 'much to the wrong' of Westmeath.[53]

45 Ibid., fol. 124. Capt. Arthur Forbes who had land in Longford and who had married the widow of Sir Claud Hamilton reported a similar meeting at Granard and stated that if they recurred 'if God would give him grace he should make the antiphonie of their mass be sung with sound of musket' (ibid. fol. 125).

46 TNA, SP 63/238, Pr 1, ff 11–12v (*CSPI, 1615–25*, 455–6); /237 fol. 122 (ibid., 432–3).

47 In March 1624 Annesley wrote to Sir Edward Conway that 'the breach of the match with Spain and the likelihood of troubles to ensue thereupon is the received belief of the discontented multitude of the kingdom' (*CSPI, 1615–25*, 473–4).

48 TNA, SP 63/237, fol. 122 (*CSPI, 1615–25*, 432–3).

49 TNA, SP 63/238, Pr 2, fol. 55 (ibid., 510–11).

50 Ibid., fol. 112.

51 *CSPI, 1615–25*, 476.

52 Ibid., 485.

53 TNA, SP 63/238, Pr 2, ff 136–6v (*CSPI, 1615–25*, 482).

There was a further report of a rising current at Belturbet at this time. A young boy living in or near the town was warned to secure his safety 'for before Mayday [1624] thou shalt see that the English are destroyed for there is help coming.'[54] In Belturbet there was a particular scare, one of the constables of the town having been warned to 'set a strong watch for there will presently be a rising'. The rector in a letter of April 17[55] to Charles Waterhouse, probably the chief officer, urged him to bring gunpowder, there being very little available in the town 'and that which is the Irish send to buy it up.' There is no evidence of this kind of apprehensiveness in Armagh.

Throughout the province provost marshals and others remained active and characteristic techniques for the preservation of order were employed.[56] However, the situation remained one merely of emergency even after war between England and Spain broke out when the humiliated suitor became king as Charles I.

As a result of the fear of invasion, however, it was decided in the summer of 1624 that 2,500 soldiers, referred to as the 'new levies' for Ireland, should be sent over from England.[57] The special needs of Ulster 'which lies most open to foreign invasion and where the inhabitants are most rebellious' were recognised when in April 1624 Sir John Bourchier recommended the erection there of two new coastal forts.[58] In 1624 also, the council of war in London regretted the alienation of the inland forts and directed that men should be sent whenever necessary to secure them 'though in private hands'.[59] They also recommended the building of a 'smale sconce at the four mile water not far distant from the castle of the Moyrie' at a cost of £200.[60]

It was felt also that Ulster colonists should be provided with arms at their own expense and that 'all the able and unsuspected persons' be enrolled, mustered, and trained. It was suggested that a captain 'of prime quality' with subordinate officers should be appointed superintendent of the planted counties, his fees to be locally raised, to train the 'enrolled soldiers' and lead them in time of danger in association with the regular army.[61] It was with

54 Ibid., ff 129–30v (ibid., 479–80).

55 Ibid.

56 A letter from William Caulfeild, Sir Toby's brother, to Falkland, 15 April 1624 is of interest with regard to the methods used in Tyrone (BL, Sloane MS 3827, ff 41–2).

57 TNA, SP 63/238, Pr 2, ff 57–63, 64–70 (copy), 72–2v (abstract) (*CSPI, 1615–25*, 511–14). At this time the army in Ireland consisted of 1,350 foot, 400 horse and a small number of warders in forts (A. Clarke, 'The army and politics in Ireland, 1625–30', *Studia Hibernica*, iv (1964), 28–9). See also Moody, *Londonderry Plantation*, 216).

58 TNA, SP 63/238, Pr 2, ff 124–5v (*CSPI, 1615–25*, 479).

59 Ibid., ff 62–3 (ibid., 512).

60 Ibid.

61 Ibid., fol. 55 (ibid., 510–11).

such plans – for the expansion of the army and the revival of the muster in Ulster – and the fears that inspired them that the reign of James I ended.

2. The inquiry of 1622

In 1618, as we have seen,[62] it was in effect recognised that the removal of the native Irish from undertakers' lands was unlikely to be effected, and therefore that their presence should be penalised and seen as a source of petty government revenue. In April 1619, by which time Pynnar's survey had indicated beyond doubt their general presence,[63] the king appointed Edward Wray, a groom of the bed-chamber, to be collector of all the fines of the Irish in Ulster for seven years paying an annual rent of £100.[64]

If this decision reflected a realistic new departure in government policy, it was but one aspect of that policy the other side of which concerned the undertakers themselves. On September 8 the king indicated[65] that although many of them had forfeited their estates by breach of conditions, all would be granted new patents if they would double their rents and pay fines to be agreed on between them and the deputy. The new patents were to remedy defective title and would not release them from performance of their conditions. If they refused the offer they could expect the 'extremetie of the law'. These two decisions form an important stage in the development of government policy, but there were to be subsequent refinements, and some years passed before new patents were taken out.

In 1620 attention was turned once again in England to the plantation.[66] On November 9 the Irish committee of the privy council report to the king on a petition referred to them by a deputation of the Ulster planters.[67] Sir James Craig and Sir John Fishe appear to have made up the delegation and though the petition has not survived it was probably the same as that presented to the commissioners of inquiry by Craig in 1622.[68] It stated what in fact were Pynnar's figures for the numbers of castles and bawns built and added that there were 30,000 British whereof 8,000 could bear arms. But it also asserted that twenty-three undertakers had sold their estates through the rigour of the conditions, and asked that in new patents they might retain Irish labourers on half of each estate in return for a doubling of rents. The committee recommended that, while disapproving

[62] Above, 110.
[63] Though the report was not despatched to England until May 7 (*CSPI, 1615–25*, 247–8).
[64] Ibid., 244; *CPRI, Jas I*, 443; Moody, *Londonderry Plantation*, 191.
[65] Marsh's Library, Dublin, MS Z4.2.6, 420–1.
[66] In June St. John was instructed to take particular care of its administration (*CSPI, 1615–25*, 287).
[67] TNA, SP 63/236, ff 19–19v (*CSPI, 1615–25*, 322–3).
[68] NLI, Rich Papers, MS 8014/3: Plantations, 11 May 1622.

of alteration of the articles of plantation, they would permit such Irish as were conformable and would take the oath of supremacy to be tenants of one-fourth of the undertakers' proportions. Should they demise more than this proportion to Irish they should forfeit the profits of such land for the time it remained in Irish occupation. No undertaker or British tenant should retain in his house any Irish servants except two for each plough used in tilling, though they might also hire masons, hedgers, ditchers, and other labourers if conformable. The undertakers were allowed until 1 May 1622 for the removal of the Irish to the segregation area on each estate. Provision was to be made for the taking of the oath of allegiance by tenants. It was also suggested that 'these favours' should only be accorded to those who had built and planted as required and withheld from others until they had done so.

In February 1621 the lord keeper directed the attorney-general on royal instructions to draw up a warrant on these lines as the basis of all regrants.[69] On July 27 the privy council considered the matter, deciding that the king should be advised to take no action until a further survey of the plantation had been carried out.[70]

It was against this background of a changing government policy that a new and comprehensive survey of the plantation was carried out in 1622. At the same time Grandison was recalled as deputy, and Falkland appointed in his place. In 1621 commissioners, mostly members of the Irish council, had reported on the 'grievances of the realm of Ireland'.[71] As to the plantations they recommended that all absentee undertakers should be required to live on their estates and build and plant, otherwise their profits should be seized. Nonetheless Ulster grantees should not be discouraged by any granting away of their lands as concealed or defectively held, and the king was requested to confirm their titles if they so desired. The change in deputy was not availed of to appoint a broadly-based commission to inquire into the entire state of Irish political and religious life.

The commissioners, appointed in March,[72] were twenty in number, about half high Irish officials and the others prominent men sent from England. Early in April they began work in Dublin, where they remained actively until the end of July and they were dissolved on November 19.[73]

69 TNA, SP 63/236, fol. 19v (endorsement).

70 *Acts privy council, 1621–3*, 28–9.

71 TNA, SP 63/236, ff 41–6v, 47–9v, 50–1v (abstracts) (*CSPI, 1615–25*, 328–30); BL, Harleian MS 3294, ff 19–25.

72 *CPRI, Jas I*, 549.

73 Exeter College, Oxford MS 95, 137; TNA, SP 63/236, fol. 211; *CSPI, 1615–25*, 345, 396; BL, Add. MS 36,775, fol. 279.

They devoted one day in the week to plantations,[74] requiring reports from government officials of whom the surveyor, and attorney-general, the auditors, and the clerk of the council were particularly taxed.[75] In this way a body of detailed information was systematised for the first time. They acquainted themselves with proprietors' names, their conditions, bonds, and covenants, and studied previous surveys particularly Pynnar's.[76] They dealt with agents and individual petitions, received deputations from the planters as a whole and made orders and decisions. They familiarised themselves with the amounts of glebe and termon and erenach lands, and ex-monastic land in some cases, as well as the details of revenue and lists of rent arrearages.[77] They were thus well equipped to conduct a perambulation of the plantation. Some of their proceedings may be discussed here, particularly those concerning our area.

Statistics of annual revenue from Ulster were assembled. The 'certain rents', those which were beyond doubt payable, from Ulster stood at £4,140. 5. 0. in 1615 and had been raised by 1621, through grants of concealments and the like, to £4,450. 1. 7.[78] 'Doubtful rents' in 1621 stood at £64. 5. 0.[79] These were largely from grants pre-dating the plantation, for example of termon lands, or from small concealments. 'Good arrears' in 1621, that is the sum arising from individual failures to pay 'certain rents' had accumulated to £1,342. 9. 5.[80] The income from the fine on native introduced in 1619 was noted,[81] as also the income, £100 per annum,[82] arising from the fine imposed on the Irish for the native custom of ploughing by the tail. This practice in Ulster was first penalised in 1606, from 1612 a fine of 10/- per plough was levied, and its collection farmed at £100 per annum.[83] Statistics for Armagh and Cavan may be presented as follows. They were not assembled in a totally systematic manner but the following table presents them, where available, under the same headings, for 1620 and 1621.

74 Exeter College, Oxford, MS 97, 3, 35.

75 Ibid., *passim*.

76 NLI, Rich Papers, MS 8014/2: Rich's notes, April 18.

77 Ibid., MSS 8013, 8014, *passim*; Exeter College, Oxford MS 95, *passim*.

78 These figures were taken from BL, Add. MS 18,022, fol. 38v. A list in NLI, Rich Papers, MS 8013/6 is £100–200 higher for the later years. However, three other documents in Rich Papers, MS 8013/3, 6, support the lower figures.

79 NLI, Rich Papers, MS 8013/3.

80 Ibid., MS 8013/6. A statement in MS 8013/3 places this at £1,272. 16. 11.

81 Ibid., MS 8013/6; BL, Add MS 18,022, fol. 38v.

82 Ibid.

83 Moody, *Londonderry Plantation*, 342–3.

	1620	1621
Armagh:		
certain rents	440. 17. 11.[84]	
good arrears	73. 0. 8.[85]	67. 2. 5.[86]
doubtful rents	2. 0. 10½[87]	
Cavan:		
certain rents	773. 5. 1¼[88]	
good arrears	63. 19. 2.[89]	193. 4. 1.[90]
doubtful rents	41. 10. 1½[91]	

The lists from which the arrears figures have been computed indicate that on the whole it was the native Irish grantees or Old English landowners who were most prevalently in arrears, though cases of land which had changed hands rapidly also feature, hence sales had affected the income of the crown as well as the progress of the plantation. Thus in Armagh arrears are listed in the cases of Art McBaron O'Neill, Henry McShane O'Neill and others of that name as well as O'Hanlon and other Irish grantees. In Cavan we find Old English proprietors in the same position. Lord Aubigny had rent unpaid as well as Peter Ameas and Sir James Craig. Rent for fairs and markets was due from the burgesses of Cavan and the archbishop of Armagh. It is not surprising in view of pre-plantation charges there that 'doubtful rents' from Cavan accounted for two-thirds of the Ulster total.

The commissioners found that some Ulster sheriffs had not accounted,[92] though also that the legal system for Ulster and Leinster was more efficiently administered than for the other two provinces.[93] They found that money had been collected in Cavan by Sir Stephen Butler towards building a sessions house.[94]

The commissioners' presence in Ireland also gave opportunity for the rehearsal of grievances. On July 3 the 'natives' of Cavan presented a petition about termon land which 'came to nothing' by the upholding of the 1610 decision that this should be episcopal property.[95] At about the same time

84 NLI, Rich Papers, MS 8013/6.
85 Ibid., MS 8013/4.
86 Ibid. There is some doubt as to the year to which this figure applies.
87 Ibid.
88 Ibid., MS 8013/6.
89 Ibid., MS 8013/4.
90 Ibid. There is some doubt as to the year to which this figure applies.
91 Ibid.
92 Ibid., MS 8013/4.
93 Ibid., MS 8013/3.
94 Ibid., MS 8014/5: Rich Journal notes, July, October, November. In Fermanagh Sir William Cole had collected £500 or £600 for this purpose (ibid.).
95 Ibid.

Conn McShane O'Neill and Sir Connor Maguire (both grantees in Fermanagh) sued for the removal of the imposition on ploughing by the tail.[96] The commissioners, however, felt that 'so barbarous a custome' was without justification. Against the assertion that English methods were impracticable they posited the practice of Sir James Hamilton in Cavan of ploughing by placing three or four horses with 'English traces' one before another. However, they felt that the best way to eradicate the custom was that the sheriffs should break ploughs used in the Irish manner rather than have fines imposed. They felt that preventive or remedial measures were preferable to penalising, but permitting the practice.[97]

A number of individual grievances were also submitted. Thus Sir Turlogh McHenry O'Neill petitioned for five 'parcels' of land in the Fews.[98] A petition from Sir Thomas Ashe was commended to London immediately after the commissioners' dissolution.[99] He claimed that he had received a grant of lands in Cavan from Queen Elizabeth[100] which he had surrendered to accommodate the plantation scheme. He claimed that St. John had made a compensation order for him, but this had not been fulfilled and he petitioned for recompense in the 'new plantations'.

The most serious problem with which the commissioners were confronted was the question of new patents for the undertakers and requiring a related recommendation on the conditions of the Irish inhabitants on undertakers' lands. On April 26[101] Sir James Craig and Sir John Fishe were requested to appear before them with evidence to support the petition they had presented to the king on this matter in 1620.[102] On May 11 Craig re-presented the proposals.[103] It was admitted in discussion that it would be impossible to 'rid out' the Irish, but it was felt that they should be confined to one-fourth part of each estate. There was also doubt as to whether the planters' agents were adequately empowered to negotiate.[104] Discussion was resumed on May 18 when both Fishe and Craig appeared, and while there was still doubt as to their competence they showed signed authorisations from the owners of all but 20,000 acres who had not yet been consulted.[105]

96 Ibid.
97 Ibid., MS 8014/5: 'heads of the king's casuall revenues'.
98 Ibid., MS 8014/5: Rich notes July 5 (difficult document).
99 TNA, SP 63/236, ff 213–14v (*CSPI, 1615–25*, 396).
100 See Cal. fiants Ir., Eliz., no. 5736.
101 Rich had made notes on the problem as early as April 18 (NLI, Rich Papers, MS 8014/2).
102 Exeter College, Oxford, MS 95, 18; NLI, Rich Papers, MS 8014/2.
103 NLI, Rich Papers, MS 8014/3: Rich's notes, May 11.
104 Ibid.
105 NLI, Rich Papers, MS 8014/3: Plantations, 18 May 1622; TNA, SP 63/236, ff 160–1v (*CSPI, 1615–25*, 357–8).

By the end of May the commissioners had reached a decision,[106] and on June 22 they submitted their proposals to the undertakers,[107] a copy being sent to London at the same time for approval.[108] In essence they accepted the scheme proposed by the Irish committee of the privy council in 1620. They agreed that one-quarter of each undertaker's estate should be 'sett out' for the Irish, who is possible should be made to dwell together in segregated communities. Only those Irish who were conformable in religion, wore English clothing, ploughed after the English manner, and would undertake to bring up their children 'in learning' or to some trade or husbandry were to be accepted as tenants in this area. Such 'receaved' tenants were to have tenures for twenty-one years or three lives, and should enclose the fourth or fifth part of their profitable land, or so much above that as was demanded of them by commissioners to be appointed for this purpose. For lands granted to Irish for a term of under twenty-one years the undertaker was to pay a fine of 10/- per family and forfeit the land for that time and any land granted to Irish for over twenty-one years was to forfeit unconditionally. These recommendations were embodied in the report.[109]

The commissioners did not make any firm recommendations as to the rents and fines to be paid following on regrants. In the letter to the privy council of June 22, however, they advised that the undertakers should be dealt with 'gentlie and fayrelie' and their new patents not laden with severe penalties for breach of conditions which could too easily be 'drawne into some subject's hands' and so be 'vexatious' to the planters. They should be required to treble their rents on the basis of the existing estimates of their acreages, suggesting that the undertakers would accept such terms rather than 'hazard' the outcome of a new measurement. A concomitant of the new arrangement, and one which would be demanded by the undertakers, would be the recall of Wray's patent and the termination of the penalties levied under it.[110] The absenteeism of Ulster planters was also criticised sharply, the commissioners stating that this must of necessity 'debilitate'

[106] Exeter College, Oxford MS 95, 57; NLI, Rich Papers, MS 8014/3: Rich's notes, May 24.

[107] NLI, Rich Papers, MS 8014/7: Propositions made by the commissioners to the undertakers.

[108] TNA, SP 63/236, ff 160–3v (*CSPI, 1615–25*, 356–8).

[109] BL, Add. MS 4756, fol. 118v. Commissioner Rich appears to have seen the segregation arrangement as in itself only temporary. He felt that, as at that moment there were said to be forty Irish to one English on the estates, the undertakers should be bound to bring in a certain number of British tenants each year, and as these increased the Irish to be excluded. He also advised that the servitors should be required to have British tenants on a fourth part of their estates (NLI, Rich Papers, MS 8014/3: Rich's notes, May 18). However, these opinions were not embodied in the report.

[110] TNA, SP 63/236, ff 160–61v. Wray's position was commended to Falkland in November (BL, Add. MS 36,775 ff 159v–80).

the strength of the colony, and pointing out that the consequent drainage of money from Ireland 'must be noe smalle detriment to the realme'.[111]

The next and final stage of the commissioners' work on plantations, turned to at the end of July, was to carry out an estate by estate survey. They received permission to do this in small groups provided that the report was made a joint responsibility.[112] They spent August viewing their allotted areas, being provided with instructions and memoranda,[113] and also receiving certificates from the planters which appear only to have survived for Armagh and Tyrone.[114] In Ulster each group was allocated two counties to examine. Three commissioners were concerned with Armagh, Caulfeild, Sir Dudley Digges, and Sir Nathaniel Rich. While Caulfeild was a landowner in the area, neither Digges nor Rich, both of whom had come from England, had local vested interests. Rich is of special interest because so many of his papers have survived.[115] He was a businessman with legal training who sustained an interest in Irish affairs as a member of the standing commission on Irish affairs set up by the privy council in 1623.[116] The commissioners for Cavan were Sir Francis Annesley and Sir James Perrot. The evidence assembled is examined below along the lines applied to earlier surveys.

In **Oneilland** as elsewhere the information available reflects the thoroughness of the inquiry. Two estates had in effect changed hands since Pynnar's survey. Heron sold his estate to Sir John Dillon, a newcomer to Ulster proprietorship who was probably not Old English, on 25 March 1621[117] and Rolleston who had mortgaged his estate to Sir Francis Annesley in 1618 had not recovered it in 1620 when the sum involved was due to be repaid.[118] Both clerical undertakers in Armagh had now relinquished control of their estates. Two of the nine owners, St. John and Obbyns, the latter then 'a prisoner in England', were non-resident.[119] Annesley was also absentee, but Rolleston resided on the estate.[120] Stanhowe, who had been a persistent absentee, was now resident.

It is clear that trends evident in 1619 had not changed. The weaker undertakers then had not substantially improved their position in the

111 Exeter College, Oxford MS 95, 79.
112 TNA, SP 63/236, ff 159–9v (*CSPI, 1615–25*, 356).
113 NLI, Rich Papers, MS 8014/7.
114 NLI, Rich Papers, MS 8013, 4.
115 Ibid.
116 V. Treadwell (ed.), 'The survey of Armagh and Tyrone, 1622', *UJA*, 3rd series, vol. 23 (1960), 127–8.
117 *Inq. cancel. Hib. repert.*, ii, Armagh (5) Chas I.
118 Below, 186.
119 BL, Add. MS 4756, fol. 108v.
120 Ibid.

interval. Thus on the Rolleston estate the commissioners noted that the buildings were 'as in Pinner's survey but decayed'.[121] Stanhowe, who had pleaded the extenuation of legal difficulties in England and was also at law with Sir John Dillon[122] had made 100,000 bricks, but had erected no stronghold.[123] The building requirements of St. John (now Lord Grandison), John Dillon, Sir John Dillon, and Sacheverall had also not been fully fulfilled.

The buildings generally show that the planters had not all adhered very closely to the required pattern. The commissioners found no more than four bawns,[124] though, on all estates except Stanhowe's, dwellings, if not defended structures, had been erected. Brownlow had replaced his ad hoc bawn of 1618–19 with one of the required type,[125] but this was a unique compliance. Cope had a 'strong house' of substantial dimensions[126] as well as a bawn with inhabited flankers elsewhere. However, many of the planters were living in smaller houses than had been expected.[127] Some were of brick, some of timber, some thatched. On John Dillon's estate the manor house was unfinished. The commissioners advised that he be pressed to complete it 'which being done will be a very good plantation'.[128] Sacheverall had leased his house and bawn and some land to the Scottish Sir Archibald Acheson who had placed a tenant there,[129] and had almost completed an alternative dwelling for his own use.[130]

The most notable change since Pynnar's time was the expansion in the size of the colony. By the most rigidly conservative calculation there were some 402 families of tenants present. This figure had been arrived at by examining the certificates of the undertakers and earlier drafts of the commissioners' report. In some cases the commissioners' scrutinisations of

121 NLI, Rich Papers, MS 8014/8: commissioners' notes on Obbyns, Stanhowe, and Annesley estates.
122 Ibid.
123 BL, Add. MS 4756, fol. 108v.
124 This must throw some doubt on Pynnar's figure of nine.
125 BL, Add. MS 4756, fol. 108.
126 See E.M. Jope, 'Moyry, Charlemont, Castleraw and Richill: fortification to architecture in the north of Ireland, 1570–1700', *UJA*, 3rd series, vol. 23 (1960), 103–4.
127 In two cases, those of Grandison and Annesley, these were described as 'small' by the commissioners.
128 TNA, Manchester papers, 30/15/2/202a. His certificate describes the house as it then was: 'Uppon this proportion is erected a bricke house 72 ft. in length within the house and 20 in breadth to which is added on the northside 27 foot in length and 20 in breadth, on the southside a porch 12 ft. more from the bottom to the top at each end a great cant window to the top of the house all the windows of freestone 2 stories, the rest of bricke the foundation of stone 3 foot and ½ thicke to the grounde table the rest of strong brick 3 foot broad in the top of the house w'ch is 40 foot high and hath 3 cornishes of freestone about the house and battlements ready. The house is not yet covered.' (NLI, Rich Papers, MS 8014/8).
129 NLI, Rich Papers, MS 8014/8: Sacheverall's certificate.
130 BL, Add. MS 4756, ff 108v–9.

the certificates, revealed in marginal notes by Rich, showed that some people claimed as tenants were absentee or departed who were nonetheless listed in the final report. In arriving at the number 402 the higher figures have been discounted in the light of the other evidence. The commissioners, however, generally did not give the number of adult males. The report ascribes 160 men to Brownlow[131] his certificate revealing 91 families.[132] John Dillon, whose 51 families were accepted by the commissioners,[133] claimed in his certificate that these contained 'no less than 300 persons ... and 100 of these all able men to do service'.[134] These figures would place the number of adult males per family in the range of 1.8 to 2. Sir John Dillon's certificate has a special value here in that it was presented in tabular form with 39, or almost all, of his families sub-divided into men, women, and children.[135] These 39 families contained 69 men or, on average, 1.77 men per family. The average family size was 5.46 persons, each family containing on average 2.08 children.[136] If one assumes the number of males per family to be in the range 1.75 to 2, the number of adult males in the barony can be suggested as lying between 700 and 800. The smaller figure, or one of slightly less, may perhaps be taken as the more accurate because some tenants sometimes held under more than one landlord.

This is a remarkably high figure, representing about a 75 per cent increase since Pynnar's inquiry. The colony, however, was by no means evenly distributed. Brownlow, Sacheverall, and Cope had the largest numbers. As to Stanhowe the report stated that there were 'not above four Englishmen on the land but it is generally inhabited with Irish as on the last survey',[137] while a preliminary draft referred to six tenants of whom three were noted as absentee, one living at Dungannon and another at Benburb.[138] Irregularities in the granting of leases were noted for Obbyns, 'a poore man',[139] and Sir John Dillon.

The report and attendant documents allows of more comment on the Oneilland colony than had been derivable from previous surveys. Brownlow's submission indicated that his village of Lurgan consisted of 47

[131] Ibid., fol. 108.

[132] TNA, Manchester papers, 30/15/2/183.

[133] BL, Add. MS 4756, fol. 109.

[134] NLI, Rich Papers, MS 8014/8: certificate of John Dillon.

[135] Ibid., /9: certificate of John Dillon.

[136] These figures indicate that colonial family sizes in Ireland were similar to those pertaining in England. See Laslett and Harrison, 'Clayworth and Cogenhoe' in Bell & Ollard (eds.), *Historical essays*, 157–84, and P. Laslett, *The World we have lost* (London 1971), *passim*.

[137] BL, Add. MS 4756, fol. 108v. His certificate claimed eleven people (NLI, Rich Papers, MS 8014/8).

[138] NLI, Rich Papers, MS 8014/8: commissioners notes on Obbyns, Stanhowe, and Annesley. Other cases of absenteeism of tenants were also revealed, e.g. one of Sacheverall's freeholders lived at Drogheda.

[139] Ibid., /7: statement on planters by Craig and Fishe, 18 May 1622.

houses occupied by a variety of artisans and others many of whom also held small holdings of land.[140] On the estate where there were 46 British tenants, there was one cooper, one glover, one shoemaker, three carpenters, three weavers, two turners, and two labourers with small acreages. The remainder were for the most part defined as yeomen or husbandmen, though a few were gentlemen. All held land, mostly not more than sixty 'accres', the majority having between ten and thirty acres, though some had less. The largest unit was that of a man who held the 'clerkes' house' and 240 acres for twenty-one years. The tenancies were generally for twenty-one or thirty-one year periods.[141] It was stated that some lived in little groupings of 'four or five houses together'.[142] Evidence of the types of tradesmen present is also available for Cope's estate. The report refers to 'sundry cottagers of occupations',[143] and amongst those listed in his certificate as undertenants were a shoemaker, a chandler, and two smiths.[144]

John Dillon's certificate throws light on the structure of his estate.[145] He had 16 ballyboes of which 4 were 'layed out' as demesne and the remainder held by tenants. Of these there were 44, though one had 7 undertenants,[14] making a total of 51 families. There were 3 freeholders holding a ballyboe each of £2 per annum. The others were tenants for three lives and occupied the remaining nine townlands. In one case as many as 11 held a ballyboe and paid rent totalling £17. 0. 8. Otherwise the numbers per ballyboe ranged from one to 6, with only one ballyboe held by an individual tenant apart from the freeholders. The total rent paid was £80. 16. 0. Dillon claimed that his tenants were each enjoined by lease to provide themselves with a musket, a pike, a sword, and a dagger. He asserted that he had no Irish tenants – a claim not inconsistent with the presence of Irish in other capacities, though the commissioners reported that there were 'few or noe' Irish on the proportion.[147]

The commissioners findings on the presence of Irish in the barony may be summarised as follows: Brownlow, 24 families; Grandison, 8 families; Obbyns, 18 families; Cope 40 families; Annesley, 12 families; Stanhowe, 24 families; Sacheverall, 49 families; John Dillon, 'few or noe Irish'; Sir John Dillon, 19 families. Sacheverall claimed to have on his estate 15 Irishmen, servants and ploughmen, 'which are conformable and have taken the oath

[140] Below, 254–5.
[141] Though see below, 268.
[142] TNA, Manchester papers, 30/15/2/183.
[143] BL, Add. MS 4756, fol. 108v.
[144] NLI, Rich Papers, MS 8014/9: certificate of Anthony Cope.
[145] Ibid., /8: certificate of John Dillon.
[146] Two of Cope's freeholders had each ten undertenants (Ibid., /9).
[147] BL, Add. MS 4756, fol. 109.

of supremacie', but Rich in a marginal note denied the conformity of 10 of these.[148] An Irishman living in Lurgan was stated to be conformable.[149] As to Stanhowe's estate the commissioners noted that it was 'generally inhabited with Irish as at the last survey'.[150] However, while the overall increase in the size of the British colony must have caused a depression in status for the Irish, it is evident that on no estate had their presence been found dispensable. The armed preparedness of the colonists is only sometimes referred to in the report.

In the Fews the picture is less fully drawn. There had been no ownership change. Sir Archibald Acheson, though not his brother, was resident, and John Hamilton did not live in this county. Sir Archibald had 132 families of tenants, his brother 26, and Hamilton 66, totalling 224, and suggesting a male colony of about 400 or almost a 50 per cent increase on the 1619 figure of 285.

The commissioners' examination of the undertakers' certificates revealed irregularities in the structure of the colony. Doubt, in particular, was cast on the freehold status of people so claimed, though these claims were accepted in the final report.[151] The five freeholders Sir Archibald Acheson listed were eroded as follows: 'a child of twelve years son of Sir Archi', 'gone into Scotland and sold', 'he lyyves not there but at Clogher and setts the land to poore men' 'no such', 'gone into Scotland two years ago and never known to be a freeholder'.[152] His brother's claim was similarly discredited.[153] It was noted with regard to two leaseholders that 'this Sr Ar. will not suffer him to enjoy quietly'.[154] In general the structure of the Acheson estates was unsound. Of 132 tenants to Sir Archibald 120 were designated as cottagers.[155]

However, given these criticisms, the increase in the colony was considerable. Evidence of tradesmen and artisans is once more available from the certificates. On Henry Acheson's estate there was a 'merchant'. For his village of Clancarny – Markethill – Sir Archibald listed 36 householders, one 'an Irish man and goes not to church'.[156] There were two

[148] NLI, Rich Papers, MS 8014/8: Sacheverell's certificate.
[149] TNA, Manchester papers, 30/15/2/183.
[150] BL, Add. MS 4756, fol. 108v.
[151] Deductions in numbers claimed were made where necessary.
[152] NLI, Rich Papers, MS 8014/9: certificate of Archibald and Henry Acheson, 7 August 1622.
[153] Ibid. One, it was noted, had been already listed as constable of Sir Archibald's town of Clancarny and was 'not known to be a freeholder', the other was hardly a freeholder since he never appeared 'upon his own charges at assizes and sessions'.
[154] Ibid.
[155] BL, Add. MS 4756, ff 109–9v.
[156] NLI, Rich Papers, MS 8014/9.

mills. The commissioners, while criticising Sir Archibald for having no freeholders, felt that 'otherwise he hath planted very well'.[157]

Sir Archibald Acheson's edifice received the commissioners' approval as 'a convenient dwelling house … environed with a bawn'.[158] On the other proportions the buildings were found inadequate. Henry Acheson had a bawn of substantial proportions but it had neither gate nor house and was 'of no use in regard it [was] so ill built'.[159] As to Hamilton they commented that 'all his building is soe ill that it is fit for nothing but to be pulled down and re-edified' adding that he had undertaken to do that and then live there.[160]

As to the Irish, the report states that on the Acheson estates there were 'noe Irish' (implying no direct tenants), but that occasionally some land was let by landlords or tenants to them for grazing. There were 48 Irish families on Hamilton's lands. The British tenants were armed, and Sir Archibald Acheson listed the following weapons as in his own possession:

> Item in the mannor howse there is now fiftye two pykes, twenty five horsemen's staves, twelve muskets, ten callevers, five longe fowleings peaces, two paire of longe rowat worke pistols, and two paire of shorte snapp worke pistols, fourteen tergetts, six bowes, two halberds, two two handed swords, twelve other swords, drum and cullers.[161]

The servitors in Orior, while resident only in the cases of Poyntz and Smith,[162] had by 1622 made a decided impact as landlords. Non-residency was mitigated for Grandison and Moore by the presence of English agents. Grandison had at this point purchased Davies's lands[163] (though the latter was taken as owner by the commissioners and submitted a certificate to them), as well as the concealed land granted to Richard Atherton who was now Grandison's agent.

Grandison's estate, perhaps the most notably developed, indicated considerable advance on the situation deplored by Pynnar. He had built a castle of lime and stone, 'strong and commodious' encompassed with a defended bawn. Within were one faucon, two brass fauconettes, and arms for forty men. Nearby there was a 'handsome' church and adjoining his house a 'pleasant park', paled around, of three miles 'compass'. There were

157 TNA, Manchester papers, 30/15/2/202a.
158 BL, Add. MS 4756, fol. 109. His submission to the commissioners provides a detailed description and has been placed in an appendix.
159 Ibid.
160 Ibid.
161 NLI, Rich Papers, MS 8014/9.
162 Smith presumably lived in Moyry fort.
163 *Inq. cancel. Hib. repert.*, ii, Armagh (7) Jas I.

two watermills, under one roof. His market town – Tandragee – was said to contain 27 houses and the householders as listed contained some four or five Irish names.[164]

Poyntz, a servitor of decidedly different type, had increased his small initial grant by 'a great quantitye of 6 or 700 ac. purchased of the natives'. He had built a 'fair' brick dwelling house surrounded by small domestic enclosures,[165] besides a bawn and stable. He had eight English families dwelling in a village – Poyntzpass – adjoining.[166]

Buildings, though not in all cases fully finished or satisfactory, existed on all estates save Davies's.[167] Smith's bawn was unoccupied 'nor [was] it of any use', but the parish minister was a tenant, and had built a 'convenient' dwelling house enclosed with a double quicksett ditch.[168]

The numbers of British in the barony cannot be stated precisely. Davies claimed seven, but their *bona fides*, with one possible exception, were demolished by the commissioners, two having 'gone to Fermanagh'. and 'generally all the land [was] planted with Irish'.[169] On Moore's and Smith's estates there was not more than one British resident each, an agent called Townley[170] and the parish minister respectively.[171] Elsewhere the immigrant population was more substantial. Poyntz was credited with 8 English families.[172] A parochial return for the parish of Munterheyney provided lists of people not referred to in the report.[173] There were at least 22 British families in Tandragee and perhaps others on Grandison's estates because this return lists 29 householders and 5 individuals by name. From Bourchier's estate there were 4 church-going British households. There were 6 British households on Annesley's lands, which were not within the competence of the commissioners. Of 11 families listed for Grandison's proportion as church-going Irish 4 had non-Irish names.[174] There must therefore have been a colony of some 100 adult males. Some were Scots having probably penetrated from Down.[175] That movement westward had attractions is indicated by the removal of the tenants from Davies's land.

164 BL, Add. MS 4756, fol. 109v; TNA, Manchester papers, 30/15/2/184, 202a.

165 'An orchard, gardens, yards, and backsides inclosed with a ditch quicksett'.

166 BL, Add. MS 4756, fol. 109v; NLI, Rich Papers, MS 8014/9.

167 It was noted that this had been granted without building stipulations in compensation for receiving only the reversion of the land granted to Art McBaron O'Neill and his wife.

168 BL, Add. MS 4756, fol. 109v.

169 NLI, Rich Papers, MS 8014/9: Davies's certificate.

170 See *CPRI, Jas I*, 582.

171 NLI, Rich Papers, MS 8014/9. He was 'all the English upon the proportion'.

172 Another source (see footnote below) lists 5 households only including 'an Enlish recusant latelye brought to church'.

173 TNA, Manchester papers, 30/15/2/182.

174 Ibid.

175 There were five households of Scots on Annesley's lands and one on Bourchier's (ibid.).

There is no evidence of any influx of Irish displaced from the neighbouring undertaker baronies. Conformity by some of the original inhabitants appears to have been limited to Grandison's estate, and in the parish of Kilsleve (including Smith's land) there was 'not one Irish that comes to church', although there were over 1,000 estimated as living in the parish.[176] The all-over numbers of Irish elude definition, though there were 'above' 200 Irish families on Davies's land.[177]

In **Loughtee** Wirrall's estate, mortgaged in 1619, was now owned by Edward Bagshaw who was clerk of the court of wards[178] and lived at Finglas outside Dublin.[179] Otherwise ownership was unchanged. Three of the seven proprietors, Taylor, Butler, and Fishe, were resident, Waldron was in England but 'dayly expected',[180] Ameas's family was present, and Mainwaring was represented by an agent.

Bawns and houses existed on all estates, but present very diverse images. Fishe's bawn was the most elaborate, being 'a strong round bawne of lyme and stone 8 foot high and 415 foote compasse built upon a rath with a chamber over the gate and a draw bridge'.[181] However, other bawns had marked deficiencies, some being merely made of sods and 'going to decay'.[182] Houses or castles were equally individualistic. Fishe's was 'strong and handsome', thirty-four feet square and four storeys high.[183] But they were not all so large, some being only two or two-and-a-half storeys. The Bagshaw house was not yet complete; Taylor's was strategically situated.[184]

The colony had not increased markedly since Pynnar's survey. Butler, who was absent as sheriff on the day of visitation, made no return for his tenantry. Elsewhere the commissioners found some 370 males resident, including 34 families in Belturbet taken as comprising 60 males. Pynnar found 439, including 139 from Butler's proportion, though excluding the uncounted residents of Belturbet. An approximate 510 may therefore be suggested for the 1622 population. These were not evenly distributed; on the Ameas, Bagshaw, and Mainwaring estates, three which had been subject to ownership change, the colony was very small.

176 NLI, Rich Papers, MS 8014/9: draft of commissioners' report on Orior.
177 Ibid.: Davies's certificate.
178 *CPRI, Jas I*, 327.
179 *Inq. cancel. Hib. repert.*, ii, Cavan (1) Chas II.
180 BL, Add. MS 4756, ff 101v–2.
181 Ibid., fol. 102.
182 Ibid., fol. 101v (Taylor's bawn).
183 Ibid., fol. 102.
184 Taylor was the only settler in our area whose place of settlement had been defined for him by the deputy and plantation commissioners as they were empowered to do for the defence of the countryside and for convenience of communications. (Chichester to Taylor, 5 October 1611, *CSPI, 1611–14*, 140–1; *Cal Carew MSS., 1603–24*, 23–4).

It is evident that the colony had been none too stable and on almost every estate tenants were noted who were absentee or had previously disposed of their lands. Of seventeen freeholders on Taylor's estate, for example, ten were non-resident as also were four of his eleven leaseholders.[185] One of two freeholders on Ameas's estate lived in Dublin and let the land 'wholy' to Irishmen.[186] As to Fishe's estate it was reported that:

> many of the first leases have been passed over from one party to another and ... the tenants have not performed their covenants of buildings and planting with their landlord as by their deeds they are tyed to doe, but some of them have and continue Irish upon the lands, whereof Sir John Fishe complaines; and others doe place poor undertenants upon it at rack'd rents.[187]

Complaints also came from the tenants. Some of Bagshaw's tenants had 'no deeds to be seen'.[188] Butler's protested that they could get 'noe reasonable bargains till the Irish be removed'.[189]

On almost all estates the presence of Irish in quantity was noted. They either held land directly from the undertakers or subsidiarily from their British tenants. On the estates of Bagshaw, Ameas, and Mainwaring the 'greatest part', or 'much' or 'most' of the land was in Irish occupation.[190]

The settlement pattern revealed in 1618–19 of village groups and dispersed dwelling receives confirmation. Only on the estates of Bagshaw and Ameas were clusters of houses absent. Waldron had a village of thirty houses with English tenants close to his own dwelling. This was probably modern Farnham where there is now a county house, but no village. In this presumably lived his thirty cottagers, each with a house and 'backside', and 'very good commons for 12 beasts grazeing and 2 acres apiece for tillage'.[191] On Fishe's estate there were five 'English-like' thatched houses close to his own dwelling,[192] probably Stradone, while Mainwaring had a 'smale' village of seven houses not all tenanted. This was subsequently named Moynehall after Mainwaring's successor as owner.[193] On Taylor's estate there were fourteen English families living near his castle – at Ballyhaise – and the rest of his tenants lived in dispersed fashion.[194]

185 BL, Add. MS 4756, fol. 101v.
186 Ibid., ff 102v–3.
187 Ibid., fol. 102.
188 Ibid., ff 102–2v.
189 Ibid., fol. 102v.
190 Ibid., ff 102–3.
191 Ibid., ff 101v–2.
192 Ibid., fol. 102.
193 Below, 172.
194 BL, Add. MS 4756, fol. 101v.

The amount of arms recorded varied immensely. Ameas's and Bagshaw's tenants had only five swords and five 'peeces' respectively. However, Waldron had 'very good arms' and a drum in his house 'besides arms which the chief tenants are bound to keep'. Taylor had the greatest variety with '4 corsletts with head pieces, 12 muskets and callivers, 7 pikes and horsemen staves, 2 long bows and 2 sheaves of arrows, and 3 halberts' in his stronghold, while Butler had 'but smale store of arms', but claimed to have distributed them amongst his tenants and others for their safety in the countryside.

On at least three estates agriculture was conspicuously energetic. Waldron and Fishe had English cattle in great numbers, Waldron also having 'very good' tillage and 'inclosures'.[195] There were now seven mills distributed between four estates; five were recorded by Pynnar. Butler had two corn mills and one fulling mill.

In **Tullyhunco** there had been no sales, but the marriage of Lady Jane Hamilton, widow of Sir Claud and mother of his minor son, to Capt. Arthur Forbes from Longford, himself a Scot, must have affected the supervision of the estate, though only his wife and 'her family' were resident at the time of inspection.[196] Of the other two owners Craig had been 'long' resident and Acheson was represented by an agent. There were now bawns on all estates, of which Acheson's only was criticised as 'already' decaying. The houses were generally substantial, two of four or four-and-a-half storeys, Craig's being again commended as 'strongly builded both for the stone work and tymber work'.[197]

It appears that there were no more than some 135 males resident, an apparent recession on Pynnar's figure and barely satisfying the required minimum of 144. Many tenants were non-resident and much of the land on all estates was in Irish occupation.[198] Only one village – Killashandra – with twenty British households, on the Hamilton estate, is mentioned.

There were many tenant complaints and there were apparent irregularities. The freeholders of the barony petitioned the commissioners 'as in all other places they did by word of mouth' to be relieved from jury service on the grounds that their freeholds were small and their rents unduly high.[199] On the Hamilton estate the inhabitants complained that they had expended money in building and planting on promise of freeholds from

[195] Ibid., ff 101v–2. On Fishe's estate there was 'good manurance'.

[196] On one of her properties there was resident a substantial freeholder in the bawn, called Lowther in the report but more likely Lawder as he appears elsewhere (*Inq. cancel. Hib. repert.*, ii, Cavan (24) Chas I; BL, Add. MS 4770, fol. 9v).

[197] BL, Add. MS 4756, fol. 103v.

[198] As to the Acheson estate, for example, it was noted that 'the most part of this proportion hath always been and is still occupied by the Irish (ibid.).

[199] Ibid.

Claud Hamilton. These promises had been unfulfilled, and now, the heir being a minor, they requested government intervention to secure their titles.[200] On Craig's estate most of the tenants had merely 'promises or short notes under Sir James his hand' rather than leases.[201] Acheson's English tenants protested against ill usage of his agent asserting that some had been deprived of their lands on pretext of forfeiture for letting to the Irish and yet the same lands had been subsequently disposed to native occupiers.[202]

On the Craig estate there was 'good manurance of tillage' and 'great store of cattle'.[203] Only one mill is mentioned, held by a leaseholder with twelve acres, on the Acheson estate. On all estates the tenants were armed or provision was made for this purpose, but the predominating weapons were pikes and 'half pikes'.

Scottish ownership in **Clankee** was affected by the sale of Sir James Hamilton's estate to Sir Henry Perse (or Piers) in September 1621.[204] Perse himself held the dissolved monastic property of Tristernagh in Westmeath, acquired by his family in 1590,[205] and was secretary to Chichester in 1607.[206] This sale did more than substitute one absentee proprietor for another. Many of the tenants, unwilling to live under the new owner, or discontented with their fortunes in Cavan, or perhaps too closely bound to Hamilton, had by 1622 left the land and returned to Clandeboy 'from whence they came'.[207] Otherwise the ownership of the barony had not changed. Bailie and John Hamilton were resident at the time of the inquiry, William Hamilton was represented by his wife and Perse had 'some servants' living in his castle.

The buildings were roughly in their 1618–19 condition, some very substantial but not all completed. The castle on the Perse estate was now 'exceedingly' well roofed, but the floors had not been installed nor the windows glazed. However, four men were at work. John Hamilton lived in one of two thatched English houses, built as 'howses of office' and within a bawn of clay and stones, but nearby there was a bawn of stone and lime in which a stone house with two vaulted towers was being constructed.[208]

There were no more than some 90 adult males among the colony in this barony. This major recession, it was roughly half of Pynnar's figure,

[200] Ibid., fol. 103.
[201] Ibid., fol. 103v.
[202] Ibid.
[203] Ibid.
[204] *Inq. cancel. Hib. repert.*, ii, Cavan (19) Chas I.
[205] Ibid., i, Westmeath (3) Eliz.
[206] *CSPI, 1606–8*, 187.
[207] BL, Add. MS 4756, fol. 100.
[208] Ibid., ff 100–100v.

must have been accounted for by the exodus of tenants back to Down following on the sale of Sir James Hamilton's estate (though it was equally apparent on all three Hamilton estates) Bailie's settlers being unchanged in numbers. There is no evidence of disturbed landlord-tenant relations, but William Hamilton had no freehold tenants. The colony appears to have been armed in at least an elementary fashion, but only John Hamilton had a supply of arms – 24 pikes, 6 horsemen's staves, and 26 muskets and callivers – in his house.[209]

There were two mills in the barony. John Hamilton and William Bailie had 'good manurance', Bailie had 'stock of cattle' on his demesne, and William Hamilton had 'some' cattle on his land 'and store of Irish upon it also'.[210] In Clankee, as elsewhere, it is manifest that the Irish were being retained on the estates. Bailie complained that his tenants let their lands to the Irish[211] though both before and after this date he himself demised land to Irish occupants on a yearly basis.[212]

The survey indicates little change in servitor ownership in Cavan since 1618–19. In **Castlerahan** the Old English lawyer, Edward Dowdall, was now the recorded owner of the estates of Fettiplace and Taaffe. Other proprietors were unchanged and absentee though Culme's family were resident on the former Ridgeway estate, Culme being himself in England. Apart from the fact that Culme had completed substantial buildings there had been no improvement here since Pynnar's perambulation. Bawns on the Dowdall and Ashe estates had a limited value through the absence of gates.

British-held land in **Tullygarvey** evinced the disadvantages of absentee ownership. The brothers Ashe had let their house and bawn – itself 'fallen down in many places' – to 'one of the Relys'.[213] The Culme-Moore partnership had been disrupted by the death of Archibald Moore, his widow and children having left it 'desolate'. This was regretted by the commissioners because their buildings at Tullyvin were 'of great strength' and had 'not been made so with out great charge'.[214]

In **Clanmahon** ownership was unchanged and was without exception absentee. Buildings were unimpressive except on the Lambert estates, and here operations had halted with the death of Sir Oliver in 1618. In Tullyhaw where only the Graham and Talbot-Culme estates were considered, building work satisfied the commissioners but only Talbot appears to have been resident.

209 Ibid.
210 Ibid., fol. 100v.
211 Ibid.
212 *Inq. cancel. Hib. repert.*, ii, Cavan (17) Chas I.
213 BL, Add. MS 4756, fol. 101.
214 Ibid.

The most general characteristic of these servitor estates was the absence of British tenantry, a condition which can have changed little over the ensuing twenty years. On Culme's estate in Castlerahan near Virginia there were, as in Pynnar's time, four British families dwelling near his bawn, one of whom kept 'a good inne', but most of the land 'being barren [was] sett to the Irish'.[215] There were only some five English families in Virginia. On the Culme and Moore estate in Tullygarvey there were but two 'poore' Englishmen on the land.[216] On one of the Lambert estates in Clanmahon there was one English 'gentleman' and an 'ancient follower' of Lambert's living in the bawn.[217] Lieutenant Rutledge, whose own property goes unmentioned in the report, was the only British tenant to Sir Richard Graham.[218] The British population can not have exceeded the figure of 30 males suggested by our examination of Pynnar's survey.

Otherwise the land was reported universally as let to the local Irish or to people from the Pale. Old English ownership in the county had thus not only been extended with the arrival of Dowdall, but Palesmen were moving in as tenantry as well, though this was doubtless also a process for which there was pre-plantation precedent in this county. Dowdall and Walter Talbot had freeholders and leaseholders from the Pale who were all recusants and Lord Lambert had leased some land and the bawn on one of his estates to a Palesman, 'one Morrice Dalton'.[219] However, the local native inhabitants formed the bulk of the tenantry on all servitor estates. It was noted in almost all cases that all the land was 'sett to Irish natives who live dispersed and plough after the Irish custom'.[220] Most of the land Ashe had acquired from Garth in Castlerahan was held by 'one head of the sept of the O'Rely'.[221] Apart then from the appearance of small numbers of Palesmen tenants holding on a leasehold basis, and likewise of British, servitor landlordry in Cavan had not been revolutionary.

By way of brief conclusion, it can be stated that a figure of approaching 1,200 was the likely British male population on undertakers' and servitors' lands in Armagh. The corresponding figure for Cavan was some 765. The English and Scottish undertakers in Cavan, owning some 130,000 acres and having planted some 735 British males, had planted much less densely than their counterparts in Armagh who with some 82,000 acres had planted near to 1,100 British males. As to relative densities, the English barony of

215 Ibid.
216 Ibid.
217 Ibid., fol. 103.
218 Ibid., fol. 104. His land was later in Culme hands.
219 Ibid., fol. 103.
220 Ibid., fol. 101.
221 Ibid.

Loughtee in Cavan was now planted about one and one-half times more densely than the two Scots' baronies. In contrast, in Armagh, Scots owners in the Fews had over twice as many dependents in relation to the acreages they owned than had the English in Oneilland.

The commissioners' general conclusion was that although some settlers had fulfilled the conditions better than others, the king's 'great bounty and godly intention' was 'generally frustrated'.[222] They particularised the defects of the different categories of grantees.[223] As to the undertakers, many were absentee, employing agents to collect their rents. They retained 'great store' of Irish on their lands to the prejudice of their British tenants. They made few *bona fide* freeholders, some being their own children, and many freeholders and leaseholders not having legally valid instruments, and so being liable to eviction, and those that were made had small quantities of land, paid high rents, and found difficulties in meeting the demands of jury service, which were consequently imposed on leaseholders and their rack-rented undertenants. Few of the undertakers had performed their building obligations within the limited time and many of the bawns built were unserviceable, some having no gates or houses within, 'and therefore of no use when nobody dwells in them'.[224] Few of the undertakers had settled their tenants in villages near their strongholds, but rather allowed them to live in dispersed fashion 'subject to the malice of any kerne to rob, kill, and burne them and their houses'.[225] Many undertakers did not have adequate arms in their houses as required. Some exacted duties and services or only let their lands from year to year contrary to the articles of plantation. Estates had been sold without license whereby some proprietors had accumulated properties 'which is a principall cause that the conditions are not performed and chiefe freeholders are extinguished'.[226]

The defects of the servitors were somewhat similar. Although many had built more than required, some had not built at all. Like the undertakers some of their bawns had 'no houses, people, or gates'. Many had not granted leases or created freeholders. Some were recusants and would not take the oath of supremacy. Some had never been resident and had only collected rents from Irish. Most of their tenants did not live in villages. The commissioners' comments on the native Irish grantees will be discussed below.[227] Finally they proposed that the undertakers should be allowed to take out new patents under the modified conditions discussed above.[228]

[222] BL, Add. MS 4756, fol. 118.
[223] Ibid., ff 118–18v.
[224] Ibid. fol. 118.
[225] Ibid.
[226] Ibid., fol. 118v.
[227] Below, 206.
[228] Above, 135.

However, in January 1623 following on the report of the commissioners a stay was put on the granting of all land in Ireland in order to prevent crown loss through dubious practices,[229] which affected grants in Ulster as elsewhere. It constituted an attempt to bring Irish affairs under more rigid supervision from England. It resulted in a temporary stoppage of the granting of the inland forts in Ulster and elicited strong complaints from Sir Thomas Dutton.[230] The stoppage as it concerned the forts was relaxed in 1624, but the attempt to curb irregularities was seriously intended, and it dovetails in with the fact that no immediate action was taken to given effect to the scheme for granting new patents to the undertakers.

In the years 1623 to 1625 three Cavan undertakers brought problems concerning their estates before the government. In May 1623 Sir Thomas Waldron petitioned the king for a regrant of his estate in order to secure substantial concealments, stating that his father, Sir Richard, had procured a king's letter of 1 December 1619 authorising a surrender and regrant but had died before taking out his new patent.[231] The matter was referred to the commissioners for Irish causes who, in November, recommended that he should receive a custodiam of the concealed lands at the same rent as applied to his other lands.[232] The other two cases had no bearing on security of title against the crown. Sir Edward Fishe and Edward Bagshaw brought forward problems concerning charges on their estates in 1624 and 1625 respectively.[233] These would have had to have been thrashed out, however, had new patents been granted at this time.

The final approval of the scheme for new patents had, despite pressure from the undertakers, to await the following reign and more expedient political circumstances. In December 1623 Falkland and his government were empowered to negotiate with the settlers in the plantations generally 'for confirmation or renewal of their estates',[234] and probably at the end of the previous year a king's letter to the lord deputy ordering the implementation of the suggested scheme for the Ulster undertakers was drafted, but apparently not dispatched to Dublin.[235] Both, at any rate, were without effect and in July 1624 three agents of the undertakers, Sir Archibald Acheson, Sir Francis Annesley, and Lord Balfour (a planter in Fermanagh) petitioned the king for an immediate implementation of the

229 *Acts privy council, 1621–23*, 395, 398, 460; TNA, SP 63/237, ff 13, 47–7v, 101–2v (*CSPI, 1615–25*, 403, 408–9, 427).

230 Above, 130.

231 TNA, SP 63/237, ff 53, 153–3v (*CSPI, 1615–25*, 411, 438).

232 Ibid.

233 TNA, SP 63/238 Pr. 2, fol. 211 (*CSPI, 1615–25*, 552, 584): Fishe; *CSPI, 1625–32*, 21: Bagshaw.

234 Rymer, *Foedera*, (Hague edn.), vol. vii, pt. iv, 89–96; see Moody, *Londonderry Plantation*, 236.

235 TNA, SP 63/236, ff 217–18v (*CSPI, 1615–25*, 396).

scheme.[236] Undertakers, they claimed, were discouraged from building, the Irish were in hopes of receiving the land back and could not be displaced, and 'many hundreds' of British families had departed, so that 'the plantation in general [had] in a useful manner relapsed'. The king referred the petition to the privy council, requiring them to give it 'all favourable expedition',[237] but no further action was taken until the following year.

3. The natives' inquiry, 1623–4

In 1623 the commissioners' recommendation of 1622 with regard to new patents was, in effect, tacitly stayed by a further directive. On December 12 the privy council instructed Falkland to issue a proclamation which would forbid the undertakers to expel any of the natives from their lands or to receive any new native tenants until further notice. He was furthermore to have carried out an inquiry by commissioners in each county into the numbers and conditions of the native Irish on each undertaker's lands.[238] The results of this inquiry, which should consider what acreage each native held from each undertaker and under what rents, either in money or in kind, and by what service and for how long, should be certified to the privy council by March 10 following at the latest. It might also come within their competence to examine the performance of the plantation conditions by the undertakers.[239] The proclamation was issued as required,[240] and commissioners chosen to carry out the inquiry in each county.[241]

The inquiries appear only to have been carried out in Armagh, Fermanagh, and Londonderry, or at least returns for these counties only, dating from February–March 1624, survive.[242] On April 21 these were transmitted to London with an accompanying letter excusing the delay.[243] The matter is referred to here to provide some further explanation of the delay in concluding the arrangement to grant new patents, but treatment of the evidence for Armagh has been deferred for inclusion in the chapter on the native Irish.[244]

[236] TNA, SP 63/238 Pr. 2, ff 78v–81v (*CSPI, 1615–25*, 518–20).
[237] Ibid.
[238] *Acts privy council, 1623–5*, 144–5; *CSPI, 1615–25*, 439–40; Moody, *Londonderry Plantation*, 217.
[239] Ibid.
[240] Steele, *Proclamations*, ii, 26.
[241] *CSPI, 1615–25*, 439–40; TNA, SP 63/238, Pr. 1, fol. 23 (*CSPI, 1615–25*, 459).
[242] TNA SP 63/238, ff 139–44 (*CSPI, 1615–25*, 482–4): the Armagh report.
[243] Ibid., ff 138–8v (*CSPI, 1615–25*, 482: letter wrongly dated).
[244] Below, 217–22.

CHAPTER 5

The Colony in a Period of Emergency, 1625–32

1. Tension and concession

The outbreak of war between England and Spain following on the accession of Charles I and lasting until 1630 raised a number of important problems in Ireland.[1] The perennial fear of insurrection or internal disturbance received an added dimension with the possibility of invasion. The reorganisation and expansion of the army thus necessitated created a major financial problem with critical political implications. The attempt to retain the loyalty of the Old English and, by extension, acquire their financial support resulted in negotiations culminating in 1628 with important concessions to them reciprocated by substantial monetary assistance. However, the significance of the war for both planter and native elements in Ulster cannot be overlooked.

The marriage negotiations in 1623, it has been seen,[2] has raised hopes in Ulster of concessions to the native population. The failure of the negotiations, with the clear possibility of war, also suggested prospects of alleviation. The reign ended with incidents or the threat of them being reported from the northern province. Ulster, where the most thorough and most recent plantation of any size was taking effect, was manifestly the greatest centre of grievance. The fact that there were a considerable number of Ulster émigrés on the continent also made it a likely landing place for an invading army in the event of war. In 1624, therefore, plans for its defence were being considered.[3] In 1626 it was suggested that a president for the province should be appointed.[4] In 1624 and 1625 a series of appointments were made whereby local landowners were commissioned as governors of their counties 'as well for the punishment and reformation of enormous and evil disposed persons as also for the defence and safety' of the colonists there.[5] No appointments for Armagh or Cavan were, however, made.

1 Clarke, 'The army and politics', *Stud. Hib.* iv, 28–53.

2 Above, 132.

3 Above, 134.

4 TNA, SP 63/243, ff 57–8v (*CSPI, 1625–32*, 144–5).

5 *CPRI, Jas I*, 591, *CSPI, 1615–25*, 548 (Fermanagh, 3 December 1624); *CPRI, Jas I*, 588–9.

Commentators in 1625 stressed the need to place a higher proportion of the army in Ulster than elsewhere. It was felt that the Irish in the north would 'provoke' war at any opportunity,[6] and follow the leadership of O'Neill or O'Donnell claimants returning from abroad.[7] It was recognised that the six planted counties were but 'thinly populated' and incapable of self defence unless reinforced and armed.[8] Armagh was mentioned as a place to be made defensible.[9] By November 1625 the deputy reported that of the army, then 4,000 strong, 1,400 foot and 150 horse had been disposed in Ulster.[10] The inland counties of Armagh and Cavan were not, however, singled out for special attention, presumably because sheltered from coastal invasion.

Fear of invasion was acute throughout the entire period. In 1627 the landing of a pirate at Killybegs in Donegal created a scare far beyond the magnitude of the incident. Falkland commented that 'though the present perrill be overblown ... yet the consideration will remayne'.[11] No invasion did come and peace was made in 1630. However, while the disposition of the Ulster garrisons indicated that they were conceived of as largely to repel attack, it was also considered necessary to maintain forces in Ulster, and to take other precautions also, to inhibit or suppress insurrection. There was, in fact, heightened unease throughout the province during the war period. Reports of incidents were widespread and active measures were taken to maintain order. All counties were affected, Armagh, perhaps, least of all.

In August 1625 a conspiracy involving McGoverns from Cavan and Maguires from Fermanagh came to light. Information had been acquired by Sir William Cole of Enniskillen and the archbishop of Cashel which was presented to the judges of assize who pursued the investigation. The plan, it appears, was to amass arms in anticipation of a Spanish landing, surprise the planters' houses (especially in Fermanagh) and repossess the confiscated lands. The judges tried four ringleaders in Enniskillen before a jury of 'good freeholders of the English' who found them all guilty. They informed Dublin of their intention to sentence them to death, unless the deputy wished to mitigate the sentence and have them sent to Dublin, but pointed out that this could only be done under strong guard because of popular

6 *CSPI, 1625–32*, 68–9.
7 Ibid.
8 Ibid.
9 Ibid.
10 *CSPI, 1625–32*, 50–1.
11 TNA, SP 63/244, fol. 271 (*CSPI, 1625–32*, 234). Spanish sources indicate that consideration was being given, or at least requested by Irish agents, to a landing on the Donegal coast or at Londonderry at this time (Jennings, *Wild Geese*, 212–13).

support.[12] The outcome is not known, but the affair convinced the deputy how seriously 'the blood [was] distempered in the veins', making it essential to overhaul the defensive arrangements for the province.[13]

While there is no indication of disorder coming to a head in Armagh at this time, a provost marshal was energetic there in the summer of 1626.[14] In the spring of 1627 reports came in to Dublin of a 'newe and dangerous rebellion' in Antrim, Down, and adjacent areas, presumably parts of north-west Armagh.[15] Edward Chichester, governor of Carrickfergus, stated that in order to counter cattle stealing and other outrages by woodkerne he had sent a company of soldiers to 'lye and cesse on their septs'.[16] Falkland, disturbed by the deterioration in Ulster which these reports suggested, pleaded that he would not be answerable for peace unless he could over-spend the concordatum allowance and stressed the need for martial law to curb lawlessness.[17] By March 1627, as further incidents from our area were reported, the deputy had made marshal appointments. Reports of 'murders and other mischiefs' from Cavan, Monaghan, and Longford, had persuaded Falkland to issue Sir Charles Coote, a man of energetic background and vice-president of Connacht,[18] with 'a large marshall commission and extraordinary trust' to regulate these areas.[19] Also, convinced that the procedures of the law were inadequate to the task of maintaining order, even when reinforced by interrogation and fines in the star chamber, he appointed Sir William Windsor to administer marshal law.[20] By July the deputy could report in favourable terms on Windsor's activities in Down, Antrim, and Armagh. Before his appointment rebels in those counties, anticipating foreign invasion, had formed into bands with the intention of forcing the British inhabitants to abandon their settlements. Windsor had, however, done much to restore order and 'slaine with the sword upwards of three score rebels'.[21] In a letter to the archbishop of Armagh in March 1627 Falkland thanked him for encouraging his tenants to make payments for the maintenance of the army. He stated that he had kept Sir Charles Coote's company away from Armagh for as long as possible and would remove it as soon as possible, however

12 *CSPI, 1625–32*, 25–37, 39–40.
13 Ibid., 34–5.
14 TNA, SP 63/242, fol. 357 (*CSPI, 1625–32*, 135).
15 TNA, SP 63/244, ff 153–9v (*CSPI, 1625–32*, 217–18).
16 Ibid., fol. 155.
17 *CSPI, 1625–32*, 217. There is evidence that provost marshals had already been engaged in other counties of Ulster by 1626 (BL, Sloane MS 3827, ff 62–3v, 65–5v).
18 Hughes, *Patentee Officers*, 31.
19 TNA, SP 63/244, ff 170–1v (*CSPI, 1625–32*, 220).
20 Ibid.
21 TNA, SP 63/244, ff 54–4v (*CSPI, 1625–32*, 248).

> your Lordship may please to understand that by the earnest intercession of some well-wishers to that county, it hath been less burdened with soldiers than any other within that province, saving only Fermanagh which is much smaller in scope than it.[22]

The use of provost marshals as an expedient for maintaining order, however, was restricted by article 33 of the Graces of May 1628.[23] This provoked a sharp complaint from Falkland which he coupled with the information that, following the death of Sir William Windsor, disorder had increased in Ulster.[24] The reply was, however, conciliatory, it being intimated that the king did not think Falkland's power had been 'in any way curtailed by the recently passed articles' and he was given full initiative in the event of a woodkerne rising.[25] No successor to Windsor appears to have been appointed, but there is also no evidence that conditions in Ulster had sufficiently improved to justify an alteration in policy. In January 1629 there were reports of outrages in Cavan (and Meath) and measures were taken against them.[26] In June Moses Hill, provost marshal of Ulster, wrote to the deputy from Stranmillis that his men were engaged as far east as Tyrone stating that there were so many that 'relieved' the woodkerne 'that they were almost ready to goe into rebellion'. He complained that neither the local justices of the peace nor the assize judges were sufficiently ruthless in executing offenders which he had been 'att great trouble and charge' in apprehending.[27] There is no further indication of unrest in either Armagh or Cavan and the conclusion of peace with Spain in 1630 removed the external stimulant.[28]

During the war years conciliation tactics had also been utilised, and some care was taken to preserve the support of well-affected Irishmen. A list of 'persons fitted to be employed against Tyrone and other Irish rebels' drawn up in 1625 included Sir Turlogh McHenry O'Neill, 'an active protestant'.[29] In February 1626 a list of people whose pensions, granted for previous support to the crown, were in arrears, was submitted by the Dublin government to the privy council as deserving of relief. These include O'Hanlons and O'Neills from Armagh.[30] In the case of one of these, Capt.

22 C.R. Elrington (ed.), *The whole works of the most reverend James Ussher, D.D.*, (Dublin 1864), xv, 372–4.

23 A. Clarke, *The Old English in Ireland, 1625* (London 1966), 249.

24 TNA, SP 63/247, ff 3, 4v (*CSPI, 1625–32*, 356).

25 Ibid., ff 42–3v (ibid., 366).

26 BL, Sloane MS 3827, fol. 155.

27 Ibid., ff 163–4v.

28 In November the earl of Cork, one of the lord justices who had succeeded Falkland, stated that he could hear of 'no one now in all Ireland unamenable to the law' (*CSPI, 1625–32*, 585).

29 Ibid., 73.

30 TNA, SP 63/242, ff 126–6v (*CSPI, 1625–32*, 96).

Patrick O'Hanlon, whose pension originated in 1603,[31] the Irish commissioners of the privy council recommended that satisfaction be given.[32] However, no payments were made to him and he renewed his petition in July 1628.[33]

In February 1627 a certain Brian O'Hogan, a native of Tyrone, who had served on the Continent, was arrested and gave evidence tending to implicate Sir Turlogh McHenry O'Neill and his family amongst others, in plots and conspiracies not precisely defined.[34] These depositions were transmitted to London,[35] where the accusations were dismissed as unlikely to be true, those concerned having been 'hitherto ... observed to live peaceably and like good subjects'. It was recommended that Falkland should instruct Lord Caulfeild to inform the accused of the allegations and let them know that the state was 'unwilling to charge good subjects without just ground' thereby to encourage them and others to remain loyal.[36] Later in the year the king intervened in O'Neill's favour, following on a petition, in a dispute for land between him and Sir Christopher Bellew of Louth.[37]

The emergency also affected the Ulster planters, and forms the background against which the undertakers were permitted to take out new patents along the lines first mooted in 1619.[38] The preservation of the goodwill of the planters was important, and it was seen in 1625 that if soldiers were cessed on Ulster quit rent payments from the province, about £4,000 per annum, would be put in hazard.[39] By 1626 soldiers had in fact been quartered there and complaints of pillaging had come in from one area.[40] In November Falkland forwarded to London a petition of the leading planters of Fermanagh representing the oppressions of soldiers quartered there.[41] Similar protests came from Londonderry, Donegal, Fermanagh, and Antrim.[42] In April 1627 a representative assembly which met in Dublin to discuss the financing of the army pointed to the distress of a barony in Ulster to indicate the general strain caused by the increased size of the army.[43] It may not be specially significant that no complaints came from Cavan or Armagh. In July 1627 Falkland concluded that a contribution of

31 Above, 20.
32 TNA, SP 63/243, ff 23–3v (*CSPI, 1625–32*, 140–41, see also 155).
33 TNA, SP 63/247, fol. 11 (ibid., 358).
34 TNA, SP 63/244, ff 84–7v, 145–6v, 148 (ibid., 209–10, 216–17).
35 Ibid., fol. 202 (ibid., 223–4).
36 Ibid., ff 210–11v (ibid., 225).
37 Below, 213.
38 Above, 135.
39 *CSPI, 1625–32*, 39–40.
40 TNA, SP 63/243, ff 126–7 (*CSPI, 1625–32*, 155).
41 Ibid., fol. 234 (ibid., 173).
42 TNA, SP 63/244, ff 5107, 68–72 (*CSPI, 1625–32*, 206–8).
43 Ibid., fol. 214 (ibid., 225).

£27,000 was required from the country towards maintaining the army. Of this, £8,250 was to be collected from the nine Ulster counties of which Armagh with £650 to pay had the smallest assessment, the share of Cavan, £900, being roughly the average for the province and identical with that required from Londonderry.[44]

It is not without some significance, then, that the undertakers' proposals for securing their titles were treated more sympathetically in these years. In February and August 1625 the English privy council considered the matter and made recommendations.[45] It was agreed that the undertakers should receive new letters patent, at doubled rents, whereby they might plant one-quarter of their estates with native Irish and the rest with British tenants. The areas reserved for Irish should be selected by special commissioners and listed by name in their patents. A clause demanding the religious conformity of the Irish tenants should not be inserted, though they should be subject to the relevant legislation of the country. The undertakers' request not to have to give security that the Irish would be completely excluded from the remaining three-quarters of their estates was conceded, but a clause should be included authorising the seizure of any land reserved for British which, found inhabited by Irish, was to be held by the king until adequate security was given that the offence would not recur. 'Good care' should be taken that the undertakers should make British freeholders and leaseholders 'truly and really' on the appropriate areas, avoiding all irregular tenures. A model grant was to be drawn up and sent to Ireland for the information of the undertakers.

On the basis of these recommendations the king sent instructions to the lord deputy on September 6 for the issuing of the new patents. In return for confirmation of their titles the undertakers were to double their rents and pay a fine at the rate of £30 per thousand acres according to the original survey. As a result Wray's commission would be withdrawn. The Irish on the reserved areas might have leases for twenty-one years or three lives, but should live in villages, wear English clothing and permit their children to be educated and learn the English language. The Irish should have removed from the remaining three-quarters of each proportion by May-day 1626.[46] In July 1626 the removal date was extended to May-day 1628.[47]

The arrangement was not given immediate effect, and in August 1627 further royal instructions were received, whereby the increased rents were

44 Ibid., /245, ff 69–87 (ibid., 250–55).
45 *Acts privy council, 1623–5*, 454–6, *1625–6*, 154–6; Moody, *Londonderry Plantation*, 236–7.
46 *CPRI, Chas I*, 100–3.
47 Ibid., 118–21; Marsh's Library, Dublin, MS Z4.2.6, 582–7.

to take effect from the following Michaelmas and the fine was to be increased to £40 per thousand acres.[48] In September the king instructed that £5 per thousand acres should be paid by the undertakers to Sir Piers Crosby and Sir Archibald Acheson who had acted as their agents in this stage of the negotiations.[49] In December a proclamation was issued for putting the new policy into effect.[50] By this the letters patent were to be issued within five months at half fees. The undertakers, however, petitioned against the increasing of the fines and requested further time before the doubled rents should become payable.[51] Their requests were admitted in article 26 of the Graces 'in regard this is the only matter wherein they receive any singular grace', though they would share equally in the payment of subsidies.[52]

At about this point, however, a much more radical scheme was put forward. A commentator in 1628[53] saw that in the last resort the success of the plantation depended on the treatment of the Irish population. The Irish would accept from the undertakers more rigorous conditions as tenants – at higher rents and on a yearly basis, a 'slavish tenancy-at-will' – than would British, hence while they might remain the British colony would not grow. To remove them, however, without provision for their re-settlement would also jeopardise the plantation through 'great clamour … if not a present invasion'.

The solution, it was felt, lay in their planned re-settlement on the lands granted, largely for this purpose, to the servitors, the bishops, and the native grantees, and this could only be done by government intervention, it could not be left to their own haphazard initiative. Commissioners should therefore be appointed to inquire into the amount of land as yet unplanted which was held by bishops, servitors, and natives and to investigate what numbers of natives yet remained on undertakers' lands. When such parallel surveys had been conducted places should be assigned to these Irish in proportion to their means to utilize them. The bishops, etc. should then be 'commanded expressly' to receive the Irish and give them specified tenures. The Irish now labouring under harsh and uncertain conditions from the undertakers would willingly take up their new lands 'whereof they may be assured to have estates'. Such a settlement, it was suggested, would ensure peace in Ulster and the king would be

48 TNA, SP 63/245, ff 125–30v (*CSPI, 1625–32*, 263–4).
49 *CSPI, 1625–32*, 273.
50 Steele, *Proclamations*, ii, 30.
51 TNA, SP 63/246, fol. 156 (*CSPI, 1625–32*, 334).
52 Ibid.
53 M. Hickson (ed.), *Ireland in the seventeenth century*, (London 1884), ii, 327–31.

> the author of that great work of uniting the English and Irish together which yet could never be done because they never live together as landlord and tenant, either in perpetuity or long leases.

Such would be 'a work of greater glory to the king than if he had brought a new people into their places'.

To give his argument further conviction he described the plantation as it then stood. Ulster was 'as yet no other than a very wilderness'. On each proportion there might be one small 'township' made by the British, but the proportions being 'wide and large the habitation of all the province is scarce visible'. The presence of the Irish who did not 'dwell together in any orderly form' deterred the expansion of the British colony. Those Irish who had received grants of land as well as being poor, were 'for the most part [such] as in time of war had relation to this state', hence they had no reputation with the mass of the native population. These tended to follow the landless 'heads of septs' and 'chiefs of creaghtes' who would now, seeing 'the times fall out so contrary to their expectations', willingly settle themselves if the proposed plan were pursued. In this way only would the 'habits, manners, and language of the English' be 'in time' introduced and the plantation reach fruition.

Such a plan might have held some possibility of a solution if put forward and acted on in 1610, but in 1628 there were a number of factors which would make its implementation difficult. The bishops and servitors at any rate had already organised their lands (the bishops for the most part having granted sixty-year leases) in ways which would not have to be completely disrupted. Furthermore, the undertakers had by now also succeeded in gaining acceptance for the compromise solution whereby the Irish might be retained on one-quarter of their estates. Also the Irish, having eluded transplantation for eighteen years, might not have accepted the scheme as cheerfully as was suggested. Had government, then, possessed the vigour to attempt to implement it there would still have been a number of associated difficulties which the proposed failed to consider.

In June the protracted negotiations were finalised and it was clear that the above proposals concerning the native Irish would not be acted upon. Falkland was ordered to issue a commission for the granting of the new patents. The rents were to be £10. 13. 4 per thousand acres and proportionably, concealed lands to be included. Fines at the rate of £30 per thousand acres were conceded. The patentee should covenant to ensure that three-quarters of his lands were planted with British tenants or used as demesne, and undertake to have two freeholders and two leaseholders at least per thousand acres. All the 'mere Irish' except artificers settled upon small 'parcels' were to be removed from this area before 1 May 1629 and any of this land granted to Irish should forfeit to the king during the time of the demise. On the other quarter of their estates the undertakers might have Irish tenants and grant leases for twenty years or more or less, though not exceeding forty-one years or three or four lives. These Irish should build and dwell together and conform to English 'habit and usage'. The limits of the Irish quarter if imprecise should be settled within six months of the patent. Any undertaker requiring it might have a commission to establish the sub-denominational names of their lands, and the amounts concealed, for exact recital in their patents. Tenants should join in the surrenders of their landlords, but should have their former estates reassured to them on appropriate increase in rent. Such undertakers as had not fulfilled their conditions of building and planting might have their new patents on condition of entering into bonds to fulfil their obligations within two years. Each patentee should covenant to have in his house five calivers or muskets and arms for five pikemen per thousand acres. The lord deputy and council should settle all disputes between patentees or patentees and others concerning their lands. British who had purchased lands from the native Irish and desired regrants should receive them. Lands might also be conveyed at the deputy's discretion to persons who had acquired them from the original undertakers. If any refused to accept the arrangement the deputy might appoint commissioners to enquire of their breaches of the plantation conditions and have their lands disposed of to more conformable persons.[54] The commission was issued on 13 August 1628.[55]

The finalisation of this arrangement coincided roughly with a new administrative arrangement for the payment of the army which evoked strong protests especially from Ulster. On 26 August 1628 it was ordered that all subsidies should be paid directly into the exchequer for central disbursement, i.e. local contributions would no longer go directly to the soldiers stationed there.[56] In July 1629 protests against this arrangement came in from many counties.[57] Phillip O'Reilly, the sheriff of Cavan, stated that that county refused absolutely to pay the sum of £334. 5. 6. demanded, and he returned a petition which begged for the removal of the imposition on account of poverty, 'the dead burying their dead and the look of death set in the face of every man.'[58] The sheriff of Armagh also returned a refusal to pay money into the exchequer lest compliance with the order should

54 TNA, SP 63/246, ff 246–8v, 251–3v (*CSPI, 1625–32*, 349–52).

55 Referred to in NAI, Lodge, Records of the rolls, v, 99.

56 Clarke, 'The army and politics', *Stud. Hib.* iv, 49–51.

57 TNA, SP 63/249, ff 59–95v (*CSPI, 1625–32*, 467–70).

58 Ibid., ff 63–5v.

establish a precedent.[59] There was also protest in the autumn of 1628 against payments towards disbanding a regiment of the army.[60] However, in 1629 the army was reduced very considerably and the conclusion of peace with Spain in 1630 eliminated much of the crisis in Ulster planter-native relations. In August 1629 the earl of Cork and lord chancellor Loftus, newly appointed lords justices after the withdrawal of Falkland, were instructed to insist on the Ulster undertakers paying their double rent and fines. So far few had taken out their new patents and the king requested a list of all who, before the end of the ensuing Michaelmas term, had not complied so that he could dispose of their forfeited property.[61]

2. The regranting of estates, 1628–32

The regranting process assembled much information about the plantation at this point not available owing to the absence of official surveys and the scarceness of estate material. A regrant of an estate was preceded in most cases by a commission of inquiry. The commissioners appointed were, where the warrants survive, made up usually of local planters and clergy, with the attorney of Ulster.[62] They were to enquire whether any part of the proportion concerned had been alienated or let to any Irish person or to any person who had not taken the oath of supremacy. Both of these were forfeitable offences. They were to investigate the precise names and quantities of all the lands concerned, and indicate the mears and bounds of the estate, setting out one-fourth part as the area to be let to the mere Irish. They should inform themselves of all concealed lands.[63] They should report on the buildings erected, the size of villages, and the number of British inhabitants.[64]

Inquisitions survive for nine properties in Cavan, and estates then in the possession of four owners in Armagh. There is almost a complete coverage of the baronies of Clankee and Tullyhunco, and evidence for four of seven proprietors in Loughtee. In Armagh, the entire Fews barony is covered and also three properties in Oneilland.

The inquisitions in themselves pose problems of interpretation. They purport to list all those tenants, British and Irish, who had not taken the oath of supremacy. There is practically no evidence – apart from Pynnar's, which may well be unreliable – that there had been any widespread taking

59 Ibid., ff 84–4v.

60 TNA, SP 63/247, ff 192–6 (*CSPI, 1625–32*, 394–5).

61 TNA, SP 63/249, fol. 9 (*CSPI, 1625–32*, 460–1).

62 Marsh's Library, Dublin, MS Z4.2.6, nos. 81, 84, 96 (estates in Cavan).

63 Ibid., no. 81: warrant for commission of inquiry into Bailie estate, Cavan, 4 December 1628.

64 Ibid., no. 84: warrant for commission of inquiry into Perse estate, 5 December 1628.

of this oath,[65] yet it might be dangerous to take the lists of tenants provided here as offending in his respect as exhaustive. Also most inquisitions purport to list only tenants who held by deed or lease and there is evidence that there were many occupying land without such security. It is only therefore where a full ascription of tenants to all the townlands of an estate, or to so many that it would not be unreasonable to assume that the remainder were held in demesne by the undertaker, that an attempt has been made to work out the relative proportions held by British and Irish tenants. Because the inquisitions do not take account of the fact that many British tenants sub-let parts of their land to native Irish, figures have been arrived at below by expressing the numbers of townlands in British and Irish tenancy as a percentage of the total listed for the estate. More precise methods would have an artificial authority.

In Armagh, an inquisition of April 1629 covering the Hamilton estate in the Fews[66] is full and informative and may, for want of other evidence, be perhaps taken to illustrate Scots' estate management methods in that barony. Of a total of some twenty-seven townlands only one and one-third were held in direct tenancy by four Irish tenants. Three of these had been granted their lands in 1625 and 1627, and the other in 1618.[67] The inquisition concluded that the estate was organised 'in full performance of the plantation'. Three townlands held by more than eleven Irish tenants in 1624 – the total of all then recorded as direct tenants to Hamilton – had been leased in 1625 and 1626 to seven Scottish tenants for periods ranging from nineteen to twenty-five years.[68] One of these townlands, held by Irish in 1624, had been the freehold of a Scot who had departed in the interval. Three other townlands granted, on the evidence of the inquisition, as freehold in 1614, were regranted in two cases as freehold in 1618 and 1626, and in one case for one year also in 1626. Thus of the four freeholds of early creation, two had become extinct and two had been renewed. Many tenures dated from 1622 and after. Apart from the two freeholds existing in 1629, three tenures were for three lives, sixteen were for twenty-one years or over (none over thirty-one), one twenty-one year lease of 1614 had been renewed for fifteen years in 1622, the remaining twenty tenures were for under twenty-one years, and in most cases for under ten years. Land held by Irish, who held on a year-to-year basis, is included in this latter category. Tenures were in many cases joint ones with occasionally for or five tenants per townland. No delimitation of an Irish area was considered necessary.

65 Above, 118.
66 *Inq. cancel. Hib. repert.*, ii, Armagh (4) Chas I.
67 His name does not appear on the 1624 list, below.
68 Below, 269.

The evidence for the three estates in Oneilland is most difficult to interpret. On Stanhowe's[69] eighteen of some twenty-four townlands were held by British, and six – one-quarter – by Irish tenants. However since eleven were held by one English tenant, John Wrench, who had let some to Irish sub-tenants,[70] direct Irish tenants numbered the same as English, there being five of each recorded. But one of the English, John Turner, would seem to have left the estate – the 1622 survey had found 'not above four English men present'[71] – his original agreement in 1611 being for one year, and some of the land being occupied by an Irish tenant in 1624.[72] The Irish all held from year to year, and of the four English (excluding Turner) one was a freeholder created in 1626, two, including Wrench, held for twenty-one years, the other from 1626, and the fourth held from March 1628. The quarter set forth for Irish occupation was in part held by Irish and in part by British tenants under lease.

An inquisition of January 1630 on the Rolleston or Annesley estate[73] adds nothing to the evidence of the 1624 inquiry which suggests that there were no Irish direct tenants. However, it and the inquisition of Sir John Dillon's lands,[74] which has no statistical value, indicate clearly that there was some amount of movement of tenants on estates. Thus, of four tenants listed for the Dillon estate whose tenures dated from 1612–16 two, one of whom was Welsh, had left the estate by 1622. One townland on the Rolleston estate, leased to an Englishman in 1612, had undergone a succession of changes before coming to John Tench of Drogheda in August 1615. In 1621 Tench received a decree against Rolleston,[75] and in May 1628 he sub-let the land to two Irish tenants, O'Quins, on a yearly basis.[76]

Some of the inquisitions also throw light on building progress. On the Acheson estate, at Coolemalish, a stone bawn forty feet in circumference with other buildings had been erected where there was only an inadequate bawn in 1622.[77] There were now three bawns on Hamilton's property,[78] and Dillon had erected a house of lime and stone, 20' by 60'[79] but, on the Stanhowe estate, there was still '*nulla edificia lapid*' erected.[80]

69 *Inq. cancel. Hib. repert.*, ii, Armagh (3) Chas I.
70 TNA, SP 63/238, fol. 142v.
71 BL, Add. MS 4756, fol. 108v.
72 Below, 266.
73 *Inq. cancel. Hib. repert.*, ii, Armagh (6) Chas I.
74 Ibid., (5) Chas I.
75 NAI, Repertories to the decrees of chancery, i, 329.
76 *Inq. cancel. Hib. repert.*, ii, Armagh (6) Chas I.
77 Ibid., (42), Chas I.
78 Ibid., (4), Chas I.
79 Ibid., (5) Chas I.
80 Ibid., (3) Chas I.

Between 14 January 1629 and 9 July 1633 ten of eleven owners of undertakers' land in Armagh took out new patents of their estates.[81] The amount of money raised in fines from nine of these regrants was £509. 6. 0.[82] The undertaker failing to comply was Sir Archibald Acheson. Acheson was later to be sharply criticised by Wentworth for his remissness as an Ulster planter.[83] The reason for Acheson's failure to take out a patent may lie in the dispute then current about his rights to the advowsons of the parish of Loughilly in which his lands fell.[84] The patents and other evidence throw light on the ownership of estates at this time.

The Stanhowe estate which had already been sharply criticised after Pynnar's survey[85] was forfeited at this time. Half of the land was restored to Henry Stanhowe who took out a patent in 1629 the remainder being granted to John Waldron, a relative of the Cavan undertakers,[86] on condition that he pay £600 to Stanhowe who had disbursed that amount on the estate.[87] This was the only estate in either county to be forfeited at this time. Waldron also acquired between June 1629[88] and January 1633,[89] when a king's letter took cognizance of the new owner, Sir John Dillon's purchase. On 8 August 1631 a king's letter was written to the lords justices instructing that Waldron be granted a patent of the Stanhowe land.[90] He did not, however, receive such a patent of this or Dillon's lands (as also of lands in Leitrim) until, after a king's letter in his favour of January,[91] July 1633.[92]

The fortunes of Michael Obbyns who had acquired Powell's estate from Rolleston were particularly dramatic. It has been seen that in 1622 he was

81 NAI, Lodge, Records of the rolls, v, 107 (Sir William Alexander), 133–5 (Sir William Brownlow), 158–60 (John Hamilton), 178 (John Dillon and Richard Cope: Armagh Public Library, Castle Dillon Papers, 28–52), 179 (Henry Stanhowe), 183–5 (Anthony Cope), 261–2 (Viscount Grandison: PRONI, PRO 1145, certified copy), 278–9 (Prudence and John Obbyns: PRONI, PRO 1147 (copy), T267 (translation)), 293–5 (John Waldron: original patent in Watson and Neill, solicitors' office, Lurgan). Sir Francis Annesley's patent, 25 November 1631, for Rolleston's Teemore was not enrolled, but is referred to in NLI, Rolleston Papers, Packing Case 112.

82 Ibid.

83 Below, 181.

84 Below, 293–5, 309–12.

85 Above, 126.

86 *CSPI, 1625–32*, 621.

87 Ibid., *1660–62*, 185, 340.

88 *Inq. cancel. Hib. repert.*, ii, Armagh (5) Chas I.

89 TNA, SP 63/254, ff 1–3 (*CSPI, 1633–47*, 1).

90 *CPRI, Chas I*, 612–13.

91 *CSPI, 1633–47*, 1.

92 NAI, Lodge, Records of the rolls, v, 293–5. Wentworth seems to have been unwilling to recognise him as an accredited undertaker, and on 20 May 1637 the king ordered that he and his son William 'be admitted into the number of planters in Ireland, they conforming themselves to the prescribed orders' (*CSPI, 1633–47*, 159).

'a prisoner in England' and his estate was neglected. He had been unable to repay an English debt of £200 to a certain Robert Horsman decreed against him in 1621 and had been outlawed at the instigation of his creditor.[93] Accordingly possession for the crown was taken of his Armagh lands and these were granted in 1626 to Horsman until the debt should be paid.[94] Obbyns died in September 1629[95] and the outcome of the judgement against him was that part of the estate, about three-quarters, was sold. His widow and son took out a patent of the remainder in July 1631[96] and this remained in Obbyns' hands up to 1641. It would appear that Richard Cope, who died in 1628 and was brother of Anthony the undertaker,[97] acquired the dispossessed portion because his sons Walter and Anthony owned much of it in 1641.[98]

The success of the Sacheverall family is somewhat ambiguous. In January 1628 Sir William Alexander,[99] took out a patent of one of Sacheverall's two small proportions.[100] Alexander appears to have had a shrewd eye for estates in difficulty having also acquired an interest in the lands of Sir James Cunningham at Carrigans in Donegal.[101] However, his ownership of Sacheverall land was temporary, and the estate was in Sacheverall hands until after 1641.[102]

Turning to Cavan, in Clankee barony, we find that approximately 62 per cent of Bailie's[103] estate was held by people of British name. The Irish tenants, holding in most cases one townland each, had their lands on a yearly basis. There were twelve British tenants, including three Bailies, and there were nine Irish tenants.[104]

On John Hamilton's small proportion of Killcloghan 44 per cent of the townlands was in British tenancy. Presumably having considerable property in Armagh he had leased the demesne. Some of his British tenants held for periods of under ten years, the Irish in all cases held for terms of one year.[105] The inquisition for the Perse estate[106] is more difficult to interpret. Only about 60 per cent of the property is accounted for and it would seem that

93 NAI, Lodge, Records of the rolls, v, 521.
94 Ibid.
95 Hill, *Plantation*, 558.
96 NAI, Lodge, Records of the rolls, v, 278–9.
97 Burke, *Peerage*, 579.
98 NAI, Books of Survey and Distribution.
99 Above, 113.
100 NAI, Lodge, Records of the rolls, v, 107.
101 Hill, *Plantation*, 507–8.
102 Below, 393.
103 On Robert Bailie see *CSPI, 1625–32*, 329.
104 *Inq. cancel. Hib. repert.*, ii, Cavan (17) Chas I: 10 April 1629.
105 Ibid., (18) Chas I: 10 April 1629.
106 Ibid., (19) Chas I.

no more than 28 per cent of the townlands was held by British tenants. However, it is evident that Perse had taken action to fill the vacuum caused by the mass removal of tenants following on the sale of the property in 1621,[107] the tenure of eight of his British tenants, mostly Englishmen, dating from the years 1627–29.

Of Fishe's estate, in Loughtee, made up of 44¾ polls, 37¼ were leased, leaving 7½, or 17 per cent of the total, as held presumably in demesne. 27¼ polls were demised to British, being 61 per cent of the total estate. The deeds of 16 polls in British hands dated from the year 1626–8. Much of the land leased at this time was held only for very short periods of one or two years. All the Irish tenants except one held on a yearly basis.[108] On the Waldron estate, there appear to have been few Irish tenants holding directly from the landlord, and where they did they seem to have held smaller areas – in one case there were four Irish tenants to a townland – than the Irish in the two Scottish baronies.[109]

Two ownership changes in Loughtee estates are revealed, both of estates of previous unstable ownership. Sir George Mainwaring had sold his estate to the bishop of Kilmore and Ardagh in October 1627 and on his death in January 1628 it had descended to his son Roger Moynes.[110] Ameas had disposed of his lands, before July 1629,[111] to John Greenham. Greenham was a Dublin lawyer,[112] a brother-in-law of Bishop Moynes, and a graduate of Emmanuel College, Cambridge.[113]

The inquisitions offer information on the state of buildings, and the sizes of villages at this stage. In Clankee the building descriptions confirm the evidence of 1622 in the cases of Perse and Bailie, and show that John Hamilton had completed building work then in progress.[114] A stone house being built on Sir Claud Hamilton's estate in Tullyhunco in 1622[115] had now been completed.[116]

As to the village development Bailieborough was now a village of fifteen 'English-like houses planted and inhabited with British families'.[117] On the Perse estate there was a town of eighteen 'English-like' houses, called

107 Above, 151.
108 *Inq. cancel. Hib. repert.*, ii, Cavan (26) Chas I.
109 NAI, Exchequer inquisitions, Ulster, Cavan, (3) Chas I, 4–22.
110 *Inq. cancel. Hib. repert.*, ii, Cavan (23) Chas I.
111 NAI, Lodge, Records of the rolls, v, 147–9.
112 Below, 314.
113 E.S. Shuckburgh (ed.), *Two biographies of William Bedell, bishop of Kilmore* (Cambridge 1902), 302, 341.
114 *Inq. cancel. Hib. repert.*, ii, Cavan (17–19) Chas I.
115 BL, Add. MS 4756, fol. 103v.
116 *Inq. cancel. Hib. repert.*, ii, Cavan (24) Chas I.
117 Ibid., (18) Chas I.

Persecourt, on the townland of Lisdrumskeagh, now Shercock.[118] The town of Killashandra on the Hamilton estate in Tullyhunco which consisted of twenty houses in 1622[119] was now – in 1629 – made up of thirty-four houses with British residents.[120] The village on the Moynes estate in Loughtee – now called Moynehall – which in 1622 when owned by Mainwaring consisted of seven houses 'but not tenants in them all'[121] – had now twenty-four houses 'and more, all inhabited with Englishe and Britishe famelies', and was recommended to be granted two annual fairs.[122] While there is no further information from which to draw a more general picture, it is clear that some villages at any rate had expanded considerably in the 1620s.

Concealments were found in greater quantity in Cavan than in Armagh. Thus small concealed areas were listed for the estates of John Hamilton and Bailie in Clankee, of Sir Francis Hamilton in Tullyhunco, and of Moynes in Loughtee. There were considerable concealments in the Waldron estate amounting to nine polls. An inquisition, not found, for the Butler estate appears to have been unsatisfactory in its treatment of concealments because in July 1631 the lords justices authorised the issuing of a new commission. It was felt that five polls in Cavan (he also had land in Fermanagh) were concealed.[123] Two polls of Sir Francis Hamilton's estate were reported to be 'wrongfullie withheld and possessed' by Sir James Craig.[124] Most of the inquisitions selected and defined the area suitable for Irish occupation; they also assembled detailed lists of sub-denominational and alternative names of places. Much of the colony on the Moynes estate appears to have been concentrated in a small area.[125]

Ten of fourteen Cavan undertakers took out patents between 20 December 1628 and 17 July 1631.[126] Most of these estates had previously been examined by commissioners and the new patents reflect that examination in the detail of topographical information, the inclusion of concealments, and in the areas allocated to Irish. The amount of money raised in fines from these ten properties was £563. 12. 0.[127] Two of three

[118] Ibid., (19), Chas I.
[119] BL, Add. MS 4756, fol. 103.
[120] *Inq. cancel. Hib. repert.*, ii, Cavan (24) Chas I.
[121] BL, Add. MS 4756, fol. 102v.
[122] *Inq. cancel. Hib. repert.*, ii, Cavan (23) Chas I.
[123] Marsh's Library, Dublin, MS Z4.2.6, no. 96.
[124] *Inq. cancel. Hib. repert.*, ii, Cavan (24) Chas I.
[125] Ibid., (23) Chas I.
[126] Detailed abstracts of these patents are found in NAI, Lodge, Records of the rolls, v, 99–100 (Bagshaw), 139–44 (Perse: NLI, D8784, attested copy), 144–7 (Bailie), 147–9 (Greenham), 158–60 (John Hamilton), 175–8 (Moyne), 181–3 (Taylor), 206–7 (Fishe), 265–71 (Craig), 273–8 (Sir Francis Hamilton).
[127] Claims for payments of arrears in Ireland were being made and ordered at this time from the additional revenue accruing from fines and increased rents (*CSPI, 1625–32*, 470, 550, 552, 564, 583).

owners in Tullyhunco, Sir Archibald Acheson failing to comply, in this way secured their estates. Three of four in Clankee, excluding William Hamilton, received new patents. Five of seven proprietors in Loughtee did likewise, neither Sir Stephen Butler nor those responsible for the Waldron estate, the owner of which was then a minor, securing new patents. Sir Stephen Butler was forbidden to take out a new patent until he had satisfied a debt to his brother.[128] That the disagreement was unresolved by December 1633 is evident from a letter of the king to Wentworth instructing him to summon Butler and his nephew (his brother being presumably dead) before him and settle the dispute.[129]

Little is known of what steps, if any, the undertakers in either county took to give effect to the segregation principle. It could, theoretically, have involved the breaking of leases of land earmarked for Irish which might have been held in leasehold by British.[130] If, however, we view the problem of the undertakers very narrowly to be that they should have no more than one-quarter of their estates held by Irish who were their direct tenants, and overlook the presence on their estates of the much more numerous groups of Irish who were either servants or workmen, or tenants to the undertakers' British tenantry, the implementing of the arrangement would not have posed great difficulties for most of the Armagh undertakers, though for many in Cavan it would have been much more difficult. An attempt has been made to work out elsewhere for Armagh,[131] using the evidence of the 1624 natives' inquiry (which may well have been conducted with leniency to the undertakers admittedly, though it does receive some confirmation from the inquisitions of the 1628–30 period), the proportion of each undertaker's estate held by direct Irish tenants. This reveals that while most had such tenants on approximately one-quarter or under of their estates only one, Sir William Brownlow, had substantially exceeded this proportion.[132] While for Cavan an inquiry of this sort has not survived or was not conducted, it is clear from the inquisitions for some estates examined above that much high proportions were held by direct Irish tenants.

In July 1630 the committee for Irish affairs of the privy council decided on punitive measures whereby the income from lands illegally held by Irish could be diverted to satisfy the arrears of two Ulster captains, themselves undertakers, Sir William Stewart of Aghintain, County Tyrone and Sir

[128] *CSPI, 1625–32*, 448.
[129] Ibid. *1633–47*, 36.
[130] See above, 140.
[131] See above, 217–22.
[132] Below, 174.

Henry Tichborne of Lifford, County Donegal.[133] The intention was that inquisitions should be held throughout the five plantation counties, excluding Londonderry, to enquire what lands in the areas for British occupation on undertakers' estates had been held in any way by Irish since the date of the letters patent, and that these lands should be granted to Stewart and Tichborne, with all rents accruing since the first breach of conditions, to hold during the king's pleasure. They should account for what rents they had received when required and 'husband and improve' the lands while they remained under their control.[134]

Inquisitions were held in both counties in the summer of 1631,[135] and in December 1631 the lands thus discovered – in all five counties – were granted to the two beneficiaries. The patent recited that the lands had reverted to the king for such term as they were granted to or occupied by the Irish. All the lands thus granted had been valued at £413. 5. 0. per annum.[136]

The inquisition for Armagh revealed that small pieces of land in three properties, all in Oneilland, were subject to confiscation. On Sir William Brownlow's estate three portions of land, the largest a townland, were revealed to be in Irish occupation contrary to his patent. On Stanhowe's estate a half townland was found to be so occupied, as was one quarter of a townland belonging to Sir William Alexander.[137]

The inquiry in Cavan revealed unsegregated Irish tenants on four estates. The amounts of land involved were considerably larger than in Armagh. In Loughtee it was found that four polls of land (one is omitted in the patent) in Moynes's portion and three polls in Fishe's were in Irish hands. In Clankee one half poll in John Hamilton's estate and twelve polls of Sir Henry Perse's were discovered in Irish occupation contrary to regulation.[138]

The completeness of the inquiry in either county is subject to some doubt. The lands itemised, with the exception of two polls on the Perse estate, appear to have been held directly by Irish occupants from the landlords. The inquiries thus, by and large, did not take account of Irish sub-tenancies at all. A subsequent inquisition on the Perse estate in Cavan in November 1632 revealed that one of his freeholders had demised two polls of land in the British area to native Irish tenants.[139] This provides a

[133] *CPRI, Chas I,* 588; referred to in NAI, Lodge, Records of the rolls, v, 526–7. In 1627 Tichborne had received a right of payment from the fines of those ploughing by the tail (*CPRI, Chas I,* 292–3).

[134] NAI, Lodge, Records of the rolls, v, 526–7.

[135] *Inq. cancel. Hib. repert.*, ii, Armagh (19) Chas I; Cavan (38) Chas I.

[136] NAI, Lodge, Records of the rolls, v, 526–7; *CPRI, Chas I,* 588.

[137] *Inq. cancel. Hib. repert.*, ii, Armagh (19) Chas I.

[138] Ibid., Cavan (38) Chas I.

[139] Ibid., Cavan (41) Chas I.

particular example of what had been a fairly general practice, continuing now despite the 1628 regulations. The government continued to be unable to enforce the modified regulations thoroughly, as it had been unable (or unwilling) to enforce the original conditions. Penalising devices, like the grant to Stewart and Tichborne, were not entirely satisfactory.

The effect of the Stewart-Tichborne grant in enforcing compliance to regulation, viewed only in the very narrow sense that the undertakers should not have Irish tenants on the British-appointed areas of their estates, is not clear owing to the tantalising dearth of estate records. By 1635 Brownlow's townland of Ballynamony, confiscated in 1631, was, at any rate, in the hands of a British tenant who paid rent to him.[140] He had therefore recovered at least part of the land confiscated, and had demised it in accordance with regulation. However, stronger and more direct measures than those adopted would have been needed to enforce complete conformity to the new conditions.

3. Population, *c.* 1630

Although the inquisitions give some picture of the estates of undertakers prior to receiving regrants, the termination of the series of government surveys in 1622 makes the presentation of a detailed picture of the colony as a whole after that a matter of difficulty. However, the survival of a muster-roll from this period, more detailed than that of 1618,[141] assists in estimating the size of the British population, at the beginning of the third decade of plantation.[142]

A renewed concern with mustering and training the 'risings out' in Ulster arose during the war years. Risings out were held in Antrim and Down in 1626.[143] In September 1628, following on royal instructions to the lord deputy of the previous July,[144] Lieutenant William Graham was appointed muster-master for Ulster and Leinster with power to demand the same fees as Alleyne had received previously.[145] Graham, a native of Cumberland and so probably a relative of the Cavan servitor family, had been responsible for the arrest and conveyance to England of 'two notorious malefactors' from Monaghan early in 1624.[146] The muster-roll commonly

140 Armagh Museum, 'A briefe survey of the severall leases and other holdings within the mannor of Brownlowes–Derry … 1667', which includes, 126–30, 'a rent-roll of Sir William Brownlowe's half years rent ending All Saints 1635'. This rental is unsatisfactory in that it states only in some cases the identity of the land leased as well as the tenant's name.

141 Above, 110–13.

142 BL, Add. MS 4770.

143 BL, Sloane MS 3827, ff 79–82 (Falkland Papers).

144 *CPRI, Chas I*, 380–1; *CSPI, 1625–32*, 367.

145 *CPRI, Chas I*, 365; NAI, Lodge, Records of the rolls, Miscellaneous Enrollments, 41.

146 *CPRI, Jas I*, 582.

dated as *c.* 1630 may then be ascribed to Graham. It is likely that he began his task on appointment, but this return is not for the first mustering; a first defaulter in Cavan is noted as having attended.[147] There is reason to suspect, however, that for Armagh at any rate its figures should be treated with some caution.

The total number of men mustered in the nine Ulster counties was 13,136.[148] Of these 926 lived in Armagh and 815 in Cavan. Fermanagh, with 913, was roughly equivalent to Armagh, but the other counties, except Monaghan with 93 and Cavan, all mustered numbers considerably exceeding 1,000, of which Londonderry with 1,930 and Down with 4,045 had the larger totals. The amount and quality of arms displayed was not reassuring. There were some 7,000 swords and 3,000 pikes, but only 700 muskets. In addition, there were 1,300 other weapons, made up of calivers, snaphances, halberts, and lances.[149] There were only 20 and 28 muskets respectively shown in Cavan and Armagh.

It seems beyond doubt that the section of the muster book for Armagh must be regarded as conservative if used as a guide to population. Professor Moody's analysis of its contents for Londonderry shows that its return for that county approximates very closely to the total of British males present,[150] but it would be dangerous to accept that this holds good for the other counties.[151] Recalcitrance in mustering was characteristic of England at this time,[152] but it is also clear that Wentworth's attitude here was a rigorous one[153] and Graham's muster return is manifestly a reflection of the greater vigour of government at this time in comparison with Alleyne's in 1618. Some of the Armagh proprietors in *c.* 1630 may have claimed that they were not required to muster more than twenty-four men per 1,000-acre proportion which had been Alleyne's assumption in 1618, though there is no evidence whatever that Graham accepted this convention ten years later.

The materials available for criticism of the Armagh section, though limited, cast doubt on its completeness. They are primarily of two types –

147 BL, Add. MS 4770, fol. 9v.

148 Ibid., fol. 283. The total for Cavan was inaccurately calculated as 795 and for Armagh as 902. The provincial total has been adjusted to take account of these faults in Graham's arithmetic.

149 Ibid.

150 Moody, *Londonderry Plantation*, 319–22.

151 The survival of a tabulated return on the population of Donegal drawn up in 1616 by a provost marshal (BL, Sloane MSS 3827, ff 62–3v) may also be noted. This return, broken down by baronies and nationalities, gives a total of 1,760 British (291 English, 1,479 Scots ('besydes the souldiers'), 5,201 Irish). The muster book gives a total of 1,258 or some 500 less, i.e. some 71.5 per cent of the provost marshal's total. The accompanying letter indicates that the provost marshal was not on good terms with at least one of the resident landlords, so he was not likely to connive at over-estimates of population.

152 Boynton, *Elizabethan Militia*, 269–87.

153 Below, 181.

inquisitions and estate papers. In using the inquisitions associated with the granting of new patents to undertakers under the 1628 arrangement it has been decided to examine whether tenants whose tenures dated from 1622 or after featured amongst those mustered. Names have not been included where it would seem likely that a person featuring on the roll was the son of a deceased tenant. It is perhaps worth noting that the inquisitions do not record British sub-tenants.

Only two inquisitions can be used in this way, those for the Hamilton estate in the Fews, and the Stanhowe estate in Oneilland. On the former it is found that 13 names, 9 of whose tenures dated from 1625 or after, were not recorded in the muster list.[154] On the Stanhowe estate where only 3 new tenures were created in this period one, the son of the owner, is not recorded.[155] Estate papers where available add further confirmation. Two rentals of the Brownlow estate in Oneilland substantially confirmed by a surviving fragment of the 1634 subsidy roll,[156] dating from 1635 and 1636 reveal in both cases 68 British tenants whereas the total of the muster roll is 42.[157] The muster master also took no account of British tenants on the lands of Trinity College. These can hardly have been numerous, but there is evidence that Caulfeild had planted British settlers on the lands he held from the college in Colure.[158] Of 56 tenants to Caulfeild's abbey lands listed in the muster book only 3 feature in a list of 16 tenants of Colure, *c.* 1641, preserved in Trinity College.[159] An examination of the estate papers of the archbishopric of Armagh from 1625 reveals some 70 names not on the muster roll.[160] Two other names emerge from a lawsuit of 1638.[161] While it is possible that some of these may have been absentee, likely absentee, and also people possibly dead and represented by sons on the muster roll have been excluded. Four names can be added from the Obbyns and Cope lands (originally Powell) in the Portadown area from a surviving fragment of the 1634 subsidy roll.[162] Thus for six estates for which evidence can be mobilised the names of some settlers not featuring on the muster roll have been recovered.[163] There were thus at least some 1,050 British males in the county at this period.

154 *Inq. cancel. Hib. repert.*, ii, Armagh (4) Chas I.
155 Ibid., (3) Chas I.
156 RCB Lib., Dublin, Libr/48, 111.
157 Armagh Museum, Brownlow Rentals, 1635 and 1636.
158 Below, 241.
159 TCD Muniment Room, Mahaffy Collection, drawer 6, from folder no. 1.
160 Armagh Archiepiscopal Registry, Rentals, post 1625; Armagh Public Library, Archbishop's manor court rolls: transcripts of the rolls pertaining to County Armagh are in PRONI, T475, 4–8, 20–48.
161 NAI, Repertories to the decrees of chancery, ii, 138.
162 PRONI, T281/7, 1.
163 Armagh Public Library, Castle Dillon Papers, 71–6.

It has to be admitted that this figure does not reconcile readily with that derived from the 1622 survey. The muster roll figure for the territory covered by the survey, i.e. excluding church land and Caulfeild's monastic property, is 712. This is close to the 685 of Pynnar but considerably lower than the approximately 1,200 arrived at from the 1622 survey. For church and monastic property the muster return lists 212 names to which have been added some 85 names, including resident on the lands of Trinity College, from other sources. If these are added to the 1622 figure there may well have been as many as 1,500 British males in the county. It is clear, at any rate, that a figure of well over 1,000 has to be suggested.

The possibility of checking this against other sources is limited. It may be noted, however, that the hearth money roll of 1664 for Armagh[164] gives the names of some 1,100 British, presumably heads of households, which must between them have contained close on 2,000 males. The census of *c.* 1659[165] provides a total of 2,393 English and Scots in the county, though it cannot be concluded that this figure was of males only.

Criticism of the Cavan return is more difficult through the absence of any substantial alternative sources. Of 6 inquisitions covering Cavan estates examined, 3, of the estates of Bailie, Fishe, and Perse, add one name each.[166] These modest additions are counteracted by the fact that three or four of those listed for Cavan town were old English. The muster return does have the limitation, not serious as far as British population is concerned, that the servitors' lands, with the exception of the estate granted to Ridgeway and now the property of the earl of Fingall, are omitted from its reckoning. It is likely that the addition of some 20 names would correct this deficiency.[167]

Graham's return for Cavan is close to the figures derived from both Pynnar's survey and the report of the 1622 commissioners. Excluding church land and the town of Cavan, the muster book indicates the presence of 745 people. For the corresponding area from Pynnar's survey the number

164 L.P. Murray (ed.), 'The County Armagh hearth money rolls, A.D. 1664', *Arch. Hib.* viii (1941), 121–202.

165 S. Pender (ed.), *A census of Ireland, circa 1659* (IMC, Dublin, 1939), 23–40.

166 *Inq. cancel. Hib. repert.*, ii, Cavan (17, 19, 26) Chas I.

167 There is only a partial survival of the 1664 hearth money roll for Cavan. Four parishes covered in whole or part in Castlerahan, reveal about 25 British names some of which are obviously post 1641 arrivals. (These extracts are presented by P. O'Connell (ed.), 'Extracts from the hearth money rolls for County Cavan', *Briefny Antiquarian Society Journal*, vol.1 no. 2 (1921), 147–8, vol. 1 no. 2 (1922), 311–12, vol. 2 no. 3 (1925–26), 288–89, and vol. 3 no. 1 (1927), 61–2. On a transcript of the roll for the barony of Tullyhunco about 183 British names occur: F.J. McKiernan, 'The hearth money rolls for the baronies of Tullyhunco and Tullyhaw, County Cavan', *Breifne* vol. 1, no. 3 (1960), 247–62.) The muster book gives 210. The Tullyhaw hearth tax return records 50 British names. The *c.* 1659 census has not survived for Cavan.

of 847 males was derived, though from the 1622 survey the figure of 765 was reached. If one adds to this the 70 people listed for church lands and the town of Cavan – a figure which includes the three of four Old English who are listed amongst 27 who appeared for Cavan – one gets a total of 835. This is identical with the *c.* 1630 total if one adds 20, as suggested, to cover servitors' lands whose sparse British population was not mustered.

It is fair to conclude that the muster roll does not indicate any substantial increase in the size of the colony after 1622. This is consistent with the general absence of evidence of immigration in the 1620s, which also holds for the 1630s. This reconciles, too, with the fact that the undertakers had pressed for, and secured sanction for, the compromise arrangement whereby part of their lands might be held by Irish tenantry. Also the emphasis in government interest in the plantation after 1622 shifts away from concern with the size of the colony.

CHAPTER 6

The Plantation under Wentworth's administration, 1634–41

Wentworth's policy to 1637

Wentworth inherited the arrangement whereby the undertakers might receive new patents in return for doubling their rents and paying a fine. When in 1633 he examined its implications he took objection on two main grounds, and felt his own initiative gravely hampered in consequence. He pointed out that the crown had lost considerable revenue in allowing the undertakers to acquire new patents without a re-measurement of their estates and a consequent increase in quit rent. The crown he asserted had thereby sustained 'shameful injury by passing in truth ten times the quantities of land expressed in their patents'.[1] Second, he felt a grave error had been made in granting their estates in 'base' soccage tenure rather than *in capite* which was

> the greatest means of drawing the subjects to depend upon his majesty. ... If the business were entire again [his] managing [he] would make it six times as beneficial for the crown and yet use the planters honourably and well.[2]

However, while admitting that little could be done to overthrow so recent a policy he was determined

> the plantation being ... one of the chief cares intrusted [to him, to] cast awhile about and search, if it were possible, to play an aftergame so well as to reduce them in these two principal respects to reason and justice.[3]

The matter achieved prominence at this time in that one Ulster undertaker – particularly relevant as a proprietor in both Armagh and Cavan – amongst others who had not previously availed themselves of the arrangement, had

[1] Wentworth to Coke, 23 October 1633 (W. Knowler (ed.), *The earl of Strafford's letters and dispatches,* (2 vols, London, 1739), i, 132).
[2] Ibid.
[3] Ibid.

desired Wentworth's warrant to initiate the process leading to a new grant. This was Sir Archibald Acheson, a powerful figure 'being considered so near in access to the king', and the warrant was refused.[4] This refusal, made in general as in particular terms, was, in effect, a breach of article 26 of the Graces which embodied the decision of 1628 to grant new patents. Thus, if he could take no immediate steps to invalidate undertakers' titles, the taking out of new patents by certain defaulters would not be allowed.

Apart, however, from imposing restrictions on individuals, notably Acheson, Wentworth's initiative in introducing a new policy for Ulster was inhibited for many years by varying political considerations.[5] Thus Wentworth, early in 1634, decided that in view of his forthcoming parliament it would be inadvisable to press them too severely to conform 'considering the truth is we must ... bow and governe the native by the planter and the planter by the native'.[6] He noted, however, the information available from Graham's muster book, observing that the Ulster colony was but 'a company of naked men', underarmed or in many cases provided with arms of 'altogether unserviceable' types such as snaphances and 'birding peeces'. His policy would be, he stated, to encourage Graham in every way, but to take no more radical action until parliamentary business had been transacted, when he would require a 'very strict' letter from the king enjoining compliance with the mustering regulations 'and all other covenants of plantation'.[7] Coke in his reply of June 30 signified acceptance of such a policy.[8] On November 27 as a tactical gesture Wentworth announced that he would no longer withhold the benefit of article 26 of the Graces from defaulting Ulster undertakers.[9]

Further cause, moreover, for procrastination of an active Ulster policy came with the decision, which had crystallised by the autumn of 1634, to carry out a plantation in Connacht. It was felt that punitive measures adopted against the Ulster settlers might deter applications for land in the west. Hence, though the penalisation of the Londoners in 1635[10] provided a precedent which Wentworth might easily have cited against the planters

4 Ibid., 132–3; Sheffield City Library, Strafford MSS, vol. v, 105, 228. Acheson had also pressed for the payment of a debt of some £750 owed to him by the crown in England.

5 Pressure was brought to bear on the county of Cavan in 1633 for reluctance to make subsidy contributions (ibid., ff 102, 4), but this involved no new departure in policy.

6 Wentworth to Cork, 31 January 1634 (Sheffield City Library, Strafford MSS, vol. v, 37–48).

7 Ibid. It may be noted that a lease made at this time by Sir Patrick Acheson (Sir Archibald died in 1634) of land in Cavan enjoined attendance at all musters and outrisings (NAI, Deeds, wills and instruments ... post mortem, vol. 25, 254–65).

8 Ibid., vol. v, fol. 242.

9 *Journals of the house of lords of the kingdom of Ireland*, vol. i, (Dublin 1779), 27 November 1634, 36–7; Clarke, *Old English*, 88.

10 Moody, *Londonderry Plantation*, 355–69.

elsewhere in Ulster, the opportunity was not availed of. Coke, in communicating the outcome of the Londoners trial to Wentworth in March 1635, had pointed out that 'we apprehend this precedent will trenche deepe not only upon the other five escheated counties but upon most plantations in that kingdome'.[11]

In the trial of the city of London one of the allegations against them was that they had procured a very considerably greater extent of land than the acreage stated in their original patent. This statement was both true and a little irrelevant since the acreage figures had been calculated not by them but by Sir William Parsons, the Irish surveyor general, and his colleagues. That the land had been grossly undermeasured was shown on the evidence of Thomas Raven, formerly the city's surveyor, who had been sent to London by Wentworth at the request of the crown in January 1635.[12] Raven had been employed by the Londoners until *c.* 1618, and from 1621 was involved with Sir Thomas Phillips of Limavady in map-making and surveying subsequently used as evidence against the Londoners at their trial.[13] In 1623, pointing out how much revenue the king had lost by conveying away lands grossly undersurveyed, he proposed that the office of king's sworn measurer should be set up in Ireland and himself appointed.[14]

The city's trial in 1635, as well as casting doubts on the probity of Parsons,[15] brought Raven and his proposals into renewed prominence. In March his scheme was recommended as having royal approval by Coke to the lord deputy[16] and in May he was despatched from England widely commended.[17] Wentworth was thus being proffered the means to put one of this two objectives for the plantation, an accurate re-survey and consequent increase of rent, into effect. However, his reply of April 7 indicated that although he had considered Raven's proposals, the plans for Ulster must be for the moment subordinated to his grant scheme for Connacht:[18]

11 Sheffield City Library, Strafford MSS, vol. ix, 261–2.

12 Ibid., vol. vi, ff 166, 167–8.

13 Moody, *Londonderry Plantation*, 112, 139, 169, 194–5, 196, 262, 275, 280, 362, 452. Raven lived in Armagh for a time and did some mapping for the archbishop.

14 TNA, SP 63/237, ff 150–51.

15 Sheffield City Library, Strafford MSS, vol. ix, 261–2. The native Irish were also critical of Parsons' procedure at the time of the plantation. A statement (in Latin) issued by the confederate catholics in 1642 claimed that he had apparently bribed those jurors who found crown title to the escheated counties (S. Kavanagh (ed.), *Commentarius Rinuccianus*, vol. i, (IMC, Dublin, 1932), 359).

16 Sheffield City Library, Strafford MSS, vol. ix, 261–2.

17 Ibid., vol. iv, 204–6, 207; vol. ix, 262–4; *CSPI, 1633–47*, 184.

18 Knowler (ed.), *Strafford's letters*, i, 405–6; Sheffield City Library, Strafford MSS, vol. ix, 13–15 of new pagination beginning after 83; see also vol. iii, 192.

> Tis most true it stands with all the reason and justice in the world the crown should be righted in this fraud of the overmeasurement which it hath suffered by ... thorough the negligence (at the best) of those ministerial officers unto whose trust the care thereof was committed. And certainly I was fully resolved to have been heard upon this subject in a season fit for it, which hitherto it hath not been, nor, in my opinion yet is. For under favour, I conceive this question would not be stirred until such times as the plantations of Connaght and Ormond were settled ... The calling for reason from others at this time [would] make the plantation land ... less esteemed and sought after ... But these plantations now in hand once settled there ought not to be an hower at after lost from vindicating the Crown in these matters, not only in the point of over-measure but in that of their tenures also.[19]

In his reply Coke accepted the deputy's 'seasonable caution' as being 'very well approved'. However, so also was Raven's proposal, 'that the saddle (as you say) may be sett on the right horse'.[20] Since the plantation scheme for Connacht proved abortive and was only abandoned in 1640,[21] the re-measurement of Ulster and consequent adjustment of rents was permanently deferred.

In 1637 and 1638 Wentworth continued to press that the prospects of future plantations should not be hazarded in any plans for Londonderry. Thus, writing to the king in April 1637, he suggested that

> truly Sir, The English which transplant themselves hither are so much the better subjects to the crown and soe much the better husbands to the ground then are the natives as they deserve to be much made of ...[22]

By 1638 the argument had acquired a further sophistication. Any redisposal of the Londoners' lands must take account of the colonists, predominantly English, who had settled there. Their harsh treatment would discourage candidates for land elsewhere, but also the province of Ulster would 'become totally possest by the Scottish' rendering them 'much harder to governe in Ulster where I assure your Majesty they are but overruly already'.[23]

The progressive abandonment of the re-measuring of Ulster can thus be seen to have been largely due to political circumstances, though the

19 Ibid.

20 Knowler (ed.), *Strafford's letters*, i, 424.

21 Kearney, *Strafford*, 190–91.

22 Knowler (ed.), *Strafford's letters,* ii, 65–6; see also Sheffield City Library, Strafford MSS, vol. x, 22 (second pagination).

23 Sheffield City Library, Strafford MSS, vol. iii, 309–12.

administrative task would also have been considerable.[24] However the plan to convert the planters' tenures to knight service was put into partial effect by means of the commission for defective titles.[25] This commission, one of Wentworth's most effective instruments, was set up by royal patent in June 1634.[26] By 1636 when the business of the commission was increasing very much in momentum Wentworth estimated that 'before the worke be finished' the revenue would be increased by £6,000 at least.[27] Also it was the purpose of the commission to convert tenures to an *in capite* basis, thereby bringing them within the competence of the court of wards with further implications of profit and power for the crown.

Early in 1637 the commission turned its attention to Ulster. On February 21 Wentworth wrote to Coke at follows:

> We have now begun to call before us at that commission the planters, natives, and servitors within the province of Ulster, where the king hath not so much as one tenure in knights service.[28]

The immediate reaction of the settlers in our area, or indeed elsewhere in the plantation counties, is not available. However, the letters of George Rawdon, the agent of Lord Conway and Killultagh for his lands at Lisburn, give a general indication. In May 1637 he reported that only two landowners in Antrim and Down had as yet submitted to the commission.[29] By June it would seem that the undertakers who had recently, under the 1628 scheme, taken out new patents had petitioned for exemption from again renewing their titles. Rawdon reported from Dublin as follows:

> The judges have argued publikally the validity of divers patents for plantation land in the north, but have not yet agreed, other judges are to argue againe in the Counsell Chamber the next week. Here [ ] great expectation of the issue but it is like [ ] must all come in and take new patents as in [ ] most of the kingdome.[30]

The details of this legal debate are not available, but by July Rawdon informed Conway that Lord Chichester was preparing to take out his patent,

24 For Falkland's appreciation of this in 1627, see below, 367.

25 For its purposes and effects see Kearney, *Strafford*, 81–4.

26 TNA, SP 63/254, ff 302–11 (*CSPI, 1633–47*, 56–7); Sheffield City Library, Strafford MSS, vol. ix, 101–7. Rules regarding the fees and other regulations were laid down by the commissioners (Bod. Lib., Carte MSS, vol. 60, ff 642–2v).

27 Sheffield City Library, Strafford MSS, vol. ix, 146–52.

28 Ibid., 209. Some Irish-owned land was held by knight's service, see below, 217, 225.

29 TNA, SP 63/256, fol. 101 (*CSPI, 1633–47*, 159).

30 Ibid., ff 110–10v (ibid., 162).

commenting that 'itt is soe tedious a worke that it makes me afraid to thinke of it'.[31] In August Wentworth communicated his expectations to Coke:

> The composition of Ulster will, I am very confident, answer expectation bringing in not only a considerable increase of revenue but gaining amongst them tenures *in capite* which (if I be not mightily mistaken) will alsone shew itself hereafter for a very great service to the Crown, and much increase the Court of Wards.[32]

2. The Commission for Defective Titles in Armagh and Cavan

Between 9 June 1638 and 24 September 1639 twenty-four landowners in Armagh took out patents under the commission for defective titles.[33] Of these thirteen were native Irish owners. Three others, including one Old English, James Fleming, were recent purchasers of small areas in the county. Of the remaining eight two, Marmaduke Symonds and Lord Caulfeild, held monastic and other land in the county, and one, Viscount Moore, was the only Orior servitor. In addition five owners of undertakers' land in Oneilland and the Fews, Henry Stanhowe, Henry Dillon, Anthony Cope, John Waldron,[34] and Sir George Acheson in this way secured their titles. Apart from the effect of increased rents and other requirements a sum of about £300 was raised in fines from these new patents.[35] It is clear that patents to a number of estates were not taken out. Explanations can be given in most cases because claims on estates which would affect title came into prominence at times when new patents might be received. We can thus assemble material which throws light on many estates at the end of the plantation period. It is clear than many owners were hampered at this stage by mortgages, debts, or charges on their estates.

The Brownlow estate in Oneilland, of which one townland had been mortgaged in 1628,[36] had run into difficulties in the 1630s. In September and October 1634 George Rawdon, Lord Conway's agent, in writing to his master, reported that Sir William Brownlow and his family had gone away in haste 'to outrun a ne exit regnum'. They had gone, he stated, to the bishopric of Durham, presumably in quest of sanctuary from creditors, and

31 Ibid., ff 120–21v (ibid., 164–5).

32 Knowler (ed.), *Strafford's letters*, ii, 89.

33 NAI, Lodge, Records of the rolls, *passim*.

34 A king's letter in favour of Waldron and his son William was written on 20 May 1637 (*CSPI, 1633–47*, 159).

35 This sum is not exact because two owners, Caulfeild and Moore, held lands outside the county and their fines are not entered on a county basis.

36 PRONI, T808/14964.

had let their house and park.[37] In December 1635 Brownlow mortgaged his estate to Alderman Sir Robert Parkhurst of the city of London, undertaking that £466 out of an annual rental of £773. 4. 6. should be paid each year to Randal Aldersey of Dublin, Parkhurst's Irish agent.[38] Parkhurst was a man with large financial interest in Ireland. As mayor of London in 1634 – he was then also governor of the Irish Society – he had clashed with the privy council over the payment of ship-money.[39] In 1642, as a member of the long parliament he 'adventured' £2,500 towards the suppression of the Irish rising.[40] He had much at stake in Ireland. He owned land in Roscommon,[41] but he seems to have been chiefly a speculative moneylender.[42] It is not surprising that in such circumstances no new patent of the estate was taken out.

The Sacheverall estate was another in a precarious financial position of which a new patent was not taken out. We have seen that Sir William Alexander received a patent of part of it in 1628.[43] This patent probably reflected his rights through a mortgage and it may well have been to buy out Alexander that Sacheverall mortgaged (or it seems, sold) areas of the estate to Rev. John Symonds, an Armagh rector,[44] between 1630 and 1636 for the sums of about £1,600.[45] While the estate is recorded as in Sacheverall hands in 1641,[46] it is clear that had Sacheverall taken out a patent under the commission for defective titles it would have had to provide for the rights of Symonds and possibly also Alexander.

Mountnorris, whose political downfall occurred in 1635–6[47] just before the commission turned its attention to Ulster, did not receive a new patent because one of the estates in Armagh, Rolleston's, in which he had an interest had become a focus of dispute at this time. It appears that in 1618 Rolleston mortgaged his property to Mountnorris (then Sir Francis Annesley), for £420, to Rolleston's use until 2 May 1620 and afterwards to Annesley's if the money involved was not repaid. The money not being paid at this date, Annesley took possession of the property, and received a patent,

37 TNA, SP 63/254, ff 437–7v (*CSPI, 1633–47*, 77, 81).
38 Armagh Museum, Brownlow leasebook, 1667, 130.
39 Moody, *Londonderry Plantation*, 356.
40 J.R. MacCormack, 'The Irish adventurers and the English civil war', *IHS*, vol. x (1956–7), 23–4, 53.
41 Kearney, *Strafford*, 101.
42 He had lent also to Phelim O'Neill, and also had an interest in a small area in Cavan (TCD, MS 832, fol. 205).
43 Above, 170.
44 Below, 311, 317.
45 *Inq. cancel. Hib. repert.*, ii, Armagh (25) Chas I.
46 NAI, Books of Survey and Distribution.
47 Kearney, *Strafford*, 70–2.

not then enrolled, in November 1631. In 1635 Rolleston commenced 'a tedious suite' in the court of chancery for the recovery of the lands. The Rolleston argument appears to have been that the redemption money had been tendered, but refused and that Mountnorris's behaviour in the whole affair had become high-handed. Mountnorris countered that his title was unquestionable, otherwise he would have not received his patent in 1631. In 1636 Rolleston petitioned Wentworth and the Irish council to adjudicate the dispute with the result that 'about' May 1637 Mountnorris was obliged to surrender the property. The case was a complex one and the extent to which Wentworth's decision was coloured by political antagonism is conjectural. At any rate it was revoked by the English parliament in 1640 and it formed part of Wentworth's impeachment. The question of the ownership of the estate was again revived before the court of claims after the Restoration and also in the early nineteenth century.[48] Neither party had secured a new patent under the commission for defective titles.

The Dillon estate raised problems for the commissioners.[49] John Dillon, the original grantee, died in 1637 his grandson and heir, Henry, having been born in 1626. The estate was encumbered in various ways. In July 1631 Dillon made a settlement whereby two-thirds of the estate should go to his son John and his successors, with provision for himself and his wife. In May 1636 Dillon and his second wife mortgaged the remainder of the estate to Lord Caulfeild for £2,000, to be repaid in seven years. On the death of John Dillon the younger his right in the two-thirds descended to his son Henry. By his will of March 1637 John Dillon the elder disposed of the mortgaged part of the estate to his wife, for her life, and various relatives. However, by 1638 complex disputes arose as to the terms under which a patent to be the mortgaged area should be issued. The commissioners, Wentworth presiding, made an order on this in June 1638 laying down the conditions under which Caulfeild should receive a patent. However, although the amount of fine and quit rent was agreed on and a fiant issued, Caulfeild did not in fact take out a patent, presumably considering that his interest was adequately guaranteed by the deed of mortgage of 1636. As a result the exchequer did not receive the new rent or the fine. It is of interest that no successful pressure was put on Caulfeild to take out this patent. Henry Dillon secured a patent of the remainder of the estate in July 1639, receiving it is free and common soccage.[50]

48 NLI, Rolleston Papers, Packing Case 112, relevant documents in folders 1–3.

49 Armagh Public Library, Castle Dillon Papers, *passim*. This, a volume of some 300 pages of transcripts, is unusually illuminating of the complexities of landownership and the role of the commissioners. See also *Inq. cancel. Hib. repert.*, ii, Armagh (40) Chas I.

50 Ibid. Caulfeild's patent of his own property was taken out in September 1639.

The affairs of the Achesons were complicated by a debt of £800 as well as family claims in 1639. Sir Archibald had died in 1634 to be succeeded by his eldest son Sir Patrick. Sir Patrick married the daughter of William Moore, clerk of the signet in England, but died without male heir in October 1638. He was succeeded by his half brother, Sir George, then ten years old.[51] The estate came immediately into public prominence. Sir William Balfour, the lieutenant of the Tower of London and a creditor of Sir Patrick to the extent of £800, pressed – with other creditors – for the payment of his debt, Lady Acheson arguing the priority of her claim to a jointure of £600. In March the king had ordered Wentworth to make a stay of other proceedings in Dublin in which Balfour was defendant because his services were needed in England.[52] However, on April 27, Balfour wrote to Wentworth from the Tower setting out his position. He stated that Sir Patrick's widow expected a jointure of £600, 'which is all the estate', although her father had not paid her portion at the time of the marriage. He would be willing to see the jointure money paid if she and her father's executors would pay their dues to the executors of Sir Patrick towards his debts. Until that had been done he entreated Wentworth not to grant her royal title to any part of the lands.[53] On April 10 Laud wrote to Wentworth on behalf of Balfour excusing his absence from Ireland and stating that the king had a good opinion of him 'and I hope deservedly in the middest of the fashion of soe many of that nation'.[54] On May 10 the king wrote stating that although he had formerly recommended Lady Acheson's suit he had since heard the petition of Balfour and the other creditors and submitted the problem to referees. He enclosed the report of the referees along with further petitions from both parties, instructing the deputy to hear and determine the case 'as you shall find agreeable to justice and equitie'.[55] Although the judgement is not available, these were the circumstances which formed the background to the new patent issued on August 5.

The presentation of case histories is excusable through the absence of more systematic materials from which to draw for a survey of the plantation on the eve of the 1641 rebellion. It is clear that a number of substantial owners of undertakers' lands had got into serious difficulties. Some had turned to British sources to raise capital, others borrowing from English settled locally. These estates presented problems to the commissioners which, in two cases, were not fully resolved in that patents were not taken

51 Burke, *Peerage*, 1039; *Inq. cancel. Hib. repert.*, ii, Armagh (29) Chas I.

52 Below, 191.

53 Sheffield City Library, Strafford letters, 19/30. These are manuscript letters additional to the transcripts usually referred to as Strafford MSS.

54 Sheffield City Library, Strafford MSS, vol. vii, 189.

55 Ibid., vol. vi (end vol.), 22. See also *CSPI, 1633–47*, 250.

out, and the object of raising government income not fulfilled. How the other proprietors in Armagh who did not compound with the commissioners eluded so doing has not been discovered.

The commission for defective titles became operative earlier in Cavan than in Armagh. Between 12 May 1637 and 30 July 1640 forty-nine landowners in the county sued out new patents.[56] Of these twenty-six were native Irish or Old English, there being four, including the earl of Westmeath, of the latter. Nine were British who had acquired small areas by purchase or otherwise, and the remainder were proprietors of undertakers' and servitors' lands. The failure of many English and Scottish undertakers and servitors in this county as in Armagh to comply is worthy of notice. However, from those who did compound a sum of about £630 was raised in fines. As in Armagh, disputes of various kinds came to light, with complainants attempting to enlist official support by having patents refused until settlements were reached.

The affairs of the Lambert family were extremely complicated at this stage. The documentation is, however, tantalisingly incomplete. Sir Oliver Lambert had died in June 1618,[57] leaving as heir a son, Charles then a minor, as well as one other son and three daughters. He was survived by his wife, Hester, daughter of Sir William Fleetwood of Middlesex, who lived until March 1639.[58] Lambert made a settlement of his estate just before his death.[59] Charles (created earl of Cavan in 1647) seems to have spent most of his mature life in England and the estate in Cavan and neighbouring counties was left to agents. Before 1632 the estate which Lambert had acquired from Jones was demised for 1,000 years – presumably a kind of mortgage – to Sir Miles Fleetwood, the widow's brother, and Sir Oliver Luke.[60] Luke was a relative of Sir Henry Wallopp and had Irish interests.[61]

By the 1630s substantial claims against the estate were being pressed, at a time when returns from the land were minimised by deficient administration. The widow and Lord Lambert brought a suit against the rent collector, Phillip O'Reilly, who was required to present a 'perfect' rent-roll, and pay three-and-a-half years rents due, it being alleged that he had caused 'the rest of the tenants' to refuse to pay their rents.[62] The claims of creditors and legatees were at the same time being pressed. The chief of

56 NAI, Lodge, Records of the rolls, v, 404–5, 417, 436, 437, 442–3, 443, 450–4, 463, 464, 474, 486, 487, 520, 572–3; vi, 6–9, 17, 34, 45–6, 55, 84, 100, 123, 134–5, 167–73, 192–3, 272–4, 322, 348–52 (see also 303 and 389), 379.

57 *Inq. cancel. Hib. repert.*, ii, Cavan (6) Jas I.

58 Burke, *Peerage*, 456.

59 NAI, Deeds, wills and instruments … post mortem, vol. 25, 201–9.

60 NAI, Lodge, Records of the rolls, v, 292–3.

61 MacCormack, 'The Irish adventurers', *IHS*, vol. x, 23.

62 NAI, Chancery salvage, N.181.

these were Sir Miles Fleetwood and Sir Oliver Luke. As early as August 1634 Wentworth undertook to Coke that 'as near as [he] could judge [he would] do right' to Lambert.[63] In the summer of 1637 a chancery suit in England between Lambert, and Fleetwood and Luke, was settled with a decree that Lambert should pay £2,400. At the same time instructions were issued that Lambert's estate in Ireland should be sold to meet this debt and Fleetwood despatched an agent with an official letter authorising the sale. However, by September Lambert had paid half the money decreed and given security for the payment of the rest and the English lord keeper instructed Wentworth, who ordered accordingly, to suspend the sale so as to allow Lambert to 'perform his promises'.[64]

This was not, however, the only claim on the estate. Jane Lambert, one of Sir Oliver's daughters, brought a suit in the Irish chancery at about this time against her mother and brother for the payment of £1,500 bequeathed to her as a marriage portion.[65] Also between July and November 1637 official letters were being written to Wentworth on behalf of Mrs. Mary Wakefield, possibly another daughter, who was also engaged in litigation with Lord Lambert.[66] In November 1638 Murtagh King, a convert to Protestantism, ordained by Bedell and employed by him in translating the Bible into Irish,[67] was summoned to Dublin to give evidence, he having been 'agent and receiver of the rents' to Sir Oliver.[68] In August 1639 Lord Lambert received leave to go to Ireland in person to deal with these problems, the king recommending him, in view of his father's services, as a person 'capable of employment'.[69] It is not surprising that under such circumstances no new patent of this estate was taken out under the commission. A small part of the estate was in the hands of the Old English Lord Dunsany in 1641.[70]

The Acheson estate in Tullyhunco was mortgaged in 1637 to Martin Basil of London for £2,000,[71] Basil receiving a patent in the following year which recited the terms of the mortgage.[72] Sir Stephen Butler's dispute with his brother about a debt, allegedly of £400,[73] had apparently been settled because a new patent was issued in September 1639 to his heir, James

[63] Knowler (ed.), *Strafford's letters*, i, 282.
[64] Sheffield City Library, Strafford MSS, vol. ix, 60, 61.
[65] NAI, Chancery salvage, I.137.
[66] Sheffield City Library, Strafford letters, 17/187, 204, 218, 271; Strafford MSS, vol. ix, 373.
[67] Shuckburgh (ed.), *William Bedell*, 339–43.
[68] Ibid., 345.
[69] Sheffield City Library, Strafford MSS, vol. vi (end vol.), 35.
[70] NAI, Books of Survey and distribution.
[71] NAI, Lodge, Records of the rolls, vi, 36–7.
[72] Ibid., 84.
[73] Above, 173.

Butler.[74] However, it is clear that the Butlers as well as the Achesons[75] had had financial dealings with Sir William Balfour, lieutenant of the Tower of London, because, in March, Balfour was defendant in a claim brought against him by Dame Mary Butler.[76] It is evident that in Cavan, as in Armagh, some proprietors had been in need of capital and had turned to sources in England to supply it.

We have seen that at the time of the 1622 inquiry an attempt was made by native Irish in Cavan to have the decision about the termon and erenach lands, made when the colony was being planned, reversed.[77] A somewhat similar, though now obscure, claim was apparently embodied in a petition, not found, submitted to London in 1635 by two members of the O'Reilly family, Hugh and James, who made claims to considerable tracts of land as having been the property of Edmund O'Reilly, the grandfather of Hugh, and apparently making some offer concerning this land which commended them to the London authorities. The matter was treated by Wentworth, however, with scant credulity. He dismissed the O'Reillys' claim as being unfounded by reference to the great office, and warned, in March 1636, that

> should we once shake that foundation all the natives would fall heavily upon us with hudge importunity and utter ruin to the British and planters there.

He urged that no encouragement should be given in England to such petitions until they had been first thoroughly investigated by the Dublin government.[78] The commissioners for defective titles were, therefore, not called upon to endorse any radical changes of ownership, thus occasioned, in the county. The case of the earl of Westmeath, with regard to his impropriations, and the attitude of the commissioners to church affairs generally, have been examined in a separate chapter.[79]

The commissioners' work provided the occasion for one longstanding claim to compensation to be discussed. Early in 1638 Thomas Nugent of Skrine, County Meath, petitioned Wentworth for compensation for land which his father, William Nugent, uncle of the earl of Westmeath, had purchased in Cavan but had surrendered at the time of plantation when it formed part of the grant to Lord Lambert, on alleged promise from

[74] NAI, Lodge, Records of the rolls, vi, 167–73.

[75] Above, 188.

[76] Sheffield City Library, Strafford MSS, vol. vi (end vol.), 17–18. Balfour was also engaged in a suit with Lord Maguire (ibid., Strafford letters, 18/5, 56).

[77] Above, 138.

[78] Sheffield City Library, Strafford MSS, vol. ix, 128–30, 158.

[79] Below, 321–2.

Chichester of compensation in a later plantation. Wentworth, in April, referred it to the commissioners for the plantation of Connacht, and later, Nugent, receiving no satisfaction addressed himself directly to the king.[80] The aim, of course, was to receive compensation in Connacht, not through the commission for defective titles.

It is evident from the above that although all estates did not come within the grips of the commissioners, that body had a profound effect in both counties. It did not only affect the landlords. In the case of the Butler estate in Cavan, at any rate, the tenants were required to make a 'reasonable and proportionable' contribution to the cost of securing the patent and towards the increase of crown rent.

However, the downfall of Wentworth's administration, and the 1641 rising came too quickly for the implications of tenures *in capite*, particularly wardship, to take wide effect.[81] The death of William, Lord Caulfeild, in December 1640[82] saw, at any rate, preliminaries concluded.[83] In January 1641 a royal letter was written to the master of the court of wards ordering that, while the heir remained a ward, his woods should be protected and his friends permitted to compound for the wardship if the master thought fit.[84] In March the mother of the ward presented a petition to the Irish house of commons[85] the terms of which are not recorded, but which presumably concerned the wardship. John Hamilton, who had estates in both counties, died in December 1639 leaving an heir, Hans aged nineteen, but he had not taken out a patent under the commission. Beyond the taking of inquisitions in March 1640[86] nothing appears to have been done to convert this situation to crown advantage. It will be seen below how aggrieved the Ulster planters were – although not all had been affected – by their treatment under the defective titles commission.

3. Ownership of British land, *c.* 1633–41

Although we have been that many estates in both counties were in an unhealthy state at this period, sales of estates were few. Sales up to about 1630 had been more numerous.

80 TNA, SP 63/256, ff 215–7 (*CSPI, 1633–47*, 186: inaccurate).

81 For confirmation see Kearney, *Strafford*, 77–81.

82 There is a partial abstract of his will in NAI, Deeds, wills and instruments … post mortem, vol. 25, 122–5.

83 An inquisition finding his property was taken at Charlemont in February 1641 (*Inq. cancel. Hib. repert.*, ii, Armagh (4) Chas I).

84 *CSPI, 1633–47*, 250.

85 *Commons jnl., Ire.*, 3 March 1641, 189.

86 *Inq. cancel. Hib. repert.*, ii, Armagh (37) Chas I, Cavan (65) Chas I.

Only one undertaker's estate, that of Fishe in Cavan, was disposed of after February 1629.[87] It was subsequently fragmented, having been in part acquired by the servitor Sir Hugh Culme or his family (Culme died in 1630[88]), the remainder being held in 1641 by five British owners, most of whom had been Fishe's tenants.[89] The most substantial of these was Thomas Burrows of Stradone.

Sales of servitors' land were more numerous. The only Armagh instance is that of the lands originally Sir Thomas Williams's which had been acquired by Capt. Smith at an early stage and which, in 1641, were held by a Mr. Roger West.[90]

In Cavan there were a number of transferences of servitors' lands. Part of the Lambert estate in Clanmahon is accredited to the Old English lord Dunsany in 1641.[91] In Tullyhaw Sir Charles Coote,[92] who was killed in action in 1642,[93] acquired the land granted to Rutledge and Brian McPhillip O'Reilly which was in Culme hands in 1638[94] and also the lands originally Pynnar's and acquired by Parsons.[95] In Castlerahan, where changes of ownership are uneasy to date, the lands of Roger Garth had passed from Sir Thomas Ashe to the new English ownership of David Kellett by 1641.[96] The Elliot estate was sold some time after 1622, only a small portion remaining in Elliot hands in 1641.[97] The remainder was acquired before 1637[98] by members of the Betagh family, a rare instance of a purchase by the Gaelic Irish, except for a small portion which was held by the Old English Lawrence Dowdall,[99] son of Edward, who had acquired considerable property in this barony. A discussion of the ownership of both counties in 1641 is provided in the conclusion.

[87] Fishe then took out a patent NAI, Lodge, Records of the rolls, v, 206–7).

[88] A. Vicars, *Index to the prerogative wills of Ireland, 1536–1810* (Dublin 1897), 116.

[89] They appear on the muster roll of *c.* 1630 (BL, Add. MS 4770, fol. 20).

[90] NAI, Books of Survey and Distribution. West, a newcomer, was possibly a relative of John West, groom of the chamber, who held a linen monopoly in Ireland (Clarke, *Old English*, 50, 58).

[91] NAI, Books of Survey and Distribution.

[92] Above, 159.

[93] Clarke, *Old English*, 211.

[94] Benjamin Culme then took out a patent (NAI, Lodge, Records of the rolls, vi, 134–5).

[95] The evidence here is contradictory. The Book of Survey and Distribution gives Culme and Parsons as owners. However, the Down Survey map ascribes it to Coote. This ascription is preferred because a deposition in 1643 by Coote's agent, responsible for ironworks there, indicates Coote ownership (TCD, MS 833, ff 223–4).

[96] NAI, Books of Survey and Distribution. Kellett lived, or had lived, at Virginia (below, 263).

[97] The Book of Survey and Distribution defines the owner, Henry Elliot as 'Ir. Pa.', but this can hardly be correct.

[98] NAI, Lodge, Records of the rolls, vi, 463–4.

[99] NAI, Books of Survey and Distribution.

4. Law and order

The Wentworth period provided little or no opportunity for Gaelic resurgence in Ulster. Although invasion was unlikely, Wentworth saw that an efficient army was an essential buttress of government, and was concerned to find it, on arrival, 'an army rather in name than in deed whether you consider their numbers, their weapons, or their discipline'.[100] He supported Graham, the muster master in carrying out his duties in Ulster.[101]

Local plots were thus not likely to be spectacular. In the spring and summer of 1634 there appears to have been a threat of rebelliousness affecting much of central Ulster, with incidents and offenders coming into prominence in the contiguous counties of Cavan and Monaghan.[102] On March 26, R. Blany, one of the Monaghan family, was instructed to 'prosecute rebels' in counties Cavan, Armagh, Monaghan, Tyrone, Fermanagh, and Louth, his authority being renewed on May 10.[103] On May 10 one Cormocke Rower O'Duffye was given protection for three months for 'discovering malefactors' in Cavan, Armagh, Monaghan, Tyrone and Fermanagh, and had it renewed for a further six months in September.[104] A number of arrests were made in Cavan at this time. On May 12 the sheriff of Cavan was given a warrant to arrest Mulmory McPhillip O'Reilly, Hugh McMulmory O'Reilly, Phillip McDonnell O'Reilly, and David McConyn,[105] some of them prominent landowners. The latter three appear to have been arrested by July 3 when a warrant was issued to the constable of Dublin Castle to receive them into custody.[106] On May 8 a similar warrant was issued for the detention there of Phillip McShane O'Reilly 'till our further pleasure be known'.[107] The most likely precipitant of these disturbances was the preparations for the parliament which met in July.

Incidents of this nature fade from sight for the remainder of the Wentworth period, though in March 1640 the provost marshal of Ulster, Sir Arthur Loftus, was commended by the king for his good services 'in discovering and bringing to justice divers rebels who much infested some parts in that our province'. Wentworth was ordered to bestow on him

[100] Knowler (ed.), *Strafford's letters*, i, 96.
[101] Graham was active in the province in September 1634 (TNA, SP 63/254, ff 436–7v (*CSPI, 1633–47*, 77)).
[102] Bod. Lib., Carte MSS, vol. 67, ff 8v–10: docquet book of Wentworth.
[103] Ibid., fol. 8v.
[104] Ibid., fol. 9.
[105] Ibid., fol. 10.
[106] Ibid.
[107] Ibid., fol. 9.

£100.[108] The area of his operations was not stated.[109] It is only from such indications that any picture of the attitudes of the Irish in our area in the years preceding 1641 can be drawn.

5. Ulster settlers and the downfall of Wentworth

Apart from the operation of the commission for defective titles, the grievances of Ulster settlers are most commonly discussed with reference to the 'black oath' imposed on the Scots. Little can be said about its impact in our area except that, of those who petitioned or were persuaded to petition for it including James Craig, William Bailie, John Hamilton, William Hamilton, Robert Maxwell and William Fullerton, landowners and clerics, were connected with our counties.[110]

With the absence of Wentworth, who was in England from October 1639, and encouraged by the growing tension in Britain, discontent in Ireland by the middle of 1640 became openly vocalised.[111] As far as Ulster landowners were concerned this had two manifestations. First and broadly, there was, the politics of pressing for the reversing of Wentworth's policies, and secondly, in a less rigorously controlled atmosphere, there were complaints from individuals, stated in petitions to the house of commons and otherwise, claiming specific grievances.

Complaints against the administration by people from our area were not numerous, but achieved telling reactions. Thus the house of commons ordered, on 4 March 1641, that the proceedings and a decree in the council about the ownership of lands in Cavan between Rev. Joseph Sing and Thomas and John Ashe had been 'altogether extrajudicial and are so … void', and that Thomas Ashe should be re-instated in the land.[112] The most spectacular personal grievance, perhaps, was that of Lord Mountnorris,

[108] Sheffield City Library, Strafford MSS, vol. vi (appended vol.), 41.

[109] In May 1639 Wentworth had reported that there were some forty 'freebooters' at large in Donegal who had committed 'burglaryes and murders' upon the English and Scots there, but he doubted not to curb them shortly (ibid, vol. x (2nd vol.), 97).

[110] Knowler (ed.), *Strafford's letters*, ii, 345; Sheffield City Library, Strafford MSS, vol. xi, 237–9.

[111] Kearney, *Strafford*, 188–92.

[112] *Commons jnl., Irel.*, 4 March 1641, 193. It may be noted that this case had in no way concerned church land. For another petition, probably concerning the court of wards, see above, 192. A petition of Dame Mary Butler to the commons, heard in June (ibid., 17 June 1641, 234), may well have concerned legal decisions taken in the previous years (above, 191). Another commons' order concerned Graham, the muster master, who was summoned before them to answer grievances. In the meantime the sheriffs of Monaghan, Down, and Antrim were not to levy his fees notwithstanding any order previously made by Wentworth (ibid., 1 March, 1641, 187–8). There were also many appeals to parliament in its judicial capacity by individuals against others, the purport of which is not easily assessed because details of the petitions are not given in the commons journals. For these see ibid., 15 February 1641, 173; 13 May 1641, 204; 29 May 1641, 219; 9 June 1641, 227; 10 July 1641, 254.

about the Rolleston estate,[113] and this formed the sixth article of Wentworth's impeachment in England.[114] He was charged with dispossessing Mountnorris 'without any legal proceedings'.[115] The court concluded that Wentworth had behaved illegally, and that in general terms he had 'exercised a tyrannical power over the estates of his majesties subjects'.[116]

The Ulster settlers also made general criticisms of the administration. The 'petition of remonstrance' adopted by the Irish commons in November 1640 contained no statement of Ulster grievances though, of the committee appointed to represent Irish grievances to the king, three were from Ulster.[117] The 'Queries' of February 1641 contained one item, no. 21,[118] concerning fairs and markets, which was a specific Ulster grievance,[119] but it had been added to a previous draft of the document.[120]

On 16 April 1641, however, the 'case of the undertakers, servitors, and natives of Ulster' was presented by the committee of the Irish parliament to the king.[121] This contained, in effect, a thorough indictment of the proceedings of the commission for defective titles. The document recited what was, in short, the official history of the plantation, that the land had been granted by King James under certain conditions and in free and common soccage, that as article 26 of the Graces the undertakers had been empowered, as they did, to take out new patents at increased rents, and that they, as also the servitors and natives, had been obliged by Wentworth to seek for new patents, under altered conditions, through the commission for defective titles.

Their grievances as a result were stated specifically. Because their estates were 'so clogged with these last tenures *in capite*' they were now unable to pay the king's rent or discharge their other obligations. Furthermore it was stated that those who had previously been granted advowsons or fairs and markets had not been allowed to include these in their patents, 'but were left open to such further advantages as might thereby be taken against them'.

The redress petitioned for was that the king should order that all patentees under the commission should be entitled to take out further new patents in which the new rents, but the old soccage tenures would feature,

113 Above, 186–7.
114 J. Rushworth (ed.), *The tryal of Thomas, earl of Strafford* (London 1680), 205–20.
115 Ibid., 205.
116 Ibid., 218; T. Salmon, *A new abridgement and critical review of the State trials* ... 2 vols. (Dublin 1737), i, 174.
117 *Commons jnl., Irel.*, 7 November 1640, 162–3; Clarke, *Old English*, 134–5. The eighth article referred to the recent treatment of the Londonderry plantation.
118 *Commons jnl., Irel.*, 26 February 1641, 175.
119 Below, 299.
120 *Commons jnl., Irel.*, 16 February 1641, 174.
121 TNA, SP 63/258, ff 256–7v, 258–9v: copy (*CSPI, 1633–47*, 272).

and that all who had not taken out patents under the commission should now do so, to hold also in soccage, but under the increased rents. All liberties and privileges, such as advowsons and fairs, originally granted, should now be regranted 'as amply as the same were … granted' in the original patents. This was presented as a compromise solution:

> By which means the king's certain revenues, with the consent and good liking of his subjects, will be much increased, his intention in the former letters patent pursued, and his royal promise in the … Graces touching the tenure as is agreeable to honour and justice, performed.[122]

On May 11 the Irish committee requested again that the subjects of the 'five escheated counties' of Ulster might have the benefit of article 26 of the Graces, and that the case of fairs and markets should be referred to the Irish parliament.[123] On May 13 the committee requested the English council to consider the creation of freeholders on the bishops' lands in Ulster whereby there would be people suitable to sit on juries and strong buildings erected for defence.[124]

The king's concession to the planters' demands came in two stages, on May 31 and July 16. On May 31 the king and council capitulated to the demands submitted on April 16.[125] On July 16 they decided that the question of fairs and markets should be decided in a test case in the court of king's bench in Ireland and then brought to the equivalent court in England and settled.[126] As to the request that freeholders be created on the estates of the Ulster bishops, the reply was that the English privy council had not seen fit to recommend it to the king because if granted the church might be prejudiced.[127] No reference was made to the regranting of advowsons.[128] On July 26 the Irish commons voted that if fairs and markets were granted along with land held in soccage tenure then those fairs and markets were not held *in capite*.[129]

In mid May a bill, sometimes called a petition, 'concerning the securing of estates' in Ulster, was 'brought into' the Irish house of commons.[130] Its

[122] Ibid.
[123] *CSPI, 1633–47*, 283–5.
[124] TNA, SP 63/259, fol. 76v (*CSPI, 1633–47*, 286).
[125] TNA, SP 63/260, ff 24–6 (*CSPI, 1633–47*, 298).
[126] Ibid., ff 12–12v (ibid., 319). A draft decision to this effect had already been drawn up on May 17 (ibid., 286).
[127] Ibid., 322.
[128] See below, 320–21.
[129] *Commons jnl., Ire.*, 26 July 1641, 271.
[130] Ibid., 14 May 1641, p. 206. It is not clear whether the Poynings's law procedure was obeyed or if it was a formal bill.

contents is not revealed, but it was probably along the same lines as the April petition. It was not, however, until the end of July that it was discussed or debated.[131] By August 4, Patrick Darcey, the Old English spokesman, had presented it to the lord justices and reported that they 'took it in good part, and would give all the furtherance they might, and would recommend it to his Majesty'.[132] The timing is of interest in that it fits in with a recent analysis of the events of this time as they concerned the Old English.[133] The winning of concessions from the king was followed by the drafting of legislation in the Irish parliament coupled with assertions of the authority of that parliament.

The Irish parliament was dissolved on August 7, to meet again in November. The Ulster settlers cannot have been unduly perturbed by delay at this stage. They had won substantial concessions from the king; it remained merely to give these statutory form. However, the outbreak of rebellion in October placed them in an unexpectedly serious predicament of an entirely different nature.

[131] Ibid., 23 July 1641, 267; July 24, 268; July 29, 276; August 2, 279; August 3, 280.
[132] Ibid., August 4, 281.
[133] Clarke, *Old English*, 138–40.

CHAPTER 7

The Native Irish and the Plantation

1. Wentworth's policy to 1637

The selecting of the native freeholders was, as we have seen, largely the function of the deputy and plantation commissioners though the English government played its part in adjudicating difficult cases.[1] Chichester saw that they must be placed in easily-controlled baronies and their lands granted

> with such equality in the partition that the contentment of the greater number may outweigh the displeasure and dissatisfaction of the smaller number of better blood.[2]

The deputy's choice was neither random nor ill-considered, the aim being to depress the social power of ruling families while giving the principal families in each county some stake in the new dispensation.[3]

In Armagh one barony, Orior, had been reserved for native freeholders (as well as servitors), though it must be remembered that the extensive lands in the Fews of Sir Turlogh McHenry O'Neill (33,704 statute acres), and in Tiranny of Sir Henry oge O'Neill were not confiscated, and two O'Hanlons in Orior were pre-plantation grantees. Lists of grantees vary in number,[4] however fifty-three owners have been found.[5] Despite Chichester's desire to preserve as much equality in sizes of estates here, as elsewhere, a small number of prominent figures received large grants. Hence Art McBaron O'Neill and his wife received a great proportion (some 7,000 acres), though with reversion to Lord Audley, and Henry McShane O'Neill a middle proportion, some 5,000 acres. The remainder received grants roughly similar in size ranging from 360 acres, current estimation, granted to Carbery McCann (815 acres), and Conn McTurlogh O'Neill (1008 acres), to about sixty acres. About a dozen received more than 300 statute acres each, but many received little more than half that amount.

1 Above, 12–14.

2 *CSPI, 1608–10*, 355–9.

3 In Donegal the natives themselves participated in the choice of grantees (*Cal. Carew MSS, 1603–24*, 61–3.

4 *Cal. Carew MSS, 1603–24*, 235–44, also in *CSPI, 1611–14*, 205–14; 'Ulster plantation papers', no. 11, *Anal. Hib.*, viii.

5 See Appendix 1.

The people thus rewarded, apart from Art McBaron and Henry McShane, were all of varying local prominence. There were some ten members of the O'Hanlon family, themselves from Orior, two being sons of Oghy oge. The others were, on the whole, required to move to this area. Six McCanns from Oneilland, including Carbery the chieftain, were grantees. Seven recipients of land were members of the McDonnell gallowglass family, two – Calvagh and Colla McArt – being the sons of Art McDonnell, chief of the gallowglass, from Clancarny in the Fews barony. There were three O'Hagans and two O'Quins, families originally from Tyrone, one O'Mulchrewe, one McMurphy, one McGilleduffe, one O'Mellan, one O'Donnelly, and one O'Donnell (probably also an O'Donnelly) among the beneficiaries.

The remaining grantees were all O'Neills. Owen McHugh [Mc Neill Mór] O'Neill was an enemy of Sir Turlogh McHenry and a claimant to the lands in the Fews.[6] He was of Toaghy in 1609,[7] the land for the most part granted to Trinity College. Felim McTurlogh Brassilogh, Turlogh oge McTurlogh Brassilogh, Cormac McTurloghe Brassilogh, and Neill McTurlogh were all sons of Turlogh Brassilogh O'Neill, a grandson of Conn, the first earl of Tyrone. Art McTurlogh, Henry McTurlogh, and Hugh McTurlogh were sons of Sir Turlogh McHenry of the Fews, and Brian McDonnell McPhelim Roe was his cousin, while Hugh McCarbery O'Neill was a distant member of the Fews sept. Donnell McHenry and his cousin Eugene Vally represented the sept of Murtagh O'Neill (d. 1471) of Clanconchy. Conn McTurlogh O'Neill was a nephew of Sir Henry Oge, and Shane McTurlogh may have been Conn's brother.[8]

Four of seven Cavan baronies, Castlerahan, Clanmahon, Tullygarvey, and Tullyhaw were divided (for the most part) amongst servitors and natives. Also land was granted to Irish in Loughtee, and in an area of Tullyhunco then regarded as in Tullyhaw. Difficulty has been experienced in locating the areas of all grants, particularly in Tullyhaw, though the amount of land they acquired collectively has been established fairly accurately.[9] The precise number of grantees also presents difficulty, but fifty-eight seems the most correct, though the lists of those allotted lands in 1610 gives only fifty-five or fifty-six.[10] We have seen that the proportion of the land owned by Irish

6 *CSPI, 1600*, 312–14.

7 *CPRI, Jas I*, 158.

8 I am especially grateful for the assistance of Mr. K.M. Nicholls of the Irish Manuscripts Commission in writing this paragraph.

9 See Appendix 1.

10 *CSPI, 1611–14*, 211–14; 'Ulster plantation papers', no. 11, *Anal. Hib.*, viii. Hill, *Plantation*, 345, treats an additional grant in 1615 to Shane McPhillip O'Reilly (*CPRI, Jas I*, 272) as if it were a grant to a second person of this name.

in both counties after the plantation – Cavan 22.5 per cent, Armagh 25 per cent – was almost identical, yet Chichester in 1610 considered that it was only in Cavan (of all the planted counties) that native grantees had received a fitting share of the land.[11] Chichester's point can be sustained when it is considered that in Armagh some 33,000 out of some 78,000 acres were held by one man, Sir Turlogh McHenry O'Neill by a pre-plantation grant, whereas in Cavan, where no such grants had been made, a more equal distribution of the land with consequently larger acreages being given to individuals (of whom also there were somewhat more than in Armagh) had taken place.

Most numerous amongst the beneficiaries were the O'Reillys, however there were some five each of the McGoverns or McGaurans, McKiernans, and Bradys, and also one or two Sheridans, one McCabe of gallowglass origin, one McTully, one O'Gowan, and one O'Moeltully. Of the O'Reillys many were descendants of Maelmora (or Mulmory) O'Reilly who died in 1565. His grandson, Mulmory McHugh Connelagh, the chieftain in Irish eyes, received a great proportion, approximately 7,000 statute acres. Mulmory oge O'Reilly, whose father Mulmory, a grandson of Hugh Connelagh, had died on the English side at the Blackwater, received an assessed 3,000 acres (over 17,000 acres statute). His uncle Capt. Hugh O'Reilly, a son of Sir John, was also a grantee, receiving almost 3,500 statute acres, and inherited Mulmory oge's lands on his death in 1617. Mulmory McPhillip, Brian McPhillip, and Shane McPhillip were all sons of Phillip, a brother of Sir John, and a son of Hugh Connelagh. Donell Backagh McShane and probably Hugh Roe McShane were sons of Shane, a son of Maelmora. Mulmory McTurlogh was a grandson of this Shane. The sons of Owen, another son of Maelmora, also feature as grantees. Hence Mulmory McOwen, Brian a Coggye [McOwen], Cahir McOwen, Donell McOwen, and Cahell McOwen his eldest son, are found as proprietors. They were not placed together, some being in Tullyhaw and some in Castlerahan. Owen McMulmory O'Reilly was a grandson of Edmund, another son of Maelmora. Mulmory McHugh McFarrall was a grandson of Farrall O'Reilly who had been a chieftain in the early sixteenth century. The other O'Reilly grantees were probably the principal men of various more distant septs.[12] In Cavan estates were considerably larger than in Armagh. None was smaller than about 150 acres, and the majority ranged from about 400 to 1,000 or even 2,000 acres.

[11] *CSPI, 1608–10*, 521–2.

[12] J. Carney (ed.), *A genealogical history of the O'Reillys* (Cavan, 1959), *passim*. I am again indebted to Mr. K.W. Nicholls for assistance.

Irish grantees who were close relatives were often separated. In Cavan, the sons of Owen O'Reilly, for example, received lands in different baronies. Henry McShane O'Neill was granted land in Armagh, whereas his half-brother, Conn McShane, was placed in Fermanagh.[13] It sometimes happened also that Irish grantees did not receive their grants in compact blocks. Mulmory McHugh Connelagh O'Reilly received lands in three different baronies. The problem may have been greater for a number of the smaller grantees who received detached townlands. Hugh roe McShane O'Reilly, for example, was granted three townlands in Castlerahan, none of which was contiguous, two were to the east of the barony and one to the west. The same happened also in Armagh where, in Orior, Owen McHugh McNeill Mór O'Neill, for example, received two separated townlands. In this case, at any rate, faults in the 'maps of the escheated counties' cannot be pleaded: they are also not adjacent on the 1609 map.[14]

One problem confronting the native Irish generally as a result of the dislocation of customary habits which the plantation entailed may be mentioned at this point. The importance of cattle as a basic unit of property and status in Gaelic Ireland is always stressed.[15] Although the chief or family leaders had the superintendence of the land belonging to the family, their personal property consisted in cattle which they hired out, in a customarily circumscribed way, to their followers. The position of the cow-lord or 'boaire' is described in detail in the early eight century law tract, the 'crith gablach'.[16] The practice was known in the early seventeenth century as 'commins'.

The suddenness of the plantation disrupted this customary arrangement as it was functioning. The 'landlords' were now to be limited to 'their own proper goods',[17] and their 'tenants' who were often not granted lands and who had cattle in this way in their possession, were either unable or unwilling to make restitution. The injustice of this quickly became apparent. Commissioners were appointed to deal with the problem in August 1610.[18] This was an attempt to remedy a grievance arising from a custom which must now cease. How efficiently the commissioners fulfilled their task is not known.[19]

13 Hill, *Plantation*, 336.

14 *Maps Ulster, 1609*, 5, 26.

15 D. Coghlan, *The ancient land tenures of Ireland* (Dublin, 1933), 65; M. & L. de Paor, *Early Christian Ireland*, 3rd edn. (London, 1961), 77–9.

16 D.A. Binchy (ed.), *Crith gablach* (Dublin, 1941), 6–8.

17 *CSPI, 1608–10*, 491; *Cal. Carew MSS, 1603–24*, 58.

18 Ibid.

19 For an indication that the problem was not immediately solved in all cases see *CSPI, 1611–14*, 390–2.

2. The fortunes of the Irish grantees

At first the Irish grantees were reluctant to commit themselves to their allotted share in the plantation. There was high expectation of foreign aid to arrive in 1611 and terminate the plantation before it got off the ground. In the autumn of 1610 the O'Quins and O'Hagans, grantees in Armagh, had declared that they would prefer to be mere tenants-at-will to the servitors and others who had adequate lands to let them than accept small grants with the onerous concomitant duties of jury service.[20] The native grantees in Tyrone and Londonderry were also dissatisfied with the size of their allotments.[21] Chichester sympathised with these complaints, and stated that he was now discredited amongst them and feared a military uprising. If any land became available in these counties it should be distributed amongst the natives.[22] In this context the stay on the removal of the natives from undertakers' land until May 1611 can be seen as a palliative to unrest.

A paradoxical situation had, however, arisen by November 1610: Art McBaron O'Neill had accepted his lands and promised to move there from Oneilland by May. His example, as Chichester wrote on December 12, was appearing to have a general effect and, coupled with the widely-publicised news that Hugh O'Neill had become blind, was causing the freeholders actively to sue out their patents, and 'accept of that little land which heretofore they so much scorned'.[23] He also suspected an ulterior motive – a keenness on the part of the grantees to remove at the appointed time, May 1611, 'hoping thereby to overthrow the work even in the foundation'.[24] Their indispensability to the undertakers had suggested to the natives a means of frustrating the infant colony which placed Chichester in a bewildering predicament.[25]

Concrete evidence of the natives' actions can be supplied. No letters patent of their allotments were taken out before November 1610. The following table shows the date ranges of natives' patents in Armagh and Cavan:[26]

20 *CSPI, 1608–10*, 499–500.
21 Ibid., 501–4.
22 Ibid.
23 Ibid., 530–1; *Cal. Carew MSS, 1603–24*, 142.
24 Ibid.
25 Ibid.
26 It is derived from *CPRI, Jas I* Hill either fails to give the dates or states them partially and so is misleading. He also omits some grantees.

Orior	13 Dec. 1610–13 June 1611
Castlerahan	25 Nov. 1610–13 Mar. 1611
Clanmahon	20 Nov. 1610–4 June 1611
Tullygarvey	25 Nov. 1610–4 June 1611
Tullyhaw	13 Mar. 1611–24 Feb. 1615

This may be no more than an indication of intention to occupy their lands. However, the majority of the native freeholders, if they had not given up hopes of ultimately overthrowing the plantation, were at least seeing the advisedness of stabilising their position under it. Also by February 1611 a similar realisation of the accomplished plantation had been borne home to Hugh O'Neill in Rome. He complained to the Spanish ambassador that the king of Spain had not intervened on his behalf with James I, and that 'consequently the English king has given his estates to Englishmen and Scots.'[27] At the end of May it was noted that the natives were more willing to leave the undertakers' lands than the undertakers were to see them go.[28] For this same reason it became essential to victual the Ulster forts for three months, because of the difficulty of obtaining supplies locally, 'by the natives removing the soldier can hardly get meat for his money.'[29]

Carew's report in September 1611, however, shows that the process of moving by the grantees still dragged. Art McBaron had by then removed with his 'tenants' from Oneilland. Carbery McCann 'cheefe of his name' had taken decisive action of a different kind in selling his grant in Orior, presumably to Poyntz whose family held it in 1641[30] and had moved to Clandeboy where he had taken lands from Conn O'Neill. None of the other Armagh grantees had moved to their lands.[31] The hiatus in ownership of this land had thus still only been filled on paper. The re-settling of those native Irish who had received land was, in fact, proceeding at a slower pace than was the process of occupation by grantees from outside the country.

In Cavan, as in Armagh, the bulk of the native freeholders, especially the smaller grantees, had not, on Carew's evidence, occupied their assignments. Eight grantees, including Mulmory oge O'Reilly, were reported to be in occupation and one, Phillip McTirlogh Brady, was about to remove. Hugh McShane O'Reilly was building a mill, and the McKiernan chief was one of two building houses. Ease of settlement was facilitated in Cavan because

27 M. Walsh, 'The last years of Hugh O'Neill, Rome 1608–1616', *Irish Sword*, vii, 29, 327–8. A year later he declared his willingness to go to Virginia 'or any other part of the world' to serve Spain and avenge himself on his enemies (ibid., 335–6).

28 *CSPI, 1611–14*, 59–60.

29 Ibid., 64.

30 NAI, Books of Survey and Distribution.

31 Lam. Pal. Lib., Carew MSS, vol. 630, fol. 68.

some did not have to move at all. Thus, it was noted, Mulmory McHugh Connelagh O'Reilly and the McGovern chief had their 'owne lande' given them under the plantation.[32] One Cavan grantee, Wony McThomas McKiernan, became a tenant to Sir James Craig in May 1611.[33]

However, that the Irish were in fact occupying their lands in 1611 and 1612 can be seen from the spate of cases between them and their neighbours, Irish and British, in these years.[34] Most of the sales which took place, beginning often very soon after this, must have resulted from other factors than initial fatalism for the future.

Bodley's survey in 1613 of the Irish patentees is too scant to offer much assistance. Only one grantee in Orior, Henry McShane O'Neill, is mentioned with the categorical statement that he had 'not strengthened his proportion with any building'.[35] In Cavan we are informed about only a minority, the larger grantees. Only in Castlerahan does he refer to the Irish collectively with the straight-forward statement that the land allocated was as yet entirely 'in statu quo prius'.[36] In Clanmahon Mulmory McHugh [Connelagh] O'Reilly had 'only digged a lime kiln and provided some small quantity of limestone to burn.'[37] However, in Tullygarvey and Tullyhaw those referred to had been at least as active as their servitor neighbours. Mulmory McPhillip O'Reilly, Capt. Hugh, and Mulmory oge had either bawns or castles under construction or completed.[38] Phelim McGovern was 'strongly seated', having begun an 'English building of lime and stone' surrounded by an improvised bawn close to his present house with promising intentions to complete his building programme.[39]

All the official surveys pass lightly over the Irish lands. In Orior Pynnar referred only to the lands of Henry McShane O'Neill, 'lately dead', which were now owned by Sir Toby Caulfeild.[40] The estate was without strong house or bawn because O'Neill had been given exemption through

32 Ibid., ff 70–70v.

33 *Inq. cancel. Hib. repert.*, ii, Cavan (27) Chas I. The man concerned, called here Eugen' McThomas Reagh is doubtless the same as Owen McTho: Reaugh listed as a grantee in Tullyhaw ('Ulster plantation papers', no. 11, *Anal. Hib.*, viii) and Owny McThomas McKiernan (*Cal. Carew MSS, 1603–24*, 241–2). He took out his patent on 4 June 1611 as Wony McThomas McKiernan (*CPRI, Jas I*, 211).

34 Above, 76–88.

35 *Hastings MSS*, iv, 177.

36 Ibid., 160.

37 Ibid., 163.

38 Ibid., 161.

39 Ibid., 165.

40 Hill, *Plantation*, 571–2. O'Neill had sold the reversion of his estate (a jointure excepted) to Sir John Bourchier and he to Sir Francis Blundell, an important government official, from whom Caulfeild has purchased it (BL, Add. MS 4756, fol. 109v).

poverty,[41] but Caulfeild now undertook to build on it.[42] It is evident that the piecemeal destruction of native freeholds was going on throughout the plantation period without government disapproval.

In Cavan Pynnar reported on eight of the more substantial grantees. These had all built strong houses with bawns and were resident. However it was noted that they were not conforming to English estate customs. Neither Mulmory McPhillip, Capt. Hugh, Mulmory oge, nor Mulmory McHugh Connelagh O'Reilly had given leasehold status to their tenants, and on some of these estates ploughing by the tail is referred to.[43] This goes some way towards confirming Chichester's apprehensions in 1610[44] that the Irish would not readily abandon their traditional customs with regard to land.

Apart from its general conclusions, the 1622 report adds nothing further in comment or coverage. They found defects in the native grantees' performance as follows: few had built other than bawns of sod 'to no purpose'; they did not make 'certain estates' to their tenants; these lived dispersed and not in 'towne reeds'; these also generally ploughed by the tail and not after the manner of the 'English Pale', as required.[45] Further comment must come from other sources and from the examination of individual cases.

We have seen that the extensive lands in Armagh of Sir Turlogh McHenry and Sir Henry oge O'Neill were not confiscated.[46] Sir Henry oge's lands – the territory of Touranny, extending also into Tyrone – represented a considerable bloc of strategically-placed, and generally profitable, land of which he had received a patent in 1605. However, to honour this would vitiate in part the overall symmetry of the plantation, but Sir Henry oge was killed in the war against O'Doherty, his oldest son Tirlogh oge having also died, his grandson and heir by English law, Phelim O'Neill, being a minor. Chichester recommended the subdivision of this land as an expedient which the king accepted in March 1612 as being for 'the quiet and good of those parts'.[47] He authorised the acceptance of a surrender from Phelim and the division of the land among the issue male, legitimate and illegitimate, of Sir Henry oge, with provision for his own and his eldest son's widow.[48]

41 BL, Add. MS 4756, fol. 109v.

42 Hill, *Plantation*, 571–2. This had not been done by 1622 when Caulfeild undertook to build after the model of Grandison at Tandragee (BL, Add. MS 4756, fol. 109v).

43 Hill, *Plantation*, 458–60, 468, 474. Hill provides a good note (459) on ploughing by the tail.

44 *CSPI, 1608–10*, 519–21.

45 BL, Add. MS 4756, fol. 118v.

46 Above, 17–18.

47 BL, Add. MS 4794, ff 253–3v; Marsh's Library, Dublin, MS Z4.2.6, 158–9; *CSPI, 1611–14*, 260; *CPRI, Jas I*, 251.

48 Ibid.

As a result the land in Armagh was broken up into seven grants to individuals, that given to Phelim's mother to descend to him.[49] These grants were made furthermore by knight's service *in capite*, and all date from 14 December 1613. The interest of this treatment of Henry oge's lands lies in the very fact that it was divided. It was clearly an intransigent decision in view of recent decisions, in 1606 and 1608, whereby the Irish landholding system had been abolished in favour of strict succession by primogeniture.[50]

So far we have been concerned with the effects of government decisions on the Irish grantees. There are a number of instances in Armagh where through administrative error grants were made to Irish that where subsequently lost through the assertion by others of primary rights. A fascinatingly complex case has been examined above.[51]

Another case of where the administration fell short in points of detail concerned the lands in Orior held by Bagnal prior to the plantation.[52] His ownership was not recorded, for example, on the 1609 map and accordingly much of the land was allotted to grantees, particularly Irish. Bagnal disputed these grants in 1612,[53] an inquiry was held locally, and he recovered the land.[54] He recovered a townland from Henry McShane O'Neill and a townland from Calvagh McDonnell who thereby lost his entire grant without compensation. In Cavan a similar situation arose, though involving much more land, whereby the baron of Delvin recovered lands which had been his from before the plantation.[55]

By about 1613, then, the share of the Irish under the plantation was decided. Although in 1610 Chichester was of the opinion that the Irish had not received an adequate share in the plantation in any county except Cavan,[56] concealments found in Orior were not granted to Irish owners.[57]

The most easily answered question concerns the amount of land lost by the Irish before 1641. It was not unusual for grantees to have sold their lands or lost them by other means, but losses by individual Irish, unlike their British counterparts, were not usually to the gain of fellow Irish and so they affected the relative proportions of landholding as well as the fortunes of individuals. In Armagh after the plantation the native Irish owned some 78,318 statute acres, or some 25.5 per cent of the total acreage of the county. In Cavan the corresponding figures at this date were 104,134

49 *CPRI, Jas I*, 262–3.
50 Moody, *Londonderry Plantation*, 26.
51 Above, 79–80.
52 Above, 85.
53 TCD, MS 806, ff 22–3.
54 *Inq. cancel. Hib. repert.*, ii, Armagh (2) Jas I. Bagnal took out a new patent in 1613 (*CPRI, Jas I*, 246–7).
55 Above, 78, 86.
56 Above, 61–2.
57 Above, 99–105.

acres, or about 22.5 per cent of the total acreage. By 1641 these shares in both counties had been substantially reduced. In Armagh the Irish then held some 59,026 acres, or about 19 per cent of the land, and in Cavan the figures were 76,640 acres, or about 16.5 per cent.

In an area of the subject where documentation is minimal the reasons for these losses cannot be given in any detail. It seems likely that some of the larger grantees were in straightened circumstances in 1610.[58] Henry McShane O'Neill, who had sold his land by an early stage, died poverty-stricken.[59] When the commissioners in 1622 investigated arrears of rents, Irish owners figures prominently.[60] Mulmory oge O'Reilly received a substantial grant principally in Tullygarvey. From a fragment of pleadings in a chancery suit it appears that as early as 1611 he sold some five denominations of land to Sir Thomas Ashe, the servitor grantee in the same barony.[61] A further suit, heard after his death, shows that he had mortgaged one townland in 1616 (in O'Reilly hands in 1641) for £34.[62] By 1641, 1,454 acres granted to him were in the possession of James Aspole (or Archbald) of an Old English family from Wicklow and 2,809 acres were owned by Sir William Hill, also Old English. In addition, smaller portions, some 1,937 acres, were owned by native Irish, Hugh Brady, Neill O'Tully, and Calle O'Gowan.[63]

Incapacity to redeem mortgages would seem to have been another reason for loss of lands. The property of Brian a'Coggy O'Reilly – 1,371 acres – in Castlerahan had been encumbered by debts and a mortgage by the time his son Farrall acquired it. It had been leased for £20 per annum, the ownership was disputed in chancery,[64] and by 1641 it was owned by Henry Hickfield or Heckett, a Protestant immigrant.[65] Abraham Dee, a Dundalk merchant,[66] who had by 1641 acquired the lands of three Armagh grantees – Shane McOghy O'Hanlon, Laughlin O'Hagan, and Phelim oge McDonnell (658 acres in all) was, in 1622, summoned into chancery by an O'Neill grantee who in about 1616 had mortgaged to him one townland

58 In 1610 Davies noted, as if it were unusual, that the commissioners had allotted to the O'Quins and the O'Hagans in Armagh portions of land 'such as the scope assigned to the natives of that county afforded' because they had 'good stock of cattle' (*CSPI, 1608–10*, 497–501). We have seen that these families considered their grants uneconomical.

59 BL, Add. MS 4756, fol. 109v.

60 Above, 138–9.

61 NAI, Chancery salvage, U.89.

62 Ibid., W.44, X.30, Z.19.

63 NAI, Books of Survey and Distribution.

64 NAI, Chancery salvage, A.347.

65 NAI, Books of Survey and Distribution.

66 NAI, Deeds, wills and instruments … post mortem, vol. 25, counties Armagh, Cavan, Donegal: County Armagh 45–8 (will, 18 July 1638).

for £30.[67] In this case, however, the land seems to have been recovered by the owner.

The sale of a piece of land originally leased can be seen in one instance. One townland – Keadew in Loughtee (233 acres) – which formed part of the grant to Walter Thomas and Patrick Brady was, in 1611, leased for twenty-one years to Richard Dowdall, an Old Englishman from Louth. In April 1613 Dowdall sold his lease to Sir Thomas Ashe who lived at Trim and held the contiguous land of Cavan abbey and he, in turn, in May of that year sold the lease (for £22) to his brother John of Kilmessan, County Meath.[68] By 1641 this land is recorded as Ashe property.[69]

In one case, in Armagh, loss of property seems to have resulted from attainder. Patrick O'Hanlon, whose patent was pre-plantation, had received a grant of 2,150 acres on condition of surrendering other property for Mountnorris fort. Now, on 15 June 1615 Sir John Kinge, the muster master general, and Sir Adam Loftus, subsequently lord chancellor, received a patent of this land.[70] It seems likely that O'Hanlon had lost his lands for treason because he was pardoned in July 1617.[71] The lands were subsequently acquired by Sir Francis Annesley and held by him in 1641.[72]

For whatever reason a substantial amount of Irish-granted land had been lost by 1641. The dating of this is not easy and, indeed, for most of it the earliest evidence of ownership change is got from the patents under the commission for defective titles in the late 1630s. Beneficiaries were of various types, British landowners extending their influence locally, British coming from outside, Old English (sometimes merchants), and, to a lesser extent, native Irish.

The acquisitions of Hugh Culme in Cavan paralleled, though on a larger scale, those of his fellow-servitor Toby Caulfeild in Armagh. Culme, or his family, acquired Irish land in Tullyhaw barony totalling some 10,837 acres (8,221 acres of which were sold to Sir Charles Coote) and in 1641 it was held by various members of his family.[73] Caulfeild acquired in Armagh the 5,000 acre estate of Henry McShane O'Neill. Sir Francis Annesley in Armagh acquired the lands of Patrick O'Hanlon and Donogh Reogh O'Hagan. Sir Garret Moore acquired 3,143 acres of natives' land in Armagh, Bourchier, or his successor Henry, earl of Bath, acquired some 168 acres. Other servitor acquisitions were those of the brothers Ashe and

[67] NAI, Chancery salvage, 2B.80.121, no. 241.

[68] NLI, Farnham Papers, MS D 20,409–20,475.

[69] NAI, Books of Survey and Distribution.

[70] *CPRI, Jas I*, 280–2.

[71] Ibid., 325.

[72] NAI, Books of Survey and Distribution.

[73] Ibid.

Sir Oliver Lambert in Cavan. The acquisitions of the Poyntz family in Orior were particularly spectacular in that a servitor who, in 1610, had received no more than 674 acres could, by 1641, show a substantial multiplication of property – all at the expense of Irish grantees. Toby Poyntz in 1641 owned some 3,744 acres acquired from fifteen Irish grantees.[74]

Local undertakers had also acquired Irish land by commercial transaction, though not on the same scale. Undertakers with estates in different baronies to the Irish had not the same incentive to contiguous expansion. In Armagh the only instance is that of Brownlow who acquired the land (584 acres) of Phelim and Brian O'Hanlon, sons of Oghy oge.[75] In Cavan, for example. Sir James Craig purchased in 1615 the lands (2,225 acres) granted to Brian McKiernan,[76] and Greenham acquired some land from Mulmory McHugh Connelagh O'Reilly.[77]

British purchasers with no previous proprietorship in these counties can also be seen. In Armagh there were three of these, John Parry, James Galbraith, and Abraham Dee. Galbraith was a Scot who owned Mongavlin in Donegal and who in 1637 acquired the lands of Ferdoragh O'Hanlon, some forty-three acres, for £20.[78] Dee was a merchant in Dundalk.[79] In Cavan such people were more numerous. Here by 1641 some 3,800 acres of land were in the hands of five new British owners. One of these estates, that of Brian McShane O'Reilly, was owned by John Chapman in 1638.[80] Chapman lived in Longford and sold the land (for £100) in 1639 to a relative William Chapman of Ballyhaise,[81] the owner in 1641, Elinor Chapman, otherwise Reynolds, was probably the widow.[82] Another purchaser, Henry Crofton was of the family of William Crofton[83] and held monastic land in Leitrim and a small area in Longford.[84] The purchases of Chapman and Crofton can be seen as a permeation of unplanted Cavan from the south and west.

[74] Ibid., Armagh and Cavan.

[75] NAI, Books of Survey and Distribution.

[76] *Inq. cancel. Hib. repert.*, ii, Cavan (27) Chas I.

[77] Ibid., (50) Chas I.

[78] NAI, Lodge, Records of the rolls, v, 400.

[79] He is stated in the Book of Survey and Distribution for Armagh to have been an 'Irish papist', but his will (NAI, Deeds, wills and instruments … post mortem, vol. 25, 45–8) gives the impression that he was Protestant.

[80] Ibid., vi, 55.

[81] NAI, Deeds, wills and instruments … post mortem, vol. 25, counties Armagh, Cavan and Donegal: County Cavan, 317–27.

[82] NAI, Books of Survey and Distribution.

[83] William Crofton had been appointed the first auditor of accounts for Ulster and Connacht in 1617 (*CPRI, Jas I*, 325).

[84] NAI, Lodge, Records of the rolls, v, 572–3.

Purchases of Irish land by British was part of a process of transformation in the ownership of the country which was to continue throughout the century. By contrast Old English acquisitions in both counties were inconsistent with the general trend. In Armagh there was only one of these, James Fleming, who was doubtless of the family which had connections with, though not land in, the county before the plantation.[85] By July 1639 he had acquired some 786 acres previously Conn McTurlogh O'Neill's.[86]

In Cavan Old English acquisitions were on a larger scale. Sir William Hill of Allenstown, a prominent Old English figure,[87] acquired in Tullygarvey some 3015 acres previously owned by Mulmory oge O'Reilly and Terence Brady, and in Loughtee 5834 acres granted to Turlogh McDonnell O'Reilly.[88] In Tullygarvey James Archbald from Wicklow had acquired 1,820 acres previously owned by Mulmory oge O'Reilly and Terence Brady.[89] Walter Talbot acquired some native land in 1612.[90] Smaller acquisitions were those of John Dowdall and Richard Fitzsimons, the former a plantation grantee.[91]

Irish also in some cases had purchased the lands of their fellows or lands granted to members of other groups. Thus part (944 acres) of the estate of Donell Backagh McShane O'Reilly (1,193 acres), acquired by Walter Talbot in 1612,[92] was sold by him to Stephen Butler in 1614,[93] but was owned by Phillip McMulmory O'Reilly in 1641.[94] In Clanmahon by 1641 Hugh McFarry O'Reilly had acquired 664 acres, part of the estate granted to Edward Nugent in 1610.[95] In Armagh the estate of some 7,000 acres granted to Art McBaron O'Neill and his wife for their lives, with reversion to Lord Audley, had, by 1641, come to Roger Moore the 1641 leader.[96] The process cannot be elucidated beyond what was recorded in 1622: that since O'Neill and Audley were dead, the land would come to Sir Piers Crosby in right of his wife, Audley's widow, on the death of O'Neill's widow.[97] Crosby was, it seems of Irish descent but his family had received

85 Above, 185.
86 NAI, Lodge, Records of the rolls, vi, 240.
87 Clarke, *Old English*, 203, 213.
88 NAI, Books of Survey and Distribution.
89 Ibid.
90 NAI, Deeds, wills and instruments … post mortem, vol. 25, counties Armagh, Cavan, Donegal: County Cavan, 239–54.
91 NAI, Books of Survey and Distribution.
92 NAI, Deeds, wills and instruments … post mortem, vol. 25, counties Armagh, Cavan, Donegal, 239–54.
93 Ibid.
94 NAI, Books of Survey and Distribution.
95 Ibid.
96 Ibid.
97 BL, Add. MS 4756, fol. 110.

land in Leix and, in 1627, he had recruited an Irish regiment to assist Buckingham in the isle of Rhe. However, by the later 1639s, he had clashed with Wentworth[98] and had probably sold his Armagh land at this stage to Moore who was also from the midlands. There were a number of other purchases, each however small, but the families of Betagh and O'Gowan in Cavan may be mentioned as having bettered themselves.[99]

The survival of joint ownership is a fascinating problem to which only a tentative treatment can be given. The evidence of a chancery suit is, however, revealing.[100] This concerns the lands granted to Brian McKiernan and conveyed by him to Sir James Craig. Five members of the McKiernan family petitioned the chancellor, then Adam Loftus, against Craig. They stated that the lands in question were the joint property of themselves and Brian McKiernan – deceased – having been 'divided and parted between them after the course and custom of gavelkind'. At the plantation they had agreed on the convenience of taking out a patent in Brian's name 'being the chief and eldest of their sept', the lands to be afterwards distributed between them. Accordingly, they stated, the land was recorded as Brian's property in the 'great office', granted to him by patent, and he conveyed to them those areas previously agreed on. Despite this, they stated, Craig induced Brian to sell it all to him without 'any valuable consideration. Craig, they stated had attempted to dispossess them one, Cahill McKiernan, having been imprisoned for a time in Cavan jail. Craig, in fact retained the land,[101] but the suit, apart from indicating that the chancery was prepared to recognise suits about gavelkind, throws light on the predicament of a family group overshadowed by a substantial non-Irish neighbour in a period of adjustment to an alien legal system.

This suit is, however, too ambiguous as a basis for generalisation. The plea of gavelkind may have been completely without justification. Conversely, if well founded, evidence of individual ownership drawn from official sources may be of no significance with regard to the survival of the older custom.

Division of estates between sons or others can be shown to have happened in a few cases. For example, in Armagh the grant to Owen McHugh O'Neill was held by Hugh oge and Hugh boy O'Neill in 1641.[102] Also in Orior the land of Brian oge O'Hagan, granted in 1610 the ownership of which was renewed in his name in 1639,[103] was ascribed

98 Kearney, *Strafford*, 62, 185, 194, 233; Clarke, *Old English*, 89, 99, 120, 169, 171, 172, 175.
99 See list of owners in Appendix.
100 NAI, Chancery salvage, N.153.
101 NAI, Books of Survey and Distribution.
102 Ibid.
103 NAI, Lodge, Records of the rolls, vi, 240.

in 1641 to Patrick and Hugh O'Hagan.[104] The Book of Survey and Distribution probably got it right that there was a joint or divided ownership of sons.[105] Strict descent by primogeniture would seem not to have been fully accepted by 1641.

The case of the Bradys, Walter, Thomas and Patrick, who received a joint patent of lands in Cavan, however, seems to indicate a strict regard for individual ownership. Members of this family, particularly Walter who was a merchant, had had long-standing contacts with the Dublin administration and probably acquired a respect for English law.[106] By 1641 the land is ascribed to individual Brady owners and the evidence of litigation in the 1630s seems to indicate concern that this should be the case.[107] The willingness of the Irish owners to utilize the British legal system was, in itself, part of an accommodation to a new legal system.

It is at this point appropriate to discuss the affairs of some prominent Irish landowners in both counties.

The large estate (some 33,000 acres) of Sir Turlogh McHenry O'Neill of the Fews was undiminished throughout the period.[108] In 1627, we have seen,[109] he was exonerated from allegations of conspiracy. Later in that year the king intervened in O'Neill's favour following on a petition in a dispute for land between him and Sir Christopher Bellew of Louth.[110] The dispute was a long-standing one about the ownership of land in the Fews, hinging on whether that barony was entirely in Armagh or partly in Louth. Bellew's claim, based on the latter contention, had been brought into chancery.[111] The king instructed, O'Neill being 'much inconvenienced', that the matter should be decided by the deputy and plantation commissioner in accordance with the great office for Armagh and that no other court should have any jurisdiction in the matter.[112] The outcome appears to have been in O'Neill's favour and in December 1628 the king authorised a regrant,

104 NAI, Books of Survey and Distribution.

105 Similarly in Cavan the same source ascribed land to Cormac McBrian and Brian oge McGowran, and the lands granted to Mulmory McPhillip O'Reilly had been divided between his sons Hugh and Edmund by 1641.

106 In 1614 he made shrewd use of the privilege of membership of parliament in having the sheriff of Cavan summoned before parliament for contempt of his privileged position (*Commons jnl., Ire.*, 8 and 19 November 1614, 21, 24).

107 In 1634 Thomas Brady by a chancery decree recovered a sum of money received by Robert Brady as rent on land in Cavan (NAI, Repertories to the decrees of chancery, ii, 127). In 1635 Patrick Brady received a decree against Richard Ashe to whom William Brady had sold two townlands. Patrick was to recover the land and pay Ashe what he had '*bona fide*' paid William (ibid.).

108 In 1619 he was in arrears with quit rent to the extent of £11 Ir. (NAI, Ferguson MSS, xii, 6).

109 Above, 161.

110 *CSPI, 1625–32*, 294–5.

111 NAI, Chancery salvage, M.27.

112 *CSPI, 1625–32*, 294–5.

which followed, for the 'entire' area in September 1629.[113] Such sympathetic treatment no doubt arose in part from the wartime situation, but, at the same time, the insistence that the dispute should be determined in accordance with the 'great office' is another instance of the determination that the foundations, geographical and otherwise, of the plantation should not be disturbed.[114]

O'Neill was one of the very few Ulster proprietors to hold his lands *in capite*, and so he was also one of the very few required to take out a licence of alienation.[115] He made a settlement of his estate in June 1639 to the use of his elder son Henry,[116] following on a licence of alienation for a fine of £133. 6. 8. in 1634,[117] and died in 1640,[118] without taking out a patent under the commission for defective titles. In May 1639 he leased portions for ninety-nine years at low rents to his second son Arthur and to Art O'Neill of Tullydonnell.[119] The names of four tenants as well as thirty-one other witnesses emerging from the settlement throw light on the type of community on the estate prior to 1641. Of the four lessees, apart from the two O'Neills above-named, one was a certain Donnogh Brady and the presence of the other, Roger Gernon, indicates contacts, no doubt long-standing, between this area and the northern part of the Pale. Of Old English or settler names amongst the witnesses seven appear: Blyke, Gamwell, Vicars, Genson, Goborne, and Bellew. However, most names were Irish and of local origin, though the appearance of one O'Reilly would indicate a contact made with Cavan probably as a result of the marriage of Henry O'Neill to a daughter of Sir John O'Reilly.[120] The estate was not encumbered by mortgage or otherwise.

The affairs of the O'Neills in Tiranny were less stable in the years before 1641. Problems are posed from the fact that Henry oge's lands extended into Tyrone, and the surviving sources are mainly legal and difficult to interpret. After the division of 1612–13 there were seven owners Tiranny, by 1641 there were only four,[121] one of whom Robert Hovendon, also a tenant to the archbishopric, who had married Phelim's mother, had not been a proprietor originally in Armagh though he did receive a grant in

[113] Ibid., 412; NAI, Lodge, Records of the rolls, v, 192.
[114] See above, 86, 191.
[115] Kearney, *Strafford*, 79, shows in tabular form how generally exempt Ulster owners were from this costly requirement in the period 1625–41.
[116] NAI, Deeds, wills and instruments … post mortem, vol. 25, 67–72.
[117] Ibid., 48–52.
[118] *Inq. cancel. Hib. repert.*, ii, Armagh (36) Chas I.
[119] NAI, Deeds, wills and instruments … post mortem, vol. 25, 52–66.
[120] *AFM*, 2403.
[121] NAI, Books of Survey and Distribution.

Tyrone. Hovendon was a member of an English family which had received land under the plantation of Leix and Offaly. His father, Henry, a remarkable figure, had been secretary and foster-brother to Hugh O'Neill.[122] In 1620 Robert Hovendon acquired the lands granted to Conn boy O'Neill,[123] and in 1631 he acquired further property from Phelim O'Neill.[124] While obviously an ambiguous figure, he retained his lands (2,364 acres) as an English Protestant in 1641.

Phelim's career was conversely one of financial decline before 1641.[125] While he retained a considerable acreage in Tyrone,[126] he had only some 1,500 acres in Tiranny in 1641, and his property was encumbered by a number of mortgages. In 1629 he seems to have persuaded his relatives to surrender their lands to him, because Carte states that on 6 May 1629 the English privy council ordered that he receive a new patent 'vesting in him all his grandfather's estate'.[127] No such new patent appears to have been taken out.[128] Although the Armagh land was not apparently mortgaged,[129] the evidence of an inquisition taken in June 1661 concerning his Tyrone lands, which is likely to be reliable, may be outlined here to indicate the extent of his debts.[130] This shows that he had raised £6,300 in mortgages between 1632 and 1640. His larger creditors were Alderman Parkhurst of London,[131] Rev. John Symonds, an Armagh rector and property-owner, and Sir Edward Bolton, son of the chancellor.[132] He had also made two long-term leases of lands to British tenants, one being to Carroll Bolton, a brother of Sir Edward, in return for an entry fine of £1,000.[133] This throws some light on the statement by Temple that O'Neill had replaced Irish by English tenants who would pay more.[134] From fragments of pleadings in chancery suits it appears that he made similar long-term leases of pieces of land to various old English tenants, Dowdalls, Plunketts, and Hamlins.[135] That Phelim was

122 J.J. Marshall, 'The Hovendens', *UJA*, 2nd series, vol. 13 (1907), 4–12, 73–83.
123 PRONI, T808/14912, 14941.
124 NAI, Deeds, wills and instruments … post mortem, vol. 25, 72–9.
125 He was, for a time, a student at Lincoln's Inn in London (T. Carte, *A collection of letters … related [to] the history … of … the duke of Ormond* (London, 1735), i, 158.
126 *Inq. cancel. Hib. repert.*, ii, Tyrone (3 and 23) Char II.
127 Carte, *Ormond*, i, 158.
128 The Phelim Roe O'Neill referred to in *CPRI, Chas I*, 547, can hardly have been Sir Phelim.
129 *Inq. cancel. Hib. repert.*, ii, Armagh (5) Chas II; Armagh Public Library, William Reeves, Memoirs of Tynan (MS volume, unfoliated).
130 *Inq. cancel. Hib. repert.*, ii, Tyrone (3) Chas II.
131 Above, 202.
132 A '1641' deponent stated that he had also mortgaged some land to Walter Cope for £800 (TCD, MS 836, fol. 23.
133 *Inq. cancel. Hib. repert.*, ii, Tyrone (3) Chas II. George Rawdon was the other tenant (ibid.).
134 J. Temple, *The history of the general rebellion in Ireland* (Cork, 1766), 26.
135 NAI, Chancery salvage, Y.53, 2B, 80, 120, no. 207.

financially embarrassed by 1641 is manifest: Carte and Temple asserted that this contributed to his decision to embark on war in 1641.[136]

The two principal O'Reilly grantees were Mulmory oge, and Mulmory McHugh Connelagh. As to Mulmory oge, we have already seen that substantial portions of his estate were dispersed. He died without heir in 1617, the remaining lands descending to his uncle Capt. Hugh, whose son, Phillip McHugh O'Reilly, owned much of them in 1641.[137] Mulmory McHugh Connelagh died in 1635 or 1636.[138] He had four sons, Edmund (or Eamon), Phillip, Hugh (d.s.p. 1637), and Hugh, the latter two being illegitimate.[139] Of this estate an area of less than 800 acres was owned by Greenham, the undertaker, in 1641, and small portions were in Old English and other hands. The remainder of the estate had been divided amongst Mulmory's heirs. Thus the 1641 owners were Phillip and Edmund, sons of Mulmory, Hugh, probably the illegitimate son, and Myles and Phillip McEdmund, sons of Edmund. Phillip McMulmory had over 6,000 acres whereas his brother Edmund appears to have had only about 100. However, his sons had some 1,750 acres between them.[140] The brothers Edmund and Phillip, and Edmund's son Myles, were prominent figures in the rising in Cavan.[141]

No simple answer can be given to the question of the prosperity of the Irish grantees on the outbreak of rebellion in 1641. In the case of one Cavan proprietor, however, a will survives which is revealing. Two brothers Shane and Phillip McPhillip O'Reilly received a joint patent of lands in Castlerahan. Phillip's share of this was about 800 acres.[142] In May 1638 he made his will (he had made a previous one in 1623) from which encumbrances on the estate emerge.[143] Half was left to his wife as a jointure as well as a lease of an additional townland which he held, and the remainder to his nephew Turlogh McShane who is recorded as owner of all in 1641.[144] His debts recorded in the will amounted to some £100. £60, charged on a townland, was to be paid to a Patrick O'Gowan, and £10, charged on another, was to be paid to Oliver Nugent who owned land in the county. Appended to the will was a schedule of 'small debts', fifty-six in all, totalling some £30. One of the larger sums was £3. 10. 0. owed to Sir

136 Carte, *Ormond*, i, 158; Temple, *General Rebellion*, 67.
137 NAI, Books of Survey and Distribution.
138 P. Walsh, *Irish chiefs and leaders* (Dublin 1960), 141–56.
139 Ibid., 157–79.
140 NAI, Books of Survey and Distribution.
141 Hamilton, *The Irish rebellion*, 149–60.
142 NAI, Books of Survey and Distribution.
143 NAI, Deeds, wills and instruments … post mortem, vol. 25, 276–83. There are gaps in the transcription. For the earlier will see ibid., 274–6.
144 NAI, Books of Survey and distribution.

James Craig. The majority of his creditors were Irish, though settler and Old English names are also prominent. Many were ladies and many lived either in Dublin or between there and Cavan. The only property on the estate referred to he left to his wife – 'all my crop of corne and two geile cowes [bullocks?] and a heifer'. Thus at the of our period one grantee's position at least was unhealthy.

3. The position of the landless Irish

The condition of the mass of the indigenous population under the plantation remains obscure. What follows is, in large part, derived from the report in 1624 of those appointed to examine the position of the Irish on undertakers' lands in Armagh.[145] No such report survived for Cavan. The Armagh inquiry was carried out at Armagh, by virtue of a commission of 27 January 1624, by Sir Francis Annesley, Charles Poyntz, and Sir Edward Trevor on February 23 before a jury consisting of seventeen people, including seven native Irish. It does not easily lend itself to numerical analysis and indeed the numerical data seems unreliable, but it is unusually informative of the conditions of the Irish and their relations with landlords and tenants of British origin.

The number of Irish found, 107+ (for two estates exact numbers are not available), is lower than the total of the commissioners in 1622, 242+. Also the amounts of rent paid or the areas of their holdings – in many cases they held less than a townland – are not always available.

The rents paid by Irish tenants were within the range of about £4 to perhaps as much as £30 per townland. Most Irish tenants held from year to year and, in a few cases, for shorter periods. There are only three cases of Irish holding for longer periods. Two Irish tenants to Sir William Brownlow held parts of four townlands at £5. 13. 0. per annum under a lease poll for twenty-one years. On the Obbyns estate four Irish held one townland at £8 per annum payable to the tenant Sir Henry Bourchier (a servitor owner in Orior) 'for a tearme'. The other case was the more complicated one of an Irishman who had acquired a seventeen-year lease of one townland on the Stanhowe estate at £2 per annum from an English tenant, which he had subsequently assigned to another English occupier for £4 per annum.

Rent payments, part in money and part in produce, were common on the Sacheverall estate. Five Irish on one townland, for example, paid as rent half of the corn and £4 for the grass. Thus, while it emerges that the Irish

[145] TNA, SP 63/263, ff 139–44 (*CSPI, 1615–25*, 482–4).

were by no means exclusively pastoral, the survey shows that very many held land, often small quantities, for grazing purposes. Pasturing rights in return for work services were prevalent on almost all estates, and almost all those defined as servants in the accompanying table owned small numbers of cattle.[146] A characteristic entry of this type can be taken from the estate of Sir John Dillon where it was found that on one townland 'Donell McCann doth reside ... as a servant to George Pinson who hath these lands in lease, and doth depasture fower or five cowes there'. Wage payments to those who feature as servants or workmen in the report were not usually made, remuneration being made in grazing rights though, in one case, a household servant to a tenant on the John Dillon estate received 6d. a week in wages and the pasture of two cows. However, the evidence of an inquiry primarily concerned with landholding by Irish cannot be taken as exhaustive on this point. On some estates Irish were found who paid for grazing in accordance with the number of cattle they placed on the land. Thus five Irish on one townland of the Stanhowe estate, which they held from a particularly substantial tenant John Wrench,[147] 'depastured' their stock there at 1d. per week per cow and 2d. per week per horse.[148]

In a few cases those who can be defined as tenants rather than workmen paid in rent and in labour services. Thus, some Irish on the Obbyns estate held land for grazing from a tenant or relative of the Rev. James Matchett, who had sold his estate to Sir Oliver St. John, and paid £1 in rent and 'work in hedging a place of wheat sowed by Matchett'.[149] The occupations of the Irish servants in those few cases where they are stated throws some light on the rural scene though may not form any basis for generalisation about the skilled attainments of the native population. However, only one appears as a craftsman, a smith under Scottish tenants on the Brownlow estate. Most commonly they appear in the care of cattle to landlords and British tenants alike and are defined as 'cowkeep', 'herd', and similarly. The one Irishman listed on the Grandison estate was employed as a 'tracker', his function evident in a predominantly unenclosed countryside.[150] However, Irish on three estates, Sir John Dillon's, John Dillon's, and Obbyns's, were engaged in land enclosing. Not only did the Irish reside on undertakers' estates in a variety of capacities but it is also clear that some undertakers, Sir Archibald

146 Goats feature in one case on the Obbyns estate.

147 Below, 266.

148 On the Cope estate some Irish paid 1½d. per week per cow, and on John Dillon's the grazing of fifteen or sixteen cattle was held for one month at 6/- in money 'or the value in work'.

149 Three Irish held part of a townland on John Dillon's estate for grazing from a widowed tenant and 'payd certaine hedging work for the same'.

150 One Irishman on a townland of the Sacheverall estate which was held by Sir Archibald Acheson was employed as a 'servant' to Acheson who held a 'stud of horses' there.

Acheson and Sir William Brownlow specifically, had Irish living in their houses as servants.

The appended table has been constructed to throw light on the status of the Irish dealt with in the report. Of a total of somewhat more than 207 people over 103, or roughly one-half, were direct tenants to undertakers, 61 were tenants to British tenants on the estates and, of the remaining 43, 18 or 19 were servants to workmen to undertakers, and 24 or 25 were servants or workmen to their tenants.[151] Although half of the Irish recorded were direct tenants sub-tenancy was apparently becoming the normal condition for Irish landholding on many estates. Only Hamilton, Brownlow, Sacheverall, Stanhowe, and Obbyns, the three latter having been criticised as planters in 1622, had substantially more Irish tenants than sub-tenants. Sub-tenancy would presuppose a willingness on the part of the Irish to pay higher rents to the undertakers than the British tenants did. They also generally paid higher rents when they were direct tenants.

Estate	Total no. of Irish	No. in 1622	No. of tenants		No. of servants		Approx. proportion of estate held by Irish direct tenants[152]
			to u'taker	to tenants	to u'taker	to tenants	
Acheson	2	some	-	-	2	-	A
Hamilton	18+	48	11+	1	2	4	A
Rolleston	7	12	-	5	2	-	A
Sacheverall	34	49	25	-	3	6	B
St. John	1	8	-	-	1	A	
Brownlow	41+	24	35+	2	3	1	C
Stanhowe	21	24	11	9	-	1	B
Dillon	8	'few or no Irish'	1	3	2	2	A
Sir J Dillon	10	19	1?	8	-	1	A
Cope	22	40	-	17	2	3	A
Obbyns	43	18	19	16	2	6	A
Totals	**207+**	**242+**	**103+**	**61**	**18**	**24**	

The column indicating the approximate proportion of each estate held in direct tenancy by Irish has been provided because the compromise agreed

[151] Where undertakers' workmen or servants had rights of pasturage they are placed in the servants, rather than tenants, column.

[152] A = under ¼; B = about ¼; C = over ¼.

to in 1628 whereby the undertakers might retain Irish on one-quarter of their estates seems to have been interpreted when in 1631 attempts were made to penalise those who had Irish on areas in excess of this as referring to Irish as direct tenants.[153]

The years around 1628 produced much discussion of the position of the Irish on undertakers lands which has been examined above.[154] The enforcement of the compromise then reached was only very partial. However, an inquisition taken in 1631[155] purporting to list lands held by Irish from Armagh undertakers in infringement of the new regulations can, perhaps, be used to indicate the predicament of Irish seeking to hold land from undertakers. The lands in question were only small fragments of three estates in Oneilland, those of Brownlow, Stanhowe, and Sir William Alexander who, at this point, held part of the Sacheverall estate.

It is of interest that though the lands occupied by Irish on Brownlow's estate in 1631 were also in Irish hands in 1624, only one of the Irish tenants in 1631 had also held his lands in 1624. Thus while the land had remained in Irish hands there is no evidence for continuity of possession in the seven-year interval. The same applies to the Stanhowe estate. Here the 'half town' of Neevore was held by Hugh duff McDonnell in 1624 and by Patrick modery O'Connellan in 1631. O'Connellan, however, had also held it in March 1629.[156] On the Alexander estate, however, Henry duffe O'Connellan who held one-quarter of Mullalellish townland in 1631 was doubtless that same Henry O'Conelan who, with four others, had held half of the townland in 1624. It seems fair to suggest that continuity of occupation, when land was held on a yearly basis, was only to be guaranteed when a tenant could outbid a fellow Irish competitor.

Further evidence that there were numbers of Irish who owned small numbers of cattle and rented grazing and other land comes from a list of the goods of felons in 1628 which were granted to the archbishop of Armagh.[157] Three such had two cows and one heifer; one cow and one garran; and one cow, two heifers, one mare, and one sucking colt respectively. Two others, as well as having two cows and four cows respectively, also had two acres and three acres of oats and other corn.

Generally up to about 1625 or so the Irish were being confined increasingly to smaller areas on each undertakers' proportion. However,

[153] Above, 173–5.
[154] Above, 161–6.
[155] *Inq. cancel. Hib. repert.*, ii, Armagh (19) Chas I.
[156] Ibid., (3) Chas I.
[157] Armagh Archiepiscopal Registry, A.2a.28/20, 13–14. The archbishop had the right to felons' goods by patent of 18 December 1616 (*CPRI, Jas I*, 314).

their share was still a substantial one, and that there was little or no immigration of British after that date is confirmed by the anxiety of the undertakers to secure permission to retain Irish tenants on one quarter of each estate. The evidence of the inquiry of 1624 and related material may thus not unreasonably be suggested as valid for the period up to 1641. On the lands of the archbishopric of Armagh a somewhat similar development can be seen,[158] which was not nearly so pronounced on the bishop's lands in Cavan or the TCD estate in Armagh[159] where, by and large, a policy of leasing to large middlemen was favoured. These, it would seem, sub-let almost exclusively to native occupants. Some servitors brought in British tenants and, in parts of Cavan and south Armagh, Old English are found, but the servitors' and natives' lands were largely occupied by native Irish. Clearly the plan to make the undertakers' baronies all-British enclaves did not result in any general movement of the Irish elsewhere and, although a scheme to facilitate this was belatedly formulated in 1628, it was not given effect. The Irish were certainly the natural sub-tenants to absentee leaseholders.

The relations of the Irish and the incoming proprietors cannot be easily generalised. As the immigrant tenant element increased, opportunities for the native population became manifestly more constricted. While the archbishop of Armagh was alleged to have wished to exclude the Irish from living near the town of Armagh, it is evident that they formed an element in the population of most towns.[160] Also it would be wrong to polarise native and settler as individually composing universally opposing elements. The plantation did not exclude all opportunities for them and some Irish have been found in rent collecting capacities[161] as well as holding office in manorial and county administration.[162] Ambiguities in relationships grew up which can be illustrated by the following instance, an undated complaint of a British tenant, George Thornton, against an Oneilland undertaker, Sacheverall.[163] Thornton complained that his house had been broken into and goods and arms stolen by 'certaine woodkerne', O'Hagans, O'Neills, and McCanns. Going into 'the creetes adjoininge' he arrested one of the delinquents, McCann, who confessed the theft. However, McCann procured his release by the intervention of Sacheverall. Thornton pressed Sacheverall to have McCann and his associates arrested and prosecuted at

[158] Below, chapter 12.
[159] Below, 348.
[160] Below, 229–56.
[161] See, for example, above 189–90.
[162] Below, 344–8.
[163] Marsh's Library, Dublin, MS Z3.1.1. no. ixvi.

the assizes. This was not done and he claimed that he had seen Sacheverall and some of them drinking and talking together on a number of occasions. This is not, however, to attempt to minimise the hardship of many who suffered the penalties of the law and, in periods of emergency, at the hands of provost marshals. The 1641 rising indicated no unnatural basic loyalties. The policy of plantation was not in their interests, even if many of the settlers were, for practical reasons, reluctant agents of that policy in its complete application.

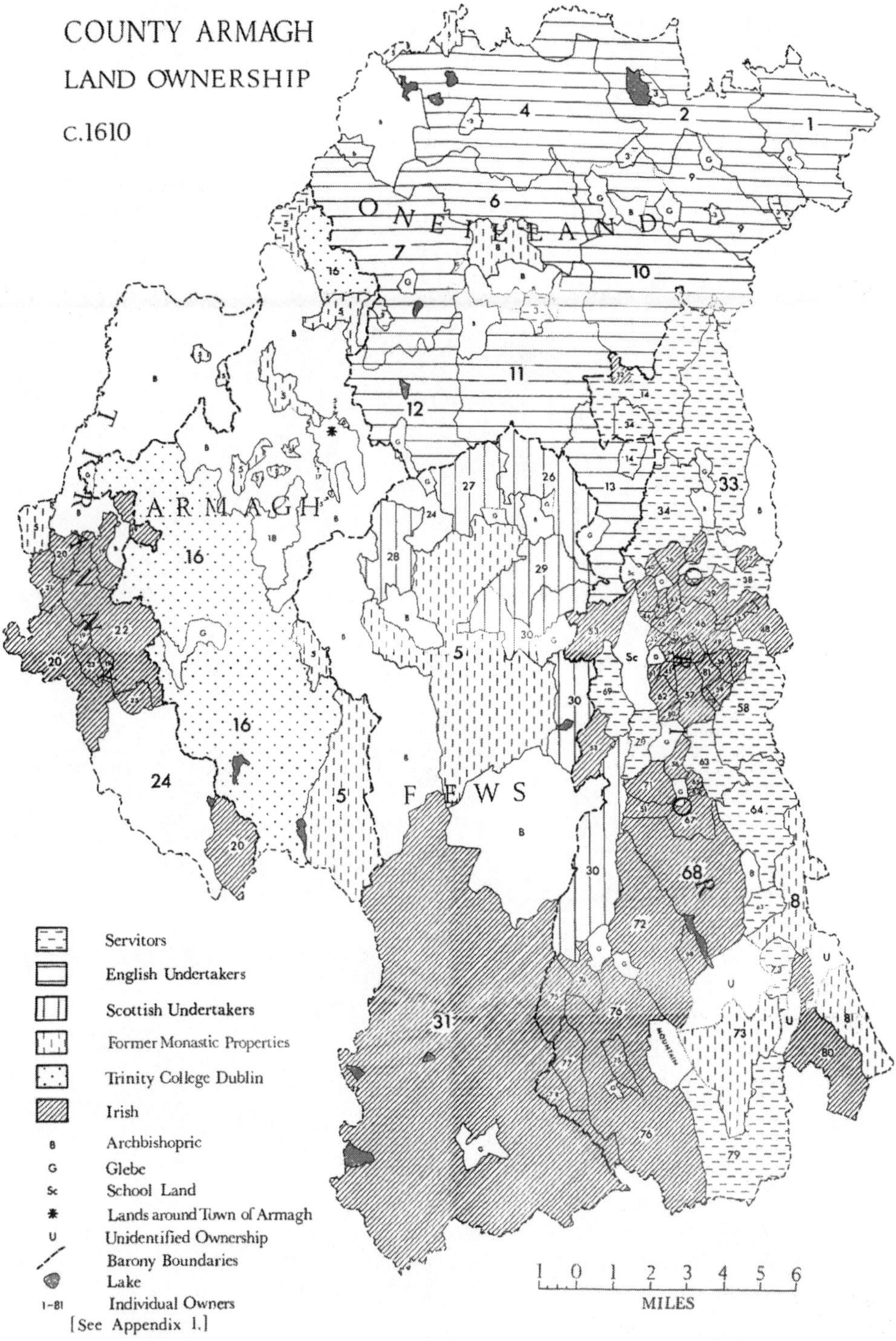

County Armagh: Landownership, *c.* 1610–*c.* 1620

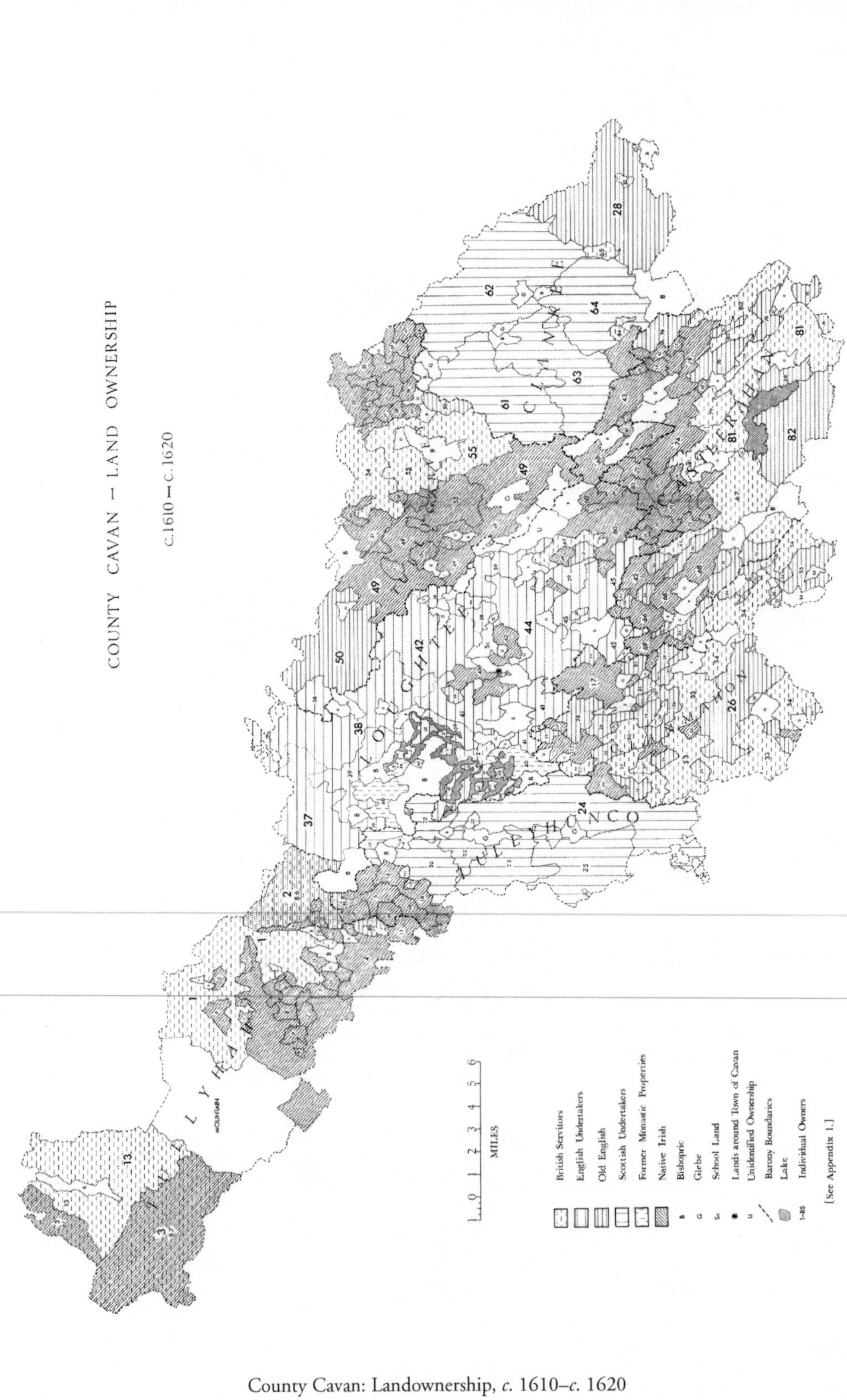

County Cavan: Landownership, *c.* 1610–*c.* 1620

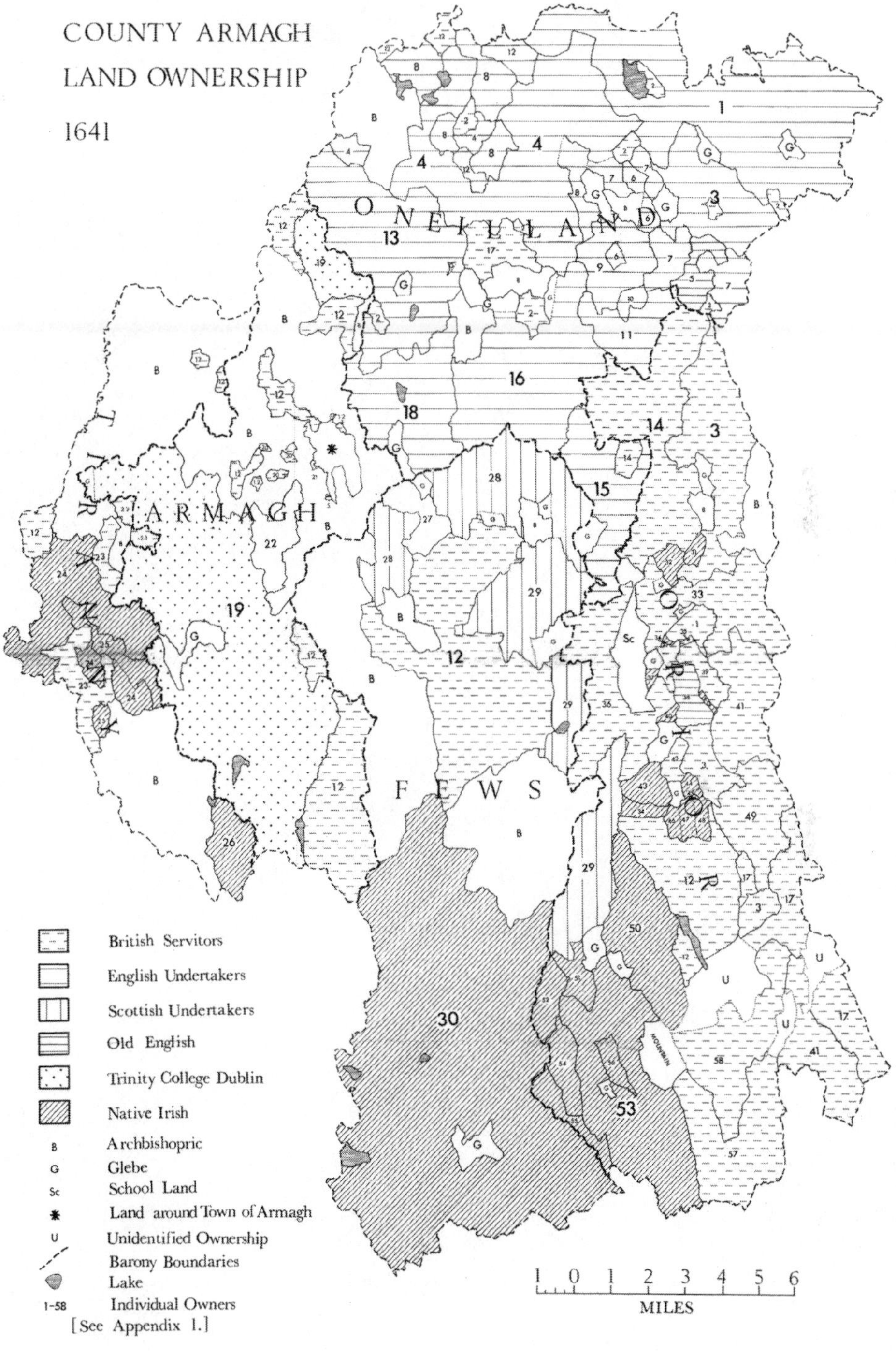
COUNTY ARMAGH
LAND OWNERSHIP
1641
ONEILLAND
ARMAGH
TIRANNY
FEWS
ORIOR
British Servitors
English Undertakers
Scottish Undertakers
Old English
Trinity College Dublin
Native Irish
B Archbishopric
G Glebe
Sc School Land
Land around Town of Armagh
U Unidentified Ownership
Barony Boundaries
Lake
1-58 Individual Owners
[See Appendix 1.]
1 0 1 2 3 4 5 6
MILES

County Armagh: Landownership, 1641

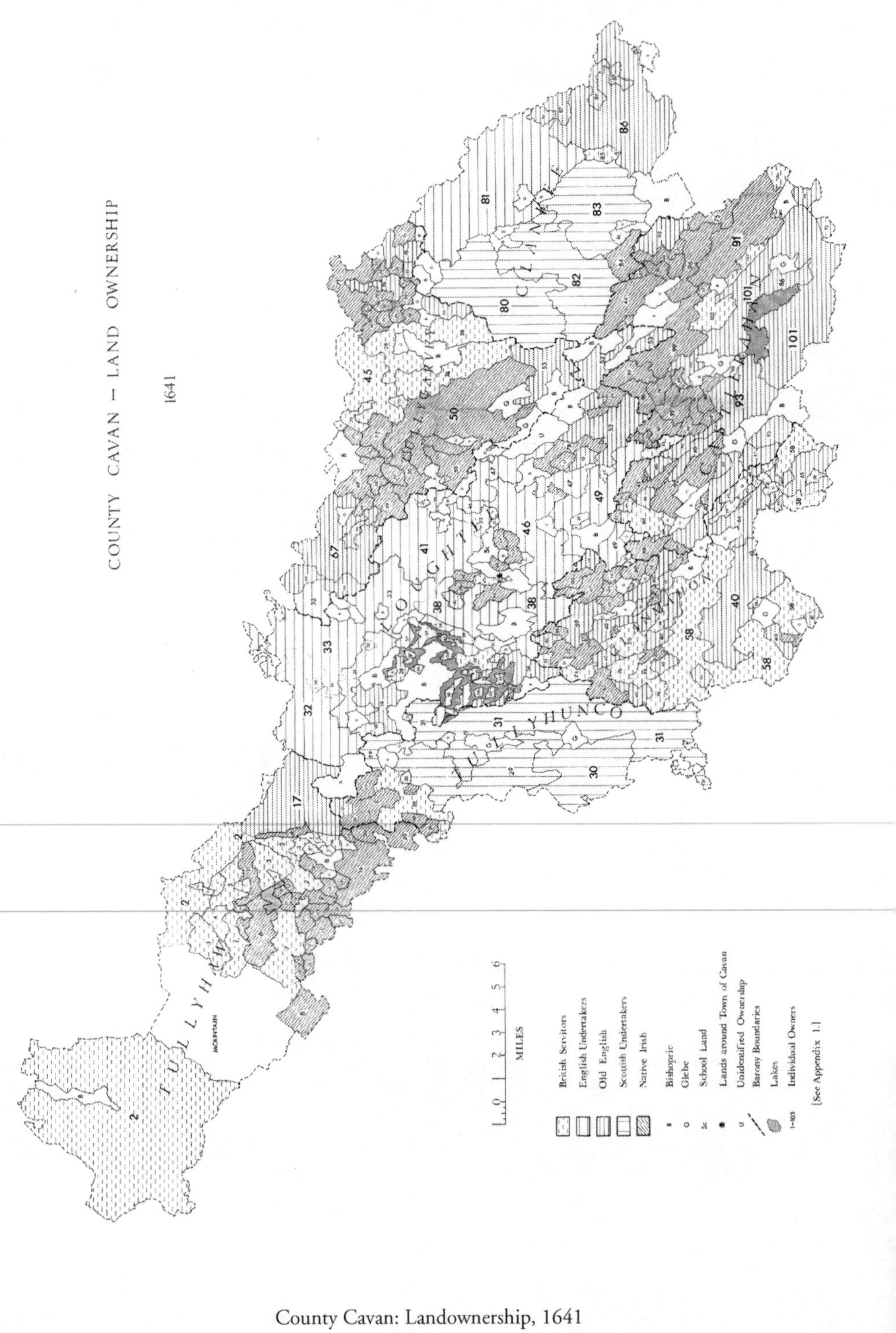

County Cavan: Landownership, 1641

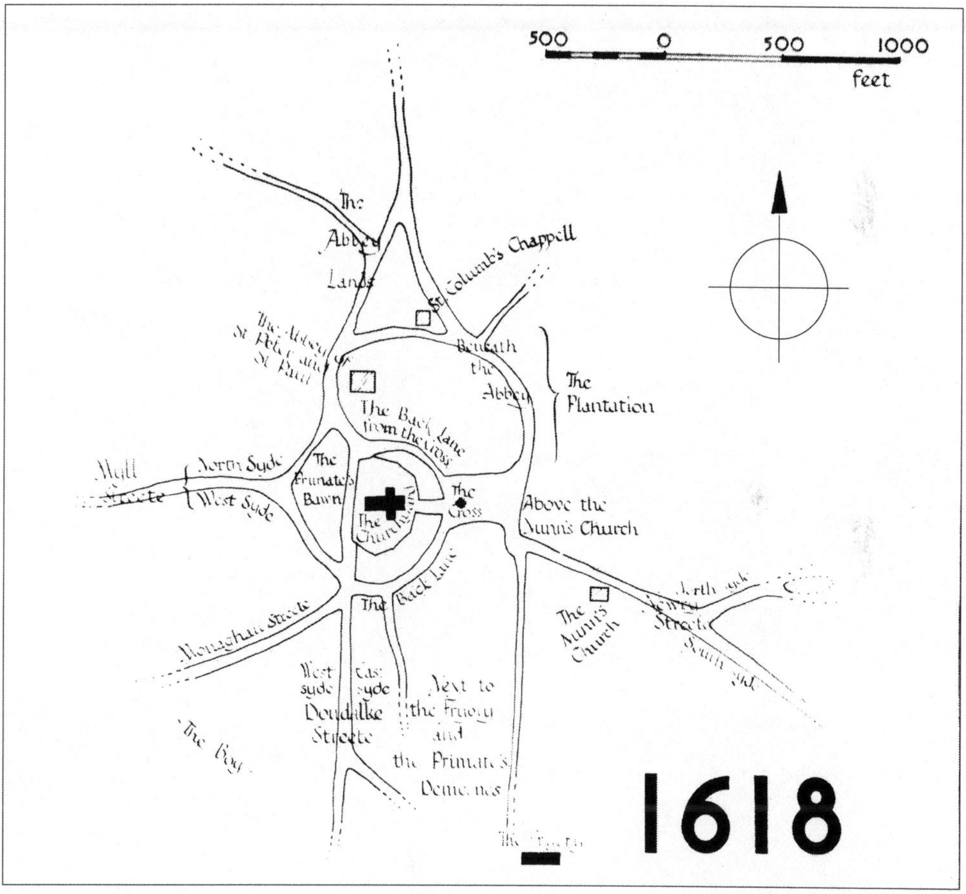

500 0 500 1000
feet
The Abbey Lands
St Columb's Chappell
Beneath the Abbey
The Plantation
The Back Lane from the Cross
The Primate's Bawn
The Churchyard
The Cross
Above the Nunn's Church
North Syde
West Syde
Monaghan Streete
The Back Lane
West syde
East syde
Doudalke Streete
Next to the Priory and the Primate's Demesnes
The Nunn's Church
Street
South syde
The Bog
1618

Reconstruction of Armagh town, 1618

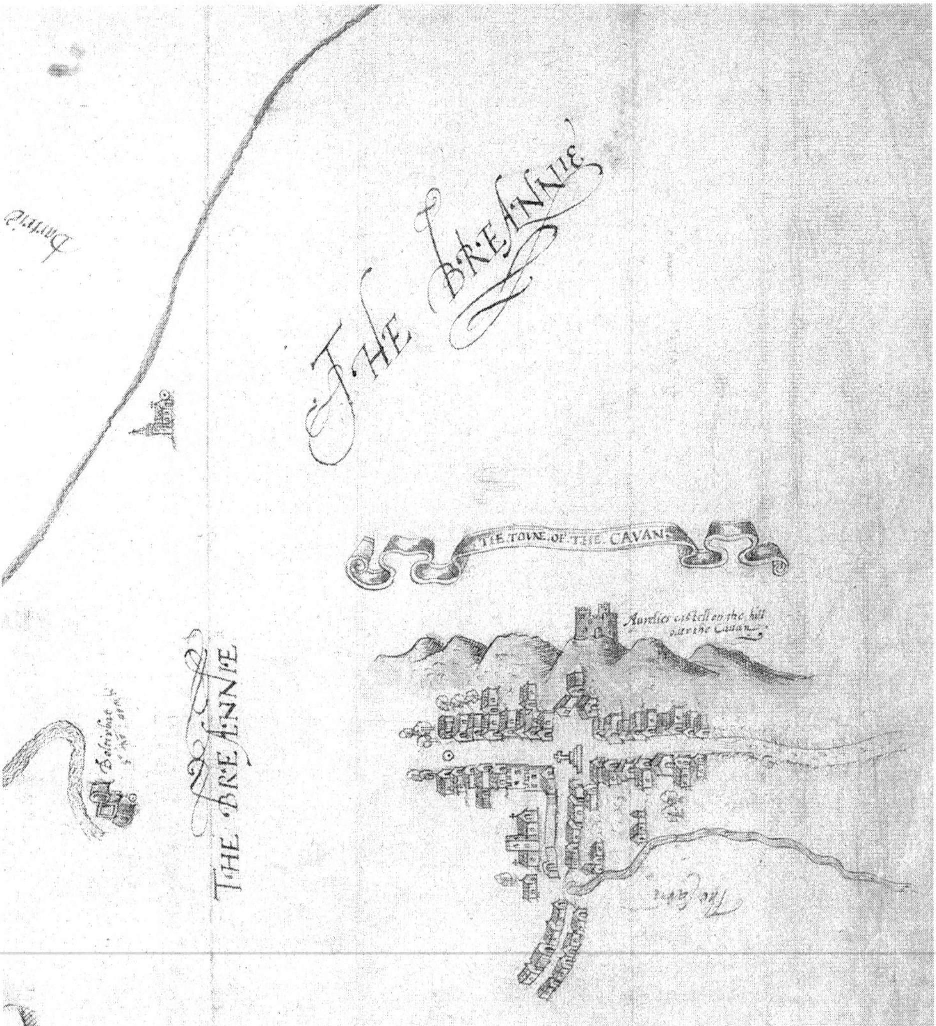

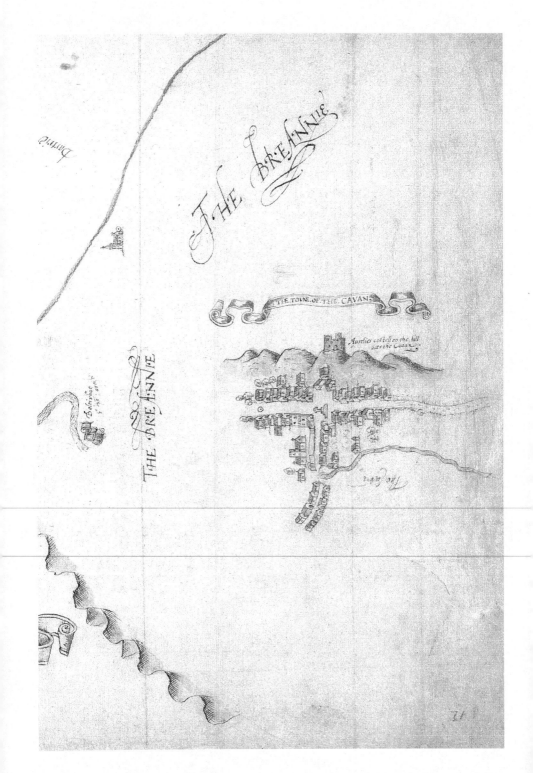

Netherclift's map of Cavan town, *c.* 1593

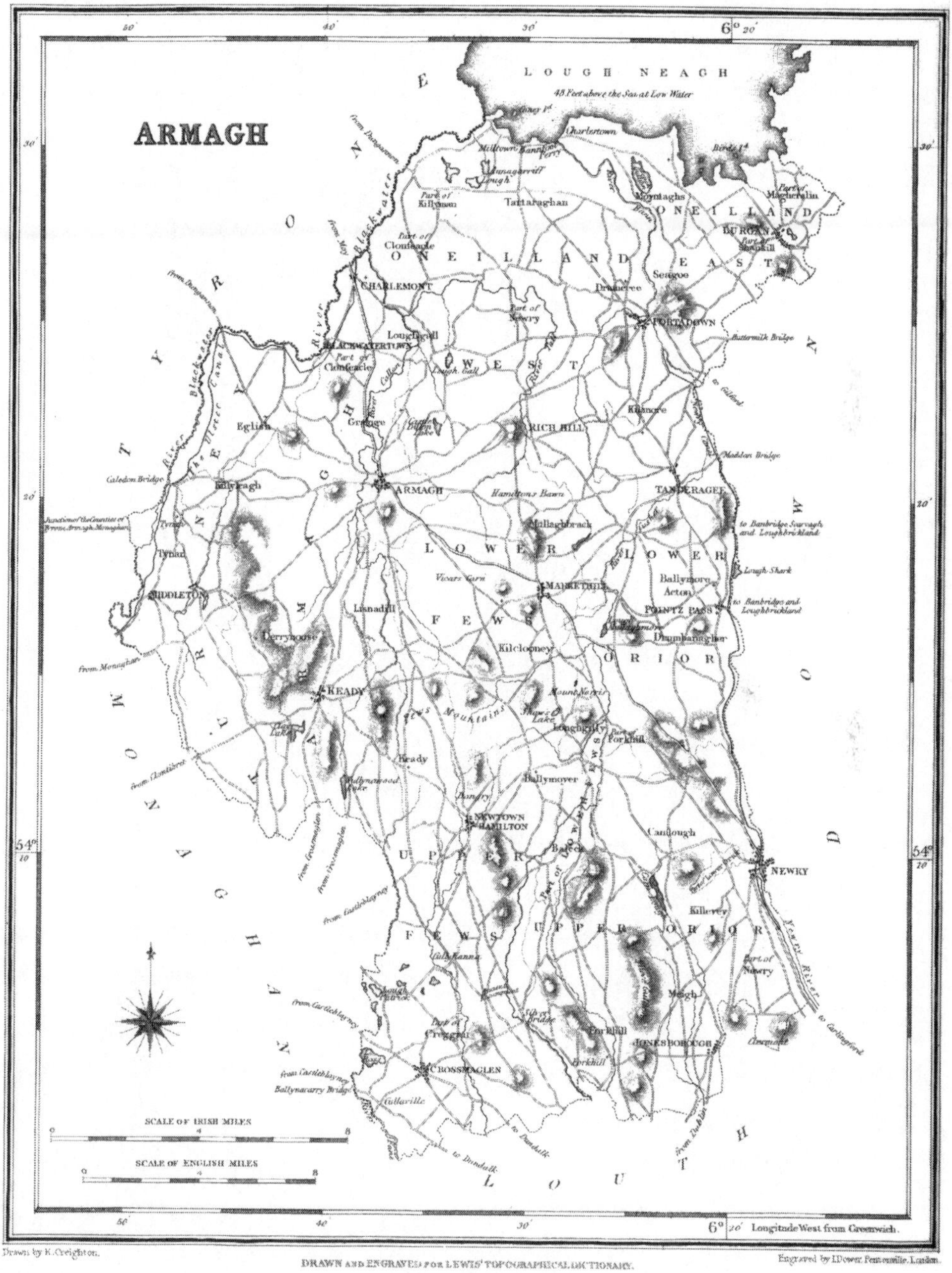

Lewis's map of County Armagh (1837)

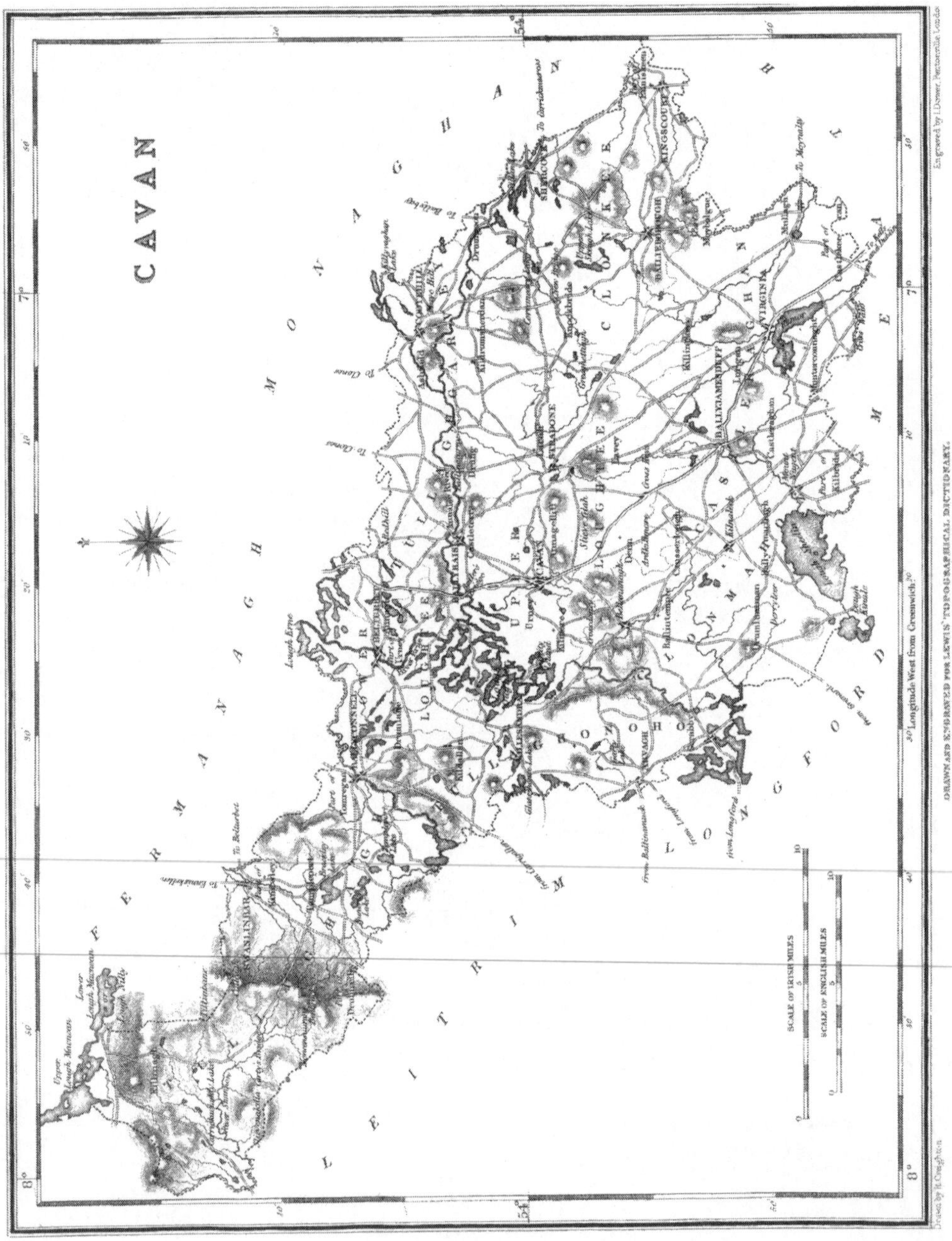

Lewis's map of County Cavan (1837)

CHAPTER 8

Towns

1. Introduction

The systematic establishment of towns as focal points for the colony in Ulster formed part of the scheme for plantation from an early stage. As early as 1590 Justice Robert Gardner and Sir Harry Wallopp had pointed to the peculiar difficulty of reforming Ulster in contrast to Munster and Connacht where there were 'some cities, many castles, towns well walled [and] well peopled with great part of th'English nation' whereas in Ulster there were 'very fewe castles, or places of defence, except in Lecale, the Newry and Knockfergus'. They went on to argue that the extension of English authority there could best be achieved by the establishment of fortified settlements on which local government institutions could be based, after the model of Philipstown and Maryborough in Leix and Offaly.[1] In the concluding stages of the Nine Years' War Mountjoy's strategy had demonstrated the value of erecting forts. The plantation scheme visualised a systematic urbanisation policy for the escheated counties.

These plantation towns were either to be settled *de novo*, or else the development of previous centres – forts or places of Gaelic origin. The 'Orders and conditions' of plantation, laid down that in each county 'a convenient number' of market and corporate towns should be established 'for the habitation and settling tradesmen and artificers'.[2] The 'Project' stated the number of towns in each county which should be incorporated. Land was reserved to be granted to each in fee farm. These corporate towns should receive rights to hold fairs and markets and other 'reasonable' liberties, including the power to return burgesses to parliament. To set them up there should be a 'leavy or presse' of tradesmen and artificers out of England. In all twenty-five such corporate towns were projected.[3]

The importance of inaugurating town life in Ulster as an integral part of the colonial scheme was thus recognised. A grant of land might in itself offer sufficient incentive to an undertaker to remove to Ulster, but it was clearly accepted that the establishment of towns was only possible through

1 Cambridge University Library, KK.1.15, vol. 1, ff 5–8.
2 Hill, *Plantation*, 78–89.
3 'Ulster plantation papers', no. 74, *Anal. Hib.*, viii.

some form of state initiative. However, in the spring of 1610 it was found that, although many aspects of the plantation had been by then considered in detail, arrangements for the foundation of towns had been neglected. It had, however, become apparent that state assistance either in the erection of houses or in the importation of townsmen had become unlikely. The question arose whether, if tradesmen were not to be 'pressed' from England, corporations should be established at all and, if so, in what way the land allotted for that purposes, then estimated as 9,600 acres, should be granted. It was decided that although the original intention of assisted or impressed settlement should be abandoned, nonetheless the projected incorporations should be proceeded with and charters to these places issued, as a means of attracting tradesmen coming over with the undertakers to live in them. Besides, the political value of such incorporations was evident because they would return burgesses to parliament 'which upon the new plantation will consist of protestants and strengthen the lower house very much'.[4]

In July 1610 further directives were issued from London. The plantation commissioners should decide how many houses should be erected for the time being in each town, lay out their sites, and assign land for further buildings. They should set out plots for churches and churchyards, and for market places and houses. They should ensure that water was conveniently available. No land was to be enclosed and appropriated to any particular householder until the town had been 'conveniently' peopled. One third of the land allotted to each town might be enclosed at the common charge to make a common meadow, the rest to be left for a common for cattle. In towns where schools were to be founded, sites should be reserved for that purpose. The deputy was to ensure that no lands appointed for towns (or schools) should be granted for other purposes. The deputy and council were to give instructions for the peopling of the towns, and the building of churches and schools 'so far as the means of the country will yield'. When the towns had grown to forty houses they should be incorporated.[5] While these orders have some interest from a planning viewpoint, on the crucial question of initial investment they embodied no more than a facile transference of responsibility from London to Dublin.

In December, when the plantation commissioners had returned to Dublin from Ulster, further problems were submitted to the privy council in London. To the question whether the corporations, the college, and the schools might plant their lands with Irish tenants it was replied that the latter two might chose their tenants 'best for their profit', but the towns were to plant with British. A further more fundamental question revealed that the

4 *CSPI, 1608–10*, 415–16.

5 *Cal. Carew MSS, 1603–24*, 56–7; *CSPI, 1608–10*, 488.

founding of towns still remained a problem to which no satisfactory solution had been found. The deputy stated his difficulties. The natives were 'indisposed and unapt' to town life. There were only a few merchants amongst them and these were wont to 'wander up and down amongst their creaghts' buying such pieces of yarn as might be for sale. Also he doubted if English or Scottish tradesmen could be brought to any of the places to be incorporated 'in any due time'. His only solution was that some 'principal gentlemen' should be appointed superintendents of the corporations to draw settlers there and to maintain order until the towns had increased to a 'sufficient' size when they should be incorporated and authority transferred to the mayors. The privy council accepted this, laying down that an undertaker or servitor near the site of each proposed town should be appointed to build houses for tradesmen, who should hold of him the fee farm of their tenements in free burgage at easy rents. The land for the town should be granted to the planter in fee farm with a time limited for the performance of his obligations, incorporation to follow subsequently.[6]

On the basis of these decisions steps were taken for the granting of the lands assigned for towns to neighbouring planters. A form of warrant for a fiant for granting boroughs was drawn up, presumably in mid 1611.[7] Grants were to follow a set pattern 'accordinge to the artickles layd downe for a burrowe towne'. The lands were to be granted in fee farm under defined rents as also markets and fairs. The clerkship of the market should vest in the patentee until the town had been incorporated, when it should then come to the chief officer of the town.[8] It was thus a year after many of the major problems of inaugurating the colony had been settled, and when almost all the land had already been granted, that a means to establish the towns had been found.

The working out of this arrangement with the prospective patrons of towns was also not, in all cases at any rate, quickly achieved. John Ridgeway, a local servitor grantee, who became patron of the proposed town at Aghanure in Cavan – subsequently Virginia – did not take out his patent

6 Lam. Pal. Lib., Carew MSS, vol. 629, ff 68–72 (*Cal. Carew MSS, 1603–24*, 141–2; *CSPI, 1611–14*, 36–7). The dating of this document in the Carew calendar is incorrect and misleading. The propositions were sent to England on 11 December 1610 and returned on 19 May 1611. (The instructions in Carew MSS vol. 629 ff 16–18v (*CSPI, 1611–14*, 63–7) are in reply to further queries sent over with Bourchier and brought back to Ireland by Carew on 13 July 1611).

7 'Ulster plantation papers', no. 52, *Anal. Hib.*, viii. The document is undated. The suggestion 1610? seems too early. It was probably drawn up following the receipt on 19 May 1611 of the directions from London, and before August 19 when the first grant (for the town of Rathmullan in County Donegal to Sir Ralph Bingley) was authorised (Bod. Lib., Carte MSS, vol. 62, fol. 19 (*CSPI 1611–14*, 96)). For the warrant for a grant of a borough [Mountnorris] to Sir Francis Annesley see'Ulster plantation papers', no. 58, *Anal. Hib.*, viii.

8 Ibid.

of the town lands until August 1612.[9] The obligations of patrons in establishing the towns can be seen in his case. He received some five townlands approximately 1,297 statute acres.[10] He undertook to 'plant and settle' on one of these townlands within four years twenty persons, English or Scottish, chiefly artificers, who should be burgesses of the town which, within the same time, should be incorporated. These burgesses were to be 'accommodated' with house and lands, ten to receive two acres each and ten one acre, in an area to be called the 'Burgess field', and a further thirty acres was to be allotted as a common to the town. The patron was also to allot 'convenient places' as sites for the town itself, and also for a church and churchyard, a market place and a public school. The patentee was licensed to hold a weekly market and an annual fair, to receive the tolls and profits of a court of pie-powder and he and his heirs to be clerks of the market.[11] One clear outcome of this arrangement whereby landlords rather than the government were made responsible for establishing the towns was that the major part of the land initially assigned as endowment of the corporations now came into private hands.

This initial recession in policy is reflected also in the number of towns eventually incorporated. Only fourteen received charters, thirteen of them in 1613, one, Derry, being a reincorporation, the other, Cavan, for peculiar reasons, having received its charter in November 1610.[12] The time lag is, in itself, of significance. As early as November 1610 the holding of a parliament was being discussed,[13] the delay in summoning it may have been in part due to the fact that the Ulster boroughs, the political support of whose Protestant burgesses was desired, had not been incorporated before 1613.

The charters of these towns had an essential simplicity and similarity. That of Cavan, in 1610, was modelled on the charter of Kells,[14] the others by and large followed a pattern contained in a 'paper booke' (not found, but referred to in the warrants for incorporation) drawn up by the privy council in London and sent to Ireland with accompanying royal letter on 26 September 1612,[15] though the charter of Derry was more complex and

9 *CPRI, Jas I*, 236.

10 He also received Lough Ramor and its fishing. The total rent of the lands and water was £1. 10. 8 (ibid.)

11 For these rights he paid a rent of 13/4 Ir. He might also keep a ferry on Lough Ramor, rent ¾ Ir. (ibid.)

12 Controversy attended the incorporation of Lifford in Donegal (Bod. Lib., Carte MSS, vol. 62, ff 212–13).

13 T.W. Moody, 'The Irish parliament under Elizabeth and James I', *PRIA*, vol. xlv, C, (1939–40), 51.

14 Bod. Lib., Carte MSS, vol. 61, fol. 497.

15 See, for example, Carte MSS, vol. 62, fol. 147 (*CSPI, 1611–14*, 338): Order for incorporation of Charlemont, County Armagh, 20 April 1613.

elaborate than those granted to the Ulster towns in general.[16] Each town area was created 'one entire and free borough' with corporate authority within it granted to a chief officer (called usually sovereign, portreeve or provost), the free burgesses, and the commons. The free burgesses were generally twelve in number.[17] The chief officers and burgesses were granted the power of 'perpetual succession', that is to say civic government was vested in a small and self-electing body. This exclusive body should elect the two members of parliament each town might return. Each charter contained the names of the first set of incorporators, to hold for life unless removed under exceptional circumstances. The commons (or assembly) was defined as all the inhabitants of the town, and such people as had been admitted freemen. The chief officer was to take the oath of supremacy as well as an oath to fulfil his duties, and was to be elected annually by the sovereign and burgesses. Each corporation could hold a weekly court of record to hear civil actions not exceeding the sum of five marks, before the chief officer. Rights to hold markets and fairs were also usual. The corporation might assemble at discretion to make bye-laws, and could impose fines or other punishments should these be disobeyed. The power of the commons was usually limited to participation in such assemblies. They might appoint from amongst themselves two serjeants at mace and such other municipal officers as were necessary.[18]

One of the most notable features of these charters is that they, necessarily, did not contain a grant of the fee farm of the town. The process, outlined above, whereby responsibility for town establishment came into private hands ensured their subordination, in varying degree, to outside authority. At best the land originally allotted for towns and subsequently granted to superintendents was leased by them to the corporators as individuals, but it never came to a corporation as a body. The original incorporators would (of course) also have been nominated by the landlord,[19] and in at least one case, Belturbet, the landlord became chief officer.[20]

The incomes of the corporations were thus from the start severely limited.[21] The financial returns from courts and fairs and markets cannot have been great and these, in some cases, had to accommodate to the

[16] For a study of the charter of Derry see Moody, *Londonderry Plantation*, 122–38.

[17] It may be noted that the grants to patrons, as seen above in the case of Virginia, envisaged twenty burgesses.

[18] References to the charters of the towns incorporated in the area under review can be seen below.

[19] In the warrant for the incorporation of Duffryn (Bangor), County Down there is the note 'Sr. James Hamilton sent thes names'. (Bod. Lib., Carte MSS, vol. 62, fol. 208). A similar note is appended to that for Donegal town (ibid., fol. 223).

[20] Bod. Lib., Carte MSS, vol. 62, fol. 167 (*CSPI, 1611–14*, 299).

[21] For a recent examination of this problem as it affected Belfast see J.C. Beckett & R.E. Glasscock (eds.), *Belfast, the origin and growth of an industrial city* (London 1967), 28, 35–6.

parallel rights of landlords to hold manor courts and fairs and markets in their own name. With a few exceptions, it may be that corporate development had not proceeded far by 1641. The statement is commonly made that because corporation records are not to hand for the period before the rising they were destroyed in 1641.[22] This need not necessarily be generally true. The size of many of the corporations, their subordination to local landlord authority, and the capacities of their early inhabitants must be considered before it is accepted without question. In some towns, of course, it is clear that this does not apply: Belfast corporation records survive from 1613,[23] Cavan had a peculiar independence from the start, Londonderry corporation records need not have started in 1673,[24] but it is hardly necessary to accept that places like Limavady, controlled by Sir Thomas Phillips and with surviving records from 1659,[25] or Armagh dominated by the archbishop, or Charlemont with its small population, had formally, regularly, and effectively exercised their privileges of assembly and bye-law-making before 1641. Few of the Ulster towns had achieved much sophistication by that date.

The retreat in government policy at the outset, in deciding to entrust the founding of towns to individual settlers, requires special emphasis. Given the resources of the early seventeenth-century state this may well have been unavoidable, but in leaving urban development to private competence, the planners incurred some responsibility for the subsequent slow and fitful growth of town life. Also the Dublin government seems not to have enforced the rules governing the size towns should be before incorporation. The surveys of Carew and Bodley have little to say on the urban aspect of the plantation; it is only with Pynnar and the 1622 report that the towns come at all under notice, and then usually with reference to their difficulties. The establishing of towns, it is suggested, was of little less importance than, and a necessary complement to, the inauguration of a rural colony.

2. Corporations in counties Armagh and Cavan

The 'Project' for the plantation recommended the incorporation of four boroughs in Armagh, and set aside 1,200 acres by the current computation as their endowment, 'to hould in fee farme as the English and Scottish undertakers'. One of these, Armagh, was long established, two, Charlemont

22 See, for example, E.M.F.-G. Boyle, *Records of the town of Limavady, 1609–1808* (Derry 1912), xv.
23 R.M. Young (ed.), *The town book of the corporation of Belfast 1613–1816* (Belfast 1892); G. Benn, *A history of the town of Belfast* (London, 1877), 188 sqq.
24 Corporation books from this date are preserved in PRONI.
25 PRONI, D663.

and Mountnorris, were the sites of recently-erected forts, and the fourth was to be a new town at Tandragee in O'Hanlon territory. For Cavan three incorporations were projected and thirty polls of land allotted for this purpose. Apart from Cavan and Belturbet a new town was to be erected 'in or neere the mydwaie between Kells and Cavan', the site to be chosen by the commissioners of plantation.[26] Of these seven, only four – Armagh and Charlemont, Cavan and Belturbet – in fact received charters. The object in this section is to examine the development of these towns, and to attempt to offer suggestions why three were not incorporated. The treatment is necessarily unsatisfactory owing to a dearth of sources from which to draw. The picture presented of each is partial and unsystematic, however it is hoped that an impression will emerge of the nature of some of the small and inceptive urban settlements of Ulster prior to the rising of 1641.

A. Armagh

In 1610 Thomas Blenerhasset described the town of Armagh as follows:

> How exceedingly wel standeth Armath, better seate for riche soyle there cannot bee, but so poore, as I doe verily thinke all the household stuffe in that citty is not worth twenty pounds, yet it is the Primate of all Ireland, and as they say for antiquitie, one of the most ancient in all Europe: it is also of so small power as forty resolute men may rob, rifle and burne it: were it a defended corporation it woulde soone be rich and religious, and the security would make one acre more worth then now twenty be. At this present time it is a more base and abiect thing, not much better than Strebane, and not able to restraine no, not the violence of the woolfe.[27]

Contemporaries concurred with his judgements both of its antiquity, ecclesiastical dignity, potential and present decay. It had suffered a half century of military significance and had only recently been de-garrisoned. Furthermore, peculiar historical circumstances had for long made it, although the ecclesiastical capital, unattractive for residence to archbishops whose cultural affiliations cut them off from the northern portion of their diocese. As a monastic centre it had had a distinguished record but in the altered circumstances of 1610 it could derive no prominence or prospects from its monastic tradition.

However, it had potential as a traditional marketing centre, and with the introduction of a Protestant colony and the rebuilding of the cathedral church, as a revived and re-orientated ecclesiastical centre as well. Its most

[26] 'Ulster plantation papers', no. 74, *Anal. Hib.*, viii, 294, E.6.
[27] Blenerhasset, 'Direction', 321.

important new function was as county capital and centre of legal sittings. However, the town which was restored and expanded in the thirty years after the plantation had, in some ways, a much greater continuity with its past, if only by reason of the smallness of its immigrant population, than Londonderry, a walled and garrisoned town with an important military role. The pre-plantation settlement fell into three areas, the Trian Sassenach to the north, the Trian Masain to the east, and the Trian Mór to the south. Dispersed throughout these trians or wards, though more densely accumulated in the central ring or hill area, were a series of ecclesiastical institutions of which the cathedral church, the abbey of St. Peter and St. Paul, the Franciscan abbey, St. Columba's church, the Culdee priory, and the nunnery of Templefartagh were perhaps the most important.[28] There was thus a nucleus of roads, paths, and sites from which the transformed town could develop.

The town for the most part fell within the manor of Armagh and was traditionally the property of the archbishopric. However, there were small areas which belonged to the abbey and monasteries, the dean, and the vicars choral.[29] Since this account is based almost exclusively on the see records, allowance must be made for a marginal incompleteness in coverage.

How negligible the impact of the reformation had been was demonstrated to the lord deputy on his visit in 1605. The archbishop, Henry Ussher, was instructed to install a minister in the town and preach and reside there himself each summer.[30] The state of the town as a civic centre must have been equally unprepossessing.[31] It is unlikely that Toby Caulfeild the grantee of the abbey had taken any immediate steps to develop the site. In 1609 it was recorded that the archbishop had recently erected a water mill 'standing upon the river of Calleyne' but there is no evidence of further development. There appears to have been only one non-Gaelic inhabitant of any standing in 1609,[32] and there is little evidence for the state of the town before the beginning of the primacy of Christopher Hampton in 1613.[33]

28 G.A. Hayes-McCoy (ed.), *Ulster and other Irish maps, c. 1600* (IMC, Dublin 1964), 111. On the origin of trians see J. Stuart, *Historical memoirs of the city of Armagh* (Newry, 1819), 143–4. The revision of this book by Rev. Ambrose Coleman, O.P. (Dublin, 1900) is less valuable for the plantation period.

29 In August 1619 the then owner of one of these monasteries, Sir Francis Annesley, was ordered by the king to surrender it, whereupon it should be granted to the archbishop (*CPRI, Jas I*, 435–6). It was so granted in July 1620 (ibid., 477–9).

30 Above, 18.

31 Bartlett's map and Bodley's map of 1609 (*Maps Ulster, 1609*, 5, 30) give some indication of the size and state of the town on the eve of plantation.

32 A certain Christopher Fleming of Armagh was a juror for the inquisition concerning the escheated lands in 1609.

33 None of the plantation surveys refer to Armagh.

In the re-development of the town the well-known device of the building lease appears to have been used. Thus we find that in November 1615 the archbishop leased an area of the city including 'all and singular the howses, ruinous edifices, creats, and ould walls' as well as plots, and parcels of land in the liberties of the town (in the area known as the 'Bende' an area of 'wast' or common grazing) then occupied by a small number both of Irish and English tenants to Theophilus Buckworth, bishop of Dromore, and Edward Dodington of Dungiven a well-known servitor and builder of the walls of Derry.[34] The object was the 'replanting and re-edifying of the decayed cyttie' and the lease was for sixty years.[35] No rent is mentioned; the lease appears to have been intended to empower Dodington, who had been the archbishop's land agent and seneschal in Tyrone since the previous year,[36] and Buckworth who, at this point, held the rectory of Armagh *in commendam* with his bishopric,[37] to act on the primate's behalf. Dodington and Buckworth proceeded to lay out the land granted to them into plots for houses within the town to each of which twenty acres of land was allotted from the previously common grazing. Lessees holdings were chosen by lot, each being a site of fifty feet in length with land behind fifty feet broad and one hundred and fifty feet in length. The tenant undertook, before 27 September 1618, to build a dwelling house, forty feet long within the walls, sixteen feet broad, the walls to be fifteen feet high with gables of brick or stone, the roofs and floors to be of oak, the house to be of two storeys and built of brick or stone and sawn timber 'according to the form of English howses and buyldings'. The garden plot – and also the twenty acres – was to be enclosed after the English manner with a ditch and hedge of two rows of quicksets. Allowances of stone and clay for bricks and timber for building and lime burning were to be made from the archbishop's lands, and the tenant, who would hold for fifty-nine years, should pay to the archbishop £2 stg rent per annum, and two fat capons at Christmas, the heriot to be 13/4. Later in 1634(?), a parcel of land was granted in Scotch street (the first time the name appears) for forty years at 5/- per annum and duties on condition to build within two years an English-type house of brick, face stone, or framed timber at least two storeys high.[38]

It is not clear how many leases were made under the original scheme. It should be noted that while longer terms were being granted than in similar

34 Moody, *Londonderry Plantation*, 275.

35 Referred to in further lease from Buckworth and Dodington to John Hall, 20 December 1615 (Armagh Public Library, cardboard box 'old leases of primate's').

36 Armagh Archiepiscopal Registry, A. 20 no. 28, fol. 28.

37 J.B. Leslie, *Armagh Clergy and parishes* (Dundalk, 1911), 42, 113, 205.

38 Indenture, 20 October 16?34 between James, archbishop of Armagh, and James Judson, bailiff of the manor of Armagh (ibid.).

building leases in London at this time, the objective was similar in both places, the landlord securing, or attempting to secure, the development of property without major investment, but forgoing any sizeable income until the determination of the first lease.[39]

By this tactic if not perhaps under this precise scheme – Dodington soon ceases to be an official of the archbishop – a number of 'plantation' houses were erected in the city. By 1622, apart from an archiepiscopal residence which had been re-built and extended at a cost of £160, eight 'fair stone' residences had been erected within the town. The costs of these had varied from £50 to £60. All were held under sixty-year leases, six, with twenty acres of land, being held at a rent of £2. 5. 0, the other two lessees holding a townland or more and paying rent accordingly. Three of the houses (including the two most expensive, and with the larger amounts of land) were held by two local clergy. Two others were held by merchants from Drogheda, Andrew Hamlin[40] and Richard Fitzsimons,[41] himself a landowner in Cavan, and one by Richard Chappell a substantial leaseholder and agent of the archbishop. Eight other plots and portions of land were held by three tenants who had as yet not build their houses, one holding five such sites.[42] In 1615 ten people are listed as 'undertakers to build',[43] and, by 1622, of twenty people who had so undertaken only seven had in fact fulfilled their obligation, and five plots, a speculation in modest scale, were held by Thomas Dawson, a burgess of the town, who later held land at Moyola (Castledawson) in Londonderry,[44] and established an iron foundry there.[45] Four of these twenty were burgesses of the town,[46] and two of these four, Dawson and Hall, had not fulfilled their building obligations by 1622. Most of the delinquents lived in small houses, usually of native type, scattered throughout the town.[47] The commissioners of inquiry in 1622 took cognizance of this building scheme[48] though their report, in common with those of Carew, Bodley, and Pynnar, made no observations on the state of the town.

39 L. Stone, *The crisis of the aristocracy, 1558–1641* (Oxford, 1965), 357–63.

40 Hamlin was mayor of Drogheda in 1609 (*CSPI, 1608–10*, 140).

41 See Moody, *Londonderry Plantation*, 151, 173.

42 Armagh Archiepiscopal Registry, B.1b.193, Royal Visitation Book for the province of Ulster, 1622, 1 (copies or alternate versions in TCD and Marsh's Library, Dublin); Rental, 1622, with amendments by James Ussher *c.* 1627 (Armagh Archiepiscopal Registry, Rent Rolls, A.2a.28/13).

43 Armagh Archiepiscopal Registry, A.2a.28/10, 36.

44 Moody, *Londonderry Plantation*, 239, 372.

45 In November 1632 he was given permission to prospect for iron ore on part of the archiepiscopal estate (Armagh Public Library, cardboard box 'old leases of primate's').

46 For a translation of the charter see Stuart, *Armagh*, 649–46.

47 Armagh Archiepiscopal Registry, A.2a.28/11, Civitas ac Villa de Armagh (Rental of 1618).

48 NLI, Rich Papers, 8013/9: Provisions in the primate's leases.

Up to 1622, then, less than 50 per cent of those who had undertaken to build in the town had done so. Until 1627, if not later, lands in the liberties and demesne adjacent to the town which it had been decided would be granted in lease to British tenants undertaking to build were being let on a yearly basis to native Irish tenants.[49] Within the town the older Gaelic inhabitants retained their houses, on a year-to-year basis, subject to piecemeal eviction if British tenants offering to build houses arrived.[50] It will be seen later that a change in policy took place in 1625.[51]

In 1615[52] there were on the archbishop's rental ninety-six houses within the town of Armagh. The annual rents (where stated) of these houses with their adjacent gardens, varied from 13/4 to 6/8. Fourteen British names occur amongst the tenants. In a very small number of cases more than one house was held in the same tenant's name, though also two tenants, always Irish, occasionally held one house.[53] From 1618 dates the only rental of our period from which a street plan can be derived.[54] The street pattern as it emerges indicates a strong continuity with the pre-plantation town.[55] The houses are mostly of Irish type, and the tenants, while predominantly Irish, appear to have been mixed together irrespective of national origin. Most of the British tenants lived in houses not markedly different from those of their Irish neighbours, but the occasional British-occupied stone house on its larger (and so more exclusive) site must have stood out. The street either followed the old roads leading from Armagh in various directions, and named appropriately Monaghan Street (now Navan Street), Dundalk Street (now Irish Street), Newry Street (now Scotch Street), or else were a group of lanes roughly following the contours of the original hill nucleus. Many of the street names were as yet in no way formalised, though it is of interest to note that English, rather than Irish, names are given. Street names implying national areas, as Irish and Scotch street, did not then formally exist nor is there clear evidence that the population was tending towards segregation. By 1641 regional segregation may well have been appearing, but it would seem wrong to speak, as Stuart does, referring to the 1620s,

49 Armagh Archiepiscopal Registry, A.2a.28/13.

50 Ibid., 5 (rental, 1622, noted by Ussher, *c.* 1627).

51 Below, 234–5.

52 The date of the first surviving rental.

53 Armagh Archiepiscopal Registry, A.2a.28/10, 28–31: Liber supervisor de anno 1615 pro ter Primat.

54 Ibid., A.2a.28/11, Civitas ac Villa de Armagh: A general survey of the town of Armagh by Mr. Thomas Crant, Xpfer Bent[ley], William Harris, and Patrick Croly, the 25 September a.d. 1618.

55 I am very grateful to Mr. H.D. McC. Reid, Vice–Principal, Armagh Royal School, for allowing me to reproduce a map based on this survey from his unpublished M.A. thesis 'The Historical Geography of Armagh' (QUB 1954).

of the citizens being divided into parties not only by religion, language and national prejudices, but by 'local position' as well.[56]

In all 123 dwelling houses come to light at this time. In addition various non-dwelling structures are referred to in the survey. Of the houses twenty-seven were held by non-Irish tenants, a small number of whom were Old English. On most of the sites there were out-buildings of various types as well. A few of the houses had only recently been erected, and it is also clear that there were many sites awaiting development. Some parcels of land adjoining the streets had been newly enclosed. The surveyors indicate that there were further houses on the abbey land, held by Caulfeild, 'of which we can get no certain knowledge'. Two 'shops', held by Irish, are referred to.[57]

We have seen that the building lease, as a device to secure the development of the town, was being granted from 1615. Up to the end of Hampton's episcopate in 1624 this had secured the erection of only a modest eight or nine 'plantation' houses, a very partial fulfilment of expectations. The town was not attracting people capable of the financial outlay demanded. As much as 500 acres around the town designed for leasing in twenty-acre units with house sites to 'gentlemen and tradesmen' remained unleased after the succession of James Ussher.[58] In expectation of applicants under the original scheme this land continued to be let piecemeal to both Irish and British on a yearly basis, the claims to a more secure tenure of the traditional occupants being necessarily overlooked.[59] Clearly the implication of such a policy for the gradual re-development of the town was the eviction of those whose house areas might be acquired. Accordingly these people – or many of them (it is not possible to state if the entire town had been in this way 'reserved for English that will build') – had been let their cottages on a year-to-year basis. However, two factors would appear to have led to the leasing of these houses or many of them. The first was simply the abortiveness of the building programme. The second was that the greater part of the British population of the town had acquired individual houses which they had expanded or rebuilt, or sites on which they had built. There may well also have been a clamour on the part of the Irish for a security of tenure, from the refusal of which, especially if it could be coupled with rent increases, it must have appeared that little could be gained.

56 Stuart, *Armagh*, 349. Stuart's suggested origin of the name English street as being derived from the old Trian Sassenach is very plausible (ibid., 144).

57 Armagh Archiepiscopal Registry, A.2a.28/11, *passim*,

58 Ibid., A.2a.28/13, 41: the true revenue of the temporalities belonging to the archbishopric of Armagh and the state thereof at the decease of Christopher Hampton. This document is of special value because it contains meticulous notes and observations, including comparisons with earlier rentals now lost, appended by Ussher, *c.* 1627.

59 Ibid., *passim*.

The decision to grant leases to the sitting tenants, Irish and British, was taken by James Ussher, and the leasing began in 1627, though there are about three instances of British residents in the town (other than those with building leases) having leased from before this date.[60] The number of unleased houses at this time is not easily established as complications had been introduced with unrecorded sub-tenancies, and the rentals are not always completely clear. A rental of *c.* 1620 claimed that the potential episcopal income from this source was £80.[61] The submission to the visitors of 1622 re-stated this figure.[62] However, Ussher has preserved a figure of £60. 2. 0 from a lost rental, and at his accession a rental for 55 houses or tenants totalled £39. 10. 9, the range of rents being from £1. 15. 4. to 6/8, the greater number paying either 13/4 or 10/-. Of these 55, 40 were native Irish.[63] On 10 September 1627 38 leases were made, each to run for 21 years.[64] Some indication of the rent increases resulting can be seen from the fact that the primate's income from these 38 tenancies was £34. 1. 4. per annum.[65] These tenants were also required to provide two fat hens each yearly at Christmas or, in some cases, two capons. The leases also required suit of court and use of the lord's mill. One of the thirty-four surviving leases contained a stipulation to build one 'faire coupled house after the English manner' within five years. At this time some familiar street names occur, Irish Street and Gallows Street, but this does not seem to indicate group segregation. However, the location of individual tenancies would be difficult to identify, and almost all the leases bear a late seventeenth- or early eighteenth-century endorsement 'the tenants being dead and the tenement not meared and bounded, not known where it lyes'. Of these 38 tenants, 25 were British. In May 1628 six further houses were leased, one to a British tenant.[66] The total annual rent from these 44 tenancies was £39. 4. 8. In the same year, there are listed 20 'cottages' in the town (6 British) which were unleased, and which appear to have paid similar rents, totalling £5. 16. 8. per annum. Thus while the decision to grant leases was not extended to all inhabitants, it does seem to have been applied to a substantial proportion of them. In 1639 the archbishop adopted a

60 Ibid., A.2a.28/13, 3. See also list of counterparts of leases made by Christopher Hampton (ibid., 43–55).

61 L.P. Murray (ed.), 'A Rent-Roll of all the Houses and Lands belonging to the See of Armagh', *Arch. Hib.* viii, 100.

62 Armagh Archiepiscopal Registry, B.1b. no. 193, 2.

63 Ibid., A.2a.28/13, 5.

64 Thirty-four of the counterparts of these leases have survived, one of which is in Ussher's own hand (Ibid., E.1.e).

65 Ibid., A.2a.28/19, 3; /20, 5–6.

66 Ibid., A.2a.28/19, 3.

middleman policy, in leasing 'most of the town' for sixty years at £58 per annum to William Hilton,[67] a baron of the exchequer, who was also lessee of the Armagh school lands.

An account of the town based on an examination of rentals has unavoidable limitations. However, they do provide valuable information. Some of them list the arrears of tenants as well as the 'charge' due, though to what extent the ratio of arrears to rent payable (in itself difficult to establish, given the account system) may be taken to indicate the prosperity of the town is, perhaps, doubtful. In 1628 a group of tenants, whose quarterly rent was £9. 18. 5, paid £9. 0. 9, i.e. were in arrears to the extent of 17. 8.[68] However, this does not present a general picture. In 1620 a rental of all, or nearly all, the houses in Armagh (other than plantation houses) revealed that, of a quarterly sum of £16. 14. 7. due, £11. 14. 3. was paid, and £5. 0. 4, or 29 per cent of the amount due, was in arrears. The influence of the wartime situation in causing this should not be wholly discounted, but it may also indicate that many townspeople were not thriving and prosperous. In three cases 'pawnes' were taken from tenants: a kettle, a horsecloth, and a 'cadaw'.[69] Thirteen of these tenants, one of them an Englishman, who had in fact left the town, whose unpaid rents came to £1. 16. 2. were designated as 'not able to pay'. Some had been 'forgiven' their rent by the archbishop, two were widows, and most of their houses were decayed.[70] The surviving rentals for the late 1630s are more difficult to interpret, but the impression is of a somewhat similar situation.[71]

The population of Armagh at the end of our period is difficult to assess. The muster roll of *c.* 1630 lists ninety British male inhabitants of the town and liberties.[72] We have seen,[73] however, that there were more British on the archbishop's estate than were listed on the muster roll. A figure of over 100 British males can therefore fairly be suggested. It must be noted, however, that Hampton's building-lease scheme had had only limited success. There were also, of course, a substantial number of native Irish living in the town. The estimated population of New York in 1630 was 300 (400 in 1640);[74] if the native element is included, Armagh cannot have been much smaller.[75]

67 Ibid., A.1b.31, Walter Dawson's rental, 1713, 3.
68 Ibid., A.1b.29/1, 2–3.
69 A rough woollen covering (OED).
70 Armagh Archiepiscopal Registry, A.1b.29/2, 1–2.
71 Ibid., A.1b.29/5, 6, 7 *passim*.
72 BL, Add. MS 4770, ff 41v–3.
73 Above, 177.
74 J.P. Greene (ed.), *Settlements to society, 1584–1763* (New York, 1966), 249.
75 In 1664, 93 householders, British and Irish, with 111 'smokestacks' were assessed for hearth-tax (Murray (ed.), 'Armagh hearth money rolls', *Arch. Hib.* vii, 121, 150–53).

The absence of will inventories and corporation records makes analysis of the social and occupational structure of the town impossible, but one does find reference to the expected occupations. Most of the leaseholders in 1627 are described as yeomen. There were also two malsters, Matthew Black and William Rastall, one of whom held a malthouse, kiln, and bar, as well as a school-house. A further malthouse was leased to one William McGerr. There was one glover, Richard Francis, and a tan house was held by a certain Richard Unddelly. The Irish family of Crawley or Croly appear to have been merchants and shop keepers.[76] Just outside the town, Matthew Ussher, a burgess and relative of the archbishop, held a mill. Roger Russell, who made the leases in 1627 on the archbishop's behalf, was a butcher who had previously moved from Moneymore in Londonderry to Armagh. While in Moneymore, an Irish deponent stated in March 1627, that Russell had frequently harboured rebels and received stolen livestock.[77] Richard Chappell,[78] at one time the archbishop's rent collector, was lessee of 'the brick p[ar]ke'. Such evidence is too slight to suggest that the British inhabitants composed the greater part of the artisans and tradesmen within the town.

Some light on one Armagh merchant comes to hand from his 'answer' in a chancery suit of post-1635. It seems that in August 1634 a certain John Rown, a Scot, came to an agreement with Sir Arthur Graham, who was then going to England, whereby the latter should purchase on his behalf £70 worth of 'stuffs', silks, buttons, and other merchandise. The goods were purchased and Rown sold them 'both in his shop and in the market place on market days'. However, litigation broke out, at first before the judges of assize at Armagh, and then in chancery, on the terms of the agreement.[79] An Armagh merchant in 1641 had a shop there and also in Loughgall.[80] There was also an English innkeeper in 1641.[81]

It was perhaps as a marketing centre that the town had most importance, and much of its life must have had a rural relevance. In 1610 it was noted that Armagh, with its markets and courts, would be a place of meeting for the colony in the county.[82] The right to hold a market in the town on Tuesdays and two fairs annually in March and August was granted to the archbishop in 1615, and a further fair on 29 June in 1634.[83] The market cross features prominently on Bartlett's map. There was both a 'new' and

[76] Armagh Archiepiscopal Registry, bundle of leases, E.1.e.
[77] TNA, SP 63/244, ff 145–6v (*CSPI, 1625–32*, 216).
[78] Memorial plaque in church of Ireland cathedral.
[79] NAI, Chancery salvage, U.66 (document damaged).
[80] TCD, MS 836, ff 57–7v.
[81] Ibid., fol. 100.
[82] *CSPI, 1608–10*, 406.
[83] Armagh Public Library, Lodge MSS, G.111.23, 5. The corporation did not receive such rights, additionally, until 1753 (ibid.).

'old' market place in 1627.[84] Being unwalled, and with the streets in many cases following the roads leading from the town, Armagh shaded with the countryside from which in various ways most of its inhabitants derived their livelihood. The land in the liberties and 'demesnes' surrounding was let in small units to many of the townsmen. The town itself must have presented a countrified image with its numerous barns, stables, orchards and gardens, many of them newly enclosed.

Apart from some ecclesiastical restoration, there can have been few buildings or institutions of civic sophistication. A sessions house, jail, and/or house of correction existed, most likely in one building.[85] In 1619 a king's letter directed that a portion of ground, 80 feet by 40 feet, should be reserved for a sessions house and jail. This was to be built 'within convenient time' upon the charge of the town and county, with whatever money had been collected already for that purpose, its custody to be committed to the sheriff of the county.[86] The royal school at Armagh can have developed very little prior to 1641.[87]

As a Protestant ecclesiastical centre the town was revived under Christopher Hampton. In 1622 the cathedral was described as follows:

> The cathedral church of Armagh which was ruined and the steeple thrown down by Shane O'Neale, the steeple built the south and northside walls with fair windows, the south and north isles roof'd and platform'd upon both sides of the church, and the great bell cast by the lo: primate.[88]

The archbishop was non-resident, though he had a house in Armagh, but the dean was not an absentee and a chapter and vicars choral were organised.

However, the ruins of the institutions of the old dispensation remained in the town and Thomas Chambers lived in the abbey.[89] Possibilities of restoration must have been in mind in 1641 and, on the evidence of the 1630 muster book, the inhabitants were ill-equipped to meet a military challenge. Although apparently the only group in the county to muster a drummer (one James Moody), no more than forty-nine men were, in any way, armed.[90]

84 Referred to in leases, 1627 (Armagh Archiepiscopal Registry, bundle of leases, E.1.e).
85 TCD, MS 836, fol. 249. The eighteenth-century jail, in a cellar under the sessions house, is described in Stuart, *Armagh*, 529–32.
86 Armagh Archiepiscopal Registry, A.1b. no. 26, 206–7.
87 Below, 411–7.
88 Armagh Archiepiscopal Registry, B.1b. no. 193, 26–7.
89 TCD, MS 836, ff 42–3. The buildings of the abbey of St. Peter and St. Paul are described in a regrant to Caulfeild (Stuart, *Armagh*, 348–9).
90 BL, Add. MS. 4770, ff 41v–2v.

The role of the corporation remains entirely indistinct. In January 1611 the lord deputy and plantation commissioners ordered the town to be incorporated and 'the Lord Prymate ... dealt with-all to make estates to certaine burgesses',[91] but incorporation did not come until 1613.[92] The first sovereign and two of the burgesses were relatives of the archbishop and most of the burgesses were resident in the town. One of them was Thomas Dawson. The corporation did not receive any grant of land. Fairs and markets, normal in plantation charters, were also not included. Its only source of income was from the right to hold a weekly court of record, with power to impose penalties of up to five marks. However, in practice, law and order in the town was maintained, perhaps exclusively, by the archbishop's manor court, held before his seneschal.[93] The episcopal landlord had been clearly unwilling to forgo any rights when the corporation was being established. It seems evident that the real source of authority within the town lay in the landlord and not the corporation.

B. Charlemont

Charlemont, also incorporated in 1613, presents a marked contrast to Armagh. On the site, near the confluence of the Blackwater and Callan rivers, there had been no previous Gaelic settlement. The town grew from the fort established by Mountjoy in 1602. A bridge was built across the river and the fortress, close to the O'Neill headquarters at Dungannon, had a special military importance. The garrison was under the energetic control of Sir Toby Caulfeild.[94]

In the years after the treaty of Mellifont the fort, rapidly erected, became decayed and, with the Flight of the Earls when fear of invasion or insurrection was again a reality, there was a concern to make Charlemont and the other Ulster forts more serviceable. In June 1607 it had been leased, with lands adjacent, for twenty-one years to Caulfeild to be maintained in good repair.[95] In 1608 Sir Josias Bodley, inspecting the Ulster defences,

91 'Ulster plantation papers', no. 27, *Anal. Hib.*, viii.

92 RIA, MS 24.Q.7, Charters of Irish towns, i, 160–72; *CPRI, Jas I*, 255 (heading only); Stuart, *Armagh*, 640–6 (translation).

93 Armagh Public Library, Manor Court Rolls.

94 Previous treatments of Charlemont have concerned themselves for the most part with its military vicissitudes and the history of the Caulfeild family. See, for example, J.J. Marshall, *History of Charlemont fort and borough ... end of Mountjoy fort* (Dungannon, 1921), 83pp; J.W. Hanna, *Annals of Charlemont* (Armagh 1846); J.P. Prendergast, 'Charlemont fort', *JRHAAI*, 4th series, vi (1883–4), 319–44; E. O'Tuat-Ghaill, 'The Fort of Charlemont in Tir-Eoghan', *UJA*, 2nd series, xviii, 1911, 47–73.

95 Above, 19.

reported that the fort and bawn were 'much decayed', but that the governor had undertaken to repair it to his requirements, at a cost of £100.[96]

The original fortress, built in two stages, is represented in Bartlett's map.[97] Within the defences there were about forty houses, mostly thatched. 'Buildings of round or elliptical ground plan were outnumbered by rectangular ones, some of them perhaps with rounded ends'.[98] Cage work was conspicuously absent. A wooden bridge with handrails, and also a float on the river, is illustrated. There is no evidence of civilian settlement nearby at this point.

The military importance of the place and the value of Sir Toby as a servitor did not go unrecognised after the plantation. In 1610, one hundred foot were lodged there. Carew, in 1611, described the fort as strongly defended and containing good houses 'buylte after the English fashion'.[99] As the place of detention of Conn O'Neill the capture of Charlemont had a special importance in 1615.[100] The conditions under which Caulfeild purchased the fort have been already described.[101] In 1641 it was captured by Sir Phelim O'Neill.

However, Charlemont did not simply remain a fortress, a symbol of military dominance. The bridge encouraged traffic and already, by the time of Carew's inquiry in 1611, there were indications of civilian activity outside and around the fort. Sir Toby himself had built a timber stable, garden, and impaled haggard outside the rampart. Also both English and Irish inhabitants had come to live there, no doubt drawing much of their livelihood from the necessities of the fort. On Carew's evidence, the 'towne' was 'replenished with many inhabitants of English and Irish who had built them good houses of copies after the best manner of the English'.[102] In 1613 the settlement was incorporated with Francis Capron as first portreeve.[103] The corporation received no grant of land. To do this would have involved the breaking of Caulfeild's lease of the fort lands. The corporation was empowered to hold a weekly court of record, make bye-laws, have a guild merchant and a common seal, and appoint two serjeants-at-mace. It was

96 James Buckley (ed.), 'Report of Sir Josias Bodley on some Ulster fortresses in 1608', *UJA*, 2nd series, xvi (1910), 62.
97 Hayes-McCoy (ed.), *Ulster maps*, iv.
98 Ibid., 7.
99 Lam. Pal. Lib., Carew MSS, vol. 630, fol. 60v.
100 Above, 106–07.
101 Above, 131.
102 Lam. Pal. Lib., Carew MSS, vol. 630, fol. 60v.
103 RIA, MS 24.Q.10, charters of Irish towns, iv, 104–15; Bod. Lib., Carte MSS, vol. 62, fol. 147; *CSPI, 1611–14*, 338 (warrant for incorporation); *CPRI, Jas I*, 255 (heading only); Marshall, *Charlemont and Mountjoy*, 14–15 (translated abstract).

also granted a free weekly market and a fair on 1 and 2 May with a court of pie powder.

It may be argued that the development of Charlemont as a civilian centre under Caulfeild's tutelage was due primarily to the fact that Sir Toby was an extensive landholder in the area. It is known that he imported tenants for his lands,[104] and some of the first burgesses, or their descendants, feature as Caulfeild tenants in the muster roll of *c.* 1630 and in a subsequent list of tenants of Colure which Caulfeild held from Trinity College.[105] Some may also have been ex-servicemen.[106]

Only a few casual snippets from the history of the town up to 1641 have survived. The muster roll does not have an independent entry,[107] but the 1664 hearth money roll records 64 names and 72 fireplaces.[108] The rural context of the town – as well, of course, as its military character – is the most obvious feature. The corporation had a fair in May and a Tuesday market, deriving from the 1613 charter, and the Caulfeild landlords had a Wednesday market and a fair in August by patent from 1622.[109] In 1626 the bridge, from which much of the civilian and military importance of the settlement derived, had become dilapidated and its replacement was raised by Caulfeild at the privy council. It was decided 'after considerable debate' that because of its local value the cost should be levied off the two adjacent counties.[110]

The relation between property holding in the town and countryside in one case is brought out in a chancery suit of *c.* 1630 between William, Lord Caulfeild, and a tenant Edward May. The suit concerned terms of rent payment and lease duration and arose in part from William's succession to Sir Toby. May had a sixty-year lease of three townlands formerly part of the abbey of St. Peter and St. Paul as well as two acres of land in Charlemont with 'certaine' houses built on it and described as 'subject to ffier and other casualtyes', and parcels of land around the town varying in size from fifty to four acres. In the town he also held a horse mill and another tenement with three acres appertaining acquired from a previous tenant under a

[104] The humble petition of the English tenants … of the Colure … to TCD (TCD, Muniment Room, Mahaffy Collection, E.79).

[105] BL, Add. MS 4770, ff 43–44; TCD, Muniment Room, Mahaffy Collection, drawer G, folder 1.

[106] Certainly some of the tenants of the archbishop of Armagh belonged to this category.

[107] Fifty-six tenants are listed for Caulfeild's lands in the county at this time (BL, Add. MS 4770, ff 43v–44v). A later document adds thirteen further names (TCD, Muniment Room, Mahaffy Collection, drawer G, folder 1).

[108] Murray (ed.), 'Armagh hearth money rolls', *Arch. Hib.* vii, 149–50.

[109] Armagh Public Library, Lodge MSS, G.111.23, 5. The volume of business on Wednesdays would probably indicate the superior authority of the Caulfeilds over the corporation.

[110] Elrington (ed.), *Ussher*, xv, 273; Marshall, *Charlemont and Mountjoy*, 16.

twenty-one year lease.[111] May, as tenant of land, mill, and cottages, was, no doubt, one of the more substantial inhabitants, but it also seems clear that the land around the town was being leased in small and irregular quantities to its inhabitants.[112] There was a tannery in Charlemont in 1641.[113]

Apart from the attraction of the site, the growth of Charlemont as a civilian centre must have depended in large part on the energy of the Caulfeilds. The pre-1641 community, however, had hardly acquired the independence, scale, or self-reliance for much corporate development.

C. Mountnorris and Tandragee

Armagh and Charlemont did have corporate status: as for Tandragee there is no indication that any steps towards incorporation were taken. Mountnorris, also intended for incorporation, never received a charter. Its origin, like that of Charlemont, was military. The fort here was established in 1600 by Mountjoy on the route between Newry and Armagh. The fortress contained fifty-three or fifty-four houses, built in most cases from wood. Thirty-six were of Irish type with a circular or elliptical ground plan, being all thatched. Twelve or thirteen followed the small English cottage style with tiled, gabled roofs, the remainder being hip-roofed.[114]

In February 1606 the fort was leased for twenty-one years to Capt. Henry Adderton,[115] and in 1608 Bodley reported that defences had been constructed in it at a cost of about 100 marks.[116] In 1611 Bodley saw Mountnorris as a place of 'special importe … and fit to be maintained and supported'. By then English and Irish inhabitants had 'resorted' there and built 'good' houses 'after the manner of the Pale, w'ch is a great releefe saftie and comforte for passengers between the Newyre and Armagh'.[117]

Its development was thus akin to that of Charlemont, and the question arises as to why it was not incorporated. Incorporation in practice had not been made dependent on size. The answer would appear to lie in the unwillingness of the leaseholder and subsequent owner of the fort and its lands, in 1613, to forgo any rights, however slight, to a corporation. It has been already seen that with the death of Adderton in 1611, the fort and, cumulatively, lands in the vicinity, came into the hands of Francis Annesley,

[111] NAI, Chancery salvage, L.65 (damaged bill).

[112] That the adjacent land was being enclosed is also suggested. In 1643 Eoin O'Neill encountered some of Monro's army in a lane leading to Charlemont 'enclosed with quicksetts' (O'Tuat-Ghaill, 'Fort of Charlemont', 56).

[113] TCD, MS 836, fol. 215.

[114] Hayes-McCoy (ed.), *Ulster maps*, 11.

[115] Above, 19.

[116] Buckley (ed.), 'Report of Sir Josias Bodley', 62.

[117] Lam. Pal. Lib., Carew MSS, vol. 630, fol. 60v.

later Lord Mountnorris.[118] After that a warrant for incorporation was issued,[119] but the matter proceeded no further, Annesley, manifestly, being unprepared to pay the fees involved. Lack of incorporation was a triumph of trivial private interest over public policy, involving the loss to the executive of two votes in parliament.

D. Cavan

Cavan was a place of some standing at the end of the sixteenth century. A map of *c.* 1593[120] shows two principal streets, corresponding to the present Main street and Bridge street. It also shows the bridge, the Franciscan monastery, the market cross, the O'Reilly castle, and about fifty houses. An inquisition in July 1601 returned that Mulmory oge O'Reilly was possessed of the castle and town, apart from the castle and land of Walter and Thomas Brady and one water mill.[121] Walter Brady, a landowner and merchant, had been appointed by the crown constable and jailer of Cavan in December 1584.[122] The town had had many contacts both with the Pale area and the Dublin administration.

Of the three projected corporations for the county, Cavan was thus a place of some size by Irish standards on the eve of colonisation.[123] Its incorporation is of special interest because the process was initiated before the arrival of colonists. In February 1610 Chichester directed the attorney-general to draw up a fiant for a charter for the town, to contain 'such reasonable liberties and franchises as ... shall seem fit and convenient', and to submit it for his consideration.[124] The matter appears to have been neglected by Davies, so that in October the deputy repeated his instructions, this time recommending that the charter should follow that of Kells, and directing that the new corporation should be granted 500 acres of land allotted to it.[125] The charter was issued on 15 November 1610.[126] The land thus granted to the corporation amounted to some 683 statute acres.

The incorporation of Cavan in November 1610 presented it with a governing body distinctively different from James I's other Ulster corporations. The first sovereign, Walter Brady, and the two portreeves, Owen [Mór] Brogan and Farrall M'Eregules, were Gaelic Irish as were most

[118] Above, 109.

[119] 'Ulster plantation papers', no. 58, *Anal. Hib.*, viii.

[120] Reproduced in P. O'Connell, *The diocese of Kilmore: its history and antiquities* (Dublin 1937), 301.

[121] NAI, Exchequer inquisitions, Ulster, Cavan, (7) Eliz., 17–24.

[122] Cal. fiants Ir., Eliz., no. 4547.

[123] Davies in 1607 described it as a 'poor Irish town' (Morley, *Ireland*, 374).

[124] Bod. Lib., Carte MSS, vol. 61, fol. 485 (*CSPI, 1608–10*, 390).

[125] Ibid., fol. 497 (ibid., 514).

[126] RIA, MS 24.Q.10, Charters of Irish towns, iv, 130–152; *CPRI, Jas I*, 180; T.S. Smyth, *The civic history of the town of Cavan* (Dublin 1938), 18–21 (abstract).

of the corporators, though Brady was thoroughly anglicised, and only two of the twelve burgesses, Hugh Culme and James Murray, were products of the plantation. Walter Talbot, who, like Culme, did not live in the town, represented the Old English landed interest. The area of the borough was to be within a one-mile circumference of Walter Brady's house, but the castle of Cavan and two polls of land appertaining was to be exempt from its jurisdiction. The sovereign was to have powers as ample as the sovereign of Kells. The corporation was empowered to appoint a recorder or town clerk with the powers of the recorders of Drogheda or Kells, and might also appoint a serjeant of the mace. The oaths of officers were laid down and recited. There might be a three-weekly court with jurisdiction to the extent of £20. A weekly market and fairs were also included in the charter, though a weekly market had also been granted to a private owner, John Bingley, in 1603, and this caused contention later.[127] In January 1611 the deputy and plantation commissioners directed that the justices of assize on their next circuit – sessions were held in the town – should ensure that the sovereign took the oath of supremacy according to the charter.[128]

From the fragmentary evidence available it seems that the corporation retained much of its Gaelic Irish character throughout the plantation period.[129] In 1627 the sovereign was Patrick Brady,[130] and in 1628 Nathaniel Dardes, a burgess of Old English origin who died *c.* 1630 and who had taken the oath of supremacy in 1612,[131] held the office.[132] It may be, however, that in the 1630s the colonial interest began to achieve a prominence. In 1633 Allan Cooke, lay-chancellor of the diocese of Kilmore, member of parliament for the town in 1634,[133] and founder of Cookstown, features as 'Superior Ville sive Oppid' Cavan',[134] and in the following year Lawrence Moore was sovereign.[135] In 1628 there was both an English and an Irish portreeve, William Moore,[136] (who held this office also in 1627)

[127] Below, 282–3.

[128] 'Ulster plantation papers', no. 27, *Anal. Hib.*, viii.

[129] The main source for what follows is a collection of leases and deeds or abstracts of them preserved amongst the Farnham Papers in the NLI (MS D 20,409–20,475, and MS 11,490/3, 4).

[130] Indenture, 20 September 1627, between corporation of Cavan and Terence O'Reilly (NLI, MS D 20,409–20,475).

[131] 'Ulster plantation papers', no. 69, *Anal. Hib.*, viii.

[132] Indenture, 1 August 1628, between corporation of Cavan and Lawrence Dardes (NLI, MS D 20,409–20,475).

[133] Kearney, *Strafford*, 257–8.

[134] Indenture, 13 September 1633, between corporation of Cavan on the one hand and William Clifford and James Gray on the other (NLI, MS D 20,409–20,475).

[135] Indenture, 28 August 1634, between corporation of Cavan and John Gibson (ibid.).

[136] Indenture, 20 September 1627, between corporation of Cavan and Terence O'Reilly (ibid.). It is possible that Moore may have been Irish. In July 1601 a list of Cavan pardons included one James O'Moore, a butcher in the town (Cal. fiants Ir., Eliz., no. 6559; *CPRI, Eliz.*, 591).

and William O'Brogan respectively.[137] In 1633 a certain John Dowdall, a Palesman in orgin, held one of these posts, though at this time the clerk of the court of the town, Edward Foherton (?), belonged to the incoming element.[138] In 1633 the recorder, William Clifford, was British.[139] Of eighteen people whose names survive as burgesses or freemen between 1627 and 1634 nine were Irish or Old English and nine British. One of these, John Gibson, was a Dublin merchant.[140] It is difficult to say if the tendency towards British dominance in the town was much further advanced by 1641. However, the sovereign then was Stephen Allen, king's attorney in Ulster, who lived in Cavan abbey,[141] and John Whitman, an English merchant, had also been sovereign.[142] After the plantation, the castle of Cavan and the abbey had come into British hands. The former was leased to Sir Thomas Rotherham, the overseer of fortifications, in 1616,[143] and subsequently became the property of Sir Oliver Lambert.[144] The abbey was granted to Sir Thomas Ashe in 1611.[145]

Certainly in comparison with Belturbet, which appears to have been larger,[146] Cavan had a special significance for native Irish elements. In 1636 a report on the state of the Catholic diocese of Kilmore stated that, although there was no city in the diocese, there was, however, one town – 'oppidum ... unicum' – Cavan, where there had been, while the Catholic religion flourished, a Franciscan monastery. Yet even now some fathers of the order lodged in private houses.[147]

In its early years the borough was rent by dispute and contention, both internal and external. In 1612 the commissioners for adjudicating disputes decided and 'quieted' differences between the townsmen, as well as four disputes for land between them and Sir Oliver Lambert, Waldron and Taylor.[148] Internal contention appears to have continued unabated however, and Bodley found 'little show of any purpose'. Two or three houses of lime and stone had been built by the townsmen, who were otherwise 'at a non

137 Indenture, 29 August 1628, between corporation of Cavan and William Moore (NLI, MS D 20,409–20,475).

138 Indenture, 13 September 1633, between corporation of Cavan on the one hand and William Clifford and James Gray on the other (ibid.).

139 Indenture, 29 August 1628, between corporation of Cavan and William Moore (ibid.).

140 Below, 247.

141 TCD, MS 832, ff 173–4.

142 TCD, MS 833, ff 273–4v.

143 *CPRI, Jas I*, 313.

144 NAI, Books of Survey and Distribution. See also *CPRI, Jas I*, 454.

145 Ibid., 199.

146 T.W. Jones (ed.), *A true relation of the Life and death of the Right Reverend Father in God William Bedell* (London, 1972), 62.

147 P.F. Moran (ed.), *Spicilegium Ossoriense,* 1st series (Dublin, 1874), 208.

148 TCD, MS 806, ff 16, 17v, 19.

plus'.[149] In 1622 it was found that dissention still prevailed, hinging on the use of the town land, and detrimental to the progress of the corporation.[150]

The use of the corporation land remains obscure throughout our period. A number of freehold grants of small areas of land along with house sites were made by the corporation from September 1611.[151] Smyth conjectures that since there is no reference to land in the corporation books which begin at 1680 it must have been alienated at an early date – possibly to burgesses.[152] It is clear now that much of the land – about 500 acres – had come into the hands of Walter Brady's family, and Robert and Patrick Brady are recorded as owners of it in 1641.[153] How they acquired this land is not clear, but the effect of it was that the Bradys were now to be in a somewhat similar position to the patrons of towns which had not been incorporated and granted land as Cavan was. The way in which the two Bradys had acquired this land was a matter of grievance to the corporators who, in March 1635, petitioned the house of commons for redress.[154] The outcome of the appeal is not known, but in July 1641 Patrick Brady petitioned for redress against the corporation.[155] It was probably through these acquisitions of the Bradys that most of the corporation land was lost.

In 1610 the town was composed, seemingly, of two streets, Castle Street and Bridge Street. However, in September 1611 a 'vicus novus' or 'new street' 'leading from the high crosse unto the Gallows Hill'[156] features in corporation deeds.[157] High street also appears, but this may merely be an alternate name.[158] The rate of town expansion appears to have been very slow, but cannot be measured with accuracy. By 1613 only two or three new houses had been built.[159] Evidence survives of nineteen freehold grants from the corporation of property in the town and its environs between September 1611 and August 1634.[160] There is no reason to suspect that these were the only grants, indeed the fact that seventeen of them date between 1624 and 1634 is noteworthy. Seven were to people of British

149 *Hastings MSS,* iv, 162.
150 BL, Add. MS 4756, fol. 104.
151 Below, 247–8.
152 Smyth, *Civic history, Cavan,* 44–5.
153 NAI, Books of Survey and Distribution. In my map and acreage figures for 1641 this land has been all accredited to the corporation.
154 *Commons jnl., Ire.*, 17 March 1635, 105; 14 April 1635, 117.
155 Ibid., 15 July 1641, 257.
156 Indenture, 13 March 1632, between Patrick Brady on the one hand, and Thomas Brady and Nicholas Garnett on the other (NLI, D 20,409–20,475).
157 Indenture (in Latin), 1 September 1611, between corporation of Cavan and Mahun O'Brogan (ibid.).
158 Indenture, 30 May 1634, between Lawrence Dardes and John Gibson (ibid.).
159 *Hastings MSS,* iv, 162.
160 NLI, Farnham Papers, D 20,409–20,475, MS 11,490/4.

name. These grants do not necessarily imply that new house were being built and, in some cases at any rate, must have been of houses already in existence. The properties in the town were usually defined as 'one house-roome messuage and freehould' with a frontage towards the street usually of seven or thirteen 'ells or Cavan slatts',[161] with gardens to the rear. The rent payable to the corporation, in three cases where it is known, was 6d. sterling (1628 and 1634) and 8d. Irish (1611) per annum. Grants of land from the corporation in six known instances ranged in size from one to four acres, the rent for two acres to two British grantees being 1/- sterling per annum.[162] All corporation grants were on condition that no part of the property should be alienated to any person other than a burgess or freeman of the town.

Between March 1632 and March 1639 thirteen Cavan freeholders, one of whom Thomas Newman who lived in Dublin, sold their property to a certain John Gibson, a Dublin merchant, who also in 1634, as a freeman of Cavan, received a grant of a 'house-roome' in Castle Street from the corporation. An absentee thus appears to have made himself perhaps the largest property owner in the town, buying out both British and Irish proprietors in almost equal numbers. For twelve of these properties he paid sums amounting to £345. 6. 8. stg in all perhaps £360. The largest component was the property of Patrick McDonagh O'Brogan, a merchant. In all he bought fifteen houses or messuages, and six freeholds in land amounting to sixteen acres.[163]

The muster roll of *c.* 1630 enters the names of twenty-seven townsmen.[164] Two of these lived outside the town and three had Old English names. Only three were armed, having three swords, one musket, one snaphance, and one pike between them. However, twenty leases and deeds of town property between 1611 and 1639, of which nineteen date from 1627, provide evidence in witnesses' signatures of forty British (of whom only six appear on the muster roll), who must have lived in the town or close by, and of under thirty Irish (including Old English) residents. There were thus perhaps some fifty British males in the town by 1641.

The association between town and countryside must have been very close. Cavan was unwalled (though there was a 'town ditch')[165] and it was

[161] Slat = yard in modern Irish.

[162] Indenture, 13 September 1633, between corporation of Cavan on one hand, and William Clifford and James Gray on the other (NLI, MS D 20,409–20,475).

[163] NLI, Farnham Papers, D 20,409–20,475, MS 11,490/3, 4.

[164] BL, Add. MS 4770, fol. 22v. In the table for the county the number 18 is mistakenly entered.

[165] Indenture, 28 August 1634, between corporation of Cavan and John Gibson (NLI, D 20,409–20,475).

a market centre. William Cole, a miller, present in 1641,[166] would have served both town and surrounding countryside. The first mayor Walter Brady, a merchant, also held land, along with two brothers, nearby. Few of the inhabitants have their occupations defined. Apart from Brady, Mahun O'Brogan was a merchant of some standing in 1611. Patrick McOwen O'Brogan and Patrick McDonagh O'Brogan were also merchants. The latter, by 1633, owned four 'messuages' in the new street and another in Castle Street which he sold to Gibson for £54.[167] These he had purchased between 1624 and 1632, two being acquired from British settlers who had received them from the corporation.[168] By 1632 Walter Brady's house, the first sovereign being by then presumably dead, was in the tenure of John Whitman, an English merchant. Between 1631 and 1633 the names of three British merchants occur, one, Nicholas Garnett, living outside the town. Hamnet (or Hamlet) Steele was an innkeeper whose wife (previously Brennan) in 1639 was the widow of another British settler, and who was often appointed to deliver seizin in property transfers. Another establishment the 'Signe of the Bull', along with four acres of land was held by Lawrence Dardes, son of Nathaniel the sovereign, until mortgaged in 1633 for £40 and sold outright in 1636 for a further £48.[169]

Cavan was, then, a county and market town, neither a military nor an ecclesiastical centre. Unlike Londonderry it was not built virtually *de novo* with the plantation, and its political structure indicates how much of the old remained in the plantation period. However, it is clear that both the economic and political balance was changing before 1641. The size of the town was not impressive nevertheless, in a list of 'chief gents in Ulster' drawn up about 1625, the sovereign of Cavan was included amongst the fifteen leading people in the county.[170]

E. Virginia

In the 'Project' it was propounded that a town should be erected, allotted land, and incorporated in County Cavan about midway between Kells and Cavan, the precise site to be chosen by the commissioners of plantation.[171] Five townlands, 619 acres by the Civil Survey (about 1,297 statute acres), were allotted for the town. There was also to be a Thursday market and a

[166] TCD, MS 833, ff 226–6v.

[167] Indenture, 17 September 1632, between Patrick O'Brogan and John Gibson; indenture 9 July 1633 between Patrick O'Brogan and John Gibson (NLI, D 20,409–20,475).

[168] Ibid.

[169] Indenture, 25 February 1636, between Lawrence Dardes and John Gibson (ibid.).

[170] PRONI, T808/15261.

[171] 'Ulster plantation papers', no. 74, *Anal. Hib.*, viii. For the original Gaelic name of the site see T.F. O'Rahilly, 'Notes on Irish place names', *Hermathena*, vol. xlviii (1933), 197–8.

fair, in June.[172] The grantees of the area, with responsibility for establishing the town and procuring its incorporation was Capt. John Ridgeway,[173] a local landowner.

It was not until August 1612 that Ridgeway, as patron, received a patent of the town lands. The conditions contained in it have already been outlined to indicate the obligations these grantees accepted.[174] He was to 'plant and settle' twenty British, who should be burgesses, within four years, and allot to each small areas of land. He should also provide sites for the town and for various public buildings – a church and churchyard, market place, and school. Apart from the land to be allotted to the burgesses, thirty acres, a further thirty acres should be designated as common. The remainder of the land became the patron's property and he also received the right to hold a weekly market and two fairs. He furthermore received Lough Ramor and its fishing, and on it he might keep a ferry.

Although by 1611 Ridgeway had imported a number of artisans to his estate,[175] at the time of Bodley's survey in 1613, coincident, as it happened, with the incorporation of the Ulster boroughs, only the site of the town, and the name Virginia had been chosen. Otherwise, there was 'nothing done'.[176] Before 1619 Ridgeway sold his estate to Capt. Hugh Culme, the obligation to build the town, and the town lands, being thus transferred.[177] From Culme the beginnings of settlement at Virginia can be traced. On Pynnar's evidence Culme had erected eight timber houses and placed in them English tenants. There was also present a minister 'which keepeth school and is a very good preacher'.[178] At this point Virginia was in no way different from the other modest villages being established under planter tutelage throughout the escheated counties. However, size had not been, in practice, a qualification for incorporation, though the grant of the town lands in trust to Ridgeway in 1612 had stipulated that within four years he should have built twenty English-type houses and placed in them twenty British families.[179] This stipulation turned out to be too onerous. The failure, however, of the incipient town in its early stages to receive a charter was due, on the one hand, to the transfer of responsibility from Ridgeway to Culme and, on the other, to government laxity in the detailed supervision of the plantation scheme.

172 NAI, Lodge, Records of the rolls, xiv, 18.
173 *CPRI, Jas I*, 236.
174 Above, 225–6.
175 Lam. Pal. Lib., Carew MSS, vol. 630, fol. 69.
176 *Hastings MSS*, iv, 160.
177 Hill, *Plantation*, 457–8.
178 Ibid.
179 *CPRI, Jas I*, 236; BL, Add. MS 4756, fol. 101.

The commissioners in 1622, Culme being absent at the time, heard complaints from the inhabitants that they had no security of tenure. The 1622 return mentions only five stone and clay houses inhabited with 'poore' families, though it states that two more houses were being built.[180] Another change of ownership came shortly afterwards placing the estate around the town, and Virginia, in the hands of the Old English Lucas Plunkett, Baron Killeen and subsequently earl of Fingall,[181] who owned land nearby.

It was under Plunkett that the inhabitants (or some of them) received grants of title to their houses and pieces of land in the area. Thus on 25 January 1625 the Rev. George Creighton of Virginia and his wife received a fee-farm grant of their house and three roods of land 'inclosed and market forth' at a rent of 5/4 per annum.[182] Later, on 30 June 1626, Plunkett leased jointly to Creighton and seven other residents of the town two of the townlands which were to have been allotted to the corporation as well as the profits of the fairs and markets for 61 years, at £17 per annum rent.[183] One of these was a weaver, another a mason, and a third a 'brasior'. Another, David Kellett, was subsequently a landholder in the area.[184] The granting of leasehold security to the residents had thus awaited the end of James's reign and after.

The fact that Virginia had not been incorporated became an issue when the commissioners for defective titles transferred their attention to Ulster. An inquiry into the extent of Plunkett land in County Cavan was held in September 1637.[185] In March 1638 Creighton on behalf of the townsmen petitioned Wentworth to cause Christopher Plunkett, Lucas's successor, to procure the incorporation of the town. The matter was referred to Lord Dillon and Sir Gerald Lowther, chief justice, and heard by them in the presence of both parties in July. They advised that Fingall should surrender the five polls of town land and receive a regrant for the purpose of incorporating the town. The corporation was to include a provost and nineteen burgesses, listed by name and presumably the total of the British inhabitants. The corporation should also receive the right to hold two fairs and a weekly market, under rent to the crown, as well as the lands and the fishing of Lough Ramor at an annual crown rent of £2. 6. 3. They went on to order that after land had been reserved for public buildings – a church, minister's house, school, schoolmaster's house, market place, and town hall

180 Ibid.

181 Date of sale is not known, but Fingall held the property in January 1625 (Indenture, 25 January 1625, between Plunkett and George Creighton, in Fingall Papers, NLI, MS 8026).

182 Indenture, 25 January 1625 (as above).

183 Indenture, 30 June 1626, between Plunkett and Creighton, etc. (NLI, MS 8026).

184 *Inq. cancel. Hib. repert.*, ii, Cavan (51) Chas I.

185 Ibid., (54) Chas I.

– the remainder, divided into equal portions, should be granted to the twenty burgesses, to be held of the earl of Fingall in free burgage at the yearly rent of twenty shillings. To effect this it was ordered that a commission should be issued to the bishop of Kilmore and others to lay out the town and lands on these principles and define places for 'convenient lanes and ways' in and about the town. The earl of Fingall should himself build the church before 9 February 1640 [?–41], and enter into a bond of £4,000 to perform the stipulations of the order as it concerned him.[186] On August 7 this adjudication was ratified in the council, and the bishop of Kilmore, Luke Dillon, Sir James Craig, and Thomas Fleming were appointed planning commissioners. The rent for the market and fairs, which were slightly adjusted, was to be £2.[187]

The commission was accordingly issued to the bishop, and emphasis was placed on defining the dimensions of the church, the thickness of its walls, and that it should be built of lime and stone and slate-roofed. Upon the return of the commission Fingall, on 7 December 1639 by order of the lords justices and council, was directed to enter into bond to fulfil his obligations. However, although the lands had thus been laid out to the inhabitants, various difficulties arose and the earl attempted to defer fulfilment of certain parts of the order. The problem was further discussed at the council in the spring. The outcome was that it was decided that Fingall should be given three years from that date (13 February 1640) for erecting the church, that he should receive all arrears and rents up to 1638 due on those parts of the town lands which had not then been leased to the inhabitants of the town, and that the grant of the market and fairs to be made to the corporation should not terminate his rights to hold those fairs and markets which had been contained in Ridgeway's patent.[188]

In achieving the postponement of his building obligation until the spring of 1643, Fingall had unwittingly achieved a much longer exemption. The 1641 rising broke out before the town was incorporated. Although the townsmen pressed their case in both the first and second courts of claims at the Restoration settlement, they were unsuccessful. They then sought redress in the court of chancery, 1668–70, and being there unsuccessful presented a petition to the house of commons with the same result.[189]

By an interesting combination of circumstances Virginia thus did not achieve corporate status. The 1622 visitation return stated that the church

[186] '1637. Proceedings at Council Table when Wentworth was Lord Deputie' (NLI, Fingall Papers, MS 8032/1).
[187] Ibid.
[188] Order of the Lord Justices and Council, 13 February 1640 (NLI, Fingall Papers, MS 8032/1).
[189] NLI, Fingall Papers, MS 8032/1, 2, 3.

for that parish was ruinous, and the recommended place in which to build was Virginia.[190] It is now clear that no such building had been erected over twenty, and perhaps over forty, years' later. Up to 1641 Virginia was a simple dwelling centre like many other plantation villages though it was somewhat strange that a projected corporation came to have an Old English landlord.

F. Belturbet

Belturbet, unlike Virginia, a place of previous Gaelic settlement was also projected for incorporation. The grantee responsible for establishing the town, and who in August 1610 received some five polls of land allocated for this purpose, was Stephen Butler. The town received its charter on 30 March 1613,[191] Stephen Butler himself being the first chief officer.[192]

Evidence of settlement, albeit on a small scale, emerges quickly. By the time of Carew's inquiry both Butler and Sir Hugh Wirrall had built houses there. Belturbet was also a centre of boat construction and Butler, Wirrall, and Ridgeway had had boats build there, one of which could carry 'twelve or fourteen' tons. Bodley stated that the town 'goeth well forward'. Both Wirrall, who was living temporarily in an 'English thatched house' in the town pending the erection of his stronghold, and Butler, on Bodley's evidence, had appointed their freeholders for the town, many of whom had already built their houses there.[193] Pynnar stated that Butler and the other undertakers of the barony of Loughtee had responsibility for planting the town and building a church. In the town he found

> houses built of cage-work all inhabited with British tenants, and most of them tradesmen, each of these having a house and garden plot, with four acres of land, and commons for certain numbers of cows and garrans.[194]

However, that the inhabitants were dissatisfied in their relations with Butler is evident. They appealed to the deputy and council for redress, and received an order in their favour.[195] On 20 May 1618, following on this order, Butler granted the town lands, with the exception of one acre called the 'Tile-Kill Yard', to the corporation at a rent of £1. 10. 0, and also a Saturday market

[190] Armagh Archiepiscopal Registry, B.1b. no. 193, 146–7.

[191] *CPRI, Jas I*, 255 (heading only).

[192] See the order for the fiant for incorporation in Bod. Lib., Carte MSS, vol. 62, fol. 167 (*CSPI, 1611–14*, 299: inaccurate).

[193] *Hastings MSS*, iv, 163; i.e. Butler, the patron, had not built the houses.

[194] Hill, *Plantation*, 465–6.

[195] Referred to in BL, Add. MS 4756, fol. 102v.

and two fairs on Ash Wednesday and St. Bartholomew's day, and a court of record every Saturday.[196]

The effect of this agreement, however, does not seem to have been satisfying. In 1622 the commissioners found that, although there were thirty-four houses all with British inhabitants, there was complaint that allocations of land had not been made. Many of the corporation claimed that they had never heard of the council order. With this knowledge at this disposal, however, they seemed more satisfied and Sir Stephen and they 'promised future love and amitie one towards another'. The commissioners hoped that this would encourage 'that well begune corporac'on which is fitt to be cherished' and stated that there was a 'great store' of protestants in and about the town. They recommended that a church should be built there.[197] The ecclesiastical visitation return embodied a similar recommendation.[198]

How the relations of the townsmen and landlord continued is not clear. However, that reasonably-sized areas of land, as well as common rights, were associated in some way with houses in the town is clear from a conveyance of 15 July 1641. This was a fine to John Madden levied by Charles Waterhouse, one of the original incorporators. By it Waterhouse conveyed to Madden six messuages, six cottages, six gardens, ten acres of arable, ten acres of meadow, ten acres of pasture, six barns, six stables, ten acres of wood and underwood, ten acres of bog and moor, and common of pasture for all kinds of beasts, in Belturbet.[199] It seems from an inquisition post mortem on Sir Stephen Butler, taken on 6 September 1639, that the Butlers exercised market and fair rights in the town.[200] The claims of the provost and burgesses over the town lands are referred to in a later inquisition of 22 August 1640.[201] There were certainly further difficulties and litigation about Belturbet corporation in the 1670s.[202]

There is little evidence for the development of the town. Wirrall lived there for a time, but had sold his estate by 1619.[203] In September 1613 a certain Richard Alsopp, merchant, of Lisduff, County Cavan, and Margaret Smith of Dublin, received licenses to keep taverns in Belturbet and Cavan.[204] In 1622 the parish minister was resident in the town though there was no

196 NAI, Co. 1822; NAI, Lodge, Records of the rolls, vi, 169 (appended to Butler's patent under commission for defective titles); *CPRI, Jas I*, 423.

197 BL, Add. MS 4756, fol. 102v.

198 Armagh Archiepiscopal Registry, B.1b. no. 193, 144–5.

199 NLI, D 10025 (in Latin).

200 *Inq. cancel. Hib. repert.*, ii, Cavan (62) Chas I.

201 Ibid., (67) Chas I.

202 NLI, D 7340.

203 Hill, *Plantation*, 464–5.

204 *CPRI, Jas I*, 261.

church there at that time.[205] Nicholas Higginson, M.A., who had been master of the Royal School, was living in Belturbet at the outbreak of the insurrection in 1641.[206] In 1624 during an insurrection scare when Belturbet was threatened, it emerges that the town had constables and a watch.[207]

However, by 1641 Belturbet was a place of some size and substance. It was larger and certainly more Protestant in character than Cavan, the county town. Bishop Bedell's son, William, writing after the Restoration, described Belturbet in his father's time as being 'the only considerable town in the whole county', but which 'yet was but as one of our ordinary market-towns here in England, having only but one church in it'. However, Cavan was 'not so big by one-half' as Belturbet.[208] A rapid examination of the 1641 depositions reveals that there were living in the town in 1641 at least five merchants,[209] one baker,[210] two carriers,[211] one gunsmith,[212] one feltmaker,[213] one shoemaker,[214] and one innkeeper who also had a tannhouse,[215] all with English names. Some of these also held land. Indeed, some substantial leaseholders and proprietors lived in the town. One of these, Thomas Taylor, was a freeholder and leaseholder on a number of Loughtee estates.[216] John Pyman and Edward Phillpott, both proprietors of land, the latter the husband of Sir Stephen Butler's widow, were also resident.[217]

3. Some other towns and villages

It has been decided to present here a discussion of other towns and villages for which some detailed evidence has survived.

A. Lurgan

Brownlow's village of Lurgan has already been mentioned in discussion of government surveys, and we have seen that it contained a church and a mill and had grown up close to the landlord's house. A document associated with the 1622 survey[218] provides a list of inhabitants and their occupations.

[205] Armagh Archiepiscopal Registry, B.1b. no. 193, 144–5.
[206] HMC, *Fifth Report*, Appendix (1876), 39.
[207] Above, 134.
[208] Jones (ed.), *Life and death of William Bedell*, 62.
[209] TCD, MS 832, ff 63v, 222; 66v–8; 131v–2; MS 833, fol. 189.
[210] Ibid., fol. 283.
[211] Ibid., MS 832, ff 125–5v; MS 833, fol. 75.
[212] Ibid., MS 832, ff 141v–3; MS 833, ff 265–6v.
[213] Ibid., MS 832, fol. 66v; MS 833, fol. 148.
[214] Ibid., MS 832, fol. 101v.
[215] Ibid., MS 832, ff 100v–101; MS 833, ff 6–6v.
[216] Ibid., MS 832, ff 97–7v.
[217] Ibid., ff 71v–2, 97–7v; MS 833, ff 182–2v.
[218] TNA, Manchester papers, 30/15/2/183.

The village then consisted of forty-seven houses, two occupied by Irishmen – one a cooper, and the other who was stated to be 'conformeable'. Of the remaining British tenants there was a mason, a butcher, a carpenter, a tanner, a smith, a weaver, and a tailor. There were two coopers, four joiners, three turners, and two shoemakers. Each had a house in the town and usually small areas of land. The other residents, apart from a labourer who held two acres, were on the whole defined as yeomen or husbandmen. It is perhaps surprising that no merchant was listed. Brownlow's Lurgan was thus a sizeable planter village, larger than Grandison's Tandragee which consisted of thirty-five 'English-lyke houses' at this time.[219]

B. Markethill

For his village of Clancarny or Markethill, Sir Archibald Acheson listed thirty-six resident householders for the commissioners in 1622.[220] These included three shoemakers, three weavers, one baker, and one carpenter. The occupations of the others were not defined, the commissioners noting against one, Patrick Sherry, that he was 'an Irish man and goes not to church'. That the town had some arrangement for the maintenance of order can be seen from the fact that one resident, Edward Johnson, is listed as constable. There was an innkeeper there in 1641.[221]

Information on other towns and villages is too slight to afford each a separate treatment. However, a few general points can be made. While it is not clear that each town appointed constables or watchmen to maintain order we have seen that Belturbet and Markethill did and, in 1641, there was a constable for Tandragee.[222] While the towns and villages were probably mostly inhabited by craftsmen or artisans and small tenants, most, as we have seen, also had some substantial residents. This was also the case in some of the small villages in Cavan. Thus, for example, Richard Cliffe, living in Killashandra in 1641, was a leaseholder of some substance.[223]

4. Conclusion

Perhaps the most obvious common characteristic of the towns in Armagh and Cavan prior to 1641 is their limited size and slow development. Much of the physical fabric of these Ulster towns, especially those which originated as forts, was of obvious British character, their alien purpose in some cases symbolised by the presence of garrisons, however small. But not

[219] *Inq. cancel. Hib. repert.*, ii, Armagh (7) Jas I.
[220] NLI, Rich Papers, MS 8014/5: Archibald Acheson's certificate.
[221] TCD, MS 836, fol. 112.
[222] Ibid., fol. 246.
[223] Ibid., MS 832, fol. 203.

all of them had such an origin, Cavan and Armagh having considerable Gaelic antiquity and retaining much of their native character, and all attracting Irish as well as immigrant inhabitants. Fundamentally they were market centres and, with the partial exception of Cavan, each was controlled by the local landlord. Many of the boroughs were not markedly different in size, character, or independence from the unincorporated landlord towns or villages.

In 1610 Blenerhasset stated that the security of the plantation would depend in large part on the establishment of 'many goodly strong corporations'. A 'scattered plantation', he argued, could never guarantee its own permanence, and it would be essential to build well-fortified towns with organised watches, 'able at any time, at an houres warning, with five hundred men well armed, to encounter all occasions'.[224] It is clear that these expectations had not been realised thirty years later. If, to the Irish, the new Ulster corporations symbolised an altered dispensation, the flimsiness of that symbolism, their pregnability, was, in most instances, demonstrated in 1641.

[224] Blenerhasset, 'Direction', 317–26.

CHAPTER 9

Rural Conditions

Rents, land values, incomes, and produce

The evidence for how rents and land values varied up to 1641 is very tentative. Government surveyors were not concerned with landlords' incomes, and legal and estate sources are very incomplete. An attempt is made here, however, to show what returns from the land were and that they were rising in our period.

At the first leasing the rents of Trinity College lands in Armagh were £5 per townland. The rents of the archbishopric at this stage ranged from £4 to £7, Irish tenants paying the higher charges. In 1611 the plantation commissioners ordered that the Armagh school lands should be let at £3 per townland.[1] In some cases, where a tenant's bargaining power was high, the early rents were even lower. Thus, much of the Stanhowe estate was leased in 1613 to a tenant at £1 and £2 per townland.[2] The townlands in Oneilland were leased at £5. 10. 0. each in *c.* 1611.[3] On the Rolleston estate many townlands were leased in small portions which makes calculation difficult. However, three were leased to Sir Francis Annesley at £1. 10. 8. each and another was leased at £5 yearly. A townland held by an Irish tenant for twenty-one years returned £30 per annum, though from what date it is not clear.[4] On the John Dillon estate the rents of eight townlands in 1622 ranged from £4. 3. 4. to £17. 0. 8. The tenants all held for three lives. Here, as was fairly general, there were more than one tenant per townland except in one case where the rent was £5. Otherwise, there were from two to eleven tenants per townland; where there were eleven the total rent was £17. 0. 8.[5]

The evidence for Cavan is somewhat similar, some rents being lower than in Armagh. Most of the land of the bishopric was leased initially for £1 per poll, though this may have been relative to the size of an entry fine.[6] Other evidence is fragmentary. Two townlands were let by Mulmory oge

1 'Ulster plantation papers', no. 27, *Anal. Hib.*, viii.
2 NAI, Chancery salvage, 2B.80.121, no. 92.
3 Ibid., X20.
4 NLI, Rolleston Papers, Packing Case 112, folder 1.
5 NLI, Rich Papers, MS 8014/8: John Dillon's certificate.
6 Below, 300.

O'Reilly before 1618 at £6 each.[7] The income from four townlands, the property of Edmund Nugent before *c.* 1630, was £5 each per annum.[8] In both counties rents may have been somewhat higher than in Londonderry.[9]

A general upward movement of rent is detected by the 1630s. The rents of the archbishop and bishops were approximately doubled, admittedly following government intervention.[10] From 1635 a small portion of Trinity College's Armagh lands was leased at £10. 2. 0. per townland, the original rate being £5.[11] By 1638 the college land in Colure returned four times its original rent.[12] From the middle 1630s the annual income of TCD from all its lands in Ulster was £1,333. 9. 6, over twice the initial figure of £632. 8. 6.[13] The rents of eight townlands of the Cope estate in May 1633 ranged from £9 to £18. For a townland occupied by Irish £30 was paid.[14] Although there is a good survival of rentals for the Brownlow estate in the 1630s rents are rarely entered by townland, however one held by British tenants returned £26. 8. 8. in 1635, though a small number of townlands particularly named returned from £6. to £10.[15]

The upward movement of rents was not limited to Armagh, for which most evidence survives. One townland in Cavan was leased in 1627 for £10.[16] Another, at Butler's Bridge, with a corn mill was leased by Sir Stephen Butler for £26 per annum before 1626.[17] Another townland on this estate was declared in 1637 to be held for £8 per annum.[18] Two townlands and a mill on the Acheson estate were leased in 1638 at £34 per annum.[19] The absence of the Civil Survey for both counties prohibits any general statement. Only one small fragment, for the Rolleston estate in Armagh, has been found. Here one townland was valued at £20 in 1640, and eight and a half at £100, or about £11. 15. 0. each.[20]

Although many estates changed hands, there is only meagre record of the sale values. Early sales, however numerous, were ill-recorded. Only the

7 NAI, Chancery salvage, B.435.
8 Ibid., H.149.
9 Moody, *Londonderry Plantation*, 333.
10 Below, 318–20.
11 Below, 337–8.
12 Below, 342.
13 Below, 339.
14 NAI, Deeds, wills and instruments … post mortem, vol. 25, 129–46; PRONI, T808/14941.
15 Armagh Museum, Brownlow Rentals, 1635.
16 NAI, Chancery salvage, K.68 (very damaged).
17 Ibid., V.61.
18 NAI, Ferguson MSS, xii, 329.
19 NAI, Deeds, wills and instruments … post mortem, vol. 25, 254–65.
20 R.J. Hunter (ed.), 'Fragments of the Civil Survey of counties Kerry, Longford, and Armagh', *Anal. Hib.*, xxiv, 231.

cost of one estate before 1620 has come to light, and this was in Fermanagh though acquired by a Cavan landowner. In 1617 Sir Stephen Butler bought the middle portion of Kilspinan from Michael Balfour for £550.[21] In February 1614 Walter Talbot sold, also to Butler, three townlands acquired from Wony McThomas McKiernan and Donell Backagh McShane O'Reilly for £50.[22] The sale in 1621 of the estate – a great and a small proportion originally granted to Aubigny in Clankee – to Sir Henry Perse for £2,300[23] appears to indicate a rise in values between Butler's purchase in 1617 for £550 of an area theoretically half the size. Of smaller areas, eight townlands in Castlerahan were sold in 1633 by Shane McPhillip O'Reilly to a fellow Irishman for £300,[24] and four, also in Cavan, were sold in 1639 for £100.[25] In 1622 four townlands and a water mill near Belturbet were sold to Butler for £400.[26] The sums that could be raised on the sale of leases are, however, also instructive. Two townlands in Toaghy, Armagh, belonging to the archbishop, and leased in 1615 for sixty years, were sold in 1622 for £49, resold in 1627 for £50, and again in 1629 for £60.[27] This would indicate rising land values.

The only other evidence is from the amounts for which property was mortgaged. In 1618 Rolleston mortgaged his entire estate in Armagh to Annesley for £420. The rental there was £140. 2. 0.[28] A townland in Orior was mortgaged about 1616 for £30,[29] and another in Cavan in 1616 for £34.[30] Brownlow in 1628 mortgaged a townland for £40.[31] Some nine townlands on the Cope estate in Armagh were apparently mortgaged in May 1633 to Mountnorris for £1,000,[32] though somewhat smaller sums were raised from parts of the Sacheverall estate at this time.[33] About eight townlands of the Castledillon estate in Armagh were mortgaged to William, Lord Caulfeild, in 1636 for £2,000.[34] In August 1637 Patrick Acheson

21 NLI, Butler Deeds, D 8896–8926, Indenture 2 March 1617 between Michael Balfour … and Sir Stephen Butler.

22 NAI, Deeds, wills and instruments … post mortem, vol. 25, 239–54.

23 *Inq. cancel. Hib. repert.*, ii, Cavan (19) Chas I.

24 Ibid., (45) Chas I.

25 NAI, Deeds, wills and instruments … post mortem, vol. 25, 317–27.

26 NLI, Deeds of sale between Charles Waterhouse and Etheldred his wife, and Sir Stephen Butler 4 May 1622 (uncatalogued).

27 Below. A lease of a townland in Cavan acquired in April 1613 by Sir Thomas Ashe was sold in May for £22 (NLI, Farnham Papers, D 20,409–20,475).

28 NLI, Rolleston Papers, Packing Case, 112, folders 1 and 2.

29 Above, 208–09.

30 Ibid.

31 PRONI, T808/14964.

32 NAI, Deeds, wills and instruments … post mortem, vol. 25, 129–46.

33 *Inq. cancel. Hib. repert.*, ii, Armagh (25) Chas I.

34 Above, 187.

mortgaged his small proportion in Cavan (where land may have had less value) for £2,000.[35] The willingness of a substantial London citizen, Sir Robert Parkhurst,[36] to lend money on the security of Ulster land in the 1630s is itself an indication of its current value. Parkhurst entered into a mortgage with Sir William Brownlow for his entire estate in 1635.[37] He also, in 1633, lent £2,000 to Sir Phelim O'Neill.[38]

The scant survival of rentals makes it possible to provide landlords' incomes in only a few cases. Incomes would, of course, vary with size of estates and the vigour of the owners. In 1635 Sir William Brownlow's annual rental was £773. 4. 6.[39] His estate was some 13,000 acres. Sir Archibald Acheson was said to have had an estate of 'some four hundred pounds sterling',[40] which was in both counties. The Rolleston rental in 1618, when the estate was mortgaged, was some £140. 2. 0.[41] The rent John Dillon received from three-quarters of his estate (the rest was demesne) in 1622 was £80. 16. 0.[42] Undertakers' incomes thus seem to have ranged from about £100 to about £800, in perhaps a few cases, per annum.

Estates in difficulties could return lower sums. The condition of the property of Peter Ameas who owned an estate in Loughtee for about ten years from 1618 can be inferred from the answer of Sir Stephen Butler to the bill of Sir Hugh Culme in a chancery suit concerning the estate.[43] Butler had acted as guarantor to Ameas for debts to Culme. He stated that the estate was worth £80 per annum, and it appears that Ameas owned no more than seven horses, four cows, six young heifers and twenty sheep.[44] At the other end of the scale there were a number of British proprietors in our area who had outside interests, and so substantial additional sources of income. Butler, for example, had land in Fermanagh. Toby Caulfeild had land in Tyrone, was a military commander, indulged in various speculative enterprises, and had a house in Dublin.[45] The incomes of Trinity College and the archbishopric are discussed elsewhere.[46]

35 *Inq. cancel. Hib. repert.*, ii, Cavan (69) Chas I.
36 Above, 186.
37 PRONI, T808/14964.
38 *Inq. cancel. Hib. repert.*, ii, Tyrone (3) Chas II.
39 Above, 186. See also PRONI, T808/14964, a chancery decree of 1654, where it is stated that the estate was worth £1,000 yearly in 1635.
40 Sir John Scott of Scotstarvet, *The staggering state of the Scots statesmen for one hundred years, viz from 1550 to 1650* (Edinburgh 1754), 74. This work was written before the end of the seventeenth century.
41 Above, 259.
42 Above, 144.
43 NAI, Chancery salvage, Q.9.
44 Ibid.
45 Below, 379.
46 Below, 324–48.

Incomes from estates ranging from about £100 to under £800 in our area may be compared with the incomes of the London companies and also with the returns from land in England. The London companies received in rent from their farmers sums ranging from £106 to £350. 10. 0. per annum.[47] The average income of 135 landowning families in Kent, including six peers and thirteen baronets, for the period 1640–1660 was £656 per annum. Of these families of Stuart origin had, on average, £602 a year and untitled gentry, accounting for nearly one-third of this sample of 135, averaged £270. Hundreds, however, had an income of under £250 per annum.[48] The sizes of estates in Kent are not available, but land was probably used more profitably than in Ulster.

We can assume that resident landlords administered their own estates. The methods devised by institutions – TCD and the archbishopric of Armagh – are examined elsewhere. Initially the undertakers were empowered to appoint deputies and we have seen that many did. Absentees employed agents whose backgrounds are, in some cases, known.

In 1613 Bodley was informed, for example, that Lord Killeen, a prominent Old English landowner in Cavan and outside, had undertaken responsibility for the lands in Cavan acquired by Sir James Hamilton from Lord Aubigny.[49] Grandison's estates in Armagh were, in 1622, administered by Richard Atherton,[50] a relative of Henry, who had been constable of Mountnorris fort. Lord Moore employed an agent Townley, presumably of the family subsequently in Louth, at this time.[51] Poyntz, an energetic servitor grantee in Orior, himself undertook the agenting of Arthur Bagnal's estate in County Down.[52] However, it was probably most common for absentee landlords to make arrangements with one of their own tenants (as indeed Atherton was to Grandison) for the supervision of their estates. This broke down, as has been seen,[53] on the Lambert estate in the 1630s where the agenting was in native Irish hands.

The importation of livestock in certain quantities free of restriction was allowed to the undertakers in 1611. For the first year the undertaker of 2,000 acres (and proportionally) might import 20 cows, 20 store cattle, 2 bulls, 100 ewes, 6 rams, 20 horses and up to 10 pigs. It is clear that some grantees did

[47] Moody, *Londonderry Plantation*, 336.

[48] Everitt, *Community of Kent*, 41, 329. The author states that the figure for Stuart families might be as low as £438 if certain families of uncertain origin are classified as Stuart (ibid., 329).

[49] *Hastings MSS,* iv, 160.

[50] TNA, Manchester papers, 30/15/2/184. Atherton's small grant of land had been acquired by Grandison.

[51] BL, Add. MS 4756, fol. 109v.

[52] NAI, Chancery salvage, G.388.

[53] Above, 189–90.

introduce British breeds, but government surveyors, not writing for posterity, recorded little of the agricultural pursuits of the colonists.

Carew found 52 English cows and 15 horses on John Dillon's land in Oneilland, 4 English cows and 8 horses on Rolleston's, and English carts and horses on Cope's, Sacheverall's, and Matchett's. In Loughtee two undertakers, Fishe and Waldron, had each two teams of English horses with English carts, but there is no reference to other imported livestock. The Scots in the Fews, except Douglas and Craig, had cattle and horses in considerable quantities, three having between them 170 cows and 47 horses and mares. For the Cavan Scots, however, there is only a reference to four horses and mares on the Auchmooty estates.[54]

Bodley refers to cattle on the estates of Dillon, Matchett, and Rolleston, though not elsewhere in Armagh. In Loughtee Butler, Taylor, Waldron, and Fishe all had livestock in quantity as had their tenants, Waldron, for example, having 'stocked his ground with English and Irish cattle'.[55] In Tullyhunco Claud Hamilton had 'above eighty head' and Craig 'a good stock of cattle'.

Pynnar makes no reference to livestock in either county and even the 1622 report is not very forthcoming. The commissioners, however, noted that, in Loughtee, Fishe had 'a great store of English cattle' as also had Waldron. In Clankee Bailie had 'stock of cattle' and William Hamilton 'some'. While not all these animals were necessarily of imported breed, it is evident that many were, and also that livestock production was a major component of the rural economy. Some of the Scots in the Fews, and some of the English in Oneilland and Loughtee emerge in the early years as particularly active in this respect.

Corn production was, of course, the other major source of income. At the end of the first year it was noted of Craig in the Fews, perhaps characteristic of the Scots, that he had 'sowne and reapte oats and barley' and begun to build a mill.[56] Bodley's survey tells us no more than that wind or water or horse mills were being erected throughout both counties. Pynnar found 'good store of tillage', two watermills, and one windmill 'all for corn' on Brownlow's estate. On Henry Acheson's in the Fews there was 'great store of tillage'. In Loughtee he found 'a little' tillage on the Waldron estate.[57] On Taylor's lands there was a water-mill 'but no great store of

54 Lam. Pal. Lib., Carew MSS, vol. 630, ff 58–63v.

55 *Hastings MSS,* iv, 162.

56 Lam. Pal. Lib., Carew MSS, vol. 630, fol. 103v.

57 The 1622 survey, otherwise unhelpful, found 'very good' tillage and 'inclosures' upon his land (BL, Add. MS 4756, ff 101v–2).

tillage'.[58] Sir Stephen Butler had two corn-mills.[59] As to all four Scots estates in Clankee he noted categorically, 'I find upon these lands good tillage and husbandry according to the English manner'.[60] In his general conclusions he stated that 'were it not for the Scottish tenants which do plough in many parts of the country, those parts may starve'.[61] Against any national propensity to produce a particular product, however, must be weighed the suitability of the soil in the area to such production.

The best available source for the rural economy is the 1641 depositions. In these, deponents usually specified their losses in terms of types of property and value. The values and quantities must be treated with caution, but, at the least, they afford evidence of the types of commodity produced, and it would seem likely also that the proportions of types of produce to each other may be taken as having some reliability. If this is the case a very rough estimate of the kind of farming practiced can be worked out. When, for example, an Oneilland farmer, John Grey, deposed that he had lost corn to the value of £100 and cattle to the same value,[62] we can assume that in October 1641 he owned these goods in equal proportions. Other goods are also usually listed and both cattle and corn frequently broken down more specifically. There is, however, the further point that corn or hay in October would be predominantly that year's crop whereas livestock could be one, two, or more years old, hence to have corn and cattle in equal proportions would imply more tillage than grazing.

Many of the depositions do not allow this kind of treatment. However, from an examination of fifteen who do for Armagh,[63] it is found that the proportions of corn to livestock were as two to three. For Cavan an examination of twenty-four depositions[64] reveals a greater concentration on grazing with the proportions of corn (with which hay is sometimes included) to livestock being as three to seven.

In the depositions there are references to English cattle, sheep, and horses in both counties.[65] One Cavan deponent claimed, amongst other animals, for the loss of twenty milch goats.[66] Pigs are listed regularly. Corn

[58] Hill, *Plantation*, 461.

[59] Ibid., 465.

[60] Ibid., 453–7.

[61] Ibid., 589. It is clear that at this time the Hamiltons were producing oats in Ulster for sale in Dublin (Lowry, *Hamilton Manuscripts*, 12).

[62] TCD, MS 836, ff 4–4v.

[63] Ibid., ff 2–3, 4–4v, 7, 11, 13, 42–3, 44–5, 46–6v, 50–51, 53–3v, 57–7v, 60–61, 69–72, 75–6v, 77–8.

[64] TCD, MS 832, ff 55–5v, 58v, 59 (2 depositions), 59v, 60–60v, 65, 69v–70, 70–71, 84–4v, 93v–4, 96–6v, 98–8v, 101–1v, 106–7, 122–5, 172, 203. MS 833., ff 6–6v, 44, 73, 124–5v, 204–6, 252.

[65] See, for example, ibid., MS 832, ff 66v, 96–6v; MS 833, ff 124–5v, 176, 204–6, 252 (Cavan); MS 836, ff 46–6v, 75–6v (Armagh).

[66] Ibid., MS 833, ff 204–6.

produced included oats, barley, wheat and rye. 'Garden roots and hearbes' were specified by one Cavan deponent[67] and peas and beans by another.[68] There is no reference to the growth of flax in either county though the widow of an Oneilland linen weaver was a deponent.[69]

Much of the rural produce must have been used or processed locally. The use of corn for beer was prevalent. One Armagh deponent who claimed corn – wheat, barley, oats, rye, and 'bear barley' – to the value of £550 stated that he had also lost his malthouses and barns.[70] A miller played an important role in rural society. The tanning of leather was also a rural industry.[71] An Oneilland tanner, for example, claimed £150 in losses of 'leather tanned and untanned'.[72] Cavan tanners made similar claims. One Cavan weaver claimed for the loss of yarn,[73] another for the loss of his weaver's tools.[74] A feltmaker in Belturbet claimed that he had lost wool to the value of £20.[75] The widow of Richard Chappell, who had been a tenant to the archbishop and lived in Armagh,[76] claimed wool to the value of £100.[77] From our examination of the occupations of village residents and tenants it has already emerged that weaving was an important activity in Armagh.[78] We have seen already that by 1619 Sir Stephen Butler had set up a fulling mill on his Cavan estate.[79] After the rising John Wheelwright of Killconny – on the Butler estate near Belturbet – who defined himself as clothier, claimed that he had lost the profits of his tuck mill worth £20 per annum.[80]

Butter, cheese, beef, bacon, and tallow were other goods which feature in the depositions. One farmer from near Belturbet claimed £54 for butter, beef, and bacon.[81] Another from near Ballyhaise claimed £40 for '3,000 (*sic*) of butter'.[82] These, however, were the larger sums. An Armagh farmer

67 Ibid.
68 Ibid., ff 66–6v.
69 Ibid., MS 836, ff 66–6v. C. Gill, *The rise of the Irish linen industry* (Oxford 1925; reprinted 1964) says little specific about the industry before 1700.
70 TCD, MS 836, ff 69–72.
71 Up to 1628 tanning could only be done under licence. This was removed by article nine of the Graces (A. Clarke, *The graces, 1625–41* (Dundalk, 1968), 19) and grants of the right to keep tanneries were made to many Ulster settlers in their patents under the 1628 arrangement.
72 TCD, MS 836, ff 2–3.
73 Ibid., MS 832, ff 49–9v.
74 Ibid., ff 99v–100v.
75 Ibid., fol. 66v.
76 Memorial tablet in St. Patrick's Church of Ireland cathedral, Armagh.
77 TCD, MS 836, ff 44–5.
78 Above, 144, 255.
79 Above, 121.
80 TCD, MS 833, fol 272.
81 Ibid., MS 832, ff 84–4v.
82 Ibid., MS 833, fol 73.

stated that he had lost £2 worth of butter and cheese,[83] and a Cavan landholder £6 worth of butter, salt, and cheese.[84] Occasionally river-fishing losses indicate another form of activity. Oliver Smith, a tenant on the Butler estate in Cavan, held fishing weirs for eels from Butler and Edward Phillpott on the river Erne and claimed to have lost fresh and salt eels to the value of £50 owing to the outbreak of the rising.[85] In Tullyhaw on Sir Charles Coote's lands an ironworks was in operation.[86]

Doubtless surplus produce was disposed of at local fairs and markets. There is evidence, too, that a carrying trade of some sort was in operation linking county Cavan with Dublin. One carrier, Thomas Poke, operated from Belturbet.[87] Another carrier, John Dewsbury of Castleterra, claimed that he had lost, due to the rebellion, six 'cars' and horses laden with butter 'which he was bringing towards Dublin' and one horse laden with tallow.[88]

2. Tenants

Two types of tenants can broadly be found: substantial middlemen as on the estates of Trinity College, the bishops' lands to a lesser extent, and occasionally elsewhere, and occupying tenants of smaller areas. The former group can be compared with the farmers of the companies' lands in Londonderry.[89]

It was on the lands of Trinity College that middlemen were most prominent and these, of whom Sir James Hamilton, Sir Toby Caulfeild, Rev. Robert Maxwell, John Temple, Sir George Wentworth, and Dr. John Harding are representative, have been discussed elsewhere.[90] They all had other Irish interests. The tenantry of the archbishopric of Armagh was more varied, but the more substantial tenants in Armagh included Caulfeild and Maxwell, Sir Edward Dodington and others who had Londonderry connections, Sir Maurice Williams, and Robert Bysse, many of them non-resident.[91] The bishops of Kilmore favoured a middleman policy more than the archbishops of Armagh, local servitors, Sir Oliver Lambert and Sir Hugh Culme featuring prominently as their tenants.[92]

Even in an individual settler's estates substantial middlemen tenants can sometimes be found. These were usually neighbouring landowners. Sir John

83 Ibid., MS 836, fol 11.
84 Ibid., MS 833, ff 124–5v.
85 Ibid., MS 832, ff 111–2v; ibid., F.3.4., fol 188.
86 Ibid., MS 833, ff 223–4.
87 Ibid., MS 832, ff 125–5v.
88 Ibid., fol 135; ibid., MS 833, fol. 144.
89 Moody, *Londonderry Plantation*, 311–14.
90 Below, chapter 11.
91 Below, chapter 12.
92 Below, 300. The school lands in both counties were also leased to middlemen.

Bourchier, servitor grantee, for example, was tenant to Richard Rolleston from 1613 of lands subsequently held by Sir Francis Annesley.[93] Sir Archibald Acheson was tenant, in 1622, to part of Sacheverall's lands in Oneilland.[94] In Cavan Sir Hugh Culme held lands from Fishe from 1617.[95] Some of these subsequently acquired the ownership of some of this land.

Tenants of this substance could sometimes hold their lands under very favourable terms. Some information about John Wrench, a great tenant on the Stanhowe estate who was not a landowner, has survived from pleadings in a chancery suit.[96] It emerges that six townlands of the estate were leased to Wrench by Edward Stanhowe, the son of the grantee, in June 1613 at £2 per townland for twenty-one years, and a further six in September for forty-one years at £1 per townland. Wrench had come from England at that time with a following of five families and met Stanhowe on the journey. In the first lease he covenanted to build six English houses and plant six English families who should be armed. The suit, initiated by Stanhowe, concerned non-payment of rent, and a claim that he had been 'allured' to live with Wrench and promised his daughter in marriage. The outcome is unknown. Wrench certainly did not introduce a colony of any size, and in 1633 he was living at Mountnorris and was then at law with Lord Mountnorris.[97]

The other category of tenants were the normal on the estates of British grantees. They can be seen as falling into three groups: freeholders, leaseholders, and cottagers.

The estating of freeholders – two per thousand acres – was a condition of plantation, the performance of which was, on the whole, a slow one. In Oneilland Carew found three freeholders on the estates of Brownlow and Matchett. By 1613 Bodley found freeholders on three other estates and inquisitions confirm that Rolleston created three freeholders in February–March 1612 and John Heron one in October.[98] However, it was not until the time of Pynnar that, more or less, the required number were found on all estates except that of Stanhowe.[99] By 1622 Stanhowe was still delinquent, but in the barony otherwise there were fifty freeholders, one an absentee. In the corresponding English barony of Loughtee in Cavan Carew found

[93] *Inq. cancel. Hib. repert.*, ii, Armagh (6) Chas I.

[94] BL, Add. MS 4756, ff 108v–9.

[95] *Inq. cancel. Hib. repert.*, ii, Cavan (26) Chas I.

[96] NAI, Chancery salvage, 2B.80.121, nos 92, 163.

[97] NAI, Ferguson MSS, xii, 215. Stanhowe, who had lived with Wrench, had apparently paid £8 yearly for his 'diet'. Wrench claimed that on some occasions he had brought clothing for Stanhowe from England.

[98] *Inq. cancel. Hib. repert.*, ii, Armagh (5, 6) Chas I.

[99] The existence of three freeholders on the estate of John Dillon, recorded by Pynnar and the commissioners, is confirmed by estate papers (Armagh Public Library, Castle Dillon Papers).

thirteen freeholders on four estates out of seven, Bodley found twenty-eight on five estates (including the previous four), but it was not until Pynnar's time that forty-one freeholders in all were found on all estates. For six estates about which information was forthcoming the 1622 commissioners reported that there were thirty-four freeholders. However, ten of these on Taylor's estate were non-resident and on Mainwaring's estate one had assigned his lands to another.[100]

The Scots were more dilatory in the estating of freeholders than the English. In the Fews neither Carew nor Bodley refer to them. Pynnar found nine on the estates of Archibald Acheson and John Hamilton,[101] but on Henry Acheson's all the tenants petitioned him to secure them their leases. The 1622 report accredited him with two freeholders and accorded eight to his brother and John Hamilton, but the minute inspection of Sir Nathaniel Rich cast doubt on the status of most of them.[102]

In Clankee Pynnar was also the first to record freeholders. He found eight on Sir James Hamilton's lands and two on each of the remaining three estates. The 1622 commissioners found two on three estates (including Sir James Hamilton's, now owned by Perse), and none on William Hamilton's. For these three estates the evidence of inquisitions must also be considered. Bailie created two freeholders, members of his family, one in November 1618 (just before Pynnar's survey), the other in 1627. The dates of John Hamilton's freehold grants are not given. On the Aubigny estate, acquired by Sir James Hamilton, four freeholds, between December 1616 and June 1621, are recorded which contrast with Pynnar's eight, and Perse created two on it in 1627 and 1629 respectively.[103]

In Tullyhunco, also, Carew and Bodley record no freeholders, but Pynnar found thirteen on three of the four estates. The 1622 commissioners again provide a lower and more likely figure of nine, of which two were non-resident.[104] The Tullyhunco freeholders petitioned the commissioners 'as in

[100] Three inquisitions suggest that the effectively smaller figure of 1622 is the more probable. Sir Nicholas Lusher created three freeholders between October 1612 and July 1615 (which confirms Pynnar) and his successor Mainwaring created one in April 1622 who, in fact, assigned his lands to Sir Hugh Culme (which confirms the 1622 report). On the Fishe estate there is evidence for the creation of no more than two (one in 1615) before 1622, as the commissioners found, and one in 1626. Waldron created one in 1612 (*Inq. cancel. Hib. repert.*, ii, Cavan (23, 26) Chas I; NAI, Exchequer inquisitions, Ulster, Cavan, (3) Chas I, 4–22).

[101] An inquisition shows that on two of the proportions then owned by Hamilton four freeholders had been created by previous owners, Craig (three in 1614) and Claud Hamilton (one in 1612). One of these had been given a further freehold by Hamilton in April 1618 (*Inq. cancel. Hib. repert.*, ii, Armagh (4) Chas I).

[102] Above, 145–6.

[103] *Inq. cancel. Hib. repert.*, ii, Cavan (17–19) Chas I.

[104] Inquisition evidence provides some confirmation. Sir Alexander Hamilton created four freeholds, February–August 1615 as the commissioners found, and on Sir Claud's estate one was created in 1623 (*Inq. cancel. Hib. repert.*, ii, Cavan (24) Chas I).

all other places they did the like by worde of mouth', to be relieved from jury service because their freeholds were 'soe smale' and their rents 'so greate'.[105]

A reason why government surveyors' figures, especially Pynnar's, for numbers of freeholders are sometimes higher than those provided by the surviving inquisitions may, perhaps, be found in a report on Brownlow's tenants in 1622.[106] Here five people are defined as 'liber tenens' and two as 'liber tenens for three lives'.[107] It can only be conjectured that these latter held their lands under leases for three lives renewable. Such a convention would guarantee a continuity of occupation somewhat equivalent perhaps to freehold status, and it may be that surveyors listed these as freeholders.

Some freeholds were certainly smaller than the plantation conditions required. As to rents, the only evidence of these comes from the estate of John Dillon in Armagh where, in 1631, three freeholders of a townland each paid £10, £12, and £13. 12. 0. respectively per annum.[108] Some freeholders were unorthodox in terms of the plantation conditions. Sir Hugh Wirrall was a freeholder to his fellow-undertaker Fishe in Loughtee.[109] Sir Hugh Culme purchased a freehold created by Sir George Mainwaring.[110] One man, Richard Lighterfoote, was freeholder to both Sir Alexander Hamilton and Sir Henry Perse.[111] Richard Hadsor, who was created a freeholder on the Aubigny estate in 1616 was a lawyer and public servant who had been proposed as an undertaker in Armagh in 1609.[112] He was clearly an absentee on this Scots-held estate and in 1621 he was bought out by the new owner Sir Henry Perse.[113] Sir William Anderson, an important member of the 1634 parliament,[114] was a freeholder to Perse, sub-let his lands to Irish, and had a local Irish agent William Kernan.[115] The scale of freeholds featured particularly on this estate. John Kennedy, estated in 1618, sold to John Crowe who, in turn, sold to Robert Madden. Madden, presumably of the Fermanagh family, leased most of his land to native Irish tenants.[116] On at least two estates, those of Bailie in Cavan and

105 BL, Add. MS 4756, fol. 103v.
106 TNA, Manchester papers, 30/15/2/183.
107 Pynnar records five freeholders, the commissioners eight.
108 Armagh Public Library, Castle Dillon Papers, 74–5.
109 *Inq. cancel. Hib. repert.*, Cavan (26) Chas I.
110 Ibid., (23) Chas I.
111 Ibid., (12, 24) Chas I.
112 *CSPI, 1608–10*, 180. In 1615 he was associated with the reorganisation of the court of wards in Ireland (H.F. Kearney, 'The court of wards and liveries in Ireland, 1622–41', *PRIA*, vol. 57, C (1955–6), 33).
113 *Inq. cancel. Hib. repert.*, Cavan (19) Chas I.
114 Kearney, *Strafford*, 247.
115 *Inq. cancel. Hib. repert.*, Cavan (38) Chas I.
116 Ibid., (41) Chas I. One other freeholder on this estate sold his lands to a second tenant who, in turn, was bought out by the new owner (ibid.).

John Dillon in Armagh, relatives of the undertakers were made freeholders. It would seem then that the freeholder section of the colony in both counties did not materialise strictly according to plan.

The second group, leaseholders, held under more diversified tenures. Indeed, it has been seen that there were many complaints that tenants had not been given documentary evidence of title at all.[117] Sizes of holdings were often very much smaller than one townland. The most common terms of leasehold were for twenty-one years, or three lives. However, it is clear that numbers of tenants held for shorter periods. On John Hamilton's Scottish estate in Armagh many held for periods of one to ten years.[118] William Bailie in Cavan also gave a number of short leases.[119] It may be that some of the Scots gave tenancies for shorter periods than the English. There were also tenancies for periods of years longer than twenty-one. John Hamilton granted four such (two per townland) in 1626 for twenty-five years and thirty-one years respectively.[120] Most of the tenants of the archbishopric of Armagh held for sixty years. Rolleston in Oneilland granted a forty-one year lease in 1612.[121] On the estate of Sir Nicholas Lusher in Loughtee, acquired by Mainwaring in 1616, there were generally long leases for periods of twenty-five, thirty-one, or forty-one years.[122] On the Butler estate in Loughtee a tenancy for eighty-seven years was granted in May 1640.[123] The balance of advantages between particular landlords and particular tenants must regularly have affected the terms of leases.

Only a small number of leases have survived, but they serve to indicate the conditions under which land was demised. A lease made by Richard Waldron in 1613 of two polls of land in Cavan required the tenant to take the oath of supremacy within six months, and to have there three British men besides himself who would also take the oath.[124] Wrench, Stanhowe's middleman, covenanted to build houses and install tenants who should be armed.[125] The archbishop of Armagh's leases in 1615 required the building of 'Englishlike' houses, and military attendance, amongst other stipulations.[126] In 1614 Sir James Hamilton, middleman to Trinity College,

[117] Above, 145–6, 148, 150–51.
[118] *Inq. cancel. Hib. repert.*, ii, Armagh (4) Chas I.
[119] Ibid., Cavan (17) Chas I.
[120] Ibid., Armagh (4) Chas I.
[121] Ibid., Armagh (6) Chas I.
[122] Ibid., Cavan (23) Chas I.
[123] Ibid., Cavan (67) Chas I.
[124] Indenture dated 18 March 1613 between Richard Waldron and Clement Cottrell (NLI, Farnham Papers, D 20,409–20,475).
[125] Above, 266.
[126] For a fuller treatment of these leases, see below 270.

undertook in his lease that he and his tenants would not build 'dispersedly or scatteringly' on the College estate.[127] John Dillon of Oneilland stated in 1622 that all his tenants were 'enjoyned by lease to finde a musket, a pike, and sworde and dagger'.[128] Rights of distraint and re-entry for non-payment of rent, and the requirements of suit of court from tenants, featured generally in leases.

A lease made in *c.* 1635 by Sir Patrick Acheson of two townlands and a mill in Cavan for twenty-one years is probably typical of leases of this period.[129] The landlord reserved all woods with free liberty to 'hawke, hunt, fish, and foule' but the tenant might cut timber of building and repairs, and underwood for 'carteboote and ploughboote'. The tenant should pay the king's rent, and £2. 10. 0. as a heriot was stipulated. The tenant should appear at all musters and outrisings and contribute, with the rest of the tenants, to a group of ten able men well armed with pike and musket for the king's service and the defence of the landlord when required. Precise enclosure stipulations were included,[130] and all houses and fences were to be maintained in good repair. He was, within seven years, to build three 'Englishlike' houses and have three British families to dwell there, and he should forfeit his lands if any were demised to Irish sub-tenants. If rent were unpaid for ten days distraint or re-entry would ensue. The landlord would support the tenant in penalising other tenants refusing, in breach of their covenants, to have their corn ground at his mill.

Two of the most important obligations placed on the undertakers by the articles of plantation were the building of houses for tenants in village groupings near the settlers' bawns, and the provision of arms for defence. Both of these were only partly fulfilled, with implications for the security and physical development of the colony.

An examination of the government surveys between 1611 and 1622 shows that most of the undertakers built small clusters of houses or villages which were occupied by their tenants, especially the cottager element. Landlord building was slow to start. Carew found few instances and these only on a small scale. Thus Sacheverall in Armagh, like Wirrall in Cavan, had built only three houses for tenants.[131] Already some tenants were deciding to build for themselves,[132] and landlords were also, at about this time, transferring building responsibilities to them. Thus, as we have seen, Wrench, Stanhowe's middleman, was required to build houses by his

[127] See below, 328.
[128] NLI, Rich Papers, MS 8014/8.
[129] NAI, Deeds, wills and instruments … post mortem, vol. 25, 254–65.
[130] Below, 278.
[131] Lam. Pal. Lib., Carew MSS, vol. 630, ff 59, 61.
[132] Ibid., ff 60, 104.

lease.[133] At the time of Bodley's survey more landlord building was taking place. In Oneilland, for example, three out of ten undertakers were engaged in building framed houses. Rolleston, on Powell's estate, had erected eight 'tenements' and had the frames of four others 'ready to be erected'.[134] Brownlow had two houses erected and other frames set up 'where his town shall be'.[135] John Dillon had built 'divers tenements' by this stage, but had also devolved responsibility in this to his tenants who were 'for the most part ... enjoined to convenient building'.[136] Even in Belturbet, which was just then incorporated and where, as a town to be incorporated, the landlord-patron was required to build houses,[137] the building-lease device was used. Thus Bodley reported that Butler, Wirrall and other undertakers had appointed their 'freeholders' for the town, 'of which divers have built already and others are preparing to build'.[138]

It was only by Pynnar's time, as we have seen,[139] that village nuclei, often very small, had been founded on most undertakers' estates in both counties, and Pynnar's report is not conclusive on whether these were built by the landlords, though it would seem that they were and that they were generally occupied by cottager elements. Many of these took root and expanded in size.[140]

It is clear, then, that there was landlord building, but also that it was inadequate to the housing needs of the colony, and that the landlords also generally succeeded in transferring much of the responsibility here to their tenants. This, in effect, gave rein to centrifugal tendencies, tenants preferring to build in dispersed fashion on their holdings rather than in central villages as the conditions of plantation required. Also, although the undertakers' estates were not as large as the companies proportions in Londonderry,[141] they were substantially larger than the planners of the colony had projected, and so it would have been very inconvenient for all the settlers on each estate to live in one village.

The outcome was a compromise, the quality of which varied from estate to estate, between village and dispersed settlement. Fishe in Loughtee had by Pynnar's time, built two villages 'consisting of ten houses the peace'.[142]

[133] Above, 269.
[134] *Hastings MSS,* iv, 174.
[135] Ibid.
[136] Ibid., 175.
[137] Above, 226.
[138] *Hastings MSS,* iv, 163. It has been seen, above, 242–4, 246, that the archbishop of Armagh used the building-lease device in Armagh with limited success.
[139] Above, 114–26.
[140] Above, 254–5, for example.
[141] Moody, *Londonderry Plantation*, 310, 455.
[142] Hill, *Plantation*, 462–4.

The tenants also did not always build in dispersed fashion. On John Dillon's estate in Oneilland Pynnar states that the tenants had made two villages and dwelled together.[143] On St. John's Oneilland estate at this time there was a small village nucleus of five houses, the rest of the tenants living 'dispersedly on the land, three or four families together'.[144] However, dispersed settlement combined with small villages became the general pattern in both counties.

This kind of pattern had implications for the security of the colony. The undertakers were required to keep arms in their strongholds for defence. Government surveyors generally pronounced themselves satisfied as we have seen with the amount of arms on most estates. Pynnar, though, criticised Adwick in Loughtee for having no arms nor 'any place to keep them in'.[145] However, the logic of dispersed as well as centralised settlement was that arms should be dispersed amongst the tenantry, and we have seen that Sir Stephen Butler, on Pynnar's evidence, had 'very good' arms for 200 men in his castle 'besides others which are dispersed to his tenants for their safeguard'.[146] Some undertakers passed on the responsibility to their tenants. Thus John Dillon of Oneilland stated in 1622 that his tenants were 'enioyned by lease to finde a musket, a pike, a sworde and dagger'.[147] The muster of *c.* 1630 produced disquieting evidence about the military preparedness of the colonists at large[148] (which runs somewhat counter to the statements of surveyors up to 1622), and Wentworth observed that the Ulster colony as but 'a company of naked men'.[149]

One of the most common sources of tension within the colony rested in disputes between landlords and tenants.[150] A number of these were brought to the court of chancery for adjudication. One damaged bill, *c.* 1635, rehearses the complaints of tenants on the Stanhowe estate whose lease apparently was not renewed and who received no compensation for improvements which had included the conversion of 'unprofitable underwoods' to pasture.[151]

From the answer of an Oneilland landlord[152] to a suit brought by two tenants after 1615 some of the details of a complicated problem emerge.

143 Ibid., 563–4.
144 Ibid., 557–8.
145 Ibid., 464–5.
146 Ibid., 465.
147 NLI, Rich Papers, MS 8014/8.
148 Above, 176.
149 Above, 181.
150 Tension between servitors and undertakers in Armagh at an early stage in the plantation has been examined, above 74–6.
151 NAI, Chancery salvage, B.377.
152 Ibid., X.20.

It seems that in 1611 two townlands had been leased to two tenants at £11 per annum. One proved to be a concealment and was granted to Trevor[153] and another area was in compensation assigned to the tenants. The two tenants subsequently, with the consent of the landlord, reached an agreement with a third, whereby they should hold one-third of the area each, and all three occupied the lands as 'tenants in common'. They did not receive individual leases. The two original tenants were in debt to the third. The partnership led to tension – 'barrattings and fallings out in very uncivil and unchristian manner' because agreement on their respective rights was not arrived at. About 1613 one of the original tenants left the estate, moving some twenty miles. The case hinged on disagreement as to the amount of compensation the landlord should give for his part of the entry fine and improvements. The landlord argued that he had offered a reasonable sum agreed to by 'indifferent men' in order 'to be able to let the same to some other'. He claimed that the affair was a bad example of his other tenants, two of whom had also left the estate, and feared that it would be noted against him in the next government survey. He stated too that since the departure of the tenant the land had been occupied by an Irishman, Murtagh McCann, allegedly by assignment, and contrary to the plantation regulations. This is an illuminating, if perhaps an extreme case, of the kind of problem which could arise at this early and unsettled stage of the plantation. Clearly tenants could move from one estate to another in search of better conditions.

There is considerable evidence, particularly in the years before 1622, for the sale of leaseholds and tenant mobility. The fate of John Brownlow, most of whose tenants had left him by 1613 'by reason of the hardness of the country',[154] was exceptional in our area as was the movement of many tenants from Sir James Hamilton's estate in Cavan when he sold it, who returned to 'dwell in the Clandeboyes from whence they came',[155] but the movement of individual tenants was not. On Fishe's estate in Loughtee, for example, it was noted in 1622 that 'many of the first leases had been passed over from one party to another' with covenants of building and planting not performed.[156] There is a case of a Cavan tenant moving to the new Leitrim plantation in 1623.[157] It seems that movement westward from Armagh was not uncommon. Two tenants of Sir John Davies in Orior had, by 1622, 'gone to Fermanagh'.[158] Two of Stanhowe's tenants had, by this time, moved

153 Above, 81, 86, 100.
154 *Hastings MSS,* iv, 174.
155 BL, Add. MS 4756, fol. 100.
156 Ibid., fol. 102.
157 Above, 133.
158 NLI, Rich Papers, MS 8014/9.

to Dungannon and Benburb.[159] Alternately, Matthew Russell moved from County Londonderry to Armagh.[160] There was doubtless some competition for tenants in the earlier years of the colony.

The British tenants on English proportions were predominantly English, those of Scottish lands predominantly Scots. However, as in Londonderry, occasional Welsh names and occasional ex-soldiers also appear. There were Scots and English on the servitors' lands in Armagh. There were also clerical tenants in both counties.[161] In 1617 Sir Hugh Culme, servitor, became a tenant for twenty-one years, to John Fishe in Loughtee.[162] He, along with other tenants on this estate who were, however, not originally landowners, subsequently acquired the ownership of parts of it. Rev. James Matchett, who sold his proportion in Oneilland, was, for a time, a tenant to Richard Rolleston in the same barony.[163] There were also absentee tenants holding speculative leases for example, Andrew Hamlin, Richard Fitzsimonds, and John Tench who held under the archbishop of Armagh.[164] Tench, who was from Drogheda, acquired a lease of a townland on Rolleston's estate in August 1615 leased by Rolleston in February 1612 to a tenant who three years later sold it to another who, in turn, had sold it to Tench.[165] Rolleston in 1621 lost a suit against Tench for possession of the land on which there was a mill.[166] Tench let the land to Irish occupiers of the O'Quinn family.[167]

As in Londonderry the smaller occupants, cottagers and tradesmen, were a very numerous group found on all estates. A wide variety of occupations were represented and they usually also had small areas of land. In Brownlow's village of Lurgan, for example, there were butchers, coopers, joiners, carpenters, turners, masons, shoemakers, tanners, blacksmiths, weavers, tailors, as well as those defined as labourers, yeomen, and husbandmen.[168] Such people were also found living in the countryside, as on the Brownlow estate also,[169] but they were more generally village dwelling. Akin to these were the British sub-tenants or undertenants and servants to whom many freeholders and leaseholders sub-let pieces of land or who were employed by them in manual capacities.

[159] Ibid., MS 8014/8: commissioners' notes on Obbyns, Stanhowe, and Annesley.
[160] Above, 237.
[161] Below, 317.
[162] *Inq. cancel. Hib. repert.*, ii, Cavan (26) Chas I.
[163] NAI, Chancery salvage, Z.23.
[164] Below, 355, 364.
[165] *Inq. cancel. Hib. repert.*, ii, Armagh (7) Chas I.
[166] NAI, Repertories to the decrees of chancery, i, 329.
[167] *Inq. cancel. Hib. repert.*, ii, Armagh (7) Chas I.
[168] TNA, Manchester papers, 30/15/2/183.
[169] Ibid.

The existence of native Irish tenants holding either directly from British landlords or as sub-tenants and being more numerous than the settler population was quite general. These were willing, or obliged, to pay rents approximately twice as large as the British, who resented their competition. The British tenants on Butler's estate in Cavan, for example, protested in 1622 that they could get 'noe reasonable bargains till the Irish be removed'.[170] Conversely, if more casuistically, the servitors, who were empowered to take Irish tenants, complained in 1611 that they had suffered through the retention of the natives on undertakers' land.

The retention of the Irish as tenants on undertakers' lands (subject in theory to regulation after 1628) was largely an economic necessity. Their presence posed a threat to the colony which, perhaps, became exacerbated as their status declined. However, it is also clear that a relationship grew up, however ambiguously based, between some British and Irish residents.[171]

The operation of the manorial system remains one of the more elusive topics in this period. It is clear, however, that manor court functioned regularly on the estates of Trinity College and the archbishopric,[172] for both of which competent seneschals were appointed. Their general existence can be suggested from the requirement in leases that tenants should do suit of court. Evidence for the existence of courts for a number of manors in Cavan and Armagh comes from the deposition of March 1642[173] of Stephen Allen, king's attorney in Ulster since 1617,[174] and who in 1641 lived in Cavan of which he was sovereign and recorder. Amongst his losses claimed – he did not assess their values – were the seneschalships of four manors in Cavan: those of Butler, Taylor, Greenham and Moynes, and of four in Armagh: those of Brownlow, Henry Cope, Sacheverall and Lord Mountnorris.[175]

Presumably conventions in the relations of landlords and tenants were also being built up or had been imported from England and Scotland. Evidence for these, however, can only be gleaned from specific instances. A rather interesting dispute involving Trinity College in which tenant right was pleaded has been examined elsewhere.[176] As has been seen above, appeal to the courts by both tenants and landlords was not uncommon when infringement of conditions was claimed.

170 BL, Add. MS 4756, fol. 102v.

171 Above, 221–2.

172 Below, 357, 361, 366.

173 TCD, MS 832, ff 173–4, 175–7.

174 Hughes, *Patentee Officers*, 2. He was involved in a protracted and, it would seem discreditable, suit about lands in Fermanagh (*CSPI, 1625–32,* 464, 533, 578, 612).

175 Ibid. In a catalogue of books and papers in the State Paper Room, Dublin Castle, published in 1819 six manor courts in Armagh and thirteen in Cavan are referred to (*Irish Record Commissioners Report, 1816–20,* 235).

176 Below, 340–41.

3. The effect on the landscape

The physical impact of the settlers on the landscape through enclosure, drainage, timber destruction and the like remains largely obscure. The physical boundaries of property in the pre-plantation period owed little or nothing to modern enclosure. Boundaries were established in terms of traditional landmarks, physical features and the like, and boundaries were a recurring preoccupation. The absence of quantitative recordings of areas, acreage surveys, and estate maps with a practical and legal application, exacerbated the problem. The maintenance of the traditional boundaries and, where new ones had to be established, the using of traditional techniques, thus had a special importance. Before the plantation the demarcation of land for forts followed such methods. In 1605, for example, an inquiry was carried out into the mears and bounds of the lands for the fort at Mountnorris, with reference to the intention of having the lands measured.[177] The plantation maps of 1609 had little or no value as a quantitative survey hence the importance of local inquiries, perambulations, and inquisitions throughout our period.

As to enclosure, there was some government interest in this, but it was not stipulated in the conditions of plantation. In 1608 Chichester expected the colonists to be 'tied ... to enclose and manure the land in a civil fashion',[178] and in 1610 it was thought they should be given four years to perform, *inter alia*, the enclosure 'with strong ditches and quickset a meet proportion of their land after the manner of England.[179]

The problem for incoming settlers was complicated by unfamiliarity with Gaelic place names,[180] and must have made for a dependence on the co-operation of the native inhabitants. A British tenant to the archbishop of Armagh, finding difficulty about the size of his tenancy, was advised to 'learne of the natives the confines of the territories and sesiages in every baliebo'.[181] It is not surprising that there was much altercation about ownership of small areas in the early years of the plantation: small areas could easily become absorbed into neighbouring estates.

Indistinctness of boundaries, facilitating dispute and encroachment, was only progressively removed by successive regrants based on the evidence of inquisition and increasing familiarity with the terrain. From this viewpoint

177 Marsh's Library, Dublin, MS Z4.2.6, 4.

178 *CSPI, 1608–10*, 64.

179 Ibid., 356.

180 It may seem at first sight surprising that there was no massive re-naming of places with more appropriate British titles. However, when it is considered that most of the Gaelic names were recorded by inquisition and map before the plantation and afterwards listed in the settlers' patents, to change them would have involved considerable trouble and uncertainty.

181 Below, 368.

the value of the new patents lies in the increasing definition of ownership they embodied. The later patents usually included a listing of sub-denominational as well as townland names. In the almost general absence of maps[182] the sworn recording and defining of mears and bounds by written description had a special importance.[183] Concern with the erection and maintenance of boundaries with marks and otherwise is not easily documented, but we see from a settlement made of the Castledillon estate in Armagh in 1631 that it was a matter of lively interest.[184]

At government level in the 1630s the need was felt to give the traditional boundaries a more permanent definition. In 1637 Wentworth issued a proclamation 'for the avoiding of the law suites concerning ... meares and bounds'.[185] It stated that through lack of enclosures encroachments took place, and facilitated the issuing of commissions of perambulation to mark out bounds. This done, a ditch four feet deep and five broad with two rows of quicksets should be made and kept in repair on penalty of punishment.

There is some evidence that this kind of enclosure of the outward bounds of estates or farms was taking place in our area even before 1637. On the archbishop of Armagh's estate some such boundary enclosure was carried out by the archbishop himself.[186] It is apparent also from the manor court rolls of the archbishopric that it was the policy of the estate that boundaries of holdings should be so defined, and it is evident from other

[182] This is not to say that there was not some estate-mapping and land-surveying done in Armagh and Cavan in our period, though there was nothing to compare at all with Raven's work in Londonderry. It will be seen below that Raven did some work for the archbishop of Armagh in the 1620s and that Trinity College required surveys to be made by its seneschal, Woodhouse. Individual owners probably felt less need for land surveys, though there is reference to a 'surveyor' being employed with regard to disputed lands near Killashandra in our period (NAI, Chancery salvage, D.9).

[183] One revealing instance comes to light from Armagh in 1617 when there was a dispute about the ownership of a townland and other parcels in Orior between Capt. Smith and Lord Moore. They appealed to the lord deputy who appointed Sir Toby Caulfeild and Sir Dudley Norton, a long-standing government official, to adjudicate. They decided that the land should be divided and the division was made under Caulfeild's supervision in the presence of Smith and Moore's agent and with the assistance of 'divers of the country' including Art McBaron O'Neill. The manner of mearing and bounding is instructive of the condition of the countryside and the methods of the time: 'Beginning at the usual foord where now a bridge is over the river in the tradeway to the Newry from Dundalke called the fower Myle Water, about two stones cast from the river, did drive a stake into the ground upon a ridge of a hill and soe driving another stake upon a right line by comerture from the first stake to a heap of stones called Firrbreage, and soe as a man's eie will direct upon a right line through a corner of a wood every eight or tenn score (*sic*) or thereabouts driving stakes till you come to a rocky mountain called the ffadd to the height of the mountain which seemeth lyke a saddle from the first rocks called Firrbreage, to w'ch all parties agreed' (Marsh's Library, Dublin, MS Z4.2.6, 537–8).

[184] Armagh Public Library, Castle Dillon Papers.

[185] Steele, *Proclamations*, ii, 36; *DKRI*, 22, 36.

[186] Below, 372.

sources that some were being so defined.[187] So far as the proclamation of 1637 is concerned, there is only one instance of its effect in our area. In a chancery suit involving lands in Cavan it was pleaded that an Old English tenant had not 'enclosed, fenced, ditched, or quicksett the outward bounds and mears of the said lands' as required by the act of state.[188]

Enclosure stipulations for tenants appear in some – though not all – of the small number of surviving leases. A lease of Sir Patrick Acheson, *c.* 1635, of lands in Cavan[189] embodied specific instructions which may also have featured in Acheson leases in Armagh. The tenant undertook to make every year:

> forty perches of good and sufficient ditches sett with the like quicksets … upon the firme ground and upon the bogge … with sallowe and such other quicksets as will thereupon best prosper … according to the manner … used in England until the [lands] be fully enclosed and ditched about and divided into convenient closes and enclosures.

He should also plant forty young oaks or ashe trees on the lands and ditches every year, and plant within seven years two gardens and orchards enclosed with a ditch 'sett with the quickesetts of white thorn and oake, ashe and crabbtrees'. The enclosure stipulations of the archbishopric of Armagh and of Trinity College have been examined elsewhere[190] and an attempt made to assess their effect.

Apart from such instances it is very difficult to present a general picture. There were even enclosed fragments before the plantation. Thus some land attached to Cavan castle was described as '14 acres enclosed by a ditch'.[191] The most that can be said is that there is some evidence of both estate and farm enclosure and also of field enclosure near settlements,[192] but that clearly it has to be stressed that there was no widespread enclosure movement.[193]

187 Below, 372.
188 NAI, Chancery salvage, K.68.
189 NAI, Deeds, wills and instruments … post mortem, vol. 25, 254–65.
190 Below, 327–8, 339–40, 357, 372.
191 *CPRI, Jas I*, 313.
192 A number of instances have been noted in the discussion of government surveys (see above, 147, 154). Some of these references are not very specific, as in the case of Sir Thomas Waldron of Loughtee who was stated in 1622 to have 'very good tillage, inclosures, and store of English cattle' (BL, Add. MS 4756, ff 101v–2). Henry Hickfield (or Hacklefield), a Cavan landowner, in a deposition concerning the 1641 rising referred to the loss of land held in lease 'being ditched and built on' (TCD, MS 833, ff 9–9v).
193 The only reference from official sources at the end of our period comes from the Book of Survey and Distribution for Cavan (230) where, in Clanmahon barony, an area of almost five profitable acres is referred to as 'Calves close', and this is also marked on the Down survey map.

The deletion of woods in Londonderry has been examined by Professor Moody.[194] Evidence for this in Armagh and Cavan is not generally forthcoming, though an attempt has been made elsewhere to examine it with regard to the estates of the archbishopric of Armagh and of Trinity College.[195] However, that the cutting of timber was fairly widespread in north Armagh would emerge from an interesting proposal put forward by an Oneilland undertaker, then in financial difficulties, in 1618.

In 1618 Rev. Richard Rolleston presented the king with a scheme for setting up sawmills in Ulster, which was received enthusiastically. It was stated that he had

> latelie found out a readye waye ... to furnish as well the undertakers as all others desirous to buylde in that kingdom with Sawen boards and tymber in more plenefull manner and att a more easye rate than heretofore hath been used, by erectinge of sawemilles for that purpose going with winde or water, a thinge not put in practise before in anye of our kingdoms yet seaming to bee verye necessary to that plantation in generall and hurtfull to none in particular.[196]

Accordingly the king directed that Rolleston should receive by patent for twenty-one years the sole right to set up such mills in any part of Ireland, provided he began to do so within two years, at a yearly rent of £20 Ir., to be remitted for the first two years. He took out his patent on 17 January 1619.[197] Such an application of power to timber processing was quite revolutionary for the British isles, although saw mills had been in use on the continent since the fifteenth century.[198] There is, however, no evidence that Rolleston exploited his grant. However, it was probably in their building and in the mobilisation of building skills that the settlers made the greatest visible effect on the landscape.

4. Fairs and markets

On the eve of the plantation a government-recognised network of fairs and markets did not exist in Ulster. A Tuesday market, to be held at Armagh, was granted to Hugh O'Neill in 1587[199] and in 1603 a grant of a weekly market at Cavan was made to John Bingley, a member of a well-known servitor

194 Moody, *Londonderry Plantation*, 113–14, 143, 146, 344, 362.
195 Below, 344–5, 346–7, 373–4.
196 James I to St. John, 21 September 1618 (BL, Add. MS 4756, ff 446v–7).
197 *CPRI, Jas I*, 412.
198 E. McCracken, 'The Irish timber trade in the seventeenth century', *Irish Forestry*, vol. xxi, no. 1, 7–20.
199 Armagh Public Library, Lodge MSS, G.111.23, 5.

family,[200] but these were the only strictly recognised facilities of this kind in either county. However, there were fairs and markets in Cavan at any rate, dating, no doubt, from far back in the Gaelic tradition, and these were recorded in the Ulster survey of 1608.[201] There was an annual fair and a weekly market at Cavan and six other annual fairs throughout the county.[202]

In a predominantly rural environment such facilities assume a special importance, enabling the exchange or sale of commodities in a competitive environment. At the same time the fair, if not the market which was held after very short intervals, provided scope for peripheral activities, entertainment and the like. Furthermore a market or fair with its temporary courts – courts of pie-powder – and public character may well have made for more orderly or honourable transacting of business. To the person or institution possessing the privilege a fair or market could be a valuable asset, providing income from dues. By Stuart times such institutions in England had a long background of use and development.[203]

Fairs also with their various social facets were deeply rooted in the Irish tradition.[204] To English government in Ireland such gatherings, unsupervised and unregulated, constituted a threat of disorder and the attempt was made to establish a network of fairs and markets in corporate towns or under the eye of planter settlements. Edmund Spenser pointed to the 'many mischiefs that have been both practiced and wrought' as a result of the traditional public assemblies, and urged the establishing of market towns 'by reason that people repairing often thither for their needs will daily see and learn civil manners of the better sort'. Private sales – 'secret bargains amongst themselves' – should be prohibited, buying and selling only to take place in

> some open market ... for now when anyone hath stolen a cow or garran he may secretly sell it in the county without privity of any, whereas if he brought it to a market town it would perhaps be known and the thief discovered.[205]

The establishment of fairs and markets would thus not only serve to curb Irish unrest, but also make for the security of property. A network of fairs

200 Marsh's Library, Dublin, MS Z4.2.6, 188.
201 J. Hogan (ed.), 'Survey of the escheated counties in Ulster, 1608', *Anal. Hib.*, iii, 151–218.
202 Ibid., 205–8.
203 Ministry of Agriculture & Fisheries, *Report on markets and fairs in England and Wales:* pt 1 – general review (London, 1927).
204 E. O'Curry, *On the manners and customs of the ancient Irish*, (1873) vol. i, ccliii–cclxi; E.E. Evans, *Irish Folk Ways* (London, 1957), 254.
205 Morley, *Ireland*, 116, 206–7.

and markets, not unexpectedly, accompanied the plantation in Ulster which was expanded and adjusted in ensuing years.

In Armagh by the 1630s thirteen centres for fairs and markets[206] had been established. The markets were weekly and the fairs varied from being quarterly to annual, usually to continue for two or three days. They were more densely distributed in the areas of British occupation, there being only one centre, created in 1629, for the whole area under Sir Turlogh McHenry O'Neill's control. It was usual for fairs to be held on saints' days, but grants always provided that they should not take place on Sundays. The patentee might hold a court of pie-powder and collect the 'usual tolls'. At Tandragee the date of a market was rearranged to a more suitable day. In May 1612 Sir Oliver St. John acquired the right to hold a Thursday market (as well as fairs) there.[207] This was surrendered in October, a new patent altering the day to Wednesday being granted in the following January.[208]

These markets and fairs were held in free and common soccage the rents varying from 5/- Ir. to £1 Ir., depending on the number that might be held in any year. The archbishop of Armagh, who had the right to hold fairs and markets in Armagh, paid no rent for the privilege though, for a grant of a market and annual fair at Tynan which he received in 1616, 13/4 Ir. in rent was required.[209] The corporation of Charlemont received a Tuesday market and a fair on May 1 and 2 by charter in 1613 without rent[210] though Toby Caulfeild, who was empowered in 1622 to hold a fair there on August 5 and a Wednesday market, paid a rent of £1.[211] Annesley was the only individual landowner in the county to acquire a fair free of rent. This was in 1618 in addition to the facilities already granted to him in 1612, with a rent charge, to be held at Mountnorris.[212] In 1622 it was found that the archbishop – who held his lands in free alms – had been in arrears with his rent for the fair at Tynan.[213] The volume of business attracted by any of these fairs and markets up to 1641 remains obscure. Surviving landlords' rentals make no reference to income from market dues or courts. It is only in 1659 that we find that the market and fairs of Lurgan, granted to the Brownlow family, were let to a middleman at £4 rent per annum.[214]

[206] NAI, Lodge, Records of the rolls, xiv, 7–9.
[207] *CPRI, Jas I*, 226.
[208] Ibid., 240.
[209] Armagh Public Library, Lodge MSS, G.111.23, 5, 7.
[210] Ibid., 5.
[211] Ibid.
[212] Ibid., 7; *CPRI, Jas I*, 234, 407.
[213] NLI, Rich Papers, MS 8014/4: doubtful rents and arrears, 1620, Ulster.
[214] Armagh Museum, Brownlow Rentals, 1659.

The provision of market facilities in Cavan was similar to Armagh. By 1631 11 places had been designated as market centres in the county.[215] As in Armagh these grants were made almost exclusively to British settlers or to corporate towns. However, two Old English landowners Gerald Fleming in Clankee and Edward Dowdall, and one Irishman also received the privilege. The Irish grantee was Brian McConnell of Drumdoon. McConnell was a footman in the royal army on whose behalf, in a dispute over land with the bishop of Kilmore, a king's letter was written to Falkland in 1629.[216] In February 1630 he was granted a patent for fairs and markets at Drumdoon.[217] Rents in Cavan ranged from 10/- to £2. Ir. No grant was made to the bishop in this county where church lands were less extensive than in Armagh.

The inquiries held in Cavan in 1629 as a result of the scheme for the regranting of undertakers' estates made, in some cases, recommendations about fairs and markets. Thus for the Hamilton estate in Tullyhunco it was recommended that 'it is and wilbe verie fitt and convenient for the inhabitants thereabouts and also the great furtherance of the plantation' that the dates of fairs and markets at Killashandra should be altered. Scrabby in the same estate was recommended as a market centre,

> there not being anie fayres or markets kept upon anie of these days or times at anie towne or place within eight mylls distance [the estimated distance of Killashandra] of the said town of Scrabagh.[218]

The new patent to Sir Francis Hamilton in 1631 embodied recognition of both recommendations.[219] A similar recommendation for a new market centre on the Moynes estate in Loughtee[220] was not, however, given effect. A change of date for one of the fairs held at Hansborough on the estate of John Hamilton in Clankee, also recommended in 1629,[221] was made in his patent of that year.[222] Such local concern with marketing facilities reflects the extent to which the plantation was becoming established.

With regard to the town of Cavan a dispute arose between the claimant under Bingley's patent of 1603 and the corporation which also received by

215 NAI, Lodge, Records of the rolls, xiv, 18–21. In the case of Killashandra, Lodge entered as a different place a grant under an alternative name.
216 NAI, Connell Papers, D19498.
217 Ibid., D19499.
218 *Inq. cancel. Hib. repert.*, ii, Cavan (24) Chas I.
219 NAI, Lodge, Records of the rolls, xiv, 18–21.
220 *Inq. cancel. Hib. repert.*, ii, Cavan (23) Chas I.
221 Ibid., (18) Chas I.
222 NAI, Lodge, Records of the rolls, xiv, 18–21.

charter in 1610 the right to hold a weekly market as well as fairs. The dispute came to a head with a chancery suit in 1624.[223] In 1622 it had been found that the burgesses had failed to pay one year's rent of 10/- for a market and two fairs.[224] The suit in 1624 offers more explanation, though the evidence surviving is only the answer of the portreeves of the town to a bill of Sir Garret Moore, Viscount Drogheda. It seems that, after 1603, Bingley had conveyed his patent to Moore, then seneschal of the county, and that he claimed the tolls of the weekly market to the exclusion of the rights of the corporation. The portreeves asserted that, in 1616, Moore had sent ten soldiers of his command to the town to collect 'in forcible manner' market tolls.[225] The dispute appears to have been unresolved – Bingley's patent being presumably overlooked when the charter was drafted – and members of the Moore family reasserted their claim as late as 1640.[226] Another dispute, also brought into chancery, concerned the fairs and markets at Killashandra, which dragged on from 1614 to 1625 or later, but it was principally concerned with the ownership of the townland in which the fairs took place.[227] Fairs and markets had thus become a valuable privilege before the end of the first generation of plantation.

The plantation thus brought a system of fairs and markets. These served the needs of the British population, but were also designed to bring the native inhabitants into civilising contact with British-conducted institutions. That they should be conducted under planter supervision had thus a special importance and may account for so few being granted to native landowners. As early as 1612 Sir John Davies reported enthusiastically about

> the care and course that hath been taken to make civil commerce and intercourse between the subjects newly reformed and brought under obedience by granting markets and fairs to be holden in their countries.[228]

Although at the time of the commission for defective titles, during Wentworth's administration, the resumption of these privileges was considered[229] they remained in private or institutional ownership as originally granted.

223 NAI, Chancery salvage, 2B.30.120, no. 96.
224 NLI, Rich Papers, 8013/4: doubtful rents and arrears, 1620, Ulster.
225 NAI, Chancery salvage, 2B.30.120, no. 96.
226 *Inq. cancel. Hib. repert.*, ii, Cavan (68) Chas I.
227 NAI, Chancery salvage, D9; 2B.80.120, no. 126; NAI, Repertories to the decrees of chancery, 30.
228 Morley, *Ireland*, 341.
229 TNA, SP 63/257, fol. 144 (*CSPI, 1633–47*, 228).

CHAPTER 10

The Church

1. Initial problems and reorganisation

The close relation between the establishing of a Protestant colony in Ulster and the effective inauguration of Protestantism there was evident from the planning stage of the colony. The aim of this chapter is to examine the setting up and operation of the church structure in Armagh and Cavan. Particular reference is made to financial aspects, and to the relationship between clergy and lay proprietors.

One of the five general principles of the project was that every proportion should be made a parish and a parish church erected. Incumbents should be endowed with glebe proportionate to the size of the estate, at the rate of sixty acres in every 1,000, and also receive the tithes.[1] A complete re-drawing of parish boundaries on logical principles was thus envisaged. Some of the settlers were also to have an influence in the choice of clergy in the church thus newly constituted. The revised articles of plantation stated that the principal undertaker within each precinct or barony should be granted one advowson.[2]

In March the 1609 the plantation commissioners were required to investigate whether one or more proportions were fit to be made a parish, and empowered to establish parish boundaries accordingly, retaining the old limits 'as far forth as it may stand with the plantation.'[3] They should also ensure that glebe assignments were close to the parish churches, and that a clause be inserted in the patents granting glebe land to forbid any alienation for longer than in incumbency.[4] At the end of June the commissioners indicated that they would prefer not to retain the old parochial system; however, in the reorganisation of the ecclesiastical geography, difficulties and delays were encountered.[5]

The impact of the reformation in Ulster had previously been slight. Some Protestant appointments had been made in the sixteenth century, but they can hardly have been rewarding in jurisdictional or financial terms.

1 'Ulster plantation papers', no. 74, *Anal. Hib.*, viii.
2 Moody, 'The revised articles', *BIHR*, xii, 178–83.
3 *CSPI, 1608–10*, 182.
4 *Cal. Carew MSS, 1603–24*, 45–6; Marsh's Library, Dublin, MS Z4.2.6, 130.
5 The sponsorship of towns and schools should be compared.

Thus Adam Loftus, appointed in 1562 archbishop of Armagh, a see only partly in Ulster, accepted translation to Dublin in 1567.[6] Owen Wood, a Welshman appointed dean of Armagh *c.* 1588, quickly acquired the archdeaconry of Meath and other benefices and, in 1601, was presented to a rectory in Wiltshire.[7] In 1605 the lord deputy and council, after a journey to Ulster, reported that the cathedral church in Armagh was 'much ruined and fallen into decay', and that there were a number of priests there 'all ordained by foreign authority'. To redress such 'enormities' they instructed the negligent archbishop, Henry Ussher, a man it was noted capable of speaking Irish, to install a minister there forthwith, and to reside and preach in Armagh 'every summer season'.[8]

A similar situation pertained in Kilmore. After the death of the government-supporting bishop, Edmund Nugent, *c.* 1550, the bishopric remained vacant until the appointment of John Garvey under Perrot in 1585. Garvey retained his archdeaconry of Meath and deanery of Christchurch, Dublin *in commendam*, becoming primate in 1590.[9] No further vacancy occurred until 1604 when the rector of Trim, Robert Draper, reputedly knowing the district, the people, and the Irish language, was appointed to both Kilmore and Ardagh, retaining his rectory *in commendam*.[10] In 1607 Sir John Davies reported that there was no 'divine service or sermon' to be heard within either of his dioceses, that the churches were in disrepair, his clergy 'barbarous' and he willing 'to make benefit out of their insufficiency, according to the proverb ... that an Irish priest is better than an milch cow'.[11] There was, however, some slight tradition of clerical conformity in Kilmore, and in this Cavan may have been unique among the six subsequently escheated counties.[12]

However, any regularised network of Protestant incumbents succeeded rather than preceded the advent of colonists.[13] In 1608 Chichester stated that the churches throughout Ulster generally were

> so defaced, and the glebe and bishops' lands so obscured, that all is confused and out of order, as if it were in a wilderness where neither Christianity nor Religion was ever heard of,

6 Leslie, *Armagh clergy*, 5.
7 Ibid., 11–12.
8 *CSPI, 1603–6*, 317.
9 NLI, Canon J.B. Leslie, biographical succession list of Kilmore diocese, MS 2685 (typescript), 7.
10 Ibid., 8.
11 Morley, *Ireland*, 377–8.
12 Clerical members of the families of O'Gowan or Smith, and Brady, appear as accepting English authority from the mid-sixteenth century (Cal. fiants Ir., Edw vi, no. 15; Cal. fiants Ir., Eliz., nos. 544, 4812; *CPRI, Eliz.*, 277–8; NAI, Chancery salvage, H.65; NLI, MS 2685, 198).
13 We have seen already that the effective dissolution of the monasteries in plantation Ulster (with the exception of those in Cavan) had also to await the seventeenth century.

and urged that immediate attention should be paid to the re-ordering and settling of the church and clergy.[14] The planning of the colony and the re-organisation of the church thus went hand in hand,[15] though many problems which arose in the succeeding thirty years sprang from the fact that no thoroughly radical reconstruction was affected.

Some brief outline of the parochial system in Armagh and Cavan on the eve of plantation must be given. In the general enquiry of 1608,[16] and again in 1609,[17] the names of the traditional parishes and how they were appropriated were recorded. The origins of these parishes, in many cases, appear to have been associated with the distribution of termon and erenach lands.[18] How confused the parochial system had become is evident from the divergence of the evidence of 1608 and 1609. For County Armagh the former source lists 12 parish churches and 4 chapels of ease.[19] The 1609 inquisition reveals 15 parishes.[20] The Book of Survey and Distribution shows Armagh as falling into 17 parishes, some of which were only partly in the county, and 2, Seagoe and Shankill, were in the diocese of Dromore.[21] The same difficulty exists for Cavan. The inquisition of 1608 lists 24 parish churches and 10 chapels.[22] From the 1609 inquisition the names of 28 parishes, and 4 chapels are derived.[23] The Book of Survey and Distribution shows the county as comprising 34 parishes in whole or in part.[24] Since the evidence of visitation returns, especially that of 1622, is discussed in this chapter, consideration is confined to those parishes or union of parishes reported on in these returns: 15 in Armagh and 23 in Cavan.[25]

With the plantation, four advowsons, two in Armagh and two in Cavan, were granted to leading settlers. Sir Anthony Cope received the advowson of Shankill rectory[26] and Sir George Douglas the advowson of the vicarage of Loughilly.[27] In Cavan Lord Aubigny received the advowson of the rectory

14 'Ulster plantation papers', no. 75, *Anal. Hib.*, viii; *CSPI, 1608–10*, 64.
15 For Hill the treatment of the church was a 'complicated question' given only passing attention (Hill, *Plantation*, 88).
16 Hogan (ed.), 'Survey … 1608', *Anal. Hib.*, iii, 151–218.
17 *Inq. cancel. Hib. repert.*, ii, App.
18 An examination of the maps of 1609 shows many of the parish churches as located within these lands. On the origins of parishes in Ireland see J. Otway-Ruthven, 'Parochial development in the rural deanery of Skreen', *JRSAI*, vol. 94, pt 2 (1964), 111–22.
19 Hogan (ed.), 'Survey … 1608', *Anal. Hib.*, iii, 213–18.
20 *Inq. cancel. Hib. repert.*, ii, App.
21 NAI, Books of Survey and Distribution.
22 Hogan (ed.), 'Survey … 1608', *Anal. Hib.*, iii, 204–13.
23 *Inq. cancel. Hib. repert.*, ii, App.
24 NAI, Books of Survey and Distribution.
25 Below, 297–304.
26 *CPRI, Jas I*, 167. This advowson might more appropriately have been granted to Brownlow.
27 Ibid., 164.

of Drumgoon (or Drumdoon),[28] and Sir Alexander Hamilton received that of the vicarage of Killashandra.[29]

Douglas did not receive the advowson of Loughilly rectory because it was already impropriate. The problem of impropriations was, of course, one in no way confined to Ulster.[30] These could be held by both clergy and laity – by the latter as a result of monastic dissolutions. Problems arising from impropriations will be discussed below. It is here necessary to outline the state of impropriations in our area. In Armagh more impropriations were in clerical hands than in lay, while in Cavan the reverse obtained.

In Armagh the prior of the vicars choral of Culdees was rector of five parishes and vicar of one. The dean was traditional rector or parson of four parishes (including Loughilly) and vicar of two, as well as having also rights of titles from some smaller areas.[31] These are the two larges ecclesiastic impropriators. The archbishop was also rector of the parish of Armagh.[32] Lay-held impropriations were less numerous. The grantee of the abbey of St.Peter and St. Paul, Caulfeild, had a number of impropriations, and the grantee of the monastery of Killeavy appears also to have had such rights.[33]

In Cavan the impropriations were predominantly in lay hands, and also predominantly in the hands of Old English catholics. Eleven rectories impropriate to the abbey of Fore had been in Nugent hands since 1567 in leasehold;[34] in 1613 Richard Nugent, baron of Delvin received an outright grant of the monastery and its rectories.[35] To the monastery at Kells, County Meath, some seven rectories in Cavan had belonged. These were leased to Gerald Fleming under Elizabeth,[36] and he received an outright grant in 1608.[37] The monastery of Drumlahen, which we have seen in speculators' hands at the end of the sixteenth century,[38] was owned by Sir James Dillon in this period. Although in the earliest lease of it, made in 1571, two rectories, Drumlahen and Killashandra, were granted,[39] and although the latest patent, in 1604, does not refer (as calendared) to rectories

28 *Inq. cancel. Hib. repert.*, ii, Cavan (19) Chas I.

29 Ibid., (24) Chas I.

30 For a discussion of this and other problems affecting the reformative church in England at this time see C. Hill, *Economic problems of the church from archbishop Whitgift to the long parliament* (Oxford 1956), *passim*.

31 This is based on the inquisition of 1609 regarding the escheated land in Armagh (*Inq. cancel. Hib. repert.*, ii, App.).

32 'Chichester Letter-Book', no. 14, *Anal. Hib.*, viii. The chancellor and treasurer of the diocese also had some impropriations.

33 *CSPI, 1611–14*, 280–81.

34 Above, 36–7.

35 *CPRI, Jas I*, 238.

36 Cal. fiants Ir., Eliz., no. 4956.

37 Above, 36–7.

38 Above, 36.

39 Cal. fiants Ir., Eliz., no. 1681; above, 37.

specifically,[40] the 1609 inquisition ascribes three rectories, including the two above mentioned, to it,[41] and this is confirmed by the 1622 visitation return.[42] Hence at the time of plantation Hamilton, like Douglas in Armagh, could receive only the advowson of the vicarage of Killashandra. Clearly almost all the Cavan rectories at this time were in lay hands. Almost all the vicarages, however, were collative by the bishop. Ecclesiastical impropriations in Cavan were few. The bishop of Kilmore was rector of the parish of Tomregan; he also had the collation of (or right of presentation to) the rectory and vicarage of Drumgoon.[43] The presentation to this parish was granted to a settler at the plantation.[44] We will examine below the government's subsequent attitude to impropriations, but we must now examine how the church was endowed with land, as the plan stipulated.

Here the government was presented with a quandary. It was important that the clergy should be resident close to their churches, i.e. that their glebe land and their churches should be in close proximity. The task would probably have been simplified had the parish clergy already had glebe land because they would doubtless have retained it as the bishops did their mensal land. But it is clear that in Armagh and Cavan, at any rate, glebe was non-existent or negligible. In an abstract of the state of landownership in Armagh in 1610, thirteen parishes are listed of which ten were without glebe, and the remaining three had only very small portions.[45] An inquiry in 1588 into the values of church livings in Cavan also suggests that they cannot have had much glebe. Most livings returned sums varying from £6 to £10 per annum, two had £12, and six ranged from £1 to £3.[46]

The problem the Dublin government had to resolve at the beginning of 1610 was whether to accept the administrative obligation of the project and redraw parish boundaries and allocate glebe as there instructed, or else to allow the existing parochial boundaries, irrational though they might now be, to continue. By January 29 Chichester had concluded that a re-structuring was hardly practicable. He approached the problem in a mood which was an apparent blend of realism and confusion. It would be difficult

> to erect new parishes before the country is better peopled and settled, for … they [would] not get the old churches rebuilt in any convenient time …[47]

40 *CPRI, Jas I*, 2–3.
41 *Inq. cancel. Hib. repert.*, ii, App.
42 TCD, MS 550, 134–65; Armagh Archiepiscopal Registry, B.1b. no. 193, 136–51.
43 *Inq. cancel. Hib. repert.*, ii, App. (1609 inquisition concerning escheated lands in Cavan).
44 Above, 287–8.
45 *CSPI, 1608–10*, 407.
46 NAI, Exchequer inquisitions, Ulster, Cavan, (3) Eliz., 4–6.
47 *CSPI, 1608–10*, 368.

Clearly he did not appreciate that if new parishes were to be created to coincide with settlers' estates new churches should be built[48] and the old ones deserted.

He had, however, an alternative plan. The bishops were at this time pressing their claims to the termon and erenach lands claims to which, as we have seen,[49] Chichester was not wildly sympathetic. On January 27 he recommended to the privy council that the bishops should be granted these lands on condition that, out of them, glebe land should be allocated to the parish churches.[50] This, he felt, would be

> but a small deduction out of the bishops great scopes; for the parishes are very large and few and without this provision the parsons and vicars cannot for the most part have any land within two or three miles of the church, and in some places further off; which is a great inconvenience.

We have seen that many of the old parish churches lay in the termon and erenach lands. In this way the desideratum that the clergy should be able to reside close to their churches could be fulfilled, and land could also be saved to gratify lay interests. If the bishops would not accept this, or the king were inclined to grant them the termon lands *in toto* then, he suggested, they should exchange amounts of termon land close to the churches for compensatory areas of forfeited lay property.[51] By March when a decision on the termon lands had been reached in England no stipulation about glebe allocations appears to have been made.[52]

The result was that glebe was allocated according to the project, but the old parish boundaries and church locations were retained. In the 1630s Bishop Bramhall is said to have told Sir William Parsons, who was surveyor-general in 1610,

> that if all the Jesuits of the church of Rome had conspired together to hinder the propagation of the gospel in Ulster they could not have contrived it more effectually than had been done in these so inconvenient assignments.[53]

48 Above, 284.

49 Above, 6, 8, 11.

50 *CSPI, 1608–10*, 358–9.

51 Ibid.

52 Ibid., 409–11. It was, however, considered proper that some part of the 'great scope of land' allotted to the bishops should be granted to deans and chapters (ibid., 415–6).

53 W.W. Wilkins (ed.), *Memoir of the life and episcopate of Dr. William Bedell* (London, 1862), 52.

However, although the land allotted as glebe was non-ecclesiastical and so, often located at a distance from the parish churches, these endowments enormously increased incumbents' incomes. In Armagh the land so allocated was some 6,561 acres or 2.1 per cent of the total acreage. In Cavan almost 14,000 acres were allocated or about 2.9 per cent of the total acreage.[54] It may be noted that the archbishop received almost 48,000 acres, some 15 per cent, in Armagh and the bishop of Kilmore some 31,785 acres, almost 7 per cent, in Cavan.[55]

Grants of these lands were not, however, immediately made. As in the establishment of towns and schools the administration faltered.[56] Most parishes in Armagh and Kilmore, and it seems in Ulster generally, had not received incumbents before 1612 or 1613, and so the issuing of patents would have been difficult. In many cases, however, the land was being used by neighbouring landowners. Indeed, some of it may have been permanently lost.[57]

In March 1615 one Armagh minister received a king's letter in his favour for the possession of glebe land and impropriate tithes which had been detained from him.[58] On April 1615 a king's letter recommended, without effect, the granting of glebe lands there to the archbishop of Armagh, to be assigned by him to the parishes.[59] In 1617 the government was obliged to take up the problem when a Donegal minister, whose glebe should have been assigned by Trinity College, appealed both to London and Dublin on behalf of himself and the other incumbents on college lands.[60] The consequent allocation of glebe from the college estate in Armagh resulted in prolonged litigation between the college and its tenant, Sir James Carroll.[61] No general conveyance of the glebe was made, though in August 1617 Parsons drew up a list of all the glebe lands throughout the northern

[54] Above, 58–9. See also NLI, Rich Papers, MS 8014/4: Sir William Parsons certificate of glebes in Ulster, 16 September 1622; also BL, Add. MS 4756, fol. 19v. In Londonderry Professor Moody has shown that incumbents received 2.8 per cent of the land (Moody, *Londonderry Plantation*, 455).

[55] Above, 58–9.

[56] In 1611 the Dublin government was instructed by London to effect exchanges of land between the bishops and the clergy to which, it was stated, some of the bishops had agreed. This was afterwards to be confirmed by act of parliament. (*CSPI, 1611–14*, 43).

[57] The *Report of … commissioners on the revenues and condition of the established church (Ireland)* (Dublin, 1868), which provides a parochial survey, appears to indicate this. William Reeves, Memoirs of Tynan, MS volume in Armagh Public Library, unfoliated, indicates this clearly for the parish of Tynan in Armagh.

[58] *CSPI, 1615–25*, 18.

[59] Armagh Archiepiscopal Registry, A.1b.26, Evidences of the see of Armagh, 204; BL, Add. MS 4794, ff 317–7v.

[60] Below, 333.

[61] Below, 334–6.

counties.[62] In August 1619 a king's letter[63] repeated the instructions of April 1615, again without effect.

The government inquiry in 1622 revealed the kind of problems which could arise for incumbents as a result of unclarified titles. The rector of Ballymore in Armagh stated that the had brought a suit before the council for the recovery of glebe land from neighbouring planters, including Lord Moore and Sir Henry Bourchier, and had been ordered to pay them £20 in compensation.[64] The commissioners, in their report, noted the king's bounty in assigning a considerable area from his 'own escheated lands' for glebe and that some of this seemed already to have been misappropriated. They recommended him to grant letters patent to the incumbents of their successors and that the Londoners and the college should also surrender land for glebe. A clause should be inserted in the patents forbidding alienations of 60 acres of glebe nearest to churches for longer than the length of incumbencies, and of the remainder for longer than 21 years.[65]

The 1622 commissioners also recommended that exchanges of glebe be made between the bishops and the incumbents, some of the parishes being

> five or six miles in length whereby the ministers and people cannot without great difficulty come to church especially in winter time and in foule weather.

However, their recommendation was not for total exchanges, but for exchanges of twenty-acre areas whereby the clergy could erect parsonage houses close to their churches.[66] In June 1623 orders based on these recommendations were submitted to the king for approval and implementation.[67]

The reign of James I ended, however, before any patents of glebe were taken out. In May 1626, twenty-one grants of glebe in Tyrone were made.[68] In July the king wrote to Falkland ordering that patents be granted of all Ulster glebe, all the incumbents in each diocese to be allowed take out a joint patent.[69] Grants then followed fairly swiftly, that to Kilmore clergy in

62 Armagh Archiepiscopal Registry, B.3a.382: large roll in Parson's hand.

63 Ibid., Evidences of the see of Armagh, 206–7.

64 TNA, Manchester papers, 30/15/2/182; Armagh Archiepiscopal Registry, B.1b.193, 29–30. The intricacies of this case have been examined above 84–5.

65 These twenty-one year leases to be to British tenants or such Irish as were church-going and the leasings to be made with the advice of the appropriate bishop. A rent of at least 1/- sterling per profitable Irish acre should be required.

66 BL, Add. MS 4756, ff 19v–20, 64.

67 TNA, SP 63/257, ff 65–9v, fairer copy: 70–75v (*CSPI, 1615–25*, 416–9).

68 *CPRI, Chas I*, 176–8. All were in one patent.

69 Armagh Archiepiscopal Registry, A.1b.26, Evidences of the see of Armagh, 109–11; Marsh's Library, Dublin, MS Z4.2.6,588–92.

January 1627[70] and to Armagh clergy in June 1628.[71] The 1622 suggestion about exchanges was not followed through and incumbents were required to build a 'sufficient mansion' of stone, thirty feet long, twenty feet high, and eighteen feet in breadth, upon their glebe.[72]

The government also did not give effect to the recommendation of the project regarding impropriations. It was there laid down that the 'whole tiethes ... of eurie parish' should be allotted to each incumbent.[73] However, impropriations would not have been surrendered without compensation. It is clear from a letter of the privy council to Chichester in August 1611 that the general recovery of impropriations in Ireland was not considered immediately practicable. He was instructed, though, to ensure that impropriators provided for the payment of ministers 'until the convocation of parliament, which will no doubt take measures to reform all great abuses'.[74]

The surrender of impropriations episcopally-held was, however, made conditional to the granting of the termon and erenach lands to the bishops. Thus, in the archbishop of Armagh's patent of 9 September 1610 his impropriations in plantation Ulster were excepted in return for the grant of the termon lands.[75] The bishops were also required to surrender their *tertiam episcopalem*, a right of tithes from all parishes, though the archbishop of Armagh and also the bishop of Kilmore had not enjoyed this right.[76] The excepting of episcopal impropriations was one thing; their surrender was another. It was only as a result of lay pressures in 1612 that episcopal impropriations in Armagh were surrendered. In Cavan, where no such pressures were brought to bear, the bishop appears to have retained the privilege. Thus the 1622 visitation described Tomregan rectory as 'the bishop's mensal'.[77] Furthermore, the Ulster bishops appear to have received the collation or presentation to (i.e the advowsons) of very many of the available appointments. We have seen that a few of these were granted to prominent undertakers. Chichester in January 1610 suggested that the

70 *CPRI, Chas I*, 186–8; NAI, Lodge, Records of the rolls, v, 32–6: dated inaccurately as 1626.

71 Armagh Archiepiscopal Registry, A.1A.11: original patent; *CPRI, Chas I*, 322–5. The Clogher patent was not taken out until February 1632 (*CPRI, Chas I*, 592–3). Similar delays took place with regard to glebes in Londonderry (Moody, *Londonderry Plantation*, 292, 362).

72 *CPRI, Chas I*, 176–8.

73 'Ulster plantation papers', no. 74, *Anal. Hib.*, viii.

74 *CSPI, 1611–14*, 96–7.

75 Abstract in Representative Church Body Library, Dublin, Libr/32, 29. In August 1610 the privy council instructed Chichester to arrange with the archbishop for the surrender of all his impropriations, and to inform them of the amount of compensation to be given (*CSPI, 1608–10*, 489–90). This, however, probably referred to impropriations in the Pale area of the archbishopric as well.

76 'Chichester Letter-Book', nos. 14 & 15, *Anal. Hib.*, viii.

77 Armagh Archiepiscopal Registry, B.1b.193, 150–51.

bishops should have the 'donation of benefices generally throughout their dioceses' except for a 'convenient number' to be granted to Trinity College[78] and some 'principal' benefices in each diocese to be in the patronage of the lord deputy.[79] The distribution of patronage was important because it would be reflected in the kinds of incumbents appointed. Bramhall was subsequently very critical of these decisions which allowed the state little influence in clerical appointments.[80] No surrenders were required in 1610 from other ecclesiastical impropriators, such as the dean or vicars choral of Armagh.

The whole question of impropriations in Armagh, especially ecclesiastical, came into prominence in 1612 as a result of lay pressures. In March 1612 the king, on the petition of Sir James Douglas and the Scots undertakers in the Fews, instructed Chichester to arrange a comprehensive series of surrenders.[81] The archbishop of Armagh and the 'rest of the bishops in the plantation' were to surrender all tithes and impropriations to the king to be disposed of 'according to the project of plantation' to the incumbents. The dean of Armagh and also the prior of the vicars choral or Culdees and the prebendaries of Armagh were also to surrender their impropriations and receive compensation from the archbishop out of the termon lands. Particularly the dean was to surrender the impropriate rectory of Loughilly, the patronage of which was to be granted to Douglas, and the incumbent vicar of that parish, James Shaw, B.D., who, it was noted, had been there since the previous July, was to be put in possession of the rectorial and vicarial tithes. When it is remembered that Douglas had been granted the advowson of the vicarage of Loughilly at the plantation it becomes clear that the whole matter of impropriations in Armagh had been made an issue as a result of a struggle between a lay Scottish planter, Douglas, and the dean, Robert Maxwell, who was also a Scot.[82]

The archbishop's surrender of impropriations took place on 20 June 1612.[83] Writing to Humphrey May on July 8, Chichester stated that these were 'but two small things', the rectory of Armagh and a rectory in Tyrone. He felt this a small return for such a large grant of land. The other Ulster-plantation bishops either had, or would be required to, resign their

[78] None of these were in Armagh. See below, 340.

[79] *CSPI, 1608–10*, 359.

[80] Below, 320–21.

[81] *CSPI, 1611–14*, 256–8. At the same time these Scottish undertakers in the Fews had sought royal support for their claim that the Armagh servitors were neglectful of obligations of defence (see above, 78–80).

[82] The dean was also in dispute at this time with Henry Acheson about the ownership of part of the land granted to Acheson. The dean vindicated his claim (see above, 85).

[83] *CPRI, Jas I*, 256.

impropriations as well which would, however, be more rewarding as they would involve the surrender of *tertiam episcopalem*. As to Armagh, he stated that those numerous benefices which were in the hands of the dean and other dignitaries of Armagh would not be surrendered 'without valuable considerations'. He had, though, possessed Shaw of the parsonage of Loughilly. This was done in the absence of the dean, who was at court, Chichester adding his fear as to 'how he [would] digest this either at his return hither or the report of it there'.[84] He had been deprived of one rectory, and there had been no general discussion of compensation for the surrender of all his impropriations.

The dean, however, soon secured an advantage. At the end of September Chichester informed the archbishop of Canterbury that Maxwell had returned to Ireland with royal letters instructing him to maintain him in possession of all his rights 'until certain mutual surrenders be first made of things' between the primate, the dean and the vicars choral.[85] The new king's letter was one of July 31[86] which required, indeed a complicated series of surrenders.

The archbishop was to surrender the territory of Derrynoose, almost 6,000 acres, which was to be conveyed to the dean[87] who, in turn, was to surrender all impropriate rectories and vicarages to the crown. The parsonage and vicarage of Armagh were to be united – the archbishop had been rector and the dean vicar – and the patronage granted to the archbishop. The prior and vicars choral should surrender their impropriations in return for reasonable compensation to be allotted by the lord chancellor.

The surrenders by the archbishop of Derrynoose[88] and, presumably, of the dean, took place accordingly. In February 1613 Chichester informed the archbishop of Canterbury of the dean's surrender of tithes and livings 'to the use of the several ministers and churches to be supplyed'.[89] The dean received his patent of lands in the same month.[90] Attention to the position of the vicars choral was, however, deferred to a later date.[91]

84 'Chichester Letter-Book', no. 14, *Anal. Hib.*, viii. No. 15, lord deputy to archbishop of Canterbury, 9 July 1612, has also been used.

85 Ibid., no. 29. Chichester, sandwiched uncomfortably between the contestants, could only note that he had and should 'incurr displeasure and obloquy of the partys in this as it is my condition to suffer unworthily in many other things besides' (ibid.).

86 *CSPI, 1611–14*, 280–81; *CPRI, Jas I*, 248–9; Armagh Archiepiscopal Registry, A.1b.26, 41; RCB Lib., Dublin, Libr./32, 5.

87 The dean was also to receive a patent of the deanery land which should include the land in dispute (ibid.).

88 *CPRI, Jas I*, 252.

89 'Chichester Letter-Book', no. 46, *Anal. Hib.*, viii.

90 *CPRI, Jas I*, 245–6; Armagh Archiepiscopal Registry, A.1b.26, 45–8.

91 Below, 306–09.

The outcome was clearly a satisfactory reorganisation of benefit to parish clergy concerned. However, the precipitating circumstances – the struggle between the dean and the Scottish undertakers – should not be overlooked. Douglas held the advowson of the vicarage of Loughilly and was manifestly determined to procure that of the rectory as well.[92] It is with this in mind that the limitations of the reorganisation, in that nothing was done about the vicars choral, should be considered.

The king's letter of 31 July 1612[93] also instructed Chichester to investigate the claims of lay impropriators in Armagh and, if they were valid, to compound with them 'that [the tithes] may be laid to the parochial ministers, according to the rules of the plantation'. There were only two such, holding dissolved monastic land, in Armagh, Sir Toby Caulfeild and Marmaduke Whitechurch,[94] though their interests were probably emotionally the stronger because of the recency of their grants and their commitment to the regime.

In the case of Caulfeild the order coincided with a further requirement – subsequently enforced – that he should surrender that portion of his abbey land which lay in County Londonderry for the benefit of the London companies' plantation.[95] In September Caulfeild went to London supported by a strong letter of commendation from the deputy[96] to argue his case in its various aspects.[97] The outcome for Caulfeild in that he was obliged to surrender the lands in Londonderry is well known,[98] but he retained possession of the tithes, and he returned from England bearing a letter requiring his appointment to the Irish privy council.[99] There is no evidence of any negotiations with Marmaduke Whitechurch.

There was no concern with impropriations in Cavan at this time. In fact in January 1613 Richard Nugent, baron of Delvin, received a new and outright grant of his Cavan rectories.[100] The ending of impropriations was thus not an energetically-pursued policy at this stage, but rather, where it happened in specific instances, it had resulted from local circumstances.

92 In October 1612 the deputy and plantation commissioners worked out an arrangement between the incumbent of Loughilly and two Irishmen, Manus and John O'Fynan, to whom the dean had disposed the tithes of rectory ('Ulster plantation papers', no. 59/d, *Anal. Hib.*, viii).

93 Above, 294.

94 Above, 20, 287.

95 Moody, *Londonderry Plantation*, 117–8.

96 'Chichester Letter-Book', no. 28, *Anal. Hib.*, viii. This can be interpreted in terms of Chichester's reaction, at this same time, to the complaints of the Scots in the Fews also against the Armagh servitors (above, 78–80).

97 Caulfeild himself stated his case in a letter to the earl of Northampton, 18 September 1612 (*CSPI, 1611–14*, 550).

98 Moody, *Londonderry Plantation*, 117.

99 *CSPI, 1611–14*, 324.

100 *CPRI, Jas I*, 238.

This is not to say that the king and the London government were not issuing general instructions and advice in these years to the Ulster bishops and their clergy, in hopes that

> the place from which heretofore the rest of the kingdom has received infection shall now become such a store ... of faithful and religious hearts, that [the king] may at all times make use of them against those that shall presume to spurn against his religious and just government.[101]

These were, to a large extent, pious gestures if taken in contrast to the failure to deal fully and completely with impropriations, as the plantation project had required. In November 1613 it was reported plainly by commissioners that the lack of clergy and the ruined state of churches – in the country at large – arose from the want of livings to sustain them as a result of impropriations.[102]

How soon did a systematic network of parish clergy appear in our area? An inquiry for Cavan in 1619, which limited itself to the period up to 9 July 1617, produced much relevant evidence.[103] Ten vicarages and three rectories had been without incumbents from the start of James's reign until 24 March 1611 and the bishop, Draper, had received the profits of them during that period. He had received the profits of four additional vicarages and one rectory from 24 March 1607 to 24 March 1611. The bishop was patron of all except two of these. Garret Fleming and his son Thomas had received the profits of one rectory, Lurgan, from 24 March 1612 until 9 July 1617. Sir James Dillon had received the profits of the vacant vicarage of Drumlahen from 24 March 1608 until 24 March 1611. The vicarage of Killashandra had been vacant from 24 March 1613 until 9 July 1617 and Claud Hamilton, its patron, had enjoyed the profits in that period. The names of only two parish clergy emerge from the inquiry. One, Nicholas O'Goven, or Smith the younger, had been admitted, prior to 1617,[104] to the vicarage of Kildrumfertan and received the emoluments of office; he had also held Castlerahan and received its profits for two years before 1617. The other, Robert Whiskens, seemingly a Cambridge graduate,[105] had held the vicarages of Annageliffe (modern Cavan) and Denn, of which the bishop was patron, for four years before 1617. Such a report suggests the unhealthy state of protestantism in Kilmore.

101 *CSPI, 1611–14*, 96–7, see also 26–7, 31–3, 142–3; *Cal. Carew MSS, 1603–24*, 127–9, 142–3.
102 *CSPI, 1611–14*, 446.
103 NAI, Exchequer inquisitions, Ulster, Cavan, (3) Jas I, 14–19.
104 The date is blank in the transcription. Leslie (NLI, MS 2685, 189) is unhelpful.
105 NLI, MS 2685, 114.

It is difficult to establish accurately the dates of appointment of many of the early seventeenth-century Kilmore clergy. Leslie's succession list[106] incorporates most of the available material, yet leaves much to be desired. However, apart from a number of Irish clergy officially appointed, there seem to have been few appointments before about 1615. Killashandra was, in fact, vacant until 1618.[107] There appear to have been just two appointments of English clergy in 1612. Both were Cambridge graduates, one having had previous parochial experience in England.[108] In 1612 the parish of Drumgoon also had a native Irish rector, Hugh McComyn.[109] It does not seem likely that in the hands of Irish clergy Protestantism would prosper, and the value of livings offered little inducement to energetic outsiders, themselves, of course, likely to be unsuitable as proselytisers.

The situation in Armagh was less complicated by massive lay-held impropriations, and it may also be Henry Ussher and Hampton were more active than bishops Draper and Moynes of Kilmore. In April 1610 a dean Robert Maxwell was presented by the crown.[110] However, it was June 1612 before a rector, James Matchett, an Englishman who had disposed of his estate in Oneilland, was appointed to Armagh parish.[111] Apart from the controversial Loughilly, where there was a vicar from 1611, no further appointments were made before 1613.[112]

2. The inquiry of 1622

The first systematic examination of the plantation church took place at the time of the inquiry of 1622. The bishops were required to conduct a visitation and present reports,[113] and the commissioners' report incorporated general recommendations.[114]

Dealing with the archbishopric of Armagh the diocesan report indicates that the archbishop, Christopher Hampton, lived at Drogheda, i.e. *inter anglicos* following medieval precedent. However, he had done much to restore his cathedral,[115] he had laid out land near Armagh for demesne, and erected buildings at Drogheda. The income of the archbishopric was stated

[106] Ibid. (typescript).
[107] Ibid.
[108] Nathaniel Hollington, vicar of Drumlane (ibid., 143) and John Bockock, vicar of Drumlease (ibid., 151).
[109] Ibid., 132.
[110] Armagh Archiepiscopal Registry, A.1b.209 (original patent); *CPRI, Jas I*, 168; Leslie, *Armagh clergy*, 13.
[111] *CPRI, Jas I*, 234.
[112] Leslie, *Armagh clergy, passim.*
[113] Armagh Archiepiscopal Registry, B.1b.193; TCD, MS 550 and MS 2629.
[114] BL, Add. MS 4756, ff 18–25v, 64–5.
[115] Above, 238.

to be £1,935. 9. 9.[116] The deanery, vacant through the death of Robert Maxwell,[117] was valued at £120 per annum. This income was from lands only and the dean had a 'poore house' in Armagh. The chapter consisted of an archdeaconry, precentorship, and treasurership. The report covers fifteen parishes or unions, of which the table below presents an abstract.[118]

Thus we see that, of the thirteen parishes for which statements of income were given, the lowest figure was £30, the highest (Armagh) £100, and the most usual £60 or £80. There is some difficulty in reconciling these with another set (b) taken from the Rich papers. These, where available, are, with one exception, higher (roughly by half) than those of the visitation, and they would clearly not be liable to clerical underestimation. The 1634 regal visitation[119] provides figures which, although in all cases except one, (Derrynoose) are higher or equal to those of the 1622 visitation, are in seven cases out of the eleven where comparison is possible lower than those of Rich and in four cases higher. In a lawsuit in 1629, however, concerning the profits of Loughilly rectory, judgement was given for £500 for the two years 1624 and 1625.[120]

Co. Armagh Parish	**Residency of incumbent**	**Annual value**		**State of Church**	**State of parsonage houses, etc.**
		(a)	(b)		
Armagh	resident curate employed	£100	£220	cathedral used 2 chapels	not built, controversial
Kilmore	resident	£80	£100	'fair church new built'	parsonage house 'new built'; also stable, barn & orchard, cost £200
Drumcree	absent curate employed	£60	£50	in repair 'but not very sufficiently'	-
Loughall	resident	£60	£100	well repaired	'sufficient' parsonage house, also orchard & housing
Loughilly	resident	£80	£120	'in building'	-

116 For a discussion of this, and the amount of it due from Armagh, see below chapter 12.

117 He is stated as having been previously resident in Armagh.

118 Armagh Archiepiscopal Registry, B.1b.193, 25–31; TCD MS 550, 26–31. Two parishes, Seagoe and Shankill, which were in the diocese of Dromore are included by using the Dromore visitation (TCD, MS 2629, 3–5). The alternative figures provided under (b) in the annual income column are derived from the papers of Sir Nathaniel Rich, one of the commissioner of inquiry (NLI, Rich Papers, 8013/9),

119 Below, 332–3.

120 NAI, Repertories to the decrees of chancery, ii, 56.

Killeavy	resident	£80	£120	'new built'	'sufficient parsonage house in churchyard. Glebe remote.
Ballymore	resident	£80	£120	'new built'	no building, controversial
Mullaghbrack	resident	£50	£100	'not wholly built'	'convenient' house
Tynan	resident	£80	£100	'new built'	'new built'
Derrynoose	resident	£80	£100	'new built'	'new built'
Creggan	non-resident; curate resident	£80	£140	in repair	'sufficient' parsonage house 'in repairing'
Derrybrocas	resident curate	£50		ruinous, chapel in good repair	-
Kilcluney	non-resident 'sufficient' curate	£30		a house only	parsonage house on the glebe
Seagoe	-	-	£70	repaired	convenient glebe
Shankill	-	-	£80	'covered'	a house

As far as the physical apparatus of protestantism was concerned the county presented a recently-changed image. Churches and parsonage houses had been in almost all cases recently built or were being built or repaired. Kilcluney and Derrybrocas were the only exceptions. In the former case the church was 'but a house instead thereof'. The church of Derrybrocas was ruinous but the chapel (at Killyman) was in good repair. For the parish of Kilmore a parsonage house, stable, and barn had been built and an orchard planted at a cost of £200. However, in five, or perhaps six, parishes parsonage houses had not been erected.[121]

The commissioners' report particularly singled out the archdiocese of Armagh. Elsewhere in Ireland parish churches were 'generally ruinous and defaced' but here many were well built and the rest under construction. This work was being done by the local recusants on the archbishop's order. They had been given three years to complete the task, to be exempt from all other penalties during that time. The commissioners felt this arrangement should be adopted throughout the country.[122]

[121] In the case of Armagh the report pleaded lay responsibility, 'the Nunn's Church in Armagh [had been] granted by his Matie to build the said house upon, but 4 or 5 years after Sir Francis Annesley took possession and intitled his Matie, and pays 16/- rent notwithstanding ye Lord of Canterbury made an order therein for the p'sons possession of that church' (Armagh Archiepiscopal Registry, B.1b.193, 28–9).

[122] BL, Add. MS 4756, fol. 65.

Of the 'handsome' parish church of Ballymore in Grandison's village of Tandragee a detailed description survives.[123] It had been built of brick in 1620 and was 60 feet long and 24 feet wide, the walls being 4 feet thick. There were three windows at each side and one at each end. Internally it was 'well seated and furnished with all things fitting'.[124] The bricks, bell, a pulpit cloth and cushion, a communion cup and 'a plate for bread' had been presented by Grandison. The rest of the cost had been borne by the primate out of the recusants' fines.

However, the church in Armagh was not without defects and difficulties. The rector of Ballymore listed thirteen families or individuals as Irish who 'come to church and receive communion', but also pointed out that of non-attending Irish in his parish there were 'nere hand 200 copple'.[125] In the parish of Killeavy there was 'not one Irish that comes to church' although there were over 1,000 estimated as living in the parish.[126] Glebe land was often distant from the parish church. The size of parishes and their territorial relationship with landlords' estates also presented difficulties.[127]

The picture presented by Kilmore diocese in 1622 was, by far, a less healthy one.[128] The total income of the united bishoprics of Kilmore and Ardagh, as Moynes reported it, was £460. 0. 0. The income of the bishopric of Kilmore was £289. 15. 0. of which £218. 15. 0. came from lands in Cavan and £10 which was paid to the bishop out of the impropriations within Cavan belonging to the priory of Fore. Within the county there were two substantial lessees of the termon and erenach lands, both servitor grantees, Lambert and Culme.[129] Both had sixty-year leases and paid at the rate of £1 per pole or townland.[130] Moynes took exception to his predecessor's leasing policy stating that the land held by Lambert for £82. 10. 0, could well be let 'without racking of tenant' for £400 more. He stated that he had recovered ten polls of mensal land leased under the same conditions to Lambert. It now yielded £50 per annum and was 'left for succession'.

The bishop was resident and his report stated that the cathedral had

[123] TNA, Manchester papers, 30/15/2/182: submission of rector; BL, Add. MS 4756, fol. 109.

[124] In the submission of Grandison's agent it is described as 'all seated round with ioyned worke' (TNA, Manchester papers, 30/15/2/184).

[125] Ibid., 182.

[126] NLI, Rich Papers, MS 8014/9: draft report on Smith estate.

[127] In a draft report of the commissioners it was noted that although the parish church of Killeavy was situated near the middle of the parish, the furthest part of the parish lay four miles from the church and the parson himself lived three and a half miles from it. He had 'only' 180 acres of glebe of which 90 were in another parish, and yet his own parish comprehended in whole or part the lands of four settlers, Caulfeild, Smith, Moore, and Grandison (ibid.).

[128] Armagh Archiepiscopal Registry, B.1b.193, 136–51; TCD, MS 550, 134–65.

[129] The lease to Culme, Moynes stated, was 'upon trust for the ... last bishop's friends and servants' (Armagh Archiepiscopal Registry, B.1b.193, 137).

[130] *CPRI, Jas I*, 215 (one of these leases).

been 'newly built and repaired' by him, having received a grant of £175 from the primate out of the recusant fines. He lived in a 'fair' house built by him at Kilmore 'the which together with the buildings of other outhouses and of seats in the chancel and body of the church of Kilmore hath cost £600'. It was noted, however, that jurisdiction was exercised within the diocese not only by the bishop's agents but also by a number of people 'being Vicars General and Commissarys established by the Pope's authority'. Both the deanery and archdeaconry were 'merely titulatory', honorary appointments without income. The dean (who appears to have been a Dublin graduate) lived in the parish of Kilmore of which he was vicar. He held also one vicarage and one rectory.[131] The archdeacon, William Andrews, lived at Belturbet and held two vicarages.

The visitation covers twenty-three parishes or unions in Cavan, that state of which can been seen in the abstract below.

Co. Cavan Parish	Residency of incumbent	Annual value	State of Church	State of parsonage houses, etc.
Annagh	rector resident at Belturbet; Ir. curate £20 p.a.	£60	ruinous; new church should be built at Belturbet	no building
Castleterra	Rector resident at Ballyhaise	£30	ruinous; new church should be built at Ballyhaise	no building; some of the glebe detained
Drumgoon	rector suspended; sequestrator	£30	ruinous	a poor Irish house
Ballintemple & Kilmore	impropriate vicar resident; Ir. curate for Ballintemple	£60	Ballintemple church ruinous; cathedral used as parish church of Kilmore	Kilmore: sufficient dwelling house & out offices built by previous dean, cost 200 marks ster at least
Urny	impropriate vicar resident at Cavan	£207	ruinous; new church should be built at Cavan	glebe inconvenient, 10 miles from church outside parish
Annageliffe	impropriate vicar resident	£13	ruinous	glebe not convenient
Denn	impropriate	£15	ruinous	glebe not convenient
Kildrumfertan	impropriate vicar not resident	£18	ruinous	glebe not convenient
Castlerahan	impropriate vicar	£9	ruinous	house built on glebe

[131] NLI, MS 2685, 27.

	not resident			
Lurgan	impropriate curate resident	£30	ruinous; new church should be built at Virginia	no building
Moybolge	impropriate vicar not resident	£12	in reasonable repair	no building
Mullaghall Killinkere	impropriate vicar resident	£20	not repaired	no building
Knockbride	impropriate vicar not resident; curate	£12	ruinous	no building
Kilcan	impropriate vicar not resident; curate	£15	not in good repair	no building; vicarages of Knockbride & Kilcan should be united
Killyserdinny	impropriate vicar not resident; curate	£20	not in good repair	no building, but cottages
Drung or Larra	impropriate vicar resident	£40	ruinous	no building
Lawey	impropriate vicar not resident	£10	ruinous	glebe not convenient, 10 miles from church
Drumlahen	impropriate vicar resident	£26 13s. 4d.	ruinous	glebe not convenient
Killdallon	impropriate vicar resident	£15	ruinous	no building
Tomregan	rectory 'mensal to bishop'; united to Killdallon	£10	ruinous	-
Killashandra	impropriate vicar resident	£50	church newly repaired	a sufficient house
Templeport	impropriate vicar not resident; curate	£20	ruinous	a timber house
Killinagh	impropriate vicar not resident; curate	£8	ruinous	no building

The impression is in marked contrast with Armagh. Almost everywhere the vice-grip of lay impropriation is evident. Only two incumbents had an income of £60 per annum, the rectory of Annagh, and the vicarages of Kilmore and Ballintemple, which appear to have been united about 1618 and were held by the deans.[132] The two incumbencies returned £50 and

£40 each, three £30, and the remainder returning less than £30 while two, Castlerahan and Killinagh, returned £9 and £8 respectively.[133] Apart from the cathedral only one church, Killashandra, had been 'newly repaired'. Most commonly they were 'ruinous' though one, Moybolge (modern Bailieborough), was 'in reasonable repair'. In four cases it was recommended that new churches should be built in the new village or urban centres of those parishes, Belturbet, Ballyhaise, Cavan, and Virginia respectively. Parsonage houses were also rare. Killashandra had a 'sufficient' house; Drumgoon 'a poor Irish house'; and for Kilmore a 'sufficient' house with outbuildings had been built by the previous dean at a cost of some 200 marks, i.e. £133. 6. 8. However, for seventeen parishes there is either no entry or the statement 'no buildings'.

The commissioners made general comments and recommendations. They commended the king's bounty in allocating land for glebe. Such afforded adequate support for a 'learned ministry', in every Ulster parish. They requested the king to grant patents of these lands to the incumbents. Where churches were decayed new buildings should be placed near to the village in, or in the centre of, every parish. They noted the large number of impropriations in the country generally, and felt it might be wise to unite many parsonages and vicarages. Because many people in Ulster eluded tithe payments, they recommended that legislation be passed in Ireland to allow redress to the clergy. The New Testament and Common Prayer Book in Irish should be used in Irish parishes. The bishops should see the church provided with learned preachers. Non-residence and pluralism in the plantation areas 'where for the most part one is sufficient to maintaine a preaching minister' were too frequently permitted. In the north of Ireland there was an adequate clericy, whereas in Connacht and other places they were 'as ignorant as poore'.[134] They commended the archbishop of Armagh's scheme for building churches by virtue of the recusants' fines.[135]

In 1623 these recommendations and others were embodied in orders and directions issued by the king for the Irish church.[136] It was laid down that no incumbent in Ulster might hold more than one benefice except under special circumstances.[137] Little was done to implement these orders, however, and in July 1626 Charles I instructed the deputy to 'settle and

132 Ibid., 27, 69, 255.

133 The Rich papers do not contain figures for this diocese.

134 The clergy on the whole were 'answerable to their incomes'.

135 BL, Add. MS 4756, ff 18v–25v.

136 TNA, SP 63/237, ff 65–9v, 70–75v (fairer copy) (*CSPI, 1615–25*, 416–19); TCD, MS 808, ff 28–40; Armagh Public Library, Meath Papers, 383–90.

137 Ibid.

establish' the church of Ireland in accordance with his father's instructions, repeating many of the directives of 1623.[138]

The reign of James I, then, had seen the establishment of Protestantism in Ulster, more effectively in Armagh than Cavan. Apart from a considerable endowment of the church at both parochial and episcopal level, the role of the state had not been great. The reformed church had taken over the traditional system, and the initially proposed redrawing of parochial boundaries had not been effected. Some clerical impropriations in Armagh had been recovered, but lay impropriations had not been effectively interfered with.

3. Financial and other problems

In December 1629 Sir Thomas Dutton informed the king that 'excepting the plantation of the church in the north of Ireland' the whole kingdom was more 'addicted to popery' than even during the wartime years at the end of the previous century.[139] However, this was a relative judgment. The church was by no means ideally established in Ulster. From about 1625 many problems presented themselves.

Tithes were a fruitful source of altercation.[140] About the end of 1614 Chichester made an order exempting the colony from certain forms of tithe in kind, particularly tithes of milk. The clergy appear to have petitioned the English privy council against this order, and Chichester was required to reconsider it.[141] He stated that the tithes so abolished had been innovations, and that the colony was only becoming established in a difficult environment. The ministers were mostly non-residents 'as having few churches in repair nor houses to dwell in' and, while making little attempt to build these, were determined to turn their livings to the greatest financial advantage, particularly at the cost of the native Irish.[142] Public order and the safety of the ministry had necessitated his order. This was furthermore only temporary, and the church in Ulster was 'far otherwise provided for than this kingdom has ever known before'.[143]

So the matter rested for the moment. In 1622 the commissioners

[138] TNA, SP 63/247, ff 25–8v (*CSPI, 1625–32*, 363–4, 687).

[139] Ibid., /249, ff 298–8v (ibid., 498–9).

[140] In 1611 it was noted in propositions then sent to England that the Ulster undertakers complained of having to make tithe payments to more than one parish minister. It was suggested that each undertaker's lands should be created a parish. The reply was that this could not be done except by act of parliament (*CSPI, 1611–14*, 27).

[141] *CSPI, 1615–25*, 16.

[142] 'who first complained of this new tithing and were animated by some of the undertakers no doubt' (ibid., 22–4). He had received a native Irish delegation of complaints.

[143] Ibid., 22–4. See also TNA, SP 63/232, ff 262–63 (*CSPI, 1611–14*, 538).

recommended that legislation should be introduced to facilitate tithe collection,[144] and on 12 July 1625 the king instructed that the Ulster clergy should receive all tithe payments and other oblations in specie, referring back to decisions made at the planning stage of the plantation, and notwithstanding disputes between clergy and laity.[145] The background to this seems to have been that in 1624 as Ulster laymen had secured an act of state limiting tithe payments there,[146] and in early 1625, after Ussher's appointment to Armagh, two Ulster clergy had been sent to England to secure its reversal.[147] However, controversy between clergy and parishioners still arose. In 1629 on a visitation of Ulster, Ussher found 'nothing so much complained of as the uncertainty of payments of tithes'.[148] He therefore drew up a 'tithing-table', a systematisation for the province of the amounts to be paid for various forms of tithes and for different clerical functions and dispatched it to Laud for the king's attention.[149] In January 1630 it was returned by the king to the Irish lords justices with orders to see it implemented.[150]

One protracted suit about tithes in Armagh is particularly illuminating of the kind of altercation which could arise between the civil and ecclesiastical wings of the colony. It was between James Matchett, rector of Kilmore and Drumcree and ex-undertaker in Oneilland, and Arthur Bagnal of Newry. The Bagnals had been granted the abbey of Newry in 1553[151] of which it appears an outlying portion of seven townlands, called the Grange, lay in Kilmore parish. The calendared patent does not refer to the lands or tithes in Armagh.[152] However, in February 1613 Arthur Bagnal received a regrant which included these lands, but does not refer to tithes.[153] The rectory had been impropriate to the deanery of Armagh until 1612, but, at about that time, the rectory and vicarage were united and Matchett was appointed. The dispute broke out immediately, but only came to a recorded crisis about 1630 when Matchett brought a suit in chancery against Bagnal.[154] Matchett argued that the seven townlands had been reputed, time out of mind, as part of the rectory. He stated that he had been to the

144 Above, 303.

145 Referred to in *CPRI, Chas I*, 550.

146 This was issued as a printed proclamation on 1 July 1624 (Grosart, *Lismore Papers*, (2nd series), iii, 118–19).

147 TNA, SP 63/249, ff 197–9v (*CSPI, 1625–32*, 481–3), Ussher to Laud, 11 September 1629.

148 Ibid.

149 Ibid. Table not now with the accompanying letter.

150 *CPRI, Chas I*, 550–2; Armagh Archiepiscopal Registry, A.1b.26, 190–91).

151 *CPRI, Eliz.*, 154–5.

152 N.B. White (ed.), *Extents of Irish monastic possessions, 1540–1* (IMC, Dublin 1943), 249, deals only with the property of the Newry monastery which lay in Louth.

153 *CPRI, Jas I*, 246–7.

154 NAI, Chancery salvage, G.388 (Matchett's bill, n.d.)

expense of building a house and 'inclosing' the glebe. His predecessors up to 1611 had enjoyed the tithes of the area but, in 1611, Capt. Edward Trevor (of Rostrevor, County Down), 'general agent' of Bagnal, had claimed the tithes and later taken them by force from the dean. The dean had appealed to the justices of assize and, on the evidence of witnesses from the area, received judgement in his favour. As a result he received the tithes 'up to surrender of his appropriation'. However, after Matchett's appointment Lieutenant Charles Poyntz became Bagnal's agent and Poyntz 'and his fellow soldiers' had then begun to collect the tithes. Matchett appealed successfully to the assizes judges against him in 1616, but Poyntz violated their orders and collected tithes valued by Matchett at £300. Matchett then took action in the consistory court at Armagh, but all his attempts to collect tithes, though assisted by sheriffs, bailiffs, constables, and other offices, had been frustrated by Poyntz who, he stated, was then sheriff of the county. Bagnal's answer has not survived. In 1628 and 1632 Bagnal had received king's letters for a regrant of his estate in Down, Louth and Armagh.[155]

In 1633 Matchett received powerful support from Archbishop Laud. In February 1632 a list of Bagnal's 'encroachments' on the church, including this, was drawn up.[156] Later Matchett presented his case in a petition to Laud,[157] and appears to have gone to England to press his case in person. He asserted that he had been informed by the English attorney general that the tithes concerned had never been granted to the Bagnals and that he had a certificate from the Irish chancery that they had never been found to belong to, or been granted to, Bagnal by any patent, and that he had received no grant of land in Armagh before 1612–13.[158] About September Laud requested Wentworth to preserve Matchett and the cause of the church 'for his adversary is potent'.[159]

An inquisition in 1657 states that all the tithes of the parish were payable to the rector,[160] so it seems Matchett had vindicated his claim. It seems also that it was a just one; at any rate there was no reference to the tithes in Bagnal's patent of 1613.[161]

We have seen that in 1612 the impropriations of the Culdean foundation in Armagh were not disturbed. The prior and vicars choral also owned seven townlands in the county (1,411 acres) as well as portions of

155 *CPRI, Chas I*, 415–17; *CSPI, 1625–32*, 624.
156 *CSPI, 1625–32*, 644.
157 TNA, SP 63/254, fol 7 (*CSPI, 1633–47*, 2).
158 Ibid. The 1609 inquisition supports Matchett's contention.
159 TNA, SP 63/254, ff 122–3v.
160 T.G.F. Paterson (ed.), 'Cromwellian inquisition as to parishes in county Armagh in 1657', *UJA*, 3rd series, vol. 2 (1939), 212–49.
161 PRONI, D1540/1/1a.

land close to the town, and the priory and dwellings in Armagh. The lands, curiously, remained undisposed by royal grant throughout the reign of James I. In August 1619 the king instructed the deputy to grant the property to the dean and chapter of Armagh 'for the erecting and maintaining of a quire of singing men and choristers' in the cathedral,[162] but no action was taken and in 1623 the king ordered that the lands be recovered and sequestered and the vicars choral appointed.[163]

In March 1626 an inquisition was held which investigated the extent of the property, found crown title to it and stated by whom it was held.[164] It was stated that the 'popish' prior and Culdees, then all dead, had 'deserted' the priory about twenty-five years previously. The inquisition indicated what the profits of the property had been since about 1605, stated who had collected these profits and, in some cases, provided the names of tenants. Thus eleven parcels of land were held largely by the archbishop's tenants – all British – at 2/- per acre.[165] Within the priory building there were two English tenants living. From about 1605 to 1608 Toby Caulfeild, as seneschal to the archbishop, received the profits of the seven townlands, amounting to £20 per annum 'because a great part of those lands lay waste and uncultivated'. After that the dean received the rents for two years and maintained 'certain' vicars choral from them. Christopher Hampton had received the rents, £47 per year, for ten years from his appointment, and devoted them to repairing the cathedral. From 1623 Rev. John Symonds had received the profits of the seven townlands, £46 per annum, and of the tenements in Armagh, £8. 6. 0. per annum, and expended a part of the rents in erecting four stalls in the cathedral. The property had thus, while remaining in clerical hands, become caught up in a general free-for-all.

The reason for the inquisition is that in December 1625 Charles I ordered the granting of the arrears of the property, for so long as they had been detained from the crown, to George Kirke, one of the grooms of the bedchamber. Kirke should also have a *custodiam* of it until vicars choral were appointed.[166] In July 1626 the king instructed Falkland to ensure that the land was used for the maintenance of vicars choral and to have the appropriations[167] made presentative parsonages, as ordered in 1612, the collation to be granted to the archbishop of Armagh.[168] Further to these

[162] Armagh Archiepiscopal Registry, A.1b.128/3.

[163] *CSPI, 1615–25*, 417.

[164] Armagh Archiepiscopal Registry, Evidences of the see of Armagh, 212–6; Armagh Public Library, Armagh Papers [Reeves transcripts], 181–87. See also *Inq. cancel. Hib. repert.*, ii, Armagh (1) Chas I (very imperfect).

[165] Thomas Raven, the cartographer, held 20 acres.

[166] *CPRI, Chas I*, 95–6.

[167] Appropriations means essentially the same as impropriation.

instructions a patent was issued on 7 April 1627 incorporating the Prior and five vicars choral and granting them the lands.[169]

The matter now assumes a complexity not easily elucidated from formal records. Kirke took out a patent on 7 June 1627, not enrolled,[170] possibly of the rectories and tithes or of the entire property.[171] From the surviving part of the evidence of a chancery suit of about this time it appears that the archbishop claimed the rectories, that other interests became involved, and that the arbitration of Sir James Fullerton was sought.[172] Kirke received the benefit of two king's letters for these and other lands on 21 August and 30 September 1628.[173] Whatever the outcome of the suit Kirke surrendered his patent on 18 March 1629.[174] An unclear interval followed until, in April 1633, the king instructed Wentworth to accept the surrender of Kirke's and also the vicars' choral previous patents so that the vicars choral could be reincorporated. The rectories were to be disappropriated and made collative, vicarages and rectories united, and a college or corporation of eight vicars choral, four choristers, and an organist to be founded, and all the lands granted to them. Their institution was to be suspended for one year and the profits spent by the primate to purchase a 'pair of organs'. In the new patent the advowsons of the rectories were to be granted to the archbishop.[175] The surrenders followed and the new patent was granted on 23 May 1634.[176]

It was thus twenty-four years after the plantation that this land had been granted in any permanent way and the vicars choral reconstituted. Some indication of the value of their lands is got from an undertaking of Burton, the prior, in 1628 (following on the 1627 patent) to grant a sixty-year lease of the seven townlands to John Dillon, the Oneilland undertaker, at an annual rent of £60.[177] An undated document, post Restoration, assessed these at 1377 acres and the annual value at £266. 1. 6.[178] However, in 1713 the vicars' choral finances were reorganised and it may be that they were not fully organised until then.[179] Kirke reimbursed himself by acquiring land at

168 *CPRI, Chas I*, 23–5; Armagh Archiepiscopal Registry, Evidences of the see of Armagh, 109–11.
169 *CPRI, Chas I*, 221.
170 Following on royal instructions of 9 September 1626 (*CSPI, 1625–32*, 154).
171 See TNA, SP 63/244, fol. 192 (*CSPI, 1625–32*, 223). In 1629 Kirke (and Porter) was involved in the recovery of impropriations (*CSPI, 1625–32*, 471).
172 NAI, Chancery salvage, G.398.
173 *CSPI, 1625–32*, 380–91.
174 NAI, Lodge, Records of the rolls, v, 299–301; Armagh Archiepiscopal Registry, Evidences of the see of Armagh, 130–3.
175 Ibid.
176 Ibid. Certified copy in TCD, Muniment Room; Cotton, *Fasti*, iii, 64–5, and v, 212 is not fully accurate.
177 Armagh Archiepiscopal Registry, A.31.39/1.
178 Ibid., A.1b.128/6.

Bray in Wicklow in 1629.[180] In 1639 Bramhall stated that a conservative estimate of the increased income to the church as a result of the rearrangement was £900.[181]

We have seen that Sir James Douglas's ambition to procure the advowson of the rectory as well as of the vicarage of Loughilly led to a general concern with impropriations in Armagh in 1612.[182] However, the advowson of the rectory (now in crown hands) was not granted to Douglas or to Sir Archibald Acheson who acquired the estate.

In 1613 John Madder, who may have been a Scot, was collated to the rectory.[183] What his relationship with Acheson was before 1624 is not clear, but in July 1625 he was presented by the crown,[184] i.e. he accepted the right of the crown against Acheson's claim. From now he was in conflict with the landlord who entered into collusion with the Scottish dean, Mackeson, about 1626. In June 1628 Madder received a chancery decree against Sir Archibald and others for £40 and costs for cattle distrained,[185] but in June 1629 Acheson recovered against Madder £500 and costs for the profits of the rectory for 1624 and 1625.[186] In 1628 Madder resigned the rectory exchanging with his successor, Dr. George Synge, for Donoghmore in Tyrone. Synge was presented by the crown, the rectory being in the king's gift and the vicarage by devolution – Madder, it was stated, 'having been presented fraudulently by Sir James Douglas' (presumably in 1613) and having resigned.[187]

Such a situation offered little satisfaction to Acheson who, about 1626, entered into collusion with the dean. In the spring of 1627 Mackeson and Acheson petitioned the king for redress against the archbishop.[188] In one of two letters from the king to Falkland of 12 May 1627,[189] he was required to investigate the truth of Acheson's and Mackeson's allegations. These were that Acheson was patron of Loughilly and had presented the dean to it in about 1626, that the archbishop had refused to admit the dean asserting

[179] T. English, *Memoir relating to the vicars-choral and organist of the cathedral church of... Armagh* (Armagh, 1800), 5 (in Armagh Public Library).

[180] *CPRI, Chas I*, 456–7, 491; *CSPI, 1625–32*, 434; NLI, Ainsworth reports, no. 319, 2516, 2517–8, 2520.

[181] E.P. Shirley (ed.), *Papers relating to the church of Ireland, 1631–39* (London 1874), 8.

[182] Above, 293–5.

[183] Leslie, *Armagh clergy*, 230, 352.

[184] *CPRI, Chas I*, 34.

[185] NAI, Repertories to the decrees of chancery, i, 31.

[186] Ibid., 56. Acheson was a master in chancery (above, 125, fn. 172).

[187] Leslie, *Armagh clergy*, 353.

[188] Referred to in King to Falkland, 12 May 1627 (Armagh Archiepiscopal Registry, Evidences of the see of Armagh, 114). No printed copy, or transcript in any other collection, of this letter has been located.

[189] Ibid.

that George Synge, his chancellor, had been previously presented 'upon a pretended lapse' (i.e. by the king) *jure devolute*, and that a suit had been commenced against the archbishop and Synge, but had been nullified by 'sinister practices'. Falkland was required, if he found the parish to be in lapse and not so before, to present the dean to it on behalf of the king.[190]

However, this was merely the first part of the dean's claim. The second, in effect, called in question the general rearrangement of the deanery which had taken place in 1612–13.[191] A second king's letter of 12 May 1627[192] referred to a further petition of Mackeson and instructed Falkland and members of the Dublin government to investigate and act on the dean's claim. The dean referred back to the 'great office' pointing out that several rectories and a vicarage had then been found to be deanery property. He made no reference to the deanery patent of 1613 and stated that these benefices had been given by the previous archbishop to others without regard to the dean's rights and that he had received no compensation for this except that, in return for Loughilly, he had been granted the territory of Derrynoose. He asserted that the archbishop's right to collate to these rectories was invalid. They were to investigate these allegations and, if found true, to restore the dean.[193]

Both arguments dovetailed neatly in that Mackeson could accept Acheson's claim to Loughilly – and so Acheson's right to present him – by asserting that the grant of Derrynoose in 1613 had been in compensation for Loughilly only. It was a neat mutual accommodation. However, it did not go unopposed. Synge justified his claim to Loughilly and received a patent in September 1628[194] and, though a lawsuit ensued, retained the rectory.[195] However, even in 1657 Sir Archibald's successor, Sir George Acheson, claimed the advowson of the rectory.[196] Throughout Ussher treated the combination of Acheson and Mackeson in a thoroughly unyielding manner. In February 1627 he informed the dean that

> when you both have tried the uttermost of your wits to subvert the good foundation laid by King James … you shall but struggle in vain with shame enough.[197]

On the related question of the property of the deanery matters proceeded

[190] Ibid.
[191] Above, 293–5.
[192] *CPRI, Chas I*, 209; *CSPI, 1625–32*, 235; Armagh Archiepiscopal Registry, Evidences of the see of Armagh, 114.
[193] Ibid.
[194] Leslie, *Armagh clergy*, 353.
[195] Ibid., 353, 356–7.
[196] Paterson (ed.), 'Cromwellian inquisition', *UJA*, 3rd series, vol. 2, 212–49.
[197] Ussher to Mr. Dean – , 1 February 1627 (Elrington (ed.), *Ussher*, xv, 388).

more slowly. However, it was found in 1628 that the cathedral chapter had never been properly constituted and the archbishop and dean and dignitaries petitioned the privy council to receive letters patent of incorporation.[198] This invalidity technically affected the leasing of episcopal land up to 1635.[199] An inquiry resulted[200] and on 27 November a king's letter to the lords justices instructed that a surrender should be accepted and a new charter issued to the dean and chapter 'for the good and quiet of the plantators of the ... archbishopric as also for the settling and establishing of the church and plantation thereof'.[201] The deanery was to be granted to Mackeson.[202]

It was not until January 1637[203] that the patent of the dean and chapter, which incorporated also a grant to the dean, was issued.[204] In the interval Mackeson had died and Peter Wentworth, a relative of the lord deputy and dean since 1637,[205] was the beneficiary of the arrangement. The delay was in part due to the working out of an arrangement between the dean and the archbishop as to what the rights of the dean should be and in part arose from the nature of that arrangement. During the period their relations were thoroughly strained.[206] The arrangement was that the dean should surrender the territory of Derrynoose to the archbishop in return for the advowson or patronage of the parish of Armagh to which the ancient parishes of Ballymoyer, Clanaul (or Eglish), and Clonconchy (or Lisnadill) had been previously united.[207] The delay was due to the fact that the grant of these to the dean, if his intention was to present himself as rector, had to await the death (or resignation) of the incumbent of that union. The incumbent, John Symonds, died in June 1637 and the dean became rector following on the patent of January 1638. The value of this Armagh union in 1634 was £300.[208] Derrynoose was leased by the archbishop at £150 per annum.[209] The dean had not, on the other hand, received back all the pre-plantation impropriations. By 1638, too, Mackeson was dead and Acheson unlikely to draw any gain from the affair. Not only was the new dean one of the

198 *CSPI, 1625–32*, 416.
199 Below, 318–9.
200 *CSPI, 1625–32*, 451, 463.
201 *CPRI, Chas I*, 565–7; Armagh Archiepiscopal Registry, Evidences of the see of Armagh, 115–16.
202 Ibid.
203 Following on royal instructions of 5 September 1637 (*CSPI, 1633–47*, 171–2).
204 RCB Lib. Dublin, Libr/32, ii, 27–29, D14; Armagh Archiepiscopal Registry, Evidences of the see of Armagh, 117–30.
205 Leslie, *Armagh clergy*, 15–16.
206 In October 1634 Ussher complained to Bishop Bramhall of the dean with which he was 'clogged' (*Hastings MSS*, iv, 63).
207 These benefices had been themselves the subject of debate in 1629 (*CSPI, 1625–32*, 453).
208 Below, 317. It was also £300 in 1640.
209 Below, chapter 12.

Wentworth circle, but the archbishop, too, received a government-sponsored tenant – Sir Philip Mainwaring.[210] On 18 October 1637 Wentworth wrote to Laud expressing satisfaction with the rearrangement:

> The business concerning the dean of Armagh is settled and with much convenience and advantage both to the primacy and the deanery, see as I conceive therein we have done a very good work for the church.[211]

In Kilmore problems of this kind did not come into prominence. The operation of the system of impropriations was not, as we have seen, disturbed. The government remained detached during the episcopates of Draper and Moynes, and protestantism made scant progress before the appointment of William Bedell, an Englishman who had been for two years provost of Trinity College, to Kilmore and Ardagh in 1629.[212] His son-in-law, Clogy, asserted that on appointment Bedell

> found such dilapidations, such disorders in his clergy and courts, and people of all sorts, as if he had come there immediately after the rebellion of the Earl of Tyrone.[213]

His son pointed to the bishop's difficulties given the face of the countryside and the dispersed nature of British settlement.[214] In a letter to Laud on 1 April 1630 Bedell transmitted his own impressions. The cathedral at Kilmore was in repair 'but without bell or steeple, font or chalice'. The parish churches were 'ruined, unroffed and unrepaired'. The people 'saving a few British planters here and there (which are not the tenth part of the remnant)' were 'obstinate recusants'[215] well served by their own clergy. Of the reformed clergy there were 'only seven or eight' in each diocese (Kilmore and Ardagh) 'of good sufficiency', and these were English and out of touch with the majority of the population 'which is no small cause of the continuance of the people in Popery still'. Pluralism was very common

[210] Below, chapter 12.

[211] Sheffield City Library, Strafford MSS, vol. vii, 36.

[212] *CSPI, 1625–32*, 447.

[213] Wilkins (ed.), *Bedell*, 34.

[214] 'His house was situate in the county of Cavan … in a county consisting altogether of hills very steep and high, the valleys between being most commonly boggs and loughs. The country was then meetly well planted with English; ut scatteringly here and there which facilitated their ruine' (Jones (ed.), *Life and death of William Bedell*, 62).

[215] However, only one incident of violence against Protestant clerical property in the area studied has emerged. In March 1623 a certain Shane O'Mulvihill of County Cavan, who had been convicted of burning the barn [presumably tithe barne] of the bishop of Kilmore, was pardoned the offence (*CPRI, Jas I*, 562).

many holding 'two, three, four, or more' vicarages each.[216]

Bedell's episcopate was conspicuous for the programme of reform to which he devoted his energies. He aimed to combat pluralism and non-residence, to rebuild parish churches and re-organise glebe land, to recover episcopal property, and to provide an effective mission to the native Irish. This latter involved the encouragement of his clergy to speak Irish, a willingness to ordain Irish natives (of which there was some tradition in Cavan), and a scheme for the translation of the Old Testament into Irish. He came into conflict with Wentworth and Laud on political and theological issues, and in his programme he achieved only a partial success.

In the administration of the episcopal estate he came into conflict with two undertakers, Sir Edward Bagshaw and Sir Francis Hamilton, and also with the widow of Moynes, his predecessor. Shortly after his appointment – a critical juncture when undertakers were taking out new patents – he petitioned Falkland and the council claiming that Bagshaw and Hamilton had occupied small areas – one was two polls – of see property.[217] The dispute with Moynes's widow was about a lease, the terms of which were considered improper, made to her and her son Roger by her husband of the Kilmore mensal land.[218] The suit was protracted and expensive,[219] and was not in fact finalised in Bedell's favour 'till just upon the breaking out of the rebellion'.[220]

The attempt to combat pluralism and non-residence can be illustrated by reference to two specific cases. The bishop himself surrendered Ardagh. One of these cases concerned the dean of Kilmore, Dr. Nicholas Bernard, an absentee and pluralist, who held the vicarages of Kilmore, Ballintemple, and Kildrumfertan, as well as the rectory of Kedy, all valued by the bishop at more than £300. 'Called to residence' by Bedell in 1636 he took out a patent to the deanery from the crown and was also allowed to be vicar of St. Peter's Drogheda.[221] Bedell pressed him to reside whereupon he resigned

[216] H.J.M. Mason, *The life of William Bedell* (London, 1843), 170–2.

[217] Wilkins (ed.), *Bedell*, 39–40.

[218] Jones (ed.), *Life and death of William Bedell*, 48.

[219] Shuckburgh (ed.), *William Bedell*, 349–51; Sheffield City Library, Strafford letters, 17/295.

[220] Jones (ed.), *Life and death of William Bedell*, 48. The surviving evidence of this suit comes almost exclusively from biographies by Bedell's relatives the impartiality of which it is difficult to assess. Clogy, his son-in-law, was very critical of Moynes, asserting that 'the former bishop ... had set up such a shop of mundination and merchandize, as if all things spiritual and temporal, belonging to episcopacy, had been ordinary vendible commodities, as in the church of Rome' (Wilkins (ed.), *Bedell*, 34). He claimed that Moynes's leases of church land to Lambert, Culme, and others, had been made without concern for his successors in return for 'great' fines and that he had sold advowsons for personal profit (ibid., 35–6). This was clearly unfair in that the leases had been made by Draper and not by Moynes (above, 316, *CPRI, Jas I*, 251), though it must also be noted that Moynes purchased an undertaker's estate in Loughtee before his death.

his livings to the crown and exchanged with Henry Jones, dean of Ardagh, in 1637.[222] Dr. Bernard, as Clogy put it, 'being then the Primate's chaplain took up his residence in Drogheda till all was lost'.[223] Bernard, then, had been dislodged, but at the same time Bedell had been frustrated. Jones's appointment was by the crown hence Bedell had lost his right of patronage. He appealed, unsuccessfully, to the deputy.[224]

To the second case Bedell devoted much attention. Bishop Moynes purchased an estate in Loughtee shortly before his death comprehending parts of two parishes. He furthermore granted the advowsons of these parishes to his brother-in-law, John Greenham, the lawyer, to the use of his family. Greenham presented a William Baillie, recently ordained by another bishop, to one of these – presumably Annageliffe (modern Cavan) which was vacant by the death of the previous incumbent in 1634,[225] – and Bedell admitted him. At this point he acquired a dispensation to hold two further parishes, and brought a presentation to Bedell for a second, Denn, shortly afterwards, to which the bishop refused to admit him. However he was instituted by the primate as metropolitan. Acrimonious and protracted litigation ensued in the clerical and other courts, and finally the dispute came directly to Bramhall and Wentworth. Baillie resigned Denn in 1637,[226] but procured the parish of Templeport from the crown on the grounds that the incumbent had forfeited his benefice through the recusancy of his wife and children, and on the further grounds that the benefice had lapsed to the crown because a previous incumbent had not been properly instituted. The incumbent was Murtagh King, an Irishman and convert, whom Bedell employed in translating the Old Testament into Irish.[227] Bedell appealed against Baillie's appointment, and Bramhall ordered that King should retain the profits of the parish to that date, empowering Baillie to proceed for his eviction or deprivation, Bedell at the same time excommunicating him. Baillie, however, proceeded against King in the Court of High Commission and the Prerogative Court, evicted him from the glebe lands, and had him arrested and harshly treated.[228] Bedell appealed sharply to Wentworth in King's favour in December 1638,[229] but seems to

221 NLI, MS 2685, 27.

222 Jones was the son of the bishop of Killala, married to Sir Hugh Culme's daughter, and brother of Col. Michael Jones (Wilkins (ed.), *Bedell*, 50).

223 Ibid.

224 Bedell to Laud, 2 September 1637 (TNA, SP 63/256, ff 137–40v; Shuckburgh (ed.), *William Bedell*, 339–43).

225 NLI, MS 2685, 49.

226 To be succeeded by Alexander Clogy, Bedell's son-in-law and biographer (ibid., 114).

227 Shuckburgh (ed.), *William Bedell*, 339–43; TNA, SP 63/256, ff 137–40v.

228 Bedell to Laud, 12 November 1638 (Shuckburgh (ed.), *William Bedell*, 344–9).

have received no support from either Laud or the Dublin administration.[230] Bedell was not in a strong position vis-à-vis the administration, and it is not clear if the dispute was resolved in his favour. In May 1639 he wrote to Laud saying that the Baillie case was not yet completed.[231] Burnet, in his biography of Bedell, states that Baillie was confirmed in his benefice,[232] though Leslie's succession list indicates no successor to King until 1661.[233]

Another of Bedell's projects was church rebuilding. The state of the churches in Cavan in 1622 has been seen,[234] little or no improvements had been effected in the interval. Two of the inquisitions concerning undertakers' estates taken in 1629 refer to the decay of the churches and the need to rebuild in more suitable places.[235] In November 1633 Bedell communicated to Wentworth a schedule of sums of money he had applotted on the Cavan parishes for the rebuilding of churches before 20 May 1634.[236] The total for twenty-four parishes was £1,199, or just less than £50 in average for each. The reaction of the laity to this can be seen in a petition to Wentworth at about this time listing their financial burdens.[237] There is only the evidence of the bishop's son and biographer to indicate the effect of the scheme:

> Moneys collected were wasted or spent, or some way converted to men's private uses, and the work neglected: with all which difficulties he so struggled and encountred that before his death all the churches were repaired and fit for the people to meet in for God's services, had the people been as willing to meet in them.[238]

We have seen that the glebe lands allotted to the parishes were, in many cases, situated remote from the parish churches. Bedell's demand that clergy reside close to their churches ran counter to the requirement that the clergy should build on their glebe. The commissioners in 1622 recommended that exchanges of land take place between the bishops and their clergy but this presented difficulty in that the episcopal lands had then been leased,

229 Wilkins (ed.), *Bedell*, 119–24.

230 Laud's response in 1637 was to offer encouragement in general terms, to venture the hope that the Irish church should not be 'an incurable body', and to point out that he had not had a vacation that summer (TNA, SP 63/256, ff 149–9v (*CSPI, 1633–47*, 172–3)).

231 *CSPI, 1633–47*, 218–9.

232 G. Burnet, *Life of Bedell* (Dublin, 1736), 97.

233 NLI, MS 2685, 321.

234 Above, 301–02.

235 *Inq. cancel. Hib. repert.*, ii, Cavan (23, 24) Chas I.

236 Sheffield City Library, Strafford letters, 20/117; Bod. Lib., Rawlinson MS D.376, fol. 231.

237 Ibid., ff 231v–2v.

238 Jones (ed.), *Life and death of William Bedell*, 60.

and it was not carried out. To effect this for Kilmore, however, at a time when new leases of episcopal property were being negotiated,[239] Bedell got a commission from Wentworth about 1636, one of the commissioners being Arthur Culme and another Bishop Bramhall.[240] The matter proceeded, apparently, almost to conclusion and an agent was sent to England to procure a new patent of the re-adjusted episcopal property.[241] The scheme foundered, as Bedell's biographers assert, as a result of the outbreak of the rising,[242] but it would seem as much from the need for new leases of the episcopal lands to be granted within a stated time.[243]

4. The policy of Wentworth and Bramhall

From 1619, at any rate, can be dated Laud's interest in the Irish church. In particular the interest concentrated on Ulster where the church was best endowed[244] and where, from 1634, John Bramhall, Laud's active supporter in Ireland, was bishop of Derry. The outcome of that interest, energetically lieutenanted, can be seen in a concerted effort to solve those financial problems which the church in Ireland shared with its English parent.[245] However, a major effect of this policy was the extent to which it provoked the opposition of the lay landowners, beneficiaries under the previous arrangement.

As a preliminary, a regal visitation of Ireland was conducted in 1633–4. The returns, though more limited than those of 1622, throw light on the state of the church at the beginning of the Wentworth administration.[246] The income of livings in Armagh and Cavan, where available, is set out in the following table. The figures given in column (b) for Armagh purport to be the income in 1640 and are taken from an inquisition of 1657.[247] With the exception of Armagh, these figures are substantially higher than those of 1634.

Co. Armagh	Income (£)	Co. Cavan	Income (£)

[239] Below, 319–22.
[240] Wilkins (ed.), *Bedell*, 52.
[241] Ibid., 53; Burnet, *Life of Bedell*, 52.
[242] Ibid.
[243] Below, 319–22.
[244] Kearney, *Strafford*, 124–5.
[245] For this see Hill, *Economic problems*.
[246] TCD, MS 1067, 3–15, 107–13, 117–25; ibid., 1040/1 (taxable valuation of Ulster benefices); NAI, RC 15/1, 2–35, 281–300; PRONI, T975/2, 1–9 (Armagh);
[247] Paterson (ed.), 'Cromwellian inquisition', *UJA*, 3rd series, vol. 2, 212–49. A corresponding inquisition for Cavan has not been located.

Parish	(a)	(b)	Parish	
Armagh	300	300	Drung or Larra	30
Loughall	90	120	Drumdoon	100
Drumcree	80		Lawey	16
Kilmore	120	200	Moybolge	10
Derrynoose	70		Killinkere	40
Tynan	80	100	Kilcan	30
Derrybrocas	60		Knockbride	20
Kilcluney	40		Annageliff	24
Killeavy	100		Deen	24
Ballymore	100	120	Lurgan	30
Mullaghbrack	80	120	Castlerahan	37
Seagoe	80	100	Drumlahen	80
Shankill	30	80	Killashandra	80
			Tomregan	60
			Kinally	100
			Killasser	40
			Killinagh	30
			Templeport	60

In both counties incomes had risen from the figures of the 1622 visitation.[248] Armagh clergy still had conspicuously higher salaries than those in Cavan. The Armagh figures compare very favourably with the values of livings in Kent at this time, to which the Cavan ones more nearly approximate, though they may perhaps have been slightly lower.[249] Also many of the clergy in our area particularly, it seems, those in Armagh also took steps to increase their incomes by leasing, or in some cases owning, land.[250]

In August 1633 Bramhall, at Wentworth's request, sent an account to Laud in general terms of the state of the church of Ireland. He concluded 'I know not whether the churches are more ruinous or the people more irreverent'.[251] A two-fold policy of reform was immediately adopted: to recover impropriations and advowsons, and to increase the rents from episcopal lands.

In Ulster the second part of the policy had the greatest success. Bramhall

[248] Above, 298–9, 301–02.

[249] C.W. Chalklin, *Seventeenth-century Kent* (London, 1965), 218–22.

[250] Bishop Moynes, as we have seen, acquired an estate in Loughtee, and Bishop Bedell in 1629 acquired a lease of part of the TCD land in Donegal (TCD, Muniment Room, shelf 2, box 28, in packet '*c.* 1610–1720'. But parochial clergy also had land interests. John Symonds, rector of Armagh, acquired by marriage the estate of Killeavy monastery and was defined by Bramhall as 'a great moneyed clerk'. Robert Maxwell, prebend of Tynan, held land in Armagh from Trinity College (below, 337). His father, the dean of Armagh, held one townland in the Fews from John Hamilton (NLI, Rich Papers, MS 8014/9). Thomas Crant held land from the archbishopric as also did Symonds (below, 360, 364). These are some examples.

[251] TNA, SP 63/254, ff 101–2v (*CSPI, 1633–47*, 16–17).

immediately set himself, with the backing of the government machine, to increase episcopal revenues from temporalities. On 20 October 1634 he wrote to Laud stating that he had made an 'amicable composition' with the tenants in his own diocese whereby the rents would be increased from £860 to £1,400 per annum as soon as an act of parliament for that purpose had been passed. The act, he stated, was to apply to the Ulster bishops as a whole 'accounting myself happy to breake the yce for their benefit'.[252] A wholesale revolution in income, statutorily based, was thus forecast and this despite the sixty-year leases then current. In return for the removal of doubts about the validity of leases (because deans and chapters who had confirmatory powers were not legally constituted), and for a general clarification of the bishops' titles against the claims of coarbs and erenachs, the tenants would be induced to make substantial increases in rent. The act, 'for the confirmation of leases made by the lord primate and other bishops in Ulster', received the royal assent on 7 April 1635. It guaranteed episcopal title to any land found by the great office and subsequently granted to the bishops, and enacted that any leases for any term not exceeding sixty years to date from the first day of the parliament made by the bishops and confirmed by the deputy and six members of the Irish council should be valid in law.[253] The act, Wentworth assured Coke would become 'of the greatest advantage ... for these bishopricks in succession as well as in present'.[254]

On February 18 Bramhall had written to Laud in explanation of the proposed legislation and, in particular, as to why the Ulster bishops should retain the right to lease for sixty years. He stated that the lands had all been escheated and that this term had been considered most conducive to 'plantation'. All the bishops had been given that right by patent and leased accordingly 'so that there is not one foot of church land (except mensals) undemised for sixty years in the six escheated counties'. The effect would be to free both bishops and tenants from suits and difficulties and would make possible a doubling of rents – 'without it not one man will surrender or improve his rents'. It would 'exceedingly' encourage the tenants to plant and improve their lands and so be of great benefit to the whole country. Finally, the bishops did not desire this power to be exercised oftener than once, nor to have longer time to exercise it than five years 'until things be settled and then to remain in the same state without brethren, who never had the like power because there never was the like occasion'.[255] The passing

252 Ibid., ff 498–9v (ibid., 37–9: misdated). It may be noted that the lands of TCD in Ulster were not included.
253 *Statutes at large passed in the parliaments held in Ireland*, ii, 102–3.
254 Sheffield City Library, Strafford MSS, vol. ix (Letters to Coke), 12.

of the bill meant that Bramhall's scheme had received Laud's blessing.[256] Five years from 1634 were provided in which to carry out negotiations with tenants, and it is clear that Bramhall pursued his task energetically.[257]

The effect of this legislation for the archbishopric of Armagh is examined in a separate chapter.[258] By October 1635 the archbishop was negotiating with his tenants. In 1636 and 1637 the new leasing arrangements were, for the most part, worked out and given official sanction though some time elapsed before they were finalised. As a result, for the lands in Armagh a 'new rent' of £1,516. 16. 0. was payable, replacing the 'old' figure of £872. 15. 0. The total income of the archbishopric, as calculated on 3 July 1639, was £3,564. 10. 0.[259]

In Kilmore Bramhall's legislation was slower to take effect. Bedell had availed of the opportunity and re-leasing afforded to attempt to make exchanges of lands with the parish clergy so that their glebes would be close to their churches.[260] This, of course, took time and caused ill-feeling between the two bishops. On 2 November 1638 Bramhall wrote to Laud requesting him to 'sharpen' Bedell with regard to the leases of his see lands. He pointed out that the statutory deadline was now being reached, 'yet upon pretence that the glebes are not settled and some other discontents he [Bedell] detracts to do it'. He stated that he had already negotiated with the two lessees of termon land, Lambert and Culme, 'by my Lord's express subsequent consent'.[261] Laud wrote to Bedell accordingly on November 20.[262] Bedell replied on December 20 stressing his difficulties; that his suit with Moynes's widow was not yet concluded; that, as to the lease to Lambert, he was in England and difficulties had been found in negotiating with him; that the lease to Culme had been arranged by Bramhall rather, it seemed, 'to accommodate others than this see'. However, the fundamental reason, he admitted, lay in the planned exchanges with the parish clergy, and he pointed out that both Bramhall and Ussher had supported that scheme originally. That was now almost arranged, and he would set himself to leasing his lands:

> In the meane tyme me thincks I am like the poore beast, that

[255] TNA, SP 63/255, ff 35–6v (*CSPI, 1633–47*, 96–7).

[256] For further details see Sheffield City Library, Strafford MSS, vol. vi, 142–3; *Hastings MSS*, iv, 62–8.

[257] TNA, SP 63/257, ff 1–1v.

[258] Below, chapter 12.

[259] Ibid.

[260] Above, 315–6.

[261] TNA, SP 63/256, fol. 288 (*CSPI, 1633–47*, 203).

[262] Referred to in reply Bedell to Laud, 20 December 1638 (Shuckburgh (ed.), *William Bedell*, 349–51), and in Laud to Bramhall, 20 November 1638 (*Hastings MSS*, iv, 79).

> travelling in a rough and unbeaten way as fast as his legs can carry him, is at once curb'd with the bitt, and putt on with the spurres because he makes no more speede.[263]

In January 1639 Bramhall complained to Laud that the settling of the glebe lands would not be completed before the statutory time limit for leases had expired.[264] However, the new leases had been made by August, and Laud wrote to Bramhall on September 2 stating his pleasure at the outcome, and his wonder 'why a man that otherwise understands himself so well should be so much his own enemy and the church's'.[265] See rentals or leases do not survive for Kilmore. However, Bramhall calculated in January 1639 that the rental of the diocese would be increased by £574 of which £274 was for lands in Cavan.[266] The previous income had been £289. 15. 0. of which £218. 15. 0. was from land in Cavan.[267]

The second objective was the recovery of impropriations and advowsons. In the country at large it appears that the crown held most of the impropriations, but leased them to laymen. The plan was to grant the leases to vicars perpetual instead, who would continue to pay the old rents to the crown.[268] In Ulster, however, impropriations were largely outright lay property, having accompanied monastic grants. In Ulster also grants of advowsons had been made to laymen, to the bishops, and to Trinity College at the time of the plantation. In August 1633 Bramhall conveyed to Laud his dissatisfaction with the policy of James I in this respect:

> it is a main prejudice to his Majesty's service, and a hindrance to the right establishment of this church, that the clergy have in a manner no dependence upon the Lord Deputy, nor he any means left to prefer those that are deserving amongst them: for besides all those advowsons which were given by that great patron of the Church, King James ... to Bishops and the College here, many also were conferr'd under the plantations (never was so good a gift so infinitely abused);[269]

He stated that Wentworth had made it his policy that no advowsons should

263 Shuckburgh (ed.), *William Bedell*, 349–51.
264 TNA, SP 63/257, ff. 1–1v (*CSPI, 1633–47*, 208).
265 *Hastings MSS*, iv, 82–4.
266 Shirley, *Papers*, 23; TNA, SP 63/256, fol. 288.
267 Above, 300.
268 Kearney, *Strafford*, 122–3; Sheffield City Library, Strafford letters, i, 383–6.
269 *The works of ... John Bramhall*, vol. 1 (Library of Anglo-Catholic Theology, Oxford 1842), i, lxxix–lxxxii.

be regranted under the commission of defective titles.[270]

The success of this policy can be seen from a report submitted to Laud from Bramhall in January 1639[271] and also from an intermediate report of 28 March 1635.[272] As to advowsons in Kilmore it was noted in the report of 1635 that the advowsons of the deanery of Kilmore, of the rectories of Annagh or Belturbet, Drumgoon and Castleterra, and of the vicarage of Killashandra, benefices valued respectively at £120, £260, or £300, £120, £40, and £100 per annum, had been recovered for the crown.[273] The circumstances of the recovery of the deanery have been already discussed.[274] Killashandra and Drumgoon had been granted out under the plantation scheme.[275] The rectory of Belturbet was intended for James Croxton,[276] Wentworth's chaplain,[277] but was granted in 1637 to Godfrey Rhodes, who was brother-in-law of Wentworth and after the Restoration bishop of Elphin.[278] Improvements in clerical income were brought about in two parishes Lurgan, or Virginia, by £60 per annum and Drumgoon by £90.[279] No advowsons in Cavan were regranted under the commission for defective titles.

The recovery of lay-held impropriations in Cavan, however, proved abortive. In May 1637 Thomas Fleming received a regrant under the commission for defective titles of all the rectories belonging to the monastery of Kells which his family had acquired.[280] However, the largest impropriator in Cavan was Richard Nugent, now earl of Westmeath.[281] In January 1639 Bramhall informed Laud that the Irish authorities were 'in a faire way' to recover the earl's impropriations 'and two hundred pounds rent to his Majestie'.[282] In April the deputy and commissioners for defective titles made an order whereby Westmeath was obliged to surrender this property.[283] However, in January 1641 Westmeath appealed to the English house of lords.[284] He stated that in March 1637 he had compounded with the commissioners for defective titles for a new patent of his entire estate

270 Ibid. See also *Hastings MSS,* iv, 76.
271 Lam. Pal. Lib., MS 943; Shirley, *Papers*, 5–24.
272 Sheffield City Library, Strafford letters, 20/175, 264.
273 Ibid.
274 Above, 301.
275 Above, 286–7.
276 TNA, SP 63/254, fol. 499; /255, ff 35–5v.
277 Kearney, *Strafford*, 115.
278 NLI, MS 2685, 50.
279 Shirley, *Papers,* 23.
280 NAI, Lodge, Records of the rolls, v, 404–5.
281 Above, 287.
282 Shirley, *Papers,* 23.
283 NAI, Lodge, Records of the rolls, vi, 303.
284 *Hastings MSS,* iv 138–9.

at the yearly rent of £277. 11. 6. of which £79. 16. 8. was a new increase. However, in June 1637 the commissioners at the instigation of the bishop of Derry and Sir George Radcliffe had ordered that he should not be allowed the rectories worth, he asserted, £500 per annum. They ordered their surrender to the crown and would allow no abatement of rent. The lords referred his petition to a committee who, on February 3, required the attendance of Radcliffe and Bramhall on March 20 following.[285] On July 19 the lords ordered that since the commissioners were not empowered to compel him to surrender the rectories but only to compound with him for a new patent, he should be restored to the possession and profits of the rectories according to his original agreement with them.[286] On August 27 the king, from Edinburgh, ordered his restoration[287] and his patent was granted on September 27.[288] In the circumstances of the year 1641 Westmeath had found sufficient leverage to defeat Bramhall's objective.

The Laudian policy in Armagh provoked less controversy than in Cavan, but had, perhaps, greater success. No advowsons were acquired for the crown, though note was taken of the fact that, earlier, the advowson of the controversial Loughilly had been recovered from the Acheson family and was in the hands of the archbishop.[289] The advowson of Shankill rectory, granted to Cope in 1610 and again in 1629,[290] does not appear to have been recovered to the crown.[291] Bramhall, however, noted that the recovery of the impropriations of the vicars choral[292] had brought to the church lands and tithes worth, he claimed, more than £900 per annum. A piece of recovered glebe was valued at £20 a year. Tithes and glebe recovered by the rector of Killeavy from Marmaduke Whitechurch, who held the Killeavy monastery, and partly paid for to (incidentally) the Rev. John Symonds, son-in-law and heir of Whitechurch, were valued at £30[293] a year. No attempt appears to have been made, however, to recover the tithes of the old impropriate parish of Tartaraghan, belonging to the abbey of St. Peter and St. Paul, and held by Lord Caulfeild. These tithes, of 19 townlands, were (in 1657) valued at £30 in 1640.[294] The Laudian policy in Armagh was

285 Ibid.; *Lords' jnl.*, iv. 14.
286 NAI, Lodge, Records of the rolls, vi, 389.
287 Ibid.
288 Ibid. His patent of lands, excluding the rectories, had been dated 30 July 1640 (ibid., vi, 348–53).
289 Shirley, *Papers*, 9.
290 NAI, Lodge, Records of the rolls, v, 183–5.
291 It may be that Cope disposed of it to Lord Conway (see TNA, SP 63/256, ff 160–61v (*CSPI, 1633–47*, 174)) and that he was not required to surrender it though, in 1657, an inquisition stated that the bishop of Down was patron (Paterson (ed.), 'Cromwellian inquisition', *UJA*, 3rd series, vol. 2, 212–49).
292 Above, 307–09.
293 Shirley, *Papers*, 7–8.

able to build on previous changes. Nothing comparable had happened in Cavan before the Wentworth period.

Such was the success of the Laudian policy in Armagh and Cavan. In January 1639 Bramhall wrote 'there is no doubt of an happy conclusion of this great worke if God bless my lord [Wentworth] among us'.[295] Within two years the political implications of their joint efforts were to be felt.

By 1641, then, despite conspicuous exceptions, long steps had been taken towards clerical financial independence. At the same time, by 1641, it was clear that protestantism only was to be the religion of the colony and, indeed, that it was likely to fragment along denominational lines. The reformation as applied to plantation Ulster had not been, in some ways, a radical one. The original thinking visualised a redrawing of parish boundaries and the abolition of impropriations. However, the old system was not dramatically altered, and we have seen that difficulties and problems continued being encountered during our thirty-year period. This chapter has attempted to examine some of these as they affected our area, concluding with a treatment of events when the clergy received powerful government backing.

[294] Paterson (ed.), 'Cromwellian inquisition', *UJA*, 3rd series, vol. 2, 212–49.
[295] TNA, SP 63/257, ff 1–1v (*CSPI, 1633–47*, 208).

CHAPTER 11

The estates of Trinity College, Dublin, in Armagh

1. Extent of lands and leasing arrangements, 1610–14

Grants to institutions formed a distinct section of the Ulster plantation arrangement. The London companies and the church were the two most substantial, but the recently-established college at Dublin was an obvious candidate for the royal bounty. The project for the plantation envisaged a grant to the college of lands in Armagh and elsewhere[1] and when plans had been finalised it received, on 29 August 1610, extensive lands in three Ulster counties.[2] In Armagh they thus acquired in the territory of Toaghy (in Armagh barony), land then estimated at 4,100 acres, and also Colure, a smaller area, rated at 600 acres. The real extent was some 22,875 acres, or 7 per cent of the land of the county.[3] They also received extensive property in Donegal and Fermanagh and nineteen advowsons, none, however, in Armagh.[4]

In procuring these lands the college had the backing of two people: James Hamilton and James Fullerton. Both were Scots who had become fellows of the college, acquired government office and, in Hamilton's case, extensive grants of land. Both were in London early in 1610 and both (particularly Fullerton) accepted responsibility for steering the college grant to its conclusion.[5] The amount to be granted became a subject of controversy arising from the decision to grant the termon and erenach lands to the bishops.[6] As a result of a case put by them, twelve townlands of

1 'Ulster plantation papers', no. 74, *Anal. Hib.*, viii.

2 Certified copy in TCD, Muniment Room (henceforth M.R.). The lands are listed in Muniment Room, Mahaffy Collection, E.40–42 (henceforth drawer and document numbers only will be cited) with marginal notes by Provost Temple.

3 It may be noted that Scots undertakers received some 5 per cent of the total acreage.

4 In writing this chapter it has been found difficult to discuss the Armagh lands separately, owing to the nature of the college's leasing policy. Some treatment of the lands in Fermanagh and Donegal is incorporated below either through necessity or because it throws light on the Armagh property. Furthermore, because the college leased to substantial middlemen and because the source materials come predominantly from the college archives, the state of the land sometimes assumes an unavoidable remoteness.

5 C.16, 19; E.26, 29.

6 Above, 6.

Toaghy were excepted from the college patent.[7] The college was required to subscribe to the same conditions of building and tenanting as undertakers,[8] not being privileged to lease to Irish tenants.[9]

The outcome for the college was such as to revolutionise its finances, and the college grace, dating from 1637, records its gratitude in fitting terms – *Jacobo ejusdem munificentissimo auctore.* Although earlier royal benefactions and private donations had begun to provide some basis for development, it had entered the seventeenth century by no means confident in its endowments. When a new provost, William Temple, assumed control in December 1609 there was, in the college 'chest', £139. 13. 11.[10] Now, in 1610, Fullerton was confident that 20,000 acres had been granted, and predicted an easy return of £500 by leasing at 6d. per acre.[11]

The urgent question for the college, important also for the development of the plantation, was how these lands could be converted to profit. Either it must manage the lands through an agent or agents, or it had to let them on satisfactory terms. Its experience with Munster land cannot have commended the former course.[12] Furthermore it had sent no agent to England or Scotland to recruit tenants and its governing body, unlike the ordinary undertakers whose conditions were similar, had no background in English rural society which would facilitate colonisation. Also the college, as an institution composed of a number of individuals, was liable to division of opinion on schemes or proposals for its land.

Apart from an offer from Hamilton, proposals to it were not numerous. Hence they requested Fullerton and Hamilton in London to procure for them permission to let to native Irish tenants. Tentative overtures were made by a group of Suffolk men (one called Wilson) to undertake the lands and Hamilton and Fullerton were also requested to conduct negotiations with them. Hamilton, however, replied on 11 January 1611 that he had

7 E.26. In a letter of 12 January 1611 Hamilton cryptically stated that 'they seeke to cutt of from you Kilmacrenan and the lands of Fermanagh' (E.29).

8 J.P. Mahaffy, *An epoch in Irish history: Trinity College, Dublin, its foundation and early fortunes, 1591–1660* (2nd edn., London, 1906), 155, is incorrect and presents a false emphasis.

9 Hamilton reluctantly gave personal bonds for the performance of these obligations which he 'perfectlie' saw would 'not be performed within the time limited for the same' (C.16), though he also pointed out that this was 'never a whitt the worse for you for their civilitie and industrie will be the bettermente of those partes and your harmony in religion good' (E.26), whereas 'the plantacon of natives would disapointe and disgrace the Colledg in the end' (E.20).

10 J.P. Mahaffy (ed.), *The particular book of Trinity College, Dublin* (London 1904) (henceforth *P.B.*), 37b; B.67. There was an additional £1,070. 5. 5. due from various sources (*P.B.*, 38).

11 C.19.

12 J.W. Stubbs, *The history of the University of Dublin, from its foundation to the end of the eighteenth century; with an appendix of original documents which, for the most part, are preserved in the college* (Dublin & London 1889), 31; notes by Temple on a roll 'The Colledge rental … Munster', n.d. (TCD, Ante room, cupboard B, shelf 5).

'nether sene nor hard of any of them', stating somewhat caustically that it seemed strange they should speak of this offer

> And yet withal you advertise that it is app'hended there to be impossible that sufficient number of English and Scottishmen should be gott to plante those landes and therefore licence is to be obtained to plant natives.[13]

Hamilton's own offer caused serious division in the college and it was only after protracted negotiations that most of the estate was finally leased to him in 1614. His proposal,[14] while it would free the college from problems of management, was hardly a generous one. He would pay 'six-fold the king's rent' over and above that rent, i.e. somewhat under £230 per annum, for the entire estate in return for a fee-farm grant. He would commence payments at Michaelmas 1612, pointing out that the crown gave four years' respite from quit rent payment.[15] He would immediately send over British tenants and workmen and would build houses 'upon special places of danger' and let the lands and houses together. All should be obliged to take the oaths of allegiance and supremacy.[16] In this way the plantation conditions would be fulfilled. Great care would be taken in the selection of tenants:

> I could lett some of your lands to some great men here, and to come captens there, but I had rather lett it to such honest men of meaner rancks, who if they do not pay me their rent shall whether they will or not, p'mit me to fetch away their distresse, then to deal with such monsiuers who being our tenants we must petition unto and intreat for our rent ...[17]

It seems that Provost Temple, Luke Challoner, and James Ussher accepted the terms though there was further negotiation about the rent.[18] Hamilton's final offer, made in December 1612 and mediated by Chichester,[19] was that for a grant in perpetuity he would pay £632 per annum. He would not waste the woods, would build 'accordingly as required' and fulfil all the plantation conditions. He would pay the rent in time of rebellion 'or so

13 E.29. The college does not ever appear to have considered the practicability of importing British tenants itself. A draft of conditions for middlemen of *c.* 1613 in Temple's hand (E.34) listed, *inter alia*, 'that they shall discharge the college from all covenants required of the undertakers'.

14 C.16.

15 E.26.

16 C16.

17 Ibid.

18 E.28/1, 2, 3; Stubbs, *University of Dublin*, 32–3.

19 E.32.

much as by a lawfull jury shalbe judged payable unless ... the wast was such for so long time as where there was nether horne nor corne'.[20]

There was, however, anxiety in the college as to the terms of the proposed bargain which led to dispute between the provost and many of the fellows. The affair may be outlined here as a detailed contemporary discussion of land-leasing policy. In the summer of 1613 the college appealed to the Dublin government, with Hamilton's assent,[21] for advice in general as to the wisdom of a fee-farm grant and, in particular, as to certain of the conditions and securities. This appeal may have been part of the provost's strategy for pushing through a transaction increasingly disapproved of by many of the fellows.

The grant of a fee-farm was considered 'a matter fitting', and it was felt that Hamilton should give assurance of part of his own lands to build six 'castles' within seven years. The college estate was thus seen as equivalent to six great proportions of plantation land to which the plantation building conditions were being applied, though here with a seven years' deadline.[22] No further securities for payment of rent were considered necessary than that the landlord should have the normal rights of distraint and re-entry.[23]

The fellows not only claimed that the rent offered was too small but put forward a substantial case against a fee-farm grant. Simply, they pointed to the dangers of inflation. If coin became 'base or scarce', if prices of goods increased, an interminable lease could be a grave disadvantage. Temple repostulated fiercely, in one case setting out his argument in syllogistic form.[24] It would not be to the college's advantage to lease at such small rents as those taking short leases would demand. He asserted that

> These Ulster lands [having] now a long tyme rested barbarous, rude, unhusbanded, indistinguished by inclosures, fences, and bounds, unfurnished of howses for habitac'on or defence, naked of all sorts of buildings for necessary use, no man of wisdome will for a short time take a lease of any proporc'on thereof.[25]

A lessee holding for a short period would 'weare out ye whole virtue and hart thereof, spoyle the woods, [and] build no more than of necessity he

20 Ibid.

21 D.15.

22 E.32.

23 E.31. Hamilton also proposed to pay one-third of his rent in provisions, but this was not accepted by Temple (B.12/2, N.7: see Mahaffy, *Epoch*, 172).

24 Drawer K. Hamilton was fully aware of the value of a fee-farm grant, having himself recommended the college to attempt to procure such an interest in neighbouring land in Armagh granted to the primate (E.26).

25 Drawer K.

must'.[26] Against the inflationary argument he attempted to prove that a long lease was, in effect, no different that a fee-farm grant.[27] Temple's other line was more a personal and political one – that the college was too profoundly indebted to Hamilton to refuse his offer. To do so would be to 'condemne us of ingratitude and dishonour'[28] and could well provoke him to seek redress in law. There were even more fundamental reasons:

> By this disgrace offred hym and by his informac'on thereof at court we shall hazard the loss of the King's favour, provoke the displeasure of the scots, [and] expose our pencon to some question … Shall he now luse the bird who hath beaten the bush so long?[29]

Four of the fellows retaliated on 28 June 1613 by entering into a bond to Sir Henry Foliot and Capt. Paul Gore, both servitors in Donegal, to accept only their offer of £700 per annum for a thirty-one year lease.[30] At this state of deadlock the provost appealed to the visitors for arbitration.[31] Their views are not known, but Hamilton did not receive a grant in perpetuity.

On 24 June 1613 articles of agreement were drawn up whereby he was to 'content himself' with a sixty-year lease at the same rent, the first payment to begin in May (*sic*) 1613.[32] The estate was seen as comprising six proportions of 2,000 acres, and on each he was to build 'a strong fort for defence'.[33] This agreement was also not finalised and it was not until 17 March 1614 that the bargain was ultimately concluded[34] after counsel's advice had been taken.[35]

On that day Hamilton received a lease for twenty-one years of the entire estate, with the exception of twelve ballyboes in Toaghy, Armagh, which were leased on the same day to William Crowe of Dublin for thirty-one years.[36] The leasing conditions were now less demanding. Sir James was to 'repair and maintaine and uphold' all castles, tenements, etc. on the property, and if he or his tenants built on the land they should not do so 'dispersedly or scatteringly.' He should not demise to any of the mere Irish or to any person who had not taken the oath of supremacy. The land was now seen as falling into thirteen units, twelve held by Hamilton, and the

26 E.30.
27 Drawer K. The fellows appear to have wanted a lease of no more than 31 years.
28 C.16/c.
29 Ibid.
30 B.13; Stubbs, *University of Dublin*, 33–4, 378–9.
31 E.32.
32 C.13; D.15; E.33.
33 C.13; E.33.
34 Counterpart of lease, in very damaged state, is in TCD, MSS Room, in Box of College leases under D.
35 Account Book, 1613–18, fol. 7v (Ante Room, Cupboard B, shelf 3). It cost £4.
36 TCD, MSS Room, in Box of College leases under D.

rent was sub-divided in terms of these units. Five of these units were in Armagh as follows:

> Colure, one unit, at £30
> Toaghy, four units, one held by Crowe, at £60 each.[37]

The total rent was £632. 8. 6. of which £270 was payable from Armagh. Crowe appears to have been a lawyer (he was in government service from 1597[38]) and his wife, Elizabeth Blount, was probably a daughter of Mountjoy.

Thus, though the college lands had been leased to middlemen some years earlier than the London companies had similarly leased their lands in Londonderry[39] the college, unlike the Londoners, had carried out no building operations or placed British occupiers on their lands, despite their common obligation to do so. The college, in fact, had expended no more than about £25 on its Ulster land up to 1614.[40] It is perhaps surprising that neither Carew nor Bodley made any reference to the college's neglect of its property. It had however, apparently, made some preliminary arrangements. Sir Toby Caulfeild must have received a caretaker grant of the Armagh lands at the end of 1610 because in June 1611 he paid £40 as part of half a year's rent.[41] In the summer of 1613 Hamilton paid £100 as rent for the Ulster lands,[42] and £200 in December.[43] His occupation must therefore have begun by 1613, and he paid £400 for the year ending May 1614.[44]

2. Tenure and profits of lands, 1614–18

On 27 June 1614 – Hamilton's lease dated from March 17 – the college was freed by king's letter from its colonising obligations. They might 'plant' the Ulster land with 'such ten'nts ether Brittish or Irishe as they shall finde

[37] The counterpart of Hamilton's lease lists only two units in Toaghy as having been leased to him but this is clearly due to an error in transcription because the college accounts and Hamilton's payment consistently indicate that he held three units and Crowe a fourth. (The accounts, in fact, usually charge the total sum to Hamilton (B.20, 26, 29).) The Donegal lands were divided into seven units (Tirhugh: 4 at £60 each, and Kilmacrenan: 3 units, 1 at £34. 8. 6. and 2 at £34), and the Fermanagh lands, Slutmulrony: 1 unit at £20.

[38] Hughes, *Patentee Officers*, 36.

[39] Moody, *Londonderry Plantation*, 446–7.

[40] Below, 344. It seemed now that the financial security of the college was guaranteed. Samuel Ward, a Cambridge don, in a letter to Ussher noted the change in its fortunes (Elrington (ed.), *Ussher*, xv, 85–6). For the year ending May 1615 its net income was computed to be £1,088, the chief items being £600 from Ulster and £388. 15. 0. annual grant from the exchequer (B.20; N.17).

[41] *P.B.*, 26b.

[42] Ibid., 85.

[43] Account book, 1613–18, fol. 3v (Ante Room, Cupboard B, shelf 3).

[44] B.22, 26.

meetest … as heretofore wee have graunted to bushopps in that province',[45] but were not to be exempt from building obligations. The estate thus became – along with the lands of servitors, natives, the church, and the schools – areas from which the native population need not be expelled. It was a technical amelioration in the conditions of the native Irish in Armagh. It was also, by the nature of the college's leasing policy, much to the advantage of Hamilton and Crowe.

It was quickly seen, nonetheless, that Hamilton could not operate virtually the entire estate himself. As early as March 26 he sold to Crowe his interest in the Fermanagh (Slutmulrony) lands.[46] In May 1615 he disposed of the entire remaining property to Sir James Carroll.[47] Carroll lived at Finglas and combined public and municipal office with mercantile pursuits and land acquisition.[48] He had business and other connections with the college from an early period.[49] Hamilton and his brothers, Carroll, and Crowe had business relationships,[50] and the Trinity estate had thus become part of their wider financial activities.

Hamilton's payment of rent was irregular, though reasonably complete.[51] At the end of his tenure he was held to be £136. 8. 6. in arrears, about one-quarter of a year's rent, but of this £60 was considered payable by Foliot, who held some of the Donegal land, and so his final debt was £76. 8. 6.[52] There is no evidence that this was ever paid.[53] How Hamilton had used the college land is not easily known.[54] His brothers, particularly William though also John, feature in the college accounts.[55] It is likely that the land was either let directly by him to the native occupiers, as at least a little of Toaghy was,[56] or else to local servitors as some of the Donegal land was to Foliot and Gore, and most likely as Colure was to Sir Toby Caulfeild. Perspective on the Hamilton disinvolvement can be got from the fact that, at this time, the family acquired estates in Armagh and Cavan.

45 F.16; BL, Add MS 4794, ff 303–3v; ibid., Add MS 36,775, ff 148–8v; *CPRI, Jas I*, 284.

46 TCD, M.R., shelf 4, box 17 in 'miscellaneous documents, mostly *c.* 1650–1750'.

47 B.22; Account Book, 1613–18, fol. 22v. Mahaffy, *Epoch*, 175, incorrectly says 1613.

48 Hughes, Patentee Officers, 24; P.B., 222; J.T. Gilbert, *Calendar of ancient records of the city of Dublin in the possession of the municipal corporation of that city* (Dublin 1889), iii, 307–8; J.P. Mahaffy, 'Attachment against Sir James Carroll, lst March 1631', *Hermathena* xi (1901), 122–5; *CPRI, Jas I*, 338–9, 358; Armagh Public Library, Cases of Lord Chancellor Bolton, no. 52.

49 *P.B.*, 24, 26, 32, 44.

50 PRONI, T808/2758; Marsh's Library, Dublin, Z4.2.6, 534–6.

51 Payments of small sums, usually under £20, were made sometimes with only intervals of days, though often of months, between them (see in particular B.22 (verso) and college accounts, *passim*).

52 B.26.

53 See *P.B.*, 171; C.30; N.28.

54 Lowry, *Hamilton Manuscripts*, does not refer to the college lands.

55 B.25; *P.B.*, 104; Bursar's Book, 1616–17, fol. 9v (Ante Room, Cupboard B, shelf 3).

56 B.21.

Carroll also proved incapable of administering the lands and, before long, surrendered his lease entirely. Litigation for non-payment of rent occupied many years. From now the lands come to be held by a number of individuals. When, in May 1618, Carroll resigned his lease[57] the Armagh lands were held as follows either from Carroll or directly from the college:

> Colure: Sir Toby Caulfeild: rent £30. Rent was being paid direct to the college from May 1616.[58] He received a twenty-one year lease from the college in May 1618.[59]
>
> Toaghy: (1) Twelve ballyboes leased to Crowe in 1614. Rent £60. Crowe transferred his interest in this land, and in Slutmulrony (Fermanagh), to Provost Temple, and rent was paid by him from Michaelmas 1614.[60] (2) Rest of estate. Held by Carroll until May 1618. Passed by him to Sir Francis Ruish.[61] Rent £180.

No improving covenants of any kind were inserted in Caulfeild's lease of Colure.

The remainder of the estate was similarly divided – the provost, several clerical ex-fellows, and local servitors becoming tenants. It was only at this time, eight years after the grant, that the essential lines of a fairly permanent leasing arrangement had been drawn – a system involving a small number of middlemen. For the college as a teaching body, unavoidably absentee, such a policy was a convenient one. However, middlemen were not the best agents of improvement, the college could not easily supervise them. Also the occupiers were at their mercy and the college was not exempted from complaints, petitions, and allegations of oppression.[62]

3. Problems of the landlord, 1617–32

In 1617, as it became apparent that Carroll would not long retain his lease, renewed friction between the provost and some of the fellows arose. In May 1617 five of the fellows petitioned the English privy council to prohibit action on the part of the provost and some of their colleagues which they felt would be to the disadvantage of the college.[63] They stated that the

57 B.59/1.

58 Account Book, 1613–18, fol. 32 (Ante Room, Cupboard B, shelf 3).

59 TCD, MSS Room, in box of college leases under D; E.35.

60 Account Book, 1613–18, fol. 13v; B.26.

61 Bursar's Book, 1616–17 (Ante Room, Cupboard B, shelf 3); TCD, MS I.4.28, 23 (this often simplifies inaccurately).

62 E.63, Basil Brooke to college, 27 January 1630; Mahaffy, *Epoch*, 171. Difficulties could also arise through the provost being tenant to his own college.

63 Stubbs, *University of Dublin*, 35.

revenue could well be doubled if the leases then in existence were allowed to run out but claimed that the provost intended to renew these leases for his own advantage. The outcome was an order of 2 November addressed to lord deputy St. John. He was instructed to inform that college that it was the king's pleasure to 'forbear' the making of any leases until the expiration of the present ones, an act of the Irish council to be passed to that effect.[64] On 8 December 1617 the provost and fellows were instructed accordingly[65] and the act of council followed on 6 January 1618.[66]

This action, however, did not sufficiently assuage the fears of the dissident fellows and further intervention from London was immediately invoked. A letter from the privy council, 20 January 1619, to the lord deputy instructed the Dublin executive to summon the provost and his associates before them and hear their case and, if necessary, take bonds for their compliance with the regulation.[67] It was further stipulated that new leases, when legitimately made, should be for no longer than twenty-one years.[68]

On February 26, the provost issued a long and testy answer to the allegations.[69] He repudiated the fellows' 'base ungrounded and undeserved suspicion' and asserted that his conscience acquitted him 'not only from all parleis and treaties' with others about demising the Ulster lands, but likewise from all intents that way. He castigated the behaviour of the fellows – their 'factious separac'on' – in conducting unconstitutional meetings and negotiations.[70] Their appeal to London represented a slight to the Dublin government, a body quite capable of dealing with 'so irregular and desperate a person' as himself. In stating what the future revenue of the college might be, the fellows had endangered the loss of its grant from the exchequer. The act of state had made no confinement to twenty-one year leases. He was not 'opposite' to the act of state and did not intend to pursue another policy 'to the overthrow of the royal foundac'on'.[71]

The next stage is a letter, 29 April, from the deputy and council to London stating that they had had the provost and all the fellows and scholars before them who had undertaken to obey the act of state and intimating that it did not appear that the provost had been 'opposite' to

64 F.31; M.R., shelf 4, box 17, from packet '1617–1745'.
65 Ibid.
66 F37/a; M.R., shelf 4, box 17, from packet '1617–1745'.
67 F.38; *Acts privy council, 1618–19*, 346–7.
68 The letter recited that this stipulation had been included in the order of 2 November 1617. This is not correct.
69 N.26/a, b, c, d. (4 drafts).
70 He deplored, in particular, the 'carriage' of Wainwright (one of the fellows) 'about the keys of the trunk'.
71 F.38.

the act or intended to break it.[72] The act of state had not, in fact, limited leases to twenty-one years. This was because in March 1617 a directive had been issued by St. John, in confirmation of one of 1609, forbidding the leasing of church or college land for longer than twenty-one years or during a clerical incumbency (except under special conditions of improvement) thereby transferring to Ireland regulations existing in England by statute to protect such lands.[73]

This was largely in internal matter. However, when in 1618 the college was summoned into the exchequer court for eight years' arrears of quit rent, £259. 8. 0., the provost was not averse to by-passing the Dublin government. The college petitioned the king, and a royal letter of April 3 declared that the college should be pressed to 'noe harder conditions' than other Ulster proprietors. They should therefore be exempt from the first four years' rent, to 1614, and be given 'reasonable time' by the deputy to pay the remainder.[74] On Jun 11 St. John so informed the barons of the exchequer, requesting that the king's letter be enrolled in their records.[75] The barons decided that the arrears of 1614–18 should be paid in four annual instalments.[76] From now the rents were paid with regularity.[77]

In 1617 a further problem arose. The plantation regulations had required that sixty acres in every thousand granted should be allotted as glebe. However, the affairs of the church were not immediately dealt with, and it was only when parish clergy had been introduced that the demand for the assignment of glebe was made.[78] The demand for the surrender of glebe by the college was made by a Donegal minister in 1617 who appealed to London and Dublin for himself and the other incumbents involved.[79] By now the college had leased its land and was reluctant to surrender any of it, or allow the claims of its tenant for consequent reductions in rent.[80]

72 F.41; TNA, SP 63/235, fol. 44 (*CSPI, 1615–25*, 247).

73 D.94. This was not the only complaint of these five fellows. In 1617 they demanded permission, *inter alia*, to examine the Ulster patent with a view to obtaining a commission from the deputy to enquire after concealments, and that two of them might go to Ulster for that purpose (N.18: a note by Temple states 'the concealments are in hand to be passed'). Whatever the share of the fellows, Temple did draw up a list of the concealments (E.23, largely in Tirhugh, one townland in Toaghy) and set in motion by petition to the deputy, October 1617 (E.37), the machinery for having them granted.

74 F.34.

75 F.37/a.

76 F.36, 37. The cost to the college of procuring this decision was nearly £20. An agent, Harry Burnett, received £14. 18. 4. for his 'imployments in England' (Account Book, 1613–18, fol. 68v). Expenses in Ireland were reduced because the remembrancer remitted his fees. However, about £2. 13. 0. was spent for ingrossing, enrolling, and in gratuities, and also a copy of Sir Walter Raleigh's *Chronicle* was given to one officer (ibid., ff 68v–9).

77 There is almost a complete set of quit rent receipts in the college archives.

78 Above, 288–90.

79 B.110.

80 B.105.

In May 1617 the college was summoned before the deputy and council[81] who ordered in June that the glebe be assigned according to the surveyor-general's certificate.[82] Parsons certified that the college should assign glebe for three Donegal parishes, and two – Tynan and Derrynoose – in Armagh.[83] The surrender of glebe in Armagh caused litigation between the college and its tenant, Carroll.[84] There was further dispute somewhat later when a fellow of the college claimed that a piece of Colure had been 'wrested' illegally from the college for glebe. He solicited the archbishop's favour, urging that while 'it well becomes you to vindicate the rights of the church … the colledge is no liss a minor than the church' and so he should 'carry an indifferent hand betwixt both'.[85] The resolution of this dispute is not known.

When in 1618 Carroll resigned his lease the college quickly found itself involved in litigation for recovery of arrears. The amount unpaid was £175 (£5 less than a year's rent) for Toaghy.[86] When the rent and *nomine poenae* were not paid within the time specified in the lease the college attempted, without effect, to distrain for non-payment. The cost to them was £2. 2. 0.[87] The outcome of a suit against Carroll in January 1619 in the exchequer is unknown.[88] He also owed other sums to the college of a highly complex nature which also caused litigation at this time,[89] but these have been segregated from treatment here. When, in 1620, negotiations commenced on the Ulster debt the college demanded £175 plus *nomine poenae* of £45 or one-quarter of the rent due.[90] Carroll argued, on February 26, that the £175 covered his loss through the assignment of glebe in Donegal and Armagh in 1617, and it was decided in March that the issue should be settled in the court of chancery.[91]

The suit about Toaghy, commenced in June 1622, focussed on whether the college or Carroll should suffer the loss of income arising from the allocation of glebe land. Trinity asserted that Carroll had been bound by

[81] Ibid.

[82] F.35.

[83] B.109.

[84] In 1624 Falkland requested the college to certify to what churches they had allocated glebe (F.47).

[85] N.47 (unsigned and undated).

[86] A sum of £43. 12. 7. from Donegal was subsequently not held to be Carroll's responsibility (B.39, 42).

[87] Account book, 1613–18, fol. 68.

[88] B.42.

[89] See B.50, 50/2, 65/2, 106, 112; C.29/c; F.45/a, b; N.20; NAI, Chancery salvage, F.36, and 2B.80.121, no. 156. These debts, however, appear to have been paid by 1626 (college accounts, *passim*)

[90] B.112.

[91] N.20.

lease to protect against all assault any part or parcel of the land, contending that their surrender of title of inheritance to the glebe had not committed him to surrender the land concerned before the expiration of his lease.[92] Carroll in his answer demanded compensation for his loss of revenue from the glebe lands claiming, in fact, for a longer time than had elapsed.[93]

The case protracted until February 1624 when a decree was issued against him for the payment of the full arrear and also £48. 2. 8. damages and £10 costs. An injunction was issued for Carroll's compliance with the decision, and an attachment was granted against him. However, Carroll 'purposely absenteth him to shun the execution of the decree' and a proclamation and commission of rebellion, and two further attachments were procured to no avail. To all a *non est inventus* was returned by the sheriff of Dublin city. On 16 June a writ *de executione decreti* was granted to instruct the sheriffs to levy from his lands and goods and property to the value decreed against him.[94] This resort was also ineffective and there the matter rested. The case has much fascination as indicating the legal process of the time and also the difficulties of enforcing legal decisions.

In 1626 the college made an offer to Carroll for payment by instalments.[95] In 1627, after Bedell had succeeded Temple as provost, Carroll offered to refer the controversy to the arbitration of the primate.[96] Neither scheme was fruitful. In 1629 the college petitioned the lord deputy not to protect Carroll,[97] and in March 1631 renewed the suit in the chancery. Carroll repeated the substance of his previous argument. He insinuated further that in the previous case he had been at the disadvantage that the provost, Temple, was also a master of the court. He claimed, too, that the other college tenants, including Temple, should have borne a proportionable share of the burden. He pointed out that the college had allowed his assignee of Toaghy, Sir Francis Ruish, an abatement of £12. 15. 0. for the glebelands and asserted that he should have received a similar abatement.[98] However, in February 1632, the court decreed as before and identical measures were instigated against him.[99]

There is no indication that any of the money claimed was recovered from Carroll, though the cost to the college of litigation against him

92 B.111 (also B.65/3).
93 B.112; NAI, Chancery salvage, 2B.80.121, no. 157.
94 C.38/c.
95 B.69.
96 *P.B.*, 98b; N.41.
97 M.R., General Registry from 1626, 21.
98 B.105.
99 B.107; document in Ante Room, Cabinet, Drawer 1; Mahaffy, 'Attachment', *Hermathena* xi, 122–5. Mahaffy misunderstood the form of an attachment, and was unaware of its significance in this case.

between 1619 and 1632 was some £55. 4. 6.[100] In addition attempts at distraint or attachment had cost £8. 11. 9, including £2. 9. 0. for three swords broken in the process.[101] Thus a sum of more than one-third the amount claimed was expended in attempts at recovery.

4. The lands in Armagh, 1618–41

When, in May 1618, Carroll resigned his lease, the Armagh lands were held either from him or the college by three tenants, Caulfeild, Temple, and Sir Francis Ruish.[102] The latter now held the larger contentious block of the Toaghy lands. Ruish was a person of servitor origin, and a privy councillor.[103] He held monastic property in Monaghan and Fermanagh,[104] but was not a local landowner like Caulfeild. He deducted from the annual rent £12. 10. 0. (2½ townlands at £5 each) to cover the loss of glebe but, while he held the lease, rents were paid with regularity.[105] Ruish died in 1623[106] and, though the rent was in arrear in 1624,[107] his widow, a substantial heiress, retained the lease and the college did not suffer from her bereavement. When she remarried to Sir John Jephson (whose first wife died in 1623) the lease was retained by them until it expired in 1635. Jephson was the second son of a Hampshire landowner who was in Ireland in a military capacity from 1598. He had married the daughter of Sir Thomas Norreys, late lord president of Munster, thereby acquiring extensive property at Mallow. In 1611, on the death of his brother, he inherited his family estate in England. He was an English MP in 1621 and 1623–5. He thus had commitments in both England and Ireland. In 1627 he was appointed governor of Portsmouth which he held until he resigned *c.* 1630 and returned to Mallow. He died in 1638.[108] Both he and Ruish were clearly absentee leaseholders.

Between 1628 and *c.* 1630 Jephson attempted to procure a new lease. These were important years in the general history of the plantation and

[100] College accounts, 1619–32, *passim* (all in Ante Room, Cupboard B, shelf 3); B.50, 51, 53, 59/1, 62, 64; C.38; N.48; document in Ante Room, Cabinet, Drawer 1. These sources preserve the costs of writs injunctions etc. This figure excludes the regular retaining fee paid to the college lawyer, and also many sums which, while not defined as arising from this suit, may well have been connected with it. The college employed seven lawyers on the case: Hilton, Finch, Sir Richard Bolton, Dowdall, Alexander, Greenham, and Powell, some of them very prominent.

[101] Account book, 1613–18, fol. 68; Accounts, 1622–3, fol. 28; Accounts, 1625, ff 16, 18v; Accounts, 1632, 31.

[102] Above, 331.

[103] *CSPI, 1615–25*, 75.

[104] *Inq. cancel. Hib. repert.*, ii, Monaghan (7) Jas I, Fermanagh (10) Chas I.

[105] College accounts, 1618–24, *passim.*

[106] *Inq. cancel. Hib. repert.*, ii, Monaghan (7) Jas I; Lodge, *Peerage* (ed. Archdall), ii, 77.

[107] Account book, 1624–25, fol. 2 (Ante Room, Cupboard B, shelf 3).

[108] M.D. Jephson, *An Anglo-Irish miscellany* (Dublin, 1964), 16–36.

Bedell's provostship, 1627–29, and the first years of Ussher's saw renewed negotiation about the college leases. Despite the act of state of 1618[109] new leases of much of the Ulster estate were granted.

In August 1628 Sir John Jephson, now about to return to Ireland, wrote to the archbishop of Armagh asking him to mediate with the provost that the lands held by his wife's late husband should not be leased to any new tenant. He was emboldened in his suit by the impression of the provost he had received from Dr. Sybbs, Sir Nathaniel Rich, and John Pym.[110] Bedell, to whom Ussher passed Jephson's letter, replied that if he would surrender his lease and accept a new one 'with reasonable increase of rent ... we are ready to treat with you'.[111] Negotiations, however, broke down despite the fact that in June 1630 Jephson wrote to Lord Dorchester, a member of the Irish committee of the privy council, pointing out that he had not insisted on the payment of debts owed to him by the king and requesting, in return, support in his dealings with Trinity College.[112]

That the college could be susceptible to pressures can be seen, however, with regard to these Toaghy lands. In March 1629 Robert Maxwell, archdeacon and ex-fellow, and tenant to Lady Ruish of two and a half townlands of Toaghy, petitioned the college to be made a direct tenant.[113] He claimed that although he held this land 'att a rack't rent' with no longer interest than what he derived from Lady Ruish, he had expended £220 in 'building and planting' there in a manner unprecedented by any of the college's 'chief tenants'. He requested that before any renewal take place he should be permitted to become 'immediatt' tenant to the college for the land he held at the expiry of the current lease.[114] On April 15 the college agreed to accept his overtures.[115] It seems, however, that Bedell's successor Robert Ussher argued in 1632 that this went counter to the act of state of 1618. Maxwell, therefore, petitioned the lords justices and council as a body best qualified to 'interpret and dispense with' their own act, to instruct the college authorities to confirm the lease 'according to equity, conscience, and their owne promise'.[116] On March 7, following on a further petition,

[109] Above, 332.

[110] John Jephson to archbishop of Armagh, 1 August 1628 (Ante Room, Cupboard B, shelf 5).

[111] Ibid. (draft reply on verso of letter).

[112] *CSPI, 1625–32*, 550.

[113] D.24.

[114] He argued amongst other things that 'others observing your carriage towards your petitioner in this particular will accordingly bee eyther incouraged or deterred from adventuringe to build upon your lands, but upon good assurance to their gaine and your loss which is neyther sought nor intended by your supl' (ibid.).

[115] M.R , General Registry from 1626, 21.

[116] Ante Room, Cabinet, Drawer 1.

the council authorised the overruling of the act in this case.[117] As a result a lease was made for twenty-one years whereby Maxwell paid five shillings a year to the college 'the surplussage of his rent to … Jephson'[118] from this date and £25. 5. 0. per annum, or £10. 2. 0. per townland, after 1635.[119]

The remainder of Toaghy was held by John Temple under Crowe's 31-year lease of 1614 and he made no offer of renewal. The Caulfeild lease of Colure was also not renewed, perhaps owing to the death of Sir Toby in 1627.

However, while the Armagh leases were not, in fact, renewed at this time, some brief mention of these renewals may be given. The re-leasing arose from overtones made by tenants unwilling to wait until the expiry of their current leases.[120] Bedell carefully managed the negotiations, soliciting Hamilton's advice which was that the college should require a doubling of rent.[121] The outcome was that new leases were granted, like Maxwell's, with very slight increases of rent for the first six years, but to be substantially increased after 1635.[122] The new leases, unlike the original ones of 1614 contained moderate improvement stipulation.[123]

It was not until the middle 1630s that leasing again became an issue. By then some of the Armagh leases had fallen in, and almost the entire Ulster estate was in fact released in the years 1635–38. From 1633, with the Wentworth administration, important changes took place in the college, which was now increasingly subject to intensified state direction. In 1632 Laud became chancellor[124] and in 1634 Robert Ussher was removed and the Laudian William Chappell appointed provost.[125] In 1637, the year in which

[117] E.64.

[118] Receipt Book, 1625–80, fol. 13v.

[119] Abstracts of leases in Ulster (M.R., Shelf 2, Box 24, from packet '*c.* 1613–1720').

[120] *P.B.*, 101b.

[121] Ibid., 103; M.R, General Registry from 1626, 23.

[122] Box of College leases under D.

[123] Thus Temple's lease of Slutmulrony stipulated that he should erect within four year years a mansion house of stone or brick at least 40 feet long, 20 feet wide within the walls, and at least two storeys high 'to be the place of principall residence within the said mannor as well for the safetie of the inhabitants upon all occasions of danger as for the keeping of all courts to be holden there' (Box of College leases under D). He also undertook to cause his tenants, if building new houses, to build near this one. During the four years the increase of rent, £2. 10. 0. per year, was to be remitted to subsidise the building, and if the house were erected within four years the increase for six years was to be discounted. This building requirement in Temple's case provides a good example of how the college's policy could be overridden by government interference. In 1632 Temple, now at court, applied to the college for a longer time in which to fulfil his building obligations. On refusal he procured a king's letter, of 17 December 1632 (*CSPI, 1625–32*, 678) requiring the satisfaction of his request. As a result the provost and fellows 'gave unto him tenne years more as he desired' (M.R., General Registry from 1626, 39–40).

[124] M.R., General Registry from 1626, 4.

[125] Stubbs, *University of Dublin*, 67.

new statutes were drawn up,[126] Wentworth required the college to admit two new senior fellows one of whom, John Harding, soon became a college tenant in Armagh.[127] Sir George Wentworth, brother of the lord deputy, acquired the benefit of another Armagh lease in 1639.[128]

While the government displayed considerable interest in one lease (in Armagh)[129] there is no evidence that the re-leasing followed from direct official interference. Although there are parallels between the college lands and those of the bishops in Ulster, the former were not included in the scheme whereby the bishop's lands were released following on an act of parliament of 1635.[130] However, some of the Armagh leases were due to fall in anyhow and there is some indication that there was competition for college land at this time.[131] A brief discussion of the re-leasing as a whole is provided because it is likely that the conditions in the new Armagh leases which have not survived were similar to those in the Donegal and Fermanagh leases now granted.[132] From this point the total annual sum due to the college from Ulster was £1,333. 9. 6, slightly over twice the 1614 figure.

These new leases or annexed schedules contained specific conditions binding on the undertenants of middlemen and the smaller direct lessors. Each tenant of a townland was to build a dwelling house of lime and stone 20 feet by 16 feet, two storeys high with chimneys and windows and also a 'kiln or oven'. Nearby should be an orchard and garden and also an 'inclosure ditcht and quicksett of twoe Irish acres to be planted with oake, ashe, or elme, round about, and not above 18 foot distant one from another'.[133] The tenant was to entertain the college seneschal for three days and nights (provided he came no more than twice a year) and assist him in laying out the bounds of his lands, as agreed to by a jury,[134] and in setting up large mearstones five perches apart 'where there is no conveniency for ditching and quicksetting'.[135] Tenants were to conform to the act of 1537

[126] Original in safe in Board Room.
[127] M.R., General Registry from 1626, 56–7.
[128] Below, 340–41.
[129] Below, 340–41.
[130] Above, 318–19
[131] The college archives contain many applications with rent offers in these years for leases of Donegal land. See four such in Ante Room, cabinet, drawer 1; also E.70, 71; N.58.
[132] Although there was some rearrangement in Donegal, where also one area was leased directly to both native Irish and immigrant tenants, the old leaseholders on the whole reacquired their lands in these counties (abstracts of college leases in Ulster: M.R., shelf 2, box 24, from packet '*c.* 1613–1720').
[133] Schedule attached to Richardson's lease of Tirhugh lands, 1637 (Box of College Leases under D). The Temple lease of Slutmulrony in particular encouraged the clearance and enclosure of unprofitable land (ibid.).
[134] Pattern draft of leases in Donegal (Ante Room, Cabinet, Drawer 2).
[135] M.R., Shelf 4, Box 17, from packet '*c.* 1620–1710'.

requiring the English language and dress.[136] Temple in his Slutmulrony lease undertook to cause Irish tenants to be removed and British substituted.[137] Tenants in Tirhugh were go grind their corn at a mill set up by a college appointee.[138] All tenants were to do suit at the college courts. Each was to provide one armed man to go one day's journey yearly when called upon.[139] The best beast must be paid as a herriot.

In Armagh, the lease of Toaghy, which Jephson's wife's late husband (Ruish) had acquired, was due to fall in in 1635. In 1634 the re-leasing of this land caused controversy between Wentworth and Sir John, the college having little or no initiative in the matter. The argument centred around – or was made to centre on – the question of tenant right. Jephson, who had applied for the lease, was the husband of Ruish's widow. Ruish's son had died unmarried in November 1629 and his three daughters, Eleanor, Mary (both married) and Anne, had become co-heirs and received a special livery of the estate.[140] Eleanor, the eldest daughter, was married to Sir Robert Loftus, eldest son of the lord chancellor.[141] Sir George Wentworth, younger brother of the lord deputy, was a suitor for Anne Ruish.[142] Who would get the lease? On 12 August 1634, in a reply to Jephson, Wentworth wrote that he had used his 'best means' to procure it for Loftus affirming that he 'never knew it a breatch of respect for a man to wish better to one than another'.[143] He agreed with Jephson that the college 'hath full liberty to choose their owne tenants', asserting that 'the right and equity of the ancient tenant dwells with them rather than with you'. He stated that the lease had now been granted to Loftus and his wife indicating that he was 'passing gladd' it had been in his power to do them a service.[144]

In a further reply to Jephson on August 22 Wentworth stated that there had been a third competitor who had offered more. He conceded that he had felt himself under an obligation to Lady Eleanor Loftus, but asserted that unquestionably 'the right of the ancient tenant' lay with her, and that both the chancellor and Jephson were 'meare strangers'. He had therefore ensured that the lease should be for the benefit of herself and her children

136 Pattern draft of leases in Donegal (Ante Room, Cabinet, Drawer 2); *Statutes at large*, i, 119–27.
137 Box of College Leases under D.
138 A specification and estimate for this mill is in Richardson Papers (Ante Room, Cupboard B, Shelf 5).
139 M.R., Shelf 2, Box 28, from packet '*c.* 1610–1720'.
140 Lodge, *Peerage* (ed. Archdall), ii, 77.
141 Ibid., vii, 247. He was M.P. for Newry in 1634 (Kearney, *Strafford*, 251–2).
142 Sheffield City Library, Strafford MSS, vol. viii, 145–56, Robert Smyth to Secretary Nicholar 3 September 1634 (*CSPI, 1633–47*, 76).
143 Earlier in the year he had refused a previous request of Jephson's (Sheffield City Library, Strafford letters, i, 251).
144 Sheffield City Library, Strafford MSS, vol. viii, 135–36.

with the remainder to Anne Ruish.[145] So the matter rested. In a letter to Wentworth in January 1635 Laud claimed that he knew of no tenant right but, as to the contestants, he felt that Loftus would be as good a tenant to 'any Church or College holding' as Jephson if the latter were 'hee yt sometimes lived at Portsmouth'.[146] The outcome was thus a vindication of tenant right, though hardly tenant right as an abstract principle. That remainder should be granted to Anne Ruish, whom Wentworth hoped would become his brother's wife, is also of interest.

These Toaghy lands, with the exception of 2½ townlands held by Maxwell, were thus leased for 21 years at £315 per annum.[147] It contained similar conditions to those in the other college leases. While the lease has not survived Loftus undertook by a bond for £1,000 to perform the conditions of his lease and also the following obligations: not to alienate his lease without licence of the college; to 'intertaine' the college seneschal when he came to hold courts for two or three days 'with horse meat and man's meate'; to preserve all timber trees on the demised lands.[148]

In April 1636 Wentworth wrote to Bramhall asking him to deal with Loftus's affairs in Toaghy and to see that the May rents were collected 'and returned with all speed'.[149] In July Sir George Wentworth wrote to thank him for his efforts.[150] The rent to the college appears to have been paid satisfactorily. However, Lady Loftus died in May 1639,[151] and Wentworth requested Bramhall to settle local difficulties about the lease.[152] In 1639 Sir George Wentworth, who had married Anne Ruish,[153] paid the rent[154] and in March 1641 Jephson's widow (Sir George's mother-in-law) paid rent due at May 1640.[155] No further payments were made before the outbreak of the rising.

No change was made in Temple's tenure of the remainder of Toaghy, the lease of 1614 not being due to expire until 1645. Maxwell's lease dating from 1632 also remained in force. The Caulfeild lease of Colure was not due to expire until 1639. However, he paid no rent after 1638 and it seems made no overtures towards renewal. In 1639 a lawyer was retained 'against

[145] Ibid., 144.

[146] Ibid., vol. vi, 142.

[147] Abstracts of College leases in Ulster (M.R., Shelf 2, Box 24, from packet '*c.* 1613–1720').

[148] M.R., Shelf 2, Box 20, from packet 'Bonds, etc. 1595–1640'.

[149] E. Berwick (ed.), *The Rawdon papers* (London, 1819), 24–6.

[150] Ibid., 27–9.

[151] Lodge, *Peerage* (ed. Archdall), vii, 247; Berwick (ed.), *Rawdon papers*, 42–6. Her husband died in October 1640 leaving one son who died in November 1640, and one daughter, born 1626 (Lodge, *Peerage* (ed. Archdall), vii, 247).

[152] Berwick (ed.), *Rawdon papers*, 45–6. The letter is not explicit.

[153] Ibid., 45.

[154] Receipt Book 1625–80, fol. 25v. This was in accordance with the lease.

[155] Ibid., fol. 26v.

my L'd Caulfeild', but presumably his death in 1640 hampered proceedings.[156] Furthermore, by 1638 it had been decided that John Harding, the nominated fellow, should have a lease of this land.[157] The rent was increased fourfold to £120 per annum.[158] The date of the lease is not known. However, the matter became complicated by ill-feeling between Harding and the English undertenants of Colure.[159] In May 1641 £96. 19. 0. was paid by Harding towards one year's rent then due[160] and the 1641 rising intervened before further payments were made or the dispute resolved though, in April 1641, three of the fellows were authorised to go to Colure to 'aske, demande, and receive' in the name of the college all rents and arrears due from the undertenants.[161] Thus the latter years of our period saw unsatisfactory returns to the college from Armagh.

The nature and fortunes of the Armagh undertenants remains obscure. Hamilton's grandiloquent offer to install a British colony did not require fulfillment with the concession to retain the natives and, while only the name of one of these has survived (Patrick Modder O'Donnelly[162]), it seems evident that the original occupiers were generally not dispossessed. Thus the muster book of *c.* 1630 has no entry for the college lands in Armagh. It is likely however that the Irish tenants had to pay high rents to the college middlemen. In a rare case where an immigrant subtenant, Rev. Robert Maxwell, held land from a college leaseholder he claimed that he held 'att a rack't rent'.[163] Carroll claimed that, as a result of the allocation of glebe land in Toaghy, he had been deprived of land for which he paid £32. 5. 0. to the college – in fact he paid £12. 10. 0. – and received himself £80 annually.[164]

Unlike Toaghy, Colure was an area which was planted with some British tenants who were introduced by Caulfeild the leaseholder. A list of these[165] preserves sixteen English names, thirteen of which had not been mustered by Caulfeild in *c.* 1630.[166] In 1641 they petitioned the college stating their grievances as a result of Harding's substitution as leaseholder.[167] They stated

156 Bursar's Accounts, 1639, 18 (Ante Room, Cupboard B, Shelf 3).
157 M.R., General Registry from 1626, 65.
158 Abstracts of college leases in Ulster (M.R., Shelf 2, Box 24, from packet '*c.* 1613–1720'); M.R., Old Receipt Book (unfoliated).
159 Below, 342–3.
160 Receipt Book, 1625–80, fol. 26v.
161 General Registry from 1640, 6.
162 B.21.
163 D.24.
164 B.105.
165 M.R., Mahaffy collection, drawer G, folder no. 1.
166 BL, Add. MS 4770, ff 43v–4v.
167 E.79 (document undated and unsigned).

that they had been brought there by Caulfeild, 'being the first English tenants that ever dwelt thereon', with promises of permanent tenancies. Now for two years they had been in continuous 'suite' with Harding, Chappell, and some of the senior fellows. As a result of Caulfeild's promises they claimed they had expended in building, hedging, and ditching 'the most p'te of their sev'all estates'. Should they now be turned out without compensation for these improvements the result would be the 'utter ruyne and destruction of att least twenty familyes'. Since Harding had begun to sue them 'a great parte' of the land had lain waste. They therefore petitioned the college, as their 'only anker and refuge', for security and fair terms. They also asked 'that ... your Worpps. would be further pleased to make such order ... that every man that inhabits on the said land may pay his own share and not some to pay all'.[168] The demand was for individual tenancies with guarantees of security. We have no indication of any action by the college before the rising presented further problems, other than to send certain of the fellows to collect the rent.[169]

5. The administration of the estate

A brief outline of the internal financial administration of the college is a necessary preliminary to this section. The college had a bursar, always a fellow and elected annually, whose duties were defined by the statutes. An auditor was also employed and the services of a lawyer were retained. The college accounts were transitional in form from the medieval to the modern in bookkeeping method.[170] They are primarily registers of day-to-day receipts and disbursements and the extraction of precise statements of profit or loss, facilitated by double-entry methods, is not easy. Bursarial fraudulence could be prevented, but an easy over-all picture of the state of the finances was not readily available. However, provosts in our period were deeply concerned with income and expenditure. Temple's management of the college's finances was thorough and painstaking. In 1628 Bedell carried out a review of the finances from foundation and drew up plans for retrenchment based on these findings.[171]

If the financial administration of the college posed problems, active and direct supervision of its land was fraught with difficulties. Although they leased, on the whole, to middlemen obliged to pay their rents at the college,

[168] Ibid.

[169] Above, 359.

[170] B.S. Yamey, H.C. Edey & H.W. Thomson, *Accounting in England and Wales, 1543–1800* (London, 1963) provides a discussion, with sources, of the impact of Italian ideas on bookkeeping.

[171] M.R., General Registry from 1626, 19, 20, 24; *P.B.*, 100b; B.67; N.45.

the college nonetheless had duties and rights requiring estate personnel. These functions were those of a seneschal: keeping manorial courts; preserving natural resources; supervising tenants' fulfilment of conditions in their leases; defining mears and bounds and defending the property against the encroachments of neighbours. An absentee landlord would also require some chorographic or cartographical investigation of new property in virtually unknown territory.

In the immediate years after the 1610 grant the college was unlikely to be exempt from the uncertainties and difficulties confronting its fellow grantees. In 1613, before the lands were leased, we find them employing an agent on unspecified tasks in the north, especially in Toaghy, and expending for this purpose £23.[172] In 1614 he received £4[173] and, earlier, in the autumn of 1610, he received a payment of £2.[174] About the background of this agent, a certain John Woodhouse, or Widdowes, subsequently an energetic estate official, little is known. In 1615 the professor of astronomy at Gresham College, London, in a scholarly letter to Ussher, asked him to convey his respects 'heartily' to Woodhouse stating that 'we have here long expected him'.[175] In 1629 he was appointed seneschal of the three Ulster manors.[176] Later, he produced two guides to Ireland with a map, one in 1647 entitled *A Guide for Strangers in the Kingdom of Ireland* ... which also included a 'true relation' of the 'massacres' of 1641, and another, *The Map of Ireland* ... in 1653, designed clearly for Cromwellian adventurers. Both were published in London.

Before his appointment in 1629, however, affairs were less systematic. In 1615 we find the college employing an Armagh man, Neale McTurlogh O'Neill, as seneschal of its lands there,[177] presumably enjoying the profits of manor courts. To the college his function seems largely to have rested in preserving timber resources. In November 1615 Temple authorised him to permit an undertenant to cut 'some competent proporc'on' of timber for his 'necessary' use 'provided that neither he nor any of his tenants sell thereof to others or make any wast in the woods'.[178] In 1617 another such agent, Brian O'Neill, appears as receiving a small sum from the college.[179] He may have been a recent graduate, or even a student, because in 1617 a 'Bernarde

[172] Account Book, 1613–18, fol. 3v (Ante Room, Cupboard B, Shelf 3). A messenger also received 7s. 6d. for carrying a letter to Sir James Hamilton (ibid.).

[173] Ibid., fol. 7v.

[174] *P.B.*, 51.

[175] Elrington (ed.), *Ussher*, xv, 88–90.

[176] Below, 345.

[177] B.21; Temple's account book, 1615, fol. 2v (Ante Room, Cupboard B, Shelf 3).

[178] B.21.

[179] Bursar's Book, 1616–17, fol. 32 (Ante Room, Cupboard B, Shelf 3).

Neile' received a stipend as 'a poore native'.[180] In 1617 some of the fellows requested leave to go to Ulster to enquire after concealments.[181]

In 1618 the college initiated action leading to the grant of a new patent of the Ulster estate on 26 July 1619.[182] Such action was paralleled in the behaviour of many undertakers in seeking regrants at this time. The only significant change was that the estate, formerly one manor, was now divided into three, called Toaghy, Slutmulrony, and Kilmacrenan. The real objective appears to have been to acquire the right to hold three manor courts and the original power to keep one such was surrendered on July 1.[183] There was obvious administrative wisdom in having three courts for three separate areas, also now no longer leased as one unit. However, the outcome was a grant to John Temple, the provost's son who supervised the lands his father held from the college in Armagh and Fermanagh, of the office of steward or seneschal of manors of Toaghy and Slutmulrony. He was to enjoy the emoluments of the courts 'without rendreinge ... any accompt for the same'.[184]

In August 1629, before Bedell resigned, the seneschalship of the Ulster manors was formally granted to John Woodhouse.[185] There had been obvious disadvantages in having as seneschal a person, John Temple, who was also a college tenant, and native Irish officials may have been considered unsatisfactory. Bedell was particularly anxious that Woodhouse should be appointed as he indicated in a letter to Dr. Ward, master of Sydney College, Cambridge, in May.[186]

The counterpart of his grant of the appointment,[187] as seneschal and surveyor, refers to the college's good opinion of him from others and, especially, from William Parsons.[188] He was given power to hold courts in the three manors, either himself or by deputy, and to enjoy the fines and profits. In return he was to provide for the college, in parchment, a '*verum superiosum descripconem et chorographiam*' of the lands concerned of Kilmacrenan and Slutmulrony within twelve months and of Toaghy within seven years. He was also to return regularly the rolls and records of the courts. This does not necessarily imply that he was to make maps (though

[180] Account Book, 1613–18, fol. 53v (ibid.).

[181] Above, 333.

[182] *CPRI, Jas I*, 410–11 (incorrectly printed as a pardon of alienation); *CSPI, 1615–25*, 254 (incorrectly dated as July 16). The recorded expenditure totals over £10, including £8 to the attorney-general for drawing up the patent (Account Book, 1613–18, ff 68v–9).

[183] *CPRI, Jas I*, 410.

[184] E.55.

[185] General Registry from 1626, 24; *P.B.*, 104.

[186] C. MacNeill (ed.), *The Tanner letters*, (IMC, Dublin 1934), 84, 88; Shuckburgh (ed.), *William Bedell*, 297–8.

[187] Ante Room, Cupboard B, Shelf 5 (in Latin).

[188] There is no indication as to what was the nature of Woodhouse's association with the surveyor-general.

a contemporary translation of his grant states that he was)[189] and if he did none have survived amongst the college papers. However, there is an undertaking under his hand, in September 1630, in which he states that he is about to 'take a surveye' of the college lands in Ulster and will not reveal any concealments to any but the provost and fellows.[190] Some indication that maps were produced is provided by the fact that five maps of the Ulster estate were in existence in 1653.[191] It may well be, then, that Woodhouse should join Raven as one of the founders of the Irish estate map tradition.

It is clear at any rate that Woodhouse was active and energetic as college agent. He immediately set about the recovery of college concealments from encroaching neighbours, particularly urgent at a time when the Ulster undertakers were taking out new patents. Woodhouse also made forceful charges against the Temples.[192] He asserted that Sir William 'would do nothing' to recover any concealed land for the college. His exposé of John Temple's behaviour amounted to a cogent questioning of the advisability of appointing as seneschal a person who was also a college middleman:

> It is not safe for the College to make their tenant seneshall for then they shall never be able to come upon the lands to enquire nor shall ever know the trew statte of theire lands, neither can punish any misdemeaner of selling of woods or wast, enquire of encheechmts, prosecute any suits, but be helld mere strangers to theire owne and never shall be able to discover anything to them.[193]

He also asserted that the Temples had done nothing to improve the lands they held in Armagh and Fermanagh. He claimed that in Slutmulrony (the Fermanagh lands):

> their is not one good house upon thirty four tatts nor any house built at theire charg, in Toaghy only a tenant hath built a house, but the said Lady and Mr. Temple's tenants have wasted all the timber woods with theire consents, and the lands of S'mulrony inhabited with kerne, and in Towaghy Patrick O'Quine whose sons

[189] TCD, MS 962, 7.

[190] N.50. The lease of Slutmulrony to Sir John Temple in 1638 reserved the right for the college's surveyor and his attendants to 'view, survey, and measure' the lands demised (box of college leases under D).

[191] A.iv/c. They were removed from the college trunk at this time along with the grant to Woodhouse and other documents relating to the Ulster estate, for consultation, by the then bursar. This was before the Down Survey. It is unlikely that they were part of the 1609 survey and there is no indication that any other cartographer had been employed. The same document also refers to another lost map of college lands in Munster.

[192] C.41.

[193] Ibid.

> with [others][194] were the principall woodkerne of Ulster and the Connylies in Mullrony.[195]

Woodhouse's recorded activities largely concerned the Fermanagh lands and a struggle with the Temples over the right to hold courts and so may only be mentioned in passing here. However, in Armagh he recovered small portions of college land from both the primate and Lord Caulfeild.[196] As to the Fermanagh lands Woodhouse claimed that the Temples and their tenants and a neighbouring undertaker, Flowerdew, were in league to have some concealed land amongst the college estate granted in a patent to Flowerdew. Woodhouse, on behalf of the college, sought protection from the deputy and council which was given, after acrimony, in limited terms and later, in 1632, had the matter also brought before the English privy council.[197] In his attempt to recover the right to hold courts from the Temples, he pursued a suit in chancery in 1630 and 1631.[198] Allegations were made on both sides that the college woods were being wasted, Temple's supporters, the O'Connellys, asserting that Brian O'Neill, now deputy to Woodhouse as seneschal of Slutmulrony, disposed of timber for profit and he making counter assertions.[199] While these problems arose largely with reference to the Fermanagh lands, it is likely that to some degree the college estate in Armagh was similarly affected.[200] Woodhouse certainly pursued his struggle with the Temples with vigour.[201] He was also involved in a variety of other activities, for example, in the recovery of college advowsons,[202] and in negotiations over leases.[203]

Woodhouse, then, is a person of some interest, tough and versatile. Such people were increasingly necessary as landlordism took root and Woodhouse is one of the few about whom details survive. It is regrettable that the maps, in existence in 1653, which may well have been his, are not now available as examples of one of the rarer by-products of Irish landlordism in this period. This section has attempted to outline the

[194] Document indecipherable. Woodhouse's hand is difficult and his reports are all undated.

[195] C.41.

[196] Ibid.; N.54.

[197] C.41; D.30; E.60, 80; F.60/a, 66; General Registry from 1626, 23; Marsh's Library, Dublin, MS Z4.2.6, fol. 730.

[198] General Registry from 1626, 29; NAI, strong room, Chancery index to ancient pleadings, 1629–34, Bills, no. 10,517.

[199] D.27, 34; E.65, 69; N.55.

[200] Certainly the college lands in Donegal were (see E.69; Articles between Provost Chappell, etc. and Woodhouse (Box of college leases under D)).

[201] He claimed that he had been threatened with physical violence by Thomas Temple and his man in 'the Coomb' in Dublin (C.41).

[202] See, for example, TCD, MS 962, 34; also E.38, 39, 39/b, c, d, e, 44.

[203] N.58.

problems of an absentee institutional landlord in administering its Ulster estate, examining the personnel and methods employed.

6. Conclusion

It can be seen that the condition of the college land in Armagh (as elsewhere in Ulster) was not profoundly affected by the change in ownership. The college originally received its lands under obligation to plant British tenants but proved incapable of fulfilling this obligation and either it, or its influential chief tenant Sir James Hamilton, procured permission to retain the native Irish as tenants. It thus, in effect, changed from being an undertaker-type to a servitor-type grantee. The college had difficulties with its early leasing arrangements – themselves a cause of controversy within the institution – both Sir James Hamilton and Sir James Carroll, to whom Hamilton transferred a lease of the greater part of the Ulster estate, leaving sums of rent unpaid. It was only by about 1618 that a leasing policy involving a small number of substantial middlemen had been evolved. In adopting such a resort it was opting for a similar policy to that favoured by the London companies in Londonderry with whom it had many similarities. Its leases to these middlemen, however, were almost entirely for twenty-one years whereas the London companies mostly leased for fifty to sixty-year terms.[204] Its leasings bear somewhat less comparison with the practice of the archbishopric of Armagh which, while it did make leases to substantial British tenants who held, however, as a result of government permission, for sixty-year terms, also leased directly, though decreasingly throughout our period, to native Irish occupiers. The bishopric of Kilmore relied much more exclusively on British chief tenants who received sixty-year leases.

There was some slight overlap in tenants in Armagh between the college and the archbishopric, but the college, unlike the archbishopric, had no overlap in tenants in Armagh with the Londoners. Both archbishopric and college in the 1630s accepted government-favoured tenantry. While the government did intervene in promoting specific tenants for college leases in the 1630s, it did not intervene on behalf of the college, as it did in the case of the Ulster bishops at this time, in any general scheme for the re-leasing of its lands. The college, in fact, with its moderate intentions to improve its lands, often got caught up in a number of situations in which private influences on the government affected, or indeed actively acted against, its policies. In its capitulation of these influences, the government was not acting in the interests of the plantation policy.

[204] Moody, *Londonderry Plantation*, 446–7.

CHAPTER 12

The estates of the archbishopric in Armagh

1. Introduction

The decision in 1610[1] to grant the termon and erenach lands to the bishops settled one of the most contentious problems with which the planners of the colony were faced. The lands the bishops received in their patents in that year included also very much smaller amounts of land traditionally appertaining to their sees, their mensal property. The land was all granted in free alms. In return for the grant of lands they were required to surrender their impropriations and rights of tithes. This should be done in a form satisfactory to the English or Irish governments, the incomes to be surrendered to come to the respective parish clergy.[2] Although it had been suggested that the bishops should surrender land for glebe so that the incumbents might have glebe land close to their churches which were, for the most part, located within the termon and erenach lands, no such surrenders were required.[3]

The patents did not make it obligatory for the bishops to plant British tenants,[4] but certain inducements were offered to them to do this in the kinds of leases they were allowed to make. The then bishops, though not their successors, were permitted to make sixty-year leases to British tenants of the termon and erenach lands.[5] This was a special relaxation of the rule defined in England by act of parliament in 1559[6] and applied to Ireland by proclamation in 1609[7] forbidding the leasing of ecclesiastical land for longer periods than twenty-one years or three lives. These sixty-year leases might only be made to British tenants, the bishops might not demise any of this

1 Above, 6–7.

2 This is based on the patent granted to the archbishop of Armagh on 6 September 1610 (Armagh Public Library, Armagh Papers, 65–116). See chapter 10 above.

3 The alternative suggestion that the bishops should exchange land with the clergy – who were allotted escheated land – was also not required.

4 See above, 329–30.

5 Armagh Public Library, Armagh Papers, 105.

6 Hill, *Economic problems*, 14–15.

7 Steele, *Proclamations*, ii, 19; *CSPI, 1608–10*, 238–9. The proclamation was re-issued in 1617 (Steele, *Proclamations*, ii, 22). The object was to prohibit the making of long leases by bishops without regard for their successors.

land to the 'mere Irish' for longer than twenty-one years or three lives. The rent to tenants, British or Irish, was to be not less than £4 per quarter. Mensal land might not be leased by the then bishops or their successors for longer than their incumbencies.[8] Should the bishops make leases contravening any of these conditions, and not revoke them within three years, the lands so demised should revert to the king.[9]

2. Extent of lands, and government policy to 1634

The extent to which the archbishopric of Armagh benefited from the granting of the termon and erenach lands was brought home to another institution competing for the royal bounty, Trinity College, when the college received less land in Armagh than it had expected. The temporalities with which the archbishopric was thus endowed or had re-confirmed by patent to Henry Ussher in September 1610[10] were spread throughout each county in the diocese, both in Ulster and the Pale, forming nine manors. The manor of Armagh, made up of the town of Armagh, the lands in the county, and the termon lands of Clonfeacle in Tyrone is, in effect, the subject of this chapter.[11] Fishing rights on the Blackwater were also granted.

The lands in Armagh were extensive, almost 48,000 acres, some 15 per cent of the total area of the county.[12] The archbishopric thus received three times as much land as the Scottish undertakers, and about three-quarters of the extent given to English undertakers. Because of the nature of the grant, it did not form a coherent block, but lay in patchwork fashion throughout the entire county.[13] The conditions under which these lands might be leased have already been outlined.

The leasing of the lands, however, both of the archbishopric and of other Ulster bishops (notably those of the bishopric of Derry), became a subject of dispute with allegations that the bishops were attempting to demise them either in perpetuity or on very long leases to the advantage of their own families. Accordingly the king intervened in April 1612 to protect the endowments of the church from 'contempt and diminution', instructing Chichester to restrain the archbishop from such action on pain of extreme

8 This throws light on Bedell's dispute with the widow of his predecessor (above, 329).

9 Armagh Public Library, Armagh Papers, 65–116.

10 Armagh Archiepiscopal Registry [henceforth in this chapter Registry], A.1a.7; A.1b.25, 53–62 (volume of transcripts); Armagh Public Library, [henceforth in this chapter Library], Meath Papers, 56–116.

11 The town has been examined separately, above, 229–39.

12 This acreage figure does not include the territory of Derrynoose (almost 6,000 acres) which, although granted in 1610, was surrendered to the dean in 1612. For the circumstances see above, 308–10.

13 See maps of Armagh in the plate section.

royal displeasure.[14] It appears that Henry Ussher had only been restrained from making a fee farm grant of 'the whole primacy' for £1,500 per annum by the intervention of the dean under the confirmatory powers of the dean and chapter.[15] It may be noted that the provost of Trinity College favoured making a similar fee-farm grant of the college lands at this time.[16]

In October 1612 the king, still conscious of the 'pernicious' behaviour of the Ulster bishops, sent Chichester rules and instructions to be followed by them in lease-making. All unconfirmed leases of the archbishop of Armagh, prejudicial to the bishopric, were to be surrendered, to be re-leased according to the restrictions in his patent. On account of the uncertainty of area estimates of lands in Armagh and Tyrone, land there should be let only by the acre, of the measure of the Pale. The better profitable land should be leased at no less than 1s. 4d. per English acre, and all profitable land at no less than 1s. per acre, 200 acres to be the most leased to any one man, and the tenant to be obliged to keep one-third in tillage if tillable. One year's rent over and above the yearly rent, should be paid to each archbishop's successor provided the previous episcopate had been of seven full years' duration. Woods, fairs, markets, courts, or fisheries should not be leased for longer than an episcopate. The preservation of woods from wastage was enjoined. British tenants should be required to have adequate arms for defence, and to live together in villages. All lettings by the archbishop should have the confirmation of the dean and chapter.[17]

In February 1613 Chichester informed the archbishop of Canterbury that he had acquainted Ussher with these directions. He gave it as his own opinion that, for the 'furtherance of the ... plantation ... and that the lands of the church should be ... well built and firmly improv'd and maintained' and given the state of Ulster which was not 'yet much different from [that] of Scythis and Barbary', it was wise that episcopal land should be leased for sixty years (or more) to men 'of fashion and of fortune'. He advised that the bishops' tenants should be pressed to increase their rents from £4 (the figure stated in the patents) to £6 a quarter, and that the bishops be pressed to re-build or build their see houses.[18]

14 *CSPI, 1611–14*, 264–5. See also 'Chichester Letter-Book', no. 7, *Anal. Hib.*, viii.

15 Registry, A.1b.31, Walter Dawson's rent roll, 1713, 11; Lodge, *Peerage* (ed. Archdall), iii, 390. Chichester stated in 1612 that he had broken a lease made by the archbishop 'not many years after the ending of the wars' for sixty-one years of see land to Sir Toby Caulfeild, procuring for Caulfeild instead a twenty-one year lease of the abbey of St. Peter and St. Paul ('Chichester Letter-Book', no. 28, *Anal. Hib.*, viii). Since Caulfeild's lease of the abbey land was made in 1607 (above, 20) this must refer to an earlier controversy.

16 Above, 326–8.

17 *CSPI, 1611–14*, 295–8.

18 'Chichester Letter-Book', no. 46, *Anal. Hib.*, viii.

The death of Henry Ussher in 1613 and the appointment of Christopher Hampton, a Cambridge D.D., brought the episcopal property again into prominence and was the occasion of a regrant. The conditions of this were established by a king's letter of 30 May 1614.[19] This recited that Ussher in his patent of 1610 had been empowered – 'to the end the said lands being for the most part waste and depopulated might be the better planted and inhabited' – on the first occasion of leasing to make leases for sixty years of all except mensal land to English or Scots tenants. It stated that Hampton had negotiated with his tenants to surrender their previous leases and to increase their rents upon condition of having regrants for sixty years. The regrant, it was stated, was required because owing to the 'imbeselinge or carelesse keepings of the ancient charters' of the see, a great part of its lands were 'unjustly deteyned' by other people. The new patent should empower Hampton, though not any of his successors, to make sixty-year leases (except of the mensal lands) to English or Scots, and leases for three lives or twenty-one years of any part of the property to English, Scots, or Irish, the rents not to be under £6 or £8 for each quarter or four balliboes. The regrant followed on 25 February 1615.[20]

Further cause of dissatisfaction to the king – in Hampton's leasing policy – came to light in 1619 perhaps as a result of inquiries at the time of Pynnar's survey. It was found that Hampton's leases had contained a proviso that if at any time there should be any 'rebellion, hostilitie, or open warres in or neere the demised lands' whereby the lessee should be unable to collect the profits, he should not be compelled to pay his rent to the archbishop. This was considered ample justification for forfeiture, and the archbishop was required to surrender his patent and take out a regrant. The tenants were also to surrender their defective leases and have them renewed for the remainder of their terms.[21] As a result of these instructions the procedures of surrender and regrant were again exercised, leading to a new patent on 3 July 1620.[22]

These surrenders and regrants had been largely the result of royal intervention arising from irregularities in the leasing arrangements. In November 1630 the archbishop received further royal permission to have a regrant.[23] This was an attempt on the part of James Ussher, who succeeded Hampton in 1624, to protect the episcopal property at a time when the

19 Registry, A.1b,26; Armagh Archiepiscopal Registry, Evidences of the see of Armagh, [John Lodge transcripts: henceforth Evidences], 50; *CSPI, 1611–14*, 479–81; *CPRI, Jas I*, 275.

20 Registry, A.2c.9 (original patent); Evidences, 52; *CPRI, Jas I*, 273–4. In November 1617 an exemplification of this patent was procured (Registry, A.1a.8).

21 Evidences, 52–4; *CPRI, Jas I*, 435.

22 Original in Armagh Public Library; Evidences, 54–78; *CPRI, Jas I*, 477–9.

23 *CSPI, 1625–32*, 587.

undertakers as a whole were renewing their titles, by acquiring a new and definitive patent of the estate. No immediate action was taken until May 1633 when the king wrote to Wentworth stating that he had been informed by the archbishop that the impreciseness in naming, distinguishing, and measuring the lands forming his estate had caused difficulties for his tenants and could make for ill-feeling with neighbouring landowners. He accordingly ordered the lord deputy to issue a commission of inquiry to define the estate in precise and exact terms.[24] The deputy concurred[25] and a detailed topographical inventory of the Armagh lands was returned by inquisition in September.[26] The regrant followed in June 1634.[27] The official history of the see property thus reveals many parallels with the civilian planters.

3. Leasing policy and profits of the lands in Armagh to 1634

Up to the changes which the plantation inaugurated the archdiocese of Armagh was divided into two units, *inter anglicos* and *inter hibernicos*, highlighting its dual character being partly in the north of the island where Irish traditions prevailed, and partly in the Pale or area of Anglo-Norman permeation. From the fourteenth century when they became invariably of non-Gaelic tradition, the primates seldom went outside the territory *inter anglicos* leaving the northern segment to be served and administered by clergy and officials of Gaelic birth. This clear-cut distinction was also marked in the primate's lands and revenues and an Irish official was maintained to administer the northern property. The income accruing from the Ulster lands was highly traditional and complex, the precise annual returns being obscure. It was also subject to diminution through political vicissitudes, raids and incursions, refusals to pay, and affected by the tensions and turmoils of the sixteenth-century Ulster situation. The task of the 'Irish official', however familiar with the local background, was not an easy one.[28] In 1591 the then custodian of the office was described by Hugh O'Neill as a 'poore old man of four score and seventeen years of age'.[29] The dislocation of the Nine Years' War must have brought added difficulties, so that the rights of the archbishopric had to be established almost *de novo* by the inquiry of 1609. The income from these Ulster lands on the eve of colonisation cannot be established owing to the disappearance,

[24] Sheffield City Library, Strafford MSS, vol. iv, 20–22; Evidences, 92–4; *CSPI, 1633–47*, 10.
[25] Knowler (ed.), *Strafford's letters*, i, 172.
[26] *Inq. cancel. Hib. repert.*, ii, Armagh (20) Chas I.
[27] Registry, A.1a.13 (original patent); Evidences, 94–108.
[28] A. Gwynn, *The medieval province of Armagh, 1470–1545* (Dundalk, 1946), 73–101.
[29] Leslie, *Armagh clergy*, 33.

or very partial survival, of rentals.[30] In 1606 an attempt was made to re-order the see finances, and a rental of that date existed in James Ussher's time. Ussher examined and listed the 'rentalta antiqua',[31] but little of the documentation which he mobilised had survived. However, it was only with the new dispensation of the Ulster church which accompanied the plantation that the finances of the northern portion of the see were reorganised effectively. The outright granting of the termon lands under the plantation revolutionised the income the archbishop could expect.

The first surviving rental of the plantation period dates from 1615.[32] It thus serves as a basis against which to examine changes, notably the progressive elimination of Irish tenants, in the succeeding twenty-five years. It can best be examined by taking each area of episcopal land separately.

In Clanaul there were forty ballyboes of which only four were in English hands held by a certain Richard Lenton for sixty years at £16 per annum. The remainder of the area, twenty-nine tenancies, was in the hands of the previous Irish occupants[33] holding usually one ballyboe each and not more than two, either for life, for the duration of the primacy, or for twenty-one years. Their rents ranged from £5[34] to £7 per ballyboe per annum, the predominating figure being £6, or £2 higher than that paid by the one English tenant who also enjoyed a longer lease. The Irish tenants, with a small number of temporary exceptions, also paid duties annually.[35] The total rent payable was £232. 18. 0. per annum. In one case two townlands were leased to a family group (the O'Corrs), otherwise individual rather than joint tenancies were the norm.[36]

In Tynan four of six ballyboes were held by an ex-serviceman, Lieutenant Robert Cowell,[37] for sixty years at £20 rent. The remainder was in the hands of five members of the McCasey family, paying £12 per annum.[38]

Of thirteen ballyboes in Clanconchy in the Fews seven were in Irish and six in non-Irish hands. The Old Irish tenants, five in number, were

30 Registry, A.2a.28, ff 1–28 comprises certain dilapidated extracts from sixteenth-century rentals but these do not provide any basis for assessing income.

31 Ibid., fol. 28.

32 Registry, A.2a.28/10 'Liber supervisor de anno 1615 pro ter du primat'. The official plantation surveys do not deal with episcopal estates.

33 The families of O'Donnelly, O'Lappan, O'Conree, O'Connor, McConnor, O'Hahy, McGrory, O'Corr, O'Finn, O'Brenigan, O'Cromy, Cuilen, McBrioge, O'Neill, and O'Donnellan.

34 For one year only, afterwards £6.

35 At the rate of '1 ox, 2 fat muttons, 4 hens, 1 fat hog, 1 barrel of barley, 1 barrel of oats and 40 loads of wood' per townland.

36 Registry, A.2a.28/10, 4–11.

37 He held a pension from the crown (*CPRI, Jas I*, 153, 279) and had land in Monaghan and also, apparently, in Down (Armagh Public Library, William Reeves, Memoirs of Tynan (MS vol., unfoliated)).

38 Registry, A.2a.28/10, 10–11.

McCaddans, O'Neills, McKiernans, and O'Flynns. Their rents ranged from £5–£8 per ballyboe with duties as in Clanaul.[39] Four of the remaining townlands were held by Richard Fitzsimonds, also a Cavan landowner, and Andrew Hamlin, Old English merchants from Drogheda.[40] One of the remaining two tenants held for 60 years. Their rents ranged from £5–£6. The total rent was at least £82 per annum.[41]

Also in the Fews, the two territories of Ballymoire and Ballymacoan, each eight ballyboes, can be examined together. Here there were no British tenants. In Ballymoire rents were as high as £9 per ballyboe with services and duties (excluding timber) in addition. Most of the land was held by the erenach family, the McImoyres, but there were also McMurphy, McGohigan, and McDonnell tenants. It appears that only one held by lease – for twenty-one years. From five tenancies, four of them joint ones, an annual income of £68. 6. 8. was due. Five ballyboes in Ballymacoan were held by the traditional McCoan occupants, not apparently by lease, the remainder being in McMurphy hands. The rent was £56, an average of £7 per ballyboe. Services and duties were also required.[42]

In Oneilland, Kilmore, ten ballyboes, was entirely in native Irish hands – O'Hagans, O'Halligans, O'Collons, O'Quins, and O'Farrans. The total rent was £55 or £5. 10. 0. per ballyboe, with duties and services also required.[43]

Doughmunter – Cullen (or Clonfeacle) in Armagh barony was made up of some seven ballyboes. The ownership of one was disputed by, and in the occupation of, Sir Toby Caulfeild. Half of the remainder was in English hands, as yet without lease, the rest being held by the original O'Cullen occupants. Rents ranged from £6. 6. 8. (to the English tenants) to £7 (to the Irish), the total being £40. 13. 4.[44]

In Toaghy, in the same barony, the archbishop held thirteen ballyboes. Four of these were in English hands for 60 and 61-year periods at £4. 10. 0. per townland, and Sir James Ware, the auditor general, appears to have been interested at this stage in leasing two others. The remaining nine ballyboes were in Irish hands, being held by the local families of Coffy, McCoddan, O'Neill, and O'Donnelly, at rents ranging from £5–£6 per annum, with duties and services, one tenant holding for twenty-one years,

39 In some cases ten days' work with a man and garran (Irish horse) was also stipulated.

40 For Fitzsimonds's connection with the Londonderry plantation see Moody, *Londonderry Plantation*, 151, 173.

41 Registry, A.2a.28/10, 12–15.

42 Ibid., 16–17.

43 Ibid., 18–19.

44 Ibid., 20–21.

the remainder being either for unspecified or brief periods. The total rent was £68.[45]

At this time the whole area of Cossvoy, eight and two-thirds ballyboes, also in Armagh barony, was held by two British tenants, John Browne and George Chambers, the latter subsequently an official of the archbishop, at approximately £4 per ballyboe. The total rent was £34. 13. 4.[46] The condition of Coscallen or Slutmellaghlin, in the same barony, also eight and two-thirds ballyboes, is more obscure, but it appears that only one ballyboe was in English hands – Chambers's – much of the remainder being held by descendants of Turlogh Brassilogh O'Neill. The rent for 7 ballyboes was £34, the remainder seemingly being occupied without payment.[47]

Five ballyboes in Derrybrocas, in Oneilland, two of which were leased to an English tenant at £9 per annum, returned £26. The remainder was held by the O'Fullan family, though it seems Sir Edward Dodington also had an interest in part of this land.[48] Two townlands in Oneilland – Drumcree – were held by an Irish tenant at £10 per annum.[49]

For the remaining segments of archiepiscopal land in the county the rental only provides a very partial coverage. For one of these, the area around the town of Armagh, many complications exist to make summary treatment difficult. Some of this was held in demesne and so not accounted for in the rental. Some was let in small parcels, which are not easily identified, and place-name changes make reconstruction problematical. Also some of this land was held by townsmen and their rents are not easily differentiated. In 1615 much of this was let from year-to-year, especially that in Irish hands. The more substantial tenants were Soloman Coffy, Owen oge O'Mellan, and Tady and Patrick Crawley (or Croly), native Irish residents, Sir Edward Dodington (then also an official of the archbishop), Matthew Ussher, burgess of the town and mill-keeper, and Rev. Thomas Crant, chancellor of the cathedral.[50] From the area accounted for a sum in excess of £63. 13. 4. was due.[51]

Remaining segments of the archbishop's lands in Armagh – Munterheyney (six ballyboes) in Orior and small areas in Oneilland and Armagh baronies – were not remunerative. An area, in Oneilland, it was noted, was 'withheld' by the adjoining undertaker Dillon. The fishing rights on the Blackwater were also as yet unleased.

45 Ibid., 22–3.
46 Ibid., 24–5. Browne was also obliged to provide timber.
47 Ibid., 24–5.
48 Ibid., 25–6.
49 Ibid., 26–7.
50 Leslie, *Armagh clergy*, 37, 85, 182.
51 Registry, A.2a.28/10, 32–4.

From this analysis of the 1615 rental certain general conclusions can be drawn. The total of rent due from the county which is clearly accounted for was £803. 4. 8. The value of duties[52] as well as income from the land unaccounted for must have made for an income of some £850. The amount of see land still in Irish hands greatly outweighed that granted to British tenants. For those Irish tenants of mensal land the plantation had thus, not so far, been revolutionary. For those of the original occupants of the termon and erenach lands the new dispensation had brought an altering of status.

The origin of the British tenants is also of some interest. Thus we find a number of ex-servicemen, Cowell, perhaps Chambers, and Sir Edward Dodington, a tenant and official to the archbishop, as he was also to one of the London companies in the west of the province. Tenants, Fitzsimonds and Hamlin, had been recruited from Drogheda, from the *inter anglicos*, and there was also a relative of the archbishop – Matthew Ussher.[53] There were a number of tenants of obvious recent arrival, though how they had been secured is not clear. These included Scots as well as English, the latter predominating.

The earliest surviving leases to British tenants of lands in Armagh made by Hampton date from June–November 1615.[54] All were for terms of sixty years, and included the forbidden proviso that, during any time of war affecting the use of the land granted, the rent should be remitted.[55] The tenancies varied in size, the largest (Kilmore) being ten townlands, none smaller than two. This was in breach of the regulation that land should be leased by the acre, no unit to be larger than 200 acres. The leases contained building stipulations. Tenants were required to build 'English-like houses of bricks, stone, or framed timber' or 'stronge and well timbered copled or Englishlike houses' and plant in them English families who should take the oath of supremacy and attend divine service. These should be built within five years or, in two cases, two years. Usually each lessee was required to build no more than one such house (and plant one tenant), though the joint lessees of Kilmore covenanted to erect two. Some leases also required the lessee to oblige his tenants to live nearby and form a village. The tenants should perambulate the mears and bounds of their lands each year and certify all encroachments to the steward of the manor court. Each tenant should have ready one 'light horse' and man armed to attend the primate

52 In the rental of 1622 the duties from the mensal lands in Clanaul were valued at £23. 12. 6. (Registry, B.1b.193, 5).

53 Son of Archbishop Henry Ussher.

54 Library, MSS Room, in box 'old leases of primate's'. Although the government commissioners in 1622 did not report on the episcopal estates, they took note of the provisions in the primate's leases (NLI, Rich Papers, 8013/9)

55 Above, 352. This provides an interesting local commentary on the war scare of 1615.

when required in time of war in Ireland and for ten days at his own cost. The tenant might fell timber and quarry stones or gravel for building on the lands, but otherwise all timber trees, quarries, and mines were reserved to the archbishop.[56] Manorial incidents, suit of court and use of the landlord's mill also featured. While some of the leases may have been renewals of previous ones,[57] many clearly were of lands previously in Irish hands, and it is of interest that these were concluded more than one year after Trinity College had leased its lands to middlemen.[58] It is clear that the Irish tenants in Clanaul had also a leasehold tenure granted by Hampton or his predecessor, holding either for the duration of the primacy, for life, or for twenty-one years.

The effect of Hampton's leases can be examined by using a rental which was included with the visitation return of 1622,[59] taken in conjunction with a slightly later rental to which elaborate notes were added by archbishop James Ussher *c.* 1627,[60] which shows the situation when Ussher succeeded Hampton. The most striking change had been in the influx of British tenants and in the increasing size of holdings.[61]

The twenty-four townlands of mensal land in Clanaul remained substantially in Irish hands. An Englishman had acquired one townland from O'Lappan (and refused to pay duties), and Conn McTurlogh O'Neill's lands had passed to Robert Hovendon – the semi-Gaelicised relative of the family.[62] Also the fishing had been leased to the Rev. Crant for £6 per annum. The yearly duties, it was noted, for those townlands yielded £23. 12. 6. However, fifteen of the sixteen townlands not mensal were now in the hands of five non-Irish tenants – one clerical (Crant), two from Drogheda (called Earlsman[63]) – under sixty-year leases from 1615 and after. This change in tenantry had not increased the rent. In fact sixty-year English leaseholders paid more than £1 per townland less than their Irish neighbours. The total annually was £231. 10. 0; it was £232. 18. 0. in 1615 when the fishing was not leased.[64]

[56] In November 1632 Thomas Dawson, then of Moyola, Londonderry, was empowered to prospect for iron ore in one are (not in Armagh) of the episcopal estate (Library, in box 'old leases of primate's').

[57] See above, 351.

[58] Above, 328.

[59] Registry, B.1b.193, 1–25.

[60] Ibid., A.2a.28/13.

[61] Difficulties arise in that tenants often held lands in different areas, and sometimes different counties, and neither the rents for townlands in any one area nor the names of places held are stated in these rentals which are in a dilapidated condition.

[62] Above, 214–15.

[63] He was a 'servant' of the archbishop.

[64] Registry, B.1b.193, 4–5; A2a.28/13, 8–12, 44–5.

In Tynan the arrival of one new British tenant reduced the amount held by the O'Caseys to one ballyboe. The rent was approximately £31.[65] In Clanconchy also only one ballyboe remained in Irish hands. One of the new tenants was Thomas Dawson, burgess of Armagh. The rent was now £69, a decrease on the 1615 figure.[66] Ten of thirteen ballyboes in Toaghy were in British hands, including Dawson and a relative of Hampton's, the rent being now reduced to £53. 1. 0. per annum.[67]

Apart from the lands around the town of Armagh these were the only areas in which Irish tenants remained. Elsewhere the interval had seen the depression of all direct Irish tenants. Both Ballymoire and Ballymacoan had been leased for sixty years to George Fairfax, the energetic seneschal to the archbishop in the later 1620s. The rent, which was also for one ballyboe near Armagh, was £114. 6. 8, or more than £10 less than when held by Irish tenants.[68] The territory of Kilmore was similarly in English hands, those of Francis and Christopher Hampton, relatives of the archbishop, at a rent (£40) which was substantially lower than the £55 previously receivable from Irish tenants.[69] The English tenants of Clonfeacle, who included a Hampton relative, held at £4 per ballyboe paying in all £29 a year.[70] Munterheyney, six ballyboes, had been leased to the servitor Charles Poyntz, at £18.[71] Cossvoy and Coscallen were both in 1622 held by British tenants, Chambers and Browne, the latter having by 1627 sold his tenancy to the Rev. John Symonds, rector of Armagh. The combined rent, £68. 13. 4, was only slightly lower than that of 1615.[72] Derrybrocas had come into the hands of an English family,[73] and Drumcree had passed from a previous English tenant to the Rev. Allan Cooke.[74]

The area around the town continued in the 1620s to be held in small or irregular portions, on a much less systematic basis. This situation pertained to some degree right up to 1641.[75] For a part of the area there is a simple explanation in the decision to allocate land in ten-acre blocks to

[65] Ibid., 6; ibid., 12, 45.
[66] Ibid., 6–7; ibid., 13–14, 45.
[67] Ibid., 8–9; ibid., 16–17, 46–7.
[68] Ibid., 7; ibid., 14.
[69] Ibid., 7; ibid., 15, 45.
[70] Ibid., 8; ibid., 15, 46. Sir Toby Caulfeild was, by 1627, paying rent for a disputed area.
[71] Ibid., 8; ibid., 16, 46.
[72] Ibid., 9; ibid., 18, 47.
[73] Ibid., 9–10; ibid., 18, 47.
[74] Registry, A.2a.28/13, 18. On Cooke's connection with Cavan see above, 256–7.
[75] Some of these lettings are of interest: In 1616 two portions of the demesne were let for one year to Crant (for meadow) and to Tady and Patrick Crawley (for blowing) (Registry, A.2a.28/10, 34). This arrangement continued from year to year. In 1628 £3. 8. 0. was received for 'grass cut' on the 'Wast' (or unlet) lands, totalling 17 acres 2 roods, in the new demesnes from five tenants, the four named being English (ibid., A.2a.28/20, 10).

houses to be erected under a building-lease scheme in the town.[76] Land so reserved was let during pleasure, pending the arrival of applicants under the scheme. Its abortiveness ensured the continuance of temporary letting arrangements. Also it was likely that much of the traditional pattern of landholding in this area of long-standing church land should survive, its contiguity to the town ensuring some degree of fragmentation. At the same time the plantation brought changes. Hampton designated some 200 acres as 'new demesnes' for the support of a rebuilt see house. Also episcopal officials and British townsmen as well as clergy began to acquire leases of land near the town. Thus, apart from the small number who took out building leases and acquired associated small areas, pieces of land came into the hands of Sir Edward Dodington, Thomas Dawson, George Fairfax, Richard Chappell, and George Chambers, all at one time or other officials of the archbishop; and clergy – Crant and Symonds. The 1622 rental suggests a sum of about £163 as the income from this area, that of 1627 about £156. Some indication of how much remained in Irish hands can be seen from the fact that about £73 was due from Irish tenants.[77]

It is clear, then, that the leases of 1615 had introduced system into the letting of the episcopal lands away from the Armagh liberties area, much of which had come into British hands for sixty-year periods. That this involved a decrease in rent returns is also apparent, £4 and £5 per ballyboe being the usual leasing figures for British tenants. In 1615 a substantial area of the estate in Armagh (excluding the city, the liberties, and Munterheyney which was then unremunerative) returned annually £739. 11. 4; after the leasings to British had taken effect no more than £667. 0. 4. was annually due. While the leases included building and other obligations, part of the explanation may well lie in Hampton's taking of entry fines from incoming tenants.[78]

The total income from land in Armagh in 1622 was £871. 10. 5.[79] This remained substantially unchanged[80] until radically altered by government intervention in the middle 1630s. The only sizeable alteration resulted from the re-leasing of the Clanaul mensal lands. These lands, predominantly in

76 Above, 231.

77 Registry, B.1b.193, 1–3; A.2a.28/13, 1–7.

78 Hampton's taking of fines was mentioned in 1635 when it was proposed that a clause forbidding this practice should be inserted in a new patent which was never taken out (Registry, A.1b.128/7).

79 The total income of the archdiocese from temporalities according to the 1622 rental was £1,935. 9. 9. (Registry, B.1b.193, 22). The 1627 rental totalled £1,903. 9. 9. (ibid., A.2a.28/13, 39).

80 See Registry, A.2a.28/16 rental *c.* 1628 drawn up by Ussher; ibid., /17 rental, *c.* 1618; ibid. /19 rental, All Saints 1628; ibid. /20 rental, Lammas 1628; A.1b.29/1 rental and arrears, Candlemas 1628; ibid /2 rental and arrears, All Saints 1629; ibid. /3 rental 1631.

Irish hands,[81] had been held by lease for the time of Hampton's primacy, at rents ranging from £5. 10. 0. to £8 per townland. On 18 June 1630 this area was re-leased for the duration of Ussher's episcopate, the rents now (apart from 4 of 24 townlands held at £6. 10. 0. each by Hovendon) were uniformly raised to £8. 10. 0. per townland. However, duties valued at £1. 2. 6. per townland[82] were not required under the new leases. These improved rents had been payable from at least 1628[83] although the leases were not 'perfected' until 1630 and had probably been negotiated at Ussher's succession. The outcome was that a sum of £148 (excluding duties) previously received was increased to £202.[84]

The nature of the accounting system makes it difficult to state if rents were paid with regularity or completely. However, in a few cases, the rentals list arrears as well as amounts due. In 1628 of a sum of £49. 17. 6. due from the area around the town, £48. 13. 0. was paid, leaving only £1. 4. 6. in arrears.[85] Of the total quarterly sum accounted for, £386. 1. 0. (for lands in Tyrone as well as Armagh), £61. 19. 11, or about 16 was at that time unpaid. In 1629 of a total quarterly sum of £456. 13. 1. accounted for (also including Tyrone entries) £98. 1. 0. was then unpaid, or some 22 of the 'charge'. On this occasion only £2 (from Hovendon) was in arrears from the block of Irish-held land in Clanaul.[86] Since the account books do not carry arrearages forward from year to year it is not possible to establish how quickly, and completely, debts were settled. Evidence of re-entry, however, is not found. It comes to light only in one case in a note appended to a rental by the meticulous Ussher as having been carried out against an English tenant in Clanaul, who subsequently re-instated himself, in December 1613.[87] Cases of violence arising from distraint for duty payments or rent against Irish tenants in Clanaul, however, feature in the manor court rolls surviving for the years 1625–27.[88] It would seem, then, that if the collection of rents presented recurrent difficulties, the archbishop's rental was not affected in a particularly serious way.

The profits of the tenants on the estate are not easily discoverable. From one case, however, they appear to have been substantial. In November 1634 Symonds recovered in chancery from the administrator of an English sub-

[81] One ballyboe was held by two English tenants, William and Edmond Brookes, 'clothworkers' (Registry, A.3a.39/10).

[82] Registry, A.2a.28/17, 3.

[83] Ibid., A1b.29/1, 4.

[84] Ibid., – /3, 2.

[85] Ibid., – /1, 3.

[86] Ibid., – /2, *passim*.

[87] Ibid., A.2a.28/13, 11.

[88] Armagh Public Library, MSS room.

tenant one year's overdue rent for one townland at the rate of £30 per year.[89] The saleable value of leasehold land is also only occasionally known. However, two townlands in Toaghy, leased for 60 years in 1615 to an English tenant, were sold to Dawson in 1622 for £40 and by him to the bishop of Dromore in 1627 for £50, to be sold two years later to a certain Francis Graves for £60.[90]

4. State intervention and re-leases

Bramhall's scheme for the re-leasing of the estates of Ulster bishops, 1634–5, has been examined elsewhere.[91] What was the effect of this legislation for the archbishopric? Between 1635 and 1637 the new leasing arrangements were worked out and given official sanction.[92] In April 1636 the terms of some of the new leases were presented to the privy council for sanction, which had been granted by May 31. On this basis negotiations with tenants continued and the proposals were submitted in detail to Wentworth early in 1637. The schedule (not fully complete) with its accompanying petition for ratification was submitted by him to Bramhall and Sir Adam Loftus and received their consent on February 28, Wentworth's confirmation following on March 2.[93] An official record of the new leases was made by the clerk of the privy council, Sir Paul Davis.[94] The leases (not found)[95] dated from 14 July 1634, though at least one was not made until 28 March 1639.[96]

A disentanglement of the precise amount of the new income from Armagh again presents the difficulty that many tenants held land outside the county. The rentals post 1636 are also less clear or detailed than those of the earlier period. However, one abstract rental states that for Armagh the 'new rent' of £1,516. 16. 0. replaced the 'old' figure of £872. 15. 0.[97] The total income of the archbishopric as calculated in July 1639 was £3,564. 10. 10.[98] In the same year the figure that Bramhall stated to land was £3,500.[99]

89 NAI, Repertories to the decrees of chancery, ii, 138.

90 Indenture, 20 June 1615, between the archbishop of Armagh and William Hayes: endorsements (Library, in box 'old leases of primate's').

91 Above, 317–9.

92 See *Hastings MSS*, iv, 70–1.

93 Certified copies of these orders are in Registry, A.3a.39/15, 19.

94 Abstract in ibid., A.1b.29/4.

95 Abstracts of them, apparently drawn up in the commonwealth period, are in ibid., A.1b.29/9 (a very dilapidated document).

96 Ibid., A.3a.39/23.

97 Ibid., A.1b.34/3, fol. 1v. This latter figure agrees substantially with my calculation of £871. 10. 5.

98 Ibid., A.1b.29/8.

99 Shirley, *Papers*, 7.

The objective of the re-leasing had been to increase income. However, it also affected the fortunes of many previous Irish tenants. In 1634 nineteen of twenty-four ballyboes in the mensal area of Clanaul remained in Irish hands by leases dating from 1630.[100] By 1640, at most, no more than four were held by Irish. The change may have been by purchase in some cases.[101] The Irish tenants may have been getting into difficulties because from 1637 the Clanaul rents (which had not been increased at this time, standing at £8. 10. 0. per townland since 1630) had been in arrears to the extent of at least £21 (of £252) per annum. In May 1640 the arrears against six Irish tenants here totalled £66. 10. 0. In 1639 Mrs. Ussher appears to have agreed to reduce their rents by £2. 2. 6. per townland but, in the same year, a change in tenancy took place.[102] The change saw the introduction of two new tenants,[103] one of whom, Sir Maurice Williams, was physician to Wentworth,[104] the other being Robert Bysse of the family of recorders of Dublin.

Elsewhere the change was less marked because it had already progressed far on the estate anyhow. An official document of 1659 lists only six major Irish tenants on the see lands. Their names had traditional associations, Neil McCoddan, Hugh Moder McCoddan, James McDonnell McCasy, Patrick O'Donnelly, Soloman Coffy, and Tady Crolly. Their combined rents in 1641 were £82. 10. 0.[105] To this, however, should be added the four townlands in Clanaul mentioned above and, perhaps, smaller areas as well. It is clear that less than one-tenth of the archbishop's income from land in Armagh derived from Irish tenants.

In February 1636, when the re-leasing negotiations were in progress, a petition for a re-lease from Tady Crowly (Crolly), who described himself as a 'native of the English Pale' indicates well the unease of these tenants. He stated that he held a house plot in Armagh and 154 acres 'farr distant' from the town. He pointed out that he had built a house at a cost of 'at least' £150, and had spent £50 on land enclosure.[106]

100 Four of the remaining five were held by Hovendon who got a new lease under the Bramhall scheme.

101 A rental in 1640 refers to two townlands having been 'bought in' by a new tenant (Registry, A.1b.29/6 and 7, 8: this document was mistakenly numbered as two in the late eighteenth century).

102 Registry, A.1b.29/6 and 7, 8.

103 Ibid., – /9, 49. These leases date from 1634, but it is clear that the land concerned was in Irish hands until 1639 (ibid. – /6 and 7, ff 7v–8). These new tenants appear to have paid £17 per townland (twice the previous rent) though this new sum may have dated from after 1641. At any rate Williams was £42. 10. 0. in arrears in 1640 (ibid., – /6 and 7, 8).

104 *CSPI, 1633–47*, 193.

105 Registry, C.1c.371, 214–2: 'Bishops Lands of Ireland and other Dignitaryes Ecclesiasticall Extracted out of Ancient Records thereof and compared with what is in Present Charge, 1659'.

106 Ibid., E.1.e, Petition of Tady Crowly to archbishop of Armagy. Crolly was also a tenant of Chambers and won a suit against him 1637–40, (NAI, Repertories to the decrees of chancery, ii, 220–21).

It should be noted too that by 1641 Old English tenants from Drogheda had also disappeared from the rental. People such as Fitzsimonds, Hamlin, Tench, and Earlsman had only a short association with the archbishopric in Armagh. Throughout the period tenancies had tended to increase in size. The archbishopric continued to draw tenants from the Londonderry plantation. Dodington's lands passed to his widow's husband[107] Sir Francis Cooke[108] and, after 1634, Tristram Beresford and George Cary were on the archbishop's rental in Armagh and Tyrone to the extent of £100 per annum.[109] Clerical leases also continued; Crant had apparently died by 1633[110] but Symonds held eleven townlands as well as houses and 'severall parkes and parcels' adjacent to the town of Armagh at a rent of £88[111] and Robert Maxwell, son of the dean of the same name, prebend of Tynan and afterwards a bishop,[112] held nine townlands (three in Tyrone) at £60 rent.[113]

It is evident that, in most cases, the Irish by 1641 had descended to the status of sub-tenants. All of Robert Maxwell's holding, for example, was sub-let to Irish occupiers, O'Caseys in Tynan, and O'Donnellans and others in Clanaul.[114] Some of the hardship for Irish inhabitants at the hands of English tenants emerges from a statement of George Fairfax, seneschal to the archbishop, in which he alleges that Sir Edward Dodington removed the natives from the land he held near Armagh 'by a p'tended command from my Lo. Primat that none might dwelle about the towne that woulde not conforme and come to church'.[115]

An additional area of land came to the archbishopric in the late 1630s. Derrynoose, sixteen ballyboes, had been granted to the archbishop in 1610 but, in a reorganisation of 1612, it was granted to the dean to revert, however, to the archbishop in a further reorganisation in 1637.[116] In July 1639 Ussher leased this land to Sir Philip Mainwaring for fifty-six years at £150 per annum.[117] The lessee was another of the Wentworth circle to

107 Moody, *Londonderry Plantation*, 447.
108 Five townlands in Armagh and eight in Tyrone, rent £110 (Registry, A.1b.29/9, 28).
109 Ibid.
110 Leslie, *Armagh clergy*, 182.
111 Registry, , A.1b.29/9, 11.
112 Leslie, *Armagh clergy*, 73.
113 Registry , A.1b.29/9, 45. In May 1639 Maxwell, though Scottish in origin, had made much of the fact in a letter to Wentworth that he was 'not in any great favour with the favourers of the covenant' (Sheffield City Library, Strafford letters, 20/136).
114 Registry , A.1b.29/9, 45.
115 Ibid., A.2a.28/11, 24–8.
116 Above, 294, 310–11.
117 Registry, A.1b.29/9, 11, 50.

become a tenant to the archbishop.[118] It does not seem likely that he paid rent regularly before 1641.[119]

Only two rentals survive – from 1639 and 1640 – to indicate how the new leasing scheme worked out before 1641.[120] These pose difficulties of interpretation, and the following conclusions are tentative. It seems clear, at any rate, that the new rents were not being regularly paid before 1639 or 1640. It appears, also, that in some cases arrears arising from the increase of rents were 'forgiven' by the archbishop. In this way Armagh and Tyrone tenants were absolved from paying about £100. The total annual rent from these two counties was some £2,300. At May 1639 arrears, apparently for the whole estate, were £476. 7. 4. or some 15 of the total rental. Clearly the see did not long enjoy its new income before the outbreak of violence in 1641 guaranteed its disruption. At the same time it should be noted that, unlike TCD, not one case of litigation with tenants for non-payment comes to light throughout the whole period. However, in 1641, when the policy of the Wentworth administration was under attack, it was proposed that the archbishop and other Ulster bishops should be required by act of parliament to create freeholders on their estates.[121]

5. The administration of the estate

It is obvious that the extension of English power to Ulster brought about a change in the relative importance of the two traditional areas, north and south, into which the archbishopric fell. The protestantism of the incoming Ulster colonists, and the extent of the lands in Ulster with which the see was endowed, both conduced to this change.

The inherited system of rent collection had recognised that an 'Irish official was best suited for a Gaelic area. From the plantation period the lands were administered more as a unit and also with more concentration – as the returns justified – on the lands previously '*inter hibernicos*'. Very quickly the dependence on a local native official disappears. The beginning of this direct interest in Ulster perhaps dates from a rental of 1606 of the 'Tenentes Armachan', no longer extant. In a list of rentals which James Ussher drew up on his appointment this was listed as the last of the 'Rentalta antiqua'. That he listed all rentals 'since the great office' as 'nova' testifies to the change.[122] Only two officials of Irish name feature in the

[118] He had been brought over from England by Wentworth and was his secretary. He sat in the 1634 and 1640 parliaments (Kearney, *Strafford*, 47, 195, 239–40). An act of parliament to confirm his lease was passed in 1640.

[119] He was charged with an arrear of £7. 10. 0. in 1639 (Registry, A.1b.29/5).

[120] Ibid.: Chappell's accounts, 1639; A.1b.29/6 and 7: Jeeve's accounts, 1639–40.

[121] TNA, SP 63/259, fol. 7v; –/26, ff 1–23v (*CSPI, 1633–47*, 285–6, 322).

[122] Registry, A.2a.28, fol. 28.

plantation period, perhaps because their familiarity with the locality was valued. One of these, Patrick Crolly, with three English people took a survey of the town of Armagh in 1618[123] and the other, Solomon Coffy, was connected with the see probably until after James Ussher's appointment.[124]

However, from the beginning of the plantation period we find a succession of English officials, seneschals, and servants. From 1614 or before, and until 1618, Sir Edward Dodington of Dungiven acted in this capacity though his accounts, extant in James Ussher's time,[125] have now disappeared. During Ussher's primacy George Fairfax argued that at an early stage some primatial land had been lost or jeopardised through Sir Toby Caulfeild, who held the abbey land, being 'both Custos Comitat., seneschal to the Lo. Primat, and powerfull in the cuntrie'. He also made allegations against Thomas Dawson.[126] In 1618 of the three Englishmen who drew up the survey of the town two were tenants and residents there and the third, Crant, was an ecclesiastic. Most of the other officials whose names and records survive were also episcopal tenants, some of substantial areas. John Jeeve, who drew up a rental *c.* 1627, appending to it a list of counterparts of leases in his keeping,[127] was a tenant to the see.[128] In 1639–40 he reappears in episcopal service. From 1625 to 1627 George Fairfax, who was a tenant of Ballymoire and Ballymacoan, was seneschal to the archbishop and manor courts were held before him not only in Armagh and Tyrone but in Louth as well.[129] Richard Chappell, who accounted for rents from 1635 to 1640 and also before 1627,[130] was also a substantial tenant.[131] Capt. George Chambers was the son of a tenant from an early stage, but his rent accounts are probably post 1641.[132] Roger Russell, who leased houses in the town of Armagh on the archbishop's behalf in 1627[133] was a tenant and burgess of the town. About Geashall, an employee of Hampton, nothing is known.[134] John Cragg and Francis Wayte, who accounted in 1628,[135] do not appear to have been tenants, but were possibly sub-tenants.

123 Ibid., A.2a.28/11.
124 Ibid., A.2a.28, fol. 28.
125 Ibid., fol. 28v.
126 Ibid., A.2a.28/11, 24–8.
127 Ibid., – /13.
128 In October 1638 Jeeve was mayor of Drogheda (NAI, Petition to Wentworth and council, June–November 1638, M. 2448, 550–51).
129 Library, Manor Court Rolls.
130 Referred to in a note by Ussher in Registry, A.2a.38/13, 9.
131 Ibid., A.1b.29/5, 6, 7.
132 Ibid., A.1b.34/3.
133 Ibid., E.1.e. On Russell see above, 237.
134 Referred to in note by Ussher in Registry, A.2a.28/13.
135 Ibid., –/20; A.1b.29/1.

How these rent collectors, in general, were paid is not known. Only in one rental, that of Francis Wayte for 1628, are disbursements recorded. He makes two relevant entries: 'for my own expenses in riding and getting his quarter's rent – £1. 17. 4.' and 'to Edmund O'Cawell and his son to help to fetch in distresses – £1. 4. 0.'[136]

Such a dependence on agents and collectors who were also tenants had obvious unsatisfactory aspects. However, at least during James Ussher's time, their work was subject to close episcopal supervision. Around 1627, Ussher, who was then engaged in a meticulous investigation of his Ulster estate, worked over John Jeeve's rental, collating it precisely with information derived from other sources. His emendations here, as well as a rental in his own hand,[137] indicate a clear personal knowledge of the estate against which the reports of his agents could be checked. In May 1640 when he was leaving the country he handed over Jeeve's 1639–40 rental to Arthur Hill, presumably of Hillsborough, a man who had no connection with the estate, with a note that the rents were to be received by in 'in my absence to my use'.[138]

Ussher, in fact, shortly after his appointment devoted considerable effort to the estate. He listed and correlated the rentals and registers from medieval times.[139] He worked over the official inquiries, the 'great office' and related documents, some of which are not now available, on which the plantation had been based, as well as the patents of the see, wresting with variant place names, and leaving invaluable critical notes.[140] To the rental of the estate which he drew up about 1628 he appended lists of the duties and heriots to which his tenants were liable.[141] A picture of Ussher as an extraordinarily painstaking investigant emerges.

Ussher, too, was particularly interested in land measurement. He wrote, apparently to Falkland, in 1627 arguing that the townlands of the estate (presumably the fragmented area near Armagh) were very much smaller than those of other proprietors. Falkland replied that an acreage measurement would present great difficulties and recommended him to continue using the traditional units:

> that error cannot be reformed without a general admeasurement and valuation of the different fertilities; for we all know that a hundred acres in a good soil, may be worth a thousand acres of land that are

[136] Ibid., A.2a.28/20, 11.
[137] Ibid., –/16; see also Elrington (ed.), *Ussher*, xv, 365–7.
[138] Ibid., A.1b.29/6 and 7, fol. 7v.
[139] Ibid., A.2a.28, ff 28–28v.
[140] Ibid., A.2a.28, after Jeeve's rental; – /13.
[141] Ibid., A.2a.28/16.

> mountainous and barren, and therefore it will surely prove a work of great difficulty and will require a long time to reduce it to any perfection, so that it is best to observe the customs in usage, until such a reformation shall be seriously debated and agreed upon.[142]

Falkland's reply is of particular interest in the light of Wentworth's view that a re-measurement of Ulster would greatly enhance the crown rent.[143] The correspondence has the further interest that Thomas Raven, the cartographer, whose advocacy of re-measurement in the Wentworth period has been noted[144] and who had suggested it as early as 1623,[145] was living in Armagh from (at least) 1625.[146] Furthermore, although the idea of re-measurement did not get state backing in 1627, Ussher himself employed Raven to map part of the estate in the Armagh area.[147] This map has since been lost.

This clarification of ownership rights had a particular relevance in view of disputes with neighbouring proprietors. A dispute with the Caulfeilds, for example, hinged on whether certain pieces of land in the Armagh area had belonged to the abbey of St. Peter and St. Paul and so should be Caulfeilds', or the primacy's. The argument is complex because it raised questions of the alternate naming of places, the confusion of denominational and sub-denominational names, and whether particular areas were whole townlands or parts. A further difficulty arises from the one-sidedness of the evidence which is set out in detail by George Fairfax, seneschal to the archbishop, whose lease included the lands in question.[148] Fairfax stated that he had been advised by 'some best hable to informe me' to 'learne of the natives the confines of the territories and sesiages in every ballebo'. His case was compounded from such evidence and a correlation of official surveys and patents. The debate is savoured somewhat by the following attempt in poetic form on the part of the lessee to mobilise sympathy for his case by depicting the sufferings of the church at the grasping hands of his fellow-English laymen:[149]

142 Elrington (ed.), *Ussher*, xv, 372–4.

143 Above, 180. The bishops, of course, did not pay quit rent.

144 Above, 182.

145 Above, 182.

146 Library, Manor Court Roll, 10 October 1625. See above 307.

147 In a note appended to Jeeve's rental Ussher states that the new demesne was 200 acres 'English measure ... whereof I have ye map delivered to me by Mr. Raven' rather than 300 acres as previously supposed (Registry, A.2a.28/13, 1).

148 Ibid., –/11, 24–28 the end pages of the 1618 rental of the town, undated and unsigned).

149 Ibid., A.2a.28/11, on verso of title page of 1618 rental. For another dispute with the Caulfeilds see St. John to Bolton, solicitor-general, 20 May 1620 (Library, with Manor Court Rolls; *CPRI, Jas I*, 274; Marsh's Library, Dublin, MS Z4.2.6, 15–16). Another case came to light in 1715 in the argument of a tenant that a piece of church land held originally in lease by George Chambers

The Estat of the Primacie
The sacred acts of kinge and state
Composed for the church
The plots of sharkinge scribes p'vert
the servitors doe lirch
And undertakers share the spoile
that cast lotts and devide
When as the souldiers would not dare
Christs garment to devide
His patrimonie rent and torne
by forged records and assigned
To Abotts and to others past
against our soverains minde
Tyrone usurpt thes since incroach
but force and fraud will faile
Witnesse the hand that Baltayar
sawe writinge on the walle.

The case, its merits aside, illustrates the difficulties of British proprietors in the inexact environment of plantation Ulster. It also indicates the dependence of the incomers, unfamiliar with Gaelic topography and land measures, on some degree of co-operation from the native inhabitants.

The archbishop is the only landlord in either county studied whose manor court records survive. By patent he was empowered to hold a court baron and court leet within each of his manors. The seneschals of these manors were to have power of oyer and terminer concerning all offences committed by any labourer or tradesman therein, with power to grant warrants of replevin, and to appoint bailiffs to issue process.[150] Court rolls survive for the years 1625–27 not only for Armagh manor, but for Donoghmore and Ardtra in Tyrone and also Termonfechan.[151] They were held before George Fairfax, seneschal to the archbishop.

The rolls begin with lists of those who had defaulted in their suit to the court, who are fined 1s. 6d. and, in some cases, 2s. 6d. each. Then follow lists of jurors. The jurisdiction of the court can be seen from the cases it heard.

and which lay next to some of the abbey land which had come to him by marriage to Sir Toby Caulfeild's niece (Lodge, *Peerage* (ed. Archdall), iii, 135), had been quickly absorbed into the abbey land and its name allowed to disappear. This, it was argued, had been contrived by Chambers or his son, Capt. Thomas, who was described as a 'cunning prying man and knew all the lands about Armagh before the '41 rebellion and as long as he lived, was protected by Sir Phelemy O'Neill in the time of that rebellion, know all the sufferings of the protestants and the carriage of the popish inhabitants thereabout better than any man alive since that time' (Registry, A.1b.25, ff 67v–8v).

150 *CPRI, Jas I*, 274.

151 Armagh Public Library, MSS Room. Transcripts (corrected from the originals) are in PRONI, T475. References below are given from the transcripts.

Very many cases are simple ones of affray, assault, effusion or blood, the majority involving Irish, but English also appeared on such charges. Some of these cases have a special interest. There are, for example, cases of violent opposition to distraint for rent or duty payments. Thus we find presentments like the following:

> Item p'sent q'd D'mus huius manerii in feodo suo apud Dromsallan – outragh p' censu sibi debit' p' Patriciu' Modd'r offin sub-ballivu' suum quedam auenam capi fecisset Patric' oge offin et Henric' offin auenam illam vi et armis scillicat cu' bacculis et cuitellis in hibernica vocat' skeanes rescusserunt et alia enormia fecerunt ad grave damn' dict D'ni et contra pacem D'ni Regis ideo sunt in m'ia – xiiis. iiid.[152]

There were many cases of anti-social behaviour. Thus we find a certain Maudelin Quash presented as a 'com'unis obiurgatrix cum vicinis suis' and fined 3s. 4d.,[153] and a certain Peirc McCasey who was 'vacabundus otiosus et [quod] recusant servire et dormit in diem et nihill laborat …'[154] The selling of bread and ale 'p' illicitas mensures', contrary to statute, is also penalised.[155] A certain Brian McCullen is presented as a 'com'm'us forstallator' and fined 2s. 6d.[156] A case of scandalisation in April 1626 brought a fine of 6s. 6d., the jury presenting

> q'd Edmundus oney O'Molmoghery in Patriciu' McCartan araim fecit et q'd dedit illi verba scandaliz vocant' p'dict' Patric' Rebello …[157]

The court also enforced conformity to its own ordinances or laid on individuals the obligation to obey manor policy. There are many judgements against people who 'nec anulat nec iugulat porcos suos contra ordinat' fact' p' hanc Cur.'.[158] It penalised failure to enclose the boundaries of properties, or imposed time limits for such enclosure. Thus, for example, it was ordered

> q'd Patric' O'Daley et Edmundus O'Mullan faciant et escorat fossatu' inter Monacree et Ahaggan citra decim' quint' diem Maii p'x' ut'm sub pena – xs.

152 PRONI, T475, 34.
153 Ibid., 8.
154 Ibid., 22.
155 Ibid., 36. In 1626 Patrick McQuaide was presented as 'co'is tipulator cervic'', and it was added 'q'd tenet malam regulam in domo suo' (ibid., 29).
156 Ibid., 46.
157 Ibid., 29.
158 Ibid., 35.

and presented

> q'd Johan Pettit de Blackwater non manutenet sepem vel fossatu' inter terram suam et terram Thom' Flinton et ordinat' est q'd Johan' p'dict' faciat et manuteneat suficient' sepem vel fossatu' ante decim' diem Maii p'x'm' sub pena – xis.[159]

There is also an interesting case of the destruction of fences.[160] The building of bridges was enjoined.[161]

Cases of theft also came within its jurisdiction. We find it present that

> Thomas Bennet serviens Richardo Scuthwicke vi et armis ... in parcum huius maerii fregit et ingressu' fecit et ex p'dict' parco vigint' vaccas cepir contra legem ...[162]

Most common, however, was the stealing of turf and timber. For example, on 10 October 1625 it was presented that Daniel McGrory entered the lands of John Earpe 'et tunc scidet et portavit ex terr p'dict' xx^{tie} loade of turfe'. He was fined 3s. 4d.[163] Numerous cases of timber cutting are dealt with. For example, on 9 April 1627 a certain Terence O'Kennan who 'succidit et vendidit arbores crescent' sup' villam Toneam' was fined 6s. 8d.[164] On one occasion the court made an order for the custody of the goods of a felon.[165]

A further function was the appointment of local officials, constables and bailiffs. Thus in 1625 we find the appointment of John Pettit of Blackwater as constable of Blackwater, Cossvoy, and Coscallen,[166] and, in the following year, a certain John Keisar was appointed and sworn to this office.[167] Constables appear to have been chosen by the courts annually for all the areas of episcopal land.[168] Sometimes an Irish constable was appointed – for example, in 1626 Arthur McPhelomy McDonnell for Ballymoire.[169]

159 Ibid., 40. See also 30, 47.

160 'Item p'sent q'd Johannis Dun transgression' fecit frangent' et comburent' sepes et domu' Edmundi O'Mullan existent' sup' sessionem [sessiogh] de Monaghcree ... ideo ip'e in m'ia – iiis. ivd. (ibid., 8).

161 Ibid., 25, 29. On once occasion the jurors presented 'q'd defectus est parcu' co'em in manerio isto et ordinat' est q'd manerium istud faciant parcu' ante festum omn' sanctor' ... sub pena – £10' (ibid., 29).

162 Ibid., 6.

163 For this and other cases see 24.

164 Ibid., 38, 45, 46.

165 Ibid., 37. The archbishop had a grant of felons' goods in his area (*CPRI, Jas I*, 314). For a list of felons' goods which came to him in 1628 see Registry, A2a.28/20, 13–14.

166 Ibid., 25, and see 31.

167 Ibid., 30.

168 See, for example, ibid., 41.

169 Ibid., 30.

Bailiffs, or sub-bailiffs, usually Irish, also appear.[170] The survival of these records epitomises well the role of the landlord in the realm of local justice and administration.

There remains the question of land use or improvement and the role of the landlord in this. The stipulations of surviving leases have already been mentioned but there is little or no evidence of how they were complied with. In 1636 Tady Crolly claimed that he had built a house at a cost of £150.[171] Certain points, however, emerge as to land enclosure. It is clear from the manor court rolls that it was the policy of the estate that the boundaries of holdings should be given permanent definition. There are numerous cases involving the failure to create or maintain such enclosures. Thus, for example, in 1627 the jurors presented that

> Thomas Hailes non fecit sepem nec fossatio inter ejus terras et terras John' Proctor, et ordinates est eu' fecisse apud cur' tent' undecimo die septembris ultim' p'terito sub pena ideo p'cept' est ballivo levari decem solidar' de bonis decti Thomas ad usu D'ni' Primat' D'ni' huius manerii.[172]

The incidence of these cases need not, of course, imply compliance with the regulation. However, there are occasional indications that enclosure of this nature – townland or farm enclosure – had been effected. In an abstract of Dawson's lease under the 1634 scheme one of his boundaries is described as 'according to a ditche drawne through the said lands fencing between the said John Dawson and the said Francis Graves'.[173] There are also references to parks or closes in the vicinity of the town.[174] In the town itself references to 'a garden plot ditched in' can also be found.[175] Crolly's statement that had 'inclosed' his holding[176] at a cost of £50 may well refer to boundary enclosure. In the rental of *c.* 1627 there is the statement about an area of land near Armagh, which had been reserved for proportions for plantation houses, that 'there was part of the outs[177] of the above 300 acres ditched by the late deceased archbishop [Hampton] which did stand his Grace in £16 sterling.'[178] However, it would be misleading to suggest that

170 Ibid., 28, 34, 44. In 1626 a certain John Russell was 'ballivus specialis' (ibd., 29).

171 Above, 363.

172 Ibid., 47.

173 Registry, A.1b.29/9, 44.

174 For example, ibid., 11, 47. 'A park of meadow containing 2 acres of thereabouts' was held by a McCodden tenant in 1628 (ibid., A.2a.28/20, 5).

175 Ibid., A.1b.29/9, 1.

176 154 acres 'of English measure after the rate of 16 (*sic*) foote to the perch' (ibid., 30).

177 Ussher appends the explanatory note 'outward fences'.

178 Registry, A.2a.28/13, 2.

there was any general enclosure movement on the estate in the first half of the seventeenth century.

One of the more difficult problems concerns the spoliation of timber on the estate. In the instructions of 1612 the preservation of woods was particularly enjoined. The destruction of timber by Elizabethan and Stuart bishops in England – who, of course, as landlords had only a life interest in the episcopal estates – had been particularly noticed and, in instructions issued by the king at Laud's prompting in 1629, the wastage of woods was strictly prohibited.[179] In Armagh primate Hampton's leasings to Irish tenants in Clanaul invariably included, amongst other duty payments, timber at the rate of forty 'loads' annually per townland.[180] The cumulative effect of this on the Clanaul woods would have been noteworthy. There is evidence, from the manor court rolls, of a reluctance to fulfil duty obligations and it also seems that duties, including wood, could be commuted for at the rate of £1. 2. 6. per townland. However, it seems that the opportunity to make money payments in lieu of duties was not generally availed of. Thus in 1628 we find a payment to the archbishop from George Chambers of £6. 13. 4. 'for duty wood he received of the tenants of Clanawle'[181] and, in the same year, he is receipted for £1 for '100 horse loads of duty wood paid to him by Mr. Robert Hovendon and was due to your Grace out of the lands of Clanaul'.[182] When the Clanaul lands were re-leased in 1630 with rent increases duty payments were no longer required. The coincidence with Laud's instructions for England (which concerned the devastation of woods on a massive scale) would seem, however, to be purely accidental, the dropping of duties being a partial compensation for substantial rent increases.[183]

There is, however, evidence that manorial timber was being cut away by private individuals. In the court rolls for Armagh manor, 1625–27, there are nine cases of penalisation of individuals who had cut timber illegally on the estate. Each was an Irishman, one features twice for this offence, and they were fined sums ranging from 2s. to 6s. 8d.[184] While it is clear, then,

179 Hill, *Economic problems*, 310–11.

180 Registry, A.2a.28/10, 4–9.

181 Ibid., A.1b.29/2, 8.

182 Ibid., A.2a.28/20, 1.

183 In his rental of *c.* 1628 Ussher noted that the Clanaul tenants had 'offered' £8 a townland, 'abating all customs save wood' (ibid., A.2a.28/16, 8). The bargain when concluded was for a simple rent payment of £8. 10. 0. per townland.

184 PRONI, T475, 5, 38, 45, 46, 47. In 1629 Ussher, in a letter to Bramhall, stated of a tenant in Tyrone that he 'should take it for a great favour at his hands, that I should have no rent paid me at all, and that he would leave my woods entire and unwasted unto my successor' (Berwick (ed.), *Rawdon papers*, 60). The tenant, Sir Thomas Staples, had also been associated with the Londonderry plantation (Moody, *Londonderry Plantation*, 328).

that the manor court made attempts to protect the woods on the estate from devastation by individuals, and also that part payment of rents in wood from some areas, particularly Clanaul, were required up to the end of the 1620s, there is no evidence, owing to the absence of account records other than rentals, to indicate or refute large-scale cutting and sale of timber by the bishops themselves.

6. Conclusion

The plantation was effective in that almost all of the episcopal land in Armagh came into British hands, the Irish having become, with a few exceptions, depressed to sub-tenancy by 1641. The archbishop's tenants were generally substantial, though they were much more numerous and held smaller areas on the whole than the middlemen to whom Trinity College leased its land. Some Old English tenants had been replaced by British by 1641. Many of the British tenants were drawn from three sources: from the Londonderry plantation, local servitors, and local clergy. Some of these were absentee, and probably not active improvers. Hampton also made leases to relatives. Government intervention in the 1630s presented the possibility of greatly increased income but also imposed a further small group of tenantry, government supporters, manifestly absentee.

And yet there were considerable numbers of British on the estate. We have seen that the British adult male population of the town of Armagh about 1630 was a least ninety and probably more than 100.[185] At least as many were on the lands in the county. The muster book of *c.*1630 listed fifty-eight British on the county lands.[186] However, some seventy additional names have been derived from estate papers and manor court rolls.[187] There was thus a British adult male population of some 230. In comparison with the lands of Trinity College, or the bishopric of Kilmore,[188] the archbishop's estates witnessed a considerable influx of population.

[185] Above, 236.

[186] BL, Add. MS 4770, ff 40v–41v.

[187] Above, 177. It has not been easy to differentiate town and countryside dwellers.

[188] The bishop of Kilmore, who had about three-fifths the acreage of the archbishop of Armagh, mustered forty-three British in *c.* 1630 (BL, Add. MS 4770, ff 21v–2, 23).

CHAPTER 13

Conclusion

1. Statistical

Commercial transactions throughout our period brought about changes in the proportions of land in each county held by the different proprietor groups. While it is necessary to differentiate ownership change from effective colonisation, as assessment of the fortunes of these groups gives some indication of the success or failure of the plantation. The situation in 1641 can best be set out in tabular form.[1]

Armagh, 1641

Proprietor groups	acreage	% of total acreage
British owners	156,944	50.51
Native Irish	59,026	19.00
Old English	1,668	0.54
Archbishopric	53,972	17.37
Trinity College, Dublin	22,875	7.36
Glebe	6,561	2.11
Other ecclesiastical proprietors	2,616	0.84
School	1,552	0.50
Mountain	987	0.32
Unidentified ownership	4,247	1.37

Cavan, 1641

Proprietor groups	acreage	% of total acreage
British owners	219,949	47.50
Native Irish	76,640	16.55
Old English	99,174	21.42
Bishopric	31,785	6.86
Glebe	13,657	2.95
School	917	0.20
Town of Cavan	683	0.15
Mountain	16,828	3.63
Unidentified ownership	1,585	0.34

[1] For the figures at the beginning of the plantation see above, 58–9.

The ecclesiastical and institutional share remained constant but, otherwise, there had been considerable change the nature of which can be compared for both counties. Individual British owners of all kinds increased their holdings in Armagh by about one-ninth, from 44.92 per cent in *c.* 1610 to 50.51 per cent in 1641. In Cavan, in contrast, their share declined very marginally from about 48.66 per cent to about 47.50 per cent. The native Irish share, however, fell in both counties, and in both by about a quarter, from 25.21 per cent to 19 per cent, in the case of Armagh, and from 22.49 per cent to 16.55 per cent in Cavan. The Old English gained in both counties, though their proportion of Armagh in 1641, where initially they had none, 0.54 per cent, was negligible. In Cavan, however, they rose from 14.62 per cent in 1610 to 21.42 per cent, or by one-half, in 1641.[2] The native Irish and old English combined had proportionately twice as much land in Cavan (37.97 per cent) than in Armagh (19.54 per cent). By that extent Protestant ownership was more firmly entrenched in Armagh than in Cavan.[3]

2. Success and failure

The greatest burden of colonisation rested with the undertakers, English and Scots. We have seen throughout the varying quality of their achievement in building, importation of tenantry, and the like. The success of the undertakers themselves, so essential to the progress of the plantation, can be measured in relation to the number of estates which changed hands. The following tables attempt to summarise the evidence. Each column indicates changes taking place in the interval since the previous date, the number of these being shown by figures 1, 2, etc. The letter M indicates that an estate was mortgaged in whole or part, and F that it was fragmented, the undertaker retaining some, or none, of the property.

2 This includes much unprofitable land. The historian of the Old English has calculated that they owned 15.6 per cent of the profitable land (Clarke, *Old English*, 236).

3 It is noteworthy that the Old English, who had been acquiring land in Cavan prior to the plantation, had, in fact, continued to gain. Some 21,000 acres of their acquisitions had been acquired from British servitor owners.

Assignees, 1610	1611	1613	1619	1622	*c.*1630	1641
Oneilland						
Saye and Seale	1					M
Sacheverall					M	
Matchett			1			
Stanhowe					F	
Powell	1		1		F	
Rolleston			M			
Dillon						M
J. Brownlow } W. Brownlow[4]						M
Warde	1			1	1	
Fews						
Douglas		1	1			
H. Acheson					1	
Craig			1			
Lawder			1			
C. Hamilton			1			
Loughtee						
Wirrall		1	1	1		
Fishe	1					F
Davies	1					
Taylor						
Waldron	2		1		1	
Snow	1		1		1	
Butler						
Clankee						
Aubigny	1			1		
Bailie						
Ralston		1				
Dunbarr			1			
Tullyhunco						
J. Auchmooty	1					
A. Auchmooty	1					
Sir A. Hamilton						
C. Hamilton	1					
Browne		1				M

4 Inherited his father's estate before 1619 (above, 116).

There was thus, in both counties, a very considerable turnover in ownership. A somewhat similar pattern of sales of servitors' lands has been seen throughout this thesis. Some of the transferences tabulated above resulted in accumulations of land in one man's hands – Sir Archibald Acheson, for example, acquiring an estate in Cavan as well as Armagh. Many of them also resulted in the introduction of new owners from Britain. But there was also a small group of new purchasers who may be classed as 'servitors of Ireland'. Conspicuous amongst these were Sir Oliver St. John, who acquired Matchett's land in Oneilland, and Edward Bagshaw, who acquired an estate in Loughtee. While such people were not exempt from the obligations of undertakers, the distinction between undertakers and servitors was beginning to break down.[5] Thus commercial transactions altered somewhat the relative shares of undertakers and servitors. These sales took place without government restriction, and are of interest in view of Chichester's opinion in 1610[6] that the servitors had received an inadequate share of the land in all counties save Cavan. The acquisition of Sir Henry Perse in Clankee is significant because it resulted in a reduction in the amount of land held by Scots' undertakers in Cavan. The noteworthy purchases – in both Armagh and Cavan – of the Hamiltons, a Scottish family well placed in Down for expansion into plantation Ulster, were, in all cases, of land originally granted to Scots.

However, it would be misleading to suggest that land in either county had fallen prey in any general way (certainly not initially) to adventurers of the type of Richard Boyle in Munster.[7] There were, of course, a number of adventurer type at the beginning, for example Lord Saye and Seale in Armagh and Lord Aubigny in Cavan,[8] but these generally sold their lands rather than expanded their interests. Boyle himself had an interest in the Cavan lands of Barrett and Lee (whose patents were prior to the plantation)[9] and also Taaffe,[10] but, while these did not retain their lands, Boyle did not acquire them. Many who received land as servitors in 1610 were *bona fide* grantees who generally retained their lands for periods comparable to the

[5] Undertakers and servitors have been classed together as 'British owners' when the shares of e ach group in 1641 were calculated, above, 375. In the maps (see plate section) indicating landownership in 1641, however, separate shadings for undertakers and servitors have been maintained. Where a proprietor owned land under undertakers' conditions it is shaded as undertakers', and where he owned land originally servitors' or acquired from any grantee other than an undertaker, it is shaded as servitors' land his ownership being indicated by a number indexed in the appropriate list of proprietors.

[6] Above, 62.

[7] For an illuminating study of the methods by which he built up a large estate see T.O. Ranger "Richard Boyle and the making of an Irish fortune', *IHS*, vol. x (1956–7), 257–97.

[8] Above, 51–6.

[9] Ranger, 'Richard Boyle', *IHS*, vol. x, 267–70.

[10] Above, 93.

undertakers. Yet there were a number of ubiquitous names and speculative activities. The accumulations of the Hamiltons – Scottish adventurers – have already been noted.[11] The doings of Francis Annesley were dubious enough. We have seen how he acquired land in Armagh with the assistance of his fellow adventurers – Kinge, Loftus, and Edgeworth.[12] He also acquired a mortgage there of undertaker Rolleston's land. In Cavan he was involved in dealings whereby almost 12,000 acres of land came into the hands of the Old English lawyer Edward Dillon.[13] However, despite many initial administrative failings (revealed, for example, in the discovery of small areas of concealed land), the plantation was so executed as to eliminate adventurer opportunities on the Munster scale. Although there were hopes in Ireland at the time of Pynnar's survey that land in Ulster would escheat,[14] the London government, though conscious of the serious defects of some of the undertakers, doubtless realised that their replacement by British already installed in Ireland offered little likelihood of improvement. Also the undertakers (a group albeit diluted by many new purchasers as we have seen) secured their position in 1628 at a time when their support of the government was desirable. New-style adventurers like Parkhurst the moneylender[15] were few, and the 1641 rising interrupted their activities.

And yet some large accumulations of land were amassed in both counties. Who amassed them and their effects on the plantation should be discussed. One, Sir William Brownlow's acquisition of his father's estate, had an inevitable quality. The acquisition of the estate originally granted to Ridgeway near Virginia in Cavan and, with it, the lands of and responsibility for, the town by Lucas Plunkett, subsequently earl of Fingall, himself a neighbouring landowner, was significant because it brought about an increase in the influence of the Old English group in that county.[16] The two most expansionist original grantees were the servitors Caulfeild in Armagh and Culme in Cavan. Caulfeild, in acquiring the 5,000-acre estate of Henry McShane O'Neill, made the more modest improvement, but he already had some 20,000 acres in Armagh and land in Tyrone as well.[17]

11 Sir James Hamilton was also, for a time, leaseholder of the TCD estate in Ulster, passing it subsequently to his associate Sir James Carroll (above, chapter 11).

12 Above, 100, 209.

13 Above, 104.

14 Above, 114–15.

15 Above, 186, 215, 260.

16 Above, 250–51.

17 He also held land in Armagh from TCD (above, chapter 11). Caulfeild also had a military position and other outside interests. He had a house in Dublin. Some indication of his financial dealings and affairs outside Ulster can be got from a letter to a Dublin agent in 1620 (Marsh's Library, Dublin, MS Z4.2.6, no. 45). Caulfeild also acquired Sandford's grant of the mountain lands in Ulster (above, 99). This patent was regarded by the author of the 'advertisements for Ireland' as detrimental to the interests of the crown, *Advertisements for Ireland,* ed. George O'Brien, (RSAI, Dublin, 1923), 17).

Culme, who began with some 4,500 acres, was involved, as has been seen, in a number of enterprises and, in 1641, his son Arthur and members of his family owned about 12,000 acres.[18] This had been acquired from both native grantees[19] and British servitors. Both were, at any rate, generally resident in Ulster. Lord Lambert, whose father Sir Oliver had an estate in Westmeath before receiving land as a servitor in Cavan, owned more than 15,000 acres there in 1641 as a result of his father's acquisitions from other servitors. He lived in England and the Cavan estate was ill-administered.[20] Furthermore, if Bishop Bedell's son-in-law, Clogy, is correct, his father and he had neglected an obligation in their original patent to build a 'citadel' at Cavan and 'a wall of defence against a sudden storm'.[21]

In fact a number of British proprietors with many outside interests or extensive lands elsewhere can be found. It is likely that their lands in plantation Ulster and the obligations which went with them would not be of primary importance to them. In Armagh St. John and Mountnorris clearly belonged to this group. Trevor and Bagnal with lands in Down and Moore, with his estate at Mellifont, were others. In Cavan the largest owner in 1641 with about 38,000 acres, Sir Charles Coote, was of this category. Coote was a prominent military figure,[22] vice-president of Connacht, and a man 'well estated in that province'.[23] His Cavan lands, recently acquired from Culme and Sir William Parsons (himself an adventurer) were originally granted to servitors (including Nicholas Pynnar) and natives. Another of Coote's type was Henry Crofton, who had acquired 1,000 acres of natives' lands,[24] and who had official and landed connections with Connacht. The Ashe brothers, servitors in Cavan, had estates in Meath, and their representative in 1641, Thomas Ashe (4,500 acres), was most likely an absentee. The ownership in both Armagh and Cavan of Sir George Acheson and Hans Hamilton necessarily led to absenteeism in one county.

The few grantees or crown-leaseholders of very small areas in both counties proved specially vulnerable. Thus, in Armagh, Richard Atherton's 105 acres were acquired by Grandison[25] and his brother's lease of the Mountnorris fort land passed – on his death – to Annesley. Similarly, in Cavan, the four smallest grantees, holding between 124 and 419 acres, did

[18] He was a leaseholder of the bishopric of Kilmore to boot (above, 300, 319).

[19] Above, 209.

[20] Above, 189–190.

[21] Wilkins (ed.), *Bedell*, 173. The patent as calendared does not refer to this stipulation (*CPRI, Jas I*, 210).

[22] Above, 159.

[23] *CSPI, 1615–25*, 449.

[24] Above, 210.

[25] Above, 146.

not retain their lands. One of these, for example, Sir Thomas Rotherham, who had a lease of the lands attached to the castle at Cavan, claimed in 1622 that he had passed his lease to Sir Oliver Lambert, who received a patent of the land as a result of negotiations conducted by St. John, the lord deputy, but had not been paid the amount agreed.[26] However, owing to the fragmentation of a few estates towards the end of our period these small owners were placed by a somewhat more numerous group of small owners in both counties and, yet, the number of British owners in both counties had declined slightly by 1641. In Cavan there were thirty-seven in 1641 (there had been thirty-nine originally) though here the amount of land in the hands of individual British owners had declined fractionally. In Armagh, where the proportion of British-owned land had increased there were thirty owners in 1641, there having been thirty-one initially. Since the increased number of small owners occupied only a small area of the land, it is clear that the effect of accumulations was not inconsiderable.

Apart entirely from the effects on the development of the plantation of ownership change, land accumulation, and absenteeism, it was considered, as early as 1618, that the success of settlement in Ulster had been jeopardised by the granting of estates which were too large. Lord deputy St. John, in proposals for the plantation of Longford, suggested that estates should be in the range of about 200 to 1,000 acres because

> experience has taught us that [in] Ulster the undertakers' buildings have not been so readily performed as was expected, nor the British brought over in sufficient numbers to inhabit those great scopes.[27]

Wentworth, planning for Connacht in 1634 and 1635, considered that estates should not be larger than 1,000 acres or, 'at most', 1,500 acres

> for I find where more have been granted the covenants of plantation are never performed nor doth it bring in half so many planters to undergoe the public service of the crown, to secure the kingdom against the natives, or to plant civility, industry, and religion amongst them ...[28]

Subsequent thinking, then, was – explicitly or implicitly – critical of the Ulster scheme. Yet it is clear that in its conception at least it reflected a considerable evolution of thought on this point of estate sizes. The

[26] NAI, Chancery salvage, 2B.80.120, no. 200.

[27] *Cal. Carew MSS, 1603–24*, 367–70.

[28] Sheffield City Library, Strafford MSS, vol. iii, 152, 180–81, 182 (ibid., Strafford letters, i, 341–2, 365).

seignories of Munster nominally 4,000 to 12,000 acres had been replaced by the propositions of Ulster in the range of 1,000 to 2,000 acres with principal undertakers, one in each barony, allowed 3,000 acres. Albeit through administrative error estates had turned out to be very much larger and the ill-effects of this disparity between planning and execution proved irremediable. And yet it remains unproven[29] that individual settlers could have succeeded, without the considerable income from native Irish tenantry which their large estates made possible, had very much smaller acreages been granted.

We have examined in earlier chapters a number of administrative failings on the part of the government which caused difficulties and uncertainties for the settlers. And yet again it is clear that the Ulster project (in our area and elsewhere) was more efficiently inaugurated than the Munster scheme. This was, admittedly, greatly facilitated by the fact that almost all the land in each county was declared confiscate and so the differentiation of forfeited and unforfeited land presented a much small problem than it did in Munster.[30] Perhaps it was for this reason, rather than because Chichester's government was markedly more efficient than that of the 1580s, that the Ulster plantation was more smoothly and more quickly inaugurated. The effect was that the initial problems of the grantees in Ulster were less staggering. Many of the Munster undertakers returned to England in 1586 because there was nobody present to receive them and allocate their lands.[31] No such frustration was in store for the Ulster undertakers in the summer of 1610. There were indeed numerous disputes about small areas between the grantees in Ulster, and the allocation of concealed land presented difficulties, but protracted litigation with native Irish or Old English claimants, so common in Munster, was only ephemeral in Ulster. This was not because the government was markedly more efficient in clarifying the rights of such claimants,[32] but because a much more comprehensive confiscation there had simplified the situation.

Despite a comparatively auspicious start to the plantation we have seen that there were many settler casualties in both Armagh and Cavan. Yet the colonising achievement was a very considerable one though, at the same

29 A study of the Longford plantation would be valuable here.

30 On the Munster plantation see D.B. Quinn, 'The Munster plantation: problems and opportunities', *JCHAS*, vol. 71, nos. 213 & 214 (1966), 19–40; idem., *Raleigh and the British empire* (London, 1947), 129–61; J. H. Andrews 'Colonisation and cartography: geographical ignorance as a factor in the Irish plantations', unpublished paper read to the International Geographical Congress, Dublin, 1964.

31 Quinn, *Raleigh*, 135.

32 See above, 78–9, 85. It should be noted also, however, that the government was able to exploit the situation regarding Sir Henry oge O'Neill's lands (above, 207).

time, the colony did not materialise in strict accord with the plantation conditions.

Stated quantitatively in terms of the size of the British population installed the plantation in our area had had a marked effect. It is also a fact that the size of the colony in Armagh was significantly larger than in Cavan. The population of Armagh in about 1630 numbered, as we have seen,[33] over 1,000 and probably as many as 1,500 British males. The population of Cavan, a county one and one-half times as large as Armagh, was, however, no more than about 835 British males. The Cavan total was, in fact, lower than any other county in plantation Ulster. The Armagh figure, however, compared very favourably with the achievement in Londonderry. The acreage of Armagh was some three-fifths that of Londonderry, a county in which there were just under 2,000 British male inhabitants.[34] In terms of real acreages the densities were very similar. However, when it is considered that undertakers (the group principally responsible for, and most generally active in, the introduction of settlers) in Armagh held only some 82,000 acres or 26 per cent of the area of the county whereas their equivalents, the companies, in Londonderry held some 291,000 acres or 57 per cent[35] it becomes clear that the achievement of private settlers in Armagh far outstripped that of the corporate bodies in Londonderry.[36] Perhaps the most distinguishing feature of the Londonderry plantation was the size attained by its two towns, Derry (500 British males) and Coleraine (300),[37] both of which far surpassed urban development in either Armagh or Cavan. Indeed, the undertakers in Cavan planted more densely than the companied did their lands in County Londonderry. To equal the companies' rate of 900 men[38] to 291,000 acres the Cavan undertakers, with 130,000 acres, should have planted somewhat over 400 men. In fact the muster return indicates that they had planted well over 600.[39] Down – privately colonised – with about 610,000 acres (almost twice the size of Armagh) and 4,045 names on the muster roll was, however, more densely settled than either Londonderry, Armagh, or Cavan.

33 Above, 175–9.
34 Moody, *Londonderry Plantation*, 322.
35 Ibid., 455.
36 It may be noted that the native Irish grantees in Armagh had half as much land again as they did in Derry at the outset of the plantation and, with some 59,000 acres, in 1641 still had somewhat more than the 52,050 acres initially allotted to natives in Derry.
37 Moody, *Londonderry Plantation*, 279.
38 Ibid., 321.
39 This figure excludes the populations of Cavan and Belturbet. For the former there is a separate entry in the muster book. The undertakers, between them, mustered 740 people. These would include the residents of Belturbet who, at most, could hardly have exceeded 100 (see above, 252–4).

The size of the Ulster colony compared very favourably with that of Munster and North America. There were about half as many British males in Armagh and Cavan as in all the Munster plantation.[40] The total population of the American colonies in 1630 has been estimated as 4,646 persons.[41] Clearly then Ulster had not only been a more successful plantation than its Munster precursor, but it had also attracted settlers on a much greater scale than concurrent efforts in America. But, whereas the North American population grew rapidly in the 1630s – though it had not exceeded 26,634 persons by 1640[42] – there is no evidence of any significant immigration to our area (or to Ireland at large) in that period. A twofold explanation can be offered. The undertakers had just procured permission to retain Irish tenantry on part of their estates and so would not seek further settlers. Also to emigrants in the 1630s – if anxious to avoid religious intolerance in England – Ireland under Wentworth and Bramhall offered no asylum, whereas America did.[43] Not only, then, was the colony on the defensive against Wentworth's administration in this decade, but it also received little or no external re-inforcement from settler arrivals. Nonetheless it must have seemed securely based.

However, there had been variations in performance between individual settlers, between settler groups, between institutional grantees, and between Armagh and Cavan. We have seen, for example, that by 1622[44] Scots and English undertakers in Armagh had planted much more densely that their counterparts in Cavan. Also the Scots in Armagh had planted twice as densely as the English undertakers in that county, while the English in Cavan had planted their barony of Loughtee more densely than were Clankee and Tullyhunco allotted initially to Scots. Such variations, interlocking factors of national and individual quality, have been examined throughout this thesis and they served to break down the planned symmetry of the plantation.

There were indeed a number of ways in which the colony did not develop according to plan. These can be listed quickly. The colony was slow in reaching its norm – the Scots in Cavan were particularly slow in starting operations. There was too much discontinuity of ownership. The stipulated pattern of settlement in village communities was only partly followed. Grantees' bawns and houses did not always measure up to requirement. The colony was not adequately armed. We have seen that the structure of

40 Quinn, 'Munster plantation', *JCHAS*, vol. 71, (1966), 38–9.

41 Greene (ed.), *Settlements*, 238.

42 Ibid.

43 Wentworth, conscious of this, was placed in somewhat of a quandary in planning his Connacht plantation (Sheffield City Library, Strafford MSS, vol. vii, 104; Kearney, *Strafford*, 101).

44 Above, 153–4.

tenantry on estates differed in varying ways from the scheme laid down in the undertakers' conditions, and that there were many disputes between landlords and tenants. One of the most striking divergences from plan was that the native Irish population was not excluded from the baronies assigned to undertakers.[45] The undertakers quickly discovered the value of the native population as tenants *in situ* who would pay higher rents than the British, and as a convenient source of manpower available for their needs.[46] Government attempts to have the undertakers honour this obligation foundered on their vested interest in its violation. The settlers' neglect of public interest for private advantage was regularly pointed to throughout our period, and it is clear that this had implications for the security of the colony. And yet it seems fair to argue that the task of removing the Irish from undertakers' lands (however short the distance might be) should have been undertaken by the government, and carried out in a planned manner.[47] Also it is possible that those undertakers who were granted land – and unknowingly received much larger acreages than they expected – might not have been able to establish settlements had they been deprived of income from the indigenous population.[48]

This is not to say, however, that there were not very definite influence areas in each county. The baronies granted to undertakers were manifestly more thoroughly planted than the other areas.[49] There were, however,

[45] It should be noted, however, that even if this rule had been enforced the baronies assigned to undertakers would still generally have contained areas from which the Irish need not be excluded – episcopal land and pieces held by pre-plantation title.

[46] Professor Quinn, in making this point about the Munster plantation, has stated that this placed the British there at an advantage *vis-à-vis* their counterparts in America who did not find the Indians so tractable to their needs and had to import African slaves if they required more labour (Quinn, 'Munster plantation', *JCHAS*, vol. 71, (1966), 28).

[47] This was suggested belatedly in 1628 (above, 163–4).

[48] One contemporary, at any rate, would have been sceptical of this argument. The author of the 'Advertisements for Ireland', *c.* 1622, claimed, speaking of the plantations generally, that 'your richer sort' of undertaker and the 'corporations here of England' (presumably a reference to the London companies) retained the natives ('because they pay them greater rents they say than the British will'), and set a bad example to the rest (George O'Brien (ed.), *Advertisements for Ireland,* (RSAI, Dublin 1923), 12).

[49] Though it is clear that the colony in all areas, however considerable in undertakers' baronies, was considerably outnumbered by the native population. In 1628 it was stated that 'although in many of the proportions … there is one small township … yet the proportions being wide and large, the habitation of all the province is scarce visible' (Hickson (ed.), *Ireland in seventeenth century,* ii, 330). Bishop Bedell's son, William, states that, during his father's episcopate, Cavan was 'meetly well planted with English, but scatteringly here and there which facilitated their ruine'. Also although there was 'a competent number of English, … the Irish were more than five times their number, and all of them obstinate papists' (Jones (ed.), *Life and death of William Bedell,* 62). However, to the Irish in Cavan, the settlers were a substantial body. A report in 1636 on the state of the Catholic diocese of Kilmore spoke of the effect of the colony on the cathedral centre of Kilmore and the county at large: 'Villa in qua sita est Eccla. Cathedralis habitores habet Anglos et assertores haereticae pravitatis, simul cum ipso Pseud-Epo.: per universam quoque Diacesim Angli mixtim, Scotique haeretici cum Catholicis natives vivunt' (Moran (ed.), *Spicilegium Ossoriense,* 208).

differences in intensity between Armagh and Cavan which may be briefly noted. The undertakers in Armagh planted more densely than those in Cavan. The servitors in Armagh[50] also introduced more British than those in Cavan, though the servitors' lands in both counties were, on the whole, Irish-occupied. The introduction of British proceeded much further on the lands of the archbishop of Armagh than it did on those of the bishopric of Kilmore. The lands of Trinity College in Armagh compare in this respect much more with those of the bishopric of Kilmore than with archiepiscopal land in Armagh. However, in Armagh some sprinkling of British tenantry usually followed British ownership, and this had proceeded very much further in Armagh than in Cavan by 1641.[51] The plantation aimed to produce a mixed society whose components would be carefully differentiated into different baronies in each county. This careful differentiation was not achieved. However in Armagh, though not in Cavan, the amount of land in British ownership increased in the thirty years before 1641.

Related to the political purpose of the plantation – to transform Ulster from being a stronghold of Gaelic particularism by the transfer of the largest proportion of the land to British owners – were social and economic objectives, to introduce 'civility' and British methods to the northern counties. An attempt has been made[52] to assess the effects of the plantation in this respect, but the almost total absence of estate papers and maps has made for only tentative conclusions. It seems clear, at any rate, that changes were confined to British-owned land. The intractability of the Irish to the adoption of British agricultural methods was often noted and, indeed, converted to crown profit through fines. Corn production and cattle raising were the two basic activities of the settlers, associated processing activities

50 Caulfeild's monastic land in Armagh can be considered as servitor in this respect. Almost all the Cavan monastic land was old English-owned.

51 On the lands owned by native Irish or old English British tenantry were extremely exceptional. Sir Turlogh McHenry O'Neill may have had a few in south Armagh (see above, 214). Otherwise the British middlemen tenants to Phelim O'Neill in Tiranny (above, 215) are all that have come to light. It is clear though that not only did some old English tenantry follow old English ownership to Cavan (above, 153) – indeed the British Lord Lambert had a Pale tenant (above, 153) – but that there were also some old English tenants in Armagh. A few of these held lands, and were generally absentee, from a number of owners (Richard Rolleston, above, 274; the archbishop of Armagh, above, 354–55, 364; Phelim O'Neill, above, 215) in different parts of the county, but there were also a number, not unexpectedly, in south Armagh bordering on Louth. We have seen that Sir Turlogh McHenry O'Neill had old English tenants (above, 214). On Bagnal's land in south Orior there was an old English tenant Patrick Babe (Armagh Public Library, Submissions of evidence to the court of claims, 1663, vol. x (unpaginated): submission of John Babe. On Babe see T. Fitzpatrick, *The bloody bridge and other papers relating to the insurrection of 1641* (Dublin 1903), 21–2).

52 See above, chapter 9.

being very common. Flour mills were built on almost all estates, brewhouses had been erected, and surplus corn, from Cavan at any rate, was sold in Dublin. There is substantial evidence for the importation of British livestock. Woollen weaving was common, though the evidence for flax is slight. Craftsmen and merchants were resident in most of the towns or villages. Only one ironworks – in north Cavan – has come to light, and the evidence about timber cutting or processing is fragmentary. It is clear that some enclosure of land had taken place and also drainage and reclamation. The compilers of the Civil Survey were particularly impressed by the achievement of the Oneilland undertakers in Armagh:

> the soyle of this barony is generally good for tillage and pasture and the finest plantation of Ulster by reason of the English nation that first planted it, most of the same being naturally subject to wett but by their industry drained and made dry.[53]

Also, despite the criticisms of the planters' building record, one of the most striking features of the plantation was the buildings they erected. Elizabethan and Jacobean England saw re-building on a considerable scale, and the settlers reproduced houses similar to those from which they came.[54] A whole range of building skills was mobilised in the Ulster environment.

The settler, then, brought much that was new to the Ulster scene – a pattern of social organisation which was alien to Gaelic tradition. A system of fairs and markets based on the planters' settlements[55] reproduced British arrangements. It was really only with the plantation, though Cavan had been nominally shired in 1579, that the English system of local government was introduced, and in county administration the settler element predominated.[56] In contrast to Munster where a presidency and council had been set up some fifteen years before it was planted, the appointment of sheriffs and constables and the holding of sessions did not systematically begin in Ulster until after O'Neill's submission in 1603: assizes were first held in Armagh in 1605 and revived in Cavan in 1606. In Cavan admittedly there was some familiarity with the English legal system from before the plantation and the office of sheriff there was, on a number of occasions in our period, occupied by persons of Old English or Gaelic Irish

[53] R. C. Simington (ed.), *The Civil Survey, 1654–56*, vol. x, miscellanea (IMC, Dublin 1961), 69.

[54] Anthony Cope in Armagh was a close relative of Sir Walter Cope who had built Cope castle – later Holland House – in the first decade of the seventeenth century (D. Hudson, *Holland House in Kensington* (London, 1967), 2–6; see also Jope, 'Moyry', *UJA*, 3rd series, vol. 23 (1960), 97–123).

[55] Above, 279–83.

[56] See below appendix 4.

origin. Yet it is clear that in both counties it was the presence of the colonists which ensured that the system was effectively introduced.[57] Its working, however, remains almost totally obscure owing to the absence of sheriffs' rolls, quarter sessions records, and constables, churchwardens, or vestry records. Yet we know that barony constables were first appointed for Armagh in 1605.[58] While only the archbishop of Armagh's manor court records survive,[59] we know that manor courts were held on a number of estates in both counties,[60] and since the archbishop's court appointed petty constables and bailiffs in the normal English way,[61] it is likely that the other courts did so also. There is evidence, too, that other county officers were appointed. In 1616 Marmaduke Whitechurch and Archibald Moore, both landowners, were collectors of fines imposed at the assizes for Armagh and Cavan respectively.[62] In 1618 Peter Ameas[63] was collector of subsidy for County Cavan.[64] In the following year Archibald Moore was receiver of the king's rents in Cavan.[65] Doubtless the unnamed 'auditour of the … county' referred to in an inquisition in 1629[66] held the same office. There was a county jail in Cavan town from before the plantation,[67] and one had been built in Armagh by 1641.[68] Sessions were probably held in these buildings, though it was noted in 1622 that Sir Stephen Butler had collected money in Cavan for building a sessions house.[69] It is clear that the maintenance of order, especially in periods of emergency, presented special problems and it was military forces (particularly those of provost marshals) at those times, rather than ordinary legal sanctions, which played the crucial role.

As far as the administration or regulation of the colony was concerned we have seen that the government faltered in a number of important respects. The enforcement of the conditions of plantation to which the individual settlers were bound was generally neglected. But it was, perhaps, in its treatment of what may be called the institutional side of the colony that the Dublin government was most lacking in vigour. We have examined in detail the procrastination which characterised government policy with

57 See above, 19.
58 Above, 18–19.
59 Above, 369–72.
60 Above, 275.
61 Above, 371.
62 TNA, SP 63/234, ff 46–7 (*CSPI, 1615–25*, 127–8).
63 Above, 120.
64 NAI, Ferguson MSS, vol. xi, 271.
65 Ibid., 284.
66 *Inq. cancel. Hib. repert.*, ii, Cavan (17) Chas I.
67 Above, 32.
68 Above, 238.
69 Above, 138.

regard to the establishment of the church,[70] towns,[71] and schools[72] in our area. It would be wrong, of course, to minimise the problems these presented since it seems fair to say that, in the planning of the colony, inadequate thought was given to their inauguration. Urban development, for example, made, as it was, a private responsibility, was, in general, slow and dependent on the fortunes of individual patrons.[73] This had important military implications, recognised in 1620 when the Leitrim plantation was being founded. Here money was reserved out of the revenue accruing from the undertakers[74] and Sir Charles Coote, vice-president of Connacht, was allocated £3,000 and charged with the building of a walled town, Jamestown.[75] This, it was noted, would

> supply the great defect in the plantation of Ulster, where there are no towns walled but Derry and Coleraine.[76]

However, in other ways the government was less exculpably negligent in its attitude to the Ulster project. The articles of plantation stated that the settlers' tenantry should be mustered twice yearly and yet it was not until 1618 that a muster master was appointed and this was due to a foreign emergency.[77] The settlers may have been themselves neglectful of military security but the government seems also to have been somewhat heedless of the danger of insurrection. While acute financial stringency offers some extenuation for the disposal of the inland forts in 1620[78] this action meant that the colony in Armagh and Cavan (and other inland counties) was left without permanent military protection.[79]

70 Above, chapter 10.

71 Above, chapter 8.

72 Below, appendix 3.

73 Virginia, as we have seen, came into Old English hands having been purchased with a servitor's estate by the earl of Fingall in 1622 from Sir Hugh Culme (NLI, Ainsworth reports, Fingall Papers, vol. 1, no. 6, 127). In 1642 Virginia was described as 'a towne of the traytor the Earle of Fingall' (J. Hogan (ed.), *Letters and papers relating to the Irish rebellion between 1642 and 1646*, (IMC, Dublin 1936), 150).

74 A special fine of £100 per 1,000 acres to be paid within five years was imposed upon the undertakers (*CSPI, 1615–25*, 336).

75 *CPRI, Jas I*, 512, 567; *CSPI, 1615–25*, 336, 448–9.

76 Ibid., 449.

77 Above, 110–11. Also there was the failure to provide machinery to facilitate the required taking of the oath of supremacy.

78 Above, 129–31.

79 There was, though, a permanent provost marshal for Ulster (Rowley Lascelles, *Liber munerum publicorum Hiberniae* (London 1852), pt. ii, 193–4), and also other appointments for specific areas were made, as has been seen, from time to time. This device of sending provost marshals to disturbed areas, at small cost, was adopted by Chichester as early as 1611 (*CSPI, 1611–14*, 156–7).

In the last resort the success of the plantation depended on the reaction of the native Irish. Although it met with intermittent localised violence, it was not disrupted by insurrection or invasion, as was that of Munster, and the fact that it grew for thirty years before receiving a major challenge made it one of the most decisive happenings in seventeenth-century Irish history. This is not to say that the Irish were not embittered by its implementation. However, finding themselves militarily incapable of immediately exterminating the colony and, also, that the undertakers were all too willing to receive them as tenants, they tended to accept for the time a situation which began to look only remotely remediable.[80] The government proved unwilling, being pressed by the undertakers, to enforce their removal from the undertakers' lands and so an ambiguous situation was not in fact resolved.[81] By remaining as tenantry and labourers they contributed substantially to making the plantation a going concern in its initial years, thereby facilitating a take-off the effect of which was to increasingly restrict their share both as owners and tenants.

The attitudes of the Irish, however, are not subject to easy generalisation. Some sporadically opted for the military solution.[82] The stealing of the settlers' livestock was a regular pursuit of wood-kerne[83] anxious to sabotage the colony. But many were prepared, in effect, to link their fortunes from year-to-year with the colonists as tenants and undertenants. Some co-operative relationships grew up at individual level, and there were even occasional intermarriages.[84] There were many who seem to have been

80 For the motives of the native grantees in accepting their lands, see above, 203–05.

81 Had the Irish decided on a concerted policy of passive resistance and withdrawn to the lands allotted to the native grantees which, in our counties (where the Irish received more than twice their allotment in Londonderry) might have been practicable, it is perhaps conceivable that the plantation would have proved much less viable in its early years and an opportunity for a negotiated restriction of its scope presented itself.

82 The collective disloyalty of the native Irish was an accepted tenet of government thinking. Wentworth formulated the value of the army, as a result, very concisely in 1636: 'the army, as of absolute necessity to that government, was rather to be re-inforced than at all diminished, as an excellent minister and assistant in the execution of all the king's writs, the great peace-maker betwixt the British and the native, betwixt the protest and the papist, and the chief securer under God and his majesty of the future and past plantations' (Carte, *Ormond*, i, 7).

83 There are also, however, instances of theft of Irish-owned livestock by British (Ferguson, 'Ulster roll', *UJA*, 1st series, i, (1853), 269).

84 Above, 98. Systematic investigation of this is impossible since parish registers have not survived. However, apart from William Brownlow's marriage to Elinor O'Doherty, two cases have been found. There was residing on Sir John Dillon's estate in Armagh in 1624 a certain 'widdow Turner, an Irishe woman' (TNA, SP 63/238, fol. 142). In 1636 a certain Daniel O'Leary who, in 1629 was a tenant on the Fishe estate in Cavan (*Inq. cancel. Hib. repert.*, ii, Cavan (26) Chas I), had as wife 'Susanna Leary, als. Partridge' (NLI, Butler Deeds, D 8896–8926: statement by Daniel O'Leary, 15 June, 1636).

prepared to accept (and use) the legal system of the colony and its social hierarchy and organisation.[85] We have found many who held office in estate or county administration and there were even some native Protestant clergy in Cavan.[86] Apart from rare instances, however, they did not accept the Protestant religion or the English language though, except of Bedell's efforts in Cavan, neither was systematically expounded to them. Finally, even weaknesses in the system of law enforcement offered some crude mitigation of the Irish position.[87]

Yet it is hard to accept the unhesitant claims of Clarendon and Temple that the Irish and the settlers formed an integrated society,[88] sharing economic prosperity, by 1641.[89] Ever since the plantation had been implemented there had been cumulative pressures on the amount of land the Irish owned or occupied. The occasional settler might acquire Irish ways,[90] but settlers and natives as groups were differentiated in many fundamental interests. However much they might begin to accept the social system, it was alien and novel (except, perhaps, to some of the Irish and the old English in Cavan) and must have often seemed hostile to them. However, intermittently they might be enforced, the Irish were subject to various penalties – for plowing by the tail, for being on undertakers' land (abolished in 1628[91]), and for recusancy.[92] Although the presence of Catholic clergy might be condoned, the temporalities had been transferred

[85] Even in 1641 the system of urban government established by charter for Armagh town was not abolished but, instead, a prominent local Irish figure, Tady Crawley or Crolly, was appointed sovereign (TCD, MS 836, fol. 65).

[86] Apart from the occasional Irish sheriff or member of parliament we have found, during the plantation period, an Irish undersheriff in Cavan in 1630 (NAI, Ferguson MSS, vol. xii, 140), Irish petty constables, bailiffs and sub-bailiffs in Armagh in the 1620s (above, 371), and Irish municipal officers in Cavan town (above, 243–8). Walter Brady presumably remained keeper of Cavan jail until his death. In July 1625 the keeper was Cale McEntire *alias* Freeman (*CPRI, Chas I*, 44–5).

[87] There are, for example, instances of jail breaks like that of the three Irish who escaped from Cavan jail in 1625 (*CPRI, Jas I*, 44–5).

[88] When, in 1627, Lieutenant Cowell, who held land in Armagh as a tenant to the archbishop (above, 354), wished to leave money in his will for charitable purposes, he designated it to be for the relief of 'the protestant poor' (Armagh Public Library, William Reeves, Memoirs of Tynan (MS volume, unfoliated)).

[89] Edward Hyde, earl of Clarendon, *The history of the rebellion and civil wars in Ireland* (London 1720), 6–10; Temple, *General Rebellion*, 25–6.

[90] Like, for example, the daughter of a County Armagh carpenter who, in 1641, 'escaped because she spoke irish and said she was an irish woman' (TCD, MS 836, fol. 92v).

[91] See above, 162–3.

[92] David Rothe, bishop of Ossory, writing in 1616, stated that in a recent year the recusancy fines for County Cavan totalled 8,000 sovereigns (P.F. Moran (ed.), *The analecta of David Rothe, bishop of Ossory* (Dublin 1884), 32. (I am grateful to Dr. Ussher, Dr. Hardy and Mr. Peacock of Magee University College for assistance in translating this and other passages from Latin sources). After the recusancy fines were granted to the archbishop of Armagh as king's almonsner in 1617 they were applied, as we have seen (above, 299–301, 303) to building Protestant churches.

to Protestant hands, and numerous ecclesiastical commentators pointed to the impoverishing effect the new dispensation had had on the Catholic church organisation. A report to Rome in 1626 stated simply that the cathedral of Armagh 'ab haereticis occupatur'.[93] A similar report in 1636 on Kilmore diocese stated that the cathedral chapter was depleted because no emoluments could be looked for.[94] The author of the *Commentarius Rinuccianus* asserted that, as a result of the plantation, Ulster – previously an 'adornment of the faith' – had turned out to be a 'cesspool of heterodox settlements'.[95] Nor were the only grievances to be articulated religious ones. A confederate declaration of 1642 pointed to the sufferings of the Irish from provost marshals and for being disarmed while the settlers were an armed colony in accordance with the rule of the plantation.[96] It must have seemed to the settlers in the 1630s, however, that the Irish could not possibly consider remedying their grievances by force. Yet, if the plantation seemed to be a success by 1641, the limitation of that success – its vulnerability in the event of concerted attack – was quickly to be demonstrated. However, by 1641, not only had the colony had thirty years of growth behind it, but the subsequent course of Irish history in the seventeenth century ensured its re-establishment.

93 B. Jennings (ed.), *Wadding Papers, 1614–38* (IMC, Dublin, 1953), 178.
94 Moran (ed.), *Spicilegium Ossoriense,* 208. See also above, 245.
95 Kavanagh (ed.), *Commentarius*, i, 201.
96 Ibid., 358–9.

APPENDIX 1

Lists of Proprietors

The following lists have been derived basically from the *Calendar of Irish patent rolls, James I* with regard to the first set for each county and from the Books of Survey and Distribution for ownership in 1641. However, in drawing up the lists indicating ownership at the outset of plantation the lists of grantees in 'Ulster Plantation Papers' nos. 11 and 21 in *Analecta Hibernica*, viii and in *Calendar of the Carew MSS, 1603–24* pp 231–44 have been correlated with material derived from the patents. All have been used to rectify occasional errors and omissions in the lists printed in Hill's *Plantation in Ulster*. Supplementary sources used have been the crown rental of *c.* 1617 (TCD, MS 570, ff 300–12) which is valuable as giving the names of assignees of lands, particularly in Cavan, granted before the plantation. Additional evidence of title or leasehold has been derived from a list in Marsh's Library, Dublin, MS Z3.2.6. The chancery inquisitions printed in *Inq. cancel. Hib. repert.*, ii, have been helpful in particular instances. The *Cal. Pat. Rolls Ire., Eliz.*, and the *Cal. Fiants Irel., Eliz.* have also been used. In the case of some of the native Irish grantees in Orior, Armagh, particularly O'Hanlons and McCanns (mistakes in whose names were made in the lists of grantees) cognizance has been taken of an order of the lord deputy of 10 January 1612 (Bodleian Library, Oxford, Carte MSS, vol. 80, fol. 630) rectifying the situation. The first lists have been given the date range *c.* 1610–*c.* 1620 to take account of small grants of concealed lands and other adjustments made within that period.

The lists for 1641 derive, in large part, from the Books of Survey and Distribution. The Quit Rent Office set (in NAI) has been chiefly used, but the Headfort and Taylor (in RIA) sets have also been consulted. The Civil Survey has not survived for either Armagh or Cavan. The 1641 ownership column of the Books of Survey and Distribution has, for Armagh and Cavan, to be treated with some caution, and a number of ascriptions of land to post 1641 owners have been rectified from other sources. Thus, for example, the Books of Survey and Distribution ascribes the Sacheverall estate in north Armagh in 1641 to Major Edward Richardson from whom Richhill derives its name. But this seems mistaken because Francis Sacheverall, son of the original grantee, whose daughter and heir

Richardson married (Burke, *Landed gentry of Ireland* (4th ed., 1958), 601), did not die until 1649 (*Inq. cancel. Hib. repert.*, ii, Armagh (1) Chas II). Similarly, Arthur Culme's lands in Cavan are ascribed to 'the heirs of Col. Arthur Culme' although Culme was still alive in October 1648 (*CSPI, 1647–60*, 32). The most generally valuable supplementary materials have been the patents issued under the commission for defective titles which are transcribed in abstract in J. Lodge, Records of the Rolls, vol. vi, preserved in NAI Inquisitions, and other miscellaneous sources have also been used.

For the methods used in establishing the acreages of estates, see appendix 2. The significance of the areas indicated by means of an asterisk is also discussed in appendix 2.

Landowners, Armagh, *c.* 1610–1620
O = Oneilland, F = Fews, Or = Orior, A = Armagh, T = Tiranny

No. on map	Barony	Owner	O.S. acreage	Acreage as granted
English undertakers:				
1	O	John Brownlow	4,817	1,500
2	O	William Brownlow	8,062	1,000
10	O	William Powell	8,656	2,000
6	O	John Heron	5,316	2,000
9	O	Rev. James Matchett	3,455	1,000
13	O	Rev. Richard Rolleston	3,430	1,000
7	O	Anthony Cope	8,365	3,000
12	O	John Dillon	4,897	1,500
11	O	Francis Sacheverall	7,499	2,000
4	O	William Stanhowe	11,747	1,500
Scottish undertakers:				
30	F, Or	Sir James Douglas	7,083	2,000
29	F	Henry Acheson	1,962	1,000
26	F	James Craig	2,634	1,000
27	F	William Lawder	2,292	1,000
28	F	Claud Hamilton	1,727	500
British servitors:				
33	Or	Sir Oliver St. John	4,806	1,500
58	Or	Sir Garret Moore	2,681	1,000
64	Or	Sir Thomas Williams	2,760	1,000
14	Or, O	Sir John Bourchier	3,685	1,000
34	Or	Francis Cooke	2,877	1,000
38	Or	Charles Poyntz	674	200

63	Or	Lord Audley	1,654	500
15	O	Richard Atherton	105	
3	O	Edward Trevor	1,773	
5	A	Sir Toby Caulfeild: Charlemont fort land		(approx.) 500
79	Or	Capt. Anthony Smith: Moyry fort land	4,447	
69	Or	Henry Atherton: Mountnorris fort land	1,134	300
70	Or	Francis Annesley	778	
73	Or	Marmaduke Whitechurch	713	
Holders of former monastic property:				
5,in*	F, A, T, O	Sir Toby Caulfeild	20,168	
73	Or	Marmaduke Whitechurch	3,276	
8	O, Or	Arthur Bagnal	5,575	
in*	A	Francis Edgeworth	(approx.) 5	
B,in*	All bars	Archbishop	47,986	
G	A, F, O, Or	Glebe	6,561	
Other ecclesiastical proprietors:				
24,in*	A, F, T	Dean	7,162	
17	A	Chancellor	9	
18,in*	A	Vicars Choral	1,426	
Sc.	Or	Armagh school land	1,552	
16	A	Trinity College, Dublin	22,875	4,700
mountain	Or	John Sandford (mountain)	987	
Native Irish:				
21	T	Turlogh oge O'Neill	561	
22	T	Brian O'Neill	3,294	
25	T	Neill O'Neill	332	
23	T	Henry & Charles O'Neill	344	
19	T	Conn boy O'Neill	1,278	
20	T	Catherine O'Neill	4,531	
76	Or	Art McBaron O'Neill	7,082	2,000
68	Or	Henry McShane O'Neill	4,910	1,500
48	Or	Turlogh groom O'Hanlon	801	140
47	Or	Shane McShane O'Hanlon	295	100
74	Or	Rory McPatrick McCann	688	120
36	Or	Rory McFerdoragh O'Hanlon	250	120
35	Or	Patrick Modder [O'Donnell]	198	120
81	Or	Laughlin O'Hagan	242	120
59	Or	Felim McOwen oge McDonnell	203	100
49	Or	Shane oge McShane roe O'Hanlon	219	120

57	Or	Conn McTurlogh [O'Neill]	1,008	360
75	Or	Owen McHugh McNeill Mor O'Neill	1,352	240
53	Or	Patrick O'Hanlon	2,150	
72	Or	Redmond O'Hanlon	3,841	
32	Or	Cormac McTurlogh Brassilogh O'Neill	168	120
42	Or	Redmond McFerdoragh O'Hanlon	140	60
43	Or	Turlogh oge McTurlogh Brassilogh O'Neill	141	60
67	Or	Mulmory O'Donnell/Art McTurlogh O'Neill/Neill McTurlogh O'Neill	754	240
37	Or	Neece Quin	181	120
46	Or	Phelim & Brian O'Hanlon	584	240
45	Or	Patrick McManus O'Hanlon & Ardell Moore O'Mulchrewe	293	120
80	Or	Donnell McHenry O'Neill/Felim McTurlogh Brassilogh O'Neill/ Eugene Vally O'Neill/Edmund oge O'Donnelly	2,708	540
55	Or	Shane McOghy O'Hanlon	213	100
54	Or	Donell McCann	167	80
39	Or	Carbery McCann	815	360
56	Or	Brian McDonnell McFelim roe O'Neill/Hugh McCarbery O'Neill/ Shane McTurlogh O'Neill	480	240
62	Or	Donogh Reogh O'Hagan	325	100
60	Or	Colla McArt McDonnell	145	120
77	Or	Donogh oge McMurphy	728	180
78	Or	Hugh McTurlogh O'Neill/Art McTurlogh O'Neill/Henry McTurlogh O'Neill	962	240
40	Or	Hugh McGilleduffe	117	120
52	Or	Cahir O'Mellan	123	100
51	Or	Hugh McBrian McCann	362	80
61	Or	Brian McMelaghlin McArt O'Neill	118	60
41	Or	Felim O'Quin	293	100
44	Or	Carbery oge McCann/Toole McFelim McCann	59	160
66	Or	Edmond Groome McDonnell	56	80
65	Or	Alexander oge McDonnell	112	83
71	Or	Brian oge O'Hagan	694	100
50	Or	Ferdoragh O'Hanlon (in 1637)	43	(20)
31	F	Sir Turlogh McHenry O'Neill	33,704	
	Or	Collo McEever McDonnell	unidentified	80
U.	Or	Unidentified ownership	4,247	

Landowners, Armagh, 1641

No. on map	Barony	Owner	O.S. acreage
British proprietors:			
1	O, Or	Sir William Brownlow	13,463
2	O	Mark Trevor	1,666
3	O, Or	Henry St. John	10,128
4	O	John Waldrom	12,101
6	O	Alse Pybus	612
7	O	Anthony Cope	2,805
8	O	Henry Stanhowe	4,013
9	O	Hamlet Oblyns	2,081
10	O	Anthony Workman	293
11	O	Walter Cope	2,004
12,in*	A, F, O, Or, T	Toby, Lord Caulfeild	26,331
13	O	Henry Cope	8,365
14	O, Or	Henry, Earl of Bath	6,730
15	O	Richard Rolleston[1]	3,430
16	O	Francis Sacheverall	7,499
17	O, Or	Arthur Bagnal	5,575
18	O	Henry Dillon	4,897
20	A	George Chambers[2]	196
23	T	Robert Hovendon	2,364
28	F	Hans Hamilton	6,653
29	F, Or	Sir George Acheson	9,045
33	Or	Toby Poyntz	4,318
36	Or	Lord Mountnorris	4,387
39	Or	Abraham Dee	658
35	Or	James Galbraith	43
41	Or	Charles, Lord Viscount Moore	5,824
42	Or	John Parry	267
49	Or	Roger West	2,760
57	Or	Richard Smith	4,447
58	Or	Marmaduke Symonds	3,989
Old English:			
5	O	Vallentine Blake	882
38	Or	James Fleming	786
19	A	Trinity College, Dublin	22,875
B,in*	All bars	Archbishopric	53,972
G	A, F, O, Or	Glebe	6,561

[1] Ownership controversial; see above, 187.

[2] Or his son, Thomas; see above, 369 fn. 149.

Other ecclesiastical proprietors:			
27,in*	A, F	Dean	1,181
21	A	Chancellor	9
22,in*	A	Vicars Choral	1,426
Sc.	Or	Armagh school land	1,552
mountain	Or	Lord Caulfeild (mountain)	987
Native Irish:			
53	Or	Roger Moore	7,082
40	Or	Keadagh McDonnell	145
37	Or	Patrick O'Mornaghan	118
51	Or	Tool McRory McCann	688
32	Or	Patrick McRory O'Hanlon	250
31	Or	Patrick O'Donnell	198
52	Or	Hugh oge O'Neill	894
56	Or	Hugh boy O'Neill	458
50	Or	Hugh boy O'Hanlon	3,841
46	Or	Mulmory McDonnell	252
47	Or	Daniel O'Neill	251
48	Or	– ? – O'Neill	251
54	Or	Donnogh oge McMurphy	728
55	Or	Brian O'Neill	962
34	Or	Hugh McBrian McCann	362
43	Or	Patrick & Hugh O'Hagan	694
44	Or	Gillaspicke McDonnell	112
45	Or	?? – McDonnell ??	56
26	T	Sir Phelim O'Neill	1,541
24	T	Turlogh oge O'Neill	5,127
25	T	Turlogh McBrian O'Neill	1,312
30	F	Sir Henry O'Neill	33,704
U	Or	Unidentified ownership	4,247

Landowners, Cavan, *c.* 1610–*c.* 1620
L = Loughtee, C = Clankee, T = Tullyhunco, Cm = Clanmahon, Cr = Castlerahan, Th = Tullyhaw, Tg = Tullygarvy

No. on map	Barony	Owner	O.S. acreage	Acreage as granted
English undertakers:				
41	L	Sir Richard Waldron	7,093	2,000
39	L	John Fishe	8,868	2,000[3]
38	L, Tg	Sir Stephen Butler	13,552	2,760

[3] Includes 284 acres, as estimated, for town of Belturbet.

44	L	Nicholas Lusher	6,619	2,000
37	L	Sir Hugh Wirrall	6,606	1,500
42	L	John Taylor	6,842	1,500
45	L	William Lusher	5,754	1,500
Scottish undertakers:				
24	T	Sir AlexanderHamilton	12,445	2,000
22	T[4]	Sir Claud Hamilton	3,406	1,000
23	T	Alexander Auchmooty	4,852	1,000
20	T	John Auchmooty	4,064	1,000
25	T	John Browne	6,424	1,000
62	C	Lord Aubigny	15,507	3,000
64	C	William Bailie	8,386	1,000
61	C	John Ralston	10,190	1,000
63	C	William Dunbar	9,345	1,000
British servitors:				
54	Tg	Sir Thomas & John Ashe	4,203	750
55	Tg	Archibald & Brent Moore	8,049	1,500
34	Cm	Sir Oliver Lambert	8,229	2,000
33	Cm	Joseph Jones	8,618	1,500
30	Cm	John Russon	1,811	500
27	Cm	Anthony Atkinson	2,170	500
80	Cr	Sir John Elliot	3,460	400
81	Cr	John Ridgeway	8,109	1,275[5]
79	Cr	Roger Garth	2,108	500
67	Cr	Sir Edmund Fettiplace	5,832	1,000
1	Th	Sir George & Sir Richard Graham	13,603	2,000
2	Th, T, L	Hugh Culme	4,580	
3	Th	Edward Rutledge	8,221	600
13	Th	Nicholas Pynnar	13,612	1,000
65	C	Sir Robert Stewart	537	
84	C	George St. George	419	
21	T	Thomas Jones	124	200
47	L	Roger Downeton	1,195	
46	L	William Binde	292	
in*	L	Sir Thomas Rotherham	141	
Holders of former monastic property:				
40	L	Sir James Dillon, earl of Roscommon	4,150	
in*	L	Sir Thomas Ashe	9	

[4] Also one small area in Loughtee.

[5] Includes 275 acres, as estimated, for the town of Virginia.

Old English:				
26	Cm, Cr, L	Richard Nugent, Baron Delvin	18,335	
31	Cm, L	Edward Nugent	1,905	462
86	Th, T	Walter Talbot	3,366	
28	C, Cm, Cr	Capt Garret Fleming	15,643	
76	Cr	Sir William Taaffe	5,832	1,000
82	Cr	Christopher Plunket, Baron Killeen	6,458	
35	Cm, Cr	Christopher Nugent	3,396	450
32	Cm	Richard Fitzsimons	209	50
50	Tg	Capt. Richard Tirrell	8,439	
B	all bars	Bishopric	31,785	
G,in*	all bars	Glebe	13,657	
Sc	L	School lands	917	
in*	L	Town of Cavan	683	
mountain	Th	John Sandford (mountain)	16,828	
Native Irish:				
51	Tg	Mulmory McPhillip O'Reilly	4,142	1,000
53	Tg	Capt. Hugh O'Reilly	3,467	1,000
59	Tg	Terence Brady	733	150
52	Tg	Morish McTully	1,321	300
57	Tg	Thomas Brady	497	150
58	Tg	Connor McShane roe [Brady]	575	150
56	Tg	Henry Betagh	2,043	262
49	Tg, L	Mulmory oge O'Reilly	17,772	3,000
17	Cm, Cr, L, T	Mulmory McHugh Connelagh O'Reilly	7,134	2,000
36	Cm	Hugh McBrian O'Reilly	271	100
29	Cm	Phillip McTurlogh Brady	1,083	300
43	Cr, L	Walter, Thomas & Patrick Brady	6,926	
75	Cr	Cahir McShane O'Reilly	1,112	300
72	Cr	Barnaby O'Reilly	977	150
71	Cr	Shane McHugh O'Reilly	2,214	475
73	Cr	Thomas McJames bane [O'Reilly]	456	50
78	Cr	Phillip McBrian McHugh O'Reilly	2,069	300
83	Cr	Owen McShane O'Reilly	1,100	200
66	Cr.	Brian a'Coggye O'Reilly	1,371	400
70	Cr	Mulmory McOwen O'Reilly	1,371	
77	Cr	Hugh roe McShane O'Reilly	742	200
69	Cr	Phillip & Shane O'Reilly	943	300
74	Cr	Shane McPhillip O'Reilly	3,273	925
68	Cr	Owen McMulmory O'Reilly	2,616	500
48	Cr, L	Hugh McGlasney [O'Reilly]	550	100
87	Th	Brian McPhillip O'Reilly	8,22	600

4	Th	Felim McGawran	2,976	1,000
5	Th, T	William O'Sheridan	1,420	
6	Th	Mulmory McTurlogh O'Reilly	1,039	200
7	Th	Brian oge McGawran	1,025	200
8	Th	Felim, Brian & Cahir, sons of Hugh O'Reilly late of Ballaghaneo	414	200
9	Th	Turlogh McHugh McBrian bane O'Reilly	452	150
10	Th	Brian McShane O'Reilly	299	300
11	Th	Donell Backagh McShane O'Reilly	193	200
12	Th	Cahir McOwen [O'Reilly]	412	100
14	Th	Callo O'Gowne	371	150
15	Th	Donell McOwen [O'Reilly]	370	150
16	Th	Shane McCabe	383	200
18	T	Brian McKiernan	2,225	400
19	T	Wony McThomas McKiernan	979	100
60	L	Turlogh McDonnell O'Reilly of Killagh	5,834	300
85	L	Shane bane O'Moeltully	222	50
	Th, C, T	Irish-owned land, owners unknown[6]	13,657	
U	L, Cm	Unidentified ownership	1,810	

Landowners, Cavan, 1641

No. on map	Barony	Owner	O.S. acreage
British owners:			
30	T	Sir George Acheson	6,424
31	T	Charles Hamilton	15,718
29	T	Sir James Craig	11,564
27	T	John Piman	371
28	T, Tg, L	Arthur Culme	7,581

[6] A number of grantees whose estates have not been identified may be listed here. They probably occupied some of this land. Baronage ascriptions are those given in the patents.

		Acreage as granted
Th	Cahill McBrian O'Reilly	100
Th	Mulmory McHugh McFarrell O'Reilly	300
Th	Cormac McGarwan	175
Th	Donnogh Magawran	75
Th	Hugh McManus oge Magawran	150
T	Donnell McFarrell oge McKiernan	100
Th	John & Connor O'Reilly	300
Th	Cahell McOwen O'Reilly	300
Cr	Donnell McBrian O'Reilly	100

7	Th	Amadis Culme	2,616
1	L	Dean Benjamin Culme	1,653
74	Tg, Cm	William Moore	5,749
45,in*	Tg, L	Thomas Ashe	4,445
72	Tg	Heirs of Joseph Singe	721
81	C	Sir Henry Perse	15,507
83	C	Sir William Bailie	8,615
80	C	Hans Hamilton	10,190
82	C	William Hamilton	9,345
85	C	? Sir Robert Stewart	537
33	Tg, L	Sir Stephen Butler	13,552
49	L	Thomas Greenham	6,536
47	L	Thomas Burrows	3,530
46	L	Roger Moynes	6,619
32	L	Sir Edward Bagshaw	6,606
41	L	Broghill Taylor	6,842
38	L	Sir Thomas Waldron	7,093
37	L	Edward Phillpott	1,142
58,in*	Cm, L	Lord Lambert	15,244
39	L	Richard Burrows	289
35	L	John Baker	133
34	L	John Sugden	468
102	Cr	George Garland	264
104	Cr	Henry Elliot	530
103	Cr	David Kellett	2,108
90	Cr	Henry Hickfield/Heckett	1,371
56	Cm	Edward Russon	1,610
55	Cm	Heirs of Dean Robinson	225
2	Th	Sir Charles Coote	38, 697
3	Th	William Graham	4,716
4	Th	Henry Crofton	1,039
19	Th	Eleanor Chapman alias Reynolds	299
Old English:			
17	Th, T	James Talbot	6,482
76	Tg	James Archbold	1,820
53	Tg, L	Sir William Hill	8,849
67	Tg	Thomas White	5,136
66	Tg	Walter Tirrell	3,303
87	C	Lord Slane	1,841
86	Cr, C	Garret Fleming	12,630
52	Cr, L	John Dowdall	689
40	Cm, Cr, L	Earl of Westmeath	18,914
36	L	Luke Dillon	4,150
101	Cr	Luke Plunket, Earl of Fingall	14,567

93	Cr	Lawrence Dowdall	13,463
57	Cm, Cr	James Nugent	1,545
64	Cm	Lord Dunsany	2,015
59	Cm	James Fleming	1,362
65	Cm	Oliver Nugent	2,141
61	Cm	Richard Fitzsimons	267
13	All bars	Bishopric	31,785
G,in*	All bars	Glebe	13,657
Sc	L	School lands	917
in*	L	Town of Cavan	683
mountain	Th	Toby, Lord Caulfeild (mountain)	16,828
Native Irish:			
60	Cm	Hugh McFarry O'Reilly	664
63	Cm	Hugh Brady	1,083
20	L, Cm, Cr, T, Th	Phillip McMulmory O'Reilly	6,145
24	Cm	Hugh O'Reilly	262
		(Myles O'Reilly	1,425
62[7]	Cm	(Phillip McEdmund O'Reilly	325
		(Edmund O'Reilly	97
51	L, Cr	Glasney O'Reilly	550
54	L	Calle O'Gowan	720
50	L, Tg	Phillip McHugh O'Reilly	12,007
44	L, Cr	Patrick Brady	4,642
43	L, Cr	Robert Brady	2,158
42	L	John Brady	79
84	C	Garret Betagh	1,222
26	T	Patrick O'Sheridan	285
25	T	Shane oge McKiernan	679
5	T, Th	Owen Sheridan	1,420
8	Th	Cormac McBrian & Brian oge McGowran	626
21	Th	Farrell McHugh McManus oge McGauran	1,083
12	Th	Gowran oge McGowran	661
9	Th	Brian oge McGawran	553
14	Th	Gillernew McGawran	821
13	Th	Henry Betagh	338
16	Th	Charles McGawran	2,976
10	Th	Shane reagh O'Reilly	770
15	Th	Thomas McGawran	494
11	Th	Charles O'Reilly	880
22	Th	Daniel McGawran	299

[7] These have been given a joint number on the map because there is a slight doubt (see above, 215–6) about the accuracy of individual allocations.

23	Th	Phelomy oge McGowran	338
18	Th	Nicholas O'Gowan	371
6	Th	Hugh O'Reilly[8]	2,220
71	Tg	Hugh McMulmory McPhillip O'Reilly	3,057
73	Tg	Edmund McMulmory McPhillip O'Reilly	1,085
77	Tg	Phillip McMulmory O'Reilly	162
70	Tg	Neil McTully	1,755
69	Tg	Phelim McHugh OpReilly	2,514
68	Tg	Hugh Brady	518
75	Tg, Cr	Henry Betagh, junior	2,536
95	Cr	Nicholas O'Reilly	977
99	Cr	Hugh O'Reilly	3,273
98	Cr	Thomas O'Reilly	456
94	Cr	James O'Reilly	2,214
88	Cr	Turlogh O'Reilly	815
91	Cr	Phillip O'Reilly	742
96	Cr	Phillip McBrian McHugh O'Reilly	2,843
92	Cr	Owen O'Reilly	2,351
89	Cr	John O'Reilly	1,055
100	Cr	Thomas Gowen	265
97	Cr	Thomas/James O'Gowen[9]	1,438
78	L, Tg	Christopher Betagh	1,472
79	Tg	James Betagh	858
	Th	Daniel McGrourke & Brian oge McGowran	unidentified
U	L	Unidentified ownership	1,585

[8] This is based on both the Headfort and Taylor sets of the Book of Survey and Distribution. The Quit Rent sent gives Gillernew McGawran (no. 14 on this list) and Hugh O'Reilly.

[9] Headfort and Taylor sets read Thomas O'Gowen. The Quit Rent set reads Jam. O'Gowran on 179 and, on 180 (on which the entry is continued), James O'Goen.

APPENDIX 2

Maps and Acreage Figures

Maps have been constructed to indicate ownership for each county at the outset of plantation and in 1641. Each proprietor has been given a number or symbol, a key to which can be found in the lists of proprietors in appendix 1. A shading system has also been devised and is explained on each map.

The 1" Ordnance Survey townland index maps have been used as a base for these maps. No previous attempt to plot the boundaries of the plantation estates, like Sampson's for Londonderry,[1] has been discovered. The process of making the maps has been an extremely laborious one of identifying and plotting the townlands of each estate. The modern barony boundaries have been used, with the exception that post-seventeenth-century divisions of baronies into 'Upper' and 'Lower' have been disregarded. These boundaries are much closer to those of the Down Survey than to those of the 1609 maps of the escheated counties the boundaries of which do not easily fit together.[2]

The problem of making the maps was exacerbated by the absence of any pre-1641 estate maps and by the fact that the Down Survey only mapped those areas which were subject to Cromwellian confiscation. It was therefore necessary to make special use of the maps of the escheated counties. Some of the difficulties involved may be mentioned here, but it is not proposed to attempt a detailed criticism of these maps.[3] The maps are poorly orientated and generally present only a very inexact representation of the individual baronies. One of the maps of Oneilland, no. 5.28, presents, in fact, a mirror-image of the area. More serious, perhaps, is the fact – arising from the poor cartographic techniques employed – that the internal orientation of the maps, i.e. the way in which townlands are mapped in relation to each other, is often faulty, thereby presenting difficulty in the superimposition of the 1609 data on to the Ordnance Survey maps. An immediate effect of these faults of orientation was that

1 Moody, *Londonderry Plantation*, 453.

2 For a minor example of this from the area studied see above 80, 83–6.

3 Various criticisms of the maps have already emerged, above, 9, 76–84.

estates which appeared as mapped to occupy a coherent area sometimes turned out, on occupation, to be illogically shaped. The maps, too, have a varying accuracy. Smaller baronies are generally more thoroughly done that larger; baronies in mountainous areas, for example Tullyhaw, are particularly defective; and the maps of County Armagh generally have been found more easy to work from than those of Cavan. The work of the map makers was, indeed, not exclusively relied on in 1610 when the patents were being issued. In Cavan the division of the land into proportions was not followed. Thus, for example, the map of Tullyhunco represents that barony as falling into four small proportions[4] whereas it was granted out as six. This arose from the revision of the conventional estimates of the Cavan polls which we have seen took place before the patents were issued. Also other sources than the maps appear to have been used when the patents were being drawn up – probably the topographical material assembled in 1608 and 1609 by inquisition – and so there is no assurance that all the places listed in the initial patents can be located on the maps. However, they can often be used to identify places the names of which had changed by the time of the Down Survey and Books of Survey and Distribution.

Many of the identifications were made without difficulty but also many required considerable persistence. However, the increasing definition of successive patents in the listing of alternative and sub-denominational names of places and in the granting of concealments made up for the difficulties of working from the first patents. Inquisitions were also of value. Knowledge of ownership changes between 1610 and 1641 sometimes facilitated working backwards from the evidence of the Books of Survey and Distribution. Estate papers, though rare except for the lands of Trinity College and the archbishopric of Armagh, were used. In the identification of church land it was possible to use the material brought together by inquisition in 1608 and 1609.

In some instances material from the later seventeenth century and after proved helpful or confirmed identifications already made. In trying to disentangle the ownership of small areas near to the town of Armagh, for example, rentals and maps in the archbishop's registry proved invaluable.[5] The identification of the Charlemont estate, including the abbey of St. Peter and St. Paul in Armagh, was also greatly facilitated by the use of estate

4 *Maps Ulster, 1609*, 4.24.

5 In particular Walter Dawson's rental, 1713; Thomas Ashe's rental, 1703 (photostat in PRONI, T848); Richard Morgan's rental, 1724; estate maps of archiepiscopal property made by William Gray in 1716 (Armagh Archiepiscopal Registry, A.1a.54–9) and by Robert Livingstone in 1773 (ibid., A.2a.44–97). A map of Mullyloughran by Henry Davison (1852) assisted in the identification of a piece of glebe land.

materials.[6] Some nineteenth-century official sources were also used, in particular the *Report of the commissioners on the revenues and condition of the established church (Ireland)* of 1868 and the *Report of the commissioners appointed to inquire into the endowments, funds, and actual condition of all schools endowed for the purpose of education in Ireland* of 1858. In cases of doubt recourse was had to the 6" sheets of the first Ordnance Survey.

The smaller grants, particularly many to the native Irish, proved most difficult to identify, though the identification of land the Irish held in 1641 was greatly facilitated by reason of its being plotted on the Down Survey maps. The precise location of the lands of about a dozen Irish grantees, all save one in Cavan, could not be established, though it is likely that those in Cavan fell within an area of land which it was possible to show had been in Irish hands. The most tantalizing fact to emerge in making the maps was that, while for many estates surviving materials made for great assurance of the accuracy of identification, for others there cannot be the same assurance, and allowance must be made for the possibility of mistaken identifications, particularly in Cavan. The mountainous barony of Tullyhaw in Cavan was the most difficult to map, and here some of the boundaries were plotted by a superimposition of the Down Survey map. Doubtful boundaries on the maps are indicated by means of dotted lines. Small areas in both counties remain unidentified.

The acreage figures have been computed from the Ordnance Survey areas of townlands. This was done because it was found that the figures given in the Books of Survey and Distribution for both counties were unreliable. While confiscable land appears to be recorded accurately enough in these books, many unforfeited estates were seriously underestimated either through an only partial listing of townlands (the Down Survey did not plot unforfeited land) or because – in some cases – only block figures for estates were presented. Thus not only are the total acreage figures of these counties defective, but also the figures for unforfeited land.

In calculating the acreage figures the method employed was to list the acreages of each townland in the estates. A calculating machine was then used to establish individual and group acreages and percentages. Townland acreages were derived for the most part from the townland index of the 1871 census.[7] The smaller acreages, provided in the 1861 index[8] of townlands south of Lough Neagh in Oneilland were preferred to those of

6 PRONI, D1644, leases Charlemont estate, 1782–1904; T971/711–41, T1176/3, T1007/291/9, D1670/2/2 (all leases, rentals, etc.); T1176/5 Maps of Charlemont estates by Thomas Noble, 1826.

7 *Census of Ireland, 1871: Alphabetical index to the townlands and towns of Ireland ...* (Dublin 1877).

8 *Census of Ireland: general alphabetical index to the townlands and towns, parishes, and baronies of Ireland* (Dublin 1861).

1871 as providing some possibility of taking account of the effects of drainage schemes and so allowing a nearer approximation to the utilizable land areas of the seventeenth century.[9] A disadvantage of this method, unavoidable because of the defects in the fugures of the Books of Survey and Distribution, is that it has not been possible to present statistics of profitable and unprofitable land. However, copies of Lewis's maps –which indicate relief and conveniently mark in barony boundaries and also the principal towns and villages – of Armagh and Cavan are presented with this thesis.[10] These give a partial assistance in the assessment of land profitability.

In all calculations the nearest acre was considered adequately accurate. The grand total achieved for Armagh, as a result of the initial set of calculations, was 310,706 acres and, for Cavan, 463,021 acres. When the townland figures were re-added when calculating the 1641 statistics slightly different total were attained as a result of different assessments of the nearest acre having been made, but the differences were slight. The Armagh total was some 250 acres smaller and the Cavan total was some 1,800 acres smaller. Because certain categories of land remained unaltered throughout the period it was thought best to use the first totals as a base for calculating the 1641 percentages also. Their accuracy is therefore marginally affected.

There is also the question of the accuracy of the totals, 310,706 and 463,021, arrived at. The acreage of Armagh, acquired by adding the barony totals of the 1871 townland index, is 329,086 acres. However, part of Lough Neagh is included in that total. The 1861 index indicates the amount of water included in each barony total. For Oneilland 16,561 acres (of Lough Neagh) were so included. The real acreage of the county is therefore 312,525 acres. There is thus, again, a small error to be admitted. Similarly, the grand total for Cavan derived from the 1871 index (477,360 acres), is in excess of the figure used as the base for calculations but, when the acreages of Lough Sheelin and Lough Ramor and other large lakes as well as the river Erne are deducted, the resulting figure is very close to that used in making calculations.

A few further explanations of how other problems encountered were overcome have to be made. Some of the original patents, especially of small areas to native Irish, included the grants to a number of individuals. The calendared versions, however, do not indicate the precise allocations of each grantee. In such cases it was not possible to indicate the boundaries of each grantee's land on maps or provide individual acreage figures. Such grantees

9 For the other exception to the use of the 1871 figures, see 409.

10 S. Lewis, *A topographical dictionary of Ireland*, 2 vols. (London, 1837).

are therefore given a single number on the maps and the total acreage of their grants also has only been provided.

There was also considerable difficulty in establishing the extent of the mountain land granted to Capt. John Sandford in each county. In Armagh the Ordnance Survey area of Slieve Gullion was accredited to Sandford because it was possible to establish the title of others to surrounding townlands, but it is known that the Ordnance Survey established the boundaries of many townlands in mountainous areas on more or less geometrical principles. Boundaries in this area of the map, following as they do those of the ordnance survey, may then be somewhat arbitrary in seventeenth-century terms. In Cavan, in Tullyhaw, the attempt was made to identify a larger area of mountain largely by a superimposition of a rather defective Down Survey map. In both cases the result may be somewhat defective, but seventeenth-century sources for title do not allow of a greater accuracy. For this reason the mountain land, though British owned, was given a separate categorisation when calculations were being made.

The acreages of townlands in the vicinity of a number of towns are taken from the 1861 townland index. This is because in the 1871 index the acreages of larger 'township' areas, meaningless in the seventeenth-century context of ownership, are given. If a townland fell entirely within the township area its name is recorded with the note 'included in – township'. If it was partly outside the township boundary, then only the extent of the area outside is indicated with the note 'remainder in – township'. The problem was, however, easily solved by recourse to the 1861 index.

The delimitation of ownership in two small areas, surrounding the towns of Armagh and Cavan, proved extremely difficult. It was therefore decided not to attempt to indicate boundaries on the maps, but rather to map in the outward bounds of these areas giving each an asterisk as index symbol. In this way it is hoped that these areas will not appear to represent individual holdings or to constitute corporation property. The boundary lines merely indicate that these are the smallest possible areas within which ownership could not be accurately plotted, especially on a map of 1" scale. There are therefore not meant to indicate that surrounding proprietors did not possess land both inside and outside them. It was, however, possible, by various means, to arrive at a reasonably accurate impression of the amount of the land so indicated which was held by each owner, and so possible to incorporate these acreage figures along with the others given above in appendix 1. When an owner possessed land, entirely or in part, within one of these areas, the indication 'in*' is given against that owner in the lists of proprietors.

The break-down of both areas arrived at for the period *c.* 1610–*c.* 1620 may be presented here, as follows:

(1) Armagh area (1,092 acres)

	acres
Archbishopric	900
Dean of Armagh	100
Vicars choral	15
Sir Toby Caulfeild (monastic property)	72
Francis Annesley (assignee of Francis Edgeworth: monastic property)	5

The only difference by 1641 was that Annesley's property had been acquired by the archbishop.

(2) Cavan area (904 acres)

	acres
Cavan corporation	683
Sir Thomas Ashe (abbey land)	9
Sir Thomas Rotherham (castle land)	141
Glebe	71

By 1641 Rotherham's land had come into Lambert hands.

In the case of glebe land, it may be noted that not all the land to which the clergy had claim (and which is recorded as glebe on the maps) may have been, in all instances, occupied by them throughout the entire period. We have seen, for example, that they did not receive their patents until the late 1620s and that some were involved in disputes with neighbouring landowners. However, during Wentworth's administration clerical problems were tackled sympathetically.[11]

Finally, while there is the possibility of error in the townland identification made, and so also in the acreage figures, both the maps and acreage figures are the result of careful investigation and are presented as an integral part of this thesis.

11 There is (at least) one case in which a substantial amount of the allocated glebe was not retained into the nineteenth century and may well have been lost in our period. This is Tynan, County Armagh (Armagh Public Library, William Reeves, Memoirs of Tynan (MS volume, unfoliated)).

APPENDIX 3

The Royal Schools in Armagh and Cavan

1. Government policy

In the planning of the colony it was decided that land should be reserved in each county to endow a school. The project recommended that fourteen polls in Cavan should be allotted to maintain a free school to be erected in Cavan town, and 720 acres in Armagh as provision for a school at Armagh.[1] The plantation commissioners were instructed in June 1609 to list the lands allocated for free schools in preparation to granting them by patent.[2] In July 1610 the commissioners, when concerned with the planning of towns, noted that a 'convenient place' must be allotted for the schools.[3] In December 1611 it was allowed that the schools being 'unapt to perform the plantation in that kind' should not be required to plant their lands with British tenants but might choose such as were best for their profit.[4]

However, the instituting of the schools was not proceeded with as a matter of urgency. It was not until January 1611 that the plantation commissioners made orders concerning the schools. It was then ordered that the land (917 statute acres) allotted for the Cavan school should be let to whoever would give most for it. They also decided that Sir Thomas Ashe, who held Cavan abbey, should be 'dealt with' for the conversion of the abbey to a parish church and a free school, and recommended that the land belonging to the castle of Cavan should be added to the school lands and the stone of the castle carried to the abbey for use in erecting the school.[5] At the same time orders were made for the Armagh school. They recommended that it should be located in the town of Armagh and that one of the sites of the friaries be used for this purpose, the income from the school lands (1,552 statute acres) to be used in erecting the school building. They further recommended that the primate should be 'dealt with' to grant

1 'Ulster plantation papers', no. 74, *Anal. Hib.*, viii.
2 Lam. Pal. Lib., Carew MSS, vol. 630, ff 7v–10v (*Cal. Carew MSS, 1603–24*, 44–8).
3 *Cal. Carew MSS, 1603–24*, 56–7.
4 Ibid., 141.
5 'Ulster plantation papers', no. 27, *Anal. Hib.*, viii.

300 acres near the school as a further endowment. The lands already allotted for the school should be let to Capt. John Bourchier and Capt. Henry Atherton at £3 per townland at least for the coming year. Both held land in Orior, the barony in which the school lands lay. The rent should be paid to the primate and used in building the school house.[6] Thus much responsibility for establishing the school would pass from the plantation commissioners to the archbishop of Armagh.

The fact that little had, as yet, been done in establishing the Ulster schools and that the Dublin government was incapable of dealing with the initial problems, was demonstrated by a king's letter of 30 January 1614[7] and, also, a letter from Chichester to the archbishop of Canterbury of 9 February 1614.[8] Chichester indicated that the government in Dublin felt the regulation of the school property was outside their competence and recommended that the school lands should be granted to the bishops, deans, and chapters in each diocese to the use of the school masters 'least they should be surreptitiously gotten from his maty. and passed to other uses … as I have already seen an offer of the like in one particular'.[9] The king's letter showed that the difficulties of Dublin were accepted in London and approved the delegation of the responsibility to the bishops for the leasing of the school lands and the nomination of schoolmasters. The bishops should therefore receive grants of the school lands, to be let to suitable persons for the use of the masters. They should not make leases for longer than twenty-one years and for less rent than £12 per quarter or four ballyboes. They should be empowered to nominate schoolmaster and recommend them to the lord deputy for appointment. Since as yet no schoolhouses had been built the deputy, with the advice of the chancellor and the archbishop of Armagh, should appoint receivers to collect the rents and disburse them for the building of schoolhouses. Only after that should the rents be received by the masters.

More than a year followed without further action until in April 1615 the king conveyed further instructions, this time for the primate alone to direct the founding of the Ulster grammar schools. Chichester was to grant all the school lands to the archbishop to be allotted by him.[10] However, Chichester's administration ended without any grant of the lands having been made, though he did, in June 1615, issue a warrant to grant them to

6 Ibid.

7 Armagh Archiepiscopal Registry, A.1b.26, 203–4 (document in full); *CSPI, 1611–14*, 467–8; *CPRI, Jas I*, 254.

8 'Chichester Letter-Book', no. 97, *Anal. Hib.*, viii. This letter must have been dispatched before receipt of the king's letter.

9 Ibid.

10 Armagh Archiepiscopal Registry, A.1b.26, 204; *CSPI, 1615–25*, 47–8; *CPRI, Jas I*, 295.

the respective bishops (rather than to the archbishop).[11] In December 1615 and in March 1618 the English privy council again took up the question of the granting of the school lands,[12] but no patents were issued. In August 1619 further instructions were issued by the king to St. John. He stated that, although the archbishop had appointed schoolmasters 'for the several schools', the lands had not been conveyed for their maintenance and were, in consequence, 'daily diminished' and the school houses not built 'to the hindrance of education and well-breeding of the gentry and youth … in learning and religion'. St. John was accordingly authorised to convey the lands to the archbishop for the use of the schoolmasters who were to be nominated by the present archbishop and afterwards by the bishops of the respective dioceses.[13] In 1622 the commissioners of inquiry discussed the question of who should have the nomination of schoolmasters for the free schools.[14] It was not until 15 December 1626 that the school lands for five counties, excluding Londonderry, were finally conveyed by patent to the archbishop to the use of the schoolmasters being not themselves 'bodies corporate or politic'.[15] No additional lands had been procured as the commissioners in 1611 had recommended.[16]

2. The schools in Armagh and Cavan

How the lands of the Armagh and Cavan schools were leased and when the income was first applied for educational purposes is not completely clear. It may be that the Armagh lands were let as the commissioners instructed in 1611, and the income from them was estimated in October of that year as likely to be £50 per annum at least,[17] however the first lease survived from 1635. In that year a lease was made whereby the archbishop and John Starky, the then schoolmaster, demised the lands to William Hilton (attorney-general for Connacht and later baron of the exchequer and justice of the common pleas)[18] for twenty-one years from 1 May 1636 at a rent of

[11] Armagh Archiepiscopal Registry, a roll in A.4b. This document is a certified statement by Sir William parsons of the school lands in each county to which Chichester added his warrant. How it came to be amongst the archbishop's muniments is not clear but its diversion there may have delayed the granting of the lands for ten years.

[12] *CSPI, 1615–25*, 102; *Acts privy council, 1618–19*, 92–3; TNA, SP 63/234, ff 185–86v (*CSPI, 1615–25*, 200–2).

[13] Armagh Archiepiscopal Registry, A.1b.128, no. 3; A.1b.26, 206–7.

[14] NLI, Rich Papers, MS 8014/3: Journal notes, 10 May 1622.

[15] Armagh Archiepiscopal Registry, A.1b.128, no. 8 (certified copy of 1701, this document is more accurate than the calendared version in *CPRI, Chas I*, 132–5); ibid., A.1b.26, 212–16.

[16] Parsons, in 1615, noted that one townland assigned for the school had been granted to Patrick O'Hanlon before the plantation but inserted a concealed townland in its place and promised to reserve any further concealment found in the area for the school.

[17] Elrington (ed.), *Ussher*, xv, 70–1.

[18] Hughes, *Patentee Officers*, 66.

£50 to be paid to the master.[19] This may well have been a second leasing, the first taking effect from 1615. The annual income from the Armagh endowment was thus no more than £50 throughout the period. The first known leasing of the Cavan lands was one for twenty-one years made in June 1637 to Matthew Maynwaring, constable of Dublin castle,[20] also at £50 per annum. Curiously this lease was not made by an episcopal custodian but by the state.[21]

The absence of school records makes it impossible to discuss the development of either institution. The Armagh school register records no students' names from before the restoration.[22] There is even slight doubt as to where the school was located, some documents placing it at Mountnorris,[23] but the weight of evidence suggests Armagh. When school buildings were erected, or the first pupils enrolled and in what numbers, or if any native Irish attended is not known for either school. Little more information than lists of masters is available in the pre-1641 period.

The first master of the Armagh school was an Englishman and a scholar of some distinction, but it is unlikely that he performed any of his duties. Thomas Lydiat, an Oxford graduate and an eminent divine, chronologer and cosmographer, had come to Ireland at Ussher's invitation and became a fellow of Trinity College in 1610.[24] He appears also to have been appointed to the Armagh school at this time but, by 1611, having apparently lost confidence in his prospects in Ireland, he was living in London and, in 1612, had entered the ministry in England.[25] In August 1611 he wrote to James Ussher from London asking for his good offices in the disposal of the school.[26] In October Ussher replied that he had found the primate, his uncle, willing to allow Lydiat receive the annual income from the lands.[27] How long Lydiat continued to receive the income as an absentee is unknown, but it would seem unlikely that any deputy was appointed or any of the money diverted towards erecting a school building. By 1615 a master had been appointed for the school at Dungannon, also in the archbishop's diocese,[28] and a 'public schoolmaster' was appointed for

19 Armagh Archiepiscopal Registry, in A.4b. On Hilton's connection with the town of Armagh see above, 236.
20 *Commons jnl., Ire.*, i, 184, 26 February 1641.
21 NAI, Lodge, Records of the rolls, vol. v, 532.
22 M.L. Ferrar, *Register of the Royal School of Armagh* (Belfast, 1933).
23 Armagh Archiepiscopal Registry, roll in A.4b.
24 C. Maxwell, *A history of Trinity College, Dublin, 1592–1892* (Dublin, 1946), 59.
25 Elrington (ed.), *Ussher*, xvi, 315–17.
26 Ibid., xc, 65–6.
27 Ibid., 70–71.
28 Armagh Archiepiscopal Registry, A.1b.26, 205.

County Fermanagh in December 1619.[29] In 1622 there were two masters and an usher in Dungannon,[30] but there is no indication of an appointment to Armagh. The first practicing master whose name survived is John Starky who is described in the 1635 lease as 'schoolmaster of the free schoole at Armagh'.[31] Starky was teaching in Dungannon in 1611 presumably moving afterwards to Armagh. At the outbreak of the 1641 rising it is recorded that Starky 'a gentleman of good parentage and parts being upwards of one hundred years of age' was put to death by drowning along with two of his daughters.[32]

The early history of the Cavan school is equally indistinct. In October 1611 the plantation commissioners made an order appointing the first master, John Robinson, who had been nominated by the bishop of Kilmore and Ardagh.[33] Robinson had graduated in Trinity College in 1605 and was a fellow in 1609.[34] By 1613 he was a 'preacher' in the diocese of Meath.[35] The next schoolmaster had had a more colourful background. Florence Nelly had been a scholar of Trinity College in 1603 and M.A. *c.*1610–11.[36] In January 1612 he was expelled from the college on the information of Sir James Carroll that he had a mistress and a bastard child.[37] In March 1613 his signature as 'Florc. Nelly schoolm'r' occurs as a witness to a lease of land in the Cavan area.[38] How long he retained this position is not known, but he was archdeacon of Tuam in 1622.[39] A certain Alexander Julius, a Scot, who received a grant of denization in September 1619[40] and was, presumably, Nelly's successor, had vacated the office through death[41] by February 1622 when John Stearne, M.A., father of the founder of the Irish College of Physicians[42] was appointed as 'schoolmaster and preceptor

29 *CPRI, Jas I*, 448.
30 NLI, Rich Papers, MS 8014/8: list of people in Dungannon.
31 Armagh Archiepiscopal Registry, in A.4b; E. Rogers, *A record of the city of Armagh* (Armagh, 1861), 25.
32 Hickson (ed.), *Ireland in seventeenth century*, i, 335 (deposition of Rev. Robert Maxwell).
33 'Ulster plantation papers', no. 51, *Anal. Hib.*, viii.
34 G.D. Burtchaell & T.U. Sadleir, *Alumni Dublinenses: a register of students, graduates, professors and provosts of Trinity College in the University of Dublin*, 2nd edn. (Dublin, 1935), 708.
35 Ibid.
36 Ibid., 613; Mahaffy, *P.B.*, 50b, 208.
37 Ibid., 22.
38 Indenture, 18 March 1613, between Richard Waldron and Clement Cottrell (NLI, Farnham Papers, MS D 20,409–20,475, bundle '41 deeds re town and county of Cavan, 1612–1805').
39 *Alumni Dublin*, 708.
40 W. Shaw (ed.), 'Letters of denization and acts of naturalisation for aliens in England and Wales', *Huguenot Society Proceedings*, xvii (1911), 329.
41 *CSPI, 1615–25*, 393. I am grateful to Mr. W. S. Ferguson, M.A., of Derry for this and the previous reference.
42 *DNB*, liv, 197.

or rector'.[43] However, by November 1624 he had resigned and Nicholas Higginson,[44] 'bachelor of arts',[45] was appointed.[46] Higginson would appear to have held office for a longer period, on 14 July 1637 being succeeded by John Bond, A.B.[47] Such a rapid-changing succession of teachers can hardly have favoured the development of the institution. The commissioners reported in 1622 that, although land had been allocated to support a school, no 'fitting school house' had been built.[48] The government order of January 1611 whereby Cavan abbey was to be converted into a school and church was not made effective – the king's attorney in Ulster, Stephen Allen, was living there in 1641.[49] The other order of 1611, that the land belonging to the castle at Cavan should be added to the school land, was also not carried out and in December 1616 it was leased to Sir Thomas Rotherham then connected with the Connacht presidency and subsequently a surveyor of fortifications.[50]

The development of grammar school education in these counties up to 1641 must have been hesitant and uneven. The absenteeism of the first Armagh master and the rapid changes of master in Cavan obviously inhibited growth and tradition. It is evident that teaching was supplied by schools other than the royal foundations, for example, in 1619 the minister of Virginia kept a school,[51] but such arrangements can hardly have made up for the deficiencies of the grammar schools. The size of the income from the school lands and the absence of any initial foundation grant from the exchequer makes it unlikely that school buildings of any size had been erected and probable that schools were held in the masters' houses. The schools might have been more immediately effective if the Dublin administration had had the capacity to take a direct interest in their supervision.[52] In proposals for the establishment or reorganisation of grammar schools drawn up at the restoration Archbishop Bramhall felt that

43 *CPRI, Jas I*, 528.
44 On Higginson see Sir Stephen Butler's will (NAI, Deeds, wills and instruments … post mortem, vol. 25, 265–70).
45 Not recorded as a TCD graduate in *Alumni Dublin.*
46 *CPRI, Jas I*, 579. Higginson was living in Belturbet in 1641.
47 Armagh Public Library, Tuam lists, 150–73.
48 BL, Add. MS 4756, fol. 104.
49 Above, 275.
50 *CPRI, Jas I*, 313.
51 Hill, *Plantation*, 458.
52 The extent of Wentworth's interest appears to have been the general statement in 1634 that all the Irish schools were 'ill governed in the most part' (Sheffield City Library, Strafford MSS, vol. vi, 19). In 1639 Bramhall hoped, in a letter to Laud, that the Derry school would be 'kept up' stating that, although king James had allotted 700 acres for it, the Londoners had never paid more than 20 marks in salary to the master (TNA, SP 63/257, ff 121–1v (*CSPI, 1633–47*, 225–6)).

an income of £100 per annum for the school or schools in each county was essential.[53]

It may be noted in conclusion that the establishment of a university for the colony was suggested but did not come to effect. The proposal was made by Bishop Montgomery of Derry, *c.* 1608

> that for the education of youth, besides grammar schools to be planted in the most commodious places endowed with som lands for the maintenance of the schoolehouse, schoolemaster, and usher, his Matie would be pleased to erect a College in Derry, or some fit place yf any be, that the youth of those parts, who have no meanes to be mayntayned in the College of Dubline, maye be civilly bred up there in the knowledge of true religion, and the liberall arts; and that his Ma'tie would be pleased to endowe the college with som fit portion of land for the maintenance of the college and of the principles and fellows of the same.[54]

The proposal did not take effect. However, the plantation did have access to the college at Dublin, itself in a struggling financial position until endowed with lands in Ulster at this time. Owing to the incomplete state of Trinity College admissions records before 1641 it is difficult to state precisely the number of students there of Ulster origin.[55] However, it would seem that they were few. Only two pupils from County Armagh feature in the register as entrants in 1639 and 1641 respectively.[56] Both had had their previous education in England.

53 *Hastings MSS,* iv, 149–50.

54 Colonel Colby, *Ordnance survey of the county of Londonderry* (Dublin 1837), i, 53. If the cost of building were considered too great, Donegal abbey might be converted for this purpose.

55 The oldest surviving admissions register dates from 1637 (TCD, MUN/V/23/2, College Admissions Registers 1637–1725). The college accounts, however, could be used to provide earlier students' names.

56 TCD, Admissions register, 1637–1724, under 15 November 1639 and 12 July 1641.

APPENDIX 4

High Sheriffs

These lists derive for the most part from two sources. Most of the Armagh names have been taken from a list which had been the property of the late Tenison Groves (now in PRONI, T808/14926) and which was published in *Portadown Times*, 21 July 1933. Most of the Cavan names come from a list in RIA, Upton MSS, 19a. This list can also be found in NLI, Canon Leslie Collection, MS 2698. Transcripts of the Summonister Rolls for either county have not been located. Where names come from other than these lists the sources are indicated in footnotes.

Armagh

1593	Oghy O'Hanlon
1606	Marmaduke Whitechurch
1607	Anthony Smith
1608	Henry Atherton
1609	Anthony Smith
1610	Robert Cowell
1611	Charles Poyntz
1612	George Chambers
1613	Charles Poyntz
1614	Charles Chambers
1615	Anthony Smith
1616	Henry Acheson
1617	Richard Atherton
1619	Richard Eaton
1621	Matthew Ussher
1622	Henry Acheson
1623	William Brownlow
1624	Anthony Cope
1625	Francis Sacheverall
1627	John Hamilton
1629	Robert Hovendon
c. 1630	Charles Poyntz[1]
1634	Walter Cope[2]

1 NAI, Chancery salvage, G.388.

2 A fragment of a docquet book of Wentworth's suggests that John Waldrom was the sheriff in this year (Bod. Lib., Carte MSS, vol. 67, fol. 6v).

c. 1635	Henry O'Neill[3]
1639	Sir Charles Poyntz
1640	Henry Stanhowe

Cavan

1584	Henry Duke
1585	Henry Duke
1587	Henry Duke
1588	Henry Duke
1589	Edward Herbert
1590	Edward Herbert
1591	Edward Herbert
1592	Edward Herbert
1593	Edward Herbert
1594	Edward Herbert
1595	Edward Herbert
1606	Sir Edward Herbert[4]
1607	Hugh Culme
1611	Hugh Culme
1612	Hugh Culme
1613	John Ridgeway
1614	John Butler
1615	James Craig
1616	John Fish
1618	Richard Lisle[5]
1619	Richard Lisle
1621	Robert Scurlock
1622	Sir Stephen Butler
1629	Phillip O'Reilly
c. 1630	Tomas Fleming[6]
1634	John Fleming
1636	Thomas Fleming
1639	William Lill[7]
1640	Francis Lawrence Devall
1641	Mulmory O'Reilly[8]

3 NAI, Ferguson MSS, vol. xii, 303.
4 It is possible that Herbert was also sheriff in 1610 (see *CSPI, 1608–10*, 547, 548).
5 This is likely to be incorrect. Hugh Culme was sheriff in June 1618 (NAI, Ferguson MSS, vol. xi, 271). Sheriffs were usually appointed in the November of the previous year (W. Notestein, *The English people on the eve of colonization, 1603–30* (New York, 1954), 202), and the compiler of this list may well have found the warrant for Lisle's appointment in 1619 and have erroneously listed him for 1618 also.
6 NAI, Ferguson MSS, vol. xii, 140.
7 NLI, MSS 2698, 49, gives Edward Gray for 1639.
8 Wilkins (ed.), *Bedell*, 167.

APPENDIX 5

A plantation house in 1622

Sir Archibald Acheson's building received the 1622 commissioners' approval as 'a convenient dwelling house ... environed with a bawne'.[1] His submission to the commissioners provides an unusually detailed description,[2] as follows:

> There is a stone bawne of six scoare foote longe and foure scoare foote wide, and ten foote high, haveinge foure flankers, three of them being fifteene foote and foureteene foote wyde, conteyninge two roomes apiece being two storyes high, all three foote thicke in the wall.
>
> Upon the east side of the said bawne is buylt a stone howse of foure scoare and ten foote longe, eighteen foote wyde and eighteen foote high in the side wall and thirty eight foote high in the three gabells, and having a rounde flanker of twentye two foote high and fourteene foote wyde, within the walls, all three foote thicke of wall, slaited, and having foure stackes of bricke chimneyes.
>
> The first storye of the said howse conteyneth a hall of 36 foote longe, a parler of eighteene foote square, a vault within the parler of fourteene foote square being the ground of the flanker, and upon the other end of the hall, a pantry of ten foote longe and of the whole wideness of the howse being eighteene foote wyde.
>
> The second storye contayneth above the hall and pantrye, two chambers, the one of twentye twoe foote longe and the other of eighteene haveinge three studies. And above the parler is another chamber of eighteene foote square, and above the flanker vault is another chamber of fourteene foote square.
>
> The third storie contayneth two chambers and a gallery within the roofe.
>
> The rest of the bawn is built about with low thatched howses once gifted, exceptinge fortye foote longe thereof reserved for an intended castle to be joined to the parler aforesaid.
>
> Without the gate is buylded a malt howse and killne of stone two stories high, and three scoare and ten foote longe and twentye foote wyde, a water mylle, barnes and other howses all thatched.

1 BL, Add MS 4756, fol 109; above, 146.

2 NLI, Rich Papers, MS 8014/9.

APPENDIX 6

Two notes on administrative matters

1. Extension of state machinery

The implementation of the plantation as a whole necessitated additional central administrative appointments or added to the responsibilities of existing officers. Ulster was now fully within the competence of the Dublin government. Assize judges now regularly went there. The first muster master was appointed in 1618.[1] In 1617 the office of auditor general was divided, William Crofton being appointed auditor for Ulster and Connacht.[2] The office of attorney general for Ulster pre-dated the plantation, the first appointment having been made in December 1603.[3] Appointments had been intermittently made of provost marshals of Ulster since 1566. However, during the plantation period this office had a special importance:

> forasmuch as the multitude of malefactors, and other loose and idle persons in … Ulster required to be corrected and repressed by some speedier and sharper means than by ordinary course of the common law

which was recognised when, in 1616, Moses Hill (first appointed in 1603) was re-appointed.[4] Occasional appointments as clerk of the crown and peace were made for Cavan from 1583, but the office for Ulster as a whole was initiated in March 1605.[5] The office of clerk of the market for Ulster as such was created in 1611.[6]

2. Licensing of ale-houses

The licensing of ale-houses, and of the making and selling of whiskey and wine, was farmed out for most of our period.[7] The number of grants of licences which have been found in the patents is not great though, of course, not all licences may have been enrolled.

1 Above, 110–11.
2 *CPRI, Jas I*, 325; Lascelles, *Liber munerum*, pt. ii, 54. However, in 1637, the offices were re-united to be held by one man (ibid.)
3 Ibid., 193.
4 Ibid., 193–4; BL, Add. MS 4794, ff 353v–4.
5 Lascelles, *Liber munerum*, pt. ii, 172–3.
6 Ibid., 146; *CPRI, Jas I*, 204.
7 The farm was withdrawn in one of the Graces in 1628 (Clarke, *The Graces*, 19).

Those for Armagh and Cavan which have been located are listed here because they throw light on the kind of people who received licences and also on the extent of land for which licences were issued. For Armagh only two licensees have come to light – the archbishop of Armagh,[8] and Sir Oliver St. John and Richard Atherton his agent.[9] St. John's licence, in 1616, was for Tandragee and the whole of barony of Orior except episcopal land.

In Cavan similar large areas were involved in most licences: John and William Hamilton for Clankee barony, December 1617;[10] Sir Claud Hamilton's widow and son for Tullyhunco, December 1617;[11] Connor and Terence O'Sheridan, the only Irish grantees, in Ballyconnell and Tullyhaw barony, also December 1617;[12] and Charles Waterhouse in Clanmahon and Loughtee, excepting Cavan town, in August 1619.[13] Licences for Cavan and Belturbet were granted in 1613 to Richard Alsopp, a local merchant, and Margaret Smith of Dublin.[14]

Only one case has come to light in the area studied of a person being fined for keeping an unlicensed tavern. This was a certain Cutherd Smythe, of Legacorry (now Richhill) County Armagh, who was fined 3s. 4d. in 1619.[15]

8 *CPRI, Jas I*, 267. It was issued in March 1614.
9 Ibid., 308.
10 Ibid., 343.
11 Ibid.
12 Ibid.
13 Ibid., 431.
14 Ibid., 261.
15 PRONI, T281/7, 1.

BIBLIOGRAPHY

MANUSCRIPT SOURCES

Inevitably, given that this thesis was completed over forty years ago and the research for it commenced in the early 1960s, aspects of this listing of manuscript sources will be out of date. Some of the archival institutions have changed name or been reorganised, and some of the manuscripts have been recatalogued. The Public Record Office of Ireland is now the National Archives of Ireland, while the Public Record Office at Kew is now The National Archives. The manuscripts that R.J. Hunter consulted in the British Museum are now part of the British Library's holdings. The Manuscripts and Archives Research Library in Trinity College, Dublin, now has responsibility for the College's manuscripts and muniments. Since the 1960s some collections have been transferred to other repositories. For instance, most of the holdings of the Archiepiscopal Registry in Armagh are now in the Public Record Office of Northern Ireland. With only a few exceptions – the application of manuscript references in place of the shelf numbers for the items listed below under Trinity College Library being the only one of significance – the following listing of manuscript sources is as originally presented by R.J. Hunter. Researchers should be aware of this and make contact with the relevant archives for further information on the sources hereafter listed.

IRELAND

Marsh's Library, Dublin

Z3.2.6	State and private papers, with material related to the granting of patents under the 1628 scheme
Z4.2.6	State papers relating to Ireland
Z2.1.1, Z3.1.1, Z3.1.3, Z3.1.9	Miscellaneous documents

National Archives of Ireland, Dublin
(formerly the Public Record Office of Ireland)

1a.53.74	Acta regia Hibernica, vol. ii

Books of survey and distribution (Quit rent office and Headfort sets)

John Lodge, Records of the rolls:

1a.53.54, 5	vols v and vi: summaries of patents of land, etc.
1a.53.63	vol. xiv: grants of fairs and markets
1a.53.64	vol. xv: index to records of the rolls
1a.53.70	vol. xxi: miscellaneous enrolments
1a.49.143, 4	Ferguson MSS, vols xi and xii

Chancery salvage (bundles A–Z and 2B.80.120, 121)

MS 2445	Letter book of lord deputy Falkland, 1629–33
M. 2448	Petition to Wentworth and council, June–November 1638

RC 15/1	Transcript, 1812, of 1634 regal visitation, dioceses of Armagh and Kilmore (2–35, 281–300)
1a.48.73	Calendar to exchequer inquisitions of the counties of Ulster
1a.48.114	Deeds, wills, and instruments appearing upon the inquisitions post mortem in the Rolls Office, vol. 25
1a.49.63, 64	Repertories to the decrees of chancery, 2 vols
1a.49.79	Repertory of exchequer decrees, 1609, 1624–67
Chancery Bill Books, Exchequer Bill Books, Indexes of ancient pleading, chancery	The large series of these, preserved in the Strong Room, have sometimes been consulted but they provide no details of pleadings in suits
Co. 1822	Sir Stephen Butler and Belturbet, 1618

National Library of Ireland, Dublin

Ainsworth reports on manuscripts in private custody (some of which are now deposited in NLI)

i	Drogheda papers
ii	Fingall papers
iii	Lennon papers
iv	Madden papers
v	Nugent papers
vi	Rolleston papers
vii	Tisdall papers
viii	Vance papers
MSS 8013, 4	Rich papers
MSS 8026, 30, 32	Fingall papers
MS 2685	Canon J.B. Leslie, biographical succession list of Kilmore diocese
MS 2698	Canon Leslie Collection

Leslie collection of will abstracts, exchequer bills, etc. mostly relating to cos. Cavan, Dublin, and Louth families, seventeenth to nineteenth centuries

MS 11,450 (Packing case 112)	Rolleston papers
MS 11,490/3, 4; D 20,409–20,475	Farnham papers
D 7340	Sir Stephen Butler and Belturbet, 1618
D 8784	Attested copy of patent to Henry Perse, 4 July 1629
D 8896–8926	Butler deeds. Also some unsorted
D 10,025	Conveyance of property in Belturbet, 15 July 1641
D 2,564–5	Drogheda papers

Representative Church Body Library, Dublin

D/6	Inquisition, 24 March 1625, concerning Culdees of Armagh

D/14	Transcript of letters patent to dean and chapter of Armagh, 23 January 1638
J.36	Transcript 1634 visitation returns
Libr./8	Canon Leslie manuscripts
Libr./27, 28	Copies of inquisition concerning parishes in Armagh, 1657 (no. 28 is fairer copy)
Libr./32	Tenison Groves transcripts
Libr./48	Transcript of subsidy roll, 1634, Shankill parish, County Armagh

Royal Irish Academy, Dublin

Books of Survey and Distribution (Taylor set)

MSS 24.Q.7, 10	Charters of Irish towns, vols I and IV
Upton MS 19a	Sheriffs of County Cavan

Trinity College Library, Dublin

MS 550	Ulster visitation book, 1622
MS 570, MS 582, MS 595	Miscellaneous papers
MS 864	Pynnar's survey
MS 806, ff. 9–31	Report of commissioners 'for deciding differences in the plantation'
MS 808	Miscellaneous papers
MS 832, MS 833	1641 depositions, Cavan
MS 836	1641 depositions, Armagh
MS 672, MS 842	Miscellaneous papers
MS 655	Miscellaneous papers
MS 805	Provost Winter's papers
MS 962	College estate papers
MS 1040	Miscellaneous papers
MS 1067	Visitatio regalis, 1633–4: transcript by Bishop William Reeves
MS 2629	Transcript by Tenison Groves of 1622 visitation Dromore diocese
Under D	Box of college leases

Trinity College Dublin, Assistant Registrar's Strong Room

College Admission's register, 1637–1725

Trinity College Dublin, Muniment Room and Ante Room

The college's archives are in a disorganised state. One group of primarily pre–1700 documents (cited below as the Mahaffy Collection) was assembled and listed by Mahaffy, and some additional sorting was done subsequently by Provost Alton and Mr. William O'Sullivan. When I worked on the college papers in 1963 I applied numbers to shelves and boxes and drew up a rough outline guide, a copy of which is deposited in the Muniment Room. The following lists give the locations of materials used in this thesis. There are other documents in the safe in the Board Room. [Note by R.J. Hunter in original thesis.]

(a) Muniment Room

Mahaffy Collection, Drawers A–G, H, K, N

Shelf 3	General Registry from 1626
Shelf 3	General Registry from 1640
Shelf 2, box 20	packets 'bonds, etc. 1595–1640', '1604–1702', 'mostly second half of 17th century'
Shelf 2, box 24	packet '*c.* 1613–1720'
Shelf 2, box 25	packet 'first half of 17th century'
Shelf 2, box 28	packets '*c.* 1610–1700', '*c.* 1610–1720', '17th century papers'
Shelf 4, box 2	
Shelf 4, box 17	packets '*c.* 1620–1710', '1617–1745', 'miscellaneous documents mostly *c.* 1650–1750'
Steel box 1	The particular book
Steel box 2	
Old Receipt book	(drawn up *c.* 1676)

(b) Ante Room

Cabinet, drawers 1, 2, 20

Cupboard B, shelf 4	'financial documents, 1618–99'
Cupboard B, shelf 5	

NORTHERN IRELAND

Armagh Archiepiscopal Registry

A.1a.7	Original patent, 6 September 1610, of lands, etc. to Archbishop Henry Ussher
A.1a.8	Exemplification, 20 November 1617, of patent of lands of archbishopric of Armagh
A.1a.11	Original patent of glebe land, Armagh diocese, 14 June 1628
A.1a.13	Original patent, 28 June 1634, to archbishop of Armagh
A.1a.54–9	Maps by William Gray, 1716
A.2a.28	Volume of rentals and other miscellaneous papers, 1608–28
A.2a.44–97	Maps by Robert Livingstone, 1773
A.3a.39	Volume of leases, etc. 1628 and after, including government material on the scheme for renewing episcopal leases, 1635

A.3a.189	Inquisition on parishes in Armagh, 1657
A.1b.24/4	Commission, February 1614, to Parsons and others to inquire into lands in escheated counties not disposed of
A.1b.25	Volume of transcripts of patents, etc., including some estate material
A.1b.26	Evidences of the see of Armagh: volume of transcripts by John Lodge
A.1b.29	Volume of rentals from 1628, abstracts of leases, lists of arrears, etc.
A.1b.31	Walter Dawson's rental, 1713
A.1b.32	Richard Morgan's rental, 1724
A.1b.34	Volume of rentals and contemporary extract from book of survey and distribution, county Armagh
A.1b.128	Volume of transcripts of patents, king's letters and other documents, concerning lands of archbishopric, free schools, vicars choral, and TCD
A.1b.209	Original patent of Robert Maxwell, 7 April 1610, to deanery of Armagh
A.4b.15	Lease of Armagh school lands, 1 October 1635
A.2c.17–20	Copies of king's letters
B.2a.216	Attested copy of patent, 23 May 1634, to vicars choral
B.2a.225	Map of vicars choral property in Armagh, 1720
B.3a.382	Roll: glebe land in escheated counties, with notes, by William parsons, 15 August 1617
B.1b.193	Ulster visitation book, 1622
C.1c.371	Volume entitled 'bishopps lands of Ireland and other dignitaryes ecclesiasticall'
Roll in A.4b	Certificate of Parsons of school lands, Ulster, with order of lord deputy, 23 June 1615
E.1.e	Bundle of 40 leases, mostly 1627

Translation of patent to Arthur Bagnal, 18 February 1613
Thomas Ashe's rental, 1703
Map of townland of Mullyloughran, by Henry Davison, 1852

Armagh Museum

Brownlow rentals

Armagh Public Library

Armagh papers	volume of transcripts by Bishop William Reeves
Rectory of Armagh	volume of transcripts by Bishop William Reeves
Jura patronatus	volume of transcripts by John Lodge
bundle q.v.x.	Notes by Lodge on vicars choral, etc.
Lodge MSS, G.111.23	Abstracts of patents and signet letters; grants of fairs and markets

Meath papers.

Volume entitled 'Tuam lists'.

1622 visitation returns (originally property of Sir James Ware).

Cases of lord chancellor Bolton.

Armagh manor court rolls.

The title, interest, and purchase of the mannor of Castle Dillon … with the coppys of the deeds and other papers … drawn up by me William Molyneux in … 1696.

Cardboard box containing collection entitled 'old leases of primate's'.

Churches of the diocese of Armagh: transcripts by Reeves.

William Reeves, Memoirs of Tynan.

Submissions of evidence to the court of claims, 1663.

Principall matters concerning the state of Ireland, collected brieflie out of soundrie writers, and observed after some opinions, by T. Haynes, 1600.

Public Record Office of Northern Ireland, Belfast

Certified copies, transcripts, Photostats, or originals of patents to various settlers, as follows:

D1540/1/1a	Bagnal
T1007/291, no. 1	Caulfield
D1345/6/1A, 1B, 2	Cope
PRO 202	Cope
PRO 1145	Grandison
PRO 1147	Obbyns
T267	Obbyns
T1303	Stanhowe
D453/1	St. John
D294/1, T529/1	Chambre documents: Audley papers

Cal 73–D778	Calendar of Trevor estate records
D999/1	Pedigree of Cope family
T107	Pedigree of Brownlow family
T281/7, p. 1	Canon Leslie collection: extract from subsidy roll, 1634, Portadown area
T475	Transcripts of Armagh manor court rolls
T625, 729/1	Transcripts and abstracts of rentals of archbishopric of Armagh
T636	Raeburn MSS. Volume of transcripts, seventeenth to nineteenth centuries largely relating to Armagh
T808/2,758, 3,871–91, 12,674, 14,912, 14,916, 14,917,	Tenison Groves MSS: transcripts of documents (many no longer extant) dealing with a number of estates as well as with ecclesiastical and legal matters; also list of sheriffs, County Armagh

14,923, 14,926, 14,930, 14, 941, 14,964, 15,261, 15,299	
T906/1, 2	Notes on Acheson family
T969–70	Transcripts of Brownlow rentals, 1635 and 1635
T975/2, 1–9	Transcript, with notes, of regal visitation of Armagh diocese, 1634, made by Tenison Groves
D266, D1644, D1670/2/2, T971/11–41, T1007/291/9, T1176/3, 5	Charlemont estate records
T1103	O'Hanlon genealogy

Watson and Neill, Solicitors, Lurgan

Brownlow papers

ENGLAND

Bodleian Library, Oxford

Carte MS vol. 61	Material relating to Ulster, 1603–11
Carte MS vol. 62	Material relating to Ulster, 1611–24
Carte MSS vols 64, 67, 77, 80	Miscellaneous material
Rawlinson MS A.237	includes survey of 1608 (in *Anal. Hib.* iii) and other Ulster material
Rawlinson MS D.376	Papers relating to Protestantism in Cavan in the 1630s

British Library, London (formerly the British Museum)

Add MS 4756	Entry book of report of commissioners of inquiry for Ireland, 1622 and letters from king and council to lord deputy of Ireland, 1616–21
Add MS 4770	Muster roll of Ulster, *c.* 1630
Add MS 4794	King's letters to lords deputy of Ireland, James I
Add MS 11,033	Falkland letter book
Add MS 18,022	Abstract of Irish revenue, 1615–21 (f. 38v)
Add MS 18,735	Muster roll of 1618
Add MS 24,200	State of Irish forts, ?1624
Add MS 36,775	King's letters to lords deputy of Ireland, James I
Add MSS 4,763, 4,819, 19,834, 21,993	Miscellaneous papers

Cott. MS Titus B.x	
Cott. MS Titus C.vii	
Harleian MS 2138	Grants to TCD (f. 76)
Harleian MS 3292	Sir Francis Blundell on plantations, 1622 (ff 40–5)
Harleian MS 3292	Sir Nathaniel Rich on plantations, 1622 (ff 19–31v)
Lansdowne MSS 151, 156, 159	
Sloane MS 1742	Description of Ireland *c.* 1605 (ff 1–47)
Sloane MS 3827	Falkland Correspondence

Cambridge University Library

KK.1.15, vol. 1	Letters relating to Ireland
Add MS 4246	

City Library, Sheffield

Strafford MSS
Strafford letters

Lambeth Palace Library, London

Carew MS 630	State papers relating to the Ulster plantation in the reign of James I
MS 943	Documents relating to the Church of Ireland in the 1630s

Library of Exeter College, Oxford

MS 95	Register of the Irish commission of 1622

Library of Hatfield House

Cecil papers vol. 127	Papers relating to *Maps, Ulster 1609* (ff 126–33v)

The National Archives, London (formerly the Public Record Office)

SP 63/226–74	State papers, Ireland, 1609–41
30/15/12/172–202a	Manchester papers

UNITED STATES OF AMERICA

Henry E. Huntington Library, California

HM 333–5	Certain considerations touching the plantations in Ireland, *c.* 1610
HM 4517	A survey of the present estate of Ireland, 1615 [both documents are only of general import]

PRINTED PRIMARY SOURCES

Acts of the privy council of England, 1613–31 (14 vols, London, 1921–64).
P. Adair, *A true relation of the rise and progress of the Presbyterian church in Ireland, 1623–70*, ed. W.D. Killen (Belfast, 1866).
J.F. Ainsworth & E. MacLysaght (eds.), 'Survey of documents in private keeping, second series, *Anal. Hib.*, xx.
F.H.A. Aalen & R.J. Hunter, 'Two early seventeenth century maps of Donegal', *JRSAI*, vol. 94, pt. 2 (1964), 199–202.
E. Berwick (ed.), *The Rawdon papers* (London, 1819).
T. Blenerhasset, *A direction for the plantation in Ulster* (London, 1610).
G. Boate, *Ireland's naturall history* (London, 1652).
E.M.F.–G. Boyle, *Records of the town of Limavady, 1609–1808* (Derry, 1912).
James Buckley (ed.), 'Report of Sir Josias Bodley on some Ulster fortresses in 1608', *UJA*, 2nd series, xvi (1910), 61–64.
G.D. Burtchaell & T.U. Sadleir, *Alumni Dublinenses: a register of students, graduates, professors and provosts of Trinity College in the University of Dublin* (2nd edn., Dublin, 1935)
Calendar of the Carew MSS, 1603–24 (London, 1867).
Calendar of Irish patent rolls, James I (Dublin, 1830).
Calendar of patent and close rolls of chancery in Ireland, Henry viii to 18th Elizabeth, ed. James Morrin (Dublin, 1861).
Calendar of patent and close rolls of chancery in Ireland, Elizabeth, 19 year to end of reign, ed. James Morrin (Dublin, 1861).
Calendar of patent and close rolls of chancery in Ireland, Charles I, years 1 to 8, ed. James Morrin (Dublin, 1864).
'Calendar to fiants of the reigns of Henry VIII–Elizabeth', *DKRI*, 7–22 (Dublin, 1875–90).
Calendar of state papers, domestic series, James I (4 vols, London, 1857–9).
Calendar of state papers relating to Ireland, 1509–1647 (19 vols, London, 1860–1901, 1905).
T. Carte, *A collection of letters ... related [to] the history ... of ... the duke of Ormond* (2 vols, London, 1735).
Census of Ireland: general alphabetical index to the townlands and towns, parishes, and baronies of Ireland (Dublin, 1861).
Census of Ireland, 1871: Alphabetical index to the townlands and towns of Ireland ... (Dublin, 1877).
H. Cotton, *Fasti Ecclesiae Hibernicae* (5 vols, Dublin, 1845–60).
W.F. Cullinan (ed.), *The Irish Statutes Revised, 1310–1800* (London, 1884)
Sir J. Davies, *A discoverie of the true causes why Ireland was never entirely subdued ... until ... his maiesties happie raigne* (London, 1612).
R. Dudley Edwards (ed.), 'Chichester letter-book, 1612–14', *Anal. Hib.*, viii (1938), 3–177.
C.R. Elrington (ed.), *The whole works of the most reverend James Ussher, D.D.*, vols 2, 11, 15, 16 (Dublin, 1864).

J.C. Erck (ed.), *A repertory of the inrollments on the patent rolls of chancery in Ireland commencing with the reign of James 1* (2 pts., Dublin, 1846–52)

C.L. Falkiner, *Illustrations of Irish history and topography, mainly of the seventeenth century* (London, 1904).

C.L. Falkiner (ed.), 'Barnaby Rich's "Remembrances of the state of Ireland, 1612"', *PRIA*, xxvi, C, no. 8 (1906), 125–142

J.F. Ferguson (ed.), 'Ulster roll of gaol delivery, 1613–18', *UJA*, 1st series, i (1853); 260–70, ii (1854), 25–28.

M.L. Ferrar, *Register of the Royal School of Armagh* (Belfast, 1933).

T. Fitzpatrick, *The bloody bridge and other papers relating to the insurrection of 1641* (Dublin, 1903).

J.R. Garstin (ed.), 'List of documents transferred from Armagh diocesan registry to the Public Record Office, Dublin', *Journal of the County Louth Archaeological Society*, vol. iii no. 4 (1915), 347–56.

J.T. Gilbert, *A contemporary history of affairs in Ireland from 1641 to 1652*, vol. i (Dublin, 1879).

J.T. Gilbert, *Calendar of ancient records of the city of Dublin in the possession of the municipal corporation of that city* (Dublin, 1889).

A.B. Grosart (ed.), *The Lismore Papers* (2 series, each 5 vols, London, 1886–8).

[Richard Hadsor], *Advertisements for Ireland*, ed. George O'Brien (RSAI, Dublin, 1923).

W. Harris, *Hibernica* (2nd edn., Dublin 1770).

G.A. Hayes–McCoy (ed.), *Ulster and other Irish maps, c .1600* (IMC, Dublin, 1964).

M. Hickson (ed.), *Ireland in the seventeenth century* (2 vols, London, 1884).

Edmund Hogan (ed.), *The Description of Ireland and the state thereof, as it is at this present in Anno 1598* (Dublin, 1878).

Historical Manuscripts Commission publications

First Report, Appendix, 1870.

Second Report, Appendix, 1871.

Third Report, Appendix, 1872.

Fifth Report, Appendix, 1876.

Eighth Report, Appendix, part ii, 1881.

Buccleugh MSS, vol. I, 1899.

Egmont MSS, vol. I, part I, 1905

Various Collections, vol. viii, 1913.

Hastings MSS, vol. iv, 1947.

Salisbury MSS, part xix, 1607, 1965.

J. Hogan (ed.), 'Survey of the escheated counties in Ulster, 1608', *Anal. Hib.*, iii (1931), 151–218.

J. Hogan (ed.), *Letters and papers relating to the Irish rebellion between 1642 and 1646* (IMC, Dublin, 1936).

H.F. Hore, 'A chorographic account of … Wexford…', *PKIAS*, new series, ii (1858), 17–21.

H.F. Hore (ed.), 'Marshal Bagenal's description of Ulster anno. 1586', *UJA*, 1st series, ii (1854), 17–21.

J.L.J. Hughes (ed.), *Patentee officers in Ireland, 1173–1826* (IMC, Dublin, 1960).

R.J. Hunter (ed.), 'Fragments of the Civil Survey of counties Kerry, Longford, and Armagh', *Anal. Hib.*, xxiv (1967), 227–31.

Inquisitionum in officio rotulorum cancellariae Hiberniae asservatarum reportorium, ii (Ultonia), (Dublin, 1829).

B. Jennings (ed.), *Wild Geese in Spanish Flanders, 1582–1700* (IMC, Dublin, 1964).

– (ed.), *Wadding Papers, 1614–38* (IMC, Dublin, 1953)

T.W. Jones (ed.), *A true relation of the Life and death of the Right Reverend Father in God William Bedell* (London, 1872).

Journals of the house of commons of the kingdom of Ireland, vol. 1, 1613–66 (Dublin, 1796).

Journals of the house of commons of the kingdom of Ireland, vol. 1, 1634–98 (Dublin, 1783).

Journals of the house of lords of the kingdom of Ireland, vol. 1 (Dublin, 1779).

S. Kavanagh (ed.), *Commentarius Rinuccianus*, vol. i (IMC, Dublin, 1932).

W. Knowler (ed.), *The earl of Strafford's letters and dispatches (*2 vols, London 1739).

Rowley Lascelles, *Liber munerum publicorum Hiberniae* (2 vols, London, 1852).

S. Lewis, *A topographical dictionary of Ireland* (2 vols, London, 1837).

Lewis's atlas comprising the counties of Ireland (London, 1837).

J. Lodge (ed.), *Desiderata curiosa Hibernica* (2 vols, Dublin, 1772).

Londonderry and the London companies, 1609–29, ed. D.A. Chart (Belfast, 1928).

T.K. Lowry (ed.), *The Hamilton manuscripts* (Belfast, 1867).

H.H.G. MacDonnell (ed.), *Chartae et statute collegii sacrosanctae et individuae trinitatis* (vol. i, 1844).

F.J. McKiernan, 'The hearth money rolls for the baronies of Tullyhunco and Tullyhaw, county Cavan', *Breifne* vol. 1, no. 3 (1960), 247–62.

E. MacLysaght (ed.), 'Survey of documents in private keeping, first series, *Anal. Hib.*, xv (1944).

–, *Guide to Irish surnames* (Dublin, 1964).

C. MacNeill (ed.), 'Calendar of Harris MSS in NLI', *Anal. Hib.*, vi (1934).

– (ed.), *The Tanner letters* (IMC, Dublin, 1934).

J.P. Mahaffy (ed.), *The particular book of Trinity College, Dublin* (London, 1904).

– (ed.), 'Attachment against Sir James Carroll, lst March 1631', *Hermathena* xi (1901), 122–25.

Maps of the Escheated Counties in Ireland [Ulster], 1609 (Ordnance Survey Office, Southampton, 1861).

Maps of the Down Survey (Ordnance Survey Office, Southampton, 1908).

Monasticon Hibernicum, ed. M. Archdall (Dublin, 1786).

C. Maxwell, *A history of Trinity College, Dublin, 1592–1892* (Dublin, 1946).

T. W. Moody (ed.), 'Ulster plantation papers, 1608–13', *Anal. Hib.*, viii (1938), 179–297.

– (ed.), 'The revised articles of the Ulster plantation, 1610', *BIHR*, xii (1935), 178–83.

P.F. Moran (ed.), *The analecta of David Rothe, bishop of Ossory* (Dublin, 1884).
– (ed.), *Spicilegium Ossoriense,* first series (Dublin, 1874).
L.P. Murray (ed.), 'The county Armagh hearth money rolls, A.D. 1664', *Arch. Hib.* viii (1941), 121–202.
– (ed.), 'A Rent–Roll of all the Houses and Lands belonging to the See of Armagh', *Arch. Hib.*, viii (1941), 99–120.
J. Nalson (ed.), *An impartial collection of the affairs of state from 1639 to the murther of king Charles I* (2 vols, London, 1682).
P. O'Connell (ed.), 'Extracts from the hearth money rolls for county Cavan', *Briefny Antiquarian Society Journal,* vol.1 no. 2 (1921), vol. 2 no. 3 (1925–26), vol. 3 no. 1 (1927).
J. O'Donovan (ed.), *Annala rioghachta Eireann; Annals of the kingdom of Ireland by the Four Masters,* vols 5 & 6 (2nd ed., Dublin, 1856).
– (ed.), *Leabhar na g-ceart or the book of rights* (Dublin, 1847).
P. O'Gallachair (ed.), 'The 1622 survey of Cavan', *Breifne,* vol. 1 (1958).
T.G.F. Paterson (ed.), 'County Armagh in 1622', *Seanchas Ardmhacha,* vol. 4 no. 1 (1960–61).
– (ed.), 'Cromwellian inquisition as to parishes in county Armagh in 1657', *UJA,* 3rd series, vol. 2 (1939).
S. Pender (ed.), *A census of Ireland, circa 1659* (IMC, Dublin, 1939).
D.B. Quinn (ed.), 'Calendar of the Irish council book, 1581–86', *Anal. Hib.*, xxiv (1967), 91–180.
Reports of the Deputy Keeper of the Records in Ireland, 7–22 (Dublin, 1875–90).
Reports of the commissioners appointed by his majesty to execute the measures recommended in an address of the house of commons respecting the public records of Ireland; with supplements and appendixes (3 vols, 1811–25).
Barnaby Rich, *A new description of Ireland* (London, 1610).
J. Rushworth (ed.), *The tryal of Thomas, earl of Strafford* (London, 1680).
T. Rymer, *Foedera*, vol. xv (London, 1728); vol. vii (Hague, 1744).
Sir John Scott of Scotstarvet, *The staggering state of the Scots statesmen for one hundred years, viz from 1550 to 1650* (Edinburgh, 1754).
W. Shaw (ed.), 'Letters of denization and acts of naturalisation for aliens in England and Wales', *Huguenot Society Proceedings,* xvii (1911).
E.P. Shirley (ed.), *Papers relating to the church of Ireland, 1631–39* (London, 1874).
E.S. Shuckburgh (ed.), *Two biographies of William Bedell, bishop of Kilmore* (Cambridge 1902).
R.C. Simington (ed.), *The Civil Survey, 1654–56,* vol. x, miscellanea (IMC, Dublin, 1961).
J. Spedding (ed.), *The letters and the life of Francis Bacon,* vols iii–vi (London, 1858).
J. Speed, *The theatre of the empire of Great Britain* (London, 1611).
Edmund Spenser, *A view of the present state of Ireland,* ed. W.L. Renwick (London, 1934).
Statutes at large passed in the parliaments held in Ireland, vols 1–2, 1310–62 (Dublin, 1786).

R.R. Steele (ed.), *Tudor and Stuart proclamations, 1485–1714* (2 vols, Oxford, 1910).

James Touchet, earl of Castlehaven, *Memoirs of the Irish wars* (London, 1684).

V. Treadwell (ed.), 'The survey of Armagh and Tyrone, 1622', *UJA*, 3rd series, vol. 23 (1960), 140–54.

A. Vicars, *Index to the prerogative wills of Ireland, 1536–1810* (Dublin, 1897).

R. Walsh (ed.), 'A memorial presented to the king of Spain on behalf of the Irish Catholics, A.D. 1619', *Archiv. Hib.*, vol. vi (1917), 27–54.

N.B. White (ed.), *Extents of Irish monastic possessions, 1540–1* (IMC, Dublin, 1943).

W.W. Wilkins (ed.), *Memoir of the life and episcopate of Dr. William Bedell* (London, 1862).

H. Wood (ed.), *The chronicle of Ireland, 1584–1608* (IMC, Dublin, 1933).

The works of… John Bramhall, vol. 1 (Library of Anglo–Catholic Theology, Oxford 1842).

R.M. Young (ed.), *The town book of the corporation of Belfast 1613–1816* (Belfast 1892).

SECONDARY SOURCES

J.A. Andrews, *Ireland in maps* (Dublin, 1961).

J.J. Auchmuty, *Irish education: a historical survey* (Dublin & London, 1937).

R. Bagwell, *Ireland under the Tudors* (3 vols, London, 1885–90).

–, *Ireland under the Stuarts* (3 vols, London, 1909–16).

J.M. Barkley, *A short history of the Presbyterian church in Ireland* (Belfast, 1959).

T.G. Barnes, *Somerset, 1625–40: a county's government during the 'Personal Rule'* (London, 1961).

J. Barry, 'The Coarb and the Twelfth–Century Reform', *Irish Ecclesiastical Record*, series 5, vol. 88 (1957), 17–25.

–, 'The Coarb in Medieval Times', *Irish Ecclesiastical Record*, series 5, vol. 89 (1958), 24–35.

–, 'The Erenagh in the Monastic Irish Church', *Irish Ecclesiastical Record*, series 5, vol. 89 (1958), 424–32.

–, 'The Lay Coarb in Medieval Times', *Irish Ecclesiastical Record*, series 5, vol. 91 (1959), 27–39.

–, 'The Appointment of Coarb and Erenagh', *Irish Ecclesiastical Record*, series 5, vol. 93 (1960), 361–5.

–, 'The extent of coarbs and erenaghs in Gaelic Ulster', *Irish Ecclesiastical Record*, series 5, vol. 94 (1960), 12–16.

–, 'The status of coarbs and erenaghs', *Irish Ecclesiastical Record*, series 5, vol. 94 (1960), 147–53.

–, 'The distinction between coarb and erenagh', *Irish Ecclesiastical Record*, series 5, vol. 94 (1960), 90–95.

–, 'The duties of coarbs and erenaghs', *Irish Ecclesiastical Record*, series 5, vol. 94 (1960), 211–18.

J.C. Beckett, *The making of modern Ireland, 1603–1923* (London, 1966).

J.C. Beckett & R.E. Glasscock (eds.), *Belfast, the origin and growth of an industrial city* (London, 1967).

H.E. Bell & R.L. Ollard (eds.), *Historical essays, 1600–1750, presented to David Ogg* (London, 1963).

G. Benn, *A history of the town of Belfast* (London, 1877).

D.A. Binchy (ed.), *Crith gablach* (Dublin, 1941).

L. Boynton, *The Elizabethan militia, 1558–1638* (London, 1967).

Burke's Peerage (103rd edn., London, 1962).

B. Burke, *Landed gentry of Ireland* (4th edn., London, 1958).

G. Burnet, *Life of Bedell* (Dublin, 1736).

H.J. Butler & H.E. Butler (eds.), *The black book of Edgeworthstown and other Edgeworth memories, 1585–1817* (London, 1927).

W.F.T. Butler, *Confiscation in Irish history* (Dublin, 1917).

–, *Gleanings from Irish history* (London, 1925).

G. Camblin, *The town of Ulster* (Belfast, 1951).

J. Carney (ed.), *A genealogical history of the O'Reillys* (Cavan, 1959).

T. Carte, *The history of the life of James, duke of Ormonde,* vol. 1 (London, 1736).

C.W. Chalklin, *Seventeenth–century Kent* (London, 1965).

R. Chambers, *Domestic annals of Scotland from the reformation to the rebellion,* vol. 1 (Edinburgh & London, 1858).

M. Clancy, 'The church lands of county Armagh: text of inquisition of 1609 – with introduction and notes', *Seanchas Ardmhacha,* vol. i, no. 1 (1954), 67–100.

A. Clarke, *The Old English in Ireland, 1625–42* (London, 1966).

–, *The graces, 1625–41* (Dundalk 1968).

–, 'The army and politics in Ireland, 1625–30', *Studia Hibernica,* iv (1964), 28–53.

D. Coghlan, *The ancient land tenures of Ireland* (Dublin, 1933).

G.E. Cokayne, *Complete peerage of England, Scotland, Ireland…* (new edn., London, 1910–1959).

Colonel Colby, *Ordnance survey of the county of Londonderry: memoir of the city and north western liberties of Londonderry* (Dublin, 1837).

A. Coleman, *Historical memoirs of the city of Armagh by James Stuart* (new edn., Dublin, 1900).

T.L. Coonan, *The Irish catholic confederacy and the puritan revolution* (Dublin, London, New York 1954).

E. Curtis, *A history of Ireland* (6th edn., London, 1950).

M. & L. de Paor, *Early Christian Ireland* (3rd edn., London, 1961).

M. Dillon, 'Ceart Ui Neill', *Studia Celtica,* i (1966).

R. Dunlop, 'Sixteenth century schemes for the plantation of Ulster', *SHR,* xxii (1925), 50–60, 115–26, 197–212.

–, 'The plantation of Munster, 1584–89', *EHR,* vol. iii (1888), 250–69.

R.D. Edwards, *Church and state in Tudor Ireland* (London & Dublin, 1935).

F.V. Emery, 'Irish geography in the seventeenth century', *Irish Geography,* vol. 3, no. 5 (1958), 263–76.

T. English, *Memoir relating to the vicars–choral and organist of the cathedral church of… Armagh* (Armagh, 1800).
E.E. Evans, *Irish Folk Ways* (London, 1957).
A. Everitt, *The community of Kent and the great rebellion, 1640–60* (Leicester, 1966).
C. Falls, *The birth of Ulster* (London, 1936).
–, *Elizabeth's Irish wars* (London, 1950).
W. Fitzgerald, *The historical geography of early Ireland* (London, 1925).
T.W. Freeman, *Ireland, its physical, historical, social and economic geography* (London, 1950).
P. Gale, *An inquiry into the ancient corporate system of Ireland* (London, 1834).
C. Gill, *The rise of the Irish linen industry* (Oxford 1925; reprinted 1964).
J.P. Greene (ed.), *Settlements to society, 1584–1763* (New York 1966).
A. Gwynn, *The medieval province of Armagh, 1470–1545* (Dundalk 1946).
E.W. Hamilton, *The Irish rebellion of 1641* (London, 1920).
–, *Elizabethan Ulster* (London, 1919).
J.W. Hanna, *Annals of Charlemont* (Armagh, 1846).
G.A. Hayes–McCoy, 'Sir John Davies in Cavan in 1606 and 1610 ', *Breifne*, vol. 1, no. 3 (1960), 177–91.
T. Healy, *Stolen waters: a page in the conquest of Ulster* (London, 1913).
C. Hill, *Economic problems of the church from archbishop Whitgift to the long parliament* (Oxford, 1956).
G. Hill, *An historical account of the plantation in Ulster…, 1608–1620* (Belfast 1877).
–, *Plantation papers* (Belfast 1889).
T. Hughes, *The history of Tynan parish, County Armagh, and other papers* (Dublin, 1910).
D. Hudson, *Holland House in Kensington* (London, 1967).
Edward Hyde, earl of Clarendon, *The history of the rebellion and civil wars in Ireland…* (London, 1720).
Irish Record Commissioners Report, 1816–20 (1819).
G. Jacob, *A new law–dictionary* (London, 1729).
M.D. Jephson, *An Anglo–Irish miscellany* (Dublin, 1964).
E.M. Jope, 'Scottish influences in the north of Ireland, castles with Scottish features 1580–1640', *UJA*, 3rd series, vol. 14 (1951), 31–47.
–, 'Moyry, Charlemont, Castleraw and Richill: fortification to architecture in the north of Ireland, 1570–1700', *UJA*, 3rd series, vol. 23 (1960), 97–123.
H.F. Kearney, *Strafford in Ireland, 1633–41* (Manchester 1959).
–, 'The court of wards and liveries in Ireland, 1622–41', *PRIA*, vol. 57 C (1955–6), 29–68.
P. Laslett, *The World we have lost* (London, 1965).
–, 'What is so special about us now' in *The Listener*, vol. LXIX, no. 1767, 7 February 1963, 235–37.
H.G. Leask, *Irish castles and castellated houses* (Dundalk 1941).
J.B. Leslie, *Armagh Clergy and parishes* (Dundalk 1911).
John Lodge, *The peerage of Ireland* ed. Mervyn Archdall (7 vols, Dublin, 1789).

J.R. MacCormack, 'The Irish adventurers and the English civil war', *IHS,* vol. x (1956–7), 21–58.

E. McCracken, 'The woodlands of Ulster in the early seventeenth century', *UJA*, 3rd series, vol. 10 (1947), 15–28.

–, 'The Irish timber trade in the seventeenth century', *Irish Forestry*, vol. xxi, no. 1 (1964), 7–20.

T. MacNevin, *The confiscation of Ulster in the reign of James I* (Dublin, 1846).

J.P. Mahaffy, *An epoch in Irish history: Trinity College, Dublin, its foundation and early fortunes, 1591–1660* (2nd edn., London, 1906).

R. Mant, *History of the church of Ireland*, vol. i (2nd edn., London, 1841).

J.J. Marshall, *History of Charlemont fort and borough ... end of Mountjoy fort* (Dungannon, 1921).

F.X. Martin, *Friar Nugent* (Rome & London, 1962).

H.J.M. Mason, *The life of William Bedell* (London, 1843).

C. Maxwell, *Irish history from contemporary sources, 1509–1610* (London, 1923).

–, 'The plantation in Ulster at the beginning of James I's reign', *The Sewanee Review*, 1923.

Ministry of Agriculture & Fisheries, *Report on markets and fairs in England and Wales*: pt 1 – general review (London, 1927).

T.W. Moody, *The Londonderry Plantation, 1609–41* (Belfast, 1939).

–, 'The treatment of the native population under the scheme for the plantation in Ulster', *IHS,* vol. 1 no. 1 (March, 1938), 59–63.

–, 'The Irish parliament under Elizabeth and James I', *PRIA*, vol. xlv, C (1939–40), 41–81.

T.W. Moody & F.X. Martin (eds.), *The course of Irish history* (Cork 1967).

B.J. Mooney & P. Keenan, *The parish of Seagoe* (Newry, 1954).

Henry Morley (ed.), *Ireland under Elizabeth and James I* (London, 1890).

L.P. Murray, 'The history of the parish of Creggan in the seventeenth and eighteenth centuries', *Journal of the County Louth Archaeological Society*, vol. viii, no. 2 (1934), 117–63.

C.P. Nettels, *The roots of American civilization* (2nd edn., London, 1963).

W. Notestein, *The English people on the eve of colonization, 1603–30* (New York 1954).

G. O'Brien, *The economic history of Ireland in the seventeenth century* (Dublin & London, 1919).

R.B. O'Brien (ed.), *Studies in Irish history, 1603–49* (Dublin, 1906).

S. O'Ceallaigh, 'A preliminary note on some of the nomenclature of the map of S.E. Ulster bound up with the maps of the escheated counties, 1610', *JRSAI*, vol. 91 (1951), 37–43.

P. O'Connell, *The diocese of Kilmore: its history and antiquities* (Dublin, 1937).

E. O'Curry, *On the manners and customs of the ancient Irish*, vol. i (1873)

J. O'Donovan, *The economic history of livestock in Ireland* (Dublin, Cork & London, 1940).

S. O'Faolain, *The great O'Neill* (London, 1942).

T.F. O'Rahilly, 'Notes on Irish place names', *Hermathena*, vol. xlviii (1933), 197–8.

J. Otway–Ruthven, 'Parochial development in the rural deanery of Skreen', *JRSAI*, vol. 94, pt 2 (1964), 111–22.

E. O'Tuat–Ghaill, 'The fort of Charlemont in Tir–Eoghan', *UJA*, vol. xvii (1911), 47–73.

A.F.S. Pearson, 'Alumni of St. Andrews and the settlement of Ulster', *UJA*, 3rd series, vol. 14 (1951), 7–14.

W. Petty, *The political anatomy of Ireland* (London, 1691).

W.A. Phillips (ed.), *History of the church of Ireland* (vols 2 & 3, London, 1933 & 1934).

K. Povey, 'The sources for bibliography of Irish history, 1500–1700', *IHS,* vol.1 (1938–9)., 393–403.

J.P. Prendergast, 'Charlemont fort', *JRHAAI,* 4th series, vi (1883–4), 319–44.

D.B. Quinn, *Raleigh and the British empire* (London, 1947).

–, 'The Munster plantation: problems and opportunities', *JCHAS*, vol. 71, nos. 213 & 214 (1966), 19–40.

T.O. Ranger, 'Richard Boyle and the making of an Irish fortune', *IHS,* vol. x (1956–7), 257–97.

–, 'Strafford in Ireland: a revaluation', *Past and Present,* no. 19 (1961), 26–45.

W. Reeves, *Ecclesiastical Antiquities of Down, Connor and Dromore* (Dublin, 1847).

–, *The ancient churches of Armagh* (Lusk, 1860).

–, 'The townland distribution of Ireland', *PRIA,* vol. vii, pt. xiv (1861), 473–90.

J.S. Reid, *History of the Presbyterian church in Ireland,* vol. i (3rd edn., London, 1853).

E. Rogers, *A record of the city of Armagh* (Armagh, 1861).

–, *Memoir of the Armagh cathedral with an account of the ancient city* (Belfast, ?1882).

–, *Topographical sketches in Armagh and Tyrone* (Armagh, 1874).

Report of the commissioners appointed to inquire into municipal corporations in Ireland (1835).

Report of the commissioners appointed to inquire into the endowments, funds, and actual condition of all schools endowed for the purpose of education in Ireland (1858).

Report of the commissioners on the revenues and condition of the established church (Ireland) (1868).

M.V. Ronan, *The Irish martyrs of the penal laws* (London, 1935).

D.B. Rutman, *Winthrop's Boston: a portrait of a puritan town, 1630–1640* (Williamsburg, Virginia 1965).

T. Salmon, *A new abridgement and critical review of the State trials …* (2 vols, Dublin, 1737).

T.S. Smyth, *The civic history of the town of Cavan* (Dublin, 1938).

–, 'Municipal charters of the town of Cavan', *Administration*, vol. 10, no. 3 (1962), 310–17.

D. Stewart, *The Scots in Ulster, the years between 1636 and 1642* (Presbyterian Historical Society of Ireland, Belfast, 1952–4).

–, *The Scots in Ulster, the years between 1636 and 1642* (Presbyterian Historical Society of Ireland, Belfast, 1955).
L. Stone, *The crisis of the aristocracy, 1558–1641* (Oxford, 1965).
J.W. Stubbs, *The history of the University of Dublin, from its foundation to the end of the eighteenth century; with an appendix of original documents which, for the most part, are preserved in the college* (Dublin & London, 1889)
J. Stuart, *Historical memoirs of the city of Armagh* (Newry, 1819).
J. Temple, *The history of the general rebellion in Ireland* (Cork 1766).
F. Tichborne, *St. Patrick's cathedral, Armagh: a short history* (1932).
P. Tohall, 'Charlemont fort, Co. Armagh', *The Irish Sword*, vol. iii, no. 12 (Summer 1958), 183–86.
V. Treadwell, 'The Irish court of wards under James I, *IHS*, vol. xii (1960), 1–27.
W. Urwick, *The early history of Trinity College, Dublin, 1591–1660* (London & Dublin, 1892).
M. Walsh, 'The last years of Hugh O'Neill, Rome 1608–1616', *Irish Sword*, vii (1965–66), 327–37.
P. Walsh, *Irish chiefs and leaders* (Dublin, 1960).
J.J. Webb, *Municipal government in Ireland* (Dublin, 1918).
C.V. Wedgwood, *Thomas Wentworth, first earl of Strafford, 1593–1641, a revaluation* (London, 1961).
P. Wilson, *The beginnings of modern Ireland* (Dublin & London, 1912).
J.B. Woodburn, *The Ulster Scot: his history and religion* (2nd edn., London, 1915).
B.S. Yamey, H.C. Edey & H.W. Thomson, *Accounting in England and Wales, 1543–1800* (London, 1963).

INDEX